Merriam-Webster's

Reader's Handbook

Merriam-Webster's Reader's Handbook

Merriam-Webster, Incorporated
Springfield, Massachusetts

A GENUINE MERRIAM-WEBSTER

The name *Webster* alone is no guarantee of excellence. It is used by a number of publishers and may serve mainly to mislead an unwary buyer.

Merriam-Webster™ is the name you should look for when you consider the purchase of dictionaries and other fine reference books. It carries the reputation of a company that has been publishing since 1831 and is your assurance of quality and authority.

Library of Congress Cataloging-in-Publication Data

Main entry under title:
Merriam-Webster's Reader's Handbook
p. cm.
ISBN 0-87779-620-3
1. Literature—Dictionaries I. Merriam-Webster, Inc.
PN41.M423 1997
803—dc21 97-26659
CIP

Made in the United States of America

123456PS:RRD999897

Preface

Merriam-Webster's Reader's Handbook is a reference work for people with an interest in the language of literature. Among its entries, one finds definitions for literary terms, literary styles and movements, and literary prizes and journals. Much of the content of the book is drawn from *Merriam-Webster's Encyclopedia of Literature,* a reference work based both on the lexical resources of Merriam-Webster and the detailed information offered by Encyclopædia Britannica. Because the *Handbook* is more narrowly focused, many of its entries have been expanded from those in the *Encyclopedia of Literature,* offering additional discussion not found in the larger book. New relevant entries also appear. Thus, the *Handbook* should serve as a worthy guide to readers, whether they be serious students or curious browsers.

Merriam-Webster's Reader's Handbook is a joint effort of Merriam-Webster, Inc., and Encyclopædia Britannica. At Merriam-Webster, the editors were assisted in producing this volume by James L. Rader, who prepared the etymologies; Brian M. Seitsema, who prepared the pronunciations; Maria A. Sansalone, Adrienne M. Scholz, and Donna L. Rickerby, who provided the cross-reference and proofreading; Peter D. Haraty and Amy West who compiled index material, and Robert D. Copeland, who managed the project through editorial and typesetting stages. Data entry was performed by Mary M. Dunn under the supervision of Veronica P. McLymont. From Encyclopædia Britannica, the editors were assisted by Kathleen Kuiper, who served as editor of the *Encyclopedia of Literature* and provided much knowledgeable and timely help in the planning of this project and during the course of the book's editing.

The plan for this book was conceived by John M. Morse, Publisher of Merriam-Webster, Inc., who himself offered invaluable help throughout the editing process.

Kathleen M. Doherty
Mary W. Cornog
Editors

Explanatory Notes

Entry Names.

Non-English Language names. In virtually all cases, vernacular usage has governed spelling. For languages not written in the Roman alphabet, the following conventions have been adopted:

Russian and other nonromanized languages have been transcribed using the systems found in the Encyclopædia Britannica.

Chinese names are romanized and alphabetized under the Pinyin rather than the Wade-Giles system, but cross-references are provided in the Wade-Giles system.

Alphabetization.

Alphabetization is letter-by-letter, not word-by-word. Thus, **literaryism** falls between **literary criticism** and **Literary Research Association.**

If *The* appears initially at the entry for a periodical title, the entry is alphabetized at the next significant word. Thus the entry **Quarterly Review, The.**

Diacritical marks, marks of punctuation, and spaces within the boldface names are ignored.

Cross-references.

Cross-references are indicated by SMALL CAPITALS. In this book, they are employed chiefly to lead the reader to further information on his or her subject of immediate inquiry.

Dates in text.

In general, dates following the titles of works indicate the date of first publication. The date following mention of a foreign-language title is the year in which the book was first published in the original language. The dates following play titles should be assumed to refer to the dates of original publication unless otherwise indicated.

Translations in text.

For non-English-language works, the date of publication is usually followed by a translation (if the title is not an obvious cognate or a proper name). Translations that appear within quotation marks are approximate renderings, as *La divina commedia* ("The Divine Comedy"). Italicized titles within parentheses indicate the work has been published in English, as *Portrait d'un inconnu* (1948; *Portrait of a Man Unknown*).

Etymologies.

Etymologies in this book are meant to provide historical and philological background for the terminology of literary studies. This work provides etymologies for common nouns, such as names of genres, verse forms and movements, but not generally for proper nouns. Etymologies are also not provided for terms whose literary significance depends on a more general sense of a word (for example, **icon**), or for terms that are obviously compounds or derivatives of words or word-forming elements with unspecialized senses (for example, **flashback** and **naturalism**).

Ordinarily, etymologies are enclosed in square brackets and placed after the pronunciation and before the body of the entry. In some entries the origin of the word is discussed in the text, and there a bracketed etymology will be lacking unless it provides additional data. An asterisk placed before a word indicates that the form can be reconstructed but is not actually attested in writing. In general, intermediate languages, remoter ancestors, and the philological detail appropriate to a dictionary of etymology have been omitted in this book, unless such information is relevant to the literary use of a term.

Pronunciation.

This book provides pronunciation respellings for most entry words. The only entry words without respellings are familiar non-literary words, such as **black humor** or **automatic writing**. The pronunciation for these words may be found in *Merriam-Webster's Collegiate Dictionary, Tenth Edition*.

When two or more variant spellings of a name have the same pronunciation, the respelling is placed after the last spelling with that pronunciation:

baihua *or* **paihua** \'bī-'hwä\

Names and terms from English literature are transcribed in a composite dialect which approximates the speech of the majority of Americans. British names are shown with variants from the Received Pronunciation of British English where this dialect differs noticeably from American speech, as at **Bard of Avon**. Foreign language names are respelled in their native pronunciation and are generally rendered in the standard dialect of the language in question. A variant labeled *Angl* is added for names with familiar anglicizations, as at **Berliner Ensemble,** and for exceptionally difficult foreign names.

Pronunciation Symbols

ə . . . . **a**noint, c**o**llide, dat**a**
ˈə, ˌə . . . . c**u**t, con**u**ndr**u**m
ə̇. . . . . biolo**gi**st, match**e**s
a. . . . . r**a**p, c**a**t, s**a**nd, l**a**mb
ā. . . . . w**ay**, p**ai**d, l**a**te, **ei**ght
ä. . . . . **o**pt, c**o**d, m**a**ch
ȧ. . . . . French *ch**a**t, t**a**ble*
ar . . . . **air**, c**are**, l**air**d
au̇. . . . . . . **ou**t, l**ou**d, t**ou**t, c**ow**
b . . . . **b**at, a**b**le, ri**b**
b̲ . . . . Spanish *Ha**b**lar, **A**vila*
ch. . . . . . . **ch**air, rea**ch**, ca**tch**er
d . . . . **d**ay, re**d**, la**dd**er
e. . . . . **e**gg, b**e**d, b**e**t
ˈē, ˌē. . . . . **ea**t, r**ee**d, fl**ee**t, p**ea**
ē. . . . . penn**y**, gen**ie**
ei . . . . Dutch ***ei**eren, d**ij**k*
f. . . . . **f**ine, cha**ff**, o**ff**ice
g . . . . **g**ate, ra**g**, ea**g**le
g̲ . . . . Spanish *la**g**o*
h . . . . **h**ot, a**h**oy
hr. . . . . . . Welsh ***rh**ad*, Icelandic ***hr**aun*
hw . . . . . . **wh**eat, **wh**en
i . . . . **i**ll, h**i**p, b**i**d
ī. . . . . **ai**sle, fr**y**, wh**i**te, w**i**de
j . . . . **j**ump, fu**dg**e, bu**dg**et
k . . . . **k**ic**k**, ba**k**er, s**c**am, as**k**
k̲. . . . . lo**ch**, Ba**ch**, German *Bu**ch***
l . . . . **l**ap, pa**l**, a**ll**ey
m . . . . **m**ake, ja**m**, ha**mm**er
n . . . . **n**ow, wi**n**, ba**nn**er
ⁿ. . . . . shows that a preceding vowel is nasalized, as in French *en* \äⁿ\
ŋ . . . . ri**ng**, si**ng**er, go**ng**
ō . . . . **oa**k, b**oa**t, t**oe**, g**o**
ȯ . . . . h**aw**k, b**aw**l, c**au**ght, **ou**ght, Ut**ah**

œ . . . . French *n**eu**f*, German *K**ö**pfe*
œ̄ . . . . French *d**eu**x*, German *L**öh**ne*
ȯi . . . . **oy**ster, t**oy**, f**oi**l
ȯr. . . . . . . **core**, b**or**n, **oar**
p . . . . **p**et, ti**p**, u**pp**er
r. . . . . **r**ut, ta**r**, e**rr**o**r**, ca**r**t
s. . . . . **s**ink, ba**ss**, la**ss**o
sh. . . . . . . **sh**in, la**sh**, pre**ss**ure
t . . . . **t**op, pa**t**, la**t**er
th . . . . **th**ird, ba**th**, Ka**th**y
t̲h̲. . . . . . . **th**is, o**th**er, ba**the**
ü . . . . **oo**ze, bl**ue**, n**oo**n
u̇ . . . . w**oo**l, t**oo**k, sh**ou**ld
ue . . . . German *B**ü**nde, f**ü**llen*
ue̅ . . . . German *k**üh**l*, French *v**ue***
v . . . . **v**eer, ro**v**e, e**v**er
w . . . . **w**ell, a**w**ash
y . . . . **y**outh, **y**et, la**w**yer
ʸ. . . . . shows palatalization of a preceding consonant, as in French *campagne* \käⁿ-ˈpänʸ\
z. . . . . **z**oo, ha**z**e, ra**z**or
zh. . . . . . . plea**sure**, deci**si**on
ʿ. . . . . indicates a consonant that is pronounced like \h\ with vibration of the vocal cords
\ \. . . . . . . reversed virgules used to mark the beginning and end of a phonetic respelling
ˈ. . . . . mark preceding a syllable with primary stress: boa \ˈbō-ə\
ˌ. . . . . mark preceding a syllable with secondary stress: beeline \ˈbē-ˌlīn\
-. . . . . mark indicating syllable divisions

A

Shakespeare led a life of allegory: his works are comments on it.
—John Keats

Abbaye group \ä-ˈbā\ A short-lived cooperative community of French writers and artists who promoted new works and who lived together in a house called L'Abbaye, in a Paris suburb, from 1906 to 1907. The group included the writers Charles Vildrac and Georges Duhamel. The house was a center of artistic activity, and other writers and artists, including Jules Romains, were associated with the group (though they were not inhabitants of the house). The Abbaye artists supported themselves by selling books that they printed on their own printing press. One of the works published by the group was the influential *La Vie unanime* (1908) by Romains. The Abbaye community was portrayed by Duhamel in his novel *Le Désert de Bièvres* (1937). *See also* UNANIMISME.

Abbey Theatre \ˈab-ē\ Dublin theater that was established in 1904. It grew out of the Irish Literary Theatre, founded in 1899 by William Butler Yeats and Isabella Augusta, Lady Gregory, and was devoted to fostering Irish poetic drama. In 1902 the Irish Literary Theatre was taken over by the Irish National Dramatic Society, which had been formed to present Irish actors in Irish plays and was led by W.G. and Frank J. Fay. In 1903 this became the Irish National Theatre Society, with which many leading figures of the IRISH LITERARY RENAISSANCE were closely associated. The quality of its productions was quickly recognized, and in 1904 an Englishwoman, Annie Horniman, a friend of Yeats, paid for the conversion of an old theater in Abbey Street, Dublin, into the Abbey Theatre. The Abbey opened in December 1904 with a bill of plays by Yeats, Lady Gregory, and John Millington Synge (who joined the other two as codirector). Founding members included the Fays, Arthur Sinclair, and Sara Allgood.

The Abbey's staging of Synge's satire *The Playboy of the Western World,* on Jan. 26, 1907, stirred up so much resentment in the audience over its portrayal of the Irish peasantry that there was a riot. When the Abbey players toured the United States for the first time in 1911, similar protests and disorders were provoked when the play opened in New York City, Boston, and Philadelphia.

In 1924, the Abbey became the first state-subsidized theater in the English-speaking world. The emergence of playwright Sean O'Casey also stimulated new interest in the theater and from 1923 to 1926 the Abbey staged three of his plays: *The Shadow of a Gunman, Juno and the Paycock,* and *The Plough and the Stars,* the last a provocative dramatization of the Easter Rising of 1916. In the early 1950s the Abbey company moved to the nearby Queen's Theatre after a fire had destroyed its playhouse. A new Abbey Theatre, housing a smaller, experimental theater, was completed in 1966 on the original site. Although the Abbey has broadened its repertoire in recent decades, it continues to rely primarily on Irish plays.

abecedarius \ˌā-bē-sē-'dar-ē-əs\ [Late Latin, alphabetical, from the names of the letters *a, b, c, d*] A type of ACROSTIC in which the first letter of each line of a poem or the first letter of the first word of each stanza taken in order forms the alphabet. Examples of these are some of the Psalms (in Hebrew), such as Psalms 25 and 34, where successive verses begin with the letters of the Hebrew alphabet in order.

Abenteuerroman \'ä-ben-ˌtȯi-ər-rō-ˌmän\ [German, literally, adventure novel] German form of the PICARESQUE NOVEL. The *Abenteuerroman* is an entertaining story of the adventures of the hero, but there is also often a serious aspect to the story. An example is the 17th-century *Der Abentheurliche Simplicissimus* (*Adventurous Simplicissimus*) by H.J.C. von Grimmelshausen. The Abenteuerroman is related to the BILDUNGSROMAN, a genre in which the subject is the formative years of the main character.

ab ovo \ab-'ō-vō\ A Latin phrase meaning literally "from the egg" that alludes to the practice of beginning a poetic narrative at the earliest possible chronological point. The Latin poet and critic Horace notes approvingly (in *Ars poetica*) that Homer does not begin a tale of the Trojan war with the twin egg from which Helen was born but rather in the middle of events. *Compare* IN MEDIAS RES.

abozzo \ə-'bȯt-sō\ [Italian] A rough sketch or draft (as of a poem).

abridged edition A version of a work that has been shortened or condensed by the omission of words, presumably without sacrifice of the principal meaning. When it is done for purposes of censorship, abridgment is known as bowdlerization. *See* BOWDLERIZE.

absolute \'ab-sə-ˌlüt, ˌab-sə-'lüt\ Being self-sufficient and free of external references or relationships. In criticism, an absolutist believes that there are inviolable standards by which a work of art should be judged and that there are certain basic and immutable values that determine worth.

abstract \ab-'strakt, 'ab-ˌstrakt\ Expressing a quality apart from an object; the word *poem* is concrete, the word *poetry* is abstract.

abstract \'ab-ˌstrakt\ A summary of points (as of a written work) usually presented in skeletal form; also, something that summarizes or concentrates the essentials of a larger thing or several things.

abstract poem Term coined by the English poet Edith Sitwell to describe a poem in which the words are chosen for their aural quality rather than specifically for their sense or meaning. An example from "Popular Song" in Sitwell's *Façade* follows:

> The red retriever-haired satyr
> Can whine and tease her and flatter,
> But Lily O'Grady,
> Silly and shady,
> In the deep shade is a lazy lady;
> Now Pompey's dead, Homer's read,
> Heliogabalus lost his head,
> And shade is on the brightest wing,
> And dust forbids the bird to sing.

absurdism \əb-ˈsər-ˌdiz-əm, -ˈzər-\ A philosophy based on the belief that humans exist in an irrational and meaningless universe and that the search for order brings one into conflict with that universe. *See also* THEATER OF THE ABSURD.

academese \ə-ˌkad-ə-ˈmēz, -ˈmēs; ˌak-əd-ə-\ A style of writing held to be characteristic of those in academic life. The term is generally pejorative, implying jargon-filled writing.

academic \ˌak-ə-ˈdem-ik\ or **academical** \-mi-kəl\ Conforming to the traditions or rules of a school, as of literature or art, or an official academy. Conventional or formalistic.

academic drama Any play written and performed at schools and colleges in England in the early 16th century. *See also* SCHOOL DRAMA.

Académie Française \à-kà-dā-ˌmē-frä^n-ˈsez\ French literary academy, established by the French first minister Cardinal de Richelieu in 1634 and incorporated in 1635, and existing, except for an interruption during the era of the French Revolution, to the present day. Its original purpose was to maintain standards of literary taste and to establish the literary language. Its membership is limited to 40. Though it has often acted as a conservative body, opposed to innovations in literary content and form, its membership has included most of the great names of French literature—e.g., Pierre Corneille, Jean Racine, Voltaire, Chateaubriand, Victor Hugo, Joseph-Ernest Renan, and Henri Bergson. In 1980 Marguerite Yourcenar became the first woman to be elected to the academy. Among numerous European literary academies, the Académie Française has consistently retained the highest prestige over the longest period of time.

academy \ə-ˈkad-ə-mē\ [Greek *Akadḗmeia, Akadēmía* a public grove and gymnasium near Athens where Plato taught, a derivative of *Akádēmos,* a legendary Attic hero after whom the grove and gymnasium were named] A society of learned individuals organized to advance art, science, literature, music, or some other cultural or intellectual area of endeavor. From its original reference in Greek to the philosophical school of Plato, the word has come to refer much more generally to an institution of learning or a group of learned persons.

At the close of the European Middle Ages, academies began to be formed in Italy, first for the study of classical and then of Italian literature. One of the earliest was the Platonic Academy, founded in Florence in 1442 by two Greek scholars under the encouragement of Cosimo de' Medici. Literary academies sprang up all over Italy in the 16th and 17th centuries; the most famous of these was the CRUSCA ACADEMY, which was founded in Florence by A.F. Grazzini in 1582.

The Académie Française, which would become Europe's best-known literary academy, began in 1635. The Royal Spanish Academy was founded in 1713 to preserve the Spanish language, and it published a landmark Spanish dictionary for that purpose.

Academies of science began to appear in the 16th century, and academies of fine arts, music, social sciences, medicine, mining, and agriculture were formed from the 18th century on. Most European countries now have at least one academy or learned society that is sponsored by or otherwise connected with the state. The academies' influence was greatest during the 17th and 18th centuries but declined during the 19th because of their tendency to resist new and unorthodox developments in science and culture.

The United States, like Great Britain, Canada, and other English-speaking countries, has no state-established academies of science or literature, a fact reflective of English beliefs that culture should basically be a matter for private initiative. The first learned society in what would become the United States was founded by Benjamin Franklin in 1743 and called the American Philosophical Society. The rival American Academy of Arts and Sciences was founded in 1779, and the National Academy of Sciences was founded in Washington, D.C., in 1863.

acatalectic \ˌā-ˌkat-ə-ˈlek-tik\ [Greek *akatálēktos,* literally, not stopping] In prosody, metrically complete (i.e., not falling short of the expected number of syllables in the last foot). It is the opposite of CATALEXIS, the suppression or absence of the final syllable of a line.

Accademia della Crusca *See* CRUSCA ACADEMY.

Accademia dell'Arcadia *See* Academy of ARCADIA.

accent \ˈak-ˌsent, -sənt\ [Latin *accentus* variation in pitch, intonation, from *ad* to, toward + *cantus* song; a calque of Greek *prosōidía*] In prosody, rhythmically significant stress on the syllables of a verse, usually at regular intervals. The word *accent* is often used interchangeably with *stress,* though some prosodists use *accent* to mean the emphasis that is determined by the normal meaning of the words while *stress* is used to mean metrical emphasis. In classical prosody, which was based on a quantitative approach to verse rather than the modern stress-based system, accent was used to determine the relative quantity and prominence of a syllable based on sound. For the Greeks, accent was explained as a difference in musical pitch, usually higher, used in the pronunciation of a word. When prosody ceased to be based on quantity, the accent changed from variation of pitch to variation of force or emphasis. *Compare* STRESS.

Accent (*in full* Accent: A Quarterly of New Literature) Literary magazine published from 1940 to 1960 at the University of Illinois. Founded by Kerker Quinn and Charles Shattuck, the journal evolved from an earlier version called *Direction* that Quinn put out in his undergraduate days. *Accent* published some of the best examples of contemporary writing by both new and established authors, including Wallace Stevens, Katherine Anne Porter, William Gass, James T. Farrell, Eudora Welty, Thomas Mann, Bertolt Brecht, and Richard Wright.

accentual-syllabic verse In prosody, the metrical system that is most commonly used in English poetry. It is based on both the number of stresses, or accents, and the number of syllables in each line of verse. A line of iambic pentameter verse, for example, consists of five feet, each of which is an iamb (an unstressed followed by a stressed syllable). Although accentual-syllabic verse is very strictly measured, variations in both accent placement and number of syllables are often allowed. *See also* METER.

accentual verse \ak-'sen-chü-wəl\ In prosody, a metrical system based only on the number of stresses or accented syllables in a line of verse. In accentual verse the total number of syllables in a line can vary as long as there are the prescribed number of accents. This system is used in Germanic poetry, including Old English and Old Norse, as well as in some English verse. The poem "What if a Much of a Which of a Wind," by E.E. Cummings, is an example of accentual verse. In the following lines from the poem the number of accents is constant at four while the number of syllables per line varies from seven to ten:

> what if a much of a which of a wind
> gives the truth to summer's lie;
> bloodies with dizzying leaves the sun
> and yanks immortal stars awry?
> Blow king to beggar and queen to seem
> (blow friend to fiend: blow space to time)
> —when skies are hanged and oceans drowned,
> the single secret will still be man

See also METER.

accismus \ak-'siz-məs\ [Greek *akkismós* prudery, a derivative of *akkízesthai* to feign ignorance] A form of irony in which a person feigns indifference to, or pretends to refuse, something he or she desires. The fox's dismissal of the grapes in the Aesop fable of the fox and the grapes is an example of accismus. A classic example is that of Caesar's initial refusal to accept the crown, a circumstance reported by one of the conspirators in William Shakespeare's *Julius Caesar*.

acephalous \ˌā-'sef-ə-ləs, ə-\ [Greek *aképhalos* headless, from *a-* not + *kephalḗ* head] *See* HEADLESS.

Acmeist \'ak-mē-ist\, *Russian* Akmeist \ˌək-mē-'ēst\, *plural* Akmeisty \-'ēs-tē\ [Russian *akmeist,* from Greek *akmḗ* highest point, acme] Member of a small group of early 20th-century Russian poets reacting against what they considered to be the vagueness and affectations of Symbolism. The Acmeist movement was formed by the poets Sergey Gorodetsky and Nikolay S. Gumilyov. They reasserted the poet as craftsman and used language freshly and with intensity. Centered in St. Petersburg, the Acmeists were associated with the review *Apollon* (1909–17). In 1912 they founded the Guild of Poets, whose most outstanding members were Anna Akhmatova and Osip Mandelshtam. Because of their preoccupation with form and their aloofness, the Acmeists were regarded with suspicion by the Soviet regime. Gumilyov was executed in 1921 for his alleged activities in an anti-Soviet conspiracy. Akhmatova was silenced during the most productive years of her life, and Mandelshtam died en route to a labor camp.

acronym \'ak-rə-ˌnim\ [Greek *ákros* outermost, at the tip + *ónyma* name] A word formed from the initial letter or letters of each of the successive parts or major parts of a compound term, such as RADAR from *ra*dio *d*etecting *a*nd *r*anging or SONAR from *so*und *na*vigation *r*anging.

acrostic \ə-'krȯs-tik\ [Greek *akrostichís,* from *ákros* outermost + *stíchos* line, verse] **1.** Short verse composition, so constructed that one or more sets of letters (such as the initial, middle, or final letters of the lines), taken consecutively, form words. An acrostic in which the initial letters form the alphabet is an ABECEDARIUS.

The word *acrostic* was first applied to the prophecies of the Erythraean Sibyl, which were written on leaves and arranged so that the initial letters of the leaves always formed a word. Acrostics were common among the Greeks of the Alexandrine period, and many of the arguments of the plays of the Latin writers Ennius and Plautus were written in acrostic verses that spelled out the titles of the plays. Medieval monks were also fond of acrostics, as were the poets of the Middle High German and Italian Renaissance periods.

An example of an acrostic is the poem in which Lewis Carroll spells out the name of Alice Liddell, for whom *Alice's Adventures in Wonderland* was written:

> A boat, beneath a sunny sky
> Lingering onward dreamily
> In an evening of July—
>
> Children three that nestle near,
> Eager eye and willing ear,
> Pleased a simple tale to hear—
>
> Long has paled that sunny sky:
> Echoes fade and memories die:
> Autumn frosts have slain July.

Still she haunts me, phantomwise,
Alice moving under skies
Never seen by waking eyes.

Children yet, the tale to hear,
Eager eye and willing ear,
Lovingly shall nestle near.

In a Wonderland they lie,
Dreaming as the days go by,
Dreaming as the summers die:

Ever drifting down the stream—
Lingering in the golden gleam—
Life, what is it but a dream?

2. A type of word puzzle utilizing the acrostic principle. A popular form is double acrostics, puzzles constructed so that not only the initial letters of the lines but in some cases also the middle or last letters form words. In the United States, a Double Crostic puzzle, devised by Elizabeth Kingsley for *The Saturday Review* in 1934, had an acrostic in the answers to the clues giving the author and title of a literary work; the letters, keyed by number to blanks like those of a crossword puzzle, spelled out a quotation.

act \ˈakt\ [Latin *actus,* literally, action, activity] One of the principal divisions of a theatrical work.

action \ˈak-shən\ [translation of Greek *práxis* (in Aristotle's *Poetics*)] **1.** A real or imaginary event or series of events forming the subject of a play, poem, or other composition. **2.** The unfolding of the events of a drama or work of fiction, also called the PLOT.

adab \ˈȧ-dȧb\ [Arabic] Islāmic concept that became a literary genre distinguished by its broad humanitarian concerns; it developed during the height of ʿAbbāsid culture in the 9th century and continued to be of importance through the Muslim Middle Ages.

The original sense of the word was simply "norm of conduct," or "custom," derived in ancient Arabia from ancestors revered as models. As such practice was deemed praiseworthy in the medieval Muslim world, *adab* acquired a further connotation of good breeding, courtesy, and urbanity.

Parallel to and growing out of this expanded social meaning of *adab* there appeared an intellectual aspect. *Adab* came to connote the knowledge of poetry, oratory, ancient Arab tribal history, rhetoric, grammar, philology, and non-Arab civilizations that qualified an individual to be called well-bred, or *adīb*. The vast and erudite *adab* literature was concerned with human achievements and was written in an expressive and flexible style that was rich in vocabulary and idiom. The best-known writers of *adab* include the 9th-century essayist al-Jāḥiẓ of Basra and his 11th-century follower Abū Hayyān at-Tawḥīdī; the 9th-century Kūfan critic, philologist, and theologian Ibn Qutaybah; and the 11th-century poet al-Maʿarrī.

As the golden age of the ʿAbbāsids declined, however, the boundaries of *adab* narrowed into belles lettres: poetry, elegant prose, anecdotal writing (*maqāmah*). In the modern Arab world, *adab* signifies literature.

adage \'ad-ij\ [Latin *adagium* proverb] A saying, often in metaphorical form, that embodies a common observation, such as "If the shoe fits, wear it," "Out of the frying pan, into the fire," or "Early to bed, early to rise, makes a man healthy, wealthy, and wise." The scholar Erasmus published a well-known collection of adages as *Adagia* in 1508. *See also* PROVERB; APHORISM.

adaptation \ˌad-ap-'tā-shən\ Something that is adapted; especially, a composition rewritten into a new form, such as a novel reworked as a film script.

ad captandum or **ad captandum vulgus** \ˌad-ˌkap-'tan-dəm-'vəl-gəs\ [Latin, for pleasing the crowd] Designed to attract or please the crowd. An argument in drama, verse, or rhetoric that is directed chiefly to the emotions is often called an argument *ad captandum*.

Adelphi, The \ə-'del-fē\, *also called* (1927–30) The New Adelphi. British literary journal founded by John Middleton Murry in 1923. The publication was more a periodical manifesto than a literary magazine. Originally dedicated to promoting the work and views of the novelist D.H. Lawrence, and of the editor himself, *The Adelphi* (from the Greek word for "brothers") attempted to reach readers beyond the traditional upper-class literary circle of the time, although this effort met with little success. In fact, Murry's radical politics, coupled with a disdain for religion as manifested in Lawrence's published declaration that "Jesus was a failure," alienated the general readers Murry had hoped to attract. Many members of the influential Bloomsbury group, including Leonard and Virginia Woolf, came to disdain both editor and journal. While the periodical published the work of W.H. Auden, T.S. Eliot, George Orwell, and W.B. Yeats, it is best known as the repository of its founder's controversial commentary on religious, political, and cultural life.

Adonic \ə-'dän-ik\ or **Adonian** \ə-'dō-nē-ən\ [Late Greek *Adṓnion* an Adonic verse, a derivative of *Adṓnis* Adonis] In classical prosody, having a meter consisting of a dactyl (– ∪ ∪) followed by a spondee (– –). It is found in dactylic contexts, and especially in aeolic and sapphic verse.

adynaton \ə-'dī-nə-ˌtän\ [Greek *adýnaton,* neuter of *adýnatos* impossible] A kind of hyperbole in which the exaggeration is so great that it refers to an impossibility, as in the following lines from Andrew Marvell's "To His Coy Mistress":

Had we but world enough, and time,
This coyness, lady, were no crime.
We would sit down, and think which way
To walk, and pass our long love's day.
Thou by the Indian Ganges' side
Shouldst rubies find; I by the tide
Of Humber would complain. I would
Love you ten years before the flood
And you should, if you please, refuse
Till the conversion of the Jews.

a-effect *See* ALIENATION EFFECT.

aeolic \ē-'äl-ik\ [Greek *Aiolikós,* literally, of the Aeolians, a people of ancient Greece] Of or relating to a group of meters used in Greek lyric poetry. "Aeolic" alludes to the poets Sappho and Alcaeus, of the Aeolian island of Lesbos, who first used these meters. Aeolic meters, such as the glyconic, typically are formed around a choriamb (– ∪ ∪ –), which may be preceded or followed (or both) by a variety of other metrical units to create a wide variety of metrical sequences. (For example, choriambic dimeter has the form – ∪ ∪ – | ⩡ – ⩡ – ; glyconic takes the form ⩡ ⩡⩡ | – ∪ ∪ – | ⩡ – .) *See also* POLYSCHEMATIST.

aesthete \'es-ˌthēt, 'ēs-\ One professing devotion to the beautiful, especially in art. The word (usually capitalized) was applied in particular to a group of English writers and artists of the late 19th century whose belief in the doctrine of Aestheticism was manifested in dandyism and affectation. This group included Oscar Wilde, Aubrey Beardsley, Arthur Symons, and Ernest Dowson.

aesthetic distance The frame of reference that an artist creates by the use of technical devices in and around the work of art to differentiate it psychologically from reality. German playwright Bertolt Brecht built his dramatic theory known in English as the alienation effect to accomplish aesthetic distance.

Aestheticism \es-'thet-ə-ˌsiz-əm, ēs-\ Late 19th-century European arts movement that centered on the doctrine that art exists for the sake of its beauty alone.

The movement began in reaction to prevailing utilitarian social philosophies and to what was perceived as the ugliness and philistinism of the industrial age. Its philosophical foundations were laid in the 18th century by Immanuel Kant, who postulated the autonomy of aesthetic standards, setting them apart from considerations of morality, utility, or pleasure. This idea was amplified by J.W. von Goethe, J.L. Tieck, and others in Germany and by Samuel Taylor Coleridge and Thomas Carlyle in England. It was popularized in France by Madame de Staël, Théophile Gautier, and the philosopher Victor Cousin, who coined the phrase *l'art pour l'art* ("art for art's sake") in 1818.

In England, the artists of the Pre-Raphaelite Brotherhood, from 1848, had sown the seeds of Aestheticism, and the work of Dante Gabriel Rossetti, Edward

Burne-Jones, and Algernon Charles Swinburne exemplified it in expressing a yearning for ideal beauty through conscious medievalism. The attitudes of the movement were also represented in the writings of Oscar Wilde and Walter Pater and the illustrations of Aubrey Beardsley in the periodical *The Yellow Book*. The painter James McNeill Whistler raised the movement's ideal of the cultivation of refined sensibility to perhaps its highest point.

Contemporary critics of Aestheticism included William Morris and John Ruskin and, in Russia, Leo Tolstoy, who questioned the value of art divorced from morality. Yet the movement focused attention on the formal aesthetics of art and contributed to the art criticism of Roger Fry and Bernard Berenson. The movement shared certain affinities with the French Symbolist movement and was a precursor of Art Nouveau. *See also* DECADENT; SYMBOLIST MOVEMENT.

affective fallacy In literary criticism, the error of judging a work on the basis of its effect on the reader. The notion of affective fallacy was described by the proponents of New Criticism as a direct challenge to impressionistic critics who argued that the reader's response to a poem is the ultimate indication of its value.

Those who support the affective criterion for judging poetry cite its long and respectable history, beginning with Aristotle's dictum that the purpose of tragedy is to evoke "terror and pity." Other proponents of the affective criterion include Edgar Allan Poe, who stated that "a poem deserves its title only inasmuch as it excites, by elevating the soul," and Emily Dickinson, who said, "If I feel physically as if the top of my head were taken off, I know that is poetry." Many modern critics continue to assert that emotional communication and response cannot be separated from the evaluation of a poem. *See also* NEW CRITICISM.

afterpiece \'af-tər-ˌpēs\ Supplementary entertainment presented after full-length plays in 18th-century England. Afterpieces usually took the form of a short comedy, farce, or pantomime and were intended to lighten the solemnity of Neoclassical drama and make the bill more attractive to audiences. Long theater programs that included interludes of music, song, and dance developed in the first 20 years of the 18th century, promoted primarily by John Rich at Lincoln's Inn Fields in order to compete with the Drury Lane. The addition of afterpieces to the regular program may also have been an attempt to attract working citizens, who often missed the early opening production and paid a reduced charge to be admitted later, usually at the end of the third act of a five-act play.

Before 1747, afterpieces were generally presented with old plays, but after that date, almost all new plays were accompanied by afterpieces as well. Although farce and pantomime were the most popular forms of afterpiece—the latter usually integrating classical themes with commedia dell'arte characters—other kinds of afterpiece occasionally were performed. These included processions, burlettas (comic operas popular in England in the second half of the 18th century) or burlesques, and ballad operas, which gained popularity after the success of John Gay's *The Beggar's Opera* in 1728.

afterword *See* EPILOGUE.

agitprop \'aj-it-ˌpräp\ Political propaganda promulgated chiefly in literature, drama, music, or art.

Agitprop or *agitpropotdel* was a shortening of the Russian *agitatsionno-propagandistsky otdel* ("agitation-propaganda section"), a department of the Central Committee, or a local committee, of the Communist Party in the Soviet Union in the years after the Bolshevik Revolution of 1917. The word is used in English to describe the work of such departments, and by extension any work, especially in the theater, that aims to educate and indoctrinate the public. It typically has a negative connotation, reflecting in part Western distaste for overt use of drama and other arts to achieve political goals.

The twin strategies of agitation and propaganda were originally elaborated by the Russian Marxist theorist Georgy Plekhanov, who defined propaganda as the promulgation of a number of ideas to an individual or small group, and agitation as the promulgation of a single idea to a large mass of people. Expanding on these notions in the pamphlet *Chto delat?* (1902; *What Is to Be Done?*), V.I. Lenin stated that the propagandist, whose primary medium was print, explained the cause of social inequities such as unemployment or hunger, while the agitator, whose primary medium was the spoken word, seized on emotional aspects of these issues to arouse the audience's indignation.

agon \'ag-ˌän, ä-'gōn\ *plural* agons *or* agones \ə-'gō-ˌnēz\ [Greek *agṓn* gathering, assembly, contest, a derivative of *ágein* to lead, bring] **1.** A contest or conflict; specifically, the dramatic conflict between the chief characters in a Greek play. In particular, in Attic comedy, debate or contest between two characters, constituting one of several formal conventions of OLD COMEDY. **2.** The struggle between protagonist and antagonist in a literary work.

agonist \'ag-ə-nist\ [Greek *agōnistḗs* contestant, combatant] A leading character (such as the PROTAGONIST or ANTAGONIST) in a literary work.

aisling \'ash-liŋ\ *plural* aislings *or* aislingi \ash-'liŋ-ē\ [Irish, vision, description of a vision] In Irish literature, a poetical or dramatic description or representation of a vision. *The Vision of Adamnán* is one of the best-known examples. In the 18th century the aisling became popular as a means of expressing support for the exiled Roman Catholic king James II of England and Ireland and for the restoration of the Roman Catholic Stuart line to the throne.

aition \'ī-tē-ˌän\ *plural* aitia \-tē-ə\ *or* aitions [Greek *aítion* cause] A tale devised to explain the origin of a religious observance.

Akutagawa Prize \ä-ˌkü-tä-'gä-wä\ Japanese literary prize awarded semiannually for the best serious work of fiction by a promising new Japanese writer. Called in Japanese the Akutagawa Ryūnosuke Shō, it is generally considered, along with the Naoki Prize, Japan's most prestigious and sought-after literary award. Short stories or novellas win the prize more frequently than do full-length novels.

The Akutagawa Prize was established in 1935 by the writer Kikuchi Kan to honor the memory of his friend and colleague, Akutagawa Ryūnosuke, an esteemed writer who had committed suicide in 1927. The prize was awarded from 1935 to 1944 and again from 1949.

alarums and excursions \ə-'lar-əmz, -'lär- . . . ik-'skər-zhənz\ Martial sounds and the movement of soldiers across the stage—used as a stage direction in Elizabethan drama.

alba \'äl-bä\ [Old Provençal, literally, dawn] A Provençal song of lament for lovers parting at dawn or of a watchman's warning to lovers at dawn. Albas were sung by the 11th- and 12th-century troubadours. Some sources consider it an early form of an aubade, though unlike the alba, an aubade is usually a celebration of the dawn. Examples of albas for which music also survives include "Reis glorios" by Guiraut de Bornelh and the anonymous "Gaite de la tor." The minnesingers, German counterparts of the troubadours, also used the form, calling it TAGELIED.

alcaic \al-'kā-ik\ Classical Greek poetic stanza composed of four lines of varied metrical feet, with five long syllables in each of the first two lines, four in the third and fourth lines, and an unaccented syllable at the beginning of the first three lines (anacrusis). The Greek alcaic stanza is scanned:

⏓ | – ⏑ | – ⏓ | – ⏑ ⏑ | – ⏑ | –
⏓ | – ⏑ | – ⏓ | – ⏑ ⏑ | – ⏑ | –
⏓ | – ⏑ | – ⏓ | – ⏑ | – ⏓
– ⏑ ⏑ | – ⏑ ⏑ | – ⏑ | – ⏓ .

Named for and perhaps invented by the poet Alcaeus, the alcaic became an important Latin verse form, especially in the *Odes* of Horace. Variations on the traditional alcaic include the use of a long initial syllable and of a spondee (– –) in the first complete foot of the first three lines.

Alcaics were adapted to English and French verse during the Renaissance and later appeared in works such as Alfred, Lord Tennyson's "Milton."

Alcmanian \alk-'mā-nē-ən\ In poetry, a metrical line named for the Greek poet Alcman. It consists of four dactyls and is scanned: – ⏑ ⏑ | – ⏑ ⏑ | – ⏑ ⏑ | – ⏑ ⏑ .

Alexander romance \ˌal-ig-'zan-dər\ Any of a body of legends about the career of Alexander the Great, told and retold with varying emphasis and purpose by succeeding ages and civilizations.

The chief source of all Alexander romance literature was a folk epic written in Greek by a Hellenized Egyptian in Alexandria during the 2nd century AD. Surviving translations and copies make its reconstruction possible. It portrayed Alexander as a national messianic hero, the natural son of an Egyptian wizard-king by the wife of Philip II of Macedon. Magic and marvels played a subsidiary part in the epic—in the story of Alexander's birth, for example, and in his meeting with the Amazons in India. In later romances, however, marvels and exotic anecdotes predominated and gradually eclipsed the historical personality. Minor episodes in the original were filled out, often through "letters" supposedly written by or to Alexander, and an independent legend about his capture of the wild peoples of Gog and Magog was incorporated into the text of many vernacular versions. An account of the Alexander legends was included in a 9th-century Old English translation of Orosius' history of the world. In the 11th century a Middle Irish Alexander romance appeared, and about 1100, the Middle High German *Annolied.* During the 12th century, Alexander appeared as a pattern of knightly chivalry in a succession of great poems, beginning with the *Roman d'Alexandre* by Albéric de Briançon. This work inspired the *Alexanderlied* by the German poet Lamprecht der Pfaffe. An Anglo-Norman poet, Thomas of Kent, wrote the *Roman de toute chevalerie* toward the end of the 12th century, and about 1275 this was remodeled to become the Middle English romance *King Alisaunder.* Italian Alexander romances began to appear during the 14th century, closely followed by versions in Swedish, Danish, Scots, and (dating from a little earlier) in the Slavic languages.

Meanwhile, Latin accounts of Alexander's legendary deeds had continued to appear, including the "letter about marvels" supposedly written by Alexander to his old tutor, Aristotle. New legends also came into being, such as one in the 12th century about Alexander's "journey to Paradise."

Eastern accounts of Alexander's fabled career paid a good deal of attention to the Gog and Magog episode, a version of this story being included in the *Qurʿān.* The Arabs, expanding Syrian versions of the legend, passed them on to the many peoples with whom they came in contact. Through them, the Persian poets, notably Neẓāmī in the 12th century, gave the stories new form. Alexander romance literature declined in the late 12th century, and, with the revival of classical scholarship during the Renaissance, historical accounts displaced it entirely.

Alexandrian \ˌal-ig-ˈzan-drē-ən\ **1.** Of, relating to, or resembling the Alexandrian school, the school of Greek literature, especially poetry, that flourished in Alexandria during the 4th century BC. **2.** In reference to a writer or literary work, overly recondite, derivative, or artificial. Also, concerned primarily with the technical perfection of language or literary form.

alexandrine \ˌal-ig-ˈzan-ˌdrēn, -drən, -ˌdrīn\ [French *alexandrin* of or pertaining to the alexandrine, from Middle French] A line of 12 syllables with a caesura, or pause, after the sixth syllable and with major stresses on the sixth and on the last syllable and one secondary accent in each half line. Because six syllables is a normal breath group and the secondary stresses can be on any other syllables in the line, the alexandrine is a flexible form, adaptable to a wide range of subjects. Its structural metrical principle is stress according to sense; the form thus lends itself to the expression of simple or complex emotions, narrative description, or grandiose patriotic sentiment. It is the most popular measure in French poetry.

The name alexandrine is probably derived from the early use of the verse in the French *Roman d'Alexandre,* a collection of romances compiled in the 12th century about the adventures of Alexander the Great. Revived in the 16th century by the poets of La Pléiade, especially Pierre de Ronsard, the alexandrine became, in the following century, the preeminent French verse form for dramatic and narrative poetry and reached its highest development in the classical tragedies of Pierre Corneille and Jean Racine. In the late 19th century, a loosening of structure occurred, notably in the work of Paul Verlaine; poets often wrote a modified alexandrine, a three-part line known as *vers romantique,* or *trimètre.*

In English versification, the alexandrine, also called iambic hexameter, contains six primary accents rather than the two major and two secondary accents of the French. Though it was introduced to England in the 16th century and was adapted to German and Dutch poetry in the 17th century, its use outside France has been limited.

Algonquin Round Table \al-ˈgän-kwən, -ˈgäŋ-\, *also called* The Round Table. Informal group of American literary men and women who met daily for lunch on weekdays at a large round table in the Algonquin Hotel in New York City during the 1920s and '30s. The Algonquin Round Table began meeting in 1919, and within a few years its participants included many of the best-known writers, journalists, and artists in New York City. Among them were Dorothy Parker, Alexander Woollcott, Heywood Broun, Robert Benchley, Robert Sherwood, George S. Kaufman, Franklin P. Adams, Marc Connelly, Harold Ross, Harpo Marx, Edna Ferber, and Russel Crouse. The Round Table became celebrated in the 1920s for its members' lively, witty conversation and urbane sophistication. After 1925, many of them were closely associated with *The New Yorker,* whose editorial offices were established on the same block. Its members gradually went their separate ways, however, and the last meeting of the Round Table took place in 1943.

alienation effect or **a-effect** \ˈā-i-ˌfekt\, *also called* distancing effect, *German* Verfremdungseffekt \fer-ˈfrem-du̇ŋks-e-ˌfekt\ *or* V-Effekt \ˈfau̇-e-ˌfekt\ Idea central to the dramatic theory of the German dramatist-director Bertolt Brecht. It involves the use of techniques designed to distance the audience from the action of the play and to provoke the audience's awareness that it is watching a performance.

Examples of such techniques include explanatory captions or illustrations projected on a screen; actors disengaging themselves from the scene to summarize, lecture, or sing songs; and stage designs that do not represent any locality but that, by exposing the lights and ropes, keep the spectators aware of being in a theater. The audience's degree of identification with characters and events is controlled, therefore, and it can more clearly perceive the "real" world reflected in the drama.

allegory \ˈal-ə-ˌgȯr-ē\ [Greek *allēgoría,* a derivative of *allēgoreîn* to speak figuratively, from *állos* other + *-ēgorein* to speak] A more or less symbolic fictional narrative that conveys a secondary meaning (or meanings) not explicitly set forth in the literal narrative. It encompasses such forms as fable, parable, and apologue and may involve either a literary or an interpretive process.

Literary allegories typically express situations, events, or abstract ideas in terms of material objects, persons, and actions or interactions. Such early writers as Plato, Cicero, Apuleius, and Augustine made use of allegory, but it became especially popular in sustained narratives of the Middle Ages. Probably the most influential allegory of that period is the *Roman de la Rose* (*Romance of the Rose*). The poem, a DREAM VISION, illustrates the allegorical technique of personification (in which a fictional character—in this case, for example, The Lover—transparently represents a concept or a type). As in most allegories, the action of the narrative "stands for" something not explicitly stated. The Lover's eventual plucking of the crimson rose, for instance, represents his conquest of his lady. Other notable examples of personification allegory are John Bunyan's *The Pilgrim's Progress* and the medieval morality play *Everyman.* Their straightforward embodiments of aspects of human nature and abstract concepts, through such characters as Knowledge, Beauty, Strength, and Death in *Everyman* and such places as Vanity Fair and the Slough of Despond in *The Pilgrim's Progress,* are typical examples of the techniques of personification allegory.

Another variant is the symbolic allegory, in which a character or material thing is not merely a transparent vehicle for an idea, but rather has a recognizable identity or a narrative autonomy apart from the message it conveys. In Dante's *Divine Comedy,* for example, the character Virgil represents both the historical author of *The Aeneid* and the human faculty of reason, the character Beatrice both the historical woman of Dante's acquaintance and the concept of divine revelation. Ranging from the simple fable to the complex, multilayered narrative, the symbolic allegory has frequently been used to represent political and historical situations and has long been popular as a vehicle for satire. In the prologue of the 14th-century English poem *Piers Plowman,* for example, the author, using the story of the mice who were afraid to bell the cat, states his views on the House of Commons' unsuccessful attempt to curb John of Gaunt's depredations. In the verse satire *Absalom and Achitophel,* John Dryden relates in heroic couplets a scriptural story that is a thinly veiled portrait of the politicians involved in an attempt to alter the succession to the English throne. A modern example of political allegory is George Orwell's *Animal Farm* (1945), which, under the guise of a fable about domestic animals who take over a farm from their human oppressor, expresses the author's disillusionment with the outcome of the Bolshevik Revolution and shows how one tyrannical system of government in Russia was merely replaced by another.

Allegory may involve an interpretive process that is separate from the creative process; that is, the term allegory can refer to a specific method of reading a text, in which characters and narrative or descriptive details are taken by the reader as an elaborate metaphor for something outside the literal story. For example, the early Church Fathers sometimes used a threefold (later fourfold) method of interpreting texts, encompassing literal, moral, and spiritual meanings. One variety of such allegorical interpretation is the typological reading of the Old Testament, in which characters and events are seen as foreshadowing specific characters and events in the New Testament. *See also* FABLE; PARABLE.

alliteration \ə-ˌlit-ə-ˈrā-shən\, *also called* head rhyme [Latin *ad* to, toward + *littera* letter; probably modeled on Latin *oblitteratio, obliteratio* effacement, obliteration, falsely taken to be a derivative of *littera*] In prosody, the repetition of consonant sounds in two or more neighboring words or syllables. In the most common form of alliteration, the initial sounds are the same, thus the alternate name head rhyme. As a poetic device, alliteration is often discussed with assonance and consonance.

Alliteration is found in many common phrases, such as "pretty as a picture" and "dead as a doornail." In its simplest form, it reinforces one or two consonantal sounds, as in this line from William Shakespeare's Sonnet XII:

> When I do count the clock that tells the time

A more complex pattern of alliteration is created when consonants both at the beginning of words and at the beginning of stressed syllables within words are repeated, as in the following line from Percy Bysshe Shelley's "Stanzas Written in Dejection Near Naples":

> The *C*ity's voice it*s*elf is *s*oft like *S*olitude's

Compare ASSONANCE; CONSONANCE.

alliterative prose \ə-ˈlit-ər-ə-tiv\ Prose that uses alliteration and some of the techniques of alliterative verse. Notable examples are from Old English and Middle English, including works by the Anglo-Saxon writer Aelfric and the so-called Katherine Group of five Middle English devotional works.

alliterative verse Early, usually unrhymed verse of the Germanic languages in which alliteration, the repetition of consonant sounds at the beginning of words or stressed syllables, is a basic structural principle rather than an occasional embellishment. Although alliteration is a common device in almost all poetry, the only Indo-European languages that used it as a governing principle, along with strict rules of accent and quantity, were Old Norse, Old English, Old Saxon, and Old High German. The Germanic alliterative line consists of two hemistichs (half lines) separated by a caesura (pause). There are one or two alliterating letters in the first half line preceding the medial caesura; these also alliterate with the first stressed syllable in the second half line. Alliteration falls on accented syllables; unaccented syllables are not effective, even if they begin with the alliterating letter.

The introduction of rhyme, derived from medieval Latin hymns, contributed to the decline of alliterative verse. In Low German, pure alliterative verse is not known to have survived after 900; and, in Old High German, rhymed verse was by that time already replacing it. In England, alliteration as a strict structural principle is not found after 1066 (the date of the Norman Conquest of Britain) except in the western part of the country. Although alliteration continued to be an important element, the alliterative line became freer: the second half line often contained more than one alliterating word, and other formalistic restrictions were gradually disregarded.

England experienced a period known as the Alliterative Revival in the late 14th century, when a series of alliterative poems appeared. These verses were freer in form than earlier alliterative verse, and such works as *Piers Plowman, Sir Gawayne and the Grene Knight,* and *Pearl* use end rhyme extensively. In these works, sometimes all the verses rhyme and sometimes the succession of alliterative verses is broken by rhymed verses grouped at roughly regular intervals. The last alliterative poem in English is usually held to be "Scottish Fielde," which deals with the Battle of Flodden in 1513.

Later Norse poets (after 900) also combined many forms of rhyme and assonance with alliteration in a variety of stanzaic forms. After 1000, Old Norse alliterative verse became practically confined to the Icelanders, among whom it continues to exist. In Celtic poetry, alliteration was from the earliest times an important, but subordinate, principle. In Welsh poetry, it gave rise to the verse form known as CYNGHANEDD.

alloeostropha \ˌal-ē-ˈäs-trə-fə\ [Greek *alloióstrophos* having irregular strophes, from *alloîos* of another sort + *strophḗ* strophe] Irregular strophes or stanzas. The term was used by John Milton to describe the irregular stanzas or strophes of the choric odes in his *Samson Agonistes.*

allonym \ˈal-ə-ˌnim\ [French *allonyme,* from Greek *állos* other + *ónyma* name] **1.** A name that is assumed by an author but that actually belongs to another person. **2.** A work published under the name of a person other than the author.

allusion \ə-ˈlü-zhən\ [Late Latin *allusio* play on words, game, a derivative of Latin *alludere* to play around, refer to mockingly, from *ad* to + *ludere* to play] In literature, an implied or indirect reference to a person, event, thing, or a part of another text. Allusion is distinguished from such devices as direct quote and imitation or parody. Most are based on the assumption that there is a body of knowledge that is shared by the author and the reader and that therefore the reader will understand the author's referent. Allusions to biblical figures and figures from classical mythology are common in Western literature for this reason. However, some authors, such as T.S. Eliot and James Joyce, deliberately use obscure and complex allusions that they know few people will understand. Similarly, an allusion can be used as a straightforward device to enhance the text by providing further meaning, but it can also be used in a more complex sense to make an ironic comment on one thing by comparing it to something that is dissimilar.

almanac \'ȯl-mə-ˌnak, 'al-\ [Medieval Latin *almanach,* from Spanish Arabic *al-manākh* the calendar] Book or table containing such items as a calendar of the days, weeks, and months of the year; a register of ecclesiastical festivals and saints' days; and a record of various astronomical phenomena, often with weather prognostications and seasonal suggestions for farmers.

Almanacs have appeared in one form or another since the beginnings of astronomy. The first printed almanac appeared in the mid-15th century, and in 1533 the French writer François Rabelais published his *Pantagrueline Prognostication,* a parody of the astrological predictions of the almanacs that were exercising a growing hold on the Renaissance mind.

The first standard almanacs were issued at Oxford. The most famous of these early English almanacs was the *Vox Stellarum* of Francis Moore, the first number of which was completed in July 1700 and contained predictions for 1701.

The first American almanacs were printed in Cambridge, Mass., under the supervision of Harvard College. Benjamin Franklin's brother James printed *The Rhode Island Almanac* in 1728, and Benjamin Franklin himself (under the nom de plume Richard Saunders) began his *Poor Richard's* almanacs, the most famous of American almanacs, in Philadelphia in 1733.

The 18th-century almanac was the forerunner of the modern magazine. It enabled the farmer to tell the time of day and to estimate the proper season for various farm chores. It also furnished much instructive and entertaining incidental information and was greatly appreciated where reading matter was scarce. A particular popular version was the *Farmer's Almanac,* later called *Old Farmer's Almanac.*

a lo divino \ˌä-lō-dē-'b̠ē-nō\ A Spanish phrase meaning literally "in the sacred style" or "in sacred terms" that in Spanish literature alludes to the recasting of a secular work as a religious work, or more generally to a treatment of a secular theme in religious terms through the use of allegory, symbolism, and metaphor. Adaptations *a lo divino* were popular during the Golden Age of Spanish literature in the 16th and 17th centuries.

alphabet rhyme \'al-fə-ˌbet\ Mnemonic verse or song used to help children learn an alphabet; such devices appear in almost every alphabetic language. Early English favorites are about 300 years old and have served as models for countless variations. One is a cumulative rhyme to which there is a printed reference as early as 1671. It often appeared in 18th-century chapbooks under the imposing name *The Tragical Death of A, Apple Pye Who was Cut in Pieces and Eat by Twenty-Five Gentlemen with whom All Little People Ought to be Very well acquainted.* It begins:

> A was an apple-pie;
> B bit it,
> C cut it,
> D dealt it, etc.

Another, known as "Tom Thumb's Alphabet," enjoyed continuous popularity. The earliest printed record of it dates to roughly 1712. In its most familiar version, the rhyme begins:

> A was an archer, who shot at a frog.
> B was a butcher, and had a great dog.

These early rhymes showed little discrimination in subject matter. Lines such as "D was a drunkard, and had a red face," "U was a Usurer took Ten per Cent," or "Y was a youth, that did not love school" were later considered to have a harmful effect on children; they were replaced by the widely taught alphabet rhyme of the 17th-century *New-England Primer,* which combined moral messages with the learning of letters:

> In Adam's fall
> We sinned all.

A simplified version of English alphabet rhyme that is popular today is one in which the alphabet is sung to the tune of "Twinkle, Twinkle, Little Star":

> A B C D E F G
> H I J K L M N O P
> Q and R and S and T
> U V W X Y Z
> Now I've said my ABC's,
> Tell me what you think of me.

altar poem *See* PATTERN POETRY.

Āḷvār \'äl-ˌvär, 'al-\ [Tamil *āṛvār,* a derivative of *āṛ-* to sink, be immersed] Any of a group of South Indian mystics who in the 7th to 10th century wandered from temple to temple singing ecstatic hymns in adoration of the Hindu god Vishnu. The songs of the Āḷvārs rank among the world's greatest devotional literature. Among the followers of the Hindu god Śiva, the counterpart of the Āḷvārs were the Nāyaṉārs.

The name Āḷvār means, in the Tamil language in which they sang, "one who is immersed in meditation of God." Their *bhakti* (religious devotion) was of an intensely passionate kind; they compared the soul to a woman who yearns for her lord's love.

The hymns of the Āḷvārs, entitled *Nālāyira Prabandham* ("Collection of 4,000 Songs"), were gathered in the 10th century by Nāthamuni, a leader of the Śrīvaiṣṇava sect

a maiore or **a majore** \'ä-mä-'yō-rē, -rā\ [Latin, from the larger] Of or relating to an IONIC foot beginning with two long syllables.

ambiguity \ˌam-bə-'gyü-ə-tē\ Use of words that allow alternative interpretations. In factual, explanatory prose, ambiguity is considered an error in reasoning or diction; in literary prose or poetry, it often functions to increase the richness and subtlety of language and to imbue it with a complexity that expands the literal meaning of the original statement. William Empson's classic *Seven Types of Ambiguity* (1930; rev. ed., 1947 and 1953) remains a useful treatment of the subject.

American Academy of Arts and Letters *also called* (1904–92) The American Academy and Institute of Arts and Letters, *original name* National Institute of Arts and Letters. Organization founded 1898 whose stated purpose is to "foster, assist and sustain an interest" in literature, art, and music. The New York-based academy has 250 members.

The academy was the inspiration of H. Holbrook Curtis, a medical doctor, and Simeon E. Baldwin, a judge. After they had organized the original 250 members, they decided (perhaps with an eye to the Académie Française's 40 "Immortals") that they had not been exclusive enough; they renamed the 250-member body an institute and from among its members were elected the academy—an elite membership of 50. The first seven members, who were elected to the academy in 1904, were the writers William Dean Howells, Mark Twain, and Edmund C. Stedman, sculptor Augustus Saint-Gaudens, painter John LaFarge, composer Edward MacDowell, and historian-statesman John Hay. The first female member of the institute was Julia Ward Howe (author of "The Battle Hymn of the Republic"), who was elected to the institute in 1907 and to the academy in 1908. She was followed by Edith Wharton in 1926. In 1992 members voted to return to a single form of membership of 250, and the merger was announced in 1993. Membership in the academy is for life. One member, Wilhelm Diederich, was expelled in 1947 for using official stationery to write anti-Semitic letters.

Committees of the organization award to selected struggling artists any of several annual monetary gifts, including the Mildred and Harold Strauss Livings (to two distinguished prose writers for a period of five consecutive years).

American Mercury \ˈmer-kyə-rē\ American monthly literary magazine known for its often satiric commentary on American life, politics, and customs. It was founded in 1924 by H.L. Mencken and George Jean Nathan.

Under the editorship of Mencken, the periodical fast gained a reputation for Mencken's vitriolic articles directed at the American public (the "booboisie") and for Nathan's excellent theatrical criticism. Its fiction and other articles were the work of the most distinguished American authors and often the sharpest satiric minds of the day. Under Eugene Lyons, the American Mercury generated much of the pressure exerted on the U.S. Congress to vote for funding of air power at the beginning of World War II. Later, the magazine passed through the hands of several publishers and over a period of time developed a militant anticommunist stand and a strident right-wing tone.

American Poetry Review, The Literary periodical founded in 1972 in Philadelphia by Stephen Berg and Stephen Parker. Issued bimonthly in a newspaper tabloid format, *The APR* sought a mass-market readership for its high-quality contributors and content. From its first issue, *The APR* spoke to a politicized generation of young people that had emerged during the 1960s, and offered an eclectic collection of serious poetry and prose by outstanding English-language writers and critics as well as works in translation from Europe, the Middle East, Africa, Latin America, and Asia. Contributors included Richard Wilbur, David Ignatow, Allen Ginsberg, Denise Levertov, Tess Gallagher, Adrienne Rich, Marge Piercy, May Swenson, William Stafford, Ntozake Shange, John Updike, Isaac Bashevis Singer, Vladimir Nabokov, Elie Wiesel, Octavio Paz, Czesław Miłosz, and Roland Barthes.

American Renaissance *also called* New England Renaissance. Period from the 1830s roughly until the end of the American Civil War in which American literature, in the wake of the Romantic movement, came of age as an expression of a national spirit.

The literary scene of the period was dominated by a group of New England writers, the BRAHMINS, notably Henry Wadsworth Longfellow, Oliver Wendell Holmes, and James Russell Lowell. They were aristocrats, steeped in foreign culture, active as professors at Harvard College, and interested in creating an American literature based on foreign models. Longfellow adapted European methods of storytelling and versifying to narrative poems dealing with American history; Holmes, in his occasional poems and his "Breakfast Table" series (1858–91), brought touches of urbanity and jocosity to polite literature; and Lowell put much of his homeland's outlook and values into verse, especially in his satirical *Biglow Papers* (1848–67).

One of the most important influences in the period was that of TRANSCENDENTALISM. This movement, centered in the village of Concord, Mass., and including among its members Ralph Waldo Emerson, Henry David Thoreau, Bronson Alcott, George Ripley, and Margaret Fuller, contributed to the founding of a new national culture based on native elements. The Transcendentalists advocated reforms in church, state, and society, fostering the rise of Free Religion and the abolition movement and the formation of various utopian communities, such as Brook Farm. The abolition movement was also bolstered by other New England writers, including the Quaker poet John Greenleaf Whittier and the novelist Harriet Beecher Stowe, whose *Uncle Tom's Cabin* (1852) dramatized the plight of the black slave.

Apart from the Transcendentalists, there emerged during this period great imaginative writers—Nathaniel Hawthorne, Herman Melville, and Walt Whitman—whose novels and poetry left a permanent imprint on American literature. Contemporary with these writers but outside the New England circle was the Southern genius Edgar Allan Poe, who later in the century had a strong impact on European literature.

a minore \ˌä-mi-ˈnō-rē, mī-, -rā\ [Latin, from the lesser] In prosody, of or relating to an IONIC foot beginning with two short syllables.

amoebean verse \ˌam-ē-ˈbē-ən, ˌam-i-\ [Greek *amoibaîos* interchanging, reciprocating] Poetry written in the form of a dialogue between two speakers. *Compare* STICHOMYTHIA. An example is the English popular ballad *Lord Randal,* which begins:

"O where ha' you been, Lord Randal, my son?
And where ha' you been, my handsome young man?"
"I ha' been at the greenwood; mother, mak my bed soon,
For I'm wearied wi' huntin', and fain wad lie down."

amorist \ˈam-ər-ist\ or **amourist** \ˈam-ər-ist, ə-ˈmu̇r-\ [Latin *amor* or French *amour* love] One who writes about romantic love.

amour courtois [French] *See* COURTLY LOVE.

amphibology \ˌam-fə-ˈbäl-ə-jē\ or **amphiboly** \am-ˈfib-ə-lē\ [Greek *amphibolía* ambiguity, a derivative of *amphíbolos* doubtful, ambiguous] A sentence or phrase susceptible of more than one interpretation, such as "Nothing is good enough for you."

amphibrach \ˈam-fə-ˌbrak\ [Greek *amphíbrachys,* literally, short at both ends, from *amphi-* around, on both sides + *brachýs* short] In prosody, a three-syllable foot consisting in quantitative verse of a long syllable between two short syllables or in accentual verse of a stressed syllable between two unstressed syllables. An example of the amphibrach is:

∪ ′ ∪
amazement.

The inverse of this meter is the amphimacer.

amphigory \ˈam-fi-ˌgȯr-ē, am-ˈfig-ə-rē\ or **amphigouri** \ˌä^{n}-fē-gü-ˈrē\ *plural* amphigories *or* amphigouris [French *amphigouri*] A nonsense verse or parody (such as those written by Edward Lear and Lewis Carroll) or any composition that appears to have meaning, but proves to have none (such as Algernon Swinburne's "Nephelidia").

amphimacer \am-ˈfim-ə-sər\ [Greek *amphímakros,* from *amphí* on both sides of, around + *makrós* long] Outmoded term once interchangeable with CRETIC.

amplification \ˌam-pli-fi-ˈkā-shən\ [Latin *amplificatio* (translation of Greek *aúxēsis*), a derivative of *amplificare* to enlarge upon, emphasize, literally, to enlarge] A rhetorical device or figure of speech that extends or enlarges a statement or idea. The subject of amplification was a matter of concern for many of the ancient rhetoricians, including Aristotle, Quintilian, and Cicero. Well-suited to epic and tragic forms, amplification is a standard device in much great literature.

anachronism \ə-ˈnak-rə-ˌniz-əm\ [Medieval Greek *anachronismós,* from Greek *aná* back + *chrónos* time] Neglect or falsification, intentional or not, of chronological relation. It is most frequently found in works of imagination that rest on a historical basis, in which appear details borrowed from a later age; e.g., a clock in William Shakespeare's *Julius Caesar*.

Anachronisms abound in early literature. With the development of modern realism, the progress of archaeological research, and the scientific approach to history, unconscious anachronism became an offense. On the other hand, a writer may deliberately introduce anachronisms to achieve a burlesque, satirical, or other desired effect; such intentional use effectively points up contrasts between the past and the present. Thus Mark Twain in his satirical novel *A Connecticut Yankee in King Arthur's Court* used anachronism to contrast homespun American ingenuity with the superstitious ineptitude of a chivalric monarchy.

anaclasis \ə-ˈnak-lə-sis\ *plural* anaclases \-ˌsēz\ [Greek *anáklasis* act of bending back, reflection] In Greek prosody, an exchange of place between a short syllable and a preceding long one that is frequent in ionic rhythms.

anacoluthon \ˌan-ə-kə-ˈlü-ˌthän\ [Late Latin, from Greek, neuter of *anakólouthos* inconsistent, anomalous] Syntactical inconsistency or incoherence within a sentence; especially, a shift in an unfinished sentence from one syntactic construction to another (as in "you really ought—well, do it your own way").

anacreontic \ə-ˌnak-rē-ˈän-tik\ **1.** In Greek prosody, one of the aeolic meters used for lyric poetry. It originated with Anacreon. The basic unit of anacreontic verse was scanned as: ∪ ∪ – ∪ – ∪ – – . **2.** A poem in imitation of or in the manner of Anacreon; especially, a drinking song or light lyric. The best-known examples in English are those of Abraham Cowley and Thomas Moore.

anacrusis \ˌan-ə-ˈkrü-sis\ *plural* anacruses \-ˌsēz\ [Greek *anákrousis* act of pushing back, beginning of a tune] In classical prosody, the up (or weak) beat, one or more syllables at the beginning of a line of poetry that are not regarded as a part of the metrical pattern of that line. Some scholars do not acknowledge this phenomenon.

anadiplosis \ˌan-ə-di-ˈplō-sis\ *plural* anadiploses \-ˌsēz\ [Greek *anadíplōsis*, literally, doubling, repetition] A device in which the last word or phrase of one clause, sentence, or line is repeated at the beginning of the next. An example is the phrase that is repeated between stanzas one and two of John Keats' poem "The Eve of St. Agnes":

> Numb were the beadsman's fingers, while he told
> His rosary, and while his frosted breath,
> Like pious incense from a censer old,
> Seem'd taking flight for heaven, without a death,
> Past the sweet Virgin's picture, while his prayer he saith.
>
> His prayer he saith, this patient, holy man:

anagnorisis \ˌan-əg-ˈnȯr-ə-sis\ [Greek *anagnṓrisis,* literally, recognition] In a literary work, the startling discovery that produces a change from ignorance to knowledge. Anagnorisis is discussed by Aristotle in the *Poetics* as an essential part of the plot of a tragedy, although it occurs in comedy, epic, and, at a later date, in the novel as well.

Anagnorisis usually involves revelation of the true identity of persons previously unknown, as when a father recognizes a stranger as his son, or vice versa. One of the finest examples occurs in Sophocles' *Oedipus the King* when a messenger reveals to Oedipus his true birth and Oedipus then recognizes his wife Jocasta as his mother, the man he slew at the crossroads as his father, and himself as the unnatural sinner who brought misfortune on Thebes. This recognition is the more artistically satisfying because it is accompanied by a PERIPETEIA ("reversal"), the shift in fortune from good to bad that moves on to the tragic catastrophe. An anagnorisis is not always accompanied by a peripeteia. In the *Odyssey,* for example, when Alcinous, ruler of Phaeacia, has his minstrel entertain a shipwrecked stranger with songs of the Trojan War, the stranger begins to weep and reveals himself as none other than Odysseus. Aristotle discusses several kinds of anagnorisis employed by dramatists. The simplest kind, used, as he says, "from poverty of wit," is recognition by scars, birthmarks, or tokens. More interesting are those that arise naturally from incidents of the plot.

anagram \ˈan-ə-ˌgram\ [Greek *anagrammatismós,* a derivative of *anagrammatízein* to transpose letters so as to form an anagram, from *aná* up + *grámma* letter] A word or phrase made by transposing the letters of another word or phrase, such as *calm* and *clam.* The construction of anagrams is of great antiquity. Their invention is often ascribed without authority to the Jews, probably because the later Hebrew writers, particularly the Kabbalists, were fond of them, asserting that "secret mysteries are woven in the numbers of letters." Anagrams were known to the Greeks and Romans, although known Latin examples of words of more than one syllable are nearly all imperfect. They were popular throughout Europe during the Middle Ages and later, particularly in France, where a certain Thomas Billon was appointed "anagrammatist to the king."

The making of anagrams was an exercise of many religious orders in the 16th and 17th centuries, and the angelical salutation "Ave Maria, gratia plena, Dominus tecum" ("Hail Mary, full of grace, the Lord is with thee") was a favorite base; it was transposed to hundreds of variations, such as, for example, "Virgo serena, pia, munda et immaculata" ("Virgin serene, holy, pure, and immaculate"). Some scientists of the 17th century—Galileo, Christiaan Huygens, and Robert Hooke, for example—embodied their discoveries in anagrams, while they were engaged in further verification, to keep others from claiming the credit.

The pseudonyms adopted by authors are often anagrams. In the 20th century, anagrams frequently were used in crossword puzzles, for both the clues and solutions.

analects \ˈan-ə-ˌlekts\ [Greek *análekta,* neuter plural of *análektos,* verbal adjective of *analégein* to gather up, collect] Selected miscellaneous written passages.

analogue or **analog** \ˈan-ə-ˌlȯg, -ˌläg\ [French *analogue,* from Greek *análogon,* neuter of *análogos* having a relationship, proportional] Something that is analogous or similar to something else. In literature the word refers to a story for which there is a counterpart or another version in other literatures. Several of the stories in Geoffrey Chaucer's *The Canterbury Tales* are versions of earlier tales that can be found in such sources as Giovanni Boccaccio's *Decameron* and John Gower's *Confessio amantis.* The French medieval beast fable *Roman de Renart* has analogues in several languages, including Flemish and German.

analytical bibliography *See* CRITICAL BIBLIOGRAPHY.

anamnesis \ˌan-am-ˈnē-sis\ [Greek *anámnēsis,* a derivative of *anamnē̆iskesthai* to recall, remember] A recalling to mind, or reminiscence. Anamnesis is often used as a narrative technique in fiction and poetry as well as in memoirs and autobiographies. A notable example is Marcel Proust's *Remembrance of Things Past.*

anapest \ˈan-ə-ˌpest\ or **anapaest** \ˈan-ə-ˌpēst\ [Greek *anápaistos,* literally, struck back (i.e., the reverse of a dactyl)] In verse, a metrical foot of three syllables, the first two being unstressed and the last being stressed (as in Edgar Allan Poe's " 'Tis the vault of thy lost Ulalume!") or the first two being short and the last being long (as in classical prosody).

First found in early Spartan marching songs, anapestic meters were widely used in Greek and Latin dramatic verse, especially for the entrance and exit of the chorus. (The classical anapest is scanned ∪ ∪ – ∪ ∪ – .) Lines composed primarily of anapestic feet, often with an additional unstressed syllable at the end of the first line, are much rarer in English verse. Because of its jog-trot rhythm, pure anapestic meter was originally used only in light or popular English verse, but after the 18th century it appeared in serious poetry. Byron used it effectively to convey a sense of excitement and galloping in "The Destruction of Sennacherib":

> ∪ ∪ ´ | ∪ ∪ ´ | ∪ ∪ ´ | ∪ ∪ ´
> The Assyr | ian came down | like a wolf | on the fold.
> ∪ ∪ ´ | ∪ ∪ ´ | ∪ ∪ ´ | ∪ ∪ ´
> And his co | horts were gleam | ing in pur | ple and gold.

In Algernon Charles Swinburne's "By the North Sea," however, anapestic trimeter conveys a more subdued effect:

> ∪ ∪ ´ | ∪ ∪ ´ | ∪ ∪ ´ | ∪
> And his hand | is not wea | ry of giv | ing.
> ∪ ∪ ´ | ∪ ∪ ´ | ∪ ∪ ´
> And the thirst | of her heart | is not fed.

anaphora \ə-'naf-ə-rə\ [Late Greek *anaphorá,* from Greek, the act of carrying back] Repetition of a word or words at the beginning of two or more successive clauses or verses especially for rhetorical or poetic effect.

An example of anaphora is the well-known passage from the Old Testament (Ecclesiastes 3:1–2) that begins:

> For everything there is a season, and a time
>   for every matter under heaven:
> a time to be born, and a time to die;
> a time to plant, and a time to pluck up
>   what is planted; . . .

Anaphora (sometimes called epanaphora) is used most effectively for emphasis in argumentative prose and sermons and in poetry, as in these lines from Shakespeare's *Hamlet:* "to die, to sleep / To sleep—perchance to dream." It is also used to great effect in such poetry as these lines from "My Cat Jeoffry" in *Jubilate Agno* written by an 18th-century English poet, Christopher Smart:

> For I will consider my Cat Jeoffry.
> For he is the servant of the Living God duly
>   and daily serving him.
> For at the first glance of the glory of God in the
>   East he worships in his way.
> For is this done by wreathing his body seven
>   times round with elegant quickness.
> For then he leaps up to catch the musk, which is
>   the blessing of God upon his prayer.

anastrophe \ə-'nas-trə-fē\ [Greek *anastrophḗ,* literally, turning back, upsetting] The deliberate inversion of the usual syntactical order of words for rhetorical effect. An example is the locution "I kid you not."

anatomy \ə-'nat-ə-mē\ [Greek *anatomḗ* dissection] A separating or dividing into parts for detailed examination, or an analysis. In literature the word has been applied to several well-known examinations of general topics, notably John Lyly's *Euphues: The Anatomy of Wit* and Robert Burton's *Anatomy of Melancholy.* The literary critic Northrop Frye, in his book *Anatomy of Criticism,* narrowed the definition of the word in literature to mean a work resembling a Menippean satire, or one in which a mass of information was brought to bear on the subject being satirized, usually a particular attitude or type of behavior.

anceps \'än-ˌcheps, 'an-ˌseps\ [Latin, equivocal, literally, facing in opposite directions] In classical prosody, a syllable in a metrical pattern that is of indeterminate length or duration, that is, one that can be either long or short. In scansion, anceps is indicated by the symbol ⏓ or × .

ancients and moderns Subject of a celebrated literary dispute that raged in France and England in the 17th century. The "ancients" maintained that the classical literature of Greece and Rome offered the only models for literary excellence; the "moderns" challenged the supremacy of the classical writers. The rise of modern science tempted some French intellectuals to assume that, if Descartes had surpassed ancient science, it might be possible to surpass other ancient arts. The first attacks on the ancients came from Cartesian circles in defense of some heroic poems by Jean Desmarets de Saint-Sorlin that were based on Christian rather than classical mythology. The dispute broke into a storm with the publication of Nicolas Boileau's *L'Art poétique* (1674), defining the case for the ancients and upholding the classical traditions of poetry. From then on, the quarrel became personal and vehement. Among the chief supporters of the moderns were Charles Perrault and Bernard de Fontenelle. Supporters of the ancients were Jean de La Fontaine and Jean de La Bruyère.

In England the quarrel continued until well into the first decade of the 18th century. In 1690 Sir William Temple's *Essay upon Ancient and Modern Learning* attacked the members of the Royal Society by rejecting the doctrine of progress and supporting the virtuosity and excellence of ancient learning. William Wotton responded to Temple's charges in his *Reflections upon Ancient and Modern Learning* (1694), which praised the moderns in most but not all branches of learning, conceding the superiority of the ancients in poetry, art, and oratory. The primary points of contention were then quickly clouded and confused, but eventually two main issues emerged: whether literature progressed from antiquity to the present as science did, and whether, if there was progress, it was linear or cyclical. These matters were seriously and vehemently discussed. Jonathan Swift, defending his patron Temple, satirized the conflict in his *Tale of a Tub* (1704) and, more importantly, in *The Battle of the Books* (1704). In 1726 Swift was to make an even more devastating attack on the Royal Society in *Gulliver's Travels,* Book III, "The Voyage to Laputa."

anecdote \'an-ik-ˌdōt\ [French, minor incident, anecdote, from Late Greek *Anékdota* (plural), title of the Byzantine historian Procopius' private history of Justinian's court, literally, unpublished things, from Greek *anékdotos* unpublished] A usually short narrative of an interesting, amusing, or biographical incident.

angry young man One of a group of young British writers of the mid-20th century whose works express the bitterness of the lower classes toward the established sociopolitical system and toward the mediocrity and hypocrisy of the middle and upper classes.

The trend that was evident in John Wain's novel *Hurry on Down* (1953) and in *Lucky Jim* (1954) by Kingsley Amis was crystallized in 1956 in the play *Look Back in Anger,* which became the representative work of the movement. When the play's 26-year-old author John Osborne was described in print as an "angry young man," the label was extended to all his contemporaries who expressed a rage at the persistence of class distinctions, a pride in their lower-class mannerisms, and a dislike for anything highbrow or "phoney." When Sir Laurence Olivier played the leading role in Osborne's second play, *The Entertainer* (1957), the angry young men were acknowledged as the dominant literary force of the decade, and they enjoyed outstanding commercial success.

Among the other writers embraced in the term are the novelists John Braine and Alan Sillitoe and the playwrights Bernard Kops and Arnold Wesker. A dominant literary force in the '50s, the movement had faded by the early 1960s.

anisometric \ˌan-ˌī-sō-ˈmet-rik\ Of verse, not having equal or corresponding poetic meters. An anisometric stanza is one composed of lines of unequal metrical length, as in William Wordsworth's "Ode: Intimations of Immortality," which begins:

> There was a time when meadow, grove, and stream,
> The earth, and every common sight,
> To me did seem
> Appareled in celestial light,
> The glory and the freshness of a dream.
> It is not now as it hath been of yore—
> Turn whereso'er I may,
> By night or day,
> The things which I have seen I now can see no more.

Compare ISOMETRIC.

annotation \ˌan-ō-ˈtā-shən\ A note added to a text by way of comment or explanation. Such a note can be added by the author or by the editor.

annual \ˈan-yü-wəl\ A publication that appears yearly. Examples include year-books and almanacs. In the early to mid-19th century a number of annual books under such titles as *The Gift* and *The Token* were published in the United States and England. They included poetry, stories, essays, and lavish illustrations by the foremost writers and illustrators of the day and were intended as giftbooks.

anonymuncule \ə-ˌnän-i-ˈməŋ-ˌkyül\ [blend of *anonymous* and *homuncule* little man, from Latin *homunculus*] An insignificant or petty anonymous writer.

Antaeus \an-ˈtē-əs\ Literary magazine founded by Paul Bowles and Daniel Halperin in 1970. It was first published in Tangier, Morocco; by its third issue (1971) Ecco Press, with offices in Tangier, London, and New York, was its publisher. Its contributing editors included William Burroughs, John Hawkes, W.S. Merwin, Muriel Rukeyser, and Tennessee Williams. Issues of the magazine often focused on particular genres or subdivisions of literature such as poetry and poetics, translation, British poetry, autobiography, and contemporary fiction. Occasionally it published long critical works, plays, and novellas. It also frequently published interviews and exchanges between leading international figures in the arts.

antagonist \an-ˈtag-ə-nist\ [Greek *antagōnístēs* opponent, rival, from *anti-* against + *agōnístēs* contestant] The principal opponent or foil of the main character in a drama or narrative. The main character is referred to as the PROTAGONIST.

antanaclasis \ˌan-tə-ˈnak-lə-sis\ [Greek *antanáklasis,* literally, reflection, echo] A word used in two or more of its possible meanings, as in the final two lines of Robert Frost's "Stopping by Woods on a Snowy Evening":

> The woods are lovely, dark, and deep,
> But I have promises to keep,
> And miles to go before I sleep,
> And miles to go before I sleep.

The first use of "sleep" refers to nocturnal rest, the second to death.

antepirrhema \ant-ˌep-ə-ˈrē-mə\ [Greek *antepírrhēma,* literally, counter-epirrhema] In ancient Greek Old Comedy, a continuation of an EPIRRHEMA following an antistrophe.

anthology \an-ˈthäl-ə-jē\ [Medieval Greek *anthología,* literally, gathering of flowers] A selection of literary, musical, or artistic works or parts of works.

One of the first major anthologies of literature was the *Anthologia Hellēnikē* ("Greek Anthology"), a renowned collection of Greek prose and poetry. The authors represented date from about 700 BC to AD 1000 and were edited variously from the 1st to the 11th centuries. Another early anthology was the *Shi jing* ("Classic of Poetry"), a collection of Chinese poetry compiled by Confucius (551–479 BC).

The first anthologies of English literature appeared in the 16th century. Among these was *Songes and Sonettes, Written by the Ryght Honorable Lorde Henry Howard Late Earle of Surrey and Other* (1557; usually known as *Tottel's Miscellany*), which first made lyric poetry available to the public. Later influential anthologies include Thomas Percy's *Reliques of Ancient English Poetry* (1765); *Des Knaben Wunderhorn* (1805–08; "The Boy's Magic Horn"), an anthology of German folk songs compiled by Clemens Brentano and Achim von Arnim; Arthur Quiller-Couch's *The Oxford Book of English Verse 1250–1900* (1900); and Francis J. Child's *The English and Scottish Popular Ballads* (1882–98).

anthropomorphism \ˌan-thrə-pə-ˈmȯr-ˌfiz-əm\ [Greek *anthrōpómorphos* of human form, from *ánthrōpos* human being + morphḗ form, shape] An interpretation of what is not human or personal in terms of human or personal characteristics; thus, the Greeks' anthropomorphisms of many of their deities.

antibacchius \ˌan-tē-bə-ˈkī-əs, ˌan-tī-\ *plural* antibacchii \-bə-ˈkī-ˌī\ A metrical foot of three syllables. In classical, particularly Latin, prosody, the first two syllables are long and the last is short (– – ∪); this foot is not used in itself as the basis for any rhythm, but rather as a variant of the bacchius. In accentual or modern prosody, the first two syllables have either primary or intermediate stress and the last is unstressed. A modern antibacchius is scanned ′ ′ ∪ . *Compare* BACCHIUS.

anticlimax \ˌan-tē-ˈklī-ˌmaks, ˌan-ˌtī-\ A figure of speech that consists of the usually sudden transition in discourse from a significant idea to a trivial or ludicrous idea. Alexander Pope's *The Rape of the Lock* uses anticlimax liberally; an example is "Here thou, great Anna, whom three realms obey,/Dost sometimes counsel take, and sometimes tea."

antihero \ˈan-tē-ˌhir-ō, ˈan-ˌtī-, -ˌhē-rō\, *also called* nonhero \ˌnän-ˈhir-ō, -ˈhē-rō\ A protagonist of a drama or narrative who is notably lacking in heroic qualities. This type of character has appeared in literature since the time of the Greek dramatists and can be found in the literary works of all nations. Examples include the title characters of Miguel de Cervantes' *Don Quixote* (Part I, 1605; Part II, 1615) and Henry Fielding's *Tom Jones* (1749). Some examples of the modern, postwar antihero, as defined by the "angry young man" generation of writers, include Joe Lampton, in John Braine's *Room at the Top* (1957), and Arthur Seaton, in Alan Sillitoe's *Saturday Night and Sunday Morning* (1958). *See also* PROTAGONIST.

antiheroine \ˌan-ˌtī-ˈher-ə-win, ˌan-tē-, -ˈhir-\ A female antihero.

antimetabole \ˌan-ˌtī-mə-ˈtab-ə-lē, ˌan-tē-\ [Greek *antimetabolḗ,* from *anti-* counter-, opposite + *metabolḗ* change] A type of chiasmus in which the repetition of two or more words in reverse order in successive clauses, as in Quintilian: "non ut edam vivo sed ut vivam edo" ("I do not live to eat but eat to live").

antinovel \ˈan-tē-ˌnäv-əl, ˈan-tī-\ [translation of French *anti-roman*] Type of avant-garde novel that marks a radical departure from the conventions of the traditional novel in that it is a work of the fictional imagination which ignores such traditional elements or properties as plot, dialogue, and human interest. In their efforts to overcome literary habits and to challenge the expectations of their readers, authors of such works deliberately frustrate conventional literary expectations, avoiding any intrusion of the author's personality, preferences, or values.

The term *antinovel* was first used by Jean-Paul Sartre in an introduction to *Portrait d'un inconnu* (1948; *Portrait of a Man Unknown*) by Nathalie Sarraute. It has also been applied to works by Claude Simon, Alain Robbe-Grillet, and Michel Butor and therefore is usually associated with the French NOUVEAU ROMAN of the 1950s and '60s. Though the word is of recent coinage, this approach to novel writing is at least as old as the work of Laurence Sterne (in whom French novelists have always been interested), as well as in the works of Virginia Woolf, James Joyce, and Samuel Beckett. Works of the same period as the *nouveau roman* but in other languages, such as *Mutmassungen über Jakob* (1959; *Speculations About Jakob*) by the German novelist Uwe Johnson and *Connecting Door* (1962) by the British author Rayner Heppenstall, also contain many of the characteristics of the antinovel—vaguely identified characters, casual arrangement of events, and ambiguity of meaning.

antiphrasis \an-'tif-rə-sis\ *plural* antiphrases \-ˌsēz\ [Greek *antíphrasis* the substitution of words with positive meaning for those with negative associations, from *anti-* against, opposite + *phrásis* way of speaking, diction] The usually ironic or humorous use of words in senses opposite to the generally accepted meanings (as in "this giant of three feet four inches").

antispast \'an-tē-ˌspast\ [Greek *antíspastos,* literally, drawn in the contrary direction] In classical prosody, the sequence ∪ – – ∪ is not itself used as the basis for any rhythm. In modern, accentual prosody, a metrical foot or system of four syllables in which an iamb (one unstressed and one stressed syllable) is followed by a trochee (one stressed and one unstressed syllable), scanned ∪ ˊ ˊ ∪.

antistrophe \an-'tis-trə-fē\ In Greek lyric odes, the second part of the traditional three-part structure. The antistrophe followed the strophe and preceded the epode. In the choral odes of Greek drama each of these parts corresponded to a specific movement of the chorus as it performed that part. During the strophe the chorus moved from right to left on the stage; during the antistrophe they reversed their movement and moved from left to right.

antithesis \an-'tith-ə-sis\ [Greek *antíthesis,* literally, opposition] A rhetorical device in which irreconcilable opposites or strongly contrasting ideas are placed in sharp juxtaposition and sustained tension, as in the phrase "they promised freedom and provided slavery."

The opposing clauses, phrases, or sentences are often roughly equal in length and balanced in parallel grammatical structures, as in the following from Abraham Lincoln's "Gettysburg Address":

> The world will little note nor long remember what we say here, but it can never forget what they did here.

In poetry, the effect of antithesis is often one of tragic irony or reversal, as in the anonymous "Bonnie George Campbell":

> Saddled and bridled
>   And booted rade he;
> A plume in his helmet,
>   A sword at his knee;
> But toom [empty] cam' his saddle
>   A' bloody to see,
> O hame cam' his gude horse
>   But never cam' he!

anti-utopia \ˈan-ˌtī-yü-ˈtō-pē-ə, ˈan-tē-\ A literary work describing an imaginary place where people lead dehumanized and often fearful lives. *See also* UTOPIA.

antonomasia \an-ˌtän-ə-ˈmā-zhē-ə\ [Greek *antonomasía,* a derivative of *antonomázein* to call by a new name, from *anti-* against, in place of + *onomázein* to name] A figure of speech in which some defining word or phrase is substituted for a person's proper name (for example, "the Bard of Avon" for William Shakespeare). In fiction, the practice of giving to a character a proper name that defines or suggests a leading quality of that character (such as Squire *Allworthy,* Doctor *Sawbones*) is also called antonomasia.

aphaeresis or **apheresis** \ə-ˈfer-ə-sis\ [Greek *aphaíresis,* literally, taking away, removal] The loss of one or more sounds or letters at the beginning of a word (such as in *round* for *around* or *coon* for *raccoon*). *Compare* APOCOPE.

aphorism \ˈaf-ə-ˌriz-əm\ [Greek *aphorismós* distinction, determination, pithy statement, a derivative of *aphorízein* to mark off, distinguish, determine] **1.** A concise statement of a principle. **2.** A terse formulation of any generally accepted truth or sentiment conveyed in a pithy, memorable statement. It is a synonym for ADAGE.

Aphorisms have been used especially in dealing with subjects for which principles and methodology developed relatively late—for example, art, agriculture, medicine, jurisprudence, and politics. The term was first used in the *Aphorisms* of Hippocrates, a long series of propositions concerning the symptoms and diagnosis of disease and the art of healing and medicine. The first aphorism, which serves as a kind of introduction to the book, runs as follows: "Life is short, Art long, Occasion sudden and dangerous, Experience deceitful, and Judgment difficult. Neither is it sufficient that the physician be ready to act what is necessary to be done by him, but the sick, and the attendants and all outward necessaries must be lightly prepared and fitted for the business."

The word gradually came to be used for the principles of other fields and finally for any statement generally accepted as true, so that it is now roughly synonymous with maxim. The poet W.H. Auden coedited *The Faber Book of Aphorisms* in 1962, and other such collections have been published since then.

apocalyptic literature \ə-ˌpäk-ə-ˈlip-tik\ Literature that expounds a prophetic revelation and especially that predicts the destruction of the world.

The term is sometimes applied specifically to a literary genre that flourished from about 200 BC to about AD 200, especially in Judaism and Christianity. Written primarily to give hope to religious groups undergoing persecution or cultural upheaval, apocalyptic works described in cryptic language interpreted by believers the sudden, dramatic intervention of God in history on behalf of the faithful elect. They further detailed the cataclysmic events that would accompany or herald God's dramatic intervention in human affairs—such as a temporary rule of the world by Satan, signs in the heavens, persecutions, wars, famines, and plagues.

Although writers of these texts also examined the present to determine whether or not current afflictions were fulfillments of past apocalyptic prophecies, they generally concentrated on the future—the overthrow of evil, the coming of a messianic figure, and the establishment of the Kingdom of God and of eternal peace and righteousness.

The Book of Daniel in the Old Testament and the Revelation to John in the New Testament represent apocalyptic writing, and several intertestamental books contain apocalyptic themes. These themes were revived in modern literature; in poetry, notably that of William Blake; in novels such as Mary Shelley's *The Last Man;* and in many works of science fiction.

apocope \ə-ˈpäk-ə-pē\ [Greek *apokopḗ,* literally, the act of cutting off, a derivative of *apokóptein* to cut off] The loss of one or more sounds or letters at the end of a word (as in *sing* from Old English *singen*). *See also* APHAERESIS.

apocrypha \ə-ˈpäk-rə-fə\ [Late Greek *apókryphos* secret, uncanonical, from Greek, hidden] **1.** *usually capitalized*; *also called* deuterocanonical \ˌdü-tə-rō-kə-ˈnä-ni-kəl, ˌdyü-\. Quasi-scriptural writings that are of doubtful authorship and authority but that are accepted as part of the canon, or approved list, of the books of some versions of the Bible, specifically the Septuagint and the Vulgate. These books are excluded from the Jewish and Protestant canons. **2.** Writings or statements of doubtful or spurious authorship. The word is used to refer to works that are attributed to an author but not accepted as part of the author's canon.

Apollon \ˌɔ-ˌpɔ-ˈlȯn\ ("Apollo") Leading Russian monthly magazine published from 1909 to 1917 in St. Petersburg. Founded by Sergey Makovsky, an art historian, and Nikolay Gumilyov, a poet, *Apollon* was dedicated to contemporary art, sculpture, poetry, and literature. Initially, the journal was associated with the Acmeist group of Russian poets, of which Gumilyov was a member. Because of this association, in its early years the magazine contained much analysis of Russian modernist literature. By 1912, however, it was primarily an art publication, featuring excellent reproductions as well as reviews of foreign and domestic avant-garde art.

Apollonian \ˌap-ə-ˈlō-nē-ən\ or **Apollonic** \ˌap-ə-ˈlän-ik\ or **Apollonistic** \ə-ˌpäl-ə-ˈnis-tik\ Of, relating to, or resembling the god Apollo. Friedrich Nietzsche used the term in his book *The Birth of Tragedy* to describe one of the two opposing tendencies or elements in Greek tragedy. According to Nietzsche, the Apollonian attributes are reason, culture, harmony, and restraint. These are opposed to the Dionysian characteristics of excess, irrationality, lack of discipline, and unbridled passion. The Apollonian and Dionysian coalesce to create the tragic story, with the Apollonian tendency represented by the dialogue and the Dionysian by the dithyrambic choruses. The drama's exhibition of the phenomena of suffering individuals (Apollonian elements) forces upon the audience "the struggle, the pain, the destruction of phenomena," which in turn communicates "the exuberant fertility of the universal." The spectators then "become, as it were, one with the infinite primordial joy in existence, and . . . we anticipate, in Dionysian ecstasy, the indestructibility and eternity of this joy." *See also* DITHYRAMB.

apologue \ˈap-ə-ˌlȯg\ [Greek *apólogos,* from *apó* from, off + *lógos* word] An allegorical narrative (such as a beast fable) that is usually intended to convey a moral.

apology \ə-ˈpäl-ə-jē\ [Greek *apología* speech in defense, from *apó* off, from + *lógos* word, speech] Autobiographical form in which a defense is the framework for a discussion by the author of his personal beliefs and viewpoints. An early example dating from the 4th century BC is Plato's *Apology,* in which Socrates answers the charges of his accusers by giving a brief history of his life and his moral commitment. Such an apology is usually a self-justification. Among the famous apologies of Western literature are *Apologie de Raimond Sebond* (1580), an essay by Montaigne, who uses a defense of the beliefs of a 15th-century Spaniard as a pretext for presenting his own views on the futility of reason; *An Apology for the Life of Mr. Colley Cibber, Comedian* (1740), in which the 18th-century English actor-manager answers his critic Alexander Pope with a summary of the achievements of his long career that is also one of the best theatrical histories of the period; and *Apologia pro Vita Sua* (1864; later retitled *History of My Religious Opinions*), in which John Henry Newman examines the religious principles that inspired his conversion to the Roman Catholic church.

apophthegm *See* APOTHEGM.

aposiopesis \ˌap-ō-ˌsī-ō-ˈpē-sis\ [Greek *aposiṓpēsis,* literally, the act of falling silent] In rhetoric, a speaker's deliberate failure to complete a sentence. Aposiopesis usually indicates speechless rage or exasperation, as in "Why, you . . . ," and sometimes implies vague threats, as in "Why, I'll . . . ." The listener is expected to complete the sentence silently and instinctively. In ancient Greek rhetoric, the aposiopesis occasionally takes the form of a pause before a change of subject or a digression.

apostrophe \ə-ˈpäs-trə-fē\ [Greek *apostrophḗ,* literally, a turning away] A rhetorical device by which a speaker turns from the audience as a whole to address a single person or thing. For example, in William Shakespeare's *Julius Caesar,* Mark Antony addresses the corpse of Caesar in the speech that begins:

> O, pardon me, thou bleeding piece of earth,
> That I am meek and gentle with these butchers!
> Thou art the ruins of the noblest man
> That ever lived in the tide of times.
> Woe to the hand that shed this costly blood!

Another example is in the first stanza of William Wordsworth's poem "Ode to Duty":

> Stern Daughter of the Voice of God!
> O Duty! if that name thou love
> Who are a light to guide, a rod
> To check the erring, and reprove;
> Thou, who art victory and law
> When empty terrors overawe;
> From vain temptations dost set free;
> And calm'st the weary strife of frail humanity!

apothegm or **apophthegm** \'ap-ə-ˌthem\ [Greek *apóphthegma,* a derivative of *apophthéngesthai* to speak out, speak one's opinion] A short, pithy, and instructive saying or formulation; an aphorism.

apparatus criticus \ˌap-ə-'rat-əs-'krit-ə-kəs, ˌap-ə-'rā-təs-\ [New Latin, critical apparatus] Supplementary data (including such additional materials as variant readings) that are provided as part of an edition of a text to be used as a basis for critical study.

applied criticism *See* PRACTICAL CRITICISM.

apposition A grammatical construction in which two usually adjacent nouns having the same referent stand in the same syntactical relation to the rest of a sentence. *The poet* and *Burns* are in apposition in "a biography of the poet Burns;" the word is also used to describe the relation of one of such a pair of nouns or noun equivalents to the other.

apprenticeship novel Biographical novel that concentrates on an individual's youth and his social and moral initiation into adulthood. The term derives from J.W. von Goethe's *Wilhelm Meisters Lehrjahre* (1795–96; *Wilhelm Meister's Apprenticeship*). It became a subgenre of the novel in German literature, where it is called BILDUNGSROMAN. Examples of the form in English include Charles Dickens' *David Copperfield* (1850) and Thomas Wolfe's *Look Homeward, Angel* (1929).

aptronym \'ap-trō-nim\ A name that fits some aspect of a character, as in Mr. Talkative and Mr. Worldly Wiseman in John Bunyan's *The Pilgrim's Progress,* or Mrs. Malaprop in Richard Brinsley Sheridan's play *The Rivals*. The term *aptronym* was allegedly coined by the American newspaper columnist Franklin P. Adams, by an anagrammatic reordering of the first letters of *patronym* (to suggest *apt*), to denote surnames that suited the occupation of the name's bearer (such as Baker for a baker).

arabesque \ˌar-ə-'besk\ [French, intricate ornament, from Italian *arabesco,* literally, ornament in the style of the Arabs] A contrived intricate pattern of verbal expression, so called by analogy with a decorative style in which flower, fruit, and sometimes animal outlines appear in elaborate patterns of interlaced lines. That these designs can sometimes suggest fantastic creatures may have given rise to another sense of the term, denoting a tale of wonder or of the supernatural. Nikolay Gogol used this sense of the word in his *Arabeski* (1835; *Arabesques*) five years before Edgar Allan Poe collected some of his tales under the title *Tales of the Grotesque and Arabesque*. Like those of Poe, Gogol's tales of hallucination, confusing reality and dream, are among his best stories ("Nevsky Prospect" and "Diary of a Madman," both 1835).

Arabic literary renaissance *Arabic* An-Naḥdah al-Adabīyah. Nineteenth-century movement aimed at creating a modern Arabic literature, inspired by contacts with the West and a renewed interest in the great classical Arabic literature.

After the Napoleonic invasion of Egypt (1798) and the subsequent establishment of an autonomous and Western-minded ruling dynasty there, many Syrian and Lebanese writers sought out the freer environment of Egypt, making it the center of the renaissance. Under the impact of the dismemberment of the Ottoman Empire after World War I and the coming of independence following World War II, the revival spread to other Arab countries.

The novel and drama, forms new to Arabic literature, were developed largely under the influence of the European works that became available in the 19th century in Arabic translation. Other genres, such as the short story, new verse forms, and the essay, owed much to Western models but had roots in classical Arabic literature.

That the renaissance succeeded in altering the direction of Arabic literature is probably attributable to two factors. The emergence of an Arabic press made writing a realistic livelihood and forced writers to abandon the traditional, ornate style of past centuries in favor of a simpler and more direct style that would appeal to a wider reading public. The spread and modernization of education further served to provide a body of readers receptive to new styles and ideas.

Arcadia \är-ˈkā-dē-ə\ or **Arcady** \ˈär-kə-dē\ *plural* Arcadias *or* Arcadies. An idealized region or scene of simple pleasure, rustic innocence, and uninterrupted quiet. The word was derived from the name of a pastoral region of ancient Greece that was represented as a rural paradise in Greek and Roman bucolic poetry. It was later used in the same sense in the literature of the Renaissance by such writers as the Italian poet Jacopo Sannazzaro and England's Sir Philip Sidney. Sidney's *Arcadia,* in its first version (written c. 1577–80), is a pastoral romance in which courtiers disguised as Amazons and shepherds make love and sing delicate experimental verses.

arcádia \ȧr-ˈkäj-ə\ Any of the 18th-century Portuguese literary societies that attempted to revive Portuguese poetry by urging a return to classicism. They were modeled after the Academy of ARCADIA, established in Rome in 1690 as an arbiter of Italian literary taste.

In 1756 António Dinis da Cruz e Silva established with others the Arcádia Lusitana, its first aim being the uprooting of *gongorismo,* a style studded with Baroque conceits and Spanish influence in general. Other prominent Arcadians included Pedro António Correia Garção, and Tomás Antônio Gonzaga, who is known for a collection of pastoral love lyrics written under the pseudonym Dirceu. Cruz e Silva's mock-heroic poem *O Hissope* (1768), about a battle between a bishop and another church official, was inspired by the French poet Nicolas Boileau's mock epic *Le Lutrin* (1674). Pedro António Correia Garção, the most prominent Arcadian, was an accomplished devotee of the Latin classical poet Horace. The bucolic verse of Dómingos dos Reis Quita signified a return to the native tradition of two centuries earlier. Sincerity and suffering spoke in the better-known *Marília de Dirceu,* pastoral love lyrics written by Tomás Antônio Gonzaga under the pseudonym Dirceu and published in three volumes (1792, 1799, 1812).

Cruz e Silva was sent to Brazil as a judge in 1776; there he helped stimulate Brazilian interest in the Arcadian movement, which flourished among the so-called Minas school of poets, including José Basílio da Gama and José de Santa Rita Durão.

In 1790 the New Arcadia was established. Its two most distinguished members were the rival poets Manuel Maria Barbosa du Bocage, who is now remembered for a few outstanding sonnets, and José Agostinho de Macedo, known for his experiments with the epic form. Curvo Semedo was another New Arcadian of merit.

Arcadia, Academy of \är-ˈkā-dē-ä\, *Italian* Accademia dell'Arcadia \äk-ä-ˈdā-myä-del-är-ˈkäd-yä\ Italian literary academy that was founded in Rome in 1690 to combat Marinism, the dominant Italian poetic style of the 17th century, named after Giambattista Marino. The Arcadians sought a more natural, simple poetic style based on the classics and particularly on Greek and Roman pastoral poetry.

The Academy of Arcadia was inspired by Queen Christina of Sweden, who, having given up her throne, gathered a literary circle in Rome. After Christina's death in 1689, her friends founded the academy to give their meetings permanence as they worked "to exterminate bad taste, and to see to it that it shall not rise again." They named the academy for Arcadia, a pastoral region of ancient Greece, and assumed Greek names themselves.

Among the founding members of the Academy of Arcadia were the classicist and critic Gian Vincenzo Gravina, Giovan Mario Crescimbeni, Giovan Battista Zappi, Alessandro Guidi, and Carlo Innocenzo Frugoni. Although most Arcadian poetry was rather pale and imitative, the academy had two outstanding writers in the 17th and 18th centuries: Paolo Rolli, who was particularly skilled in *canzonetti,* and Pietro Metastasio, one of the greatest lyricists and librettists in Italian literature. Gabriello Chiabrera, who experimented with metrical forms, was also an Arcadian, as were Gabriele Rossetti (the father of the English poets Dante Gabriel and Christina Rossetti) and Pope Leo XIII, an accomplished poet who wrote a poem for the academy's 200th anniversary.

The Academy of Arcadia was an important influence in the simplification of Italian poetry and inspired the establishment in Italy of many Arcadian colonies that did not have a specifically literary purpose but sought a return to a pastoral existence.

In 1925 the academy was made an academic and historical institute and was renamed the Accademia Letteraria Italiana.

Arcady *See* ARCADIA.

archaic \är-ˈkā-ik\ [Greek *archaïkós* old-fashioned] Of a writer or literary work, characterized by the intentional use of old-fashioned language.

archetypal criticism \ˌär-kə-ˈtī-pəl\ A form of literary criticism that is concerned with the discovery and analysis of the original pattern or model for themes, motifs, and characters in poetry and prose.

This approach to literature is based on the idea that narratives are structured in accordance with an underlying archetypal model: the specific plot and characters are important insofar as they allude to a traditional plot or figure or to patterns that have recurred with wide implications in human history. An archetypal critic, for example, on examining Katherine Anne Porter's story "Flowering Judas," would note that it echoes and ironically inverts the traditional Christian legend of Judas Iscariot.

Archetypal criticism was effectively founded with the publication of the multivolume work *The Golden Bough* by British anthropologist and folklorist J.G. Frazer. The theories of the psychologist Carl Jung also contributed to the underlying principles of such criticism. Other important works on the subject are *Archetypal Patterns in Poetry* (1934) by Maud Bodkin and Northrop Frye's *Anatomy of Criticism* (1957).

archetype \ˈär-kə-ˌtīp\ [Greek *archétypon* original pattern] A primordial image, character, or pattern of circumstances that recurs throughout literature and thought consistently enough to be considered universal. The term was adopted by literary critics from the writings of the psychologist Carl Jung, who formulated a theory of the collective unconscious. For Jung, the varieties of human experience have somehow been genetically coded and transferred to successive generations. Originating in pre-logical thought, these primordial image patterns and situations evoke startlingly similar feelings in both reader and author.

The laurel and olive branches, the snake, whale, eagle, and vulture all are archetypal symbols. An example of an archetypal theme in literature is that of initiation, the passage from innocence to experience; archetypal characters that recur in literature include the blood brother, rebel, wise grandparent, generous thief, duplicitous clergyman, and prostitute with a heart of gold.

archilochean \ˌär-kə-ˈlō-kē-ən\ In classical poetry, one of several different verse forms ascribed to the Greek poet Archilochus, including the greater archilochean (a line composed of a dactylic tetrapody followed by a trochaic tripody) and the lesser archilochean (a dactylic tripody catalectic). This line was the chief component of a larger metrical unit called the archilochean strophe. In its most frequent form this strophe consisted of six lines: a dactylic hexameter followed by a lesser archilochean, another dactylic hexameter followed by an iambelegus, and a greater archilochean followed by an iambic trimeter catalectic.

arch-poet \ˌärch-ˈpō-ət\ A chief poet.

arena theater *See* THEATER-IN-THE-ROUND.

aretalogy \ˌar-ə-ˈtal-ə-jē\ [Greek *aretalogía* celebration of miraculous deeds, from *aretaí* miraculous deeds, wonders + *légein* to say, speak] A narrative of the miraculous deeds of a god or hero.

argument \ˈär-gyə-mənt\ [Latin *argumentum*] **1.** *also called* argumentation A form of rhetorical expression that is intended to convince or persuade. **2.** An abstract or summary of a literary work. **3.** The subject matter or central idea of a literary work.

aristarch \ˈar-əs-ˌtärk\ A severe critic. The term is derived from the name of the Greek grammarian and critic Aristarchus, who was known for his harsh judgments.

aristophanean \ə-ˌris-tō-ˈfan-ē-ən\ In classical prosody, an aeolic meter that scans as – ∪ ∪ – | ∪ – – . It frequently follows a similar line that is a syllable longer: – ∪ ∪ – | ∪ – ∪ – . The name of the meter alludes to its use by the comic dramatist Aristophanes.

aristophanic *See* PHERECRATEAN.

Armageddon \ˌär-mə-ˈged-ən\ The site or time of a final conclusive battle between the forces of good and evil. The scene of the battle is described in the New Testament, Revelation to John, chapter 16: 14–16.

arsis \ˈär-sis\ *plural* arses \-ˌsēz\ [Greek *ársis,* act of raising or lifting, raising of the foot in beating time] **1.** The lighter or shorter part of a poetic foot especially in quantitative verse. **2.** The accented or longer part of a poetic foot especially in accentual verse. Compare THESIS.

The Latin meaning, in which *arsis* refers to the accented part of the foot, has been retained in modern prosody.

ars poetica \ˈärz-pō-ˈet-i-kə\ *plural* ars poeticas. Any treatise that, in the manner of Horace's *Ars Poetica,* authoritatively sets down principles of poetic composition.

arte mayor \ˈär-tā-mä-ˈyōr\ [Spanish, short for *versos* (*coplas*) *de arte mayor,* literally, verses of greater art] Spanish verse form consisting of eight-syllable lines, later changed to 12 syllables, usually arranged in eight-line stanzas with a rhyme scheme of *abbaacca*. The form originated in the late 13th to the early 14th century and was used for most serious poetry in the 15th century. It fell out of general use by the 16th century.

arte menor \'är-tā-mā-'nōr\ [Spanish, short for *versos de arte menor,* literally, verses of lesser art] In Spanish poetry, a line of two to eight syllables and usually only one accent, most often on the penultimate syllable. Because of the general nature of the form, it has been used for many different types of poetry, from traditional verse narratives to popular songs.

art for art's sake A slogan translated from the French *l'art pour l'art,* which was coined in the early 19th century by the French philosopher Victor Cousin. The phrase expresses the belief held by many writers and artists, especially those associated with Aestheticism, that art needs no justification, that it need serve no political, didactic, or other end. *See also* AESTHETICISM.

Arthurian legend \är-'thůr-ē-ən\ The body of stories and medieval romances, known as the Matter of Britain, centering on the legendary king Arthur. The stories chronicled Arthur's birth, the adventures of his knights, and the adulterous love between his knight Sir Lancelot and his queen, Guinevere. This liaison and the largely unsuccessful quest for the Holy Grail (the vessel used by Christ at the Last Supper) brought about the dissolution of the knightly fellowship, the death of Arthur, and the destruction of his kingdom.

Stories about Arthur and his court had been popular in Wales before the 11th century; they won fame in Europe partly through the *Historia regum Britanniae,* a pseudo-chronicle written between 1135 and 1139 by Geoffrey of Monmouth. The *Historia* celebrates a glorious and triumphant king who defeated a Roman army in eastern France but was mortally wounded in battle during a rebellion at home led by his nephew Mordred. Some features of Geoffrey's story were marvelous fabrications, while certain others were medieval adaptations of the Celtic tales. The concept of Arthur as a world conqueror was clearly inspired by legends surrounding great leaders such as Alexander the Great and Charlemagne. Later writers in the chronicle tradition, notably Wace of Jersey and Layamon, filled out certain details, especially in connection with Arthur's knightly fellowship.

The literary development of Arthurian legend flourished early in France, where Breton storytellers had orally transmitted the heroic accounts that their Briton ancestors had carried with them into France. Drawing from such Celtic material, Chrétien de Troyes in the late 12th century made Arthur the ruler of a realm of marvels in five romances of adventure. Chrétien's *Perceval* is the first extant Arthurian romance to treat the theme of the Grail.

Prose romances of the 13th century began to explore two major themes: the winning of the Grail and the love story of Lancelot and Guinevere. An early prose romance centering on Lancelot seems to have become the kernel of the Prose *Lancelot,* a section of the cyclic work known as the Vulgate cycle (*c.* 1210–30). The Lancelot theme was connected with the Grail story through Lancelot's son, the pure knight Sir Galahad, who achieved the vision of God through the Grail as fully as is possible in this life, whereas Sir Lancelot was impeded in his progress along the mystic way because of his adultery with Guinevere. Another branch of the Vulgate cycle was based on a very early 13th-century verse romance, *Merlin,* by Robert de Boron, that had told of Arthur's birth and childhood and his winning of the crown by drawing a magic sword from a stone. The writers of the Vulgate cycle (thought to be a group of Cistercian monks) turned this into prose, adding a pseudo-historical narrative dealing with Arthur's military exploits. A final branch of the Vulgate cycle contained an account of Arthur's Roman campaign and war with Mordred, to which was added a story of Lancelot's renewed adultery with Guinevere and the disastrous war between Lancelot and Sir Gawain that ensued. A later prose romance, known as the post-Vulgate Grail romance (*c.* 1240), combined Arthurian legend with material from the Tristan romance.

The legend told in the Vulgate cycle and post-Vulgate romance was transmitted to English-speaking readers in Thomas Malory's late 15th-century prose work *Le Morte Darthur.* At the same time, there was renewed interest in Geoffrey of Monmouth's *Historia,* and the fictitious kings of Britain became more or less incorporated with official national mythology. The legend remained alive during the 17th century, though interest in it was by then confined to England. Of merely antiquarian interest during the 18th century, it again figured in literature during Victorian times, notably in Alfred, Lord Tennyson's *Idylls of the King* and, in quite a different vein, in Mark Twain's *A Connecticut Yankee in King Arthur's Court.* The Arthurian legend continued to be retold in the 20th century by writers such as Edwin Arlington Robinson, who wrote an Arthurian trilogy, and T.H. White, who wrote a series of novels collected as *The Once and Future King* (1958) which were made into the popular musical *Camelot* (1960) by Alan Lerner and Frederick Loewe. A later treatment is Marion Zimmer Bradley's *The Mists of Avalon* (1982).

Arzamas society \ˌər-ˌzə-ˈmàs\ Russian literary circle (flourished 1815–18) formed for the semi-serious purpose of ridiculing the conservative "Lovers of the Russian Word," who wished to keep the modern Russian language firmly tied to Old Church Slavonic. They took the name Arzamas from a small city in east-central Russia; it was the setting of a work by Dmitry Bludov that satirized the language conservatives.

The Arzamas circle supported the work begun by Nikolay Karamzin, who advocated the stylistic revision of written Russian. The members of Arzamas included the poets Vasily A. Zhukovsky, Konstantin Batyushkov, the young Aleksandr Pushkin, and many others. Though their Arzamas activities were limited to composing burlesques of the archaic Slavonic style—and some of the works they produced as Arzamas members were among the best of those years—it was their adoption of the new style in their subsequent serious works that permanently influenced the formation of the modern Russian literary language.

ascending rhythm *See* RISING RHYTHM.

asclepiad \ə-ˈsklē-pē-əd, -ˌad\ [Greek *Asklēpiádeios*] A Greek lyric verse later used by Latin poets such as Catullus, Horace, and Seneca. The asclepiad consisted of an aeolic nucleus, a choriamb to which were added more choriambs and iambic or trochaic elements at the end of each line. A version with four choriambs is known as the *greater asclepiad,* a version with three choriambs, the *lesser choriamb*. The form was named for the 3rd-century-BC Greek poet Asclepiades.

Asiaticism \ˌā-zhē-ˈat-ə-ˌsiz-əm, ˌā-shē-\ A literary style characterized by excessive ornamentation or emotionalism.

aside \ə-ˈsīd\ An actor's speech heard by the audience but supposedly not by other characters.

assonance \ˈas-ə-nəns\ [Latin *assonare* to make a sound in accompaniment, respond] **1.** Resemblance of sound in words or syllables, such as the sound of *i* in *ring* and *hit*. **2.** Relatively close juxtaposition of similar sounds, especially of vowels. **3.** *also called* vowel rhyme. In prosody, repetition of stressed vowel sounds within words with different end consonants, as in the phrase "quite like." In this sense, assonance is to be distinguished from regular rhyme, in which initial consonants differ but both vowel and end-consonant sounds are identical, as in the phrase "quite right."

Many common phrases, such as "mad as a hatter," "free as a breeze," or "high as a kite," owe their appeal to assonance. As a poetic device, internal assonance is usually combined with ALLITERATION (repetition of initial consonant sounds) and CONSONANCE (repetition of end or medial consonant sounds) to enrich the texture of the poetic line. Sometimes a single vowel sound is repeated, as in the opening line of Thomas Hood's "Autumn":

> I saw old Autumn in the misty morn

Sometimes two or more vowel sounds are repeated, as in the opening lines of Percy Bysshe Shelley's "The Indian Serenade":

> *I* ar*i*se from dr*ea*ms of th*ee*
> In the first sw*ee*t sl*ee*p of n*i*ght

Assonance at the end of a line, producing an impure, or off, rhyme, is found in *La Chanson de Roland* and most French verses composed before the introduction of pure rhyme into French verse in the 12th century. Assonance remains a feature of Spanish and Portuguese poetry. In English verse, it is frequently found in the traditional ballads, where its use may have been careless or unavoidable. The last verse of "Sir Patrick Spens" is an example:

> Haf owre, haf owre to Aberdour,
> It's fiftie fadom deip:
> And thair lies guid Sir Patrick Spence,
> Wi' the Scots lords at his feit.

Otherwise, it was rarely used in English as a deliberate technique until the late 19th and 20th centuries, when it appears in the works of Gerard Manley Hopkins and Wilfred Owen. Their use of assonance instead of end rhyme was often adopted by such poets as W.H. Auden, Stephen Spender, and Dylan Thomas.

Aṣṭchāp \'äsh-tə-ˌchäp\ [Sanskrit *aṣṭā* eight + Hindi *chāp* seal] Group of 16th-century Hindi poets, four of whom were disciples of the Vaishnava leader Vallabha, and four of his son and successor, Viṭṭhala. The greatest of the group was Sūrdās, a blind singer whose descriptions of the exploits of the child-god Krishna are the highlights of his collection of poetry called the *Sūrsāgar,* a work that is deeply loved throughout the Hindi-speaking areas of northern India. It is particularly rich in its details of daily life and in its sensitive depiction of human emotion, especially the parent's for the child and the maiden's for her lover. Other members of the Aṣṭchāp group were Paramānanddās, Nanddās, Kṛṣṇadās, Govindswāmī, Kumbhandās, Chitaswāmī, and Caturbhujdās.

astrophic \ˌā-'strōf-ik, -'sträf-\ **1.** Of stanzas or stanzaic structure, arranged in series without regular repetition of stanzaic units. The term can also refer to stanzas that are irregular in arrangement. **2.** Not arranged or divided into strophes or stanzas.

asynartetic \ˌā-ˌsin-är-'tet-ik\ [Greek *asynártētos,* literally, disconnected] Of a line of verse, containing different or unconnected rhythmic units, as in the first two lines of one of John Donne's sonnets:

> Batter my heart, three-personed God; for You
> As yet but knock, breathe, shine, and seek to mend;

The term can be applied more specifically to a line in which the two parts that are separated by the caesura have different rhythms or to a line with a diaeresis or hiatus at the caesura so that a quasi independence of the two members is effected.

asyndeton \ə-'sin-də-ˌtän, ˌā-\ [Greek *asýndeton,* from neuter of *asýndetos* without conjunctions, literally, unconnected] Omission of the conjunctions that ordinarily join coordinate words or clauses, as in the phrase "I came, I saw, I conquered" or in Matthew Arnold's poem *The Scholar Gipsy:*

> Thou hast not lived, why should'st thou perish, so?
> Thou hadst *one* aim, *one* business, *one* desire;
> Else wert thou long since numbered with the dead!

Athenaeum, The \ˌath-ə-'nē-əm\ Influential literary and critical journal, founded in London by James S. Buckingham. A successor to a general monthly magazine of the same name (published 1807–09), *The Athenaeum* appeared weekly from Jan. 2, 1828, until Feb. 11, 1921, when it merged with *The Nation.* Published for the next 10 years as *The Nation and Athenaeum,* the journal was absorbed in 1931 by *The New Statesman.*

Subtitled "A Journal of Literature, Science, the Fine Arts, Music, and the Drama," *The Athenaeum* sought to be considered the literary and intellectual forum through which the best contemporary intellectuals, poets, and writers could present their ideas. It maintained its authoritativeness and reputation throughout its 93 years as an independent literary chronicle.

Among contributors in the 19th century were Robert Browning, Thomas Carlyle, Thomas Hood, Charles Lamb, and Walter Pater. Twentieth-century contributors included T.S. Eliot, Robert Graves, Thomas Hardy, Katherine Mansfield, John Middleton Murry (also editor, 1919–21), and Virginia Woolf.

athetesis \ˌath-ə-ˈtē-sis\ *plural* atheteses \-ˌsēz\ [Greek *athétēsis,* literally, abolition, annulling] In literary criticism, the rejecting or marking of a passage (in a poem, for example) as spurious.

Atlantic, The, *also called* (1857–1932, 1971–81) The Atlantic Monthly. Monthly journal of literature and opinion, founded in 1857 by Moses Dresser Phillips and published in Boston. One of the oldest and most respected of American reviews, *The Atlantic* has long been noted for the quality of its contents. Its long line of distinguished editors and authors included James Russell Lowell, Ralph Waldo Emerson, Henry Wadsworth Longfellow, and Oliver Wendell Holmes. In 1869, the magazine caused a scandal when it published an article by Harriet Beecher Stowe about Lord Byron and his scandalous personal life. She intended the article to "arrest Byron's influence upon the young," but it fascinated young readers, whose outraged parents cancelled 15,000 subscriptions.

In the early 1920s, *The Atlantic Monthly* expanded its scope to political affairs, featuring articles by such figures as Theodore Roosevelt, Woodrow Wilson, and Booker T. Washington. The high quality of its literature—including serialized novels, best-sellers among them—and its literary criticism have preserved the magazine's reputation as a lively literary periodical with a moderate worldview.

Atlantic Club *See* SATURDAY CLUB.

atmosphere \ˈat-mə-ˌsfir\ The overall aesthetic effect of a work of art, or a dominant mood or emotional effect or appeal. The opening paragraph of Edgar Allan Poe's story "The Fall of the House of Usher," for example, establishes the tone of gloom and desolation that pervades the rest of the story.

atticism \ˈat-ə-ˌsiz-əm\ A witty or well-turned phrase. The word refers to the characteristic literary style of Attic Greek, which was simple yet refined and elegant.

aubade \ō-ˈbäd\ [French, ultimately from Old Provençal *albada,* a derivative of *alba* dawn] *also called* dawn song **1.** A song or poem greeting the dawn. **2.** A morning love song, or, more specifically, a song or poem of lovers parting at daybreak. *See also* ALBA; TAGELIED.

Aufklärung *See* ENLIGHTENMENT.

Augustan Age \ȯ-ˈgəs-tən\ One of the most illustrious periods in Latin literary history, from approximately 43 BC to AD 18; together with the preceding CICERONIAN PERIOD, it forms the Golden Age of Latin literature. Marked by civil peace and prosperity, the age reached its highest literary expression in poetry, producing a polished and sophisticated verse generally addressed to a patron or to the emperor Augustus and dealing with themes of patriotism, love, and nature. One decade alone, 29 to 19 BC, saw the publication of Virgil's *Georgics* and the completion of the *Aeneid;* the appearance of Horace's *Odes,* Books I–III, and *Epistles,* Book I; the elegies (Books I–III) of Sextus Propertius; and Books I–II of the elegies of Tibullus. Also during those 10 years, Livy began his monumental history of Rome, and another historian, Pollio, was writing his important but lost history of recent events. Ovid, the author of *Metamorphoses,* a mythological history of the world from the creation to the Augustan Age, was the last great writer of the Golden Age; his death in exile in AD 17 marked the close of the period.

By extension, the name Augustan Age also is applied to a "classical" period in the literature of any nation, especially to the 18th century in England and, less frequently, to the 17th century in France. Some critics prefer to limit the English Augustan Age to a period covered by the reign of Queen Anne (1702–14), when writers such as Alexander Pope, Joseph Addison, Sir Richard Steele, John Gay, and Matthew Prior flourished. Others, however, would extend it backward to include John Dryden and forward to take in Samuel Johnson.

aureate \ˈȯr-ē-ət, -ˌāt\ [Middle English *aureat* golden, splendid, probably coined on the basis of Latin *auratus* gilded and *aureus* golden] Marked by a style that is affected, pompous, and heavily ornamental, that uses rhetorical flourishes excessively, and that often employs interlarded foreign words and phrases. The style is often associated with the 15th-century French, English, and Scottish writers.

Ausonian \ȯ-ˈsō-nē-ən\ Pertaining to Ausonia, a name used in ancient Greek and Latin verse for Italy. On the classical model, *Ausonian* has been used in English as a poetic substitute for "Italian."

author \ˈȯ-thər\ [ultimately from Latin *auctor* authorizer, responsible agent, originator, maker] One who is the source of some form of intellectual or creative work; especially, one who composes a book, article, poem, play, or other literary work intended for publication. Usually a distinction is made between an author and others (such as a compiler, an editor, or a translator) who assemble, organize, or manipulate literary materials. Sometimes, however, the title of author is given to one who compiles material (as for publication) in such a way that the finished compilation can be regarded as a relatively original work.

authorcraft \ˈȯ-thər-ˌkraft\ Skill in or practice of authorship.

authoress \'ȯ-thər-əs, 'ȯ-thrəs\ A female author—now usually replaced by *author*.

authorship \'ȯ-thər-ˌship\ **1.** The profession of writing. **2.** The source (as the author) of a piece of writing, music, or art. **3.** The state or act of writing, creating, or causing.

autobiography \ˌȯt-ō-bī-'äg-rə-fē, -bē-\ The biography of oneself narrated by oneself. Autobiographical works can take many forms, from the intimate writings made during life that were not necessarily intended for publication (including letters, diaries, journals, memoirs, and reminiscences), to the formal autobiography.

Formal autobiographies offer a special kind of biographical truth: a life, reshaped by recollection, with all of recollection's conscious and unconscious omissions and distortions. The novelist Graham Greene said that, for this reason, an autobiography is only "a sort of life" and used the phrase as the title for his own autobiography (1971).

There are but few and scattered examples of autobiographical literature in antiquity and the Middle Ages. In the 2nd century BC the Chinese classical historian Sima Qian included a brief account of himself in the *Shiji,* "Historical Records." It is stretching a point to include, from the 1st century BC, the letters of Cicero (or, in the early Christian era, the letters of St. Paul); and Julius Caesar's *Commentaries* tell little about Caesar, though they present a masterly picture of the conquest of Gaul and the operations of the Roman military machine at its most efficient. Generally speaking, autobiography began with the Renaissance in the 15th century. One of the first examples was written in England by Margery Kempe.

In her old age Margery Kempe, a religious mystic of Lynn in Norfolk, dictated an account of her bustling, far-faring life, which, however concerned with religious experience, racily reveals her somewhat abrasive personality and the impact she made upon her fellows. The first full-scale formal autobiography was written a generation later by a celebrated humanist publicist of the age, Enea Silvio Piccolomini, after he was elevated to the papacy, in 1458, as Pius II. Later celebrated autobiographers include Benvenuto Cellini, Lord Herbert of Cherbury, Benjamin Franklin, and Jean-Jacques Rousseau. In the first book of his autobiography—misleadingly named *Commentarii,* in evident imitation of Caesar—Pius II traces his career up to becoming pope; the succeeding 11 books (and a fragment of a 12th, which breaks off a few months before his death in 1464) present a panorama of the age.

The neglected autobiography of the Italian physician and astrologer Gironimo Cardano, a work of great charm, and the celebrated adventures of the goldsmith and sculptor Benvenuto Cellini in Italy of the 16th century; the uninhibited autobiography of the English historian and diplomat Lord Herbert of Cherbury, in the early 17th; and Colley Cibber's *Apology for The Life of Colley Cibber,* a playwright in the early 18th—these are representative examples of biographical literature from the Renaissance to the Age of Enlightenment. The latter period itself produced three works that are especially notable for their very different reflections of the spirit of the times as well as of the personalities of their authors: the urbane autobiography of Edward Gibbon, the great historian; the plainspoken, vigorous success story of an American who possessed all the talents, Benjamin Franklin; and the somewhat morbid introspection of a revolutionary Swiss-French political and social theorist, the *Confessions* of J. J. Rousseau—the latter leading to two autobiographical explorations in poetry during the Romantic period in England, William Wordsworth's *Prelude* and Lord Byron's *Childe Harold,* cantos III and IV.

There are roughly four different kinds of autobiography: thematic, religious, intellectual, and fictionalized. The first grouping includes books with such diverse purposes as *The Americanization of Edward Bok* (1920) and Adolf Hitler's *Mein Kampf* (1925, 1927). Religious autobiography claims a number of great works, ranging from *The Confessions* of St. Augustine in the Middle Ages to the autobiographical chapters of Thomas Carlyle's *Sartor Resartus* and John Cardinal Newman's beautifully wrought *Apologia* in the 19th century. That century and the early 20th saw the creation of several intellectual autobiographies, including the severely analytical *Autobiography* of the philosopher John S. Mill and *The Education of Henry Adams*. Finally, somewhat analogous to the novel as biography is the autobiography thinly disguised as, or transformed into, the novel. This group includes such works as Samuel Butler's *The Way of All Flesh* (1903), James Joyce's *A Portrait of the Artist as a Young Man* (1916), George Santayana's *The Last Puritan* (1935), and the novels of Thomas Wolfe.

automatic writing Writing produced without conscious intention and sometimes without awareness, as if of telepathic or spiritualistic origin. The phenomenon may occur when the subject is in an alert waking state or in a hypnotic trance. What is produced may be unrelated words, fragments of poetry, epithets, puns, obscenities, or well-organized fantasies. During the late 19th century, at the height of popular interest in the phenomenon, inspiration for automatic writing was generally attributed to external or supernatural forces. Since the advent, around 1900, of theories of personality that postulate unconscious (or subconscious) as well as conscious motivation, the inspiration for automatic writing has been assumed to be completely internal.

Modern psychodynamic theories of personality propose that traits, attitudes, motives, impulses, and memories that are incompatible with the person's conscious awareness may be dissociated from awareness and rarely expressed overtly in the course of normal waking behavior. These elements may be revealed, however, in the content of automatic writing. Automatic writing thus became popular with some writers in the early decades of the 20th century. Gertrude Stein, for example, practiced the technique as a student; it was employed by many of the Surrealist writers (notably the French poet Robert Desnos), who considered the unconscious mind to be the wellspring of imagination.

auto sacramental *Spanish* 'aü-tō-ˌsäk-rä-men-'täl, *Portuguese* 'aü-tü-sȧ-krȧ-'men-tȧl, -taü\\ [Spanish, literally, sacramental play] *plural* autos sacramentales.

A short play on a sacred or biblical subject, similar to a miracle or morality play. The genre reached its height in the 17th century with *autos* written by the Spanish playwright Pedro Calderón de la Barca. Performed out of doors as part of the Corpus Christi feast day celebrations, *autos* were short allegorical plays in verse dealing with some aspect of the mystery of the Holy Eucharist, which the feast of Corpus Christi solemnly celebrated. They derived from tableaus that had been part of the procession accompanying the Eucharist as it was carried through the streets at Corpus Christi. The tableaus became animated, then developed a dramatic form, and finally were detached from the Eucharistic procession to form one of their own. Mounted on carts, they were pulled to selected places in the municipality, and the actors presented their *autos,* one after another, much as the scriptural plays of the Netherlands and northern England had been presented on pageant wagons during the Middle Ages. Expenses for these superbly set and dressed *autos* were paid by the municipality.

These little plays had begun to appear in the late 16th century, but they were at first rough and primitive, a rustic form of pious entertainment. Important names in the development of the *autos* into works of polished art were a bookseller from Valencia, Juan de Timoneda, and the playwrights Jose de Valdivielso (*c.* 1560–1638) and his contemporary Lope de Vega. It was Calderón, however, who seized the opportunity allegory offered for covering a wide range of nonsacramental subjects, and he took the *auto* form to new heights of artistic achievement.

Accused of displaying irreverence toward the sacrament during the 18th century, their performance was in 1765 prohibited by royal decree. Some 20th-century poets have imitated their form and have written secularized versions of the old *autos.*

autotelism \ˌȯt-ō-ˈtel-ˌiz-əm, -ˈtēl-\ [Greek *autotelḗs* complete in itself] The belief that a work of art, especially a work of literature, is an end in itself or provides its own justification and does not exist to serve a moral or didactic purpose. It was adopted by proponents of New Criticism and is similar to the "art for art's sake" doctrine of the AESTHETICISM movement of the late 19th century.

avant-garde \ˌä-ˌvän-ˈgärd, ˌa-, -ˌvänt-; ə-ˌvänt-\ [French, vanguard] An intelligentsia that develops new or experimental concepts, especially in the arts.

Awangarda Krakowska \ȧ-vȧŋ-ˈgȧr-dȧ-krȧ-ˈkȯf-skȧ\ [Polish, literally, Kraków avant-garde] Avant-garde Polish literary movement launched at Kraków in 1922 that led to a regeneration of poetic technique and a renewed interest in Polish folklore and pre-17th-century Polish literature. Influenced by revolutionary trends in poetry, particularly Futurism, in France, Italy, and Spain, the Awangarda movement opposed the emphasis on lyricism and the anti-intellectualism of the contemporary SKAMANDER group. Associated with the Awangarda were Julian Przyboś, one of the outstanding poets of the post-World

War II period; Adam Ważyk, poet, essayist, prose writer, and brilliant translator; and Józef Czechowicz, who assimilated traditional and regional elements to the new style.

awdl \'au̇d-əl\ *plural* awdlau \'au̇d-ˌlī\ [Welsh, song, ode] In Welsh verse, a long ode characterized by alliterative verse and internal rhyme. By the 13th century the awdl had developed into the intricate system of consonant and vowel correspondence, or consonant correspondence and internal rhyme, called CYNGHANEDD. Twenty-four strict bardic meters were available to the poet; only four bardic meters are still commonly used. The *awdl* was, by the 15th century, the vehicle for many outstanding Welsh poems. It remains the predominant form in the annual national eisteddfod (bard and minstrel competition), where since 1887 a wooden chair (the chair is the Welsh bard's highest honor) has been awarded to the writer of the winning *awdl*. Despite the criticism advanced by some that the form is obsolete, *awdlau* of high poetic merit are still occasionally written.

B

There is no Frigate like a Book
To take us Lands away
—Emily Dickinson

bacchius \ba-ˈkī-əs\ *plural* bacchii \-ˈkī-ˌī\ [Greek *Bakcheîos,* from *Bakcheîos* (adjective) of Bacchus] A metrical foot of three syllables. In classical prosody the first is short and the others long (∪ – –). In accentual or modern prosody, the first syllable is unstressed and the other two have either primary or intermediate stress. A modern bacchius is scanned ∪ ˊ ˊ. *Compare* ANTIBACCHIUS.

backflash *See* FLASHBACK.

Bagutta Prize \bä-ˈgüt-tä\ Italian literary prize that is awarded annually to the author of the best book of the year. Established in 1927, it is named after the Milan trattoria in which the award ceremony is held. The prize recognizes authors in several genres, including novels and works of poetry and journalism, and carries an award of 1,000,000 lire.

baihua or **pai-hua** \ˈbī-ˈhwä\ [Chinese *báihuà*] In Chinese literature, vernacular style of Chinese that was adopted as a written language in a movement to revitalize the classical Chinese literary language and make literature more accessible to the average citizen. Started in 1917 by the philosopher and historian Hu Shi, the *baihua* literary movement succeeded in making *baihua* the language of textbooks, periodicals, newspapers, and public documents, as well as producing a flood of new literature in the vernacular. By 1922 the government had proclaimed *baihua* the national language. Traditionally considered inferior to *guwen, baihua* had long been studiously avoided for creative writing. *Compare* GUWEN.

Baker Street Irregulars \ˈbā-kər\ A group of devotees of the fictional detective Sherlock Holmes who founded a fan club in New York City in 1933. They took their name from that of a gang of boys who appear in three of the Sherlock Holmes mystery stories written by Sir Arthur Conan Doyle and who do occasional errand running and discreet snooping for Holmes. The gang took its name from the name of the street on which Holmes resides. Chapters of this organization, loosely organized throughout the United States, were known as "scion societies." Individual clubs took their names from the Sherlock Holmes stories, such as the Hounds of the Baskerville of Chicago or the Red-Headed

League of Westtown, Pa. As of 1980, approximately 200 such clubs existed in the United States. Similar groups were organized in many countries.

The Baker Street Journal, devoted entirely to Holmesiana, footnoted scholarship about the detective, and minute dissection of his cases, was published by the Baker Street Irregulars.

balance \'bal-əns\ The juxtaposition in writing of syntactically parallel constructions containing similar, contrasting, or opposing ideas (such as the statement "To err is human; to forgive, divine").

ballad \'bal-əd\ [Old French *balade,* from Old Provençal *ballada* dance, song sung while dancing, a derivative of *ballar* to dance] A form of short narrative folk song, the distinctive style of which crystallized in Europe during the late Middle Ages. The ballad has been preserved as a musical and literary form up to modern times. It was originally part of the oral tradition, and the oral form has been preserved as the folk ballad, while a written, literary ballad evolved from that tradition.

Typically, the folk ballad (or standard ballad) tells a compact tale in a style that achieves bold, sensational effects through deliberate starkness and abruptness. Despite a rigid economy of narrative, it employs a variety of devices to prolong highly charged moments in the story and to thicken the emotional atmosphere, the most common being a frequent repetition of some key word, line, or phrase.

Because folk ballads have thrived among people who do not rely on a written language and are freshly created from memory at each performance, they are subject to constant variation in both text and tune. In terms of subject matter, they exhibit fascination with supernatural happenings, with the fate of lovers (usually, though not always, tragic), with crime and its punishment, and with apocryphal legends (the chief stuff of religious balladry), among other topics.

The ballad genre in its present form can scarcely have existed before about 1100. The oldest ballad in Francis J. Child's definitive compilation, *The English and Scottish Popular Ballads* (1882–98), dates from 1300, but as an oral form the ballad did not need to be written down in order to be performed or preserved. Indeed, to ask for the date of a ballad displays a misunderstanding of the very nature of balladry. Behind each recorded ballad one can detect the workings of tradition upon some earlier form of the same work.

Some scholars—notably those of the "communal school," led by F.B. Gummere and G.L. Kittredge—have argued that ballads are the result of collective composition; others (those of the "individualist school," led by W.J. Courthope and Louise Pound) have argued that each is the work of an individual composer.

Significant traditions of balladry exist in England, Scotland, Ireland, the United States, France, Denmark, Germany, Russia, Greece, and Spain. Their formal characteristics vary from one area to another: British and American ballads, for instance, are invariably rhymed and divided into stanzas (strophes). The Russian ballads (*byliny*) are unrhymed and astrophic; the Spanish *romances* and the Danish *viser* employ assonance rather than rhyme, but the latter are strophic while the former are not.

Unlike the strictly impersonal folk ballad, the literary ballad calls attention to itself and to its composer. Early ballads of this sort were the work of professional entertainers employed in wealthy households from the Middle Ages until the 17th century, and many of these pieces glorify noble families. The older Robin Hood ballads, celebrating traditional yeoman virtues, are also examples of minstrel propaganda. Broadside ballads are urban adaptations of the folk ballad, and are the work of hack poets commemorating some sensational item of topical interest. They appeared on crudely printed handbills (called broadsheets or broadsides) in the 16th to 19th century. Sophisticated imitations of broadside ballads, usually penned for purposes of jocular satire, were popular in the 18th and 19th centuries, enjoying a special vogue after the publication in 1765 of Thomas Percy's *Reliques of Ancient English Poetry*. The modern literary ballad recalls in its rhythmic and narrative elements the traditions of folk balladry. Among the well-known poets who have written their own literary ballads are Sir Walter Scott, Samuel Taylor Coleridge, John Keats, and Heinrich Heine.

ballade \bə-ˈläd, ba-\ [Middle French *balade,* literally, ballad] One of several *formes fixes* ("fixed forms") in French lyric poetry and song, cultivated particularly in the 14th and 15th centuries. (*Compare* RONDEAU; VIRELAI.) Strictly, the ballade consists of three stanzas and a shortened final dedicatory stanza. All the stanzas have the same rhyme scheme and the same final line, which thus forms a refrain. Different forms have been used for the ballade stanza, but the most common is eight lines with a rhyme scheme of *ababbcbc* for the first three stanzas and four lines rhyming *bcbc* for the final dedicatory stanza. The last stanza is called the prince (because that is usually its first word) or the envoi. The *chant royale* is similar to the ballade but has five main stanzas.

The general shape of the ballade is present in the poetry of many ages and regions. The odes of the Greek poet Pindar (5th century BC) have the same stanza form with their strophe, antistrophe, and epode. Much of the art song of the 16th century in Germany is cast in a similar form, though normally without the envoi, or the refrain line. In its purest form, however, the ballade is found only in France and England. The immediate precursors of the ballade can be found in the monophonic songs of the TROUBADOURS (poet-musicians using the Provençal language), which frequently employ a similar stanza pattern with an envoi. They normally have more than three stanzas, however, and the refrain line, if there is one, is often not the last line of the stanza. In the later 13th century the standard form appears more and more frequently in the French songs of the trouvères (the northern counterparts of the troubadours). The history of the polyphonic ballade begins with Guillaume de Machaut, the leading French poet and composer of the 14th century. He wrote more songs in this than in any other form. In his work can be seen the gradual emergence of a standard manner of setting a ballade.

The ballade was the most expansive of the *formes fixes*. The texts more often contained elaborate symbolism and classical references than did those of the other *formes fixes*. Later in the 14th century, the ballade was used for the most solemn and formal songs: the celebration of special patrons, the commemoration of magnificent occasions, the declarations of love in the highest style.

In the 15th century the form became less popular. The foremost Burgundian composer, Guillaume Dufay, wrote few ballades, almost all of which can be connected with specific occasions and all early in his life. Later in the century, musical ballades were rare except in the work of English composers. Among the two greatest songwriters of the later 15th century, Antoine Busnois wrote no ballades, and Jean d'Ockeghem wrote just one—on the occasion of the death of another famed song composer, Gilles Binchois, in 1460.

The form gradually disappeared among the poets, too, only to reappear spasmodically in the work of later writers as a conscious archaism. But there are fine examples from the 15th century among the work of Alain Chartier, Charles, Duke d'Orléans, and Jean Molinet; and François Villon's best-known poem is a ballade with the refrain line "Mais où sont les neiges d'antan?" ("But where are the snows of yesteryear?"). English writers who have used the form include Austin Dobson, Andrew Lang, W.E. Henley, and Algernon Charles Swinburne.

ballade royal \bɔ-'läd-'rȯi-əl, bȧ-'lȧd-rwä-'yȧl\ *plural* ballade royals [Middle French, royal ballade] A ballade written in rhyme royal stanzas (stanzas of seven 10-syllable lines rhyming *ababbcc*).

ballad meter The meter common in English ballads consisting chiefly of iambic lines of seven accents, each arranged in rhymed pairs and usually printed as the four-line BALLAD STANZA. *See also* COMMON METER.

balladmonger \'bal-əd-ˌmäŋ-gər, -ˌməŋ-gər\ A poor or inferior poet.

ballad revival Late 18th- and early 19th-century movement within English and German literary circles that was characterized by a renewal of interest in folk poetry. In reality the ballad revival was a rediscovery and new appreciation of the merits of popular poetry.

The trend that began in England in 1711 with the publication of Joseph Addison's *Spectator* papers cautiously defending "the darling Songs of the common People" crystallized in 1765 with the publication of Thomas Percy's *Reliques of Ancient English Poetry,* a collection of English and Scottish traditional ballads. The *Reliques* and a flood of subsequent collections, including Sir Walter Scott's three-volume *Minstrelsy of the Scottish Border* (1802–03), had great impact and provided the English Romantic poets with an alternative to outworn Neoclassical models as a source of inspiration. In Germany the influential philosopher-critic J.G. von Herder conferred an almost mystical distinction on the ballad as the genuine expression of the spirit of the folk. The collection of lyrical and narrative folk songs entitled *Des Knaben Wunderhorn* (1805–08; "The Boy's Magic Horn"), edited by Clemens Brentano and Achim von Arnim, was the dominant influence on German poetry throughout the 19th century.

ballad stanza A verse stanza common in English ballads that consists of two lines in ballad meter, usually printed as a four-line stanza with a rhyme scheme of *abcb,* as in *The Wife of Usher's Well,* which begins:

> There lived a wife at Usher's Well,
>   And a wealthy wife was she;
> She had three stout and stalwart sons,
>   And sent them o'er the sea.

banns \'banz\[plural of *bann* originally a spelling variant of *ban* proclamation, prohibition] *obsolete* The proclamation or prologue of a play.

barcarole or **barcarolle** \'bär-kə-ˌrōl\ [Italian dialect (Venice) *barcarola* gondolier's song, ultimately a derivative of *barca* boat] A Venetian boat song characterized by the alternation of a strong and weak beat that suggests a rowing rhythm; or more generally, any poem or song connected with boats or water and whose sound suggests the movement of water.

bard \'bärd\ [Middle English (Scots), from Scottish Gaelic and Irish] A poet, especially one who writes impassioned, lyrical, or epic verse.

Bards were originally Celtic composers of eulogy and satire, or more generally, tribal poet-singers gifted in composing and reciting verses on heroes and their deeds. In Gaul the institution gradually disappeared, whereas in Ireland and Wales it survived. The Irish bard through chanting preserved a tradition of poetic eulogy. In Wales, where the word *bardd* has always been used for poet, the bardic order was codified into distinct grades in the 10th century. Despite a decline of the order toward the end of the European Middle Ages, the Welsh tradition persisted and is celebrated in the annual National Eisteddfod, an assembly of poets and musicians.

Bard of Avon, The \'av-ən, *commonly* 'āv-ən, -ˌän\, *also called* The Bard. A byname of William Shakespeare.

bardolater \bär-'däl-ə-tər\ or **bardolatrist** \bär-'däl-ə-trist\ [*Bard* (*of Avon*), nickname of Shakespeare + id*olater*] One who idolizes William Shakespeare.

Baroque \bə-'rōk, ba-, -'räk, -'rȯk\ [French, probably from Middle French *barroque* irregularly shaped (of a pearl), from Portuguese *barroco* irregularly shaped pearl] A style of literary composition prevalent in most Western countries from the late 16th century to the early 18th century and marked typically by complexity and elaborateness of form and by the use of bizarre, calculatedly ingenious, and sometimes intentionally ambiguous imagery. *Compare* EUPHUISM.

basis \'bā-sis\ *plural* bases \-ˌsēz\ [Greek *básis* metrical unit, measured movement, literally, the act of stepping, step] **1.** A step in a march or dance; the lifting and lowering of the foot, or arsis plus thesis. **2.** Two syllables or the first foot in some ancient verse that serve to introduce the line or stanza and often admit more variation from the norm of the line than appears in subsequent feet. *Compare* ARSIS; THESIS.

bathos \'bā-thäs, -thōs\ [Greek *báthos* depth] The unsuccessful, and therefore ludicrous, attempt to portray pathos in art, i.e., to evoke pity, sympathy, or sorrow. The term was first used in this sense by Alexander Pope in his treatise *Peri Bathous; or, The Art of Sinking in Poetry* (1728). Bathos may result from an inappropriately dignified treatment of the commonplace, the use of elevated language and imagery to describe trivial subject matter, or greatly exaggerated pathos (emotion provoked by genuine suffering). It can also be seen as an unintentional anticlimax.

Even great poets occasionally lapse into bathos as did William Wordsworth in "Simon Lee," which contains the following lines:

> Few months of life has he in store
> As he to you will tell,
> For still, the more he works, the more
> Do his weak ankles swell.

battle piece A work (such as a painting, musical composition, or poem) concerned with or descriptive of a battle. Alfred, Lord Tennyson's "The Charge of the Light Brigade" is an example of the genre.

beast epic A long verse narrative with climactic epic construction comprising beast tales, or stories of animals represented as acting with human feelings and motives. Although individual episodes may be drawn from fables, the beast epic differs from the fable not only in length but also in putting less emphasis on a moral. Instead it provides a satiric commentary on human society.

The earliest European beast epics were written in Latin, but vernacular epics in French, German, and Dutch existed in the late Middle Ages. Among the most famous are the 10th- and 11th-century cycles in which the hero is Reynard the Fox. The cycle includes the tale of the Fox and Chanticleer the Cock, the basis of "The Nun's Priest's Tale" in Geoffrey Chaucer's *The Canterbury Tales*. John Dryden used the beast epic as the framework of his poem *The Hind and the Panther* (1687).

beast fable A prose or verse fable or short story that usually has a moral. In beast fables, animal characters are represented as acting with human feelings and motives. Among the best-known examples in Western literature are those attributed to the legendary Greek author Aesop. The best-known Asian collection of beast fables is the *Pañca-tantra* of India.

beast tale A prose or verse narrative similar to the beast fable in that it portrays animal characters acting as humans, but unlike the fable in that it usually lacks a moral. Joel Chandler Harris' *Uncle Remus: His Songs and His Sayings* (1880) derived many episodes from beast tales carried to the United States by

African slaves. *Animal Farm* (1945), an anti-utopian satire by George Orwell, is a modern adaptation of the beast tale.

beat \'bēt\ A metrical or rhythmic stress in poetry or music. The word can also refer to the overall rhythmic effect of these stresses.

Beat movement \'bēt\ American social and literary movement originating in the 1950s and centered in the bohemian artists' communities of San Francisco's North Beach, southern California's Venice West, and New York City's Greenwich Village. Its adherents, self-styled as "beat" (originally meaning "weary," but later also connoting a musical sense, a "beatific" spirituality, and other meanings) and derisively called "beatniks," expressed their alienation from conventional, or "square," society by adopting an almost uniform style of seedy dress, "cool"—detached, ironic—manners, and "hip" vocabulary borrowed from jazz musicians. Generally apolitical and indifferent to social problems, they advocated personal release, purification, and illumination through the heightened sensory awareness that might be induced by drugs, jazz, sex, or the disciplines of Zen Buddhism. Apologists for the Beats, among them Paul Goodman (*Growing Up Absurd,* 1960), found the joylessness and purposelessness of modern society sufficient justification for both withdrawal and protest.

Beat poets—including Gregory Corso, Lawrence Ferlinghetti, Allen Ginsberg, Gary Snyder, and Philip Whalen—sought to liberate poetry from academic preciosity and bring it "back to the streets." They read their poetry, sometimes to the accompaniment of progressive jazz, in such Beat strongholds as the Coexistence Bagel Shop and Ferlinghetti's City Lights bookstore in San Francisco. Their verse was frequently chaotic and liberally sprinkled with obscenities but was sometimes, as in the case of Ginsberg's *Howl* (1956), ruggedly powerful and moving. Ginsberg and other major figures of the movement, such as the novelist Jack Kerouac, advocated a type of free, unstructured composition in which the writer put down thoughts and feelings without plan or revision—to convey the immediacy of experience—an approach that led to the production of much undisciplined and incoherent verbiage on the part of their imitators. By about 1960, when the faddish notoriety of the movement had begun to fade, it had produced a number of interesting and promising writers and the Beat movement had paved the way for acceptance of other unorthodox and previously ignored writers, such as the BLACK MOUNTAIN POETS and the novelist William Burroughs.

bedtime story A simple story for young children, usually about animals, which are often portrayed anthropomorphically.

beginning rhyme Rhyme at the beginning of successive lines of verse. Lines 3 and 4 of Robert Herrick's "To Daffodils" demonstrate beginning rhyme:

> As yet the early-rising sun
> Has not attained his noon.

The term is also used as a synonym for ALLITERATION.

Bell, The Irish literary magazine, founded in October 1940 by Sean O'Faolain, its editor until 1946. From its first issue, which included works by such writers as Frank O'Connor, Elizabeth Bowen, Jack B. Yeats, Flann O'Brien, and O'Faolain, *The Bell* published stories, poetry, essays, and book and theater reviews by Ireland's most celebrated modern writers.

The Bell was, during World War II, Ireland's sole organ of political liberalism and was particularly critical of the wartime censorship of books. Peadar O'Donnell became editor in 1946, guiding *The Bell* toward an increasingly radical political stance that gradually alienated its Irish reading public. Publication ended with issue 131, in December 1954.

belles lettres \ˌbel-ˈlet, -ˈlet-rə, *French* bel-ˈletr *with* r *as a uvular trill*\ [French *belles-lettres,* literally, beautiful letters] Literature that is an end in itself and is not practical or purely informative. The term can refer generally to poetry, fiction, drama, etc., or more specifically to light, entertaining, sophisticated literature. It is also often used to refer to literary studies, particularly essays.

Berliner Ensemble \ber-ˈlē-nər, *Angl* bər-ˈlin-ər\ Theatrical company founded in 1949 in East Berlin by the German playwright and poet Bertolt Brecht as a branch of the Deutsches Theater, where Brecht had directed a production of his *Mutter Courage und ihre Kinder* (*Mother Courage and Her Children*) in January 1949. Originally designed as a touring company, the ensemble was composed primarily of younger members of the Deutsches Theater with Helene Weigel, Brecht's wife, as its leading actress and codirector. The company devoted itself to works written or adapted by Brecht and worked in Brecht's style of epic theater, which influenced directors throughout western Europe and the United States. In 1954 the Berliner Ensemble moved to the Theater am Schiffbauerdamm, where it was established as an independent state theater.

Besserungsstück \ˈbes-ər-u̇ŋk-ˌshtu̵ek\ [German, literally, improvement play] A genre of play popular in Vienna in the early 19th century. A form of *Volksstück,* a play written in local dialect for popular audiences, the *Besserungsstück* was concerned with the improvement in or remedy of some fault of the main character. Examples include several plays by Joseph Gleich, a minor but prolific Austrian dramatist of the period.

bestiary \ˈbes-chē-ˌer-ē, ˈbēs-\ [Medieval Latin *bestiarium,* a derivative of Latin *bestia* beast] A medieval European work in verse or prose, often illustrated, that consisted of a collection of stories, each based on a description of certain qualities of the subject, usually an animal or a plant. The stories were allegories, used for moral and religious instruction and admonition.

The numerous manuscripts of medieval bestiaries ultimately are derived from the Greek *Physiologus,* a text compiled by an unknown author before the middle of the 2nd century AD. It consists of stories based on the "facts" of natural science as accepted by someone called Physiologus (Latin: "Naturalist") and on the compiler's own religious ideas.

The *Physiologus* consists of 48 sections, each dealing with one creature, plant, or other subject and each linked to a biblical text. It probably originated in Alexandria and, in some manuscripts, is ascribed to one or the other of the 4th-century bishops St. Basil the Great and Epiphanius of Constantia, though it must be older. The stories may derive from popular fables about animals and plants. Some Indian influence is clear and India may be the source of the story of the unicorn, which became very popular in the West. Many attributes that have become traditionally associated with real or mythical creatures derive from the bestiaries: e.g., the phoenix's burning itself to be born again, the parental love of the pelican, and the hedgehog's collecting its stores for the winter with its prickles.

The popularity of the *Physiologus,* which was second only to the Bible in circulation in the early Middle Ages, is clear from the existence of many early translations. It was translated into Ethiopic, Syriac, Arabic, Coptic, and Armenian. Early translations from the Greek also were made into Georgian and into Slavic languages.

Translations of the *Physiologus* were also made from Latin into Anglo-Saxon before 1000. The only surviving Middle English *Bestiary* dates from the 13th century. It, and other lost Middle English and Anglo-Norman versions, influenced the development of the beast fable. Early translations into Flemish and German influenced the satirical BEAST EPIC. Bestiaries were popular in France and the Low Countries (Belgium, the Netherlands, and Luxembourg) in the 13th century and a 14th-century French Bestiaire d'amour applied the allegory to love. An Italian translation of the *Physiologus,* known as the *Bestiario toscano,* was made in the 13th century.

Many of the medieval bestiaries were illustrated; the earliest known illustrated manuscript is from the 9th century. Illustrations accompanying other medieval manuscripts are often based on illustrations in the *Physiologus,* as are sculptures and carvings (especially in churches) and frescoes and paintings well into the Renaissance period.

The religious sections of the *Physiologus* (and of the bestiaries that were derived from it) are concerned primarily with abstinence and chastity; they also warn against heresies. The frequently abstruse stories to which these admonitions were added were often based on misconceptions about the facts of natural history: e.g., the stag is described as drowning its enemy, the snake, in its den.

best-seller \ˈbest-ˈsel-ər\ Book that, for a time, leads all others of its kind in sales, a designation that serves as an index of popular literary taste and judgment.

The best-seller list was initiated in 1895, when *Bookman,* an American magazine of literature and criticism, began publication. Its list was compiled from reports of sales at bookstores throughout the country. Similar lists began to appear in other literary magazines and in metropolitan newspapers. In the United States, the lists most commonly considered authoritative are those published in *Publishers Weekly* and *The New York Times*. The practice spread from the

United States; the British list generally considered most authoritative is that of *The Sunday Times* (London), reprinted in *Bookseller*. In the compilation of such lists, the works of William Shakespeare, the Bible, and direct-mail and book-club sales are excluded.

The all-time best-seller in the English-speaking world—said to be unequaled in sales—is the Bible. Indeed, in the United States, in the period since 1895, the only book that has outsold it in a given month is Margaret Mitchell's *Gone with the Wind* (1936), a historical novel set in the South during the American Civil War and Reconstruction periods.

bhakti poetry \'bək-tē\ In Indian literature, poetry inspired by or reflecting bhakti (religious devotion), a mystical Hindu movement that emphasizes the intense emotional attachment and love of a devotee toward a personal god. The way of bhakti (bhakti-marga) is contrasted with other means of achieving salvation, such as knowledge (jnana-marga), ritual and good works (karma-marga), and ascetic disciplines of the body; it is claimed by its supporters to be a superior way, as well as one open to all, regardless of sex or caste.

An emotional attraction toward a personal god began to be expressed in the early 7th century. It was furthered by the Indian epics—the *Mahābhārata* and the *Rāmāyaṇa*—and by the *Purāṇas*, encyclopedic texts that recount legends of the various incarnations and appearances of the deities, their genealogies, and the devotional practices accorded them.

The fervor of the 7th–10th-century hymnists of South India, the Āḻvārs and the Nāyaṉārs, which were known as bhakti sects also traveled north, until in time bhakti became an extremely widespread and popular part of Hindu religious life, inspiring a substantial quantity of superb religious poetry and art.

During the medieval period (12th to mid-18th century), the various possible relationships of the worshiper to God—based on the analogy of human sentiments, such as that felt by a servant toward his master, friend toward a friend, parent toward a child, child toward a parent, and woman toward her beloved—were explored in separate schools. In Bengal the 15th–16th-century mystic Caitanya stressed the passionate yearning of a woman for her beloved, while his contemporary Vallabha delighted in the exploits of Krishna as the divine child, as well as Krishna as the divine lover. Tulsīdās' retelling of the Rāma legend in the *Rāmcaritmānas* focused on the sentiment of friendship and loyalty. The synthesis in the medieval period of bhakti ideas with Ṣūfī (mystical) elements from Islām can be discovered in the writings of such poet-saints as Kabīr.

bibliography \ˌbib-lē-'äg-rə-fē\ [Greek *bibliographía* the copying of books, from *biblíon* book + plus; *gráphein* to write] **1.** The history, identification, or description of writings or publications. **2.** A list often with descriptive or critical notes of writings relating to a particular subject, period, or author. In a closely related use, the word can also refer to a list of works written by an author or printed by a publishing house. **3.** The works or a list of the works referred to in a text or consulted by the author in its production. *See also* CRITICAL BIBLIOGRAPHY; DESCRIPTIVE BIBLIOGRAPHY.

bibliotics \ˌbib-lē-ˈä-tiks\ [Greek *biblíon* book + the English suffix *-otics* (probably modeled on *semiotics* the study of signs)] The scientific study of handwriting, documents, and writing materials especially to determine authenticity or authorship.

biform \ˈbī-ˌfȯrm\ [Latin *biformis*] Having or appearing in two dissimilar guises. The term is used of characters in classical mythology that appeared to mortals in other than their customary bodily form. Zeus, for example, often took other forms; he appeared to Leda as a swan and to Europa in the form of a white bull.

bildungsroman \ˈbil-ˌdu̇ŋz-rō-ˌmän, *German* -ˌdu̇ŋs-\ *plural* bildungsromane \-rō-ˌmän-ə\ *or* bildungsromans [German, literally, novel of formation] A class of novel in German literature that deals with the formative years of the main character.

The folklore tale of the dunce who goes out into the world seeking adventure and learns wisdom the hard way was raised to literary heights in Wolfram von Eschenbach's medieval epic *Parzival* and in Hans Grimmelshausen's picaresque tale *Der Abentheurliche Simplicissimus* (1669; "The Adventurous Simplicissimus"). The first novelistic development of this theme was J.W. von Goethe's *Wilhelm Meisters Lehrjahre* (1795–96; *Wilhelm Meister's Apprenticeship*), and it remains the classic example of the type. Other examples are Adalbert Stifter's *Nachsommer* (1857; "Indian Summer") and Gottfried Keller's *Der grüne Heinrich* (1854–55; *Green Henry*). The bildungsroman ends on a positive note, though it may be tempered by resignation and nostalgia. If the grandiose dreams of the hero's youth are over, so are many foolish mistakes and painful disappointments, and a life of usefulness lies ahead.

A common variation of the bildungsroman is the KÜNSTLERROMAN, a novel that deals with the formative years of an artist. Other variations are the *Erziehungsroman* ("novel of upbringing") and the *Entwicklungsroman* ("novel of character development"), although the differences between these terms and the bildungsroman are so slight that they are sometimes used interchangeably.

biocritical \ˌbī-ō-ˈkrit-i-kəl\ [*bio*graphical + *critical*] Of, relating to, or being a study of the life and work of someone (such as a writer).

biography \bī-ˈäg-rə-fē, bē-\ [Late Greek *biographía,* from Greek *bíos* life + *gráphein* to write] Form of nonfictional literature, the subject of which is the life of an individual. In general, the form is considered to include autobiography, in which the author recounts his or her own history.

The earliest biographical writing probably consisted of funeral speeches and inscriptions, usually praising the life and example of the deceased. From this evolved the laudatory and exemplary biography with its associated problems of uncritical or distorted interpretation of available evidence. Such lives are still found, but they have produced their own antithesis in the denunciatory or debunking biography of which Lytton Strachey's *Eminent Victorians* (1918) is a famous modern example.

The origins of modern biography as a distinct genre lie not with eulogy or admiring accounts of great sages and saints but with Plutarch's moralizing lives of prominent Greeks and Romans and Suetonius' gossipy lives of the Caesars, which quote documentary sources. While kings and leaders attracted biographical attention as a part of the general historical record of their times, few lives of common individuals were considered for themselves until the 16th century. In England in the 17th century, William Roper's life of Thomas More is an important example, and Izaak Walton and John Aubrey also produced brief biographies of writers and eminent persons. But the major developments of English biography came in the 18th century with Samuel Johnson's critical *Lives of the English Poets* and James Boswell's massive *Life of Johnson,* which combines detailed records of conversation and behavior with considerable psychological insight. This provided the model for exhaustive, monumental 19th-century biographies such as A.P. Stanley's *Life of Arnold* and John Morley's *Gladstone*. Thomas Carlyle's conviction that history was the history of great men demonstrated the general belief of the time that biographical writing was an important method of understanding society and its institutions. In modern times, impatience with Victorian reticence and deference and the development of psychoanalysis have sometimes led to a more penetrating and comprehensive understanding of the biographical subject. Leon Edel's massive *Henry James* is a good example. Another modern development has been the group biography of a family or small body of close associates, such as Rebecca Fraser's *The Brontës*.

Biographical and autobiographical writing can easily pass into fiction when rational inference or conjecture pass over into imaginative reconstruction or frank invention or when the biographical subject itself is wholly or partly imaginary.

black aesthetic movement *also called* black arts movement. Period of artistic and literary development among black Americans in the 1960s and early '70s. Based on the cultural politics of black nationalism, the movement sought to create a populist art form to promote the idea of black separatism. Many adherents viewed the artist as an activist responsible for the formation of racially separate publishing houses, theater troupes, and study groups. The literature of the movement, generally written in black English vernacular and confrontational in tone, addressed such issues as interracial tension, sociopolitical awareness, and the relevance of African history and culture to blacks in the United States.

Leading theorists of the black aesthetic movement included Houston A. Baker, Jr.; Henry Louis Gates, Jr.; Addison Gayle, Jr., editor of the anthology *The Black Aesthetic* (1971); Hoyt W. Fuller, editor of the journal *Negro Digest* (which became *Black World* in 1970); and LeRoi Jones and Larry Neal, editors of *Black Fire: An Anthology of Afro-American Writing* (1968). Jones, later known as Amiri Baraka, wrote the critically acclaimed play *Dutchman* (1964) and founded the Black Arts Repertory Theatre in Harlem (1965). Haki R. Madhubuti, known as Don L. Lee until 1973, became one of the movement's most popular writers with the publication of *Think Black* (1967) and *Black Pride* (1968). Characterized by an acute self-awareness, the movement produced such autobiographical works as *The Autobiography of Malcolm X* (1965) by Alex Haley, *Soul On Ice* (1968) by Eldridge Cleaver, and *Angela Davis: An Autobiography* (1974). Other notable writers were Toni Morrison, Ishmael Reed, Ntozake Shange, Sonia Sanchez, Alice Walker, and June Jordan.

Blackfriars Theatre \\'blak-ˌfrī-ərz\\ Either of two separate London theaters, the second famed as the winter quarters (after 1608) of the King's Men, the company of actors for whom William Shakespeare served as chief playwright.

black humor [translation of French *humour noir*] Humor marked by the use of morbid, ironic, or grotesquely comic episodes that ridicule human folly. A comic work that employs black humor is a black comedy.

Although the French Surrealist André Breton published his *Anthologie de l'humour noir* ("Anthology of Black Humor," frequently enlarged and reprinted) in 1940, the term did not come into common use until the 1960s. Among the best-known novelists to employ black humor were Nathanael West, Vladimir Nabokov, and Joseph Heller. An outstanding example of black comedy is Heller's *Catch-22* (1961). Other novelists who mined the same vein included Kurt Vonnegut, particularly in *Slaughterhouse Five* (1969); Thomas Pynchon, in *V* (1963) and *Gravity's Rainbow* (1973); and Bruce Jay Friedman in *Stern* (1962). The term black comedy also was applied to a number of playwrights in the THEATER OF THE ABSURD, especially to Eugène Ionesco, as in *La Leçon* (1951; *The Lesson*) and *Les Chaises* (1952; *The Chairs*).

Antecedents to black comedy include the comedies of Aristophanes (5th–4th century BC), François Rabelais' *Pantagruel* (1532), Jonathan Swift's "A Modest Proposal" (1729), and Voltaire's *Candide* (1759).

Black Mountain poets A loosely associated group of poets that formed an important part of the advance guard of American poetry in the 1950s. They published innovative yet disciplined poetry in the *Black Mountain Review* (1954–57), which became a leading forum of experimental verse. The group grew up around the poets Robert Creeley, Robert Duncan, and Charles Olson while they were teaching at Black Mountain College in North Carolina.

Turning away from the poetic tradition espoused by T.S. Eliot, the Black Mountain poets emulated the freer style of William Carlos Williams. Charles Olson's essay *Projective Verse* (1950) became their manifesto. Olson emphasized the creative process, in which the poet's energy is transferred through the poem to the reader. Inherent in this new poetry was the reliance upon decidedly American conversational language.

Much of the group's early work was published in the magazine *Origin*

(1951–56). Dissatisfied with the lack of critical material in that magazine, Creeley and Olson established the *Black Mountain Review,* and Creeley edited it while living in Majorca, Spain. It featured the work of Williams and Duncan, as well as Paul Blackburn, Denise Levertov, Gary Snyder, and many others who later helped shape poetry in America. The magazine was significant, too, for its emphasis on American-oriented, nonacademic verse.

Black Orpheus \'ȯr-ˌfyüs, -fē-əs\ Literary journal founded in 1957 in Lagos, Nigeria, to encourage the production and discussion of contemporary African writing. The journal was founded by Ulli Beier, a German teaching at the University of Ibadan, and published by the Nigerian Ministry of Education. *Black Orpheus* published articles about African literature, music, sculpture, and other art forms. Although it underwent major changes in editorial leadership and aesthetic and political philosophy, it always held to its initial purpose of encouraging contemporary African writing in the English language. Also included in its statement of purpose was the publication in English translation of works by African writers in French, Portuguese, and Spanish. Works by black American and West Indian authors also appeared, as did examples of literature from the African oral tradition. In time the journal published works from virtually all areas of Africa. In the 1970s and '80s publication became sporadic.

Among authors who were published in the journal were Wole Soyinka, Gabriel Okara, and John Pepper Clark from Nigeria; Peter Abrahams and Dennis Brutus from South Africa; and LeRoi Jones from the United States.

black theater In the United States, dramatic movement encompassing plays written by, for, and about blacks. The minstrel shows of the early 19th century are believed by some to be the roots of black theater, but initially they were written by whites, acted by whites in blackface, and performed for white audiences. After the American Civil War, blacks began to perform in minstrel shows, and by the turn of the century they were producing black musicals, many of which were written, produced, and acted entirely by blacks. The first known play by an American black was James Brown's *King Shotaway* (1823). William Wells Brown's *Escape; or, A Leap for Freedom* (1858) was the first black play published, but the first real success of a black dramatist was Angelina W. Grimké's *Rachel* (1916).

Black theater flourished during the HARLEM RENAISSANCE of the 1920s and '30s. Experimental groups and black theater companies emerged in Chicago, New York City, and Washington, D.C. Among these was the Ethiopian Art Theatre, which established Paul Robeson as America's foremost black actor. Garland Anderson's play *Appearances* (1925) was the first play of black authorship to be produced on Broadway, but black theater did not experience a Broadway hit until Langston Hughes' *Mulatto* (1935) won wide acclaim. In that same year the Federal Theatre Project was founded, providing a training ground for blacks. In the late 1930s, black community theaters began to appear, revealing talents such as those of Ossie Davis and Ruby Dee. By 1940 black theater was firmly grounded in the American Negro Theater and the Negro Playwrights' Company.

After World War II black theater grew more progressive, more radical, and more militant, reflecting the ideals of black revolution and seeking to establish a mythology and symbolism apart from white culture. Councils were organized to abolish racial stereotypes in theater and to integrate black playwrights into the mainstream of American dramaturgy. Lorraine Hansberry's *A Raisin in the Sun* (1959) and other successful black plays of the 1950s portrayed the difficulty blacks had in maintaining an identity in a society that degraded them.

The 1960s saw the emergence of a new black theater, angrier and more defiant than its predecessors, with LeRoi Jones, known later as Amiri Baraka, as its strongest proponent. Baraka's plays, including the award-winning *Dutchman* (1964), depicted whites' exploitation of blacks. He established the Black Arts Repertory Theatre in Harlem in 1965 and inspired playwright Ed Bullins and others seeking to create a strong "black aesthetic" in American theater. Another playwright of this era was Ntozake Shange.

In the 1970s several black musicals were widely produced. In the early 1980s Charles Fuller's *A Soldier's Play* won a Pulitzer Prize, an award later given also to the powerful and prolific dramatist August Wilson.

Blackwood's Magazine \'blak-ˌwu̇dz\ Monthly publication that was an important literary force in 19th-century England. William Blackwood, Scottish founder of the publishing firm William Blackwood and Sons, Ltd., launched the *Edinburgh Monthly Magazine* in April 1817 as a Tory counterpart to the Whig-inclined *Edinburgh Review*. His magazine was retitled *Blackwood's Edinburgh Magazine* in October 1817 and was styled simply *Blackwood's Magazine* from 1906 until it ceased publication in 1980.

In its first year of publication writers John Gibson Lockhart, James Hogg, and John Wilson quickly made *Blackwood's* notorious throughout England with their biblical parody "Translations from an Ancient Chaldee Manuscript." Libel suits filed by victims of its satires also helped to make *Blackwood's* famous. Unlike its competitors, *Blackwood's* published short fiction and serialized novels; Thomas De Quincey, George Eliot, Joseph Conrad, and Alfred Noyes were among its contributors. It declined in influence, however, during the 20th century.

blank verse Unrhymed verse, specifically unrhymed iambic pentameter, the preeminent dramatic and narrative verse form in English. It is also the standard form for dramatic verse in Italian and German. Its richness and versatility depend on the skill of the poet in varying the stresses and the position of the caesura (pause) in each line, in catching the shifting tonal qualities and emotional overtones of the language, and in arranging lines into thought groups and paragraphs.

Adapted from unrhymed Greek and Latin heroic verse, blank verse was introduced in 16th-century Italy along with other classical meters. The Italian humanist Francesco Maria Molza attempted the writing of consecutive unrhymed verse in 1514 in his translation of Virgil's *Aeneid.* Other experiments in 16th-century Italy were the tragedy *Sofonisba* (written 1514–15) by Gian Giorgio Trissino and the didactic poem *Le api* (1539) by Giovanni Rucellai. Rucellai was the first to use the term *versi sciolti,* which was translated into English as "blank verse." It soon became the standard meter of Italian Renaissance drama and was used in such major works as the comedies of Ludovico Ariosto, *L'Aminta* of Torquato Tasso, and the *Il pastor fido* of Battista Guarini.

Henry Howard, Earl of Surrey, introduced the meter, along with the sonnet and other Italian humanist verse forms, to England in the early 16th century. Thomas Sackville and Thomas Norton used blank verse for the first English tragic drama, *Gorboduc* (first performed 1561), and Christopher Marlowe developed its musical qualities and emotional power in *Tamburlaine, Doctor Faustus,* and *Edward II.* William Shakespeare transformed the line and the instrument of blank verse into the vehicle for the greatest English dramatic poetry. In his early plays, he combined it with prose and a 10-syllable rhymed couplet; he later employed a blank verse dependent on stress rather than on syllabic length. Shakespeare's poetic expression in his later plays, such as *Hamlet, King Lear, Othello, Macbeth,* and *The Winter's Tale,* is supple, approximating the rhythms of speech, yet capable of conveying the subtlest human delight, grief, or perplexity.

After a period of debasement, blank verse was restored to its former grandeur by John Milton in *Paradise Lost* (1667). Milton's verse is intellectually complex, yet flexible, using inversions, Latinized words, and all manner of stress, line length, variation of pause, and paragraphing to gain descriptive and dramatic effect. In the 18th century, James Thomson used blank verse in his long descriptive poem *The Seasons*, and Edward Young's *Night Thoughts* uses it with power and passion. Later, William Wordsworth wrote his autobiography of the poetic spirit, *The Prelude* (completed 1805–06; published 1850), in blank verse; Percy Bysshe Shelley used it in his drama *The Cenci* (1819), as did John Keats in *Hyperion* (1820). The form's extreme flexibility can be seen in its range from the high tragedy of Shakespeare to the low-keyed, conversational tone of Robert Frost in *A Masque of Reason* (1945).

Blank verse was established in German drama by Gotthold Lessing's *Nathan der Weise* (1779). Examples of its use are found in the writings of J.W. von Goethe, Friedrich von Schiller, and Gerhart Hauptmann. It was also used extensively in Swedish, Russian, and Polish dramatic verse. *Compare* FREE VERSE.

blason \blȧ-ˈsō^{n}\ [French, from Middle French, eulogy, reproach, literally, coat of arms] A type of catalog verse in which something is either praised or blamed through a detailed listing of its faults or attributes. The word is normally used more specifically to refer to a type of verse in which aspects of the beloved's appearance are enumerated. This type of *blason* was said to have been invented by the French poet Clément Marot in 1536.

blood \'bləd\ *British* A lurid work of fiction; especially a cheap and ill-written book of adventure or crime. The word is a short form of *blood-and-thunder book*.

bloodcurdler \'bləd-ˌkərd-ə-lər\ A gruesome, melodramatic theatrical or literary production.

bloods *See* PENNY DREADFUL.

Bloomsbury group \'blümz-bə-rē, -ˌber-ē\ Name given to a coterie of English writers, philosophers, and artists who frequently met between about 1907 and 1930 at the houses of Clive and Vanessa Bell and of Vanessa's brother and sister Adrian and Virginia Stephen (later Virginia Woolf) in the Bloomsbury district of London, the area around the British Museum. They discussed aesthetic and philosophical questions in a spirit of agnosticism and were strongly influenced by G.E. Moore's *Principia Ethica* (1903) and by A.N. Whitehead's and Bertrand Russell's *Principia Mathematica* (1910–13), in the light of which they searched for definitions of the good, the true, and the beautiful and questioned accepted ideas with a "comprehensive irreverence" for all kinds of sham.

Nearly all the male members of the group had been at Trinity or King's College, Cambridge, with another brother Thoby Stephen, who had introduced them to Vanessa and Virginia. Most of them had been "Apostles," or members of the "society," a select, semisecret university club for the discussion of serious questions, founded at Cambridge in the late 1820s by J.F.D. Maurice and John Sterling.

The Bloomsbury group included the novelist E.M. Forster, the biographer Lytton Strachey, the art critic Clive Bell, the painters Vanessa Bell and Duncan Grant, the economist John Maynard Keynes, the Fabian writer Leonard Woolf, and the novelist and critic Virginia Woolf. Other members were Desmond Macarthy, Arthur Waley, Saxon Sidney-Turner, Robert Trevelyan, Francis Birrell, J.T. Sheppard (later provost of King's College), and the critic Raymond Mortimer and the sculptor Stephen Tomlin, both Oxford men. Bertrand Russell, Aldous Huxley, and T.S. Eliot were sometimes associated with the group, as was the economist Gerald Shove. The group survived World War I but by the early 1930s had ceased to exist in its original form, having by that time merged with the general intellectual life of London, Oxford, and Cambridge. Although its members shared certain ideas and values, the Bloomsbury group did not constitute a school. Its significance lies in the number of talented persons associated with it.

blues stanza Three-line stanza form associated originally with blues music developed by African-Americans. It is used to express a melancholy feeling or a complaint and involves frequent repetition, especially in the first two lines.

Bluestocking \'blü-ˌstäk-iŋ\ Any of a group of ladies who in mid-18th-century England held "conversations" to which they invited men of letters and members of the aristocracy with literary interests. The word has come to be applied derisively to a woman who affects literary or learned interests. The Bluestockings attempted to replace social evenings spent playing cards with something more intellectual. The term probably originated when Mrs. Elizabeth Vesey invited the learned Benjamin Stillingfleet to one of her parties; he declined because he lacked appropriate dress, whereupon she told him to come "in his blue stockings"—the ordinary worsted stockings he was wearing at the time. He did so, and Bluestocking (or Bas Bleu) society became a nickname for the group.

The group was never a society in any formal sense. Mrs. Vesey and Mrs. Elizabeth Montagu became leaders of the literary ladies. Others included Madame d'Arblay (the diarist and novelist better known as Fanny Burney), Mrs. Frances Boscawen, Mrs. Hester Chapone, Mrs. Elizabeth Carter, Mrs. Mary Delany, and Miss Hannah More, whose poem "The Bas Bleu, or, Conversation" (1786) supplies valuable inside information about them. Guests included Samuel Johnson, James Boswell, David Garrick, George Lyttleton, and Horace Walpole (who called the women "petticoteries").

blurb \'blərb\ A short publicity notice (as on a book jacket). It is generally accepted that the word was coined in 1914 by the American humorist Gelett Burgess.

boasting poem Type of poem common in oral literature in which a character brags about personal exploits or great deeds. It can also be part of a longer written work, as in the Old English poem *Beowulf.* The *farsa* of the African Oromo people is a form of boasting poem.

bob and wheel \'bäb . . . 'hwēl, 'wēl\ In alliterative verse, a group of typically five rhymed lines following a section of unrhymed lines, often at the end of a strophe. The bob is the first line in the group and is shorter than the rest; the wheel is the quatrain that follows the bob.

bodice ripper A historical or gothic romance typically featuring scenes in which the heroine is subjected to sexual violence.

Bokmål or **Bokmaal** \'bůk-ˌmȯl, 'bōk-\, *also called* Riksmål \'riks-ˌmȯl\ A literary form of Norwegian developed by the gradual reform of written Danish in conformity to Norwegian usage. Bokmål means in Norwegian "book language" and Riksmål approximately "official language" (literally, "language of the kingdom"). *Compare* NYNORSK.

Bollingen Prize \'bō-liŋ-ən\ Award for achievement in American poetry, originally conferred by the Library of Congress with funds established in 1948 by the philanthropist Paul Mellon. An admirer of the psychoanalyst Carl Jung, Mellon named the prize after the Swiss town where Jung spent his summers. In 1949 the first award was made for *The Pisan Cantos* to Ezra Pound, who was then under indictment for treason for his World War II broadcasts from Italy, which were anti-Semitic and pro-fascist. A bitter controversy ensued in the press, and the Library of Congress was requested by a congressional committee to disassociate itself from the award. In 1950 the award was transferred to the Yale University Library, under the auspices of which it has since been administered. Originally annual, it became biennial in 1964. In 1961 the Bollingen Foundation also established a prize for translation.

bombast \ˈbäm-ˌbast\ Pretentious, inflated speech or writing. The now obsolete literal sense of the word was "cotton padding."

book \ˈbu̇k\ [Old English *bōc*] **1.** A set of written sheets of skin or paper or tablets of wood or ivory. **2.** A set of written, printed, or blank sheets bound together into a volume. **3.** A long written or printed literary composition. **4.** A major division of a treatise or literary work. **5.** A libretto or the script of a play.

The form, content, and provisions for making books have varied widely during their long history, but, generally speaking, a book is a written (or printed) message of considerable length, meant for public circulation and recorded on materials that are light yet durable enough to afford comparatively easy portability. Its primary purpose is to announce, expound, preserve, and transmit knowledge and information between people.

The papyrus roll of ancient Egypt is more nearly the direct ancestor of the modern book than is the clay tablet of the ancient Sumerians, Babylonians, Assyrians, and Hittites; examples of both date to about 3000 BC. The Chinese, somewhat later, independently created an extensive scholarship based on books. Primitive Chinese books were made of wood or bamboo strips bound together with cords. The emperor Shi Huangdi attempted to blot out publishing by burning books in 213 BC, but the tradition of book scholarship was nurtured under the Han dynasty (206 BC to AD 220). In AD 175, Confucian texts began to be carved into stone tablets and preserved by rubbings. Lampblack ink was introduced in China in AD 400 and printing from wooden blocks in the 6th century.

The Greeks adopted the papyrus roll and passed it on to the Romans. The parchment or vellum codex, which had superseded the papyrus roll by AD 400, was a revolutionary change in the form of the book. The advantages of the codex were that its series of pages enabled the reader to open to any point in the text, that both sides of the leaf could carry information, and that longer texts could be bound in a single volume. The medieval parchment or vellum leaves were prepared from the skins of animals. By the 15th century paper manuscripts were common. In medieval Europe, monasteries characteristically had libraries and scriptoria, places in which scribes copied books. The manuscript books produced there were the models for the first printed books.

The spread of printing was rapid in the second half of the 15th century. The availability of books and the increasing speed with which ideas and information could be disseminated made possible a revolution in thought and scholarship. Technical achievements, such as the development of offset printing, improved many aspects of book culture, but for sheer efficiency of storage and retrieval and rapidity of dissemination, the book was challenged in the mid to late 20th century by developments in electronic media.

Booker Prize \'bu̇k-ər\, *formerly* Booker McConnell Prize \mə-'kän-əl\ Prestigious British award given annually to a full-length novel; those eligible include English-language writers from the United Kingdom, the Commonwealth countries, the Republic of Ireland, and South Africa. Booker McConnell, a multinational company, established the award in 1968 to provide a counterpart to the Prix Goncourt in France. The prize became the subject of controversy on occasion. In 1984 Salman Rushdie, a former winner, described the judging committee as "Killjoyces" and "Anti-Prousts"; the committee chairman stated that he had not read the fiction of James Joyce and Marcel Proust, and did not want to award the prize to writers like them. Well-known winners in addition to Rushdie include V.S. Naipaul, Nadine Gordimer, Ruth Prawer Jhabvala, Iris Murdoch, J.M. Coetzee, A.S. Byatt, Kingsley Amis, Penelope Lively, Ben Okri, Michael Ondaatje, and Barry Unsworth.

In 1992 the first Booker Russian Novel Prize was awarded, to Mark Kharitonov for "Lines of Fate."

***Books Abroad* International Prize for Literature** *See* NEWSTADT PRIZE.

border ballad Type of spirited heroic ballad celebrating the raids, feuds, seductions, and elopements on the lawless border between England and Scotland in the 15th and 16th centuries. Among the better-known border ballads are "Johnny Cock," "Jock o' the Side," "Hobie Noble," and "The Bonny Earl of Murray." Though a few deal with events of historical importance, most are concerned with the personal retributions of the outlaws and robber clans who maintained their own grim code on the border. *See also* CORONACH.

boustrophedon \ˌbüs-trə-'fē-ˌdän, -dən\ [Greek *boustrophēdón,* literally, turning like oxen (in plowing)] The writing of alternate lines in opposite directions, one line from left to right and the next from right to left. Some Etruscan texts are written in boustrophedon style, as are some Greek ones of about the 6th century BC.

bouts-rimés \ˌbü-ˌrē-'mā, -'māz\ [French, literally, rhymed ends] Rhyming words or syllables to which verses are to be written; or the literary game of making verses from a list of rhyming words supplied by another person. The game, which requires that the rhymes follow a given order and that the result make some sense, is said to have been invented by the minor French poet Dulot in the early 17th century. Its wide popularity inspired at least one notable tour de force, an extended satirical poem by the French poet Jean-François Sarasin, entitled *Dulot vaincu* (1654; "Dulot Defeated"). The fad was revived in the 19th century when Alexandre Dumas (*père*) invited French poets and versifiers to try their skill with given sets of rhymes and published the results in 1865.

In 19th-century England, John Keats is said to have produced his charming poem "On the Grasshopper and Cricket" (1816) in a bouts-rimés competition with his friend Leigh Hunt, and Dante Gabriel Rossetti and his brother William tested their ingenuity and improved their rhyming facility by filling in verses from bouts-rimés. Most of William's poems in the Pre-Raphaelite magazine *The Germ* were bouts-rimés experiments. *See also* CRAMBO.

bowdlerize \'bōd-lə-ˌrīz, 'bau̇d-\ To remove matter considered indelicate or otherwise objectionable by expurgation or alteration. Thomas Bowdler was an English doctor of medicine, philanthropist, and man of letters, known for his *Family Shakspeare* (1818), in which, by expurgation and paraphrase, he aimed to provide an edition of the plays suitable for a father to read aloud to his family without fear of offending their susceptibilities or corrupting their minds. The first edition, the title of which was spelled *The Family Shakespeare* (1807), contained a selection of 20 plays that probably were expurgated by Bowdler's sister, Harriet. Although criticized for tampering with Shakespeare's text, Bowdler deserves a certain amount of credit for making the plays well known to a wide audience. The word *bowdlerize* was current by the mid-1830s as a synonym for expurgate, and it is now used in a pejorative sense.

boys' company *See* CHILDREN'S COMPANY.

Brahmin \'bräm-ən\ Member of any of several New England families of aristocratic and cultural pretensions, from which came some of the most distinguished American literati of the 19th century. Originally a humorous reference to the Brahmans, the highest caste of Hindu society, the term came to be applied to a number of prominent New England writers, including Oliver Wendell Holmes, Henry Wadsworth Longfellow, and James Russell Lowell. All three were educated in Europe and became associated with Harvard University.

Assuming the role of arbiters of literary taste, the Brahmins made Boston the literary capital of America in their day. Though they espoused democratic ideals, they remained aesthetically conservative. In an age that brought forth the masterpieces of Ralph Waldo Emerson, Henry David Thoreau, Nathaniel Hawthorne, Herman Melville, Walt Whitman, Edgar Allan Poe, and Mark Twain, they advocated a genteel, rational humanism, quite out of step with their brilliant contemporaries. Nevertheless, the Brahmins exerted the main influence on American literary taste until the 1890s.

break \'brāk\ **1.** Discontinuity in the flow or tone of a composition. A notable change of subject matter, attitude, or treatment. **2.** A pause or interruption (as a caesura or diaeresis) within or at the end of a verse.

Bremer Beiträger \'brā-mər-'bī-ˌtreg-ər\ Group of mid-18th-century German writers, among them Johann Elias Schlegel, who objected to the restrictive, Neoclassical principles laid down in 1730 by Johann Christoph Gottsched, according to which "good" literature was to be produced and judged. They demanded room for the play of genius and inspiration. Their organ was the *Bremer Beiträge* (1745–48).

Breton lay \'bret-ən\ *Middle English* lai Breton. A short medieval French narrative poem usually based upon Celtic legends.

The form is so called because Breton professional storytellers supposedly recited similar poems, though none are extant. The Breton lay is typically a short, rhymed romance recounting a love story; it includes supernatural, mythological, chivalric, and fairy-tale elements, mythology transformed by medieval chivalry, and the Celtic idea of faerie, the land of enchantment. Derived from the late 12th-century French lays of Marie de France, it was adapted into English in the late 13th century and became very popular. The few extant English Breton lays include *Sir Gowther* (*c.* 1400); the incomplete, early 14th-century *Lai le Freine; Sir Orfeo,* a recasting of the Orpheus and Eurydice story; the 14th-century *Sir Launfal,* or *Launfalus Miles,* an Arthurian romance by Thomas Chestre; *Sir Emare,* of the late 14th or early 15th century, on the theme of the constant wife; and the 15th-century *Sir Landeval.* Some of Geoffrey Chaucer's *Canterbury Tales* are derived from Breton lays. *See also* LAY.

brevis brevians \ˈbrev-is-ˈbrev-ē-ˌanz\ [New Latin, literally, short (syllable) shortening (the following syllable)] In classical prosody, especially that of Latin comedy, the tendency to make a long syllable short when it follows a short syllable and is adjacent to an accented syllable.

brevis in longo \ˈbrev-is-in-ˈlȯŋ-gō\ [New Latin, short for *syllaba brevis in elemento longo* short syllable in a long element] In classical prosody, the presence of a short syllable in the final position in a line of verse where there is normally a long syllable.

brevity \ˈbrev-i-tē\ A short piece (as of writing, music).

bridge \ˈbrij\ A passage, section, or scene in a literary or dramatic work serving as a transition between two other more significant passages, sections, or scenes.

broadside \ˈbrȯd-ˌsīd\ **1.** A sizable sheet of paper printed usually on one side only. **2.** Something (especially a broadside ballad) printed on a broadside usually for general sale or distribution.

broadside ballad A descriptive or narrative verse or song, commonly in a simple ballad form, on a popular theme, and sung or recited in public places or printed on broadsides for sale in the streets.

Broadside ballads appeared shortly after the invention of printing in the 15th century and were hawked in the streets, fairs, and marketplaces of Europe into the 19th century. Typical broadsides included hack-written topical ballads on recent crimes, executions, or disasters. Many ballads passed into the oral tradition from broadside origins. Although older texts were often "beautified" by the addition of flowery, sentimental, or moralizing language, broadsides also preserved versions of traditional ballads that might otherwise have disappeared from popular tradition. *See also* GOOD-NIGHT.

broken-backed line A line truncated in the middle. The term is used especially of John Lydgate's poetry, many lines of which have nine syllables and appear to lack an unstressed syllable at the medial break or caesura.

broken rhyme **1.** Rhyme in which one of the rhyming elements is actually two words (i.e., "gutteral" with "sputter all"). **2.** Rhyme involving division of a word by the break between two lines in order to end a line with a rhyme provided by the first part of the word, as in the second stanza of Gerard Manley Hopkins' untitled poem that begins "No worst, there is none. Pitched past pitch of grief":

> My cries heave, herds-long; huddle in a main, a chief-
> woe, world-sorrow; on an age-old anvil wince and sing—
> Then lull, then leave off. Fury had shrieked 'No ling-
> ering! Let me be fell: force I must be brief'.

Edward Lear provides another example in stanza 6 of "How Pleasant to Know Mr. Lear":

> When he walks in a waterproof white,
> The children run after him so!
> Calling out, 'He's come out in his night-
> gown, that crazy old Englishman, oh!'

Brook Farm \'bru̇k\, *in full* The Brook Farm Institute of Agriculture and Education. A utopian experiment in communal living that lasted from 1841 to 1847. The farm itself was located in West Roxbury, Mass., near Boston. It was organized and virtually directed by George Ripley, a former Unitarian minister, editor of *The Dial* (a critical literary monthly) and a leader in the Transcendental Club, an informal gathering of intellectuals of the Boston area.

The project was financed by the sale of stock, a purchaser of one share automatically becoming a member of the institute. Among the original shareholders in the project were Charles A. Dana and Nathaniel Hawthorne. Ralph Waldo Emerson, Bronson Alcott, Margaret Fuller, Elizabeth Peabody, Theodore Parker, and Orestes A. Brownson were among its interested visitors.

Although communal living proved to have disadvantages (Hawthorne found that he was unable to write there and left after six months), for a while the project seemed to prosper. But disaster struck when the members put all available funds into the construction of a large central building that burned to the ground as its completion was being celebrated. Though the colony struggled on for a while, the enterprise gradually failed; the land and buildings were sold in 1849.

Hawthorne's *The Blithedale Romance* (1852) is a fictional treatment of some aspects of the Brook Farm setting.

Broom \'brüm\ Important international magazine of the arts, founded by Harold A. Loeb as a showcase for experimental writing, criticism, and graphic arts. Published in English, though issued from Rome and Berlin before all operations were moved to New York City, the magazine was initially edited by Loeb and Alfred Kreymborg and published from November 1921 through January

1924. *Broom* published works by Guillaume Apollinaire, Malcolm Cowley, E.E. Cummings, Robert Graves, Luigi Pirandello, Jean Toomer, and William Carlos Williams, among others. Graphic artists whose works were published included Pablo Picasso, Juan Gris, George Grosz, Paul Klee, and Henri Matisse.

Brut \'brüt\ Any of several medieval chronicles of Britain tracing the history and legend of the country from the time of the mythical Brutus, descendant of Aeneas and founder of Britain. The *Roman de Brut* (1155) by the Anglo-Norman author Wace was one such chronicle. Perhaps the outstanding adaptation of the story is Layamon's *Brut* (*c.* 1200), written in Middle English; it lent a distinctly Germanic and heroic flavor to the story and signaled the revival of English literature after the Norman Conquest of 1066.

bucoliast \byü-'kō-lē-ast\ *obsolete* A pastoral poet.

bucolic \byü-'kä-lik\ [Greek *bukolikós,* a derivative of *boukólos* cowherd] Of or relating to shepherds or herdsmen, or typical of rural life. In literature the word refers to a type of pastoral writing that deals with rural life in a formal and fanciful style. *See also* PASTORAL.

bucolic diaeresis or **bucolic caesura** *See* DIAERESIS.

Bulletin \'bu̇l-ə-tin\ Leading Australian literary journal founded in 1880 by J.F. Archibald and John Haynes. Based in Sydney, N.S.W., the *Bulletin* had its major success from 1886 to 1903 under Archibald's direction. Key elements in its success were its radical political position and its humor. Perhaps the most significant legacy of the journal was the emphasis on stories and poetry by Australian writers; this policy encouraged cultural nationalism and reflected unique Australian values. Archibald also urged his writers to write about life in the Australian outback. The *Bulletin* was an important outlet for many Australian fiction writers and poets, and its literary review section, "The Red Page," was also influential. Over time the journal became increasingly conservative, and its writers and cartoonists often promulgated racist stereotypes; in 1908 "Australia for the White Man" became its slogan, and remained so until 1960. Declining sales led to a change in content, and after 1960 the *Bulletin* became a news magazine.

bunraku \'bu̇n-rä-kü\ [Japanese] Japanese traditional puppet theater in which nearly life-size dolls act out a chanted dramatic narrative, called *jōruri,* to the accompaniment of a small samisen (or *shamisen;* three-stringed Japanese lute). The term bunraku derives from the name of a troupe organized by puppet master Uemura Bunrakuken in the early 19th century; the term for puppetry is *ayatsuri,* and puppetry theater is more accurately rendered *ayatsuri jōruri.*

The puppets are trunkless and elaborately costumed. Principal dolls require three manipulators. The chief handler, wearing 18th-century dress, operates the head and right hand, moving the eyes, eyebrows, lips, and fingers. Two helpers, dressed and hooded in black to make themselves invisible, operate the left hand and the legs and feet (or in the case of female dolls, the movements of the kimono). Puppet theater reached its height in the 18th century with the plays of Chikamatsu Monzaemon. Its fortunes rose and fell with the quality of *jōruri* writers. *See also* JŌRURI.

burlesque \bər-'lesk\ [French, from the adjective *burlesque* mocking, burlesque in style, from Italian *burlesco,* a derivative of *burla* joke, harmless prank] In literature, comic imitation of a serious literary or artistic form that relies on an extravagant incongruity between a subject and its treatment. In burlesque the serious is treated lightly and the frivolous seriously; genuine emotion is sentimentalized, and trivial emotions are elevated to a dignified plane. Burlesque is closely related to parody, in which the language and style of a particular author, poem, or other work is mimicked, although burlesque is generally broader and coarser.

The long history of burlesque includes such early examples in Greece as *Batrachomyomachia* (*The Battle of the Frogs and Mice*), an anonymous burlesque of Homer, and the comedies of Aristophanes (5th–4th century BC). The long-winded medieval romance is satirized in Geoffrey Chaucer's 14th-century "The Tale of Sir Thopas"; the Charlemagne story and the whole theme of chivalry is mocked in the epic-style *Morgante* by Luigi Pulci. Italian burlesque of the 15th century attacked the concept of chivalry as a dying aristocratic notion lacking in common sense, and it thus anticipates Miguel de Cervantes' novel *Don Quixote* which is, however, of a size and seriousness that takes it out of the realm of burlesque. In the France of Louis XIV, burlesque was used in the "battle of the ancients and moderns" over the relative merits of modern and classical literature. The *Virgile travesty* (1648–53) of Paul Scarron is one of the best known of many burlesque or antiheroic epics on classical or even sacred themes.

English burlesque is chiefly dramatic, notable exceptions being Samuel Butler's satiric poem *Hudibras* (1663–78), an indictment of Puritan hypocrisy; the mock-heroic couplets of John Dryden and Alexander Pope; and the prose burlesques of Jonathan Swift and Henry Fielding. *The Rehearsal* (1671), a play by George Villiers, the 2nd Duke of Buckingham, mocks the Restoration drama of Dryden and Thomas Otway. John Gay's *The Beggar's Opera* (1728), Henry Fielding's *Tom Thumb* (1730), Richard Brinsley Sheridan's *The Critic* (1779), and Henry Carey's "most tragical tragedy" *Chrononhotonthologos* (1734) are the outstanding survivals from an age when burlesque was cruelly satirical and often defamatory. The heroic Bombardinion's lines in the following fragment from Carey's play resemble the more kindly, punning Victorian burlesque, however:

> Go call a coach, and let a coach be called;
> And let the man who calls it be the caller;
> And in his calling, let him nothing call,
> But coach! coach! coach! Oh! for a coach,
> ye gods!

Authors of Victorian burlesque—light entertainment with music and with plots frivolously modeled on those of history, literature, or classical mythology—included H.J. Byron, J.R. Planché, and W.S. Gilbert (before his partnership with Arthur Sullivan). Before the end of the 19th century, burlesque had largely yielded in popular favor to other forms.

Burns meter or **Burns stanza** In poetry, a stanza often used by Robert Burns and other Scottish poets. The stanza consists of six lines rhyming *aaabab* of which the fourth and sixth are regularly iambic dimeters and the others iambic tetrameters, as in Burns' *Holy Willie's Prayer:*

> I bless and praise thy matchless might,
> Whan thousands thou hast left in night,
> That I am here afore thy sight,
> For gifts an' grace
> A burnin' an' a shinin' light,
> To a' this place.

buskin \'bəs-kin\ [probably modification of Middle French *brouzequin* kind of foot covering] A thick-soled boot worn by actors in ancient Greek tragedies. Because of the association the term has come to mean tragedy. It is contrasted with sock, which refers to the foot covering worn by actors in comedies.

bylina \bə̇-'lē-nə\ *plural* byliny \-nē\ *or* bylinas [Russian, adaptation of Old Russian *bylina,* a word occurring only in *The Song of Igor's Campaign* and taken to mean "tale of a past event"] Traditional form of Old Russian and Russian heroic narrative poetry transmitted orally.

The term *bylina* came into use in the 1830s as a scholarly name for what is popularly called a *starina.* Although byliny originated about the 10th century during the Kievan period of Russian history, or possibly earlier, they were first written down about the 17th century. Byliny have been classified into several groupings or cycles, the largest of which deals with the golden age of Kiev in the 10th to 12th century. The byliny of this cycle center on the deeds of Prince Vladimir I and a group of heroes called the bogatyrs. One of the favorite heroes is the independent peasant Ilya of Murom, who defended the Kievan Rus from the Tatar khans. Although these ancient songs are no longer known around Kiev, they were discovered in the 19th century in the repertoire of people living around Lake Onega in the remote northwestern regions of European Russia. They are also known in the far northeastern outposts of Siberia.

Other byliny, dealing with all periods of Ukrainian and Russian history, have been collected throughout the country. They may relate events from the reigns of Ivan the Terrible or Peter the Great, or deal with the Cossack rebels Stenka Razin and Yemelyan Ivanovich Pugachov. A 20th-century bylina, the *Tale of Lenin,* converts the chief events of the Russian Revolution of 1917 into a formulaic hero tale. Taken together, byliny constitute a folk history in which facts and sympathies are often at variance with official history.

Byliny may have originated with professional court minstrels, but they are now circulated and created by non-specialists. With the spread of literacy the art of composing and chanting byliny is less vital than it once was.

C

When he can in one Couplet fix
More Sense than I can do in Six
—Jonathan Swift

caballine \'kab-ə-ˌlīn, -lin\ [Latin *fons caballinus,* literally, horse's spring, an epithet of Hippocrene] Of a fountain, imparting poetic inspiration. The source of this derivation is the ancient belief that the Muses' spring, Hippocrene (from Greek *hippos,* horse, and *krēnē,* fountain), came from a hoofprint of the winged horse Pegasus.

caccia \'kät-chä\ [Italian, literally, chase, hunt] Italian verse and musical form popular mainly in the mid-14th to mid-15th centuries. The caccia texts consisted of short, free-verse lyrics describing realistic, animated scenes such as the hunt or the market place, and horn calls, bird calls, shouts, and dialogue frequently enlivened the musical settings. Very few poems of this type have survived. The musical form consisted of two voices in strict canon at the unison (that is, in strict melodic initiation at the same pitch), and often of a noncanonic third part, composed of long notes that underlay the canonic voices, followed by a ritornello (short, recurrent instrumental passage).

The caccia is related in name to a 14th-century French genre, the chace, a setting of a text in three-part canon. The English catch, a type of round, may derive its name from caccia.

cacophony \kə-'käf-ə-nē, -'kȯf-, -'kaf-\ [Greek *kakophōnía,* from *kakós* bad + *phōnḗ* sound] Harsh or discordant sound; specifically, harshness in the sound of words or phrases. It is opposite in meaning from EUPHONY. Cacophony is usually produced by combinations of words that require a staccato, explosive delivery. Used skillfully, intentional cacophony can vitalize the content of imagery. Three lines from Walt Whitman's "The Dalliance of the Eagles" illustrate cacophony:

> The clinching interlocking claws, a living, fierce, gyrating wheel,
> Four beating wings, two beaks, a swirling mass tight grappling,
> In tumbling turning clustering loops, straight downward falling

cadence \'kā-dəns\ [Medieval Latin *cadentia,* literally, falling motion] **1.** A rhythmic sequence or flow of sounds in language; specifically, a particular rhythmic sequence distinctive of an individual author or literary composition. **2.** The rising or falling order of strong, long, or stressed syllables and weak, short, or unstressed syllables. *Compare* ARSIS; IONIC; METER. **3.** An unmetrical or irregular arrangement of stressed and unstressed syllables in prose or free verse that is based on natural stress groups.

caesura or **cesura** \si-ˈzyu̇r-ə, -ˈzhu̇r-ə\ *plural* caesuras *or* caesurae \-ˈzyu̇r-ē, -ˈzhu̇r-ē\ [Late Latin, literally, the act of cutting or felling; a calque of Greek *tomḗ* caesura, literally, cutting] **1.** In Greek and Latin prosody, a break in the flow of sound within a verse that is caused by ending a word within a foot (arma vi/rumque ca/no ‖ Tro/jae qui/ primus ab/oris). It is represented in scansion by the sign ‖. It is usually distinguished from DIAERESIS, in which the word ending and the foot ending coincide. Individual types are often distinguished in classical prosody, thus hephthemimeral caesura indicates a caesura occurring after the seventh half foot; penthemimeral caesura, occurring after the fifth half foot; and trithemimeral caesura, occurring after the third half foot. In this prosody, the caesura is strictly a metrical element, not an element of expression. **2.** In modern prosody, a pause within a poetic line that breaks the regularity of the metrical pattern. The caesura sometimes is used to emphasize the formal metrical construction of a line, but it more often introduces the cadence of natural speech patterns and habits of phrasing into the metrical scheme. The caesura may coincide with conventional punctuation marks, as in the following line from William Shakespeare, in which a strong pause is demanded after each comma for rhetorical expression:

> This blessed plot, ‖ this earth, ‖ this realm,
> ‖ this England,

The caesura is not necessarily set off by punctuation, however, as in this line from John Keats:

> Thou foster-child of silence ‖ and slow time,

In Germanic and Old English alliterative poetry, the caesura was a formal device dividing each line centrally into two half lines as in this example from "The Battle of Maldon":

> Hige sceal þe heardra,
> hearte þe cenre,
> mod sceal þe mare,
> þe ure mægen lytlaþ

> (Mind must be firmer, ‖ heart the more
> fierce,
> Courage the greater, ‖ as our strength
> diminishes.)

In Romance and Neoclassical verse, the caesura occurs most frequently in the middle of the line (medial caesura), but in modern verse its place is flexible, and it may occur near the beginning of one line (an initial caesura) or near the end of the next (terminal caesura). There also may be several caesuras within a single line. Thus, it has the effect of interposing the informal and irregular patterns of speech as a subtle counterpoint to the poem's regular rhythm; it prevents metrical monotony and emphasizes the meaning of lines.

Types of caesura that are differentiated in modern prosody are the *masculine caesura,* a caesura that follows a stressed or long syllable, and the *feminine caesura,* which follows an unstressed or short syllable. The feminine caesura is further divided into the epic caesura and the lyric caesura. An *epic caesura* is a feminine caesura that follows an extra unstressed syllable that has been inserted in accentual iambic meter. An epic caesura occurs in these lines from Shakespeare's *Macbeth:* "but how of Cawdor? || The Thane of Cawdor lives." The *lyric caesura* is a feminine caesura that follows an unstressed syllable normally required by the meter. It can be seen in A.E. Housman's "they cease not fighting || east and west."

Caldecott Medal \ˈkal-də-ˌkät, *commonly* ˈkäl-\ Annual prize awarded "to the artist of the most distinguished American picture book for children." It was established in 1938 by Frederic G. Melcher, chairman of the board of the R.R. Bowker Publishing Company, and named for the 19th-century English illustrator Randolph Caldecott. It is presented at the annual conference of the American Library Association along with the Newbery Medal for children's literature.

Cambridge critics \ˈkām-brij\ Group of critics who were a major influence in English literary studies from the mid-1920s and who established an intellectually rigorous school of critical standards in the field of literature. Their approach to literary criticism was influenced by the distinguished work in other fields that was going on at Cambridge in the 1920s: Ernest Rutherford's scientific work in the Cavendish Laboratory, John Maynard Keynes' economic theories, and, especially, Ludwig Wittgenstein's ventures in philosophy, linguistic analysis, and semantics.

The leaders of the group were I.A. Richards and F.R. Leavis of the University of Cambridge and Richards' pupil William Empson. C.K. Ogden, a writer and linguist, was associated with Richards in linguistic studies (*The Meaning of Meaning,* 1923) at Cambridge. These critics' treatment of literature was based upon a close examination of the literary text, as exemplified in two seminal books by Richards, *Principles of Literary Criticism* (1924) and *Practical Criticism* (1929), and upon their belief in a close relationship of literature to social issues. This view was part of a larger criticism of life, which was treated by Leavis in such books as *Culture and Environment* (1933) and *The Great Tradition* (1948), a work on the English novel. Leavis' quarterly *Scrutiny* (1932–53) was devoted to both aspects, and its contributors—among them L.C. Knights, Denys Thompson, and Leavis' wife, Q.D. Leavis (*Fiction and the Reading Public,* 1932)—made notable contributions to criticism. William Empson's *Seven Types of Ambiguity* (1930) and *The Structure of Complex Words* (1951) demonstrated the scope of criticism stemming from linguistic analysis. Cambridge criticism conformed to no special type, but its analytical bent, astringency, and disdain of merely appreciative writing sprang from its creators' formidable training and interests in philosophy, linguistics, psychology, and social sciences and from their immense reading in literature. *See also* NEW CRITICISM.

cameo \ˈkam-ē-ˌō\ A usually brief literary or dramatic piece that brings into delicate or sharp relief the character of a person, place, or event.

campus novel A novel set on a university campus, usually written by someone who is or was an academic. Examples include Kingsley Amis' *Lucky Jim* (1954), John Barth's *Giles Goat-Boy* (1966), and Robertson Davies' *The Rebel Angels* (1981).

cancioneiro *Spanish* ˌkän-thē-ō-ˈnā-rō, *Portuguese* ˌkȧ^{n}n-syō-ˈnā-rü\ [Portuguese *cancioneiro,* from Spanish *cancionero,* a derivative of *canción* song] A Spanish or Portuguese collection of songs and poems, usually by several authors. The earliest examples of Portuguese-Galician poetry, composed from the 12th to the 14th century, were collected during the 14th and 15th centuries into three manuscript songbooks: the *Cancioneiro da Ajuda,* the *Cancioneiro da Vaticana,* and the *Cancioneiro de Colocci-Brancuti* (or *da Bíblioteca Nacional de Lisboa*). The 2,000 poems in these books can be classified by content into three major categories: (1) the *cantigas de amigo,* laments of women for their lovers, dealing with sad partings, grief, and patient waiting and containing descriptions of nature that are permeated with *saudade* (the melancholy tone characteristic of Portuguese poetry); (2) the *cantigas de amor,* in which the pining lover is a man; and (3) the *cantigas de escárnio e maldizer,* ribald satires on contemporary themes. The collections also contain occasional religious songs extolling the miracles of the Virgin. Among the 200 composers to whom these poems are attributed are the Portuguese king Dinis (died 1325) and his illegitimate son Alfonso Sanches.

The later *Cancioneiro Geral* (1516), compiled by Garcia de Resende, contains nearly 1,000 *cantigas* in Portuguese and Castilian. Dealing with love and satiric themes, the verses are more intricate and sophisticated than those in the earlier collections and show evidence of Spanish and Italian influence.

The Portuguese *cantigas* stimulated the development of Spanish lyrical poetry, also collected into *cancioneros*. Outstanding among the Spanish examples are the *Cancionero de Baena* (1445), a collection of 583 poems made by Juan Alfonso Baena that shows the influence of the Portuguese lyric but is more intellectual, using symbol, allegory, and classical allusion in the treatment of themes of high moral, philosophical, or political intent, and the *Cancionero general* (1511), a collection of late medieval lyrics made by Hernando del Castillo.

caṅkam literature \ˈchäŋ-gäm\, caṅkam *also spelled* śaṅgam \ˈshäŋ-gäm\ The earliest writings in Tamil, thought to have been produced in three *caṅkams*, or literary academies, in Madurai, India, from the 1st to the 4th century AD. The *Tolkāppiyam,* a book of grammar and rhetoric, was compiled along with eight anthologies (*Eṭṭuttokai*) of secular poetry: *Kuruntokai, Narriṇai, Akanāṉūru, Aiṅkurunūru, Kalittakai, Puranāṉūru, Patirruppattu,* and *Paripāṭal.* The poems are probably unique in early Indian literature, which is otherwise almost entirely religious. Two topics, love and the praise of kings and their deeds, predominate. Many of the verses, especially those written about noble deeds, display great freshness and vigor, and they are singularly free of the elaborate literary conceits of much other early and medieval literature of India. As largely secular works, they are also free of the complex mythical allusions that are characteristic of most Indian art forms. Among the rare instances of religious works in *caṅkam* writing, *Pattupāṭṭu* ("The Ten Long Poems") contains the earliest Indian poem of personal devotion to a god, and *Paripāṭal* contains poems about Vishnu, Śiva, and Murugaṉ.

canon \'kan-ən\ [Greek *kanṓn* rod, measuring line, rule, standard] **1.** An authoritative list of books accepted as Holy Scripture. **2.** The authoritative works of a writer. **3.** A sanctioned or accepted group or body of related works.

The question of a canon of Western literature was widely discussed in American education during the 1980s and '90s. Those who sought greater inclusion of works by women and by members of nondominant ethnic groups were accused by conservative critics of sacrificing standards of quality for the sake of inclusiveness.

cantar \kän-'tär\ [Spanish, song, poem set to music, a noun derivative of *cantar* to sing] In Spanish literature, originally, the lyrics of a song. The word was later used for a number of different poetic forms. In modern times it has been used specifically for an octosyllabic quatrain in which assonance occurs in the even-numbered lines and the odd-numbered lines are unrhymed with the accent falling on the last syllable.

The *cantar de gesta* was a medieval narrative epic poem similar to the French chanson de geste though with somewhat longer lines arranged in irregular stanzas, each based on a single recurring rhyme. The *Cantar de mio Cid* is the most famous example. The *cantar de pandeiro* is a Galician folksong arranged in three-line stanzas.

canterbury tale or **canterbury story** \'kan-tər-ˌber-ē, -bə-rē\ **1.** A cock-and-bull story, a yarn, or a fable. **2.** A long, tedious tale. Both senses are derived from *The Canterbury Tales* of Geoffrey Chaucer.

canto \'kan-tō\ [Italian, act of singing, song, poem, division of a poem] One of the major divisions of an epic poem or other long narrative poem. As its etymology suggests, it probably originally indicated a portion of a poem that could be sung or chanted by a minstrel at one sitting. Though early oral epics, such as Homer's, are divided into discrete sections, the name canto was first adopted for these divisions by the Italian poets Dante, Matteo Maria Boiardo, and Ludovico Ariosto. The first long English poem to be divided into cantos was Edmund Spenser's *The Faerie Queene* (1590–1609). Lord Byron structured his long poems *Childe Harold's Pilgrimage* (1812–18) and *Don Juan* (1819–24) in cantos. An ambitious unfinished epic by the American poet Ezra Pound is known as *The Cantos*.

canvas or **canvass** \ˈkan-vəs\ The background, setting, or scope of a historical or fictional account or narrative. The metaphor, which is drawn from painting, seems to have originated in the 18th century.

canzone \kan-ˈzō-nē, känt-ˈsō-nā\ or **canzona** \-nä\ [Italian, from Latin *cantio* song] **1.** A medieval Italian or Provençal lyric poem in stanzaic form. Masters of the form included Petrarch, Dante, Torquato Tasso, and Guido Cavalcanti. **2.** An elaborately constructed ode suited to musical setting.

cardinal sins *See* SEVEN DEADLY SINS.

caricature \ˈkar-ə-kə-ˌchu̇r, -ˌchər, -ˌtyu̇r, -ˌtu̇r\ [Italian *caricatura* exaggeration, caricature, literally, the act of loading, a derivative of *caricare* to load, pile up, increase] A representation characterized by exaggeration. The effect is usually produced by means of deliberate oversimplification and often ludicrous distortion of characteristics. Thus, Lady Bracknell in Oscar Wilde's *The Importance of Being Earnest* and the unrepentant Ebenezer Scrooge in Charles Dickens' *A Christmas Carol* may be considered caricatures.

carmen \ˈkär-mən\ *plural* carmina \-mə-nə\ [Latin, incantation, song, poem] A song, poem, or incantation. *See* POEM; INCANTATION.

carmen figuratum [New Latin, shaped poem] *See* PATTERN POETRY.

carmina Fescennina *See* FESCENNINE VERSE.

carpe diem \ˈkär-pā-ˈdē-ˌem, -pē, ˈdī-, -əm\ Latin phrase (meaning literally "pluck the day!"), used by the Roman poet Horace to express the idea that one should enjoy life while one can. The sentiment has been expressed in many literatures, especially in 16th- and 17th-century English poetry. Two of the best-known examples are in Robert Herrick's "To the Virgins, to Make Much of Time" and Andrew Marvell's "To His Coy Mistress."

cast \ˈkast\ The set of characters in a narrative.

Castalia \ka-ˈstā-lyə, -lē-ə\ or **Castalie** \ˈkas-tə-lē\ A source of poetic inspiration. Castalia was the name of a nymph who threw herself into or was transformed into a spring to evade the pursuit of Apollo. The spring then was named Castalia for her, and it was a source of inspiration for Apollo and for the Muses. The Muses were sometimes called Castalides because of their association with the spring.

casual \ˈkazh-ə-wəl\ An essay written in a familiar, often humorous style. The word is usually associated with the style of essay that was cultivated at *The New Yorker* magazine.

catachresis \ˌkat-ə-ˈkrē-sis\ [Greek *katáchrēsis,* a derivative of *katachrêsthai* to make use of, use up, misuse] Use of the wrong word for the context; specifically, use of a forced and especially paradoxical figure of speech (such as "blind mouths").

catalexis \ˌkat-ə-ˈlek-sis\, *plural* catalexes \-ˌsēz\ [Greek *katálēxis* final syllable, close of a rhetorical period, a derivative of *katalḗgein* to leave off, stop] Omission of one or more syllables in the last foot of a line in metrical verse. Thus if the chief meter of a poem is iambic tetrameter and a line scans ∪ ′ | ∪ ′ | ∪ ′ | ∪ ′ | ∪ |, that line is catalectic. *Compare* HYPERMETRIC.

catalog verse or **catalogue verse** \ˈkat-ə-ˌlȯg, -ˌläg\ Verse that presents a list of people, objects, or abstract qualities. Such verse exists in almost all literatures and is of ancient origin. The genealogical lists in the Bible and the lists of heroes in epics such as Homer's *Iliad* are types of catalog verse, as are more modern poems such as Gerard Manley Hopkins' "Pied Beauty," which begins:

> Glory be to God for dappled things—
>   For skies of couple-colour as a brinded cow;
>   For rose-moles all in stipple upon trout that swim;
> Fresh-firecoal chestnut-falls; finches' wings;
>   Landscape plotted and pieced—fold, fallow, and plough;
>   And áll trádes, their gear and tackle and trim.

catastasis \kə-ˈtas-tə-sis\, *plural* catastases \-ˌsēz\ [Greek *katástasis* settlement, state, condition] **1.** The dramatic complication that immediately precedes the climax of a play. **2.** The climax of a play. *Compare* CATASTROPHE; EPITASIS; PROTASIS.

catastrophe \kə-ˈtas-trə-fē\ [Greek *katastrophḗ* end of a tragedy, end, close, a derivative of *katastréphein* to turn down, overturn] The final action that completes the unraveling of the plot in a play, especially in a tragedy. Catastrophe is a synonym of DENOUEMENT. The term is sometimes applied to a similar action in a novel or story.

catch \ˈkach, ˈkech\ In prosody, an extra unstressed syllable at the beginning of a line that should start with a stressed syllable in order to fit the meter.

catharsis \kə-ˈthär-sis\ *plural* catharses \-ˌsēz\ The purification or purgation of the emotions (especially pity and fear) primarily through art. The term, derived from the medical term *katharsis* ("purgation" or "cleansing"), was used as a metaphor by Aristotle (*Poetics*) to describe the effects of true dramatic tragedy on the spectator. Aristotle states that the purpose of tragedy is to arouse "terror and pity" and thereby effect the catharsis of these emotions.

Aristotle's meaning has been the subject of critical debate over the centuries. The 18th-century German dramatist and literary critic Gotthold Lessing held that catharsis converts excess emotions into virtuous dispositions. Other critics saw tragedy as a moral lesson in which the fear and pity excited by the tragic hero's fate serve to warn the spectator not similarly to tempt providence. The interpretation generally accepted is that, through experiencing fear vicariously in a controlled situation, the spectator's own anxieties are directed outward, and, through sympathetic identification with the tragic protagonist, his or her insight and outlook are enlarged. Tragedy then has a healthful and humanizing effect on the spectator or reader.

causerie \ˌkōz-ˈrē, ˌkō-zə-\ [French, literally, chat, conversation] In literature, a short, informal essay, often on a literary topic. This sense of the word is derived from the title of a series of essays by the French author Charles-Augustin Sainte-Beuve, *Causeries du lundi.*

Cavalier poet \ˌkav-ə-ˈlir\ Any of a group of English gentlemen poets who were Cavaliers (supporters of Charles I [1625–49] during the English Civil Wars, as opposed to the Roundheads, who supported Parliament). They counted the writing of polished and elegant lyrics as only one of their many accomplishments as soldiers, courtiers, gallants, and wits. The term embraces Richard Lovelace, Thomas Carew, Sir John Suckling, Edmund Waller, and Robert Herrick. Although Herrick, a clergyman, was detached from the court, his short, fluent, graceful lyrics on love and dalliance and his carpe diem ("seize the day") philosophy ("Gather ye rosebuds while ye may") are typical of the Cavalier style. Besides writing love lyrics addressed to mistresses with fanciful names like Anthea, Althea, or Amarantha, the Cavaliers occasionally wrote of war, honor, and their duty to the king. Sometimes they deftly combined all these themes, as in Richard Lovelace's well-known poem "To Lucasta, Going to the Wars," which ends,

> I could not love thee, dear, so much
> Loved I not honour more.

Celtic revival *also called* Celtic Twilight. Mystical element in the GAELIC REVIVAL and especially the IRISH LITERARY RENAISSANCE, Irish literary movements of the 19th century. Originating in Romanticism and sustained by Irish nationalism, Celtic revival literature was characterized by an emphasis on Irish myth and legend combined with a moody sense of gothic mystery, supernatural magic, and romantic melancholy.

Notable proponents of the Celtic revival were Æ (George Russell) and William Butler Yeats, who compiled a volume of folklore called *The Celtic Twilight* (1893; revised and enlarged 1902). Other authors who made use of the Celtic revival were Thomas Love Peacock, Alfred, Lord Tennyson, and Gerard Manley Hopkins. The movement faded with the development of realism in Irish literature at the turn of the century.

cénacle \ˈsen-ə-kəl, *French* sā-ˈnȧkl\ [French, literally, the room where Christ and his apostles had the Last Supper, from Latin *cenaculum* upper story, dining room] A type of literary coterie formed around various early leaders of the

Romantic movement in France, replacing the salon as a place for writers to read and discuss their works. An early cénacle formed around Victor Hugo after the founding of the short-lived but influential *La Muse française*. When the review ceased publication in 1824, the young contributors shifted to the salon of Charles Nodier, who was then librarian of the Arsenal Library, second of the great French libraries. The activities of this group, which included Hugo, Alphonse de Lamartine, Alfred de Vigny, and Alfred de Musset, are described in the *Mémoires* of Alexandre Dumas *père*. Three years later, Hugo and the critic Charles-Augustin Sainte-Beuve formed a cénacle at Hugo's house on the rue Notre-Dame-des-Champs, where other young writers, including Prosper Mérimée, Théophile Gautier, and Gérard de Nerval, joined the group. The entourage of Gautier, Nerval, and Petrus Borel, the more turbulent, bohemian Romantics, became known as the Petit Cénacle. When Hugo's poetic drama *Hernani* was performed in 1830, their clamor and applause in support of the play overwhelmed the scorn of the traditionalists who had come to disparage it, thus ending the battle of the Romantics—the so-called battle of *Hernani*—and bringing about the demise of the outmoded dramatic conventions of classicism.

censorship \ˈsen-sər-ˌship\ The suppression or prohibition of anything that is considered objectionable or subversive of the common good.

In Christendom one of the most notable forms of censorship was the *Index librorum prohibitorum,* by which the Roman Catholic church for centuries policed the literature available to its followers. The struggle against censorship in the Anglo-American world began to take its modern form in the 17th and 18th centuries. Of special importance was John Milton's *Areopagitica* (1644), in which he argued against a government's right to license (or previously restrain) publication. Milton's definition of freedom of the press, however, did not preclude the condemnation of material after publication.

cento \ˈsen-ˌtō\, *plural* centones \sen-ˈtō-nēz\, centoes, *or* centos [Latin, patchwork quilt or curtain] An often poetic patchwork composition of words, phrases, or lines from other works. An early example is Decimus Magnus Ausonius' *Cento nuptialis,* a patchwork in which lines of Virgil are pieced together to form a shockingly explicit account of the consummation of a marriage. This type of composition, sometimes known as a collage or pastiche, is still written, some notable examples being works by practitioners of Dada and Surrealism.

ceremonial oratory *See* EPIDEICTIC ORATORY.

Cervantes Prize \ther-ˈb̠än-tās, *Angl* sər-ˈvän-tēz, -ˈvan-\, *in full* Premio de Literatura en Lengua Castellana Miguel de Cervantes. Literary award established in 1976 by the Spanish Ministry of Culture. It is the most prestigious and remunerative award given for Spanish-language literature. The Cervantes Prize is presented to an author whose work as a whole is judged to have most enriched Spanish culture. The award of 10 million Spanish pesetas is given annually and cannot be divided.

cesura *See* CAESURA.

chain of being *See* GREAT CHAIN OF BEING.

Chamberlain's Men \'chām-bər-lin\, *also called* The Lord Chamberlain's Men. An English theatrical company, the most important company of players in Elizabethan and Jacobean England. William Shakespeare was intimately connected with the company for most of his professional career as a dramatist.

The company's early history is somewhat complicated. A company known as Hunsdon's Men, whose patron was Henry Carey, 1st Lord Hunsdon, is traceable to 1564–67. Hunsdon took office as Lord Chamberlain in 1585, and another company (The Lord Chamberlain's Men) under his patronage is traceable to 1590. Two years later the theaters closed because of plague; when they reopened in 1594, a good deal of reorganization and amalgamation between various theater companies took place and a strong Lord Chamberlain's company emerged. After their patron's death in 1596, the company came under the protection of his son, the 2nd Lord Hunsdon, who himself became Lord Chamberlain in 1597. The company was known as The Lord Chamberlain's Men until the accession of James I in March 1603, when, by letters patent, it was taken under royal patronage and henceforth known as the King's Men.

The records of performances given at court show that it was by far the most favored of the theatrical companies. Its only rival was a company known during Elizabeth I's reign as the Admiral's Men and after that as Prince Henry's Men. Although the company frequently toured outside of London, its base remained in London, from 1599 to 1608 at the Globe Theatre. Shakespeare was the company's principal dramatist (he also acted with them), but works by Ben Jonson, Thomas Dekker, and the partnership of Francis Beaumont and John Fletcher were also presented. The company ceased to exist when, at the outbreak of the English Civil Wars in 1642, the theaters were closed and remained so until the Restoration 18 years later.

changga [Korean, song, singing] *See* PYŎLGOK.

chanson \shäⁿ-'sōⁿ\ [French, song] French art song of the Middle Ages and the Renaissance. The chanson before 1500 is preserved mostly in large manuscript collections.

Dating back to the 12th century, the monophonic chanson reached its greatest popularity with the trouvères of the 13th century, and it occurs as late as the lays of the composer and poet Guillaume de Machaut in the 14th century. Only the melodies survive. The monophonic chansons show the development of intricate musical-poetic forms deriving from the songs of the troubadours, who were slightly earlier counterparts of the trouvères. These forms were eventually simplified to become the three *formes fixes* ("fixed forms") of the accompanied chanson. *See also* BALLADE; RONDEAU; VIRELAY.

chanson à personnages \shäⁿ-sōⁿ-ȧ-per-sō-'nȧzh\ [French, literally, song with characters] Medieval French song in the form of a dialogue, often between a husband and a wife, a knight and a shepherdess, or lovers parting at dawn. Specific forms of such chansons include the pastourelle and the aubade.

chanson de geste \shä^{n}'-sō^{n}-də-'zhest\, *plural* chansons de geste *same*\ [French, literally, song of heroic deeds] Any of several Old French epic poems that form the core of the Charlemagne legends.

More than 80 chansons de geste have survived in manuscripts dating from the 12th to 15th centuries, but they deal chiefly with events of the 8th and 9th centuries during the reigns of Charlemagne and his successors. In general, the poems contain a core of historical truth overlain with legendary accretions. Whether they were composed under the inspiration of the events they narrate and survived for generations in oral tradition, or whether they were the independent compositions of professional poets of a later date, is still a disputed question. A few poems have authors' names, but most are anonymous.

Chansons de geste are composed in lines of 10 or 12 syllables grouped into *laisses* (irregular stanzas) based on assonance or, later, rhyme. The poems' lengths range from approximately 1,500 to more than 18,000 lines. They contain exemplary stories of warfare, often pitting Franks against Saracens, that fire the emotions with their insistent rhythms.

The fictional background of the chansons is the struggle of Christian France against a conventionalized polytheistic or idolatrous "Muslim" enemy. The emperor Charlemagne is portrayed as the champion of Christendom. He is surrounded by his court of Twelve Noble Peers, among whom are Roland, Oliver, Ogier the Dane, and Archbishop Turpin.

Besides the stories grouped around Charlemagne, there is a subordinate cycle of 24 poems which concerns Guillaume d'Orange, a loyal and long-suffering supporter of Charlemagne's weak son, Louis the Pious. Another cycle deals with the wars of such powerful barons as Doon de Mayence, Girart de Roussillon, Ogier the Dane, and Raoul de Cambrai.

The earlier chansons are heroic in spirit and theme. They focus on great battles or feuds and on the legal and moral niceties of feudal allegiances. After the 13th century, elements of romance and courtly love came to be introduced, and the austere early poems were supplemented by *enfances* (youthful exploits) of the heroes and fictitious adventures of their ancestors and descendants.

The masterpiece and probably the earliest of the chansons de geste is the 4,000-line *Chanson de Roland*. Appearing at the threshold of French epic literature, *Roland* was the formative influence on the rest of the chansons de geste. The chansons, in turn, spread throughout Europe. They strongly influenced Spanish heroic poetry such as the mid-12th-century Spanish epic *Cantar de mio Cid* ("Song of the Cid"). In Italy stories about Orlando and Rinaldo (Roland and Oliver) were very popular and formed the basis for the Renaissance epics *Orlando innamorato* (Matteo Boiardo; 1483) and *Orlando furioso* (Ludovico Ariosto; 1532). In the 13th century the German poet Wolfram von Eschenbach based his epic *Willehalm* on Guillaume d'Orange, and the chansons were recorded in prose in the Icelandic *Karlamagnús saga*. Charlemagne legends, referred to as "the matter of France," were long staple subjects of romance.

In the 20th century the chansons continued to enjoy a strange afterlife in folk ballads of the Brazilian hinterlands, called *literatura de la corda* ("literature on a string") because, in pamphlet form, they were formerly hung from strings and sold in marketplaces. Frequently in these ballads, through a misunderstanding of a Portuguese homonym, Charlemagne is surrounded by a company of 24 knights; i.e., "Twelve Noble Pairs."

chanson de toile \shä^{n}-sō^{n}-də-ˈtwȧl\ Early form of French lyric poetry dating from the beginning of the 12th century. The poems consisted of short monorhyme stanzas with a refrain. The Old French phrase *chançon de toile* (literally, "linen song") alluded to songs sung over needlework.

chansonnier \ˌshä^{n}-sən-ˈyā\ [French, a derivative of *chanson* song] **1.** A writer or singer of chansons; especially, a cabaret singer. **2.** A collection of songs or of verses for singing.

chantefable \shä^{n}t-ˈfȧbl, *Angl* -ˈfäb-lə\ [French, from Old French (Picard dialect) *cantefable,* literally, (it) sings (and it) narrates] A medieval tale of adventure told in alternating sections of sung verse and recited prose. The word itself was used—and perhaps coined—by the anonymous author of the 13th-century French work *Aucassin et Nicolette* in its concluding lines: "No cantefable prent fin" ("Our *chantefable* is drawing to a close"). It is the sole surviving example of the genre.

chant royal \ˌshä^{n}-rwä-ˈyȧl\, *plural* chants royaux \ˌshä^{n}-rwä-ˈyō\ [French, literally, royal song] A fixed form of verse, an elaboration of the ballade that was developed by French poets of the 13th to 15th centuries.

The chant royal is composed of five stanzas, identical in arrangement, of 11 lines each, and of an envoi (a short, fixed final stanza) of 5 lines. All the stanzas are written on the five rhymes exhibited in the first stanza, the entire poem, therefore, consisting of 60 lines in the course of which five rhymes are repeated. The rhyme scheme is *ababccddede*.

Because of its length and the rigidity of its form, the chant royal was more suitable than the ballade for solemn themes, such as the exploits of a noble hero or the praise of the Virgin Mary. Like the ballade, the chant royal had variations. As the *serventois,* for example, a poem in honor of the Virgin Mary, the chant royal early acquired, then lost, a refrain. Other variations on the chant royal were the *amoureuse* ("love poem"), the *sotte amoureuse* ("playful love poem"), and the *sotte chanson* ("comic poem").

In Old French, the most admired chants royaux are those of Clément Marot; his *Chant royal chrétien,* with its refrain "Santé au corps et Paradis à l'âme" ("Health to the body and Paradise to the soul"), was well known. The 17th-century fabulist Jean de La Fontaine was the last exponent of the chant royal before its eclipse.

Known only in French literature during its development, the chant royal was introduced into England by Sir Edmund Gosse in his poem "The Praise of Dionysus" (1877). Since then, it has been adapted by a number of English-language poets, but its solemn or religious tone is a thing of the past. It is now largely used for *vers de société* (urbane, ironic poetry).

chapbook \'chap-ˌbu̇k\ A small, inexpensive stitched book or pamphlet formerly sold by itinerant dealers, or chapmen, in western Europe and in North America. Most chapbooks were 5 1/2 by 4 1/4 inches (14 by 11 cm) in size and were made up of four pages (or multiples of four), illustrated with woodcuts. They contained tales of popular heroes, legend and folklore, jests, reports of notorious crimes, ballads, almanacs, nursery rhymes, school lessons, farces, biblical tales, dream lore, and other popular matter. The texts were mostly crude and anonymous, but they formed the major part of secular reading and now serve as a guide to the manners and morals of their times.

Many of the earliest English and German chapbooks derived from French examples, which began to appear at the end of the 15th century. The *Volksbücher* (a type of chapbook) began to flourish in Germany in the mid-16th century. Some were prose versions of medieval German verse romances; others contained tales of foreign origin. Whatever their sources, they satisfied a need for light literature that persisted long after the 16th century. In colonial America they were imported from England and were produced locally. When religious and other more serious tracts appeared, and as publication of inexpensive magazines developed in the early 19th century, chapbooks lost popularity and went into eclipse. With the rebirth of the small press in the late 20th century and the resurgence of letterpress use in fine printing, chapbooks began to reappear in specialty bookstores.

character \'kar-ik-tər\ [Greek *charaktḗr* stamp, mark, characteristic, character] **1.** A descriptive, often satiric analysis (usually in the form of a short literary sketch) of a human virtue or vice or of a general type of human character. In 17th-century English and French literature, the quality of a particular place or thing may also be analyzed. A representative human (such as a busybody, an old man, a country bumpkin) usually is made to stand for the trait, quality, or type. *See also* CHARACTER WRITER. **2.** Personality as represented or realized in fiction or drama. **3.** One of the persons of a drama or novel. **4.** Characterization, especially in fiction or drama.

characterization \ˌkar-ik-tə-rə-'zā-shən, -ˌrī-\ The representation in fiction or drama of human character or personality.

character study **1.** Analysis or portrayal in literature of the traits of character of an individual. **2.** A brief narrative or sketch devoted primarily to the examination of character.

character writer Any of the writers who produced a type of character sketch that was popular in 17th-century England and France.

Their writings stemmed from a series of character sketches produced by the Greek philosopher and teacher Theophrastus (fl. *c.* 372 BC). These sketches may have been part of a larger work and probably were written with the intention of instructing and amusing his students of rhetoric. Theophrastus' technique was to define an undesirable personal quality (such as vanity or stinginess) and then to describe the characteristic speech and behavior of the person who exemplified it. His work was introduced to Europe during the Renaissance in an edition of 1529; admiring his wit and insight into human failings, a number of contemporary writers imitated his example. They included, in France, Jean de La Bruyère, and, in England, Joseph Hall, Sir Thomas Overbury, John Earle, and Samuel Butler.

charactonym \'kar-ik-tə-ˌnim\ [*charact*er + *-onym* (as in *toponym*)] A name of a fictional character that suggests a distinctive trait of that character. Examples of charactonyms include Mistress Quickly and Caspar Milquetoast.

charm \'chärm\ [Old French *charme,* from Latin *carmen* ritual utterance, incantation, song] A practice or expression believed to have magic power, similar to an incantation or a spell. Charms are among the earliest examples of written literature. Among the charms written in Old English are those against a dwarf and against the theft of cattle.

chase literature Literature in which suspense is created by the action of pursuit.

chaser \'chā-sər\ A literary work or portion of a literary work that is of a light or mollifying nature in comparison with that which it follows or accompanies. The metaphor may stem from the practice of following the consumption of strong alcoholic drink with consumption of a less potent beverage or, occasionally, with food.

chasten \'chā-sən\ To prune a work of art or literature of excess, pretense, or falsity; to refine.

chastushka \chʸi-'stüsh-kə\ [Russian, a derivative of *chastyĭ* frequent, in quick succession; probably originally referring to the refrain of a song] A rhymed folk verse usually composed of four lines. The chastushka is traditional in form but often has political or topical content.

chef d'oeuvre \shā-'dœvr *with* r *as a uvular trill, Angl* -'dərv\, *plural* chefs d'oeuvre *same*\ [French *chef-d'oeuvre,* literally, leading work] A masterpiece, especially in literature or art.

Chester plays \'ches-tər\ A 14th-century cycle of 25 scriptural, or mystery, plays, performed at the prosperous city of Chester, in the north of England, during the Middle Ages. They are traditionally dated about 1325, but a date of about 1375 has also been suggested. They were presented on three successive days at Corpus Christi, a religious feast day that falls in summer. On the first day there was a performance of plays 1–9 (from the Fall of Lucifer, through key episodes in the Old Testament, up to the Nativity and the Adoration of the Wise Men); on the second day a performance of plays 10–18 (including the Flight into Egypt, Jesus' ministry, the Passion and Crucifixion, the Descent into Hell, and the arrival in paradise of the virtuous who had died before the Redemption had been achieved); and, finally, on the third day a performance of plays 19–25 (including the Resurrection, the Ascension, the Descent of the Holy Spirit, the coming of the Antichrist, and the Last Judgment).

The Chester plays are rich in content, yet tell the great story of human redemption more simply than the other surviving cycles of York, Wakefield, and "N-Town." The text, containing more than 11,000 lines of verse, has been preserved in five manuscripts, which are kept in the Bodleian Library, Oxford; the Huntington Library, California, U.S.; and the British Museum, London. The Chester cycle was published by the Early English Text Society (1892–1916). *See also* MYSTERY PLAY.

cheville \shə-ˈvē\ [French, literally, peg] A redundant word or phrase used to fill out a sentence or verse.

chiasmus \kī-ˈaz-məs, kē-\ [Greek *chiasmós,* literally, the act of placing crosswise, a derivative of *chiázein* to mark with an X (the letter chi), place crosswise] An inverted relationship between the syntactic elements of parallel phrases (as in Oliver Goldsmith's "to stop too fearful, and too faint to go").

Chicago critics \shi-ˈkäg-ō, -ˈkȯg-\, *also called* The Chicago school. A group of pluralist, formalist American literary critics—including Richard McKeon, Elder Olson, R.S. Crane, and Norman Maclean—that exerted a significant influence in the development of modern American criticism. The group associated from the 1940s with the University of Chicago, agreed with the proponents of New Criticism on the importance of textual analysis but held that the emphasis on language alone was limiting. They often were called "Aristotelian" or, more accurately, "Neo-Aristotelian" because of their concern with form and genre. Their approach emphasized an evaluation of the author's solutions to specific problems in the construction of a text.

One of the most complete discussions of the Chicago critics is found in *Critics and Criticism: Ancient and Modern* (1952), edited by Crane. A full exposition of the theoretical basis of the group's method is to be found in Crane's study *The Languages of Criticism and the Structure of Poetry* (1953). Wayne C. Booth, one of the younger Chicago critics, applied the group's principles to fiction in *The Rhetoric of Fiction* (1961) and expanded its theories in later works.

Chicago literary renaissance \shi-ˈkäg-ō, -ˈkȯg-\ The flourishing of literary activity in Chicago during the period from approximately 1912 to 1925. The leading writers of this renaissance—Theodore Dreiser, Sherwood Anderson, Edger Lee Masters, and Carl Sandburg—realistically depicted the contemporary urban environment, condemning the loss of traditional rural values in the increasingly industrialized and materialistic American society. They mourned the failure of the romantic promise that hard work would automatically bring material and spiritual rewards. Most of these writers were originally from small Midwestern towns and were deeply affected by the regional writing of the 1890s that foreshadowed the realism of 20th-century literature. The renaissance also encompassed the revitalization of journalism as a literary medium; writers such as Floyd Dell, Anderson, Dreiser, and Sandburg all were associated at one time with Chicago newspapers.

The Little Theatre, established in Chicago in 1912 by Maurice Browne, became an important outlet for the creative talents of young playwrights. The first stirrings of the Chicago renaissance were felt after the World's Columbian Exhibition of 1893. The Little Room, a literary group that included both artists and patrons of the arts, encouraged literary activity. *The Dial* magazine, established in 1880, grew to be a respected literary organ. Henry Blake Fuller and Robert Herrick, who belonged to the genteel tradition, wrote several novels that foreshadowed the later realistic novels of Dreiser and Anderson. Hamlin Garland, already famous for novels on the bleakness of rural life in the Midwest, was associated briefly with the Little Room.

The appearance of Dreiser's naturalistic novel *Sister Carrie* (1900), Masters' collection of poetic epitaphs entitled *Spoon River Anthology* (1915), Sandburg's *Chicago Poems* (1916), and Anderson's *Winesburg, Ohio* (1919) marked the height of the Chicago renaissance. Two Chicago literary magazines—*Poetry: A Magazine of Verse,* founded in 1912 by Harriet Monroe, and *The Little Review* (1914–29), founded by Margaret Anderson—published exciting new verse by such local poets as Vachel Lindsay, Masters, and Sandburg. Dell, a journalist associated with the *Friday Literary Review* (1909–11), the weekly literary supplement to the *Chicago Evening Post,* was the center of a vital literary circle that included Dreiser, Sherwood Anderson, Margaret Anderson, and Monroe.

After World War I the writers began to disperse, and by the Great Depression of the 1930s the Chicago literary renaissance had ended.

Chicago school, The *See* CHICAGO CRITICS.

childe \'chīld\ [spelling variant of *child*] *archaic* A youth of noble birth or a youth in training to be a knight. In literature the word is often used as a title, as in the character Childe Roland of Robert Browning's poem "Childe Roland to the Dark Tower Came" and Lord Byron's *Childe Harold's Pilgrimage.*

children's company *also called* boys' company. Any of a number of troupes of boy actors whose performances enjoyed great popularity in Elizabethan England. The young actors were drawn primarily from choir schools attached to the great chapels and cathedrals, where they received musical training and were taught to perform in religious dramas and classical Latin plays. By the time of Henry VIII, groups such as the Children of the Chapel and the Children of Paul's were often called upon to present plays and to take part in ceremonies and pageants at court. During the reign of Queen Elizabeth I, these groups were formed into highly professional companies, usually consisting of from 8 to 12 boys, who gave public performances outside the court.

In the late 16th and early 17th centuries, these companies were so popular that they posed a serious threat to the professional men's companies. Children acted in the first Blackfriars Theatre (*c.* 1576–80), and in 1600 a syndicate representing the Children of the Chapel acquired a lease on the second Blackfriars Theatre, where the boys performed many important plays, including those of John Marston and Ben Jonson. By about 1610 the children's companies had greatly declined in popularity.

children's literature The body of written works and accompanying illustrations produced to entertain or instruct young people. The genre encompasses a wide range of works, including acknowledged classics of world literature, picture books and easy-to-read stories written expressly for children, and fairy tales, lullabies, fables, folk songs, and other primarily orally transmitted materials.

Children's literature emerged as a distinct and independent form only in the second half of the 18th century. Its late development may be traced to low literacy rates, the prohibitive cost of bookmaking, and the general perception of children as simply diminutive or miniature adults.

One of the first printed works of children's literature was the Czech educator John Amos Comenius' *Orbis Sensualium Pictus* (1658; *The Visible World in Pictures*), a teaching device that was also the first picture book for children. It was the first such work to acknowledge that children are different from adults in many respects. The work considered to be the first novel written specifically for children is *The History of Little Goody Two-Shoes* (1765). One of the earliest and most enduring classics of children's literature is the collection of nursery rhymes known as *Mother Goose,* the first English edition of which appeared in 1781. Children's literature blossomed in the 19th century, particularly in England and the United States, into a rich and complex genre serving children of all ages, from toddlers to adolescents.

Among the more famous 19th-century works are *Alice's Adventures in Wonderland* (1865) by Lewis Carroll, *Treasure Island* (1883) by Robert Louis Stevenson, and *The Adventures of Huckleberry Finn* (1884) by Mark Twain. Illustrations became a major part of children's books in the 19th century and were used, as they are now, to interest children in the stories and to help them visualize the characters and the action. The first modern picture book for children was *The Tale of Peter Rabbit* (1902) by Beatrix Potter. From its beginnings in Germany with *Des Knaben Wunderhorn* (1805–08; "The Boy's Magic Horn")—folk tales collected by Achim von Arnim and Clemens Brentano—and in France with Jean de La Fontaine's *Fables* (1668–94), children's literature emerged in the 20th century as a major genre in the Germanic- and Romance-language countries of Europe, as well as in the Soviet Union. Folktales, myths, and legends—not particularly geared to children—make up the major portion of stories for children in most other cultures. No book written for children was published in Japan until 1891, when Iwaya Sazanami's *Koganemaru* appeared.

Children's literature reached its fullest development in the 20th century. The high level of literacy in many developed nations guaranteed an audience of young readers numbering in the tens of millions. The production of cheap hardcover and paperback books, the spread of children's bookshops, improvement of library services, the growth of serious attempts at reviewing children's books, and sophisticated marketing techniques have all combined to give greater access to, and information about, children's literature. The genre now embraces a child's imaginative world and daily environment, as well as certain ideas and sentiments characteristic of it. The inhabitants of this world are not only children themselves but animated objects, plants, and grammatical and mathematical abstractions; toys, dolls, and puppets; real and chimerical animals; miniature or magnified humans; supernatural and fantasy figures; creatures of fairy tale, myth, and legend; and adults as seen through a child's eyes. Late 20th-century children's literature almost rivals the diversity of popular adult literature.

ching-hsi *See* JINGXI.

chōka \'chō-kä\ [Japanese] A form of waka (Japanese court poetry of the 6th to 14th century) consisting of alternating lines of five and seven syllables and ending with an extra line of seven syllables. The length is indefinite. *See also* WAKA.

choliamb \'kō-lē-ˌam, -ˌamb\ or **choliambus** \ˌkō-lē-'am-bəs\, *plural* choliambs *or* choliambi \ˌkō-lē-'am-ˌbī, -ˌbē\ [Greek *chōlíambos,* from *chōlós* lame + *íambos* iamb], *also called* scazon. In classical prosody, an iambic trimeter verse of six feet or three metra having a spondee in the last foot. It scans as: ⏑ – ⏑ – | ⏓ – ⏑ – | ⏑ – – –.

choral speaking Ensemble speaking by a group often using various voice combinations and contrasts to bring out the meaning or tonal beauty of a passage of poetry or prose.

choreion \'kȯr-ē-ˌän\ [Greek *choreîos,* from *choreîos* (adjective) of a chorus] In classical prosody, a trochee (– ⏑). The term was originally used especially of the trochee or the iamb when resolved into the tribrach (a metrical foot of three short syllables).

choriamb \ˌkȯr-ē-'am, -'amb\ or **choriambus** \ˌkȯr-ē-'am-bəs\, *plural* choriambi \-'am-ˌbī\ *or* choriambuses [Greek *choríambos,* from *choreîos* choreus + *íambos* iamb] In prosody, a metrical unit of four syllables. The choriamb was frequently used by the Greek poets Sappho and Alcaeus and by the Latin poet Horace. In classical prosody, a choriamb is scanned – ⏑ ⏑ – ; it is sometimes used by itself to form a complete system but is more often found as the nucleus of a colon such as a glyconic or another aeolic pattern. The corresponding pattern of cadence in accentual prosody is scanned ˊ ⏑ ⏑ ˊ. Its use as a sustained pattern is rare in modern poetry, but examples can be found, for example, in J.W. von Goethe's *Pandora* (which is written in choriambic dimeter) and in Algernon Charles Swinburne's *Choriambics.*

chorus \'kȯr-əs\ [Greek *chorós* dance, place for dancing, group of dancers and singers, chorus] In classical Greek drama, a group of actors who described and commented upon the main action of a play with song, dance, and recitation. Greek tragedy had its beginnings in choral performances, in which a group of 50 men danced and sang dithyrambs—lyric hymns in praise of the god Dionysus. In the middle of the 6th century BC, the poet Thespis reputedly became the first true actor when he engaged in dialogue with the chorus leader. Choral performances continued to dominate the early plays until the time of Aeschylus (5th–4th century BC), who added a second actor and reduced the chorus from 50 to 12 performers. Sophocles, who added a third actor, increased the chorus to 15 but reduced its role to one of commentary in most of his plays. The chorus in Greek comedy numbered 24, and its function was displaced eventually by interspersed songs. The distinction between the passivity of the chorus and the activity of the actors is central to the artistry of the Greek tragedies. While the tragic protagonists act out their defiance of the limits prescribed by the gods for mortals, the chorus expresses the fears, hopes, and judgment of the average citizens.

As the importance of the actors increased, the choral odes became fewer in number and tended to have less importance in the plot, until at last they became mere decorative interludes separating the acts. During the Renaissance the role of the chorus was revised. In the drama of Elizabethan England, for example, the name chorus designated a single person, often the speaker of the prologue and epilogue, as in Christopher Marlowe's *Doctor Faustus*. The use of the group chorus was revived in a number of modern plays, such as Eugene O'Neill's *Mourning Becomes Electra* (1931) and T.S. Eliot's *Murder in the Cathedral* (1935).

chosism \ˈshō-ˌziz-əm\ [French *chosisme,* a derivative of *chose* thing] A literary style involving the detailed description of things, used particularly by such French authors as Michel Butor and Alain Robbe-Grillet and others associated with the *nouveau roman.*

chrestomathy \kres ˈtäm ə thē\ [Greek *chrēstomátheia,* from *chrēstós* useful + *-matheia,* a derivative of *matheîn, manthánein* to learn] A volume of selected passages or stories of an author.

chronicle \ˈkrän-i-kəl\ [Middle English *cronicle,* from Anglo-French, alteration of Old French *chronique,* from Late Latin *chronica,* from Greek *chroniká* annals, chronology, from neuter plural of *chronikós* of time, a derivative of *chrónos* time] A usually continuous historical account of events arranged in order of time without analysis or interpretation. Examples of such accounts date from Greek and Roman times, but the best-known examples were written or compiled in the Middle Ages and the Renaissance. These were composed in prose or verse, and in addition to providing valuable information about the period they covered, they were used as sources by William Shakespeare and other playwrights. Examples include the Anglo-Saxon Chronicle, Geoffrey of Monmouth's *Historia regum Britanniae* (*History of the Kings of Britain*), Andrew of Wyntoun's *Orygynale Cronykil,* and Raphael Holinshed's *Chronicles of England, Scotlande, and Irelande.*

chronicle play or **chronicle history** *also called* history play. A play with a theme from history, consisting usually of loosely connected episodes chronologically arranged. Chronicle plays often emphasize the public welfare by pointing to the past as a lesson for the present.

The genre is characterized by its assumption of a national consciousness in its audience. It has flourished in times of intensely nationalistic feeling, notably in England from the 1580s until the 1630s, when it fell out of fashion. Early chronicle plays had such titles as *The Famous Victories of Henry the Fifth, The Life and Death of Jacke Straw, The Troublesome Raigne of John King of England,* and *The True Tragedie of Richard III.* The genre came to maturity with the work of Christopher Marlowe (*Edward II*) and William Shakespeare (especially *Henry VI,* Parts 2 and 3).

In *An Apology for Actors* (1612) the dramatist Thomas Heywood wrote that chronicle plays

> are writ with this ayme, and carryed with this methode, to teach their subjects obedience to their king, to shew the people the untimely ends of such as have moved tumults, commotions, and insurrections, to present them with the flourishing estate of such as live in obedience, exhorting them to allegeance, dehorting them from all trayterous and fellonious stratagems.

Elizabethan dramatists drew their material from the wealth of chronicle writing for which the age is renowned, notably Edward Hall's *The Union of the Two Noble and Illustrate Famelies of Lancastre and York* and Raphael Holinshed's *Chronicles of England, Scotlande, and Irelande.* The genre was a natural development from the didactic MORALITY PLAY of the Middle Ages. In a forerunner of the chronicle play, John Bale's *Kynge Johan,* all the characters except the king himself are allegorical and have names such as Widow England, Sedition, and Private Wealth.

No age has matched the Elizabethan, either in England or elsewhere, in this kind of play. But chronicle plays are still sometimes written—for example, by the 20th-century English playwright John Arden *(Left-Handed Liberty, Armstrong's Last Goodnight)*—and the genre corresponds in many respects, especially in its didactic purpose and episodic structure, with the influential EPIC THEATER of Bertolt Brecht in 20th-century Germany.

Chuangzao she *See* CREATION SOCIETY.

chuanqi or **ch'uan-ch'i** \'chwän-'chē\ [Chinese *chuánqí*] Form of traditional Chinese operatic drama that developed from the *nanxi* in the late 14th century. *Chuanqi* alternated with the *zaju* as the major form of Chinese drama until the 16th century, when *kunqu,* a particular style of *chuanqi,* began to dominate serious Chinese drama. Highly subject to regional variations in language and music, *chuanqi* became popular throughout southern China. The average *chuanqi* was characterized by 30 to 50 changes of scene; the frequent and free change of end rhymes in arias; singing parts that were probably more languorous than those of the *zaju* and were distributed among many actors (not just the hero and heroine); and plots often taken from popular accounts of historical figures or from contemporary life.

chüeh-chü *See* JUEJU.

ci or **tz'u** \'chə̇\ [Chinese (Beijing dialect) *cí*] In Chinese poetry, song form characterized by lines of unequal length, with prescribed rhyme schemes and tonal patterns, each bearing the name of a musical air. The varying line lengths are comparable to the natural rhythm of speech and therefore easily understood when sung. First sung by ordinary people, they were popularized by professional women singers and attracted the attention of poets during the Tang dynasty (618–907). The *ci* served as a major vehicle for Song dynasty (960–1279) verse.

It was not, however, until the transitional period of the Five Dynasties (907–960), a time of division and strife, that *ci* became the major vehicle of lyrical expression. Of *ci* poets in this period, the greatest was Li Yu, last monarch of the Nan Tang (Southern Tang), who was seized in 976 as the new Sung dynasty consolidated its power. Li Yu's *ci* poetry is saturated with a tragic nostalgia for better days in the South; it is suffused with sadness—a depth of feeling notably absent from earlier *ci,* which had been sung at parties and banquets. The following is typical, translated by Jerome Ch'en and Michael Bullock:

> Lin hua xie liao chun hong
> Tai chong chong
> Wu nai zhao lai han yu wan lai feng
> Yan zhi lei
> Xiang liu zui
> Ji shi chong
> Zi shi ren sheng chang hen shui chang dong
>
> (The red of the spring orchard has faded.
> Far too soon!
> The blame is often laid
>   on the chilling rain at dawn
>   and the wind at dusk.
> The rouged tears
> That intoxicate and hold in thrall—
> When will they fall again?
> As a river drifts toward the east
> So painful life passes to its bitter end.)

Ciceronian period \ˌsis-ə-'rō-nē-ən\ The first great age of Latin literature, from approximately 70 to 43 BC; together with the following AUGUSTAN AGE, it forms the Golden Age of Latin literature. The political and literary scene was dominated by Cicero, a statesman, orator, poet, critic, and philosopher who perfected the Latin language as a literary medium, expressing abstract and complicated thoughts with clarity and creating the important quantitative prose rhythm. Cicero's influence on Latin prose was so great that subsequent prose—not only in Latin but in later vernacular languages up to the 19th century—was either a reaction against or a return to his style. Other outstanding figures of the Ciceronian period are Julius Caesar, notable for political oratory and vivid military narratives; Marcus Terentius Varro, who wrote on topics as varied as farming and the Latin language; and Sallust, who opposed Cicero's style and espoused one later imitated by Seneca, Tacitus, and Juvenal. Among Ciceronian poets are Catullus, the first master of the Latin love lyric, and Lucretius, the author of the long didactic poem *De rerum natura* (*On the Nature of Things*).

cielito \ˌsē-e-ˈlē-tō, ˌthē-\ Poetic form associated with gaucho literature, consisting of an octosyllabic quatrain written in colloquial language and rhyming in the second and fourth lines. The Uruguayan poet Bartolomé Hidalgo was especially known for his poems in this form. The form takes its name from the frequent use of the word *cielito* (Spanish: "darling," literally "little heaven") in refrains.

cinquain \ˈsiŋ-ˌkān\ [Middle French, from *cinq* five + *-ain,* suffix forming nouns from numerals] A five-line stanza. An American poet, Adelaide Crapsey (1878–1914), applied the term in particular to a five-line verse form of specific meter that she developed. Analogous to the Japanese verse forms haiku and tanka, it has two syllables in its first and last lines and four, six, and eight in the intervening three lines and generally has an iambic cadence. Two examples are her poems "The Warning":

> Just now,
> Out of the strange
> Still dusk . . . as strange, as still . . .
> A white moth flew. Why am I grown
> So cold?

and "November Night":

> Listen . . .
> With faint dry sound
> Like steps of passing ghosts,
> The leaves, frost-crisp'd, break from the trees
> And fall.

cinquecento \ˌchēŋ-kwā-ˈchen-tō\ [Italian, literally, five hundred, short for *mille cinquecento* the year 1500] The 16th century; specifically, the 16th-century period in Italian literature and art.

circular tale A factitious jocular narrative indefinitely repeated in which the last element leads to repetition of the first.

circumbendibus \ˌsər-kəm-ˈben-di-bəs\ [Latin *circum* round about + English *bend* + Latin *-ibus,* ablative plural ending] An indirect or roundabout course, especially one taken in writing or speech.

circumlocution \ˌsər-kəm-lō-ˈkyü-shən\ [Latin *circumlocutio,* from *circum* around + *locutio* speech, expression; a calque of Greek *períphrasis*] **1.** *also called* PERIPHRASIS The use of an unnecessarily large number of words to express an idea. **2.** Evasion in speech.

citizen comedy A form of drama produced in the early 17th century in England. Such comedies were set in London and portrayed the everyday life of the middle classes. Examples include Ben Jonson's *Bartholomew Fair* (1614) and Thomas Middleton's *A Chaste Mayd in Cheape-side* (1630).

City Dionysia *See* GREAT DIONYSIA.

civic poetry A 19th-century Russian literary movement whose proponents held that poetry should serve social and civic purposes and that poets should be accepted as integral members of the community. The movement was led by Nikolay Alekseyevich Nekrasov, and many of its adherents were noted for their caustic satires against the government. Many of these poets wrote for liberal journals, notably *Sovremennik* ("The Contemporary"), under Nekrasov's editorship in 1846–66. The movement was influential in reviving Russian poetry, which had become neglected in Russian literature. The civic poets, most of whom came from the lower classes, emphasized the political possibilities of poetry and introduced the culture of the common people into the national verse. They were innovative in their use of language and in their realistic portrayal of characters. One of the most important of the civic poets was the Decembrist Kondraty Fyodorovich Ryleyev, who expressed abhorrence of czarist oppression and glorified death in the struggle against it. Other major civic poets included Nikolay Dobrolyubov, Ivan Nikitin, and Ivan Aksakov.

classic \ˈklas-ik\ [French *classique,* from Latin *classicus* belonging to the highest of the five classes of Roman citizens] **1.** A literary work of ancient Greece or Rome. **2.** A work of enduring excellence or the author of such a work.

classicism \ˈklas-ə-ˌsiz-əm\ **1.** The principles, historical tradition, aesthetic attitudes, or style of the literature of Greece and Rome in antiquity. In the context of the tradition, classicism refers either to the work produced in antiquity or to later works inspired by those of antiquity; NEOCLASSICISM always refers to the art produced later but inspired by antiquity. The terms are sometimes used interchangeably. **2.** Classical scholarship. **3.** Adherence to or practice of the virtues thought to be characteristic of classicism or to be universally and enduringly valid (such as formal elegance and correctness, simplicity, dignity, restraint, order, proportion). The term is often opposed to ROMANTICISM.

Periods of classicism in literature have generally coincided with the classical periods in the visual arts. In literature, for instance, the first major revival of classicism occurred during the Renaissance, when Cicero's prose was especially imitated. France in the 17th century developed a rich and diversified classicism in literature, as it did in the visual arts. The dramatists Pierre Corneille and Jean Racine, together with the philosophers Blaise Pascal and René Descartes, were particularly important. In England, classicism in literature arose later than in France and reached its zenith in the 18th-century writings of John Dryden and Alexander Pope. G.E. Lessing, J.W. von Goethe, and Friedrich Schiller were major figures in the German classical literary movement. In the early 20th century, T.S. Eliot and proponents of New Criticism were sometimes considered classicists because they valued restraint and because they emphasized form and discipline. *Compare* AUGUSTAN AGE.

clausula \'klȯ-zhə-lə\ *plural* clausulae \-ˌlē\ [Latin, ending, close of a rhetorical period, a derivative of *claudere* to close] In Greek and Latin rhetoric, the rhythmic close to a sentence or clause, or a terminal cadence. The clausula is especially important in ancient and medieval Latin prose rhythm; most of the clausulae in Cicero's speeches, for example, follow a specific pattern and distinctly avoid certain types of rhythmic endings. The final words of a speech were an important element of its effectiveness. Thus the quantity of syllables became the basis on which to establish a regular metrical sequence. Certain endings were regarded as strong; others were avoided as weak.

clerihew \'kler-i-ˌhyü\ A light verse quatrain in lines usually of varying length, rhyming *aabb,* and usually dealing with a person named in the initial rhyme.

This type of comic biographical verse form was invented by Edmund Clerihew Bentley, who introduced it in *Biography for Beginners* (1905) and continued in *More Biography* (1929) and *Baseless Biography* (1939). The humor of the form lies in its purposefully flat-footed inadequacy: both the verse and its treatment of the subject are off the mark, as though they were the work of a reluctant schoolchild. It is written as a four-line verse of two rhyming couplets, the first line almost invariably ending with the name of the subject:

> After dinner, Erasmus
> Told Colet not to be "blas'mous"
> Which Colet, with some heat
> Requested him to repeat.

The number of accents in the line is irregular, and one line is usually extended to tease the ear. Another requisite of the successful clerihew is an awkward rhyme, as in Bentley's "Cervantes":

> The people of Spain think Cervantes
> Equal to half-a-dozen Dantes:
> An opinion resented most bitterly
> By the people of Italy.

Some of the best clerihews were written by Sir Francis Meynell, W.H. Auden, and Clifton Fadiman.

cliché or **cliche** \klē-'shā, 'klē-ˌshā, kli-'\ [French, literally, stereotype (in printing)] **1.** A trite or stereotyped phrase or expression. **2.** The idea expressed by a cliché. **3.** A hackneyed theme, plot, or situation in fiction or drama.

cliff-hanger \'klif-ˌhaŋ-ər\ An adventure serial or melodrama; especially one presented in installments each of which ends in suspense.

climax \'klī-ˌmaks\ [Greek *klîmax,* literally, ladder] **1.** A figure of speech in which a number of phrases or sentences are arranged in ascending order of rhetorical forcefulness. The following passage from Herman Melville's *Moby Dick* is an example:

> All that most maddens and torments; all that stirs up the lees of things; all truth with malice in it; all that cracks the sinews and cakes the brain; all the subtle demonisms of life and thought; all evil, to crazy Ahab, were visibly personified and made practically assailable in Moby Dick.

2. The last and highest member of a rhetorical climax. **3.** The point of highest dramatic tension or a major turning point in the action of a play, story, or other literary composition. In the structure of a play the climax, or crisis, is the decisive moment, or turning point, at which the rising action of the play is reversed to falling action. It may or may not coincide with the highest point of emotional interest in the drama. In the influential pyramidal outline of five-act dramatic structure, advanced by the German playwright Gustav Freytag in *Die Technik des Dramas,* the climax, in the sense of crisis, occurs close to the conclusion of the third act. By the end of the 19th century, when the traditional five-act drama was abandoned in favor of the three-act, both the crisis and the emotional climax were placed close to the end of the play.

clinch \'klinch\ *archaic* A pun or play on words.

cloak-and-dagger Dealing in intrigue and action of a romantic and melodramatic kind, usually with characters in a colorful historical setting and involving espionage, duels, pursuit, and rescue.

cloak-and-sword [translation of Spanish (*comedia de*) *capa y espada* cloak-and-sword comedy] Dealing in fictional or semifictional romance and adventure of the nobility in a period when swordplay and colorful elaborate dress were common.

The term specifically refers to a type of 17th-century Spanish play of upper middle-class manners and intrigue. The name derives from the cloak and sword that were part of the typical street dress of students, soldiers, and cavaliers, the favorite heroes. The type was anticipated by the plays of Bartolomé de Torres Naharro, but its popularity was established by the inventive dramas of Lope de Vega and Tirso de Molina. The extremely complicated plots deal with the frustration of an idealized love by the conventional Spanish *pundonor* ("point of honor"). The affairs of the lady and her gallant are mirrored or parodied in the actions of the servants; the hero's valet (the *gracioso*) also supplies a common-sense commentary on the manners of his master. After many misunderstandings, duels, renunciations, and false alarms about honor, the plays usually end happily with several marriages.

close \ˈklōz\ The concluding passage, as of a speech or play.

closed couplet A rhymed couplet in which the sense is complete. *See* COUPLET.

closet drama A drama suited primarily for reading rather than production.

Examples of the genre include John Milton's *Samson Agonistes* (1671) and Thomas Hardy's *The Dynasts* (three parts, 1903–08). Closet drama is not to be confused with readers' theater, in which actors read or recite without decor before an audience.

Club, The *also called* The Literary Club. A group of men who beginning in 1764 met regularly for supper and conversation. The Club was founded (at the suggestion of Joshua Reynolds), presided over, and frequently dominated by Samuel Johnson. Among the original members, besides Reynolds and Johnson, were Edmund Burke, Topham Beauclerk, Bennet Langton, and Oliver Goldsmith. Later additions included James Boswell, Edward Gibbon, Adam Smith, and David Garrick. The Club continued to meet for many years, with Sir Walter Scott and Alfred, Lord Tennyson among its later members.

cockneyism \ˈkäk-nē-ˌiz-əm\ The writing or the qualities of the writing of the 19th-century English authors John Keats, Percy Bysshe Shelley, William Hazlitt, and Leigh Hunt. The term was used disparagingly by some contemporaries, especially the Scottish critic John Lockhart, in reference to the fact that these writers lived in, or were natives of, London, as the term *cockney* was a derogatory term for Londoners in general.

coda \ˈkō-də\ A concluding portion of a literary or dramatic work; usually, a portion or scene that rounds off or integrates preceding themes or ideas.

codex \ˈkō-ˌdeks\ *plural* codices \ˈkōd-ə-ˌsēz, ˈkäd-\ [Latin *caudex, codex* tree trunk, book made originally of wooden tablets] A manuscript book, especially of Scripture, early literature, or ancient mythological or historical annals.

The earliest type of manuscript in the form of a modern book (i.e., a collection of pages stitched together along one side), the codex replaced the earlier rolls of papyrus and wax tablets. The codex had several advantages over the roll, or scroll. It could be opened at once to any point in the text, it enabled one to write on both sides of the leaf, and it could contain long texts. The difference can be illustrated with copies of the Bible. While the Gospel According to Matthew nearly reached the practical limit of a roll, a common codex included the four Gospels and the Book of Acts bound together, and complete Bibles were not uncommon.

The eventual triumph of the codex over other manuscript packages is ultimately attributable to cultural and technological changes—i.e., the rise of Christianity, with its demand for more and larger books, and the availability of first parchment and then paper. The oldest extant Greek codex, said to date from the 4th century, is the Codex Sinaiticus, a biblical manuscript written in Greek. Also important is the Codex Alexandrinus, a Greek text of the Bible probably produced in the 5th century and now preserved in the British Library, London. The term codex aureus describes a volume that includes gold letters written on sheets that have been stained with a purple dye called murex. Existing examples of the codex aureus date from the 8th and 9th centuries.

In a completely separate development, codices also were made by pre-Columbian peoples of Mesoamerica after about AD 1000. These books contained pictographs and ideograms rather than written script. They dealt with the ritual calendar, divination, ceremonies, and speculations on the gods and the universe. Among these codices are the Vienna Codex, the Dresden Codex, the Codex Colombino, and the Codex Fejérváry-Mayer, all believed to have been produced before the Spanish conquest of the region. Certain collections of formulas or standards are also referred to as codices; for example, the Codex Alimentarius and the *British Pharmaceutical Codex.*

Colégio Nordestino *See* NORTHEASTERN SCHOOL.

collation \kə-ˈlā-shən, kä-, kō-\ [Latin *collatio* placing together, comparison] **1.** A comparison of manuscripts or editions of a text in order to determine the original version or the condition or authenticity of a particular copy. The term may also be used to refer to the conclusions drawn and recorded from such a comparison. **2.** The bibliographical description of a book expressed in a formula in which information about size, signatures, and pagination is represented by symbols.

collectanea \ˌkä-lek-ˈtā-nē-ə\ [Latin, neuter plural of *collectaneus* collected] Collected writings or literary items forming a collection.

collected edition A uniform, usually complete edition of an author's work.

collective biography A volume containing biographies of a number of people. The best-known classical example is Plutarch's *Parallel Lives* (*Bioi parallēloi*), which describes the characters and recounts the deeds of many prominent Greeks and Romans, including soldiers, statesmen, orators, and legislators. A modern example is Phyllis Rose's *Parallel Lives,* a study of several Victorian couples. *See also* BIOGRAPHY.

collective unconscious A form of the unconscious (that part of the mind containing memories and impulses of which the individual is not aware) common to humanity as a whole and originating in the inherited structure of the brain. The term was introduced in German as *collektive Unbewusstes* by psychiatrist Carl Jung. He distinguished the collective unconscious from the personal unconscious, which arises from the experience of the individual. According to Jung, the collective unconscious contains archetypes, or universal primordial images and ideas. Thus, ARCHETYPAL CRITICISM regularly identifies literary power with the presence of certain themes that run through the myths and beliefs of all cultures. *See also* ARCHETYPE.

colometry \kə-ˈläm-ə-trē\ [Medieval Greek *kōlometría,* from Greek *kôlon* part of a strophe + *-metria,* a derivative of *métron* measure] A measurement or division (as of a manuscript) by colons (rhythmic units).

colon \ˈkō-lən\ *plural* colons *or* cola \ˈkō-lə\ [Greek *kôlon* limb, part of a strophe, clause of a sentence] **1.** A rhythmic unit of an utterance; specifically, in Greek or Latin verse, a rhythmic measure of lyric meter ("lyric" in the sense of verse that is sung, rather than recited or chanted), with a recognizable recurring pattern. Also, the different parts that make up an asynarteton, a verse made up of two or more metrical units that follow each other without a pause, but are separated by diaeresis, the demanded or recommended ending of a word between two metra or feet. **2.** In prose, a division (by sense or rhythm) of an utterance that is smaller and less independent than the sentence and larger and less dependent than the phrase.

colophon \ˈkäl-ə-ˌfän, -fən\ [Greek *kolophṓn* summit, finishing touch] An inscription placed at the end of a book or manuscript, usually with facts that relate to its production. These details might include the name of the printer and the date and place of printing. Colophons are found in some manuscripts and books made as long ago as the 6th century AD. In medieval and Renaissance manuscripts, a colophon was occasionally added by the scribe and provided facts such as his name and the date and place of his completion of the work, sometimes accompanied by an expression of pious thanks for the end of his task.

The printer's colophon grew from this practice; it often included such information as the title of the book, the date and place of printing, the name and house device of the printer, and a bit of self-advertisement. The first such printed colophon occurs in the Mainz Psalter produced by Johann Fust and Peter Schöffer in 1457 and is translated as follows:

> The present copy of the Psalms, adorned with beauty of capital letters and sufficiently picked out with rubrics, has thus been fashioned by an ingenious method of printing and stamping without any driving of the pen, and to the worship of God has been diligently completed by Johannes Fust, citizen of Mainz, and Peter Schoeffer of Gernsheym, in the year of the Lord 1457 on the Vigil of the Assumption [i.e., August 14].

In some printed books, the scribe's colophon was carried over and printed instead of or with the printer's colophon. When they stood alone these were distinguished from colophons and called explicits. When the two were combined the term colophon was retained. Such colophons are important sources of information for the origin of early printed books.

Printed colophons soon became more elaborate, however, evolving into a means whereby the printer might praise the book at length and even insert a short essay upon its merits. Ultimately, by about 1480, part of the contents of the colophon was transferred to the blank cover page at the front of the book.

In most countries, the colophon appears on the page opposite the title page and consists of a one-sentence statement that the book was printed by a given printer at a given location. Fine editions often retain the former practice, including colophons stating the typeface, paper, and other production details on the last page. *Compare* EXPLICIT.

color \ˈkəl-ər\ **1.** *archaic* Rhetorical ornaments of language. Stylistic decorations, especially figures of speech. **2.** Vividness or variety of emotional effects of language (such as those of sound and image) in prose or poetry.

columbiad \kə-ˈləm-bē-ˌad\ [New Latin *Columbia* United States + English *-ad* (as in *Iliad, Dunciad*)] Any of certain epics recounting the European settlement and growth of the United States. It may have been derived from *La Colombiade, ou la foi portée au nouveau monde,* a poem by the French author Marie Anne Fiquet de Boccage. A relatively well-known example is *The Columbiad* (1807; an extensive revision of *The Vision of Columbus,* 1787), by Joel Barlow.

comedia \kō-ˈmāth-yä\ [Spanish, comedy] A Spanish regular-verse drama or comedy. Specific forms included the *comedia de capa y espada,* a cloak-and-sword comedy of love and intrigue, and the *comedia de figurón,* a form in which the emphasis is placed on one particular character who is presented as an exaggerated personification of a vice or flaw. *See also* COMEDY.

Comédie-Française \kō-mā-ˈdē-frä^{n}-ˈsez\, *formally* Le Théâtre-Français, *also called* La Maison de Molière. National theater of France and the world's longest established national theater. It is chiefly associated with the plays of Molière.

After the death of Molière in 1673, his company of actors joined forces with a company playing at the Théâtre du Marais, the resulting company being known as the Théâtre Guénégaud. In 1680 the company that has survived as the Comédie-Française was founded when the Guénégaud company merged with that at the Hôtel de Bourgogne, to become the only professional French company then playing in Paris.

After the French Revolution, in 1791, one group within the company established separate headquarters at the present home of the Comédie-Française in what is now the Place de Théâtre-Français, while the more conservative group remained at the original site as the Théâtre de la Nation. In 1803 the Comédie-Française was again reconstituted, this time under Napoleon's administration. A decree issued by him while in Moscow in 1812 established the rules under which the Comédie-Française was to function.

Throughout its long history, the Comédie-Française has exercised a lasting influence on the development of French theater, arts, and letters. It has given the world some of the theater's most illustrious actors: François-Joseph Talma, Adrienne Lecouvreur, Sarah Bernhardt, and Jean-Louis Barrault. Although it remains a theater primarily rooted in past traditions, after the appointment of Pierre Dux as its head in 1970 the Comédie-Française also began to introduce the work of new playwrights, directors, and stage designers.

Comédie-Italienne \kō-mā-ˈdē-ē-tȧl-ˈyen\ Troupe of Paris-based Italian actors of the Italian COMMEDIA DELL'ARTE. The Comédie-Italienne was established under Louis XIV's royal grant in 1680 and was given the name to distinguish the plays performed by Italian players from those performed by the Comédie-Française, the French national theater troupe.

Italian commedia dell'arte companies had appeared in France from the 16th century. In 1697 the Comédie-Italienne offended the king with their satire on his second wife; they were banished from France until 1716, after Louis' death.

Prior to their banishment, the Comédie-Italienne had increasingly interspersed French words, phrases, and sometimes whole scenes into productions. After the troupe received official sanction from Louis XIV to use French, the Comédie-Italienne became a new market for French dramatists. Allowed in 1716 to return to France, the Italian players increasingly performed French works by French dramatists, particularly those of Pierre Marivaux, and from that time only some of the spirit of the commedia dell'arte—foreign flavor and the ribaldry, drolleries, pantomime, as well as some of the characters—remained.

French actors began to replace the Italians. As tastes changed, Comédie-Italienne productions turned toward opéra-bouffe (comic opera). In 1801 the company merged with a former rival, the Théâtre Feydeau, to form the Opéra-Comique, and the Comédie-Italienne was dissolved.

comédie larmoyante \kō-mā-ˈdē-lȧr-mwȧ-ˈyä^{n}t\ [French, literally, tearful comedy] Eighteenth-century genre of French sentimental drama that formed a bridge between the decaying tradition of aristocratic Neoclassical tragedy and the rise of serious bourgeois drama. Such comedies made no pretense of being amusing; virtuous characters were subjected to distressing domestic crises, but even if the play ended unhappily, virtue was rewarded. If the heroine died, for example, her "moral" triumph was made clear to the audience.

The form is best exemplified in the 40 or so verse plays of Pierre-Claude Nivelle de La Chaussée, such as *Le Préjugé à la mode* (1735; "Fashionable Prejudice"). The effect of the *comédie larmoyante* was to blur the distinctions between comedy and tragedy, drive both from the French stage, and form the basis for the DRAME BOURGEOIS, realistic contemporary comedy heralded by Denis Diderot's *Le Fils naturel* (1757; *Dorval; or, The Test of Virtue*).

comedy \ˈkäm-ə-dē\ [Greek *kōmōidía,* a derivative of *kōmōidós* singer in a revel, from *kômos* band of revelers, revel + *-ōidos,* a derivative of *aeídein* to sing] The genre of dramatic literature that deals with the light or the amusing or with the serious and profound in a light, familiar, or satirical manner. *Compare* TRAGEDY.

As a genre, comedy dates to the 5th century BC, when it was associated originally with the revels that were part of the worship of the Greek god Dionysus. The first period of ancient Greek comedy, known as OLD COMEDY, is represented by the plays of Aristophanes, most of which satirized public officials and events. A transitional period followed. NEW COMEDY, which came into vogue beginning about 320 BC, shifted the focus to ordinary citizens who were portrayed as stock characters. The plots, too, followed a formula, usually a story of young love, as seen in the works of Menander. These works were later adapted by the Romans Terence and Plautus, who produced almost the only other examples of comedy in classical literature. It was not until the end of the Middle Ages that comedy reappeared in literature in any lasting form.

The medieval meaning of the word *comedy* was simply a story with a happy ending. Thus some of Geoffrey Chaucer's tales are called comedies, and Dante used the term in that sense in the title of his poem *La divina commedia*. Modern usage combines this sense with that in which Renaissance scholars applied it to the ancient comedies.

Consideration of the form as it actually exists suggests that what might be regarded as different kinds of comedy derive fundamentally from differences in the attitude of authors toward their subjects. When an author's intention is to ridicule, satirical comedy emerges; when ridicule is turned on individuals, the result is the comedy of character; satire of social convention and within social convention creates the comedy of manners; social comedy concerns the structure of society itself; and satire of conventional thinking produces the comedy of ideas. Progress from troubles to the triumph of love in a happy outcome produces romantic comedy. The comedy of intrigue derives from a dominant intention of providing amusement and excitement with an intricate plot of reversals with artificial, contrived situations. Such is the comedy of Spain as seen in the works of such dramatists as Lope de Vega and Tirso de Molina. Where the author wants to exploit potentially serious issues merely sentimentally—without approaching the truly tragic aspects of the subject or examining its underlying significance—sentimental comedy results. Tragicomedy (or sometimes comitragedy) combines elements of the tragic and the comedic. In the 20th century, a mordant form of humor, so-called black humor (or black comedy), and absurdism reflected existentialist concerns. Musical comedy, in which true comedy is often subservient to broad farce and spectacular effects, has been popular in Great Britain and the United States since the late 19th century.

comedy drama Serious drama with comedy interspersed.

comedy of character Comedy in which the emphasis is on characterization rather than plot or lines. *Compare* COMEDY OF SITUATION.

comedy of humors A dramatic genre most closely associated with the English playwright Ben Jonson from the late 16th century. The term derives from the Latin *humor* (more properly *umor*), meaning "fluid." Medieval and Renaissance medical theory held that the human body had a balance of four fluids, or humors: blood, phlegm, yellow bile (choler), and black bile (melancholy). When properly balanced, these humors were thought to give the individual a healthy mind in a healthy body. Variant mixtures of these humors determined an individual's "complexion," or temperament, physical and intellectual qualities, and disposition.

Each of these complexions—sanguine, phlegmatic, choleric, and melancholic—had specific characteristics, so that the words carried much weight which they have since lost: the choleric man, for example, was not only quick to anger but also yellow-faced, lean, hairy, proud, ambitious, revengeful, and shrewd.

In his play *Every Man Out of his Humour* (1600), Jonson explains that the system of humors governing the body may by metaphor be applied to the general disposition, so that a peculiar quality may so possess one as to cause particular actions. Jonson's characters usually represent one humor and, thus unbalanced, are basically caricatures.

comedy of intrigue A comedy of situation in which complicated conspiracies and stratagems dominate the plot.

The complex plots and subplots of comedies of intrigue are often based on ridiculous and contrived situations with large doses of farcical humor. An example of comedy of intrigue is William Shakespeare's *Comedy of Errors,* a humorous exploitation of the confusion resulting from twin masters and their twin servants, itself a version of two plays—*Menaechmi* and *Amphitruo*—by the Roman comedy writer Plautus (*c.* 254–184 BC). In the hands of a master such as Molière, the comedy of intrigue often shades into a comedy of manners. Thus, *Le Médecin malgré lui* (1666; *The Doctor in Spite of Himself*), which begins as a farce based on the simple joke of mistaking the ne'er-do-well woodcutter Sganarelle for a doctor, gradually becomes a satire on learned pretension and bourgeois credulity as Sganarelle fulfills his role as a doctor with great success.

comedy of manners Witty, cerebral form of drama that satirizes the manners and fashions of a particular social class or set.

A comedy of manners is concerned with social usage and the ability (or inability) of certain characters to meet social standards. Often the governing social standard is morally trivial but exacting. The plot of such a comedy, usually concerning an illicit love affair or similarly scandalous matter, is subordinate to the play's brittle atmosphere, witty dialogue, and pungent commentary on human foibles.

Usually written by sophisticated authors for members of their own coterie or social class, the comedy of manners has historically thrived in periods and societies that combined material prosperity and moral latitude. Such was the case in ancient Greece when Menander (*c.* 342–*c.* 292 BC) inaugurated NEW COMEDY, the forerunner of comedy of manners. Menander's graceful style, elaborate plots, and stock characters were imitated by the Roman dramatists Plautus (*c.* 254–184 BC) and Terence (*c.* 195–159 BC), whose comedies were widely known and copied during the Renaissance.

One of the greatest exponents of the comedy of manners was Molière, who satirized the hypocrisy and pretension of 17th-century French society in such plays as *L'École des femmes* (1663; *The School for Wives*) and *Le Misanthrope* (1667; *The Misanthrope*).

In England the comedy of manners had its great day during the Restoration period. Although influenced by Ben Jonson's comedy of humors, the Restoration comedy of manners was lighter, defter, and more vivacious in tone. Playwrights declared themselves against affected wit and acquired follies and satirized these qualities in caricature characters with label-like names such as Sir Fopling Flutter (in Sir George Etherege's *The Man of Mode,* 1676) and Tattle (in William Congreve's *The Old Bachelour,* 1693). The masterpieces of the genre were the witty, cynical, and epigrammatic plays of William Wycherley (*The Country-Wife,* 1675) and Congreve (*The Way of the World,* 1700). In the late 18th century Oliver Goldsmith (*She Stoops to Conquer,* 1773) and Richard Brinsley Sheridan (*The Rivals,* 1775; *The School for Scandal,* 1777) revived the form.

The tradition of elaborate, artificial plotting and epigrammatic dialogue was carried on by the Anglo-Irish playwright Oscar Wilde in *Lady Windermere's Fan* (1893) and *The Importance of Being Earnest* (1899). In the 20th century the comedy of manners reappeared in the witty, sophisticated drawing-room plays of the British dramatists Noël Coward and W. Somerset Maugham and the Americans Philip Barry and S.N. Behrman.

comedy of situation Comedy in which the comic effect depends chiefly upon the involvement of the main characters in a predicament or ludicrous complex of circumstances. *Compare* COMEDY OF CHARACTER.

comic relief or **comedy relief** A release of emotional or other tension resulting from a comic episode or item interposed in the midst of serious or tragic elements (as in drama); also, something that causes such relief.

comitragedy \ˌkäm-i-ˈtraj-ə-dē\ Tragedy with an element of comedy. *See also* TRAGICOMEDY.

comma \ˈkäm-ə\ [Latin, from Greek *kómma* clause, literally, something cut off, a derivative of *kóptein* to cut off] **1.** In Greek and Latin prosody or rhetoric, a short phrase or word group smaller than a colon; a fragment of a few words or metrical feet. **2.** *obsolete* A clause or short section of a treatise or argument.

commedia dell'arte \kōm-ˈmā-dyä-del-ˈlär-tā\ [Italian, comedy of art] Italian theatrical form that flourished throughout Europe from the 16th through the 18th century. Outside of Italy, the form had its greatest success in France, where it became the COMÉDIE-ITALIENNE. In England, certain elements of commedia dell'arte were naturalized in the harlequinade in pantomime and in the Punch-

and-Judy show, a puppet play involving the commedia dell'arte character Punch.

The commedia dell'arte emphasized ensemble acting; its improvisations were set in a firm framework of masks and stock situations, and its plots were frequently borrowed from the classical literary tradition of the commedia erudita, or literary drama. Despite contemporary depictions of scenarios and masks and descriptions of particular presentations, impressions today of what the commedia dell'arte was like are secondhand.

Professional companies of actors arose in the 16th century. These recruited unorganized strolling players, acrobats, street entertainers, and a few better-educated adventurers, and they experimented with forms suited to popular taste: vernacular dialects, plenty of comic action, and recognizable characters derived from the exaggeration or parody of regional or stock fictional types. The actors, relying on their wits and capacity to create atmosphere and convey character with little scenery or costume, gave the commedia dell'arte its impulse and character.

The first date certainly associated with an Italian commedia dell'arte troupe is 1545. The most famous early company was the Gelosi, headed by Francesco Andreini and his wife, Isabella; the Gelosi performed from about 1568 to 1604. Others included the Desiosi (formed 1595), the Comici Confidènti (1574–1621), and the Uniti (first mentioned 1574). The first mention of a company in France is in 1570–71. The Gelosi, summoned to Blois in 1577 by the king, later returned to Paris, and the Parisians embraced the Italian theater, supporting resident Italian troupes who developed additional French characters. The Italian players were also popular in England, Spain, and Bavaria.

Each commedia dell'arte company had a stock of scenarios, commonplace books of soliloquies and witty exchanges, and about a dozen actors. Most players created their own masks to represent the standardized characters they played, or they developed masks already established. For an understanding of the commedia dell'arte, the mask is more important than the player.

A typical scenario involved a young couple's love being thwarted by their parents. The scenario used symmetrical pairs of characters: two elderly men, two lovers, two *zanni* (madcap servants), a maidservant, a soldier, and extras. The lovers, who played unmasked, were scarcely true commedia dell'arte characters Another character without a mask was Columbine, a saucy servant girl. Pantaloon was a Venetian merchant: serious, rarely consciously comic, and prone to long tirades and good advice. Dottore was, in origin, a Bolognese lawyer; gullible and lecherous, he spoke in a pedantic mixture of Italian and Latin.

Other characters began as stock masks and developed into well-known characters in the hands of the most talented players. Capitano developed as a caricature of the Spanish braggart soldier, boasting of exploits abroad, running away from danger at home. He was turned into Scaramouche (Scaramuccia) and altered to suit French taste. The *zanni* were characterized by shrewdness and self-interest; much of their success depended on improvised action and topical jokes. Harlequin (Arlecchino), one of the *zanni*, was created as a witty servant, nimble and gay: as a lover he became capricious, often heartless. Pedrolino was his counterpart. Doltish yet honest, he was often the victim of his fellow comedians' pranks. As Pierrot, his winsome character carried over into later French pantomimes. The *zanni* used certain tricks of their trade: practical jokes (*burle*)—often the fool, thinking he had tricked the clown, had the tables turned on him by a rustic wit as clever, if not so nimble, as his own—and comic business (*lazzi*).

Commedia dell'arte began to decline as the rich verbal humor of the regional dialects was lost on foreign audiences; physical comedy came to dominate the performance, and, as the comic business became routine, it lost its vitality. The characters became fixed and no longer reflected the conditions of real life, thus losing an important comic element. The efforts of such playwrights as Carlo Goldoni to reform Italian drama sealed the fate of the decaying commedia dell'arte. Goldoni borrowed from the older style to create a new, more realistic form of Italian comedy, and audiences greeted the new comedy with enthusiasm.

The commedia dell'arte's last traces entered into pantomime as introduced in England in 1702. It was taken from England to Copenhagen (1801), where, at the Tivoli Gardens, it still survives.

A more important, if less obvious, legacy of the commedia dell'arte is its influence on other dramatic forms. Visiting commedia dell'arte troupes inspired national comedic drama in Germany, eastern Europe, and Spain. Other national dramatic forms absorbed the comic routines and plot devices of the commedia. Molière, who worked with Italian troupes in France, and Ben Jonson and William Shakespeare in England incorporated characters and devices from the commedia dell'arte in their written works. European puppet shows, the English harlequinade, French pantomime, and the cinematic slapstick of Charlie Chaplin all recall commedia dell'arte at its best.

commedia erudita \kōm-ˈmā-dyä-ā-rü-ˈdē-tä\ [Italian, literally, erudite comedy] Sixteenth-century Italian comedy played from a text written in Latin or Italian and based on the scholarly works of earlier Italian and ancient Roman authors. *Compare* COMMEDIA DELL'ARTE.

Because the language used in the commedia erudita was not easily comprehensible to the general public, the plays were performed for the nobility, usually by nonprofessional actors (*dilettanti*). Sources for commedia erudita included the comedies of the Roman dramatists Plautus and Terence and works of the 14th-century Italian humanist Giovanni Boccaccio. Other dramas were contributed by Ludovico Ariosto, considered the best writer of early Italian vernacular comedy and a principal figure in the establishment of this literary form; the philosopher-playwright Giambattista della Porta, author of a number of stinging satires; and Niccolò Machiavelli, whose *La mandragola* (first dated publication 1524; "The Mandrake") was one of the outstanding comedies of the century.

Themes, motifs, situations, and the use of stock characters by the commedia erudita greatly influenced the commedia dell'arte, whose repertoires, especially in northern Italy, resembled the commedia erudita in their tight structures based on the three dramatic unities (time, place, action).

commentary \'käm-ən-ˌter-ē\ [Latin *commentarius, commentarium* notebook, commentary] **1.** *usually plural* An explanatory treatise. **2.** *usually plural* A record of a set of events usually written by a participant and marked by less formality and elaborateness than a history. **3.** A systematic series of explanations or interpretations of a text.

common meter or **common measure**, *abbreviated* C.M., *also called* hymnal stanza. A meter used in English ballads that is equivalent to ballad meter, though ballad meter is often less regular and more conversational than common meter. Whereas ballad meter usually has a variable number of unaccented syllables, common meter consists of regular iambic lines with an equal number of stressed and unstressed syllables. The song "Amazing Grace" by John Newton is an example of common meter, as can be seen in the following verse:

> Amazing grace! how sweet the sound.
> That saved a wretch like me!
> I once was lost, but now am found,
> Was blind, but now I see.

See also BALLAD METER.

common particular meter or **common particular measure** A variation of ballad meter in which the four-stress lines are doubled to produce a stanza of six lines in tail-rhyme arrangement (i.e., with short lines rhyming). The number of stresses in the lines is thus 4, 4, 3, 4, 4, 3.

commonplace \'käm-ən-ˌplās\ [translation of Latin *locus communis* passage of a speech not directly concerned with the issue at hand, general observation, translation of Greek *koinòs tópos*] **1.** *obsolete* A passage of general significance that may be applied to particular cases. **2.** *obsolete* The theme, topic, or text of a discourse. **3.** *archaic* A striking or especially noticeable passage; usually, such a passage entered in a commonplace book. **4.** *obsolete* A commonplace book.

commonplace book A book of literary passages, cogent quotations, occasional thoughts, or other memorabilia.

commos *See* KOMMOS.

Compagnia dei Gelosi *See* GELOSI.

companion piece A work (as of literature) that is associated with and complements another.

complaint \kəm-'plānt\, *also called* plaint \'plānt\ A formerly popular variety of poem that laments or protests unrequited love or tells of personal misfortune, misery, or injustice. Works of this type include Rutebeuf's *La Complainte Rutebeuf* (late 13th century) and Pierre de Ronsard's "Complainte contre fortune" (1559).

complication \ˌkäm-plə-ˈkā-shən\ A situation or a detail of character that enters into and complicates the main thread of a plot.

composition \ˌkäm-pə-ˈzish-ən\ The construction of a literary work, especially with reference to its degree of success in meeting criteria of correctness, order, or proportion.

conceit \kən-ˈsēt\ An elaborate or strained metaphor. This sense of the word *conceit,* which originally meant "idea" or "concept," was influenced by Italian *concetto,* which from its original sense "concept" came to denote a fanciful metaphor. The Petrarchan conceit, especially popular with Renaissance writers of sonnets, is a hyperbolic comparison made generally by a suffering lover of his beautiful and cruel mistress to some physical object; e.g., a tomb, the ocean, the sun. The metaphysical conceit, associated with the Metaphysical poets of the 17th century, is a more intricate and intellectual device. It sets up an analogy, usually between one entity's spiritual qualities and an object in the physical world, that sometimes controls the whole structure of the poem. For example, in the following stanzas from "A Valediction: Forbidding Mourning," John Donne compares two lovers' souls to a draftsman's compass:

> If they be two, they are two so
> As stiffe twin compasses are two,
> Thy soule the fixt foot, makes no show
> To move, but doth, if the'other doe.
>
> And though it in the center sit,
> Yet when the other far doth rome,
> It leanes, and hearkens after it,
> And growes erect, as that comes home.

Conceits often were so far-fetched as to become absurd, degenerating in the hands of lesser poets into strained ornamentation. With the advent of Romanticism they fell into disfavor along with other poetic artifices. In the late 19th century they were revived by the French Symbolists and are commonly found, although in brief and condensed form, in the works of such poets as Emily Dickinson, T.S. Eliot, and Ezra Pound.

conceptismo \ˌkōn-thep-ˈtēz-mō, -sep-\ or **conceptism** \ˈkän-ˌsep-ˌtiz-əm\ [Spanish *conceptismo,* a derivative of *concepto* concept, conceit, ingenious expression] In Spanish literature, an obscurely allusive style cultivated by essayists, especially satirists, in the 17th century. *Conceptismo* was characterized by the use of striking metaphors, either expressed concisely and epigrammatically or elaborated into lengthy conceits.

Concerned primarily with the stripping off of appearances in a witty manner, *conceptismo* found its best expression in the satirical essay. Its chief exponents were Francisco Gómez de Quevedo, who is generally considered the master satirist of his age, in *Sueños* (1627; *Dreams*), and Baltasar Gracián, the theoretician of *conceptismo,* who codified its stylistic precepts in *Agudeza y arte de ingenio* (1642; 2nd edition, 1648; "Subtlety and the Art of Genius"). By the middle of the century, however, the style had lost its original vitality as it became more rigid and mannered. *Compare* CULTERANISMO.

concetto \kən-'chet-ō\ *plural* concetti \-'chet-ē\ [Italian, notion, idea, literary conceit, from Late Latin *conceptus* thought, concept] A conceit, especially in literary style.

concinnity \kən-'sin-ə-tē\ [Latin *concinnitas,* a derivative of *concinnus* neatly arranged, elegant] Harmony or fitness in the adaptation of parts to a whole or to each other. The term is often used to mean studied elegance of design or arrangement and is used especially of literary style.

concision \kən-'sizh-ən\ The quality or state of being concise, used especially of literary style.

concordance \kən-'kȯr-dəns, kän-\ [Medieval Latin *concordantiae* index containing parallel occurrences of a word or passage in Scripture, plural of *concordantia* agreement, harmony] An alphabetical index of the principal words in a book or the works of an author with their immediate contexts.

concrete Naming a real thing or class of things; the word *poem* is concrete, the word *poetry* is abstract.

concrete poetry [translation of Portuguese *poesia concreta* or German *konkrete Dichtung*] Poetry in which the poet's intent is conveyed by graphic patterns of letters, words, or symbols rather than by the meaning of words in conventional arrangement. The writer of concrete poetry uses typeface and other typographical elements in such a way that chosen units—letter fragments, punctuation marks, graphemes (letters), morphemes (any meaningful linguistic unit), syllables, or words —and graphic spaces form an evocative picture. The origins of concrete poetry are roughly contemporary with those of *musique concrète,* an experimental technique of musical composition.

Max Bill and Eugen Gomringer were among the early practitioners of concrete poetry. The Vienna Group of Hans Carl Artmann, Gerhard Rühm, and Konrad Bayer also promoted concrete poetry, as did Ernst Jandl and Friederike Mayröcker. The movement drew inspiration from Dada, Surrealism, and other early 20th-century movements. Concrete poetry has an extreme visual bias and in this way is usually distinguished from PATTERN POETRY. It attempts to move away from a purely verbal concept of verse toward what its proponents call "verbivocovisual expression," incorporating geometric and graphic elements into the poetic act or process. It often cannot be read aloud to any effect, and its essence lies in its appearance on the page, not in the words or typographic units that form it. Concrete poetry is still produced in many countries, including Brazil, France, the United States, and the United Kingdom. Notable contemporary concrete poets include Haroldo de Campos and Augusto de Campos.

confection \kən-ˈfek-shən\ An artistic or literary work marked by artificiality or lack of sincerity; a work made up of unsuitable or incongruous elements that are combined without real unification or feeling of purpose.

Confederation group \kən-ˌfed-ə-ˈrā-shən\ Canadian English-language poets of the late 19th century whose work expressed the national consciousness inspired by the Confederation of 1867. Their transcendental and romantic view of the Canadian landscape dominated Canadian poetry until the 20th century. The Confederation group is also called the Maple Tree school because of the love characteristically shown for that dominant feature of the Canadian landscape. The group includes four poets, all born between 1860 and 1862: Charles G.D. Roberts, whose *Orion, and Other Poems* (1880) heralded the movement; Bliss Carman, who wrote lyric poems on nature, love, and the open road; Archibald Lampman, known for his vivid descriptions of nature; and Duncan Campbell Scott, who composed ballads and dramas of the northern Ontario wilderness.

The group's members used traditional poetic forms, and they all reacted to the growing industrialization of Canada by retreating to the as yet unspoiled wilderness.

confession \kən-ˈfesh-ən\ In literature, an autobiography, either real or fictitious, in which intimate and hidden details of the subject's life are revealed.

The first outstanding example of the genre, written about AD 400, was *The Confessions* of St. Augustine, a painstaking examination of Augustine's progress from juvenile sinfulness and youthful debauchery to conversion to Christianity and the triumph of the spirit over the flesh. Other notable examples include Thomas De Quincey's *Confessions of an English Opium-Eater* (1822), which reveals the writer's early life and his gradual addiction to drugs, and *Confessions* (1782–89), the intimate autobiography of Jean-Jacques Rousseau. The 20th-century French writer André Gide used the form to great effect in such works as *Si le grain ne meurt* (1920 and 1924; *If It Die . . .*), an account of his life from birth to marriage.

Such 20th-century poets as John Berryman, Robert Lowell, Sylvia Plath, and Anne Sexton wrote poetry in the confessional vein, revealing intensely personal, often painful perceptions and feelings.

confessional \kən-ˈfesh-ə-nəl\ Of, relating to, or being intimately autobiographical writing or fiction.

conflate \kən-ˈflāt\ In literature, to combine two readings of a text into a composite whole. To produce a composite reading or text by conflation.

conflict \'kän-ˌflikt\ In drama or fiction, the opposition of persons or forces upon which the dramatic action depends.

Connecticut wit *See* HARTFORD WIT.

consonance \'kän-sə-nəns\ [Latin *consonantia* concord, harmony], *also called* consonant-rhyme. Recurrence or repetition of identical or similar consonants; specifically, the correspondence of end or intermediate consonants unaccompanied by like correspondence of vowels at the ends of two or more syllables, words, or other units of composition.

As a poetic device, consonance is often combined with assonance (the repetition of stressed vowel sounds within words with different end consonants) and alliteration (the repetition of initial consonant sounds). Consonance is also occasionally used as an off-rhyme, but it is most commonly found as an internal sound effect, as in William Shakespeare's song "The ousel co*ck* so bla*ck* of hue" or in "The curfew to*ll*s the kne*ll* of parting day" from Thomas Gray's "An Elegy Written in a Country Church Yard." *Compare* ALLITERATION; ASSONANCE.

Contact Literary magazine founded in 1920 by American author Robert McAlmon, aided by poet William Carlos Williams. Devoted to avant-garde writing of the period, it led to McAlmon's important Contact Editions book-publishing enterprise.

Contact began in New York as a mimeographed magazine and relocated to Paris in 1921 following McAlmon's marriage to English author Bryher (Annie Winifred Ellerman). Four issues were published in 1920–21 and a fifth in 1923. Contributors included Kay Boyle, H.D., Marianne Moore, Ezra Pound, Wallace Stevens, and Glenway Wescott. Meanwhile, in 1922 McAlmon had himself published his short-story collection *A Hasty Bunch.* This, his contacts with fellow expatriate writers in Paris, and a large gift of money from his father-in-law led McAlmon to establish a book-publishing venture. Contact Editions books began to appear in 1923. Over the years McAlmon issued works by himself and Bryher; Williams' *Spring and All;* Ernest Hemingway's first book; *The Making of Americans* by Gertrude Stein; and *Contact Collection of Contemporary Writers,* an anthology including works by James Joyce and Ford Madox Ford. Nathanael West's novel *The Dream Life of Balso Snell* (1931) was the last Contact book. Williams and West revived *Contact* magazine for three issues in the United States in 1932, publishing prose by S.J. Perelman, James T. Farrell, and McAlmon and poetry by E.E. Cummings and Louis Zukofsky.

contamination \kən-ˌtam-ə-'nā-shən\ In manuscript tradition, a blending whereby a single manuscript contains readings belonging to different groups. In literature, a blending of legends or stories that results in new combinations of incident or in modifications of plot.

conte \'kōnt, 'kōⁿt\ *plural* contes *same or* 'kōnts\ [French, a derivative of *conter* to relate] **1.** A short tale especially of adventure. *Compare* SHORT STORY. **2.** A narrative that is somewhat shorter than the average novel but longer than a short story.

conteur \kōn-'tər, kōⁿ-\ *plural* conteurs *same or* -'tərz\ [French, a derivative of *conter* to relate] A reciter or composer of contes. A storyteller.

context \'kän-ˌtekst\ [Latin *contextus* connection, structure, literally, the act of weaving together, a derivative of *contexere* to weave together] **1.** *obsolete* A written composition. **2.** The parts of a discourse that surround a word or passage and can throw light on its meaning.

continuation \kən-ˌtin-yə-'wā-shən\ **1.** A book begun by one writer and continued by another; also, the portion of such a book that continues the original part. **2.** A work (such as a periodical or numbered monograph) that is issued in successive parts; also, one of the parts.

contraction \kən-'trak-shən\ In classical prosody, the substitution of one long syllable for two short ones, as when a spondee (– –) appears as a contracted form of the dactyl (– ∪ ∪). The word is contrasted with RESOLUTION. *See also* PROSODY; SCANSION.

convention \kən-'ven-chən\ An established technique, practice, or device in literature or the theater. Dramatic conventions include the willing suspension of disbelief, the use of stock characters, and the use of soliloquy.

conversation piece A piece of writing (such as a play) that depends for its effect chiefly upon the wit or excellent quality of its dialogue. The term is also used to describe a poem that has a light, informal tone despite its serious subject. Examples include Samuel Taylor Coleridge's "The Nightingale," William Wordsworth's "Tintern Abbey," and W.H. Auden's "September 1, 1939."

Corinthian \kə-'rin-thē-ən\ Elegant and ornate in style or manner, especially in literary style. The allusion is to the reputed elegance of the art of ancient Corinth.

corn \'kȯrn\ Something (such as writing, music, or acting) that is corny (mawkishly old-fashioned or tiresomely simple and sentimental).

Cornhill Magazine, The \ˌkȯrn-'hil\ Long-lived British literary periodical (1860–1975) that specialized in publishing novels in serial form and was renowned for its uniformly high literary quality. Its founder and first editor was William Makepeace Thackeray. It was the first literary magazine to achieve a circulation of 100,000. *The Cornhill Magazine* suspended publication from 1940 to 1943 during the height of World War II, resuming in January 1944.

Among the major novelists, poets, and critical writers whose work appeared in the periodical were George Eliot, Thomas Hardy, Alfred, Lord Tennyson, Robert Browning, Algernon Swinburne, John Ruskin, and Leslie Stephen, who also served as the magazine's editor (1871–82).

coronach \'kȯr-ə-nək, 'kär-\ [Scottish Gaelic *corronach* and Irish *coránach*] In Scottish and Irish tradition, choral lament or outcry for the dead; also, a funeral song sung or uttered by women. Though observers frequently reported hearing such songs in Ireland or in the Scottish Highlands, no such songs have been recorded. The Scottish border ballad "The Bonny Earl of Murray" was supposedly composed in the tradition of the coronach. It begins:

> Ye Highlands, and ye Lawlands,
> Oh where have you been?
> They have slain the Earl of Murray,
> And they layd him on the green.

corpus \'kȯr-pəs\ *plural* corpora \'kȯr-pə-rə\ [Latin, body] The whole body or total amount of writings of a particular kind or on a particular subject (as the total production of a writer [*compare* OEUVRE] or the whole of the literature on a subject).

correct \kə-'rekt\ Of literary or artistic style, conforming to recognized conventions or an established mode.

correption \kə-'rep-shən\ [Latin *correptio* shortening of a vowel or syllable, a derivative of *corripere* to pronounce a syllable short, literally, to reduce, diminish] In classical prosody, the shortening of a final long vowel or diphthong when the next word begins with a vowel. The device occurs most often in the works of Homer.

corrupt \kə-'rəpt\ To alter from the original or correct form or version (as by error, omission, or addition).

cosmogonic myth *See* CREATION MYTH.

costumbrismo \ˌkȯs-tu̇m-'brēz-mō\ [Spanish, a derivative of *costumbre* custom, manner] In Spanish literature, a movement that emphasized the depiction of the everyday manners and customs of a particular social or provincial milieu. Although the origins of *costumbrismo* go back to the Golden Age of Spanish literature in the 16th and 17th centuries, it grew into a major force in the literature of the first half of the 19th century, first in verse and then in prose sketches called *cuadros de costumbres* ("scenes of customs") that stressed detailed descriptions of typical regional characters and social conduct, often with a satirical or philosophical intent.

Among its early practitioners were Mariano José de Larra, who wrote about Madrid, and Serafín Estébanez Calderón, who wrote about Andalusia. Significant *costumbrista* writers of the last half of the 19th century included Fernán Caballero, and Pedro Antonio de Alarcón, both of whom wrote novels set in Andalusia, and José María de Pereda, who wrote about the mountainous region of northern Castile.

Costumbrismo's lasting importance lies in its influence on the development of the regional novel in Spain and Latin America.

couch \'kau̇ch\ To place or compose in a specified kind of language. It means much the same as "to word" or "to phrase."

counterpoint \'kau̇n-tər-ˌpȯint\ Any artistic arrangement or device using significant contrast or interplay of distinguishable elements; specifically, motions in dance juxtaposed rhythmically and visually against the music or against other motions by parts of the body or groups of dancers. The term was adapted by literary critics to denote metrical variation in poetry.

counterpoint rhythm Rhythm that includes so much metrical inversion that the prevailing cadence ceases at times to prevail and so that a complex rhythm results from the conjunction of the basic cadence with its inversion. The term was applied by Gerard Manley Hopkins particularly to the work of John Milton, whose choruses in *Samson Agonistes* were for Hopkins an excellent example of counterpoint rhythm. *See also* INVERSION; SUBSTITUTION.

counterturn \'kau̇n-tər-ˌtərn\ [translation of Greek *antistrophḗ*] An unexpected turn or development in the action of a play, especially at the climax.

coup de theatre \ˌkü-də-tā-'ätr *with* r *as a uvular trill*\ *plural* coups de theatre *same*\ [French *coup de théâtre,* literally, stroke of theater] **1.** A sudden sensational turn in a play; also, a sudden dramatic effect or turn of events. **2.** A theatrical success.

couplet \'kəp-lət\ [Middle French, a derivative of *couple* pair] Two successive lines of verse marked usually by rhythmic correspondence, rhyme, or the inclusion of a self-contained utterance. In classical prosody, the synonym *distich* is often preferred.

A couplet in which the sense is relatively independent is a *closed couplet;* a couplet that cannot stand alone is an *open couplet.* In a closed couplet, each of the two lines may be end-stopped (that is, both sense and meter end in a pause at a line's end); alternatively, the meaning of the first line may continue to the second (this is called *enjambment*).

Couplets are most frequently used as units of composition in long poems; but, since they lend themselves to pithy, epigrammatic statements, they are often composed as independent poems or function as parts of other verse forms. William Shakespeare concluded his sonnets with a couplet. In French narrative and dramatic poetry, the rhyming alexandrine (12-syllable line) is the dominant couplet form, and German and Dutch verse of the 17th and 18th centuries reflects the influence of the alexandrine couplet. The term *couplet* is also commonly substituted for *stanza* in French versification. A "square couplet," for example, is a stanza of eight lines, with each line composed of eight syllables. The preeminent English couplet is the *heroic couplet,* two rhyming lines of iambic pentameter with a caesura (pause), usually in the middle of each line. Couplets were also frequently introduced into the blank verse of Elizabethan and Jacobean drama for heightened dramatic emphasis at the conclusion of a long speech or in running dialogue, as in the following example from Shakespeare's *Richard II:*

> Think what you will, we seize into our hands
> His plate, his goods, his money, and his lands.

courtesy literature \'kər-tə-sē, 'kȯr-\ Literature comprising courtesy books and similar pieces. Though it was essentially a book of etiquette, the typical courtesy book was in fact much more than a guide to manners. It concerned the establishment of a philosophy of life, a code of principles and ethical behavior by which to live.

The earliest courtesy literature was written in Italian and German in the 13th century. By the end of 17th century, much courtesy literature had begun to evolve into the literature of proper behavior and was designed more to produce the veneer of civility than to educate the whole person.

courtly love *French* amour courtois \ȧ-mür-kür-'twä\ A late medieval, highly conventionalized code that prescribed the behavior and emotions of ladies and their lovers. *Amour courtois* also provided the theme of an extensive courtly medieval literature that began with the troubadour poetry of Aquitaine and Provence in southern France toward the end of the 11th century.

The courtly lover existed to serve his lady. His love was invariably adulterous, upper-class marriage at that time being usually the result of economic interest or the seal of a power alliance. The lover ultimately saw himself as serving the all-powerful god of love and worshiping his lady-saint. Faithlessness was the one mortal sin.

The Roman poet Ovid undoubtedly provided inspiration in the developing concept of courtly love. His *Ars Amatoria* (*The Art of Love*) had pictured the lover as the slave of passion—sighing, trembling, growing pale and sleepless, even dying for love. The Ovidian lover's adoration was calculated to win sensual rewards; the courtly lover, however, while displaying the same outward signs of passion, was usually willing to love his lady from afar.

The idea of courtly love spread swiftly across Europe, and a decisive influence in this transmission was Eleanor of Aquitaine, wife first to Louis VII of France and then to Henry II of England, who inspired some of the best poetry of Bernard de Ventadour, among the last and finest of troubadour poets. Eleanor's daughter Marie of Champagne encouraged the composition of Chrétien de Troyes' courtly romance *Lancelot, ou Le Chevalier de la charrette*. Soon afterward the doctrine of courtly love was "codified" in a three-book treatise by André le Chapelain. In the 13th century a long allegorical poem, the *Roman de la rose,* expressed the concept of a lover suspended between happiness and despair.

Courtly love soon pervaded the literatures of Europe. The German minnesinger lyrics and court epics such as Gottfried von Strassburg's *Tristan und Isolde* are evidence of its power. Italian poetry embodied the courtly ideals as early as the 12th century, and during the 14th century their essence was distilled in Petrarch's sonnets to Laura. But perhaps more significantly, Dante had earlier managed to fuse courtly love and mystical vision: his Beatrice was, in life, his earthly inspiration, and in *La divina commedia* she became his spiritual guide to the mysteries of Paradise. Courtly love was also a vital influential force on most medieval literature in England, but there it came to be adopted as part of the courtship ritual leading to marriage.

courtly makar or **courtly maker** *See* MAKAR.

courtyard theater Any temporary or permanent theater structure established in an inn's courtyard in England or a residential courtyard (*corrale*) in Spain. The first reference to the courtyard theater is from the mid-16th century. The size and shape of the stage varied, and in most theaters of this type the audiences stood. Because there was no roof, performances were always held in the afternoon and were frequently canceled because of inclement weather.

Cowleyan ode \'kaů-lē-ən\ *See* IRREGULAR ODE.

cradle book A book printed before 1501. *See* INCUNABULUM.

crambo \'kram-bō\ *plural* cramboes. A game in which one player gives a word or line of verse to be matched in rhyme by other players. The word *crambo,* altered from the earlier *crambe,* apparently alludes to the proverbial Latin phrase *crambe repetita* ("dull repetition," literally, "repeated [i.e., re-served] cabbage"). *Compare* BOUTS-RIMÉS.

crasis \'kras-is\ *plural* crases \-ēz\ [Greek *krâsis,* literally, mixing, blending] In classical Greek, the contraction of two vowels or diphthongs at the end of one word and the beginning of an immediately following word, as *kán* for *kaì án* or *houmós* for *ho emós*. Crasis is especially common in some lyric poetry and in Old Comedy. The term sometimes refers to word-internal contraction in Latin, as *nīl* from *nihil.*

Creacionismo \ˌkrā-ä-syō-'nēz-mō, -thyō-\ [Spanish, a derivative of *creación* creation] A short-lived experimental literary movement founded about 1916 in Paris by the Chilean poet Vicente Huidobro.

For *Creacionistas,* the function of the poet was to create an autonomous, highly personal, imaginary world rather than to describe the world of nature. Creationist poets boldly juxtaposed images and metaphors and often used an original vocabulary, frequently combining words idiosyncratically or irrationally. The movement strongly influenced the generation of avant-garde poets in France, Spain, and Latin America—notably the Spanish poets Gerardo Diego and Juan Larrea—during the period immediately after World War I. Huidobro generally is considered to be the movement's most important poet.

create \krē-'āt, 'krē-ˌāt\ To produce a work of art or of dramatic interpretation along new or unconventional lines.

creation myth \krē-ˈā-shən\ or **cosmogonic myth** \ˌkäz-mə-ˈgän-ik\ A symbolic narrative of the beginning of the world as understood in a particular tradition and community. Creation myths are of central importance for the valuations of the world, for the orientation of the individual in the universe, and for the basic patterns of life and culture.

As the myth par excellence, the creation myth is the model for all other myths of the origins of cultural practices and artifacts. Many rituals may be thought of as dramatizations of the creation myth, performed to underscore and highlight the effectiveness of the myth in ordering and safeguarding the culture and its way of life. In addition, a culture's modes of artistic expression—the gestures and dance of ritual and the imagery of the visual and verbal arts—find their models and meanings in the myths of creation.

The major cosmogonic myths include those that feature a supreme creator deity, those that describe the emergence of the world through various stages of development, and those that view the world as the offspring of primordial parents.

Creation Society *Chinese* Chuangzao she \ˈjwaŋ-ˈdzau̇-ˈshə\. Chinese literary society founded in 1921 by Zhang Ziping, Guo Moruo, and a number of other Chinese writers studying in Japan. At first, the group advocated the idea of "art for art's sake"; the works produced by its members, notably Guo, Tian Han, and Yu Dafu, were influenced by Western Romanticism and were highly individualistic and subjective. In 1924, however, Guo, the society's leading figure, converted to Marxism. The Creation Society subsequently evolved into China's first Marxist literary society and began to advocate proletarian literature. *See also* LITERARY RESEARCH ASSOCIATION.

Crepuscolarismo \ˌkrā-pü-ˌskō-lä-ˈrēz-mō\ [Italian, a derivative of *crepuscolare* of the twilight, after *poeti crepuscolari* or *i crepuscolari,* the members of the group, literally, twilight poets] A movement of early 20th-century Italian poets whose work was characterized by disillusionment, nostalgia, a taste for simple things, and a direct, unadorned style. Like Futurism, a contemporaneous movement, *Crepuscolarismo* reflected the influence of European Decadence and was a reaction to the florid ornamental language of Gabriele D'Annunzio. It differed from the militant Futurist movement in its passivity, but both movements expressed the same spirit of desolation, and many *crepuscolari* later became *futuristi.*

The movement was named in a 1910 article, "Poesie crepuscolare," by the critic Giuseppe Borgese, who saw in their poetry the twilight of D'Annunzio's day. The main poets associated with it were Guido Gozzano, Fausto Maria Martini, Sergio Corazzini, Marino Moretti, and Aldo Palazzeschi; the last two poets later became notable writers of fiction. Of the poets, Gozzano's work was notably strong in descriptive power, stylistically skillful, and quietly humorous. Most of the poets were sentimental and nostalgic, stressing their boredom and loneliness and the tedium of their lives. Though it died out in the second decade of the 20th century, *Crepuscolarismo* was an important influence in returning Italian poetry to simple language and simple subjects.

Crescent Moon Society *Chinese* Xinyue she \'shin-'yue̅-'shə\ Chinese literary society that was influential during the 1920s. An offshoot of the earlier Creation Society, this group of Chinese poets was led by the British-educated Xu Zhimo and the American-educated Wen Yiduo, both of whom created new forms based on Western models.

cretic \'krē-tik\ [Greek *Krētikós,* from *Krētikós* (adjective) Cretan] In prosody, a three-syllable foot consisting in quantitative verse of a short syllable between two long syllables (– ∪ –) or in accentual verse of an unstressed syllable between two stressed syllables (´ ∪ ´). An example is the word *twenty-two.* The inverse of this meter is the amphibrach.

crib \'krib\ [English argot *crib* to pilfer] **1.** In literature, a key to an understanding of a literary work; especially, an explication of a work that follows the text line by line or page by page. *Compare* EXPLICATION DE TEXTE. **2.** A small theft or something stolen. Often used as a synonym for plagiarism.

crime novel Subgenre of the DETECTIVE STORY in which the focus of the work is on the environment and psychology of the criminal. Prominent writers of the genre include John Wainwright, Colin Watson, Nicholas Freeling, Ruth Rendell, Jessica Mann, Mickey Spillane, and Patricia Highsmith. Crime novels differ from police procedurals, which are written from the point of view of the criminal investigator.

criollismo \ˌkrē-ō-'yēz-mō, -ōl-\ [Spanish, a derivative of *criollo* person native to the Americas, Creole] Preoccupation in the arts and especially the literature of Latin America with native scenes and types; especially, nationalistic preoccupation with such matter. The gaucho literature of Argentina was a form of criollismo. Writers associated with the movement included Tomás Carrasquilla, Rufino Blanco Fombona, Benito Lynch, and Ricardo Güiraldes.

crisis \'krī-sis\ *plural* crises \-ˌsēz\ *or* crisises [Greek *krísis* decision, event, turning point] The decisive moment in the course of the action of a play or other work of fiction. *Compare* CLIMAX; RESOLUTION.

Crisis, The (*in full* The Crisis: A Record of the Darker Races) Monthly magazine published by the National Association for the Advancement of Colored People (NAACP). It was founded in 1910 and, for its first 24 years, edited by W.E.B. Du Bois; by the end of its first decade it had achieved a monthly circulation of 100,000 copies. In its pages, Du Bois displayed the evolution of his thought from his early, hopeful insistence on racial justice to his resigned call for black separatism.

The Crisis was an important medium for the young black writers of the Harlem Renaissance, especially from 1919 to 1926, when Jessie Redmon Fauset was its literary editor. The writers she discovered or encouraged included the poets Arna Bontemps, Langston Hughes, and Countee Cullen and the novelist-poet Jean Toomer. Under Fauset's literary guidance *The Crisis,* along with the magazine *Opportunity,* was the leading publisher of young black authors. After Fauset's departure *The Crisis* was unable to sustain its high literary standards.

Criterion, The English literary review published primarily as a quarterly magazine from 1922 to 1939. It was founded by T.S. Eliot, whose poem *The Waste Land* was published in the first issue.

The magazine was published briefly as *The Criterion, The New Criterion,* and *The Monthly Criterion* but reverted to its original title and to its quarterly schedule in September 1928. In January 1939 it ceased publication because of, in Eliot's words, "a depression of spirits" due to "the present state of public affairs."

Considered by some critics to reflect fascist leanings, *The Criterion* published poems, short fiction, essays, and reviews; among its contributors were W.H. Auden, Ezra Pound, and Stephen Spender. Works by European writers such as Marcel Proust and Jean Cocteau had their first publication in *The Criterion.*

critic \'krit-ik\ [Latin *criticus,* from Greek *kritikós,* from *kritikós* (adjective) discerning, critical, a derivative of *kritós,* verbal adjective of *krínein* to distinguish, judge] One who expresses a reasoned opinion on any matter especially involving a judgment of its value, truth, righteousness, beauty, or technique. Also, one who engages, often professionally, in the analysis, evaluation, or appreciation of works of art. *See also* CRITICISM.

critical bibliography or **analytical bibliography** The systematic study and description of books as tangible objects.

The field of critical bibliography grew largely from the study of incunabula (books printed in the first 50 years after the invention of printing, i.e., before 1501). The earliest printed books display the individual styles of their printers in such features as the type used, the typesetting, and the layout of the pages. These were used to deduce the order of individual books in a printer's total production and hence their approximate dates. For books lacking a printer's mark, these same stylistic variants were often used to attribute a book to a particular printer.

The two most significant studies in the development of critical bibliography are William Blades' *The Life and Typography of William Caxton* (1861–63), in which typographical details were used to arrange the publications of England's first printer in chronological order, and Henry Bradshaw's special study of 15th-century books printed in the Netherlands. Bradshaw's method was still more widely applied by Robert Proctor, who assigned the incunabula in the library of the British Museum (now part of the British Library) and the Bodleian Library at Oxford to countries and towns of origin and to particular printers. Proctor meticulously examined all the features of a book—paper, type, makeup, ornamentation, sewing, binding, manuscript notes, and marks of ownership—and, by publishing his descriptions of these books, firmly established this method of study, which was later applied to books by 16th- and 17th-century English authors. In one of the earliest examples of this method in action, the question of the priority between the two 1609 issues of William Shakespeare's *Troilus and Cressida* was resolved.

Critical Journal, The *See* THE EDINBURGH REVIEW.

criticaster \'krit-i-ˌkas-tər\ An inferior or petty critic.

criticism \'krit-ə-ˌsiz-əm\ **1.** The art of evaluating or analyzing works of art or literature. *See* LITERARY CRITICISM. **2.** The scientific investigation of literary documents (as the Bible) in regard to such matters as origin, text, composition, or history.

critique \kri-'tēk\ [French] An act of criticizing; especially, a critical examination or estimate of a thing or situation (as a work of art or literature) with a view to determining its nature and limitations or its conformity to standards.

Crusca Academy \'krüs-kə\ (Accademia della Crusca \äk-kä-'dā-myä-del-lä-'krüs-kä\; "Academy of the Chaff") Italian literary academy founded in Florence in 1582 for the purpose of purifying Tuscan, the literary language of the Italian Renaissance. Partially through the efforts of its members, the Tuscan dialect, particularly as it had been employed by Petrarch and Boccaccio, became the model for Italian literature in the 16th and 17th centuries.

Founded by five members of the Florentine Academy, with the purpose of sifting the impure language (*crusca,* literally, "bran" or "chaff") from the pure, the Crusca Academy set itself up immediately as the arbiter of the literature of its time. Cruscans wrote many commentaries on Petrarch and Boccaccio, their models for linguistic usage. They compiled dictionaries and lists of acceptable phrases and images from these authors; and translated many works into what they judged to be pure Tuscan. Members of the academy became known as linguistic conservatives, and in 1612 they began publication of their official dictionary, *Vocabolario degli Accademici della Crusca,* which continues to be published. Though the academy was suppressed in the late 18th century, Napoleon reestablished it in 1808, and it gained autonomy in 1811.

In the early 20th century, legislation by the Italian government limited the academy to the publication of classical authors and linguistic documents and periodicals.

crux \'krəks\ [Latin, cross, torture] A puzzling, confusing, difficult, or unsolved problem, as for example a scholarly question about the literal meaning of a word or line in a work of literature.

cubism \'kyü-ˌbiz-əm\ [French *cubisme,* a derivative of *cube* cube] A style of art that stresses abstract structure at the expense of the pictorial (or in writing, the narrative). Written attempts to produce cubist effects used bizarre associations and dissociations in imagery, the simultaneous evocation of several points of view toward the material, and other devices. One of the better-known practitioners of literary cubism was the writer Gertrude Stein, whose good friend Pablo Picasso had helped invent the cubist style. Stein's experiments in *Tender*

Buttons (1914), while obscure and virtually impossible to decode, provide the occasional telling or evocative phrase.

culteranismo \ˌkůl-ter-ä-ˈnēz-mō\ [Spanish] In Spanish literature, an esoteric style of writing that attempted to elevate poetic language and themes by re-Latinizing them, using classical allusions, vocabulary, syntax, and word order. The name *culterano* for a practitioner of this style is a derivative of *culto* ("cult"), which was perhaps modeled with a mixture of humor and disdain on *luterano* ("Lutheran").

Announced as a theory by Luis Carillo y Sotomayor in 1611 with his *Libro de la erudición poética* ("Book of Poetic Erudition"), *culteranismo* reached its height in the 17th century with the poetry of Luis de Góngora. Góngora's complex imagery, unusual grammatical constructions, and obscure mythological allusions in *Soledades* (1613; "Solitudes") carried *culteranismo* to such extremes that *gongorismo* entered the language as a synonym for literary affectation. Lesser imitators of Góngora deliberately cultivated obscurity in their work, thus overshadowing the original aim of the style, which was to create a poetry that would be timeless and universally appealing.

After 300 years of almost universal ridicule, *culteranismo* was rediscovered by early 20th-century avant-garde poets in Spain as a fruitful method of poetic expression, and Góngora himself was reevaluated by modern critics as one of Spain's greatest poets.

culture myth A myth that accounts for the discovery of arts and sciences.

curtain-raiser \ˈkərt-ən-ˌrā-zər\ A short play, usually of one scene, that is presented before the main full-length drama.

curtal sonnet \ˈkər-təl\ A curtailed or contracted sonnet; specifically, a sonnet of 11 lines rhyming *abcabc dcbdc* or *abcabc dbcdc* with the last line a tail, or half a line. The term was used by Gerard Manley Hopkins to describe the form that he used in such poems as "Pied Beauty" and "Peace." *Curtal* is a now obsolete word meaning "shortened."

cutback \ˈkət-ˌbak\ A shift from a chronological order in narration to events that took place earlier than those last presented. *Compare* FLASHBACK.

cyberpunk \ˈsīb-ər-ˌpəŋk\ A science-fiction subgenre comprising works characterized by countercultural antiheroes trapped in a dehumanized, high-tech future.

The word cyberpunk was coined by writer Bruce Bethke, who wrote a story with that title in 1982. He derived the term from the words *cybernetics,* the science of replacing human functions with computerized ones, and *punk,* the cacophonous music and nihilistic sensibility that developed in youth culture during the 1970s and '80s. Science-fiction editor Gardner Dozois is generally credited with popularizing the term.

The roots of cyberpunk extend past Bethke's tale to the technological fiction of the 1940s and '50s, to the writings of Samuel R. Delany and others who took up themes of alienation in a high-tech future, and to the criticism of Bruce Sterling, who in the 1970s called for science fiction that addressed the social and scientific concerns of the day. Not until the publication of William Gibson's 1984 novel *Neuromancer,* however, did cyberpunk take off as a movement within the genre. With its renegade "cowboy" hero and its creation of cyberspace, an omnipresent mind-altering computer network, the book exemplified cyberpunk concerns. Other members of the cyberpunk school included Sterling, John Shirley, and Rudy Rucker.

Science-fiction critics credited cyberpunk with revitalizing the genre. The movement also influenced popular culture in the mid- and late-1980s, spawning in 1987 a clever computer-animated television series, "Max Headroom."

cycle \ˈsī-kəl\ [Greek *kýklos,* literally, ring, circle] **1.** A group or series of works (such as poems, plays, novels, or songs) that treat the same theme. **2.** The complete series of poetic or prose narratives (usually of different authorship) that deal typically with the exploits of legendary heroes and heroines and their associates.

The term cyclic poems was first used in late classical times to refer to the independent poems that appeared after Homer to supplement his account of the Trojan War and the heroes' homecomings. Another classical Greek cycle is the "Theban" group, dealing with Oedipus and his descendants. The Theban cycle is best known through Sophocles' tragedies *Oedipus the King, Antigone,* and *Oedipus at Colonus* and Aeschylus' *Seven Against Thebes.*

Medieval romance is classified into three major cycles: the Matter of Rome the great, the Matter of France, and the Matter of Britain ("matter" here is a literal translation of the French matière, referring to subject matter, theme, topic, etc.). The Matter of Rome, a misnomer, refers to all tales derived from Latin classics. The Matter of France includes the stories of Charlemagne and his Twelve Noble Peers. The Matter of Britain refers to stories of King Arthur and his knights, the Tristram stories, and independent tales having an English background, such as *Guy of Warwick.*

Groups of mystery plays that were regularly performed in various towns in England were also known as cycles. (*See* CHESTER PLAYS; N-TOWN PLAYS; WAKEFIELD PLAYS; YORK PLAYS.)

The word cycle is also used for a series of poems, plays, or novels that are linked in theme, such as Émile Zola's Rougon-Macquart cycle of 20 novels (1871–93), which traces the history of a family.

cyclic poets The post-Homeric poets who composed epics on the Trojan War and its heroes.

cynghanedd \ˌkəŋ-ˈhän-eth\ *plural* cynganeddion \ˌkəŋ-ä-ˈneth-yȯn\ [Welsh, literally, consonance, harmony] In Welsh poetry, a strict, intricate system of alliteration and internal rhyme that is obligatory in the 24 strict meters of Welsh bardic verse.

Cynghanedd had developed by the 13th century from the prosodic devices of the early bards and was formally codified at the Caerwys Eisteddfod (assembly of bards) of 1524. The device thus became an obligatory adornment of poems in the strict (classical bardic) meters. There are four fundamental types of cynghanedd, but within these there are a number of refinements and variations. Characteristic of all but the simplest form is a rule of serial alliteration that requires the same consonants to occur in the same order in relation to the main stress in each half of a line, as in the following couplet:

> Dwyn ei géiniog / dan gẃynaw
> d n g n d ng n
>
> Rhoi angen ún / rhewng y ńaw
> rh ng n rh ng n
>
> ("He brings his penny home amid complaints and sets one person's need among the nine.")

When skillfully used, cynghanedd is capable of conveying an almost unlimited variety of subtle effects.

cywydd \'kə-ˌwit͟h\ *plural* cywyddau \kə-'wə-ˌt͟hī\ [Welsh] A Welsh verse form, a short ode in rhyming couplets (or occasionally triplets) using CYNGHANEDD (a complex system of alliteration and internal rhyme). Especially, a verse that consists of couplets of seven-syllable lines with varying cynghanedd and terminal rhymes that fall alternately on accented and on unaccented syllables.

Developed in the 14th century in South Wales by Dafydd ap Gwilym, the cywydd shows affinities with forms used by the earlier *bardd teulu* ("bard of the [king's] war band"), the second grade in the Welsh bardic system, and with those of the French trouvère and jongleur. It was the leading Welsh verse form from the 14th to the early 17th century; its golden age was from the mid-14th to the mid-15th century. It was revived, with other bardic forms, by the classical school of Welsh poets in the mid-18th century and again in the 19th century. It remains in use by those modern Welsh poets who prefer strict (i.e., classical) forms to the free meters that are derived from Welsh folk song and from English verse.

D

I never travel without my diary. One should always have something sensational to read in the train.
—Oscar Wilde

dactyl \'dak-təl\ [Greek *dáktylos,* literally, finger; from the fact that the syllables of the metrical foot are three in number like the joints of the finger] In prosody, a metrical foot of three syllables, the first being stressed and the last two being unstressed (as in "take her up tenderly"). A falling cadence, the dactyl is scanned – ∪ ∪ (long, short, short) in classical prosody or ´ ∪ ∪ (stressed, unstressed, unstressed) in English prosody. The scansion may also be written óoo. *Compare* ANAPEST.

Probably the oldest and most common meter in classical verse is the dactylic hexameter, the meter of Homer's *Iliad* and *Odyssey* and of other ancient epics. Dactylic meters are fairly rare in English verse, one difficulty being that the prolonged use of the dactyl tends to distort normal word accent, giving the lines a jerky movement. They appeared with regularity only after poets such as Robert Browning and Algernon Charles Swinburne successfully used the form in the 19th century. Dactylic rhythm produces a lilting movement as in the following example from Lord Byron's *Bride of Abydos:*

´ ∪ ∪ ´ ∪ ∪ ´ ∪ ∪ ´ ∪
Know ye the | land where the | cypress and | myrtle.

This line exhibits catalexis, the common variation of omitting an unstressed syllable at the end of a line.

dactylo-epitrite \ˌdak-tə-lō-'ep-i-ˌtrīt\ In classical prosody, the metrical compound associated particularly with the poets Pindar and Bacchylides. It consists of various combinations of the hemiepes (– ∪ ∪ | – ∪ ∪ | –) and the cretic (– ∪ –), often linked by an anceps syllable.

Dada \'dä-dä\ or **Dadaism** \'dä-dä-ˌiz-əm\ [French, from *dada,* child's word for a horse] Nihilistic movement in the arts that flourished chiefly in France, Switzerland, and Germany from 1916 to about 1920 and that was based on principles of deliberate irrationality, anarchy, and cynicism and the rejection of laws of beauty and social organization.

The most widely accepted account of the movement's naming concerns a meeting held in 1916 at Hugo Ball's Cabaret (Café) Voltaire in Zürich, during which a paper knife inserted into a French–German dictionary pointed to the word *dada;* this word was seized upon by the group as appropriate for their anti-aesthetic creations and protest activities, which were engendered by disgust for bourgeois values and despair over World War I.

In the United States the movement was centered in New York at Alfred Stieglitz's gallery, "291," and at the studio of the Walter Arensbergs, both wealthy patrons of the arts. There Dada-like activities, arising independently but paralleling those in Zürich, were engaged in by such chiefly visual artists as Man Ray and Francis Picabia. Both through their art and through such publications as *The Blind Man, Rongwrong,* and *New York Dada,* the artists attempted to demolish current aesthetic standards. Traveling between the United States and Europe, Picabia became a link between the Dada groups in New York City, Zürich, and Paris; his Dada periodical, *291,* was published in Barcelona, New York City, Zürich, and Paris from 1917 through 1924.

In 1917 the Dada movement was transmitted to Berlin, where it took on a more political character. One of the chief means of expression used by these artists was the photomontage, which consists of fragments of pasted photographs combined with printed messages. Like the groups in New York City and Zürich, the Berlin artists staged public meetings, shocking and enraging the audience with their antics. They, too, issued Dada publications: *Club Dada, Der Dada, Jedermann sein eigner Fussball* ("Everyman His Own Football"), and *Dada Almanach.* The First International Dada Fair was held in Berlin in June 1920.

Dada activities were also carried on in other German cities. In Cologne in 1919 and 1920, the chief participants were Max Ernst and Johannes Baargeld. Also affiliated with Dada was Kurt Schwitters of Hannover, who gave the name Merz to his collages, constructions, and literary productions. Although Schwitters used Dadaistic material—bits of rubbish—to create his works, he achieved a refined, aesthetic effect that was uncharacteristic of Dada anti-art.

In Paris Dada took on a literary emphasis under one of its founders, the poet Tristan Tzara. Most notable among the numerous Dada pamphlets and reviews was *Littérature* (published 1919–24), which contained writings by André Breton, Louis Aragon, Philippe Soupault, and Paul Éluard. After 1922, however, Dada faded and many Dadaists grew interested in SURREALISM.

Dada had far-reaching effects on the art of the 20th century. Its preoccupation with the bizarre, the irrational, and the fantastic bore fruit in the Surrealist movement. Dada artists' techniques of creation involving accident and chance were later employed by the artists in other movements.

dance of death *also called* danse macabre \ˈdäns-mə-ˈkäb, -ˈkä-brə, -ˈkä-bər\ *or* skeleton dance. Medieval allegorical concept of the all-conquering and equalizing power of death, expressed in the drama, poetry, music, and visual arts of western Europe mainly in the late Middle Ages. Strictly speaking, it is a literary or pictorial representation of a procession or dance of both living and dead figures, the living arranged in order of their rank, from pope and emperor to child, clerk, and hermit, and the dead leading them to the grave. The dance of death had its origins in late 13th- or early 14th-century poems that combined the essential ideas of the inevitability and the impartiality of death. The concept probably gained momentum in the late Middle Ages as a result of the obsession with death inspired by the Black Death in the mid-14th century and the devastation of the Hundred Years' War (1337–1453) between France and England. The mime dance and the morality play undoubtedly contributed to the development of its form.

The earliest known example of the fully developed dance of death concept was a series of paintings (1424–25) with explanatory verses painted on the walls of a building in the Cimetière des Innocents in Paris. The work was destroyed in 1699, but a reproduction or free rendering can be seen in the woodcuts of the Paris printer Guy Marchant (1485), and the explanatory verses have been preserved in a translation by the English poet John Lydgate. All other picture cycles on the theme were derived directly or indirectly from that of the Innocents. In 1523–26 the German artist Hans Holbein the Younger made a series of drawings of the subject, perhaps the culminating point in the pictorial evolution of the dance of death.

The proliferation of literary versions of the dance of death included a 15th-century Spanish masterpiece, the poem "La danza general de la muerte," which was inspired by the verses at the Innocents and by several German poems. Though depictions of the dance of death declined after the 16th century, much later literature, including works by Miguel de Cervantes, J.W. von Goethe, Robert Browning, Thomas Beddoes, Hugo von Hofmannsthal, August Strindberg, Federico García Lorca, and W.H. Auden, contains references to the theme.

The concept of the dance of death lost its awesome hold in the Renaissance, but the universality of the theme inspired its revival in French 19th-century Romantic literature and in 19th- and 20th-century music. In 1956 it was effectively used as the visual climax of Ingmar Bergman's motion picture *The Seventh Seal.*

dandyism \'dan-dē-ˌiz-əm\ A literary and artistic style of the latter part of the 19th century marked by artificiality and excessive refinement.

danse macabre *See* DANCE OF DEATH.

Dantist \'dan-tist, 'dän-\ A Dante scholar.

dawn song Any of several genres of song or poem greeting the dawn. *See* ALBA; AUBADE; TAGELIED.

débat \dā-'bä\ [French, literally, debate, altercation] **1.** A type of literary composition popular especially in medieval times in which two or more usually allegorical characters discuss or debate some subject, most often a question of love, morality, or politics, and then refer the question to a judge. *Compare* TENSON. **2.** An extended discussion, debate, or philosophical argument between two characters in a work of literature. George Bernard Shaw incorporated such discussions into several of his plays, including *Major Barbara.*

decadence \'dek-ə-dəns, di-'kā-\ A period of decline or deterioration of art or literature that follows an era of great achievement. Examples include the SILVER

AGE of Latin literature, which began about AD 18 following the end of the Golden Age, and the Decadent movement at the end of the 19th century in France and England.

Decadent \'dek-ə-dənt, di-'kā-\ [French *décadent,* literally, person living in a decadent period] Any of several poets of the end of the 19th century, including the French Symbolist poets in particular and their contemporaries in England, the later generation of the Aesthetic movement. Both the Symbolists and the Aesthetes aspired to set literature and art free from all influences. They emphasized the idea of art for art's sake, seeing art as autonomous and opposed to nature as well as to the materialistic preoccupations of industrialized society. They therefore stressed the bizarre and the incongruous and artificial in their work as well as their personal lives. In both, the freedom of some members' morals helped to enlarge the connotation of the term, which is almost equivalent to fin de siècle.

Decadence was primarily associated with poetry, but its psychological basis is well illustrated in Joris-Karl Huysmans' novel *À rebours* (1884; *Against the Grain*) and the trilogy *Le Culte du moi* (1888–91) by Maurice Barrès. The impetus to Decadent poetry came partly from the study of Charles Baudelaire and partly from the works of Stéphane Mallarmé and Paul Verlaine.

In Verlaine's work two impressions predominate: that only the self is important, and that the function of poetry is to preserve moments of extreme sensation and unique impression. These were the features, together with experiments in form, on which the younger generation of poets seized in the 1880s. The poetic movement found its best exponent in Jules Laforgue, who brought together a subjectivism and pessimism fed by his studies in contemporary German philosophy and a genius for harnessing effects of poetic contrast. The review *Le Décadent,* whose title consecrated a label originally coined by hostile critics, was founded in 1886.

In England the Decadents were the poets of the 1890s—Arthur Symons, Oscar Wilde, Ernest Dowson, and Lionel Johnson, who were members of the Rhymers' Club or contributors to the avant-garde journal *The Yellow Book. Compare* AESTHETICISM; SYMBOLIST MOVEMENT.

decadentismo \ˌdā-kä-dān-'tēz-mō\ or **Decadentism** [Italian, from French *décadentisme,* a derivative of *décadent* decadent] Italian artistic movement that derived its name but not all its characteristics from the French and English Decadents, who flourished in the last 10 years of the 19th century. Writers of the Italian movement, which did not have the cohesion usual in such cases, generally reacted against the tenets of positivism and the belief in scientific rationalism and the significance of society as a whole. They instead stressed instinct, the irrational, the subconscious, and the individual.

The writers of the movement—Antonio Fogazzaro, Giovanni Pascoli, Gabriele D'Annunzio, Italo Svevo, and Luigi Pirandello—differed greatly from each other in style and philosophical approach, but they all created highly subjective pictures of society and the world.

The critic Benedetto Croce attacked the movement early in the 20th century. Its reputation was somewhat restored by Walter Binni after World War II, but it was attacked once again by the Marxist critic Carlo Salinari in the 1960s.

decameter \də-ˈkam-ə-tər\ [Greek *dekámetron,* from *déka* ten + *métron* meter, measure] In prosody, a poetic line of 10 feet.

decastich \ˈdek-ə-ˌstik\ [Greek *déka* ten + *stíchos* line, verse] A poem or stanza of 10 lines.

decasyllable \ˈdek-ə-ˌsil-ə-bel\ In prosody, a line of verse having 10 syllables.

decency \ˈdē-sən-sē\ **1.** Literary decorum or its observance. **2.** The established conventions of literary decorum often with special reference to syntactical or grammatical propriety.

deconstruction \ˌdē-kən-ˈstrək-shən\ A method of literary criticism which assumes that language refers only to itself rather than to an extratextual reality and which asserts multiple conflicting interpretations of a text and bases such interpretations on the philosophical, political, or social implications of the use of language in the text rather than on the author's intention.

Deconstruction was initiated by French critic Jacques Derrida, who in a series of books published beginning in the late 1960s launched a major critique of traditional Western metaphysics. He introduced the words *déconstruire* ("to deconstruct") and *déconstruction* ("deconstruction") in *De la grammatologie* (1967). Like Sigmund Freud's psychological theories and Karl Marx's political theories, Derrida's deconstructive strategies, which expand on Ferdinand de Saussure's insistence on the arbitrariness of the verbal sign, have subsequently established themselves as an important part of postmodernism, especially in poststructural literary theory and text analysis. Though the deconstructive principles of Derrida and later critics are well established, they remain somewhat controversial.

The deconstruction of philosophy involves the questioning of the many hierarchical oppositions—such as cause and effect, presence and absence, speech ("phonocentrism") and writing—in order to expose the bias (the privileged terms) of those tacit assumptions on which Western metaphysics rest. Deconstruction takes apart the logic of language in which authors make their claims, a process that reveals how all texts undermine themselves in that every text includes unconscious "traces" of other positions exactly opposite to that which it sets out to uphold. Deconstruction undermines "logocentrism" (literally, a focus on the word, the original and originating word in relation to which other concepts such as truth, identity, and certainty can be validated; but understood more generally as a belief in reason and rationality, the belief that meaning inheres in the world independently of any human attempt to represent it in words). It follows from this view that the "meaning" of a text bears only accidental relationship to the author's conscious intentions. One of the effects of deconstructive criticism has been a loosening of language from concepts and referents.

To many American scholars deconstruction seemed a logical step beyond

NEW CRITICISM (with its strong emphasis on text), and it was readily accepted and enlarged upon at Yale University by such proponents as Paul de Man and J. Hillis Miller. Some of the other figures who, to a greater or lesser degree, have associated themselves with deconstruction are Geoffrey Hartman, Catherine Belsey, Harold Bloom, Eugenio Donato, Shoshana Felman, Michel Foucault, Barbara Johnson, Edward Said, Jonathan Culler, and Gayatri Spivak. *See also* POSTSTRUCTURALISM.

decorum \di-ˈkȯr-əm\ [Latin (Cicero's translation of Greek *prépon*), neuter of *decorus* becoming, suitable, decent] Literary and dramatic propriety especially as formulated and practiced by the Neoclassicists. The concept of literary propriety, in its simplest stage of development, was outlined by Aristotle. In later classical criticism, the Roman poet Horace maintained that, to retain its unity, a work of art must be consistent in every aspect: the subject or theme must be dealt with in the proper diction, meter, form, and tone. Farcical characters, for example, should speak in a manner befitting their social position, kings should intone with the elegance and dignity commensurate with their rank.

dedication \ˌded-ə-ˈkā-shən\ A name and often a message prefixed to a literary, musical, or artistic production. Formerly, a dedication was used to testify to the artist's respect for a patron and often recommended the work to the patron's favor. Contemporary dedications usually express admiration or affection for a person or for a cause.

dedication copy The copy of a book presented by its author to the person to whom it is dedicated.

definitive \də-ˈfin-i-tiv\ Most authoritative, reliable, and complete. The word is used in reference to research, scholarship, or criticism, especially of a biographical or historical study, or of a text or edition of a literary work or author.

deictic \ˈdīk-tik, ˈdāk-\ [Greek *deiktikós* able to show, derivative of *deiktós,* verbal adjective of *deiknýnai* to show] Showing or pointing out directly. The words *this, that,* and *those* have a deictic function.

deliberative oratory According to Aristotle, a type of suasive speech designed to advise political assemblies. One of the most impressive deliberative orators was Demosthenes, an Athenian lawyer, soldier, and statesman. In one of his greatest speeches, "On the Crown," he defended himself against the charge by his political rival Aeschines that he had no right to the golden crown granted him for his services to Athens. So brilliant was Demosthenes' defense of his public actions and principles that Aeschines, who was also a powerful orator, left Athens for Rhodes in defeat. *Compare* EPIDEICTIC ORATORY; FORENSIC ORATORY.

Della-Cruscan \ˌdel-ə-ˈkrüs-kən\ **1.** Of, relating to, or resembling the Italian Accademia della Crusca, which was founded in 1582 for the cultivation of the Italian language and literature, or the literary style it championed. **2.** Of, relating to, or resembling a school of English writers of pretentious, affected, rhetorically ornate poetry in the late 18th century. The school was centered on Robert Merry, who belonged to the Italian academy, and was satirized by William Gifford in *The Baviad* (1791) and *The Maeviad* (1795). **3.** Affectedly pedantic—used of writings or literary style.

Delphin \ˈdel-fin\ Of or relating to the Delphin classics, an edition of the Latin classics prepared in the reign of Louis XIV of France. The name originated from a Latin inscription on the title page of the books, *in usum serenissimi Delphini* ("for the use of the most serene Dauphin").

demythologize \ˌdē-mi-ˈthäl-ə-ˌjīz\ To divest a written work of mythological forms in order to uncover the meaning underlying such forms. Also, to separate the meaning of a writing from the mythological forms in which it is expressed. The term may also be used to refer to the interpretation of a work's mythological elements in order to uncover the meaning of the work.

denouement \ˌdā-nü-ˈmä^{n}, dā-ˈnü-ˌmä^{n}\ [French *dénouement,* literally, the action of untying] The events following the climax of the plot. The final outcome, result, or unraveling of the main dramatic complication in a play or other work of literature.

descending rhythm *See* FALLING RHYTHM.

descort \des-ˈkȯr\ [Old French & Old Provençal, literally, quarrel, discord] **1.** A synonym for LAY, a medieval Provençal lyric in which the stanzas are unlike. **2.** A poem in medieval Provençal literature with stanzas in different languages.

description Composition intended primarily to present to the mind or imagination graphically and in detail a unit of objective or subjective experience.

descriptive bibliography or **enumerative bibliography** Bibliography in which the primary purpose is to organize detailed information, item by item, culled from a mass of materials in a systematic way so that others can have access to useful information. In the earliest bibliographies, the organizing principle was simply that of compiling all the works of a given writer, either a writer's list of his own works (autobibliography) or a biographer's lists of his subjects' writings.

Early Western autobibliographies include those by the 2nd-century Greek physician Galen and by the Venerable Bede. One of the first biographers to include bibliographies in his lives of church writers was St. Jerome in his *De viris illustribus* ("Concerning Famous Men"), in the 4th century. With the invention of printing in the 15th century, books proliferated, and the organization of information about them became both more necessary and more practical. As early as 1545 the idea of a universal bibliography aroused the German-Swiss writer

Conrad Gesner to compile his *Bibliotheca universalis* of all past and present writers. Part of his plan, completed in 1555, was to divide entries into categories of knowledge. His attempts at both universality and classification earned him the title "father of bibliography."

The vast numbers of books published as part of the modern knowledge explosion require elaborate methods of classification. Widely used systems are the Dewey Decimal Classification, the Library of Congress Classification, and the Universal Decimal Classification. In the last quarter of the 20th century, the widespread use of computers in processing such systematized information revived the possibility of creating a universal bibliography, including articles in periodicals. The problems threatening its implementation, besides those of worldwide standardization of cataloging entries and programming multilanguage materials, are the usual modern ones of cost, labor, and storage. What is meeting the need for comprehensive banks of recorded bibliographic data are the published catalogs of the great comprehensive libraries such as the British Library and Bibliothèque Nationale and the practice of producing and distributing information about newly published materials in machine-readable form, notably by the U.S. Library of Congress.

design \di-ˈzīn\ A conceptual outline or sketch according to which the elements of a literary or dramatic composition or series are arranged.

detective story Type of popular literature dealing with the step-by-step investigation and solution of a crime, usually murder.

The traditional elements of the detective story are: (1) the seemingly perfect crime; (2) the wrongly accused suspect at whom circumstantial evidence points; (3) the bungling of dim-witted police; (4) the greater powers of observation and superior mind of the detective; and (5) the startling and unexpected denouement, in which the detective reveals how he or she has ascertained the identity of the culprit. Detective stories frequently operate on the principle that superficially convincing evidence is ultimately irrelevant. Usually it is also axiomatic that the clues from which a logical solution to the problem can be reached be fairly presented to the reader at exactly the same time that the sleuth receives them and that the sleuth deduce the solution to the puzzle from a logical interpretation of these clues.

The first detective story was "The Murders in the Rue Morgue" by Edgar Allan Poe, published in April 1841. The profession of detective had come into being only a few decades earlier, and Poe is generally thought to have been influenced by the *Mémoires* (1828–29) of François-Eugène Vidocq, who in 1817 founded the world's first detective bureau, in Paris. The detective story soon expanded to novel length. The French author Émile Gaboriau's *L'Affaire Lerouge* (1866) was an enormously successful novel that had several sequels. Wilkie Collins' *The Moonstone* (1868) remains one of the finest English detective novels. Anna Katharine Green became one of the first American detective novelists with *The Leavenworth Case* (1878). *The Mystery of a Hansom Cab* (1886) by the Australian Fergus Hume was a phenomenal commercial success.

The greatest of all fictional detectives, Sherlock Holmes, made his first appearance in Sir Arthur Conan Doyle's novel *A Study in Scarlet* (1887) and continued into the 20th century in such collections of stories as *The Memoirs of Sherlock Holmes* (1894) and the longer *The Hound of the Baskervilles* (1902). So great was the appeal of Sherlock Holmes' detecting style that the death of Conan Doyle did little to end Holmes' career; several writers, often expanding upon circumstances mentioned in the original works, have attempted to carry on the Holmesian tradition.

The early years of the 20th century produced a number of distinguished detective novels, among them Mary Roberts Rinehart's *The Circular Staircase* (1908) and G.K. Chesterton's *The Innocence of Father Brown* (1911). From 1920 on, the names of many fictional detectives became household words, including Hercule Poirot and Miss Marple (creations of Agatha Christie), Lord Peter Wimsey (created by Dorothy L. Sayers), Philo Vance (created by S.S. Van Dine), and Ellery Queen (created by Frederic Dannay and Manfred B. Lee).

The 1930s was the golden age of the detective novel, particularly as seen in the books of Dashiell Hammett, in whose work the character of the detective became as important as the "whodunit" aspect of ratiocination had been earlier. *The Thin Man* (1932), with Nick and Nora Charles, was more in the conventional vein, with the added fillip of detection by a witty married couple. Successors to Hammett included Raymond Chandler and Ross Macdonald, who also emphasized the characters of their tough but humane detectives Philip Marlowe and Lew Archer, respectively. At the end of the 1940s, Mickey Spillane preserved the hard-boiled crime fiction approach but emphasized sex and sadism.

The introduction of the mass-produced paperback book in the late 1930s made the detective story readily accessible to a wide public. Among the writers who capitalized on this new market were Erle Stanley Gardner, whose criminal lawyer Perry Mason unravelled crimes in court; Rex Stout, with his fat, orchid-raising detective Nero Wolfe; and Frances and Richard Lockridge, with their bright married couple, Mr. and Mrs. North. In France, Georges Simenon created Inspector Jules Maigret, one of the best-known detectives since Sherlock Holmes. Other detective-story writers included Nicholas Blake (pseudonym of the poet C. Day-Lewis), Michael Innes, Ngaio Marsh, Josephine Tey, and John Dickson Carr. The 1980s and '90s saw a large number of female writers—notably Sara Paretsky and Sue Grafton—whose works often featured women sleuths.

The Mystery Writers of America, a professional organization founded in 1945 to elevate the standards of mystery writing, including the detective story, has exerted an important influence through its annual Edgar Allan Poe Awards for excellence. After the advent of the Cold War had increased interest in espionage and international intrigue, the suspense novel made some inroads on the popularity of the detective story, but the heirs of Poe and Conan Doyle still commanded a large readership. *See also* MYSTERY STORY; HARD-BOILED FICTION.

deus ex machina \ˈdā-əs-ˌeks-ˈmak-i-nə, -ˈmäk-; -mə-ˈshē-nə\ [New Latin, literally, a god from a machine, translation of Greek *apò mēchanês theós* (Demosthenes) or *theòs ek mēchanês* (Menander)] A person or thing that appears or is introduced into a situation suddenly and unexpectedly and provides an artificial or contrived solution to an apparently insoluble difficulty.

The term was first used in ancient Greek and Roman drama, where it meant the timely appearance of a god to unravel and resolve the plot. The deus ex machina was named for the convention of having the god appear in the sky, an effect achieved by means of a crane (Greek: *mēchanē*). The dramatic device dates from the 5th century BC; a god appears in Sophocles' *Philoctetes* and in most of the plays of Euripides to solve a crisis by divine intervention.

Since ancient times, the phrase has also been applied to an unexpected savior, or to an improbable event that brings order out of chaos (for example, in a western film the arrival, in time to avert tragedy, of the U.S. Cavalry).

deuterocanonical *See* APOCRYPHA.

device \də-ˈvīs\ Something (such as a figure of speech or a special method of narration) designed to achieve a particular effect.

diablerie \dē-ˈäb-lə-rē\ [French, literally, devilry, manifestations of the devil or of devils] A representation in words or pictures of black magic or of dealings with the devil. Among the literary works that contain such representations are Nathaniel Hawthorne's "Young Goodman Brown" and Sylvia Townsend Warner's *Lolly Willowes.*

diaeresis or **dieresis** \dī-ˈer-ə-sis, -ˈir-\ *plural* diaereses *or* diereses \-ˌsēz\ [Greek *diaíresis,* literally, the act of dividing, division] **1.** The resolution of one syllable into two, especially by separating the vowel elements of a diphthong and, by extension, two adjacent vowels, as in the word c*oo*peration; it is also the mark placed over a vowel to indicate that it is pronounced as a separate syllable, as in *naïve* or *Brontë.* **2.** In classical prosody, the break in a line of verse that occurs when the completion of a metrical foot coincides with the end of a word. A diaeresis after the fourth foot in a dactylic hexameter, especially common in pastoral poetry, is called a bucolic diaeresis or bucolic caesura. *Compare* CAESURA.

Dial, The Quarterly journal published between July 1840 and April 1844 and associated with the New England Transcendentalist movement. Edited first by Margaret Fuller and later by Ralph Waldo Emerson, *The Dial* printed poems and essays by Emerson, Fuller, Henry David Thoreau, and Bronson Alcott, among others. Although the magazine often suffered from undeveloped material and a lack of consensus about its purpose, it was an important vehicle for Transcendental philosophy. *See also* TRANSCENDENTALISM.

Dial, The Literary magazine founded in Chicago by Francis F. Browne and published from 1880 to 1929. It moved to New York City in 1918. Intended as a forum in which to carry on the tradition of the Transcendentalist journal of the same name, *The Dial* became famous for introducing some of the best new writing and artwork of the early 20th century. In its heyday it published works by Thomas Mann, T.S. Eliot, Sherwood Anderson, Djuna Barnes, D.H. Lawrence, and E.E. Cummings, among others. Line drawings by Henri de Toulouse-Lautrec, Pablo Picasso, and Marc Chagall also appeared in its pages. The prestigious succession of its editors included Conrad Aiken, Van Wyck Brooks, Scofield Thayer, and Marianne Moore.

dialectic \ˌdī-ə-ˈlek-tik\ [Greek *dialektikḗ* discussion and reasoning by dialogue, from feminine of *dialektikós,* adjective derivative of *diálektos* discussion, debate] Any systematic reasoning, exposition, or argument, especially in literature, that juxtaposes opposed or contradictory ideas and usually seeks to resolve their conflict. The Socratic method of question and answer as displayed in Plato's dialogues is an example. The term can also mean the play of ideas, cunning or hairsplitting disputation, or argumentative skill.

dialogue or **dialog** \ˈdī-ə-ˌlȯg, -ˌläg\ [Latin *dialogus,* from Greek *diálogos* conversation, a derivative of *dialégesthai* to converse] **1.** A written composition in which two or more characters are represented as conversing or reasoning on some topic. **2.** The conversational element of literary or dramatic composition.

As a literary form, a dialogue is a carefully organized exposition, by means of invented conversation, of contrasting philosophical or intellectual attitudes. The oldest known dialogues are the Sicilian mimes, written in rhythmic prose by Sophron of Syracuse in the early 5th century BC. Although none of these has survived, Plato knew and admired them. But the form of philosophic dialogue that he perfected by 400 BC was sufficiently original to be an independent literary creation. With due attention to characterization and the dramatic situations from which the discussions arise, Plato's dialogues develop dialectically the main tenets of Platonic philosophy. From Lucian in the 2nd century AD the dialogue acquired a new tone and function. His influential *Dialogues of the Dead,* with their coolly satirical tone, inspired innumerable imitations in England and France during the 17th and 18th centuries, e.g., dialogues by the French writers Bernard de Fontenelle (1683) and François Fénelon (1700–12).

The revival of interest in Plato during the Renaissance encouraged numerous imitations and adaptations of the Platonic dialogue. In Spain, Juan de Valdés used it to discuss problems of patriotism and humanism in 1533, and Vincenzo Carducci, theories of painting in 1633. In Italy, dialogues on the Platonic model were written by Torquato Tasso in 1580, Giordano Bruno in 1584, and Galileo in 1632. The Renaissance also adapted the dialogue form to uses unsuspected by either Plato or Lucian, such as the teaching of languages.

In the 16th and 17th centuries, the dialogue lent itself easily and frequently to the presentation of controversial religious, political, and economic ideas. George Berkeley's *Three Dialogues Between Hylas and Philonous* (1713) is perhaps the best of the English imitations of Plato. The best-known 19th-century examples of the form are Walter Savage Landor's *Imaginary Conversations* (vols. 1 and 2, 1824; vol. 3, 1828; thereafter sporadically to 1853), sensitive re-creations of such historical personages as Dante and Beatrice. André Gide's *Interviews imaginaires* (1943), which explore the psychology of the supposed participants, and George Santayana's *Dialogues in Limbo* (1925) illustrate the survival of this ancient form in the 20th century.

diamb \'dī-ˌam, -ˌamb\ or **diiamb** \ˌdī-'ī-ˌam, -ˌamb\ [Greek *diíambos*] In prosody, a metrical foot consisting of two iambs, or an iambic dipody reckoned as a single compound foot (◡ ⁄ ◡ ⁄).

diary \'dī-ə-rē\, *also called* journal \'jər-nəl\ [Latin *diarium,* a derivative of *dies* day] A record of events, transactions, or observations kept daily or at frequent intervals; especially a daily record of personal activities, reflections, or feelings. Written primarily for the writer's use alone, the diary usually offers a frankness not found in writing done for publication.

The diary form began to flower in the late Renaissance. In addition to revealing the diarist's personality, diaries are important for the recording of social and political history. For example, *Journal d'un bourgeois de Paris,* kept by an anonymous French priest from 1409 to 1431 and continued by another hand to 1449, is invaluable to the historian of the reigns of Charles VI and Charles VII. Attention to historical events also characterizes *Memorials of the English Affairs* by the lawyer and parliamentarian Bulstrode Whitelocke (1605–75) and the diary of the French Marquis de Dangeau (1638–1720), which spans the years 1684 to his death. The English diarist John Evelyn is surpassed only by the greatest diarist of all, Samuel Pepys, whose diary from Jan. 1, 1660 to May 31, 1669, gives both an astonishingly frank picture of his foibles and frailties and a stunning picture of life in London, at the court and the theater, in his own household, and in his Navy office.

An 18th-century diary of extraordinary emotional interest was that of Jonathan Swift, published as *Journal to Stella* (written 1710–13; published posthumously 1766–68). It is a surprising amalgam of ambition, affection, wit, and freakishness. Other notable English diaries of the late 18th century were those of the novelist Fanny Burney, published posthumously in 1842–46, and James Boswell's *Journal of a Tour to the Hebrides* (1785), a genuine diary though somewhat expanded, which was one of the first diaries to be published in its author's lifetime.

Interest in the diary increased greatly in the first part of the 19th century. Those of unusual literary interest, all published posthumously, include the *Journal* of Sir Walter Scott (1890), the *Journals* of Dorothy Wordsworth (1855), and the diary of Henry Crabb Robinson (1869). The latter contained much biographical material on his literary acquaintances, who included Goethe, Schiller, Wordsworth, and Coleridge. The posthumous publication of the diaries of the Russian artist Marie Bashkirtseff produced a great sensation in 1887, as did the publication of the diary of the Goncourt brothers, beginning in 1888.

André Gide's journal was published in several volumes in his lifetime. Other notable examples from the 20th century, all published posthumously, include the *Journal* of Katherine Mansfield (1927), *Het Achterhuis* (1947; *The Diary of a Young Girl*) by Anne Frank, and the five-volume *Diary of Virginia Woolf* (1977–84).

diastole \dī-ˈas-tə-lē\ [Greek *diastolḗ* the act of expanding or dilating] In prosody, the lengthening of a short quantity or syllable for metric regularity. It is the opposite of SYSTOLE.

dichoree \ˌdī-ˈkȯr-ē, ˌdī-kȯr-ˈē\ [Greek *dichóreios,* from *di-* two + *choreîos* choreus] *See* DITROCHEE.

dichronous \ˈdī-krō-nəs\ [Greek *díchronos,* from *di-* two + *chrónos* time] In classical prosody, capable of being occupied by either a long or a short syllable, or a syllable that can be scanned as either long or short. *See also* ANCEPS.

Dickensian \di-ˈken-zē-ən\ Characteristic of or having the qualities of the writings of Charles Dickens with respect to humor and pathos in the portrayal of odd, often extravagant, and picturesque character types usually from the lower economic strata of 19th-century English society.

dicolon \dī-ˈkō-lən\ *plural* dicola \-ˈkō-lə\ A verse or rhythmic period having two colons.

diction \ˈdik-shən\ [Latin *dictio* oratorical style, literally, the act of speaking, a derivative of *dicere* to say] Choice of words, especially with regard to correctness, clearness, or effectiveness. Any of the four generally accepted levels of diction—formal, informal, colloquial, or slang—may be correct in a particular context but incorrect in another or when mixed unintentionally. Most ideas have a number of alternate words that the writer can select to suit a particular purpose. "Children," "kids," "youngsters," "youths," and "brats," for example, all have different evocative values.

The widest scope for literary style is offered at the level of word choice. Phrases such as "the little house," "the diminutive house," and "the petite house" have overlapping or synonymous meanings; but "little" may suggest endearment as well as size; "diminutive," good construction; and "petite," prettiness. Writers such as Samuel Johnson, who believed that great thoughts were always general and that it was not the business of poets to "number the streaks of the tulips," use general, abstract, nonemotive words. Other writers, however, prefer particular, concrete, and emotive words and take advantage of the evocative values of technical, dialect, colloquial, or archaic terms when it suits their purpose. George Meredith used the archaic "damsel" to suggest the immaturity of a heroine; Ronald Firbank, in "Mrs. Henedge lived in a small house with killing stairs just off Chesham Place" (*Vainglory,* 1915), uses "killing" colloquially, in contrast to the standard words around it.

didactic \dī-ˈdak-tik, di-\ or **didactical** \-ti-kəl\ [Greek *didaktikós* apt at teaching] Of literature or other art, intended to convey instruction and information.

The word is often used to refer to texts that are overburdened with instructive or factual matter to the exclusion of graceful and pleasing detail so that they are pompously dull and erudite. Some literature, however, is both entertaining and consciously didactic, as for example proverbs and gnomic poetry.

didascaly \dī-'das-kə-lē, di-\ [Greek *didaskalía* teaching, instruction, a derivative of *didáskalos* teacher] The instruction or training of the chorus in ancient Greek drama. The Greek plural noun *didaskaliai* ("instructions") came to refer to records of dramatic performances, containing names of authors and dates, in the form of the original inscriptions or as later published by Alexandrian scholars.

diectasis \dī-'ek-tə-sis\ [Greek *dia-* through, completely + *éktasis* stretching, lengthening of a short syllable] In prosody, lengthening by an interpolated syllable.

dieresis *See* DIAERESIS.

digest \'dī-ˌjest\ [Latin *digesta* systematic arrangement of laws, from neuter plural of *digestus,* past participle of *digerere* to disperse, arrange, organize] **1.** A summation or condensation of a body of information on a specific subject, such as a periodical devoted to condensed versions of previously published works. **2.** A product of digestion, such as a literary condensation or abridgment.

digression \dī-'gresh-ən, di-\ [Latin *digressio,* a derivative of *digredi* to go off, digress] **1.** The act of digressing, or turning aside from the main subject of attention, in a discourse or other usually organized literary work. The writers Laurence Sterne and Jonathan Swift were particularly well known for their use of this technique. **2.** The portion of the discourse in which such a change of topic is made.

diiamb *See* DIAMB.

dilemma tale *also called* judgment tale. Typical African form of short story that has a morally ambiguous ending, thus allowing the audience to comment or speculate upon the correct solution to the problem posed in the tale. Issues raised include conflicts of loyalty, the necessity of choosing a just response to a difficult situation, and the question of where to lay the blame when several parties seem equally guilty. An example is the story of a young boy who in a time of crisis must choose between loyalty to his own father, who is a cruel and unjust man, and loyalty to the kindly foster father who brought him up.

Another tale deals with a man who died while hunting an ox to feed his three wives. The first wife learns through a dream what has happened to him, the second leads her fellow wives to the place where he died, and the third restores him to life. The audience must decide which of the three most deserves his praise.

A third tale has a tortoise as central character. Tortoise wishes to be thought of as equal in power and authority to Hippopotamus and Elephant. When his boastings reach their ears, however, they snub him by saying he is only a small being of no account. So Tortoise challenges both of them to a tug of war and through a trick pits them against each other, thus winning from each the grudging consent that he is their equal. The audience must decide exactly how equal the three of them are.

A final example is the Wolof tale of three brothers, all married to the same girl, who journey together to a strange land. One night the girl is murdered by a robber, and the eldest brother, with whom she is sleeping, is condemned to death on suspicion. He begs leave to visit his father before he dies. When he is late in returning, the second brother offers to die in his place, but as he is about to be executed, the third brother steps forward and "confesses" that he is the murderer. At that moment the eldest brother rides in, just in time to embrace his fate. Which of the brothers, the listeners are asked, is the most noble?

As these examples show, dilemma tales function both as instruction and entertainment, and they help to establish social norms for the audience.

dime novel A type of inexpensive, usually paperback, melodramatic novel of adventure popular in the United States roughly between 1860 and 1915; it often featured a western theme. One of the best-known authors of such works was E.Z.C. Judson, whose stories, some based on his own adventures, were written under the pseudonym of Ned Buntline. The dime novels were eventually replaced by pulp magazines. *Compare* PENNY DREADFUL.

dimeter \ˈdim-ə-tər\ In prosody, a line consisting of two metrical feet or of two dipodies.

dingdong \ˈdiŋ-ˌdȯŋ, -ˌdäŋ\ A verse or poem having a singsong monotonous character, such as a jingle.

diplasic \dī-ˈplas-ik, -ˈplaz-\ [Greek *diplásios* twofold, double] *in classical prosody* **1.** Two to one in proportion, that is, having a thesis twice the length of the arsis. **2.** Containing the repetition of a metrical pattern.

diplomatic \ˈdip-lə-ˈmat-ik\ Exactly reproducing the original, as in a *diplomatic* edition of a text. The word *diplomatic* originally meant "pertaining to the original copies of official documents," a diploma being originally any official document. *Compare* PARADIPLOMATIC.

dipody \ˈdip-ə-dē\ [Greek *dipodía,* a derivative of *dípous* two-footed, from *di-* two + *pod-, poús* foot] In classical prosody, a pair of metrical feet that is taken as a single unit. Trochaic, iambic, and anapestic verse are all measured by dipodies. In them, a monometer consists of one dipody (or two feet), a dimeter of four feet, a trimeter of six feet, and a tetrameter of eight feet. When trochaic or iambic verse is measured by single feet it is called tripody (three feet), tetrapody (four feet), hexapody (six feet).

dirge \'dərj\ [Middle English *dirige, derge,* from Latin *dirige* (singular imperative of *dirigere* to direct), the first word of an antiphon in the Office of the Dead adapted from Psalm 5:9 (Vulgate)] **1.** A song or hymn of grief or lamentation; especially, one intended to accompany funeral or memorial rites. **2.** A piece of writing resembling a dirge in being expressive of deep and solemn grief or sense of loss; especially, a poem of this kind. *Compare* ELEGY.

discourse \'dis-ˌkȯrs\ Formal and orderly and usually extended expression of thought on a subject. Also, a linguistic unit (such as a conversation or story) larger than a sentence.

diseme \'dī-ˌsēm\ [Greek *dísēmos* having two beats or morae, from *di-* two + *sêma* sign] In classical prosody, a long syllable that is regarded as two short ones. This may be scanned ⏑̲ ⏑̲ in resolution, when a normally long syllable becomes two shorts, or ⏑̄ ⏑̄ in contraction, when two normally short syllables become one long.

dispositio \ˌdis-pə-'zish-ē-ˌō, -'zit-\ [Latin, literally, arrangement] The rhetorical and logical arrangement of the matter or the discrete elements of a discourse, especially in classical and Renaissance rhetorical systems.

disputatio \ˌdis-pü-'tä-tē-ō\ *plural* disputationes \-ˌtä-tē-'ō-ˌnās\ [Latin, discussion, dispute] Disputation, especially in medieval or Renaissance rhetorical principle or practice.

disquisition \ˌdis-kwə-'zish-ən\ [Latin *disquisitio* inquiry] A formal or systematic inquiry into or discussion of a subject; specifically, an elaborate analytical or explanatory essay or discussion.

dissociation of sensibility Phrase used by T.S. Eliot in the essay "The Metaphysical Poets" (1921) to explain the change that occurred in English poetry after the heyday of the Metaphysical poets. According to Eliot, the dissociation of sensibility was a result of the natural development of poetry after the Metaphysical poets, who had felt "their thought as immediately as the odour of a rose"; this phenomenon—the "direct sensuous apprehension of thought," or the fusion of thought and feeling—which Eliot called a mechanism of sensibility, was lost by later poets. Eliot gave evidence of the dissociation of sensibility in the more elevated language and cruder emotions of later poets.

distancing effect *See* ALIENATION EFFECT.

distich \'dis-tik\ [Greek *dístichon,* from neuter of *dístichos* having two rows, of two verses, from *di-* two + *stíchos* row, line, verse] A strophic unit of two lines.

disyllabic \ˌdī-sə-'lab-ik, ˌdis-ə-\ Consisting of or having two syllables.

dit \'dē\ *plural* dits \'dē, 'dēz\ [Old French, word, speech, dit, from past participle of *dire* to say] A short, usually didactic, sometimes satirical poem in medieval French literature often dealing with simple subjects.

dithyramb \ˈdith-i-ˌram, -ˌramb\ [Greek *dithýrambos*] A choric poem, chant, or hymn of ancient Greece sung by revelers at the festival in honor of the god Dionysus.

The form originated about the 7th century BC in the songs of banqueters under the leadership of a man who, according to Archilochus, was "wit-stricken by the thunderbolt of wine." It was contrasted with the more sober paean, sung in honor of Apollo. The dithyramb began to achieve literary distinction about 600 BC, when the poet Arion composed works of this type, gave them names, and formally presented them at the Great Dionysia competitions at Corinth. These presentations consisted of a dithyrambic song accompanied by circular dances performed around the altar of Dionysus by choruses composed of 50 men and boys; the whole proceeding was accompanied by reed flutes and was led by the speaker of a prologue.

By the end of the 6th century BC, the dithyramb was a fully recognized literary genre. Its most famous exponent was Lasus of Hermione (b. *c.* 548), who is said to have been one of Pindar's teachers. The great age of the dithyramb was also the great age of Greek choral lyric poetry in general; Simonides of Ceos, Pindar, and Bacchylides all composed them. Of Simonides' and Pindar's dithyrambs, little is known; but two of Bacchylides' are complete, and there are considerable fragments of several others. Bacchylides' Ode 18 is unusual in that it contains a dialogue between a chorus and a soloist. This attempt to increase the dramatic interest of the narrative may explain why the classical dithyramb gave way to the more vivid methods of tragedy.

From about 450 BC onward, dithyrambic poets employed ever-more-startling devices of language and music, until for ancient literary critics "dithyrambic" acquired the connotations of "turgid" and "bombastic." True dithyrambs are rare in modern poetry, although John Dryden's "Alexander's Feast" (1697) may be said to bear a coincidental resemblance to the form.

Dithyramb may also refer to any poem in an inspired wild irregular strain, or to a statement or piece of writing in an exalted impassioned style usually in praise of a particular subject.

ditrochee \ˌdī-ˈtrō-kē\ A double trochee; a trochaic dipody reckoned as a single measure or compound foot

divan or **diwan** \di-ˈvan, -ˈvän; dī-ˈvan, ˈdī-ˌvan\ [Turkish, from Persian *dīwān* council, account book, collection of poems] A collection of poems especially in Persian or Arabic; specifically, a series of poems by one author, such as the *Dīvān* of Moḥammad Shams od-Dīn Ḥāfeẓ.

dizain \dē-ˈzaⁿ, *Angl* di-ˈzān\ or **dizaine** \dē-ˈzan\ [French *dizain,* from Middle French, a derivative of *dix* ten] A French poem or stanza of 10 octosyllabic or decasyllabic lines.

dochmiac \ˈdäk-mē-ˌak\ or **dochmius** \-mē-əs\ *plural* dochmii \-mē-ˌī\ [Greek *dóchmios,* from *dochmós, dóchmios* slanted, oblique] In classical prosody, a foot of five syllables typically having the first and fourth short and the rest long

(∪ – – ∪ –). Dochmiac verse is based on this pattern and occurs mainly in Greek drama.

documentary novel \ˌdäk-yü-ˈmen-tə-rē\ Fiction that features a large amount of documentary material such as newspaper stories, trial transcripts, and legal reports. Examples include the works of Theodore Dreiser.

documentary theater *See* THEATER OF FACT.

dodecasyllable \ˌdō-ˌdek-ə-ˈsil-ə-bəl\ [Greek *dṓdeka* twelve] In poetry, a line of 12 syllables.

dodrans \ˈdō-ˌdranz\ [Latin, three quarters] In classical prosody, a unit of six syllables of aeolic meter. The nucleus of a dodrans is a choriamb, which is either preceded or followed by an iamb or a trochee. Thus dodrans is scanned as ⏓ ⏓ – ∪ ∪ – or – ∪ ∪ – ⏓ ⏓ .

doggerel or **doggrel** \ˈdȯg-ə-rəl, ˈdȯg-rəl, ˈdäg-\ [Middle English (*rym*) *dogerel,* perhaps a derivative of *dogge* dog] Verse that is loosely constructed and often metrically irregular. (The term is sometimes used as an epithet for trivial or bad poetry.)

Doggerel appears in most literatures and societies as a useful form for comedy and satire. It is characteristic of the rhymes of children's games from ancient times to the present and of most nursery rhymes.

One of the earliest uses of the word is found in the 14th century in the works of Geoffrey Chaucer, who applied the term "rym doggerel" to his "Tale of Sir Thopas," a burlesque of the long-winded medieval romance.

John Skelton, caught in the transition between Chaucer's medieval language and the beginning of the English Renaissance, wrote verse long considered to be doggerel. He defended himself in *Colin Clout:*

> For though my rhyme be ragged,
> Tattered and jagged,
> Rudely rain-beaten,
> Rusty and moth-eaten,
> If ye take well therewith,
> It hath in it some pith.

Doggerel has been employed in the comic verse of such poets as Samuel Butler, Jonathan Swift, and Ogden Nash, and it is commonly heard in limericks and nonsense verse, popular songs, and commercial jingles.

In German, doggerel is called *Knüttelvers* (literally "cudgel verse"). It was popular during the Renaissance and was later used for comic effect by such poets as J.W. von Goethe and Friedrich von Schiller.

Dokumentartheater or **dokumentarisches Theater** *See* THEATER OF FACT.

dolce stil nuovo \ˈdōl-chā-stēl-ˈnwō-vō\ or **dolce stil novo** \ˈnō-vō\ [Italian, literally, sweet new style] The style of a group of 13th–14th-century Italian poets, mostly Florentines, whose vernacular sonnets, canzones, and ballate celebrate a spiritual and idealized view of love and womanhood in a way that was considered sincere, delicate, and musical. The Bolognese poet Guido Guinizelli is considered a forerunner of the *stilnovisti* ("writers of the new style"), and the most brilliant poets of the group are Guido Cavalcanti and Dante himself (in his lyric works). The most prominent minor poet associated with the group is Cino da Pistoia; others are Lapo Gianni, Gianni Alfani, and Dino Frescobaldi.

Several influences prepared the way for the development of the *dolce stil nuovo:* the troubadour poetry of Provence, which celebrated courtly love and used poetic forms that evolved into the Italian sonnet and canzone; the simplicity and mysticism of St. Francis and his followers; the 13th-century Sicilian school of poets, who created the sonnet and canzone from Provençal forms and who were the first poets in Italy to use the vernacular; and the philosophical doctrines of Thomism, Aristotelianism, and Platonism, with which all the *stilnovisti* had contact. Guinizelli's contribution was his own gentle style of poetry as well as an exalted view of woman and love, which he presented in the canzone "Al cor gentil ripara sempre amore" ("Within the gentle heart Love shelters him").

The genius of Dante and Cavalcanti brought the movement to its full power. Dante pointed out in *Il convivio* ("The Banquet") that he deliberately chose sweet and musical language for his love poetry, and the lovely lyrics to Beatrice that interlace *La vita nuova* ("The New Life") amply prove his success. His notion of love is a very exalted one: even while she was alive, Beatrice was pictured as an angelic presence, and after her death, Dante gave her the role of his divine guide in *La divina commedia* ("The Divine Comedy"). The beatific quality suffusing Dante's love for Beatrice is somewhat different from that which his "first friend," Cavalcanti, expresses in his emotional, often anguished, love lyrics.

Cavalcanti, the poet of the complexities of love, contributed some of the most stunning examples of the *dolce stil nuovo,* as for example the sonnet that begins "Who is she coming, whom all gaze upon." Cavalcanti was also the author of a famous and difficult canzone analyzing the nature of love, called "Donna mi prega" ("A lady entreats me"). It suggests the notion that love exists when a man encounters a woman who corresponds to an ideal image in his mind and ceases to exist when this correspondence of images ceases.

The influence of the *stilnovisti* was felt for centuries; their impact can be seen on the poetry of Petrarch and Lorenzo de' Medici (who consciously imitated them), as well as that of Michelangelo, Pietro Bembo, Torquato Tasso, Dante Gabriel Rossetti, and Ezra Pound.

domestic tragedy Drama in which the tragic protagonists are ordinary middle-class or lower-class individuals, in contrast to classical and Neoclassical tragedy, in which the protagonists are of kingly or aristocratic rank and their downfall is an affair of state as well as a personal matter. The earliest known examples of domestic tragedy are three anonymous late Elizabethan dramas: *Arden of Feversham* (*c.* 1591), the story of the murder of Mr. Arden by his wife and her lover and their subsequent execution; *A Warning for Faire Women* (1599), which deals with the murder of a merchant by his wife; and *A Yorkshire Tragedy* (*c.* 1606), in which a father destroys his family. To these may be added Thomas Heywood's less sensational but no less tragic *A Woman Kilde with Kindnesse* (1607). Domestic tragedy did not take hold, however, until reintroduced in the 18th century by George Lillo with *The London Merchant; or, The History of George Barnwell* (1731). The popularity of this sordid drama of an apprentice who murders his uncle-guardian influenced domestic tragedy in France and Germany; in the latter, G.E. Lessing, in his *Hamburgische Dramaturgie* (1767–69), paved the way for its critical acceptance.

Domestic tragedy found its mature expression in the plays of Henrik Ibsen toward the end of the 19th century. In earlier domestic dramas by other playwrights the protagonists were sometimes villains and at other times merely pathetic, but the bourgeois heroes of Ibsen's *Brand* (1866), *Rosmersholm* (1886), *The Master Builder* (1892), and *When We Dead Awaken* (1899) are endowed with some of the isolated grandeur of the heroes of classical tragedy.

The tragedy *Woyzeck,* written in 1836 by the German dramatist Georg Büchner, took as its subject the poor and oppressed. *Woyzeck,* however, was well in advance of its time, since domestic tragedy set in the milieu of the lower classes did not come to the fore until the turn of the 20th century with such works as Gerhart Hauptmann's *Die Weber* (1892; *The Weavers*) and *Rose Bernd* (1903). Examples of 20th-century domestic tragedies are Arthur Miller's *Death of a Salesman* (1949) and Eugene O'Neill's *Long Day's Journey into Night* (1956).

donnée \dȯ-ˈnā\ *plural* données *same or* -ˈnāz\ [French, from feminine past participle of *donner* to give] The set of assumptions (such as a widely held belief or a body of common knowledge) or a given subject or motif (such as a plot situation or a quirk of character) on which a work of fiction or drama proceeds.

doppelgänger \ˈdäp-əl-ˌgaŋ-ər, *German* ˈdȯp-əl-ˌgeŋ-ər\ [German, from *doppel-* double + *-gänger* goer; coined by Jean Paul in the novel *Siebenkäs* (1796)] In German folklore, a wraith, or apparition, of a living person, as distinguished from a ghost. The concept of the existence of a spirit double, an exact but usually invisible replica of every person, bird, or beast, is an ancient and widespread belief. To meet one's double is a sign that one's death is imminent. The doppelgänger became a popular symbol in 18th- and 19th-century horror literature, and the theme took on considerable complexity. One of the masters of the double figure was the German writer of fantastic tales E.T.A. Hoffmann. His first novel, *Die Elixiere des Teufels,* 2 vol. (1815–16; *The Devil's Elixir*), was one of the earliest expositions of the theme. Another, perhaps better-known, version of the doppelgänger occurs in Fyodor Dostoyevsky's novel *Dvoynik*

(1846; *The Double*), in which a poor clerk, Golyadkin, driven to madness by poverty and unrequited love, encounters his own wraith, who succeeds in everything at which Golyadkin has failed. Finally the wraith succeeds in disposing of his original.

Other themes related to the doppelgänger theme in folklore and literature include the mirror image, the shadow image, and the multiple personality.

double ballade A ballade having six stanzas and usually an envoi, or shortened final dedicatory stanza. *See also* BALLADE.

double dactyls *also called* higgledy-piggledy \ˌhig-əl-dē-ˈpig-əl-dē\ *or* jiggery-pokery \ˌjig-ə-rē-ˈpō-kə-rē\ A light-verse form consisting of eight lines of two dactyls each, arranged in two stanzas. The first line of the poem must be a jingle, often "Higgledy-piggledy" or "Jiggery-pokery"; the second line must be a name; the last lines of each stanza are truncated and they should rhyme; and one line in the second stanza must consist of a single word. The following example by R. McHenry illustrates the form:

> Higgledy-piggledy
> Emily Dickinson
> Amherst had nothing more
> Noble than she.
>
> 'Sconced in her house with the
> Curtains pulled back just so:
> Monochromatically
> Serving up tea.

Double Dealer, The American literary magazine founded in New Orleans, La., and published from January 1921 until May 1926. From July 1921 it was subtitled *A National Magazine from the South.*

The Double Dealer, sometimes rendered *The Double-Dealer,* was named after a William Congreve play. Enjoying the support of H.L. Mencken and Sherwood Anderson, it was the first magazine to publish the fiction of Ernest Hemingway (May 1922) and the second magazine to publish William Faulkner's verse (June 1922). It also helped launch the careers of Hart Crane, Thornton Wilder, Jean Toomer, and Kenneth Fearing. Among the other writers it published were Robert Penn Warren, Edmund Wilson, Amy Lowell, John Crowe Ransom, Richard Aldington, Hilda Doolittle (H.D.), Joseph Campbell, Mary Austin, and Ben Hecht.

double rhyme *See* FEMININE RHYME.

drama \ˈdräm-ə, ˈdram-\ [Greek *drâma* deed, action on the stage, play, a derivative of *drân* to do, act] A composition in verse or prose intended to portray life or character or to tell a story usually involving conflicts and emotions through action and dialogue and typically designed for theatrical performance. *See also* COMEDY; TRAGEDY.

dramatic irony A plot device; a type of IRONY that is produced when the audience's or reader's knowledge of events or individuals surpasses that of the characters. The words and actions of the characters therefore take on a different meaning for the audience or reader than they have for the play's characters. This may happen when, for example, a character reacts in an inappropriate or foolish way or when a character lacks self-awareness and thus acts under false assumptions.

The device abounds in works of tragedy. In the Oedipus cycle, for example, the audience knows that Oedipus' acts are tragic mistakes long before he recognizes his own errors. Later writers who mastered dramatic irony include William Shakespeare (as in Othello's trust of Iago), Voltaire, Jonathan Swift, Henry Fielding, Thomas Hardy, and Henry James. Dramatic irony can also be seen in such works as O. Henry's short story "The Gift of the Magi." In Anton Chekhov's story "Lady with the Dog," an accomplished Don Juan engages in a routine flirtation only to find himself seduced into a passionate lifelong commitment to a woman who is no different from all the others.

dramatic literature The texts of plays that can be read, as distinct from being seen and heard in performance.

The relationship between dramatic text and performance is complex. In the case of the Greek dramatists of the 5th century BC, the texts now available are a small selection made by later copying and preservation. Scholars cannot ascertain how, precisely, these are related to the compositions made available for the original productions. The problem here as in many later periods is the relation between the words written to be spoken or sung by the performers and the many other elements of dramatic composition—in movement, in scene and costume, and occasionally in music—the performance would include. Some of these can be inferred from the particular styles of writing, but most have to be studied from other kinds of surviving accounts.

In the drama of the English Renaissance few plays were published as literary works, but the importance of the dramatic writing of the period eventually established many of the plays as texts. In later periods, and notably from the 19th century onward, it became habitual to include in the written text of a play, and especially in its independently published form, details not only of scene and stage movement but also of the appearance of the characters and of the states of mind intended to accompany or to punctuate the spoken words. Some of these later texts of plays resemble, in part, the printed modes of novels or short stories.

There is no doubt that the printed texts of plays, in any of these forms, can be read as literature. Many of them are now regarded as being among the great works of literature of the world: Aeschylus' Oresteia trilogy, Shakespeare's *King Lear,* Henrik Ibsen's *Peer Gynt*. Yet it is then easy to forget that they are always a particular form of writing, for several voices and for action. It can be reasonably claimed that one gains the essential meanings of a play from the printed text alone, but there are cases when a plain silent reading from the text may miss some significant points. It is possible, for example, to read the Greek plays, especially in translation, without realizing that this or that "speech" was in fact sung, by a single actor or by the two halves of the chorus. In what are called the "soliloquies" of Shakespeare it is possible, from the printed text, to suppose that these are forms of "private thought," when in fact, within the well understood dramatic conventions of the period, they were spoken aloud, directly or indirectly, to audiences. In many other cases the physical movements and relations that were part of the essential composition may be missed altogether, or only vaguely apprehended, from the apparently self-sufficient text of the words spoken and its minimal "stage directions."

Most drama is a form of writing for oral and actual performance, and it is in periods when imaginative writing has been taken to be coterminous with "literature," and particularly with printed literature, that some of its elements have been most persistently misunderstood. The phrase dramatic literature has elements in common with the phrase oral literature, especially in times such as the present when the silent reading of print has come to seem the normal means for the reception and study of imaginative writing. The name for work within these conditions—"literature"—was applied to these other forms of writing intended primarily for oral communication. The need for understanding the conditions of oral performance is now more widely recognized. At the same time, given this recognition, the texts of the great plays are still read as dramatic literature, with a proper emphasis on the distinguishing features of the dramatic.

Remnants of the art of drama before it occurs as text, or dramatic literature, may be seen in the storytelling traditions of ancient cultures, in which gesture and often dance and song, as well as the individual style of the storyteller, are essential elements of the narrative.

dramatic monologue A poem written in the form of a speech of an individual character to an imaginary audience; it compresses into a single vivid scene a narrative sense of the speaker's history and psychological insight into his character. Though the form is chiefly associated with Robert Browning, who raised it to a highly sophisticated level in such poems as "My Last Duchess," "The Bishop Orders His Tomb at St. Praxed's Church," and "Fra Lippo Lippi," it is actually much older. Many Old English poems are dramatic monologues—for instance, "The Wanderer" and "The Seafarer." The form is also common in folk ballads, a tradition that Robert Burns imitated with broad satiric effect in "Holy Willie's Prayer."

Browning's contribution to the form is one of subtlety of characterization and complexity of the dramatic situation, which the reader gradually pieces together from the casual remarks or digressions of the speaker. The subject discussed is usually far less interesting than what is inadvertently revealed about the speaker himself. In "My Last Duchess," an Italian aristocrat shows off a painting of his late wife and in passing remarks reveals his cruelty to her.

The dramatic monologue form parallels the novelistic experiments with point of view in which the reader is left to assess the intelligence and reliability of the narrator. Later poets who successfully used the form were Ezra Pound ("The River Merchant's Wife: A Letter"), T.S. Eliot ("Love Song of J. Alfred Prufrock"), and Robert Frost ("The Pauper Witch of Grafton"). *Compare* SOLILOQUY.

dramatic unities The unity of time, unity of place, and unity of action. *See* UNITY.

dramatism \'dram-ə-ˌtiz-əm, 'dräm-\ A technique of analysis of language and thought as basically modes of action rather than as means of conveying information. It is associated with the critic Kenneth Burke.

dramatis personae \'dram-ə-tis-pər-'sō-nē, 'dräm-, -ˌnī\ [New Latin] **1.** The characters or actors in a drama. **2.** *singular in construction* A list of the characters or actors in a drama.

dramatist \'dram-ə-tist, 'dräm-\ *See* PLAYWRIGHT.

dramatization \ˌdram-ə-tə-'zā-shən, ˌdräm-\ An adaptation for theatrical presentation.

dramaturge \'dram-ə-ˌtərj, 'dräm-\ [German *Dramaturg,* from Greek *dramatourgós* contriver (taken to mean literally "dramatist"), from *dramat-, drâma* drama, play + *-ourgos* maker] A specialist in dramaturgy. The term is sometimes used specifically to mean an individual employed by a theater company as an adviser in choosing and interpreting the plays it presents.

dramaturgy \'dram-ə-ˌtər-jē, 'dräm-\ [German *Dramaturgie,* from Greek *dramatourgía* dramatic composition, action of a play, from *dramat-, drâma* drama, play + *-ourgia* making, production] The art or technique of dramatic composition or theatrical representation. In this sense English *dramaturgy* and French *dramaturgie* are both borrowed from German *Dramaturgie,* a word used by the German dramatist and critic Gotthold Lessing in an influential series of essays entitled *Hamburgische Dramaturgie* ("The Hamburg Dramaturgy") published from 1767 to 1769.

drame bourgeois \ˌdråm-bürzh-'wå\ [French, bourgeois drama] Type of play that enjoyed brief popularity in France in the late 18th century. Written for and about the middle class and based upon the theories of the French essayist and encyclopedist Denis Diderot, the *drame bourgeois* was conceived of as occupying a place between tragedy and comedy. It was designed as a serious depiction of middle-class problems, especially social abuses, but usually included a conventional happy ending. Diderot wrote two *drames* illustrating his theories, *Le Fils naturel* (1757; *Dorval; or, The Test of Virtue*) and *Le Père de famille* (1758; *The Father*), adapting them from the earlier *comédie larmoyante* ("tearful comedy") of Pierre-Claude Nivelle de La Chaussée.

The form was also espoused by Pierre-Augustin Caron de Beaumarchais in his *Essai sur le genre dramatique sérieux* (1767). He also wrote several *drames,* among them the sequel to *Le Mariage de Figaro*. Most of the plays in this genre, including those of Diderot's successors, Michel-Jean Sedaine and Louis-Sébastien Mercier, are regarded by critics today as sentimental and humorless, full of inflated dialogue and pompous sermonizing. *Drame bourgeois,* however, was important to the development of French acting; it led to more natural styles of speech and gesture and attempted greater historical accuracy in costumes and scenery. Diderot and his followers are also seen as distant precursors of the earliest writers of a drama known as the problem play.

drawing-room comedy Theatrical genre popular in the early 20th century, so called because the plays were usually set indoors, often actually in a drawing room. Such comedies generally portrayed upper-class society and were a form of COMEDY OF MANNERS. The plays of George Bernard Shaw, Noël Coward, and Philip Barry are examples of the genre.

dreadful \'dred-fəl\ A cheap and sensational story or periodical; especially, a story of crime or desperadoes such as was popular in mid-to-late Victorian England. *See also* PENNY DREADFUL.

dream vision *also called* dream allegory. A type of poetic narrative or narrative framework that was especially popular in medieval literature. It was so named because the poet pictured himself falling asleep and envisioning in his dream a series of allegorical people and events. The device made more acceptable the fantastic and sometimes bizarre world of personifications and symbolic objects characteristic of medieval allegory.

Well-known dream visions include the first part of *Roman de la rose* (13th century); Geoffrey Chaucer's *Book of the Duchesse* (1369/70); *Pearl* (late 14th century); *Piers Plowman* (*c.* 1362–*c.* 1387), attributed to William Langland; William Dunbar's *The Thrissill and the Rois* and *The Goldyn Targe* (early 16th century); and John Bunyan's *The Pilgrim's Progress* (1678).

droll \'drōl\ A short comical scene performed in an English public house during the mid-17th century when the theaters were closed by the government and the performance of plays was not permitted. Drolls, or droll humors, often consisted of scenes adapted from full-length plays, such as one concerning Bottom the Weaver from William Shakespeare's *A Midsummer Night's Dream,* though they were sometimes improvised by the actors.

drollery \'drōl-ə-rē\ An artistic or intellectual production of a light and humorous character.

drott-kvaett \'drōt-ˌkvet\ [Old Norse *drōtt-kvætt,* from neuter of *drōttkvæthr* composed in drott-kvaett meter, from *drōtt* retinue + *kvæthi* poem] A medieval Scandinavian verse form used in skaldic poetry. Drott-kvaett consists of stanzas of eight regular lines, each of which has three stresses and ends with a trochee. The form exhibits a complex pattern of internal and terminal rhyme, alliteration, and especially alternation of consonance with full rhyme at the ends of lines.

Drum South African literary magazine, published in English monthly from 1951, that focused on the concerns of black writers. Originating in Sophiatown, a black neighborhood near Johannesburg, it came to symbolize an era of protest literature that vehemently opposed the apartheid legislation of the 1950s. Together with the companion publication *Trust,* the journal circulated in several African nations.

Drum launched the careers of such writers as Can Themba and Nat Nakasa. Other early contributors included Bloke Modisane, Es'kia Mphahlele, Jordan K. Ngubane, and Alex La Guma.

duan \'dü-ən, 'thü-\ [Irish and Scottish Gaelic] A poem or song in Irish and Scottish Gaelic literature. The word was used by James Macpherson for major divisions of his Ossianic verse and hence was taken to be the Scottish Gaelic equivalent of "canto."

duologue \'dü-ə-ˌlȯg, -ˌläg\ [Latin *duo* two + English *-logue* (as in *dialogue*)] **1.** A dialogue between two persons. **2.** A dramatic or musical piece for two participants.

duple \'dü-pəl, 'dyü-\ In prosody, consisting of a meter based on disyllabic feet.

dystopia \ˌdis-'tō-pē-ə\ [*dys-* bad + u*topia*], *also called* anti-utopia. An imaginary place where people lead dehumanized and often fearful lives. *Compare* UTOPIA.

E

What is an Epigram? A dwarfish whole,
Its body brevity, and wit its soul
—Samuel Taylor Coleridge

echo \'ek-ō\ In literature, the repetition of a sound, syllable, word, or phrase for rhetorical or poetic purposes. Assonance, consonance, and all rhymes are types of echo.

echo verse Verse in which repetition of the end of a line or stanza imitates an echo. The repetition usually constitutes the entire following line and changes the meaning of the part being repeated. This device was popular in the 16th and 17th centuries in France, England, and Italy, particularly in pastoral poetry and drama. The best-known examples are George Herbert's poem "Heaven" and Jonathan Swift's "A Gentle Echo on Woman."

eclogue \'ek-ˌlȯg, -ˌläg\ [Latin *ecloga* short extract from a literary work, short poem, from Greek *eklogḗ* extract from a literary work, literally, choice, selection] A short, usually pastoral, poem in the form of a dialogue or soliloquy. The eclogue first appeared as a specifically pastoral form in the idylls of the Greek poet Theocritus (*c.* 310–250 BC), generally recognized as the inventor of pastoral poetry. The Roman poet Virgil (70–19 BC) adopted the form for his 10 *Eclogues,* also known as *Bucolics*. The eclogue was revived during the Renaissance by the Italians Dante, Petrarch, Giovanni Boccaccio, and Battista Spagnoli (also called Baptista Mantuanas or Mantuan) whose *Latin-language Eclogues* (1498) were read and imitated for more than a century.

Edmund Spenser's series of 12 eclogues, *The Shepheardes Calender* (1579), is considered the first outstanding pastoral poem in English. By the 17th century less formal eclogues were being written by such poets as Richard Lovelace, Robert Herrick, and Andrew Marvell. Marvell's "Nymph Complaining for the Death of her Fawn" (1681) climaxed the eclogue tradition of combining rural freshness with learned imitation. In the 18th century English poets began to use the eclogue for ironic verse on nonpastoral subjects, such as in Jonathan Swift's "A Town Eclogue. 1710. Scene, The Royal Exchange." Since then a distinction has been made between the terms *eclogue* and *pastoral,* with *eclogue* referring only to the dialogue or soliloquy form.

The eclogue eventually fell from favor, but it has occasionally been revived for special purposes by modern poets, as in Louis MacNeice's ironic eclogues in his *Collected Poems, 1925–1948* (1949). *See also* IDYLL.

École de Genéve *See* GENEVA SCHOOL.

ecthlipsis \ek-'thlip-sis\ *plural* ecthlipses \-ˌsēz\ [Greek *ekthlípsis* loss of a sound or letter in a word, literally, the act of squeezing out, a derivative of *ekthlíbein* to squeeze out] In Latin prosody, the elision or suppression of a final *m* and a preceding short vowel before a word beginning with *h* or a vowel.

Eddic \'ed-ik\ or **Eddaic** \e-'dā-ik\ **1.** Of or relating to the Old Norse *Edda,* a 13th-century collection of mythological, heroic, and gnomic poems, many of which were composed at a much earlier date. **2.** Having the characteristics of the alliterative strophic poetry of the *Edda* that is relatively simple in syntax and imagery. *Compare* SKALDIC POETRY.

Edinburgh Review, The \'ed-in-ˌbər-ə\ (*in full* The Edinburgh Review, or The Critical Journal) Scottish magazine that was published from 1802 to 1929 and which contributed to the development of the modern periodical and to modern standards of literary criticism. *The Edinburgh Review* was founded by Francis Jeffrey, Sydney Smith, and Henry Brougham as a quarterly publication, with Jeffrey as its first and longtime editor. It was intended as an outlet for liberal views in Edinburgh. The magazine soon earned wide esteem for its political and literary criticism, and by 1818 it had attained a circulation of 13,500. Its contributors included the novelist Sir Walter Scott, the essayist William Hazlitt, the historian Thomas Babington Macaulay, the educator Thomas Arnold, and the legal historian Sir James Stephen. *The Edinburgh Review*'s prestige and authority among British periodicals during the 19th century were matched only by that of *The Quarterly Review.*

edition \ə-'dish-ən\ [Latin *editio* published version of a literary work, literally, the act of emitting or bringing forth] **1.** A set of copies differing in some way from others of the same published text, as in a paperback edition or an illustrated edition. **2.** The whole number of bound copies of a work printed from a single setting of type or from plates made therefrom. The term *edition* is usually distinguished from *printing;* a printing refers to one continuous operation of the printing process, and thus a single edition may have several printings if the same plates are used more than once. **3.** A printed work that has the same title as an earlier production but with substantial changes in or additions to the text.

editio princeps \ā-'dit-ē-ˌō-'prin-ˌkeps, ə-'dish-ē-ˌō-'prin-ˌseps\ *plural* editiones principes \ā-ˌdit-ē-'ō-ˌnās-'prin-ki-ˌpās, ə-ˌdish-ē-'ō-nēz-'prin-sə-ˌpēz \[New Latin, literally, first edition] The first printed edition especially of a work that circulated in manuscript before printing became common.

education novel Genre popular in the late 18th and early 19th centuries in which a plan of education was set forth for a young person. The education novel was similar to the BILDUNGSROMAN but less well developed in terms of characters and plot and narrower in scope. Examples include Henry Brooke's *The Fool of Quality* and Jean-Jacques Rousseau's *Émile.*

Egoist, The Avant-garde British literary periodical founded in 1914 by Harriet Shaw Weaver and Dora Marsden as a feminist paper named *The New*

Freewoman: An Individualist Review. The periodical changed its name as well as its direction under the editorial influence of Ezra Pound. *The Egoist* published articles on all the modern arts and became known as the journal of Imagist poets. James Joyce's novel *A Portrait of the Artist as a Young Man* was first published there in 1914–15. Weaver and Marsden alternated the chief editorship. Richard Aldington and his wife, the Imagist poet H.D., were assistant editors, as was T.S. Eliot. Initially issued every two weeks, *The Egoist* became a monthly periodical until it ceased publication at the end of 1919.

eisteddfod \ī-ˈsteth-ˌvōd, ā-\, *plural* eisteddfods *or* eisteddfodau \-ˌsteth-ˈvō-ˌdī\ [Welsh, literally, session] Formal assembly of Welsh bards and minstrels that originated in the traditions of court bards of medieval times. The modern National Eisteddfod, revived in the 19th century and held each summer alternately in a site in North or South Wales, has been broadened to include awards for music, prose, drama, and art, but the chairing and investiture of the winning poet remains its high point.

Earlier assemblies were competitions of musicians (especially harpists) and poets from which new musical, literary, and oratorical forms emerged. The assembly at Carmarthen in 1451 is famous for establishing the arrangement of the strict meters of Welsh poetry in forms that are still authoritative. In the 17th century the custom fell into disuse, though poetry remained a popular art and a form of eisteddfod survived in informal gatherings of rhymesters who met to compose verses on impromptu subjects. In the 18th century, when local eisteddfods were revived, it was apparent that many farmers and workers were still sufficiently skilled in the complicated craftsmanship of bardic versification to win prizes. In the 19th century the eisteddfod exerted a dominant influence on Welsh poetry through its annual national assembly and a number of local competitions. Though the bardic forms were preserved, the quality of eisteddfod poetry was normally mediocre and degenerated to its lowest level in the late 19th century. The subjects assigned for the competition were celebrations of Welsh history or the Welsh countryside, biblical subjects such as the Resurrection, or abstract subjects such as almsgiving. Such poetry was necessarily impersonal and resulted in lengthy, descriptive compositions in which form was the major concern and content and emotional depth were secondary. With World War I and the Depression of the 1930s, many Welsh poets turned to more personal poetry, and the eisteddfod became primarily a forum for a youthful poet to gain a hearing. *See also* AWDL.

elegiac \ˌel-ə-ˈjī-ək, -ˌak; i-ˈlē-jē-ˌak\ or **elegiacal** \ˌel-ə-ˈjī-ə-kəl\ [Greek *elegeiakós*, a derivative of *elegeîon* elegiac couplet, elegy] **1.** In classical prosody, of, relating to, consisting of, or noted for verse written in elegiac meter. **2.** Of or relating to the period in Greece around the 7th century BC when poetry written in elegiac meter flourished. **3.** Of, relating to, befitting, or comprising elegy or an elegy; especially, expressing sorrow or lamentation, often for something past.

elegiac meter \ˌel-ə-ˈjī-ək, -ˌak; i-ˈlē-jē-ˌak\ **1.** In classical prosody, a distich (two lines), the first line of which is a dactylic hexameter and the second of which is often misleadingly called pentameter (it lacks the arsis, or short elements, in the third and sixth feet). In actuality, the second line is made up of two hemiepe, or two and a half dactyls followed by another two and a half dactyls. Elegiac meter is scanned:

– ∪ ∪ | – ∪ ∪ | – ∪ ∪ | – ∪ ∪ | – ∪ ∪ | – –
– ∪ ∪ | – ∪ ∪ | – | – ∪ ∪ | – ∪ ∪ | –.

2. The meter characteristic of a kinah, a Hebrew elegy or dirge. *Compare* KINAH METER.

elegiac stanza In poetry, a quatrain in iambic pentameter with alternate lines rhyming. The older and more general term for this is heroic stanza, but the form became associated specifically with elegiac poetry when Thomas Gray used it to perfection in *An Elegy Written in a Country Church Yard* (1751). From the mid-18th to the mid-19th century the form was usually used for elegiac verse, of which the best-known example is Gray's poem, which begins:

The curfew tolls the knell of parting day,
  The lowing herd wind slowly o'er the lea,
The plowman homeward plods his weary way,
  And leaves the world to darkness and to me.

elegiambus \ˌel-ə-ˌjī-ˈam-bəs\ *plural* elegiambi \-ˌbī\ [Late Greek *elegíambos,* from Greek *elegeîon* elegiac couplet + *íambos* iamb] In classical prosody, a verse composed of the dactylic – ∪ ∪ – ∪ ∪ –, as in the elegiac pentameter, and iambics. It is sometimes applied to the length – ∪ ∪ – ∪ ∪ – | ∪ – ∪ – –.

elegy \ˈel-ə-jē\ [Greek *elegeía, elegeîon* elegiac couplet, elegy, a derivative of *élegos* song accompanied by the flute] **1.** A poem in elegiac couplets. **2.** A song or poem expressing sorrow or lamentation, especially for one who is dead. **3.** A pensive or reflective poem that is usually nostalgic or melancholy.

In classical literature an elegy was simply any poem written in the elegiac meter (alternating lines of dactylic hexameter and pentameter) and was not restricted as to subject. Though some classical elegies were laments, many others were love poems. In some modern literatures, such as German, in which the classical elegiac meter has been adapted to the language, the term elegy refers to this meter, rather than to the poem's content. Thus, Rainer Maria Rilke's famous *Duineser Elegien* are not laments; they deal with the poet's search for spiritual values. In English literature since the 16th century, however, an elegy has come to mean specifically a poem of lamentation. It may be written in any meter the poet chooses.

A distinct kind of elegy is the pastoral elegy, which borrows the classical convention of representing its subject as an idealized shepherd in an idealized pastoral background and follows a rather formal pattern. It begins with an expression of grief and an invocation to the Muse to aid the poet in expressing his suffering. It usually contains a funeral procession, a description of sympathetic mourning throughout nature, and musings on the unkindness of death. It ends with acceptance, often a very affirmative justification, of nature's law. The outstanding example of the English pastoral elegy is John Milton's "Lycidas" (1638), written to commemorate the death of Edward King, a college friend. Other notable pastoral elegies are Percy Bysshe Shelley's *Adonais* (1821), on the death of John Keats, and Matthew Arnold's "Thyrsis" (1867), on the death of the poet Arthur Hugh Clough.

Other elegies observe no set patterns or conventions. In the 18th century the English GRAVEYARD SCHOOL of poets wrote generalized reflections on death and immortality combining gloomy, sometimes ghoulish imagery of human impermanence with philosophical speculation. Representative works are Edward Young's *Night Thoughts* (1742–45) and Robert Blair's *The Grave* (1743), but the best known of these poems is Thomas Gray's more tastefully subdued creation *An Elegy Written in a Country Church Yard* (1751), which pays tribute to the generations of humble and unknown villagers buried in the church cemetery. In the United States, a counterpart to the graveyard mode is found in William Cullen Bryant's "Thanatopsis" (1817). A wholly new treatment of the conventional pathetic fallacy of attributing grief to nature is achieved in Walt Whitman's "When Lilacs Last in the Dooryard Bloom'd" (1865).

In modern poetry the elegy remains a frequent and important poetic statement. Its range and variation can be seen in such poems as A.E. Housman's "To an Athlete Dying Young," W.H. Auden's "In Memory of W.B. Yeats," E.E. Cummings' "my father moved through dooms of love," John Peale Bishop's "The Hours" (on F. Scott Fitzgerald), and Robert Lowell's "The Quaker Graveyard in Nantucket."

elision \i-ˈlizh-ən\ [Late Latin *elisio* (translation of Greek *ékthlipsis*), a derivative of Latin *elidere* to eject, force out] In prosody, the slurring or omission of a final unstressed vowel that precedes either another vowel or a weak consonant sound, as in the word *heav'n*. It may also be the dropping of a consonant between vowels, as in the word *o'er* for *over*. Elision is used to fit words into a metrical scheme, to smooth the rhythm of a poem, or to ease the pronunciation of words. In classical Greek poetry, an apostrophe (') is substituted for an elided letter, as it is frequently in English verse. In Latin, however, the elided vowel or consonant remains, but it is ignored in scanning the line.

Elizabethan literature The body of works written during the reign of Elizabeth I of England (1558–1603), probably the most splendid age in the history of English literature. Elizabethan literature encompasses the work of Sir Philip Sidney, Edmund Spenser, Roger Ascham, Bishop Richard Hooker, Christopher Marlowe, William Shakespeare, and others. The epithet Elizabethan can only suggest the immense vitality and richness of English literature produced in the late 16th and early 17th centuries and does not describe any special characteristic of the writing. The Elizabethan Age saw the flowering of poetry (the sonnet, the Spenserian stanza, dramatic blank verse), was a golden age of drama (especially for the plays of Shakespeare), and inspired a wide variety of splendid prose (from historical chronicles, versions of the Holy Scriptures, pamphlets, and literary criticism to the first English novels). From about the beginning of the 17th century a sudden darkening of tone became noticeable in most forms of literary expression, especially in drama, and the change more or less coincided with the death of Elizabeth. English literature during the reign of James I (1603–25) is properly called Jacobean. But, insofar as 16th-century themes and patterns were carried over into the 17th century, the writing from the earlier part of his reign, at least, is sometimes referred to as "Jacobethan."

ellipsis \i-ˈlip-sis, e-\ [Greek *élleipsis,* literally, a falling short, defect, a derivative of *elleípein* to leave out, fall short] The omission of one or more words that are understood but that must be supplied to make a construction semantically complete, as in "No! I am not Prince Hamlet, nor was meant to be" from T.S. Eliot's poem "The Love Song of J. Alfred Prufrock."

elliptical \i-ˈlip-tik-əl\ or **elliptic** \i-ˈlip-tik\ **1.** Of, relating to, or marked by extreme economy of speech or writing. The style is exemplified in W.H. Auden's poem "This Lunar Beauty":

> But this was never
> A ghost's endeavor
> Nor finished this,
> Was ghost at ease;
> And till it pass
> Love shall not near
> The sweetness here
> Nor sorrow take
> His endless look.

2. Of or relating to deliberate obscurity (as of literary or conversational style).

elocution \ˌel-ə-ˈkyü-shən\ [Latin *elocutio* expression of an idea in words] *archaic* **1.** Literary style or expression. **2.** Impressive writing or style; eloquence.

eloge \ā-ˈlōzh, -ˈlȯzh\ *plural* eloges [Middle French, eulogy, from Latin *elogium* elegiac couplet, epitaph] A panegyrical, or laudatory, funeral oration. The term is also an archaic synonym for EULOGY.

emblem book Collection of symbolic pictures, usually accompanied by mottoes and expositions in verse and often also by a prose commentary. Derived from the medieval allegory and bestiary, the emblem book developed as a pictorial-literary genre in 16th-century Italy and became popular throughout western Europe in the 17th century.

The father of emblem literature was the 16th-century Italian lawyer and humanist Andrea Alciato, whose *Emblemata* (Latin; 1531) appeared in translation and in more than 150 editions. The Plantin press specialized in emblem literature, publishing at Antwerp in 1564 the *Emblemata* of the Hungarian physician and historian Johannes Sambucus; in 1565, that of the Dutch physician Hadrianus Junius (Adriaen de Jonghe); and, at Leiden, the early English emblem book of Geoffrey Whitney, *Choice of Emblemes* (1585), an anthology of emblems from Alciato, Junius, and others. English emblem books were either printed in the Netherlands or made by combining English text with foreign engravings, as in the English edition of the *Amorum Emblemata, Figuris Aeneis Incisa* (1608) of Octavius Vaenius (Otto van Veen), an important early Dutch emblem book.

The Netherlands became the center of the vogue. Vaenius' *Amorum Emblemata* presented metaphors from Ovid and other Latin erotic poets with pictorial representation. The Dutch emblem books were widely translated, plagiarized, and reprinted with different text or engravings. From polyglot editions, begun by Daniël Heinsius' verses in Dutch and Latin and later in French, publication of emblem books became an international enterprise. Books of love emblems were exchanged by lovers and formed attractive little encyclopedias of those "questions of love" that had been the erudite pastime of the academies throughout the Renaissance. Meanwhile, the Dutch emblematists had turned to religious emblems, serving Calvinists as well as Jesuits, who used them for propaganda. In Vaenius' *Amoris Divini Emblemata* (1615), quotations from St. Augustine replace those of Ovid and Cupid reappears as the soul's preceptor.

The only English emblem book to achieve widespread popularity was the *Emblemes and Hieroglyphikes* (1635) of Francis Quarles, with plates from the *Pia Desideria* and *Typus Mundi* (1627), popular Jesuit emblem books.

emend \ē-ˈmend\ **1.** To correct (a written work) usually by textual alterations. **2.** To alter (a literary work) to serve a purpose different from the original.

empyrean \ˌem-ˌpī-ˈrē-ən, -pə-; em-ˈpir-ē-ən, -ˈpī-rē-\ [Late Greek *empýrios* belonging to the highest celestial sphere, from Greek *en* in + *pŷr* fire] The highest heaven or heavenly sphere in ancient and medieval cosmology usually consisting of fire or light. The word was used chiefly by Christian writers (such as John Milton) to signify the true and ultimate heavenly paradise. In a more general sense, it refers to an ideal place or state.

enallage \en-ˈal-ə-jē\ [Greek *enallagḗ,* literally, interchange, derivative of *enallássein* to exchange] A substitution of one part of speech for another or of one gender, number, case, person, tense, mode, or voice of the same word for another.

enchiridion also **encheiridion** \ˌen-ˌkī-ˈrid-ē-ən, ˌen-kə-\ *plural* enchiridia *also* encheiridia \-ˈrid-ē-ə\ [Greek *encheirídion,* from *en* in + *cheír* hand] A handbook or a manual.

enclosed rhyme *also called* enclosing rhyme. In poetry, the rhyming pattern *abba* found in certain quatrains, such as the first verse of Matthew Arnold's "Shakespeare":

Others abide our question. Thou art free.
We ask and ask—thou smilest and art still,
Out-topping knowledge. For the loftiest hill,
Who to the stars uncrowns his majesty, . . .

encomiologic \en-ˌkō-mē-ə-ˈläj-ik\ [Greek *enkōmiologikón* meter used in encomia, from *enkṓmion* encomium + *lógos* word, utterance] Of or having to do with a compound verse in Greek and Latin prosody that is made up of two and a half dactylic feet followed by two and a half iambic feet:

– ∪ ∪ – ∪ ∪ – ∪ – ∪ – ⏓.

encomium \en-ˈkō-mē-əm\ *plural* encomia \-mē-ə\ [Greek *enkṓmion* laudatory ode, panegyric] A prose or poetic work in which a person, thing, or abstract idea is glorified. The term originally meant a Greek choral song honoring the winners of the Olympian and other games and sung at the victory celebration at the end of the games. The Greek writers Simonides of Ceos and Pindar wrote some of the earliest of these original encomia. The term later took on the broader meaning of any composition of a laudatory nature. Verse forms of the encomium include the EPINICION and the ODE.

end rhyme In poetry, a rhyme that occurs in the last syllables of verses, as in stanza one of Robert Frost's "Stopping by Woods on a Snowy Evening":

Whose woods these are I think I know,
His house is in the village, though;
He will not see me stopping here
To watch his woods fill up with snow.

End rhyme is the most common type of rhyme in English poetry. *Compare* BEGINNING RHYME; INTERNAL RHYME.

end-stopped \ˈend-ˌstäpt\ In poetry, marked by a grammatical pause at the end of a line, as in these lines from Alexander Pope's *An Essay on Criticism:*

A little learning is a dangerous thing;
Drink deep, or taste not the Pierian spring.
There shallow draughts intoxicate the brain,
And drinking largely sobers us again.

Compare ENJAMBMENT; RUN-ON.

English sonnet *See* SHAKESPEAREAN SONNET.

englyn \ˈeŋ-lin\ *plural* englyns *or* englynion \eŋ-ˈlən-yȯn\ [Welsh] A group of strict Welsh poetic meters. The most popular form is the *englyn unodl union* ("direct monorhyme englyn"), which is a combination of a CYWYDD, a type of rhyming couplet, and another form and is written in an intricate pattern of alliteration and rhyme called CYNGHANEDD. The *englyn unodl union* consists of 30 syllables in lines of 10, 6, 7, and 7 syllables. In this form the last syllables of the last three lines rhyme with the 6th, 7th, 8th, or 9th syllable of the first line. The various forms of englyns were among the 24 strict bardic meters available to Welsh poets from about the 14th century.

enjambment or **enjambement** \en-ˈjam-mənt, ä^{n}-zhä^{n}b-ˈmä^{n}\ [French *enjambement,* literally, the act of striding over, a derivative of *enjamber* to stride over, straddle, encroach on], *also called* run-on. In prosody, the continuation of the sense of a phrase beyond the end of a line of verse. T.S. Eliot used enjambment in the opening lines of his poem *The Waste Land:*

> April is the cruelest month, breeding
> Lilacs out of the dead land, mixing
> Memory and desire, stirring
> Dull roots with spring rain.
> Winter kept us warm, covering
> Earth in forgetful snow, feeding
> A little life with dried tubers.

Compare END-STOPPED.

Enlightenment \en-ˈlīt-ən-mənt\, *French* Siècle des Lumières \syekl-də-lūēm-ˈyer\ ("Age of the Enlightened"), *German* Aufklärung \au̇f-ˈkler-u̇ŋ\ A European intellectual movement of the 17th and 18th centuries in which ideas concerning God, reason, nature, and humankind were synthesized into a worldview that gained wide assent and that instigated revolutionary developments in art, philosophy, and politics. Central to Enlightenment thought were the use and the celebration of reason, the power by which the individual understands the universe and improves the human condition. The goals of the rational individual were considered to be knowledge, freedom, and happiness.

The Enlightenment produced the first modern secularized theories of psychology and ethics. John Locke conceived of the human mind as being at birth a tabula rasa, a blank slate on which experience wrote freely and boldly, creating the individual character according to the individual experience of the world. Supposed innate qualities, such as goodness or original sin, had no reality. In a darker vein, Thomas Hobbes portrayed humans as moved solely by considerations of personal pleasure and pain. The notion of the individual as neither good nor bad but interested principally in survival and the maximization of pleasure led to radical political theories. Where the state had once been viewed as an earthly approximation of an eternal order, with the city of man modeled on the city of God, now it came to be seen as a mutually beneficial human arrangement aimed at protecting the natural rights and self-interest of each individual.

The idea of society as a social contract, however, contrasted sharply with the realities of actual societies. Thus the Enlightenment became critical, reforming, and eventually revolutionary. Locke and Jeremy Bentham in England, Jean-Jacques Rousseau, Montesquieu, and Voltaire in France, and Thomas Jefferson in America all contributed to an evolving critique of the arbitrary, authoritarian state and to sketching the outline of a higher form of social organization, based on natural rights and functioning as a political democracy. Such powerful ideas found expression as reform in England and as revolution in France and America.

The Enlightenment expired as the victim of its own excesses. The celebration of abstract reason provoked contrary spirits to begin exploring the world of sensation and emotion in the cultural movement known as Romanticism. The Reign of Terror that followed the French Revolution severely tested the belief that humans could govern themselves. The high optimism that marked much of Enlightenment thought, however, survived as one of the movement's most enduring legacies: the belief that human history is a record of general progress.

enoplion \e-ˈnäp-lē-ˌän, -ən\ [Greek *rhythmòs kat' enóplion* martial rhythm] A hemiepes preceded by one or two short syllables or a long syllable, or any of a variety of aeolic lines that expand by the addition of dactyls; this latter form is also known as a *prosodiac.*

entrelacement \ˌän-trə-ˌläs-ˈmäⁿ, -ˈmänt\ [French, act or product of interlacing, a derivative of *enterlacer* to interlace] Literary technique in which several simultaneous stories are interlaced in one larger narrative. This technique allows digression and presents opportunities for moral and ironic commentary while not disturbing the unity of the whole.

Entwicklungsroman \ent-ˈvik-ˌlüŋz-rō-ˌmän, *German* -ˌlüŋs-\ [German, from *Entwicklung* development + *Roman* novel] *See* BILDUNGSROMAN.

enumerative bibliography *See* DESCRIPTIVE BIBLIOGRAPHY.

envelope \ˈen-və-ˌlōp, ˈän-\ In poetry, a device in which a line or a stanza is repeated so as to enclose a section of verse, as in Sir Thomas Wyat's "Is it Possible?":

> Is it possible
> That so high debate,
> So sharp, so sore, and of such rate,
> Should end so soon and was begun so late?
> Is it possible?

The term can also be used for a quatrain with a rhyme scheme of *abba* because the rhymes of the first and last lines can be said to enclose the other lines.

envoi or **envoy** \ˈen-ˌvȯi, ˈän-\ [French *envoi,* from Middle French *envoy,* literally, the act of sending, dispatch] The usually explanatory or commendatory concluding remarks to a poem, essay, or book; specifically, a short, fixed final stanza of a poem (such as a BALLADE) pointing the moral and usually addressing the person to whom the poem is written. Although they are most often associated with the ballade and chant royal—i.e., French poetic forms—envois have also been used by several English poets, including Geoffrey Chaucer, Robert Southey, and Algernon Charles Swinburne.

epanalepsis \ˌep-ə-nə-ˈlep-sis\ [Greek *epanálēpsis* resumption, repetition, a derivative of *epanalambánein* to take up again, repeat] Repetition of a word or phrase after intervening language, as in the first line of Algernon Charles Swinburne's "Itylus":

> Swallow, my sister, O sister swallow,
> How can thine heart be full of the spring?

epanodos \e-ˈpan-ə-ˌdäs\ [Greek *epánodos* recapitulation, literally, ascent, return] A figure of speech in which a word is repeated within a sentence, as in "Because I do not hope to turn again/Because I do not hope" from T.S. Eliot's poem "Ash Wednesday."

epic \ˈep-ik\ [from *epic,* adjective, pertaining to an epic, from Latin *epicus,* from Greek *epikós,* a derivative of *épē* lines, verses, epic poetry, plural of *épos* word] Long narrative poem in an elevated style that celebrates heroic achievement and treats themes of historical, national, religious, or legendary significance. It is to be distinguished from the briefer heroic lay, the less elevated, less ambitious folktale and ballad, and the more consistently extravagant and fantastic medieval romance, although in the narrative poetry of Ludovico Ariosto, Matteo Boiardo, and Edmund Spenser the categories tend to merge. One may also distinguish "primary" (also called traditional or classical) epic, shaped from the legends and traditions of a heroic age and part of the oral tradition of literature, from "secondary" (or literary) epic, which was written down from the beginning and was self-consciously produced by sophisticated poets who adapted aspects of traditional epic for specific literary and ideological purposes. Homer's *Iliad* and *Odyssey* are primary epics; Virgil's *Aeneid* and John Milton's *Paradise Lost* are secondary epics.

Although the Mesopotamian verse-narratives of Gilgamesh, dating from the 3rd millennium BC, may constitute the earliest epic, the Homeric poems, which assumed their final form in the period 900–750 BC, are usually regarded as the first important epics and the main source of epic conventions and characteristics in the secondary epics of western Europe. It is now generally agreed that such Homeric features as descriptive set pieces, stock epithets, and formulaic phrases and lines for recurring elements of the poem are attributable to narrative and metrical convenience in improvised oral composition and transmission.

The main aspects of epic convention are the centrality of a hero—sometimes semidivine—of military, national, or religious importance; an extensive, perhaps even cosmic, geographical setting; heroic battle; extended and often exotic journeying; and the involvement of supernatural beings, such as gods, angels, or demons, in the action. Epics tend to treat familiar and traditional subjects. They usually begin with a statement of the subject, invoking the assistance of a muse, and then plunge into the middle of the story, filling in the earlier stages later on with retrospective narrative by figures within the poem. Catalogs and processions of heroes, often associated with specific localities, are common, and when such heroes speak it is often in set speeches delivered in formal circumstances. Epic narrative is often enriched by extended epic similes that go beyond an initial point of correspondence to elaborate a whole scene or episode drawn from a different area of experience.

The self-consciousness of literary epic and its cultural context in a post-heroic age encourage an element of criticism, ironic deployment, or even parody of standard epic materials and conventions. This is already present in the *Aeneid* in which epic battle may be brutal and degrading as well as heroic, and Milton in *Paradise Lost* attributes to his villain Satan many of the characteristics of the old warring hero of epic tradition. The heroic world with its formal conventions, supernatural "machinery," and epoch-making events may be used as a framework to recount trivial, squalid, or irreverent matters for satiric purposes in poems such as Alexander Pope's *The Rape of the Lock* and *The Dunciad* and Lord Byron's *Don Juan*. Henry Fielding exploited the dignity and structure of epic and a sense of its incongruity with contemporary experience with comic effect in *Tom Jones,* while later novels such as James Joyce's *Ulysses* have achieved epic stature by re-creating the Homeric story. William Wordsworth's autobiographical poem *The Prelude* aspires to epic seriousness and uses the blank-verse medium of Milton's *Paradise Lost* for its portrait of an evolving poetic imagination.

Primary epics registering heroic experience in the vernacular languages of Europe continued to appear long after Virgil popularized secondary epic. The Spanish *Cantar de mio Cid* celebrates the hero of the wars against the Moors in the 11th century; the French *La Chanson de Roland* (12th century) commemorates an 8th-century battle in the Pyrenees between Charlemagne's army and the Saracens; the 13th-century German *Nibelungenlied* recounts a story deriving ultimately from the war between the Burgundians and the Huns in the 5th century; and the Anglo-Saxon *Beowulf* refers to historical characters and events of the 6th century as it describes Beowulf's struggles against the monsters that threaten the heroic fellowship of the mead hall. But long before these poems assumed the form in which they now exist, the historical elements in them had passed into myth and were influenced by legends from other periods and traditions. The *Kalevala* ("Land of Heroes"), the Finnish national poem, is a synthetic primary epic (first published in 1835) composed by Elias Lönnrott, who incorporated ancient orally transmitted lays into a single narrative structure.

The epic poem was generally regarded as a superseded form in the 20th century, but the scope and majesty of the genre were occasionally suggested by works in other forms, such as Frank Norris' unfinished trilogy of novels *The Epic of the Wheat* (1901–03), Sergei Eisenstein's film *Ivan the Terrible* (Part I,

1944; Part II, completed 1946, banned until 1958), and the fantasy trilogy *The Lord of the Rings* (1954–55), a prose work by the Oxford University philologist J.R.R. Tolkien that reflects the flavor and forms of Norse saga and Anglo-Saxon poetry in its epic narrative set of adventures and quests in the realm of Middle Earth.

epic caesura A type of feminine caesura. *See* CAESURA.

epic drama *See* EPIC THEATER.

epicede \ˈep-ə-ˌsēd\ or **epicedium** \ˌep-ə-ˈsē-dē-əm\ *plural* epicedes *or* epicedia \-dē-ə\ [Greek *epikḗdeion,* from *epí* on, upon + *kêdos* funeral rites, mourning] In ancient Greece, a funeral song or ode that was performed in the presence of the corpse, as opposed to a dirge, which could be sung anywhere.

epic simile *also called* Homeric simile. An extended simile often running to several lines used typically in epic poetry to intensify the heroic stature of the subject and to serve as decoration. Two examples from the *Iliad* follow:

> As when the shudder of the west wind suddenly rising
> scatters across the water, and the water darkens beneath it,
> so darkening were settled the ranks of Achaians and Trojans
> in the plain.

and

> But swift Aias the son of Oïleus would not at all now
> take his stand apart from Telamonian Aias,
> not even a little; but as two wine-coloured oxen straining
> with even force drag the compacted plough through the fallow land,
> and for both of them at the base of the horns the dense sweat gushes;
> only the width of the polished yoke keeps a space between them
> as they toil down the furrow till the share cuts the edge of the ploughland;
> so these took their stand in battle, close to each other.

epic theater *also called* epic drama; *German* episches Theater \ˈā-pē-shəs-tā-ˈät-ər\ Form of drama presenting a series of loosely connected scenes that avoid illusion and often interrupt the action to address the audience directly with analysis or argument (as by a narrator) or with documentation (as by a film). Epic theater is now most often associated with the dramatic theory and practice evolved by the playwright-director Bertolt Brecht in Germany from the 1920s onward. Its dramatic antecedents include the episodic structure and didactic nature of plays by the 19th-century German Georg Büchner, the pre-Expressionist drama of the German Frank Wedekind, and the Expressionist theater of the German directors Erwin Piscator (with whom Brecht collaborated in 1927) and Leopold Jessner, both of whom made exuberant use of the technical effects that came to characterize epic theater.

Brecht's perspective was Marxian, and his intention was to appeal to his audience's intellect in presenting moral problems and in reflecting contemporary social realities on stage. He wished to block their emotional responses and to hinder their tendency to empathize with the characters and to get caught up in the action. To this end, he used "alienating," or "distancing," effects to cause the audience to think objectively about the play, to reflect on its argument, and to draw conclusions and pass intellectual judgment upon it. A similar concept was the Living Newspaper, which later became part of the tradition of epic theater. *See also* ALIENATION EFFECT; LIVING NEWSPAPER.

epideictic oratory \ˌep-ə-ˈdīk-tik\ [Greek *epideiktikós* for display, declamatory, a derivative of *epideiknýnai* to show off, display], *also called* ceremonial oratory. According to Aristotle, a type of suasive speech designed primarily for rhetorical effect. Epideictic oratory was panegyrical, declamatory, and demonstrative. Its aim was to condemn or to eulogize an individual, a cause, occasion, movement, city, or state. An outstanding example of this type of speech is a funeral oration by Pericles in honor of those killed in the first year of the Peloponnesian War. *Compare* DELIBERATIVE ORATORY; FORENSIC ORATORY.

epigram \ˈep-ə-ˌgram\ [Greek *epígramma* inscription, short poem, epigram, a derivative of *epigráphein* to write on, inscribe] A short poem treating concisely, pointedly, and often satirically a single thought or event and often ending with a witticism or ingenious turn of thought. By extension the term is also applied to a terse, sage, or witty, often paradoxical saying, usually in the form of a generalization.

Originally an inscription suitable for carving on a monument, the term took on its current meaning by about the 1st century BC. Many of the poems of the period that were collected in the Greek Anthology are examples of the verse form. Catullus (*c.* 84–*c.* 54 BC) originated the Latin epigram, and it was given final form by Martial (*c.* AD 40–103) in some 1,500 pungent and often indecent verses that served as models for French and English epigrammatists of the 17th and 18th centuries.

The epigram was revived by Renaissance scholars and poets such as the French poet Clément Marot, who wrote epigrams in both Latin and the vernacular. In England the form took shape somewhat later, notably in the hands of Ben Jonson and his followers; one of these was Robert Herrick, writer of such graceful examples as the following:

> I saw a Flie within a Beade
> Of Amber cleanly buried:
> The Urne was little, but the room
> More rich than *Cleopatra's* Tombe.

As the century progressed, both English and French epigrams became more astringent and closer in spirit to Martial. The *Maximes* (1665) of François VI, Duke de La Rochefoucauld, marked one of the high points of the epigram in French. It influenced such later practitioners as Voltaire. In England,

John Dryden, Alexander Pope, and Jonathan Swift produced some of the most memorable epigrams of their time.

Samuel Taylor Coleridge, writing at the beginning of the 19th century, produced an epigram that neatly sums up the form:

> What is an Epigram? A dwarfish whole,
> Its body brevity, and wit its soul.

The epigram engaged German taste in the 18th and early 19th centuries, culminating in J.W. von Goethe's *Zahme Xenien* (1820; "Gentle Epigrams"). Among later masters of the English epigram were Oscar Wilde and George Bernard Shaw. Wilde became famous for such remarks as "A cynic is a man who knows the price of everything and the value of nothing." Shaw, in his *Annajanska* (1919), commented that "All great truths begin as blasphemies."

epigraph \ˈep-ə-ˌgraf \ [Greek *epigraphḗ*, a derivative of *epigráphein* to write on, inscribe] **1.** An inscription on a statue, a building, or a coin. **2.** A quotation set at the beginning of a literary work (such as a novel) or a division of a work to suggest its theme.

epilogue or **epilog** \ˈep-ə-ˌlȯg, -ˌläg\ [Greek *epílogos* concluding part of a speech or play, a derivative of *epilégein* to say in addition] **1.** The conclusion or final part of a nondramatic literary work that serves typically to round out or complete the design of the work—also called *afterword* \ˈaf-tər-ˌwərd\. *Compare* FOREWORD; PREFACE. **2.** A speech often in verse addressed to the audience by one or more of the actors at the end of a play, such as that at the end of William Shakespeare's *Henry VIII:*

> 'Tis ten to one this play can never please
> All that are here. Some come to take their ease,
> And sleep an act or two; but those, we fear,
> We have frighted with our trumpets; so 'tis clear,
> They'll say 'tis naught; others, to hear the city
> Abused extremely, and to cry, "That's witty!"
> Which we have not done neither. That, I fear,
> All the expected good we're like to hear
> For this play at this time is only in
> The merciful construction of good women;
> For such a one we show'd 'em. If they smile,
> And say 'twill do, I know, within a while
> All the best men are ours; for 'tis ill hap,
> If they hold when their ladies bid 'em clap.

The epilogue, at its best, was a witty piece intended to send the audience home in good humor. Its form in the English theater was established by Ben Jonson in *Cynthia's Revels* (*c.* 1600). Jonson's epilogues typically asserted the merits of his play and defended it from anticipated criticism.

The heyday of the prologue and epilogue in the English theater was the Restoration period. From 1660 to the decline of the drama in the reign of Queen Anne, scarcely a play was produced in London without a prologue and epilogue. Playwrights asked their friends to write these poems for them. Poems supplied by writers of established reputation conferred prestige on the works of novices. Epilogues were rarely written after the 18th century. *Compare* PROLOGUE. **3.** The final scene of a play whose main action is set within a framework, such as Bertolt Brecht's *The Caucasian Chalk Circle*.

epinicion \ˌep-ə-ˈnis-ē-ˌän, -ˈnish-\ or **epinikion** \-ˈnik-ē-ˌän, -ˈnēk-\ *plural* epinicia *or* epinikia \-ē-ə\ [Greek *epiníkion,* from *epí* on, upon + *níkē* victory] A song of triumph or a choral lyric ode in honor of a victor in war or in the great Hellenic games. An epinicion was performed as part of the celebration on the victor's triumphal return to the city.

The epinicion had a basis in improvised celebration, but the form as it has survived is highly literary. One of the earliest examples extant is an ode for an Olympic victory in 520 BC that was written by Simonides of Ceos. Though the epinicion's structure is not fixed, there is a certain uniformity in content and arrangement. The occasion demands a reference to the victor and the nature and place of his victory; to this may be added reference to victories of members of his family or, in the case of athletic victory, a compliment to his trainer. Generally there is a myth, more or less elaborate and relevant to the occasion. A gnomic element is also included.

The epinicion did not use traditional lines or stanzas, but the meter was formed afresh for each poem and was never used again in exactly the same form. The strophes, or stanzas, either single or in systems of three, were repeated throughout the poem, and often their form was related to the accompanying dance. Its performance required a trained choir and musicians skilled in the lute and the lyre. The epinicion reached its zenith in the odes of Pindar (518 or 522 to after 446 BC). Those of a younger contemporary, Bacchylides, signaled the end of the form's popularity. *See also* ODE.

epiphany \i-ˈpif-ə-nē\ [Greek *epipháneia* appearance, manifestation of a deity, a derivative of *epiphaínesthai* to come into view, appear] **1.** A usually sudden manifestation or perception of the essential nature or meaning of something; an intuitive grasp of reality through something usually simple and striking (such as a commonplace event or person). **2.** A literary representation of an epiphany, or a symbolically revealing work or part of a work. The use of the word in relation to literature is associated particularly with James Joyce because of his description of the concept in a draft of the work that became *A Portrait of the Artist as a Young Man* and because of the occurrence of epiphanies throughout his works.

epirrhema \ˌep-i-ˈrē-mə\ [Greek *epírrhēma,* from *epí* on, following + *rhêma* something spoken, word] In ancient Greek Old Comedy, an address usually about public affairs. It was spoken by the leader of one-half of the chorus after that half of the chorus had sung an ode. It was part of the parabasis, or performance by the chorus, during an interlude in the action of the play.

episches Theater *See* EPIC THEATER.

episode \'ep-i-ˌsōd\ [Greek *epeisódion* parenthetic addition in a poem or play, episode, from *epí* on, following + *eísodos* entrance] A usually brief unit of action in a dramatic or literary work, such as the part of an ancient Greek tragedy between two choric songs and equivalent to any developed situation in a modern play; a developed situation that is integral to but separable from a continuous narrative (such as a novel or play); or one of a series of loosely connected stories or scenes.

epistle \i-'pis-əl\ [Latin *epistula,* literally, letter, dispatch, from Greek *epistolḗ* message, dispatch, letter, a derivative of *epistéllein* to send to, order] A composition in prose or poetry written in the form of a letter to a particular person or group.

In literature there are two basic traditions of verse epistles, one derived from Horace's *Epistles* and the other from Ovid's *Epistulae heroidum* (better known as *Heroides*). The tradition based on Horace first addresses moral and philosophical themes and has been the most popular form since the Renaissance. The form that developed from Ovid deals with romantic and sentimental subjects; it was more popular than the Horatian form during the European Middle Ages. Well-known examples of the Horatian form are the letters of Paul the Apostle (the Pauline epistles incorporated into the Bible), which greatly aided the growth of Christianity into a world religion, and such works as Alexander Pope's "An Epistle to Dr. Arbuthnot." Other writers who have used the form include Ben Jonson, John Dryden, and William Congreve, as well as W.H. Auden and Louis MacNeice more recently.

epistolary literature *See* LETTER.

epistolary novel \i-'pis-tə-ˌler-ē, ˌep-i-'stōl-ə-rē\ A novel told through the medium of letters written by one or more of the characters. Originating with Samuel Richardson's *Pamela* (1740), the story of a servant girl's victorious struggle against her master's attempts to seduce her, the epistolary novel was one of the earliest forms of novel to be developed. It remained one of the most popular up to the 19th century. The epistolary novel's reliance on subjective points of view makes it the forerunner of the modern psychological novel.

The advantages of the novel in letter form are that it presents an intimate view of the character's thoughts and feelings without interference from the author and that it conveys the shape of events to come with dramatic immediacy. Also, the presentation of events from several points of view lends the story dimension and verisimilitude. Though the method was most often a vehicle for the SENTIMENTAL NOVEL, it was used in other types of novels as well. Of the outstanding examples of the form, Richardson's *Clarissa* (1747–48) has tragic intensity,

Tobias Smollett's *Humphry Clinker* (1771) is a picaresque comedy and social commentary, and Fanny Burney's *Evelina* (1778) is a novel of manners. Jean-Jacques Rousseau used the form as a vehicle for his ideas on marriage and education in *La Nouvelle Héloïse* (1761), and J.W. von Goethe used it for his statement of Romantic despair, *Die Leiden des jungen Werthers* (1774). The letter novel of Pierre Choderlos de Laclos, *Les Liaisons dangereuses* (1782), is a work of penetrating and realistic psychology. Aagje Deken and Betje Wolff wrote the first Dutch novel, *Sara Burgerhart* (1782), in the epistolary style after Richardson. This work was unsentimental and its characterizations subtle.

Some disadvantages of the form were apparent from the outset. The servant girl Pamela's remarkable literary powers and her propensity for writing on all occasions were cruelly burlesqued in Henry Fielding's *Shamela* (1741), which pictures his heroine in bed scribbling, "I hear him coming in at the Door," as her seducer enters the room. From 1800 on, the popularity of the form declined, though novels combining letters with journals and narrative were still common. In the 20th century, letter fiction was often used to exploit the linguistic humor and unintentional character revelations of such semiliterates as the fatuous ballplayer hero of Ring Lardner's *You Know Me Al* (1916).

epistolography \i-ˌpis-tə-ˈläg-rə-fē\ The art or practice of writing epistles, or letters.

epistrophe \e-ˈpis-trə-fē\ [Greek *epistrophḗ* the act of turning about] Repetition of a word or expression at the end of successive phrases, clauses, sentences, or verses, especially for rhetorical or poetic effect, as in Abraham Lincoln's "of the people, by the people, for the people." *Compare* ANAPHORA.

epitaph \ˈep-ə-ˌtaf\ [Latin *epitaphium* inscription on a tomb, funeral oration, from Greek *epitáphios* funeral oration, from *epí* on, upon + *táphos* funeral rites, grave, tomb] An inscription in verse or prose upon a tomb; and, by extension, anything written as if to be inscribed on a tomb.

Probably the earliest surviving are those written on the sarcophagi and coffins of the ancient Egyptians. Ancient Greek epitaphs are often of considerable literary interest, deep and tender in feeling, rich and varied in expression, and epigrammatic in form. They are usually in elegiac verse, though many of the later epitaphs are in prose. Among the most familiar epitaphs are those, ascribed to Simonides of Ceos (*c.* 556–*c.* 468 BC), on the heroes of Thermopylae, the most famous of which has been translated thus:

> Go tell the Spartans, thou that passest by
> That here, obedient to their laws, we lie.

Roman epitaphs, in contrast to the Greek, contained as a rule nothing beyond a record of facts with little variation.

An inscription commonly found is "may the earth lie light upon thee." A satirical inversion of this is seen in the epitaph by Abel Evans (1679–1737) on the architect Sir John Vanbrugh:

> Lie heavy on him, Earth! for he
> Laid many heavy loads on thee.

Many Roman epitaphs included a denunciation on any who should violate the sepulcher; a similar later denunciation is found on William Shakespeare's tomb:

> Good friend, for Jesus' sake forbear
> To dig the dust enclosed here;
> Blest be the man that spares these stones,
> And curst be he that moves my bones.

The oldest existing British epitaphs are those of the Roman occupiers and are, of course, in Latin, which continued for many centuries to be the preferred language for epitaphs. The earliest epitaphs in English churches are usually a simple statement of name and rank, with a hic jacet ("here lies"). In the 13th century, French came into use (on, for example, the tomb of Henry III at Westminster) and English about the middle of the 14th century, but as late as 1776, Dr. Johnson, asked to write an English epitaph for Oliver Goldsmith, replied that he would never consent to disgrace the walls of Westminster Abbey with an English inscription. A familiar 18th-century epitaph was the one of 12 lines ending Thomas Gray's *An Elegy Written in a Country Church Yard.* Perhaps the most noted modern epitaph was that written by William Butler Yeats for himself in "Under Ben Bulben":

> Cast a cold eye
> On life, on death.
> Horseman, pass by!

Most of the epitaphs that have survived from before the Reformation were inscribed upon brasses. By Elizabethan times, however, epitaphs upon stone monuments, in English, became much more common and began to assume a more literary character. Thomas Nashe tells how, by the end of the 16th century, the writing of verse epitaphs had become a trade. Many of the best-known epitaphs are primarily literary memorials, not necessarily intended to be placed on a tomb. Among the finest are those by William Browne, Ben Jonson, Robert Herrick, John Milton, and Robert Louis Stevenson. Alexander Pope wrote several epitaphs; they inspired one of the few monographs on the subject—Samuel Johnson's examination of them in *The Universal Visiter* for May 1756.

Semiliteracy often produces epitaphs that are comic through grammatical accident—for example, "Erected to the memory of/John MacFarlane/Drowned in the Water of Leith/By a few affectionate friends." Far more common, though, are deliberately witty epitaphs, a type abounding in Britain and the United States in the form of acrostics, palindromes, riddles, and puns on names and professions. Benjamin Franklin's epitaph for himself plays on his trade as a printer, hoping that he will "appear once more in a new and more beautiful edition, corrected and amended by the Author"; and that of the antiquary Thomas Fuller has the inscription "Fuller's Earth."

Many offer some wry comment, such as John Gay's

> Life is a jest, and all things show it;
> I thought so once, and now I know it.

The epitaph was also seen as an opportunity for epigrammatic satire, as in the Earl of Rochester's lines on Charles II: "He never said a foolish thing / Nor ever did a wise one."

The art of the epitaph was largely lost in the 20th century. Some notable examples of humorous epitaphs were suggested, however, by the 20th-century writer and wit Dorothy Parker; they include "I told you I was sick" and "If you can read this, you're standing too close."

epitasis \ə-ˈpit-ə-sis\ *plural* epitases \-ˌsēz\ [Late Greek *epítasis,* from Greek, stretching, increase in intensity] The part of a play that develops the main action and that leads to the catastrophe or denouement. *Compare* CATASTASIS; PROTASIS.

epithalamium \ˌep-ə-thə-ˈlā-mē-əm\ or **epithalamion** \-mē-ən, -ˌän\ or **epithalamy** \-ˈthal-ə-mē\ *plural* epithalamiums *or* epithalamia \-thə-ˈlā-mē-ə\ *or* epithalamies [Greek *epithalámion,* from *epí* on, upon + *thálamos* room, bridal chamber] A nuptial song or poem in honor or praise of a bride and bridegroom.

In ancient Greece the singing of such songs was a traditional way of invoking good fortune on the marriage and often of indulging in ribaldry. By derivation, the epithalamium should be sung at the marriage chamber, but the word is also used for the song sung during the wedding procession, containing repeated invocations to Hymen (Hymenaeus), the Greek god of marriage. No special meter has been associated with the epithalamium either in antiquity or in modern times.

The earliest evidence for literary epithalamiums are the fragments from Sappho's seventh book (*c.* 600 BC). The earliest surviving Latin epithalamiums are three by Catullus (*c.* 84–*c.* 54 BC). In the most original, Catullus tried to fuse the native Fescennine verse (a jocular, often obscene form of sung dialogue sometimes used at wedding feasts) with the Greek form of marriage song.

Epithalamiums based on classical models were written during the Renaissance by Torquato Tasso in Italy and Pierre de Ronsard in France. Among English poets of the same period, Richard Crashaw, John Donne, Sir Philip Sidney, and Ben Jonson used the form. Edmund Spenser's *Epithalamion,* written for his second marriage in 1595, is considered by some critics to be the finest example of the form in English.

Anonymous 17th-century epithalamiums are extant. In the 19th century, epithalamiums were written by Gerard Manley Hopkins and Edmund Gosse, and in the 20th, by such poets as A.E. Housman.

epithet \'ep-ə-ˌthet, -thət\ [Greek *epítheton* adjective, epithet, from neuter of *epíthetos* adjectival, literally, additional, added] An adjective or phrase that is used to express the characteristic of a person or thing, such as Ivan the Terrible. In literature, the term is considered an element of poetic diction, or something that distinguishes the language of poetry from ordinary language. Homer used certain epithets so regularly that they became a standard part of the name of the thing or person described, as in "rosy-fingered Dawn" and "gray-eyed Athena." The device was used by many later poets, including John Keats in his sonnet "On First Looking Into Chapman's Homer":

> Oft of one wide expanse had I been told
> That deep-browed Homer ruled as his demesne; . . .

epitome \i-'pit-ə-mē\ [Greek *epitomḗ,* a derivative of *epitémnein* to cut short, abridge] **1.** A summary or an abridgment of a written work. **2.** A brief presentation of a broad topic, or a compendium. **3.** A brief statement expressing the essence of something.

epitrite \'ep-ə-ˌtrīt\ [Greek *epítritos,* from *epítritos* (adjective) containing a whole and a third, having a ratio of 4:3, having three long syllables and one short, from *epí* on, upon + *trítos* third] In classical prosody, a foot consisting of one short and three long syllables, usually in the sequence – ∪ – –. The epitrite is not used as the basis of any rhythm in Latin verse, though it did appear as a rhythm for the clausulae of Ciceronian orations. *Compare* PAEON. Four forms of the epitrite were distinguished, depending on the position of the short syllable: first (∪ – – –), second (– ∪ – –), third (– – ∪ –), and fourth (– – – ∪).

epizeuxis \ˌep-ə-'zük-sis\ [Greek *epízeuxis* repetition, literally, the act of fastening together] In literature, a form of repetition in which a word is repeated immediately for emphasis, as in the first and last lines of "Hark, Hark! the Lark," a song in William Shakespeare's *Cymbeline:*

> Hark, hark! the lark at heaven's gate sings,
> And Phoebus gins arise,
> His steeds to water at those springs
> On chaliced flowers that lies;
> And winking Mary-buds begin
> To ope their golden eyes:
> With every thing that pretty is,
> My lady sweet, arise:
> Arise, arise!

Epoch American literary journal founded in 1947. *Epoch* published fiction and poetry of high caliber by unknown as well as established writers. Its first issue contained works by E.E. Cummings and John Ciardi. Subsequent issues included the writings of, among others, Hayden Carruth, David Ignatow, Anne Sexton, May Swenson, Diane Ackerman, William Kennedy, Leslie Fiedler, Ray Bradbury, Joyce Carol Oates, Philip Roth, Richard Farina, and Thomas Pynchon.

Baxter Hathaway served as editor from 1947 to 1976; after his retirement the issues had varying single and group editors. From the second issue of Volume 3, Hathaway shared editorship with an informal editorial board, some of whose members included William Dickey, Harvey Shapiro, and A.R. Ammons. Beginning with its Spring 1956 issue, when publication was taken over by Cornell University, *Epoch* published two or three times yearly. Later issues were devoted in large measure to special topics, such as "A Symposium on the Theory and Practice of the Line in Contemporary Poetry," whose participants included Margaret Atwood, Allen Ginsberg, Seamus Heaney, Denise Levertov, Howard Nemerov, and May Swenson.

epode \'ep-ˌōd\ [Greek *epōidós,* from *epōidós* (adjective) sung or said after] **1.** A verse form composed of two lines differing in construction and often in meter, the second shorter than the first. **2.** In Greek lyric odes, the third part of the three-part structure of the poem, following the strophe and the antistrophe.

eponym \'ep-ə-ˌnim\ [Greek *epṓnymos* person whose name has been given to something, from *epṓnymos* (adjective) giving one's name to something, surnamed, from *epí* on, upon + *ónoma, ónyma* name] One for whom or which something is or is believed to be named. The word can refer, for example, to the usually mythical ancestor or totem animal or object that a social group (such as a tribe) holds to be the origin of its name. In its most familiar use, *eponym* denotes a person for whom a place or thing is named, as in describing James Monroe as the eponym of Monrovia, Liberia. The derivative adjective is *eponymous*. An eponymous hero of a work of literature is one whose name is the title of the work, such as Anne Brontë's *Agnes Grey,* Charles Dickens' *David Copperfield,* and John Fowles' *Daniel Martin.*

epopee \'ep-ə-ˌpē\ [French *épopée,* from Greek *epopoiía,* a derivative of *epopoiós* epic poet, from *épē* epic poetry + *poieîn* to make] An epic, especially an epic poem.

epos \'ep-ˌäs\ [Greek *épos* word, speech, tale] **1.** An epic. **2.** A body of poetry expressing the tradition of a people; specifically, a number of poems that treat an epic theme but are not formally united.

epyllion \e-'pil-ē-ən, -ˌän\ *plural* epyllia \-ē-ə\ *or* epyllions [Greek *epýllion* short verse, short epic poem, diminutive of *épos* word, speech, line of verse] A brief narrative poem in dactylic hexameter, usually dealing with mythological and romantic themes. The epyllion is characterized by lively description, scholarly allusion, and an elevated tone similar to that of the epic.

Such poems were especially popular during the Greek Alexandrian period (*c.* 4th–3rd century BC), as seen in the works of Callimachus and Theocritus, although the term *epyllion* was not applied to them until the 19th century. Late

Republican and early Augustan Latin poetry, such as Catullus' poem on the marriage of Peleus and Thetis and Ovid's *Metamorphoses* (c. AD 1–8), reflect the influence of the epyllion, as do medieval European troubadour songs and modern Greek Klephtic songs. William Shakespeare's *Lucrece* and Matthew Arnold's "Sohrab and Rustum" are examples of epyllions in English.

equivalence \i-ˈkwiv-ə-ləns\ or **equivalency** \-lən-sē\ *plural* equivalences *or* equivalencies. In classical prosody, the principle that one long syllable is equal to two short ones. The principle is used as the basis for SUBSTITUTION in quantitative verse.

Ercles vein \ˈər-kləz, -ˌklēz; ˈär-kləz\ A rousing, somewhat bombastic manner of public speaking or writing. In William Shakespeare's *A Midsummer Night's Dream* (Act I, scene 2), "Ercles' vein" is Bottom's expression for the style of speech he considers appropriate to the character of "Ercles," i.e., Hercules.

Ermetismo *See* HERMETICISM.

Ern Malley hoax \ˈərn-ˈmal-ē\ Literary fraud perpetrated in 1943–44 on the Australian literary periodical *Angry Penguins* by two antimodern poets, James McAuley and Harold Stewart. In order to parody what the hoaxers saw as the meaninglessness of experimental verse and to discredit the magazine and its editor Max Harris, the two wrote to *Angry Penguins* under the name Ethel Malley, the sister of a deceased mechanic and poet named Ernest (Ern) Malley. Claiming to have found the poetry in her late brother's effects, "Miss Malley" submitted some 17 poems to the magazine for an opinion as to their worth. Harris received the work enthusiastically, publishing a special edition of the magazine and a volume of the collected poems under the title *The Darkening Ecliptic* (1944). About nine months after first contacting the magazine, McAuley and Stewart revealed their hoax, listing as the sources of Malley's poetry patches of William Shakespeare, medical journals, government reports, and other random text. The generally unsympathetic press made much of the event. Despite the efforts of McAuley and Stewart, however, at least some of the verses can be considered to have merit, and the Malley poetry and its worth continue to be subjects of debate.

erotica \i-ˈrät-i-kə\ [Greek *erōtiká,* plural of *erōtikós* erotic, pertaining to sexual love, a derivative of *erōt-, érōs* sexual love] Literary or artistic works having an erotic theme; especially, books treating of sexual love in a sensuous or voluptuous manner. The word erotica typically applies to works in which the sexual element is regarded as part of the larger aesthetic aspect. It is usually distinguished from pornography, which can also have literary merit but which is usually understood to have sexual arousal as its main purpose. *Compare* PORNOGRAPHY.

There are erotic elements in literary works of all times and all countries. Among the best-known examples of erotic literature are the *Kāma-sūtra* and other Sanskrit literature from about the 5th century AD, Persian lyric poems called ghazels, Ovid's *Ars Amatoria,* parts of Geoffrey Chaucer's *The Canterbury Tales,* Giovanni Boccaccio's *Decameron,* the 16th-century Chinese novel

Jin ping, William Shakespeare's *Venus and Adonis,* the writings of the Marquis de Sade, and D.H. Lawrence's *Lady Chatterley's Lover.*

Erziehungsroman \ert-ˈsē-ˌu̇ŋz-rō-ˌmän, *German* -ˌu̇ŋs-\ [German, literally, novel of upbringing] *See* BILDUNGSROMAN.

Escola Velha \esh-ˈkō-lə-ˈväl-yə\ [Portuguese, literally, old school] Spanish dramatists in the early 16th century who were influenced by the Portuguese dramatist Gil Vicente. Their designation as a school was the work of later critics. Although in form Vicente was a medieval dramatist, his skill in comedy and character portrayal and the varied subject matter of his plays made him a forerunner of the modern drama. He wrote 12 of 44 plays entirely in Spanish and 18 more in both Spanish and Portuguese, but the Inquisition proved to be the death of popular theater in Portugal and Vicente's real influence was felt in Spain. Playwrights stimulated by Vicente's innovations included Alfonso Álvares and Baltasar Dias, who wrote popular religious plays; António Ribeiro Chiado and his brother Jerónimo Ribeiro, writers of satirical farces; and António Prestes and Simão Machado, who evinced a knowledge of folklore and the peasant life.

esemplastic \ˌes-ˌem-ˈplas-tik, -əm-\ [Greek *es, eis* into + *hén,* neuter of *heîs* one + *plastikós* capable of molding, plastic] Shaping or having the power to shape disparate things into a unified whole. The word, coined by Samuel Taylor Coleridge to describe a faculty of the imagination, was probably suggested by *Ineinsbildung,* a term used by the German philosopher Friedrich Schelling.

Esquire \ˈes-ˌkwīr\ American monthly magazine, founded in 1933 by Arnold Gingrich, that began production as an oversized magazine for men, featuring drawings of scantily clad young women and winning its right to do so in court. It later abandoned its titillating role but continued to cultivate the image of refined taste.

Esquire's early notoriety became the subject of a celebrated court case. In 1943 Frank C. Walker, the U.S. postmaster general, attempted to withdraw the magazine's second-class mailing privileges (an economic rate generally considered essential to a magazine's survival) on the grounds that *Esquire* was "not devoted to useful information" worthy of the mail subsidy. Gingrich and his associates protested, enlisting writers in their defense; he brought suit against Walker and in 1946 won his case in the U.S. Supreme Court.

Esquire was a pioneer in the use of unconventional topics and feature stories. As it began to publish the work of Thomas Wolfe, Ernest Hemingway, William Faulkner, John Steinbeck, Truman Capote, and Norman Mailer, the magazine's risqué image and its once racy air gradually receded. It provided an outlet for new writers of fiction and nonfiction, and its topical features, satiric humor, and excellent book, movie, and music reviews filled a void between literary and opinion periodicals in the American market. Although the magazine continued to emphasize clothing and advertising directed to men, *Esquire* evolved into a general-audience publication.

essay \'es-ˌā\ [Middle French *essai,* literally, trial, test] An analytic, interpretive, or critical literary composition usually much shorter and less systematic and formal than a dissertation or thesis and usually dealing with its subject from a limited and often personal point of view.

Some early treatises—such as those of Cicero on the pleasantness of old age or on the art of "divination," Seneca on anger or clemency, and Plutarch on the passing of oracles—presage to a certain degree the form and tone of the essay, but not until the Renaissance, with its increasing assertion of the self, was the flexible and deliberately nonchalant and versatile form of the essay perfected by Montaigne.

Choosing the name *essai* to emphasize that his compositions were attempts or endeavors, a groping toward the expression of his personal thoughts and experiences, Montaigne used the essay as a means of self-discovery. Later writers who most nearly recall the charm of Montaigne include, in England, Robert Burton, though his whimsicality is more erudite, Sir Thomas Browne, and Laurence Sterne, and in France, with more self-consciousness, André Gide and Jean Cocteau.

At the beginning of the 17th century, social manners, the cultivation of politeness, and the training of an accomplished gentleman became the theme of many essayists. This theme was first exploited by the Italian Baldassare Castiglione in his *Il libro del cortegiano* (1528; *The Book of the Courtier*). The influence of the essay and of genres allied to it, such as maxims, portraits, and sketches, proved second to none in molding the behavior of the cultured classes, first in Italy, then in France, and, through French influence, in most of Europe in the 17th century. Among those who pursued this theme was the 17th-century Spanish Jesuit Baltasar Gracián in his essays on the art of worldly wisdom.

With the advent of a keener political awareness with the age of Enlightenment, in the 18th century the essay became all-important as the vehicle for a criticism of society and of religion. Because of its flexibility, its brevity, and its potential both for ambiguity and for allusions to current events and conditions, it was an ideal tool for philosophical reformers. *The Federalist Papers* in America and the tracts of the French Revolutionaries are among the countless examples of attempts during this period to improve the human condition through the essay.

The genre also became the favored tool of traditionalists of the 18th and 19th centuries, such as Burke and Coleridge, who looked to the short, provocative essay as the most potent means of educating the masses. French Catholics, German pietists, and a number of individual English and American authors confided to the essay their dismay at what they saw as modern vulgarity and a breakdown of the coherence of the Western tradition. Essays such as Paul Elmer More's long series of *Shelburne Essays* (published between 1904 and 1935), T.S. Eliot's *After Strange Gods* (1934) and *Notes Towards the Definition of Culture* (1948), and others that attempted to reinterpret and redefine culture, established the genre as the most fitting to express the genteel tradition at odds with the democracy of the new world.

While in several countries the essay became the chosen vehicle of literary and social criticism, in other countries the genre became semipolitical, earnestly nationalistic, and often polemical, playful, or bitter. Essayists such as Robert Louis Stevenson and Willa Cather wrote with grace on several lighter subjects, and many writers mastered the essay as a form of literary criticism.

Ernest Renan, one of the most accomplished French masters of the essay, found relief from his philosophical and historical studies in his half-ironical considerations on love, and Anatole France, his disciple, and hosts of others have alternated playful essays with others of high seriousness. Izaak Walton's *The Compleat Angler* (1953), however, enjoys the status of a minor classic, and the best of the modern Dutch essayists, Johan Huizinga (1872–1945), reflected with acuteness on *Homo ludens,* or man at play. A Frenchman, Jean Prévost (1901–44), who was to die as a hero of the Resistance to the German occupation of France during World War II, opened his career as an essayist with precise and arresting analyses of the *Plaisirs des sports* (1925). But there are surprisingly few very significant works, except in chapters of novels or in short stories, on the joys of hunting, bullfighting, swimming, or even, since Anthelme Brillat-Savarin's overpraised essay, *Physiologie du goût* (1825; "The Physiology of Taste") on gourmet enjoyment of the table.

Serious speculations, on the other hand, have overburdened the modern essay, especially in German and in French. The several volumes of Jean-Paul Sartre's *Situations,* published from 1947 on, constitute the most weighty and, in the first two volumes in particular, the most original body of essay writing of the middle of the 20th century. Albert Camus' *Mythe de Sisyphe* (1942; *Myth of Sisyphus*) and his subsequent *Homme révolté* (1951; *The Rebel*) consist of grave, but inconsistent and often unconvincing, essays loosely linked together. Émile Chartier (1868–1951), under the pseudonym Alain, exercised a lasting influence over the young through the disjointed, urbane, and occasionally provoking reflections scattered through volume after volume of his essays, entitled *Propos.*

Apart from philosophical speculation, many modern essays have examined the character of nations. In the 20th century, the masters of this type of essay included Salvador de Madariaga in Spanish, Hermann Keyserling in German, and Elie Faure in French. The Spanish-born essayist George Santayana was one of the most accomplished masters of written English prose; because of his cosmopolitan culture and the subtlety of his insights, he was one of the most percipient analysts of the English and of the American character.

Noteworthy essayists of the 20th century have been numerous since the 1940s, when articles in most journals tended to become shorter and to strive for more immediate effect. As a result, the general reader grew accustomed to being attacked rather than seduced. Still, the 20th century could boast of the critical essays of Virginia Woolf, Edmund Wilson, Albert Thibaudet, and Charles du Bos.

ethos \'ē-ˌthäs, -ˌthȯs\ [Greek *êthos* disposition, character] In rhetoric, the character or emotions of a speaker or writer that are expressed in the attempt to persuade an audience. It is distinguished from pathos, which is the emotion the speaker or writer hopes to induce in the audience. The two words were distinguished in a broader sense by ancient classical authors, who used *pathos* when referring to the violent emotions and *ethos* to mean the calmer ones. Ethos was the natural disposition or moral character, an abiding quality, and pathos a temporary and often violent emotional state. For Renaissance writers the distinction was a different one: ethos described character and pathos an emotional appeal.

euhemerism \yü-'hēm-ə-ˌriz-əm, -'hem-\ **1.** A theory held by the 4th-century-BC Greek mythographer Euhemerus that the gods of mythology were but deified mortals. **2.** Interpretation of myths as traditional accounts of historical persons and events. The word *euhemeristic* is applied to such explanations of primitive myths.

There is no doubt an element of truth in the euhemeristic approach, for, among the Romans, the gradual deification of ancestors and emperors was a prominent feature of religious development. Among preliterate people, family and tribal gods sometimes originate as great chiefs and warriors. But euhemerism is not accepted by students of comparative religion as the sole or even chief explanation of the origin of gods.

eulogy \'yü-lə-jē\ [Greek *eulogía* praise, eulogy, from *eu-* well + *lógos* word, speech] A composition or an oration in commendation of someone or something (such as of the character and accomplishments of a deceased person); a synonym for ENCOMIUM.

eumolpique \œ̄-mȯl-'pēk\ [French, from Greek *eúmolpos* sweetly singing, from *eu-* well + *mélpein* to sing] Poetic measure devised by the French poet and composer Antoine Fabre d'Olivet (1767–1825). It consists of two unrhymed alexandrines (lines of iambic hexameter), the first verse of 12 syllables ending in masculine (stressed) rhyme, the second of 13 syllables ending in feminine (unstressed) rhyme. It scans as:

∪ – | ∪ – | ∪ – | ∪ – | ∪ – | ∪ –
∪ – | ∪ – | ∪ – | ∪ – | ∪ – | ∪ – | ∪.

euphemism \'yü-fə-ˌmiz-əm\ [Greek *euphēmismós,* a derivative of *euphēmízesthai* to use words of good omen, from *eu-* good + *phēmízein* to spread a report, name, call] The substitution of an agreeable or inoffensive expression for one that may offend or suggest something unpleasant.

euphony \'yü-fə-nē\ [Greek *euphōnía,* a derivative of *eúphōnos* sweet-voiced, musical, from *eu-* well + *phōnḗ* sound of the voice, voice] Pleasing, harmonious, or sweet sound, the acoustic effect produced by words so formed and combined as to please the ear. Euphony is achieved through the use of vowel sounds in words of generally serene imagery. Vowels are considered more euphonious than consonants and back vowels (ü, u̇, ō, ȯ) more euphonious than front vowels (ē, i, ā, e). Liquid consonants and the semivowel sounds (l, m, n, r, y, w) are also considered euphonious. An example may be seen in Alfred Tennyson's "The Lotos-Eaters": "The mild-eyed melancholy Lotos-eaters came." Euphony is the opposite of CACOPHONY.

euphuism \ˈyü-fyü-ˌiz-əm\ An elegant Elizabethan literary style marked by excessive use of balance, antithesis, and alliteration and by frequent use of similes drawn from mythology and nature. The word is also used to convey artificial elegance of language. It was derived from the name of a character in the prose romances *Euphues: The Anatomy of Wit* (1578) and *Euphues and his England* (1580) by the English author John Lyly. Although the style soon fell out of fashion, it played an important role in the development of English prose. It appeared at a time of experimentation with prose styles, and it offered prose that was lighter and more fanciful than previous writing. The influence of euphuism can be seen in the works of such writers as Robert Greene and William Shakespeare, both of whom imitated the style in some works and parodied it in others.

Eupolidean \ˌyü-ˌpäl-ə-ˈdē-ən, -pəl-; ˌyü-pə-ˈlid-ē-ən\ [Greek *eupolídeion,* from neuter of *eupolídeios* in the style of Eupolis] In classical prosody, the characteristic meter used by the Greek writer Eupolis (5th century BC). The meter was used, e.g., by Aristophanes, as a stichic length (measured by line rather than by stanza) as well as in strophic verse. It consists either of the aeolic pattern | ⏖ ⏒ – ⏓ | – ∪ ∪ – in which four variable syllables precede the choriambic nucleus (– ∪ ∪ –) and create what is called *choriambic dimeter,* or the same pattern lacking the final syllable (catalectic). A full Eupolidean line is scanned:

⏖ ⏒ – ⏓ | – ∪ ∪ – | ⏓ ⏒ – ⏓ | – ∪ –.

Evergreen Review Literary magazine published from 1957 to 1973 in the United States. Its editor, Barney Rosset, developed the progressive periodical into a forum for radical expression of ideas on topics from sex to politics. The magazine was known for publishing erotic—some said pornographic—material. Some of the more noteworthy contributors to the magazine included Che Guevara, Vladimir Nabokov, Jack Kerouac, Allen Ginsberg, Samuel Beckett, Henry Miller, and E.E. Cummings.

examen \ig-ˈzā-mən\ [Late Latin, examination] A critical study (such as of a writer or a phenomenon).

Examiner, The Influential British magazine that was known for its radical, reformist positions on significant issues of the time, including opposition to the slave trade and support of Roman Catholic emancipation. It was published weekly from 1808 until 1881. Among its notable contributors were John Keats, Percy Bysshe Shelley, and William Hazlitt, poets who were attacked by other major periodicals of the day, including *Blackwood's Magazine* and *The Quarterly Review*. Leigh Hunt, who cofounded *The Examiner* with his brother John, was its editor until 1821. The brothers were fined and imprisoned for two years after the March 22, 1812, issue of the magazine described the unpopular prince regent as a fat, 50-year-old "Adonis."

excerpt \ˈek-ˌsərpt, ˈeg-ˌzərpt\ [Latin *excerptum,* from neuter of *excerptus,* past participle of *excerpere* to pick out, select] A selection or fragment (such as from a writing or a work of music); a chosen portion or sample.

excursion [Latin *excursio* sortie, sally] Part of a stage direction. *See* ALARUMS AND EXCURSIONS.

exegesis \ˌek-sə-ˈjē-sis, ˈek-sə-ˌjē-\ *plural* exegeses \-ˌsēz\ [Greek *exḗgēsis,* a derivative of *exēgeîsthai* to explain, interpret] An explanation or interpretation of a portion of Scripture.

Doctrinal and polemical intentions often influence interpretive results; a given text may yield a number of very different interpretations according to the exegetical presuppositions and techniques applied to it. The study of these methodological principles themselves constitutes the field of HERMENEUTICS.

Although at times the Hebrew and Greek of the Bible have been treated as sacred languages, and the history contained in the text has been regarded as somehow different from "ordinary" history, most forms of biblical exegesis employed in the modern era are applicable to many other bodies of literature. *Textual criticism* is concerned with establishing, as far as is possible, the original texts of the biblical books through the critical comparison of the various early materials available. *Philological criticism* is the study of the biblical languages in respect to grammar, vocabulary, and style to ensure that they may be translated as faithfully as possible. *Literary criticism* classifies the various biblical texts according to their literary genre. It also attempts to use internal and external evidence to establish the literary genre, date, authorship, and intended audience of the various biblical texts. For example, different strains of tradition in the Pentateuch (the first five books of the Hebrew Bible) have been connected with different stages in the development of Israelite religion. *Tradition criticism* attempts to analyze the various sources of the biblical materials in such a way as to discover the oral traditions that lie behind them and to trace their gradual development. *Form criticism,* to some extent an offshoot of tradition criticism, the major exegetical method of the 20th century, assumes that literary material, written or oral, takes certain forms according to the function the material serves within the community which preserves it. The content of a given narrative is an indication both of its form—miracle story, controversy, or conversion story, for example—and of the narrative's use within the life of the community. *Redaction criticism* examines the way the various pieces of the tradition have been assembled into the final literary composition by an author or editor. The arrangement and modification of these pieces of tradition can reveal something of the author's intentions and the means by which these intentions were hoped to be achieved. *Historical criticism* places the biblical documents within their historical context and examines them in the light of contemporary documents.

The word exegesis has also been used in a more general sense to mean an analysis of any literary text. *See* EXPLICATION DE TEXTE.

exemplum \ig-'zem-pləm, eg-\ *plural* exempla \-plə\ [Late Latin, from Latin, model, example] An anecdote or short narrative used to point to a moral or sustain an argument. Exempla were used in medieval sermons and were eventually incorporated into literature in such works as Geoffrey Chaucer's "The Nun's Priest's Tale" and "The Pardoner's Tale."

existentialism \ˌek-si-'sten-chə-ˌliz-əm, ˌeg-zi-\ [German *Existentialismus,* a derivative of *existentiell* grounded in existence, existential] A family of philosophies devoted to an interpretation of human existence in the world that stresses its concreteness and its problematic character. As a self-conscious movement it is primarily a 20th-century phenomenon, embracing the theories of Martin Heidegger, Karl Jaspers, Jean-Paul Sartre, Gabriel Marcel, and Maurice Merleau-Ponty, but its characteristic features occurred earlier, especially in the 19th-century thinkers Friedrich Nietzsche and Søren Kierkegaard.

Existentialism is largely a coherent development within traditional philosophy. It rejects traditional epistemology and the attempts to ground human knowledge in the external world, however. According to existentialists, human beings are not solely or even primarily knowers; they also care, desire, manipulate, and, above all, choose and act. Second, the self, or ego, required by some if not all traditional epistemological doctrines, is not a fundamental entity but rather emerges from experience.

It is an important tenet of existentialism that the individual is not a detached observer of the world, but "in the world." A person "exists" in a special sense in which entities like stones and trees do not; a human being is "open" to the world and to objects in it. Yet there is no distinct realm of consciousness on the basis of which one might infer, project, or doubt the existence of external objects.

Further, humans, unlike other entities, make themselves what they are by choices, choices of ways of life (Kierkegaard) or of particular actions (Sartre). Even when one seems simply to be acting out a "given" role or following "given" values—given, for example, by God or by society—one is in fact choosing to do so. It does not follow that the choices available are unlimited.

Existentialism had an enormous influence outside philosophy, on, for example, psychology and theology. The importance of specific situations and autonomous choices implies that existential truths can be conveyed in drama and fiction as well as in direct philosophical discourse; the concerns of the movement have inspired a large body of imaginative literature, such as that of Sartre, Albert Camus, and Simone de Beauvoir. Existentialist writers are characterized by their concern with "being," which contrasts not only with knowing but also with abstract concepts, which cannot fully capture what is individual and specific. Because one's choices cannot, in the existentialist view, be rationally grounded, they do not propose, except incidentally, an ethic in the sense of a set of rules or values, but rather a framework in which action and choice are to be viewed. This framework does not tell one what to choose, but it does imply that there are right and wrong ways of choosing. One can be authentic or inauthentic, act in bad faith or with sincerity. It is especially in the face of death, struggle, guilt, or anxiety that one becomes aware of one's responsibility as an agent, as well as of the ultimate inexplicability of the world in which one must act. The existential movement also provided a means of articulating and interpreting these same themes as discerned in works of literature from all periods (e.g., Sophocles, William Shakespeare, Fyodor Dostoyevsky, William Faulkner).

exodos \'ek-sə-ˌdäs, 'eg-zə-\ [Greek *éxodos,* literally, close, end, departure, exit] The last part of a Greek drama. The exodus follows the last song of the chorus, and it is during the exodus that the deus ex machina appears.

exordium \eg-'zȯr-dē-əm\ *plural* exordiums *or* exordia \-dē-ə\ [Latin, literally, warp laid on a loom before the web is begun, starting point] The introductory part of a discourse or composition. The term originally referred specifically to one of the traditional divisions of a speech established by classical rhetoricians.

explication de texte \ek-splē-kä-'syōⁿ-də-'tekst\ *plural* explications de texte *same*\ [French, literally, explanation of text] **1.** A method of literary criticism involving a detailed examination of each part of a work, such as structure, style, and imagery, and an exposition of the relationship of these parts to each other and to the whole work. The method was originally used to teach literature in France and has since become a tool for use by literary critics in other countries, particularly by practitioners of New Criticism. **2.** A critical analysis employing explication de texte.

explicit \'eks-pli-sit, -kit\ A device added to the end of some manuscripts and incunabula by the author or scribe and providing such information as the title of the work and the name or initials of its author or scribe. Explicits were soon incorporated into or completely replaced by the COLOPHON, information about the printer, printing materials, and typeface, and, often, the printer's emblem.

In medieval Latin works, the word *explicit* meant "here ends. . . ." Originally, it may have been an abbreviation for *explicitus est liber* ("the book is unrolled"), but by analogy with *incipit* ("here begins . . ."), it was taken as a present-tense, third-singular verb form.

exposition A setting forth of a meaning or purpose of a writing or discourse.

Expressionism \ek-'spresh-ə-ˌniz-əm\ An artistic theory or practice of the late 19th and early 20th centuries in which the subjective or subconscious thoughts and emotions of the artist, the struggle of abstract forces, or the inner realities of life are presented by a wide variety of nonnaturalistic techniques that include abstraction, distortion, exaggeration, primitivism, fantasy, and symbolism. It arose as a reaction against complaints of materialism, complacent bourgeois prosperity, rapid mechanization and urbanization, and the domination of the family within pre-World War I European society.

In forging a drama of social protest, Expressionist writers were concerned with general truths rather than with particular situations; hence they explored the predicaments of representative symbolic types rather than of fully developed individualized characters. Emphasis in Expressionist drama is laid not on the outer world, which is merely sketched in and barely defined in place or time, but on the internal, on an individual's mental state; hence the imitation of life is replaced by the ecstatic evocation of states of mind. The leading character in an Expressionist play often delivers long monologues couched in a concentrated, elliptical, almost telegrammatic language that explores youth's spiritual malaise, its revolt against the older generation, and the various political or revolutionary remedies that present themselves. The leading character's inner development is explored through a series of loosely linked tableaux, or "stations," in which traditional values are shunned and a higher spiritual vision of life is sought.

August Strindberg and Frank Wedekind were notable forerunners of Expressionist drama, but the first full-fledged Expressionist play was Reinhard Johannes Sorge's *Der Bettler* ("The Beggar"), which was written in 1912 but not performed until 1917. The other principal playwrights of the movement were Georg Kaiser, Ernst Toller, Paul Kornfeld, Fritz von Unruh, and Walter Hasenclever, all of Germany. Outside Germany, playwrights who used Expressionist dramatic techniques included the American authors Eugene O'Neill and Elmer Rice.

Expressionist poetry, which arose at the same time as its dramatic counterpart, was similarly nonreferential and sought an ecstatic, hymnlike lyricism that would have considerable associative power. This condensed, stripped-down poetry, utilizing strings of nouns with only a few adjectives and infinitive verbs, eliminated narrative and description to get at the essence of feeling. The principal Expressionist poets were Georg Heym, Ernst Stadler, August Stramm, Gottfried Benn, Georg Trakl, Else Lasker-Schüler, and Franz Werfel. The dominant theme of Expressionist verse was horror over urban life and apocalyptic visions of the collapse of civilization.

The decline of Expressionism was hastened by the vagueness of its longing for a better world, by its use of highly poetic language, and in general by the intensely personal and inaccessible nature of its mode of presentation. In Germany, the movement was effectively killed by the Nazi regime, which labeled Expressionism decadent and forbade its exhibition and publication.

expurgate \ˈek-spər-ˌgāt\ To expunge obscene or otherwise objectionable parts of a written or dramatic work before publication or presentation.

extraliterary \ˌek-strə-ˈlit-ə-ˌrer-ē\ Lying outside what is literary, or lying outside the province of literature.

extrametrical \ˌek-strə-ˈmet-ri-kəl\ In prosody, exceeding the usual or prescribed number of syllables in a given meter. Also, in reference to a syllable or syllables not counted in metrical analysis. In the following final couplet from a sonnet by William Shakespeare, the ending syllables are extrametrical:

> Yet him for this my love no whit disdaineth;
> Suns of the world may stain when heaven's sun staineth.

extravaganza \ek-ˌstrav-ə-ˈgan-zə\ [Italian *estravaganza, stravaganza,* literally, extravagance] **1.** A literary or musical work marked by extreme freedom of style and structure and usually by elements of burlesque or parody, such as Samuel Butler's *Hudibras.* **2.** An elaborate and spectacular theatrical production. The term once specifically referred to a type of 19th-century English drama made popular by J.R. Planché, a British playwright and antiquary who wrote fanciful portrayals of fairy tales and other poetic subjects based on similar French productions. Planché's productions included dancing and music and influenced such later writers as W.S. Gilbert.

eye dialect The use of misspellings that are based on standard pronunciations (such as *sez* for *says* or *kow* for *cow*) but are usually intended to suggest a speaker's illiteracy or his use of generally nonstandard pronunciations. It is sometimes used in literature for comic effect.

eye rhyme In poetry, an imperfect rhyme in which two words are spelled similarly but pronounced differently (such as *move* and *love, bough* and *though, come* and *home,* and *laughter* and *daughter*). Some of these (such as *flood* and *brood*) are referred to as historical rhymes because at one time they probably had the same pronunciation.

F

Writing free verse is like playing tennis with the net down.
—Robert Frost

fable \'fā-bəl\ [Old French, from Latin *fabula* talk, narrative, fable] **1.** A story of supernatural or marvelous happenings (as in legend, myth, or folklore). **2.** A narration intended to enforce a useful truth; especially, one in which animals or inanimate objects speak and act like human beings. The fable differs from the ordinary folktale in that it has a moral—or lesson for behavior— that is woven into the story and often explicitly formulated at the end.

The Western tradition of the fable effectively began in Greece with tales ascribed to Aesop, almost certainly a legendary figure. The Aesopian fables emphasize the social interactions of human beings, and the morals they draw tend to embody advice on the best way to deal with the competitive realities of life. One of the shortest Aesopian fables says: "A vixen sneered at a lioness because she never bore more than one cub. 'Only one,' the lioness replied, 'but a lion.' " Modern editions contain up to 200 "Aesop" fables, but there is no way of tracing their actual origins. Among the classical authors who developed the Aesopian model were the Roman poet Horace, the Greek biographer Plutarch, and the Greek satirist Lucian.

Fable flourished in the European Middle Ages, as did all forms of allegory. A notable collection of fables was made in the late 12th century by Marie de France. The medieval fable gave rise to an expanded form known as the BEAST EPIC—a lengthy, episodic animal story replete with hero, villain, victim, and an endless stream of heroic endeavor, parodying epic grandeur. The most famous of these is a 12th-century group of related tales called Roman de Renart whose hero is Renart, or Reynard, the Fox (German: Reinhart Fuchs), a symbol of cunning. In the Renaissance, Edmund Spenser made use of this kind of material in "Prosopopoia, or Mother Hubberd's Tale" (1591). Later, John Dryden's poem *The Hind and the Panther* (1687) revived the beast epic as an allegorical framework for serious theological debate.

The fable has traditionally been of modest length, however. The shorter form reached its zenith in 17th-century France in the work of Jean de La Fontaine, whose theme was the folly of human vanity. His first collection of Fables in 1668 followed the Aesopian pattern, but his later ones, accumulated during the next 25 years, satirized the court and its bureaucrats, the church, the rising bourgeoisie—indeed, the whole human scene. His influence was felt throughout

Europe, and in the Romantic period his outstanding successor was the Russian Ivan Andreyevich Krylov.

In the 19th century fable found a new audience with the rise of literature for children. Among the celebrated authors who employed the form were Lewis Carroll, Kenneth Grahame, Rudyard Kipling, Hilaire Belloc, Joel Chandler Harris, Beatrix Potter, and, though not writing primarily for children, Hans Christian Andersen, Oscar Wilde, Antoine de Saint-Exupéry, J.R.R. Tolkien, and James Thurber.

The oral tradition of fable in India may date as far back as the 5th century BC. The *Pañca-tantra,* a Sanskrit compilation of beast fables, has survived only in an 8th-century Arabic translation known as the *Kalīlah wa Dimnah,* after two jackals that figure in one of the tales. It was translated into many languages including Hebrew, from which in the 13th century John of Capua made a Latin version.

In China the full development of fable was hindered by traditions of thought that prohibited the Chinese from accepting any notion of animals behaving and thinking as humans. Between the 4th and the 6th century, however, Chinese Buddhists adapted fables from Buddhist India as a way to further the understanding of religious doctrines. Their compilation is known as *Boyu jing*.

In Japan the 8th-century histories *Kojiki,* ("Records of Ancient Matters") and *Nihon shoki* ("Chronicles of Japan") are studded with fables, many on the theme of small but intelligent animals getting the better of large and stupid ones. The form reached its height in the Kamakura period (1192–1333). In the 16th century, Jesuit missionaries introduced Aesop's fables into Japan, and their influence has persisted into modern times. *See also* FOLKTALE.

fabliau \'fab-lē-ˌō\ or **fableau** \fa-'blō\ *plural* fabliaux \-ˌō, -ˌōz\ *or* fableaux \-'blō, -'blōz\ [French, from Old French (Picard dialect) *fabliau* (in other dialects *fablel, fableau*), diminutive of *fable* fable] A short metrical tale made popular in medieval France by the jongleurs, or professional storytellers. Fabliaux were characterized by vivid detail and realistic observation and were usually comic, coarse, and often cynical, especially in their treatment of women.

About 150 fabliaux are extant. Many are based on simple jokes or puns—such as one called *Estula,* which can either be a person's name or mean "Are you there?"—or on wry situations, such as one in which a man is rescued from drowning but has his eye put out by the boat hook that saves him. The majority of fabliaux are erotic, and the merriment often depends on situations and adventures that are either indecorous or frankly obscene. Recurring characters include the cuckold and his wife, the lover, and the naughty priest. The theme of guile is often treated, frequently to show the deceiver deceived.

It was once widely held that fabliaux represented the literature of the bourgeois and common people. This, however, is unlikely, since they frequently contain a substantial element of burlesque (or mockery and parody) that depends, for its appreciation, on considerable knowledge of courtly society, love, and manners. They also presuppose something like scorn for those of humble rank who ape their betters.

Some of the subject matter in the fabliaux has parallels in other times and other countries: many of the plots stem from folklore, some have classical affinities, and a few can be traced to Oriental sources. But many of the tales are so simple that they could have arisen spontaneously. The earliest fabliau, *Richeut,* dates from about 1175, but the main period of their composition was the 13th century, extending into the first half of the 14th. Most fabliaux are 200 to 400 lines in length, though there are extremes of fewer than 20 lines and of more than 1,300. Their authors included amateur writers (notably Philippe de Beaumanoir) and professionals (e.g., Jehan Bodel and Rutebeuf). Verse tales analogous to the fabliaux exist in other languages. Geoffrey Chaucer's "The Reeve's Tale," for example, is based on a known fabliau, and several of the other comic *Canterbury Tales* also may have origins in fabliaux.

fabula \ˈfab-yə-lə, ˈfäb-yu̇-lä\ *plural* fabulae \-ˌlē, -ˌlī\ [Latin] In addition to meaning "talk," "story," or "fable," Latin *fabula* was a general word for "play"; particular types included the *fabula Atellana* \ˌat-ə-ˈlän-ə\, *fabula crepidata* \ˌkrā-pi-ˈdät-ə\, *fabula palliata* \ˌpäl-ē-ˈät-ə\, *fabula praetexta* \prē-ˈteks-tə\, and *fabula togata* \tō-ˈgät-ə\.

The *fabula Atellana* ("Atellan play") was the earliest form of native farce in ancient Italy. These fabulae were presumably rustic improvisational comedies featuring masked stock characters. The farces derived their name from the town Atella in Campania and seem to have originated among speakers of the Oscan language. They became a popular entertainment in ancient republican and early imperial Rome, by which time they were performed in Latin but possibly spiced with Oscan words and place-names. Originally based on scenarios handed down by tradition, they became a literary genre in the 1st century BC, but only a few fragments survive of works by Lucian Pomponius of Bononia, Novius, and other writers. They feature stock characters, including Maccus, the clown; Bucco ("Fat-cheeks"), the simpleton; and Pappus, the old fool; Dossennus, whose name has been taken to mean hunchback; and Manducus, perhaps meaning the glutton. There is no record of these farces after the 1st century AD, but certain of the stock characters of the 16th-century Italian commedia dell'arte reflect the influence of the Atellan plays.

The *fabula crepidata* was a form of Roman tragedy based on Greek models. The name was derived from the *crepida,* a kind of thick-soled Greek shoe presumably worn by the actors.

The *fabula palliata* was an ancient Roman comedy based on Greek New Comedy and treating a Greek subject. The name derives from *pallium,* a cloak, and means roughly "play in Greek dress." The form was developed by the playwright Gnaeus Naevius in the 3rd century BC.

The *fabulae palliatae* retained the Greek stock characters and conventionalized plots of romantic intrigue as a framework for the satire of everyday contemporary life. These comedies became more than mere translation in the works of Plautus and Terence, who introduced Roman manners and customs, Italian place-names, and Latin puns into the Greek form, writing in a style that is characterized by boisterous humor, nimbleness and suppleness of diction, and high spirits. Terence, though closer in spirit to his Greek originals, often combined materials from two different plays into one. His style is graceful and correct, more polished but less lively than that of Plautus, and his characters are well delineated. Statius Caecilius, famed for his emotional power and well-constructed plots, is another prominent representative. It is through the *fabulae palliatae* of Plautus and Terence that Greek New Comedy was preserved and influenced succeeding generations of comedy in Europe from the Renaissance on.

The *fabula praetexta,* or *fabula praetextata,* was an ancient Roman drama with a theme from Roman history or legend. It was introduced in the 3rd century BC and took its name from the *praetexta,* an outer garment bordered with purple worn by Roman officials.

The *fabula togata* (from the Roman *toga,* hence "play in Roman dress") replaced the *fabula palliata* by about the 2nd century BC. The *togata* form was also a comedy based on Greek models, but it featured Roman life and characters. No complete work of this form survives.

fabulist \ˈfab-yü-list\ A creator or writer of fables.

facetiae \fə-ˈsē-shē-ˌē, -ˌī\ [Latin, cleverness, wittiness, plural of *facetia* joke] Witty or humorous writings or sayings.

faction \ˈfak-shən\ [blend of *fact* and *fiction*] Literary work based on fact but using the narrative techniques of fiction. *See also* NONFICTION NOVEL.

fair copy A neat and exact copy of a written work, especially of a corrected or revised draft of a document.

fairy tale *also called* fairy story **1.** A simple narrative dealing with supernatural beings (such as fairies, magicians, ogres, or dragons) that is typically of folk origin and written or told for the amusement of children. **2.** A more sophisticated narrative containing supernatural or obviously improbable events, scenes, and personages and often having a whimsical, satirical, or moralistic character.

The term embraces such popular folktales (also called MÄRCHEN) as "Cinderella" and "Puss in Boots" and art fairy tales (*Kunstmärchen*) of later invention, such as *The Happy Prince* (1888), by the Irish writer Oscar Wilde. It is often difficult to distinguish between tales of literary and oral origin, because folktales have received literary treatment from early times, and, conversely, literary tales can often be traced back into the oral tradition. Early Italian collections such as *Le piacevoli notti* (1550, vol. 1; 1553, vol. 2; "The Pleasant Nights") of Gianfrancesco Straparòla and the *Il pentamerone* (1636; orig. pub. [1634] in Neapolitan dialect as *Lo cunto de li cunti* ["The Story of Stories"]) of Giambattista Basile contain reworkings in a highly literary style of such stories as "Snow White," "Sleeping Beauty," and "The Maiden in the Tower."

A later French collection, Charles Perrault's *Contes de ma mère l'oye* (1697; *Tales of Mother Goose*), including "Cinderella," "Little Red Riding Hood," and "Beauty and the Beast," remains faithful to the oral tradition, while the *Kinder- und Hausmärchen* (1812–15; "Children's and Household Tales"; generally known as *Grimm's Fairy Tales*) of the Brothers Grimm are transcribed directly from oral renderings (although often from literate informants). The influence of Perrault and the Grimms has been very great, and their versions have been commonly adopted as nursery tales among literate people in the West. For example, Grimm's "Rumpelstiltskin" has replaced the native English "Tom Tit Tot," and Perrault's "Cinderella" has replaced "Cap o' Rushes," once almost equally popular in oral tradition.

Art fairy tales were cultivated in the period of German Romanticism by J.W. von Goethe, Ludwig Tieck, Clemens Brentano, and E.T.A. Hoffmann and in Victorian England by John Ruskin (*The King of the Golden River,* 1851) and Charles Kingsley (*The Water-Babies,* 1863), but few of these tales have found permanent popularity. The master of the art fairy tale, whose works rank with the traditional stories in universal popularity, is the Danish writer Hans Christian Andersen. Though his stories have their roots in folk legend, they are personal in style and contain elements of autobiography and contemporary social satire.

Twentieth-century psychologists, notably Sigmund Freud, Carl Jung, and Bruno Bettelheim, have interpreted elements of the fairy tale as manifestations of universal fears and desires. In *The Uses of Enchantment* (1976), Bettelheim asserted that the apparently cruel and arbitrary nature of many folk fairy stories is actually an instructive reflection of the child's natural and necessary "killing off" of successive phases of development and initiation.

fakelore \ˈfāk-ˌlōr\ [blend of *fake* and *folklore*] Imitation folklore (such as tales or songs) created to pass as genuinely traditional.

falling action In a play or other work of literature, the events that follow the climax and lead to the catastrophe or denouement. It is in contrast to *rising action,* the events leading up to the plot's climax.

falling rhythm *also called* descending rhythm. In prosody, rhythm established by a metric foot in which the first syllable is accented, as in trochaic and dactylic feet. It is the opposite of rising, or ascending, rhythm. *See also* CADENCE.

family sagas *See* ICELANDERS' SAGAS.

fancy \ˈfan-sē\ [ME *fantsy,* contraction of *fantasie* imagination, mental image, ultimately from Greek *phantasía,* a derivative of *phantázein* to make visible, present to the mind] **1.** The power of conception and representation used in artistic expression (such as through the use of figures of speech by a poet). Sometimes used as a synonym for imagination, especially in the sense of the power of conceiving and giving artistic form to that which is not existent, known, or experienced. **2.** The invention of the novel and the unreal by recombining the elements found in reality so that life is represented in alien surroundings or essentially changed in natural physical and mental constitution (as in centaurs or giants)—distinguished from *imagination.* **3.** The conceiving power that concerns itself with imagery (as figures of speech and details of a decorative design); synonymous with *conceit.*

The concepts of fancy and imagination have always been closely related, but at least since the Middle Ages distinctions have been made between the two. In some countries, such as Italy and Germany, fancy was associated with creativity and was considered a higher or greater quality than imagination. In England, John Dryden, Sir Joshua Reynolds, David Hume, and others set forth views of the differences, generally giving imagination a broader and more important role than fancy. For most, however, the terms were virtually synonymous until the Romantic period of the late 18th and early 19th century, when Samuel Taylor Coleridge stated the theory that has had the most lasting influence. According to Coleridge, imagination is the faculty associated with creativity and the power to shape and unify, while fancy, dependent on and inferior to imagination, is merely "associative."

fantasy or **phantasy** \ˈfan-tə-sē, -zē\ Imaginative fiction dependent for effect on strangeness of setting (such as other worlds or times) and of characters (such as supernatural or unnatural beings). Examples include William Shakespeare's *A Midsummer Night's Dream,* Jonathan Swift's *Gulliver's Travels,* J.R.R. Tolkien's *The Lord of the Rings* trilogy, and T.H. White's *The Once and Future King.* Science fiction can be seen as a form of fantasy, but the terms are not interchangeable, as science fiction usually is set in the future and is based on some aspect of science or technology while fantasy is set in an imaginary world and features the magic of mythical beings.

farce \ˈfärs\ **1.** A light dramatic composition that uses highly improbable situations, stereotyped characters, extravagant exaggeration, and violent horseplay. Also, the class or form of drama made up of such compositions. **2.** The broad humor characteristic of theatrical farce. Also, a passage containing such comic element.

Farce is generally regarded as intellectually and aesthetically inferior to comedy in its crude characterizations and implausible plots, but it has been sustained by its popularity in performance. Antecedents of farce are found in ancient Greek and Roman theater, both in the comedies of Aristophanes and Plautus and in the popular native Italian *fabula Atellana,* entertainments in which the actors played stock character types—such as glutton, greybeard, and clown—who were caught in exaggerated situations.

It was in 15th-century France that the term *farce* was first used to describe the elements of clowning, acrobatics, caricature, and indecency found together within a single form of entertainment. Such pieces were initially bits of impromptu buffoonery inserted by actors into the texts of religious plays—hence the use of the Old French word *farce,* "stuffing." Such works were afterward written independently, the most amusing of the extant texts being *Maistre*

Pierre Pathelin (c. 1470). French farce spread quickly throughout Europe, notable examples being the interludes of John Heywood in 16th-century England. William Shakespeare and Molière eventually came to use elements of farce in their comedies.

Farce remained popular throughout the 18th and 19th centuries; in France, Eugène-Marin Labiche's *Le Chapeau de paille d'Italie* (1851; *The Italian Straw Hat*) and Georges Feydeau's *La Puce à l'oreille* (1907; *A Flea in Her Ear*) were notable successes. Farce also surfaced in music hall, vaudeville, and boulevard entertainments.

Farce survived in the late 19th and early 20th centuries in such plays as *Charley's Aunt* (1892) by Brandon Thomas and found new expression in film comedies with Charlie Chaplin, the Keystone Kops, and the Marx Brothers. The farces presented at the Aldwych Theatre, London, between the world wars were enormously popular, and numerous successful television comedy shows attest to the durability of the form. Farce continued to be produced in theaters throughout the 20th century. Two examples from the second half of the century are the Italian Dario Fo's *Morte accidentale di un anarchico* (1974; *Accidental Death of an Anarchist*) and Michael Frayn's *Noises Off* (1982).

farce-comedy Comedy of a marked farcical character or a comic work that employs elements of farce. Examples include Oscar Wilde's *The Importance of Being Earnest* and several of William Shakespeare's plays.

farceur \fär-'sər\ [French] A writer or actor of farce.

farsa \'fär-sä\ [Oromo (Cushitic language of East Africa) *faarsaa* singer, song] *See* BOASTING POEM.

fashionable novel Early 19th-century subgenre of the comedy of manners portraying the English upper class, usually by members of that class. One author particularly known for his fashionable novels was Theodore Hook.

fast \'fast\ Of a dramatic or literary work, holding the reader's interest by reason of sustained conflict, vivid writing, or the rapid advancement of the story.

Fastnachtsspiel \'fäst-ˌnäk̲t-ˌshpēl\ *plural* Fastnachtsspiele \-ˌshpē-lə\ [German, from *Fastnacht* Shrove Tuesday + *Spiel* play] Carnival or Shrovetide play that emerged in the 15th century as the first truly secular drama of pre-Reformation Germany. Usually performed on platform stages in the open air by amateur actors, students, and artisans, the *Fastnachtsspiele* consisted of a mixture of popular and religious elements—broad farce and abbreviated morality plays—that reflected the tastes of a predominantly bourgeois audience. The plays often contained satirical attacks on greedy clergymen and other traditional dislikes of the German burghers, an element that relates them to the Feast of Fools (a medieval festival during which ecclesiastical ritual was parodied) and the French *sotie*. In addition to features borrowed from liturgical drama and bits of comedy that were no doubt brought in by the wandering minstrels, the

Fastnachtsspiele, according to many scholars, contain themes and influences from German folk traditions of the pre-Christian era.

Hans Rosenplüt of Nürnberg and his younger contemporary Hans Folz of Worms, who also settled in Nürnberg, were the most notable purveyors of *Fastnachtsspiele* in the mid-15th century, their plays being formless, uninhibited comedy. In the 16th century the plays reached a level of greater respectability when Hans Sachs wrote many *Fastnachtsspiele* among his 208 plays. He is also said to have directed and acted in them.

fate tragedy or **fate drama** (German: *Schicksalstragödie*) A type of play especially popular in early 19th-century Germany in which a malignant destiny drives the protagonist to commit a horrible crime, often unsuspectingly. Adolf Müllner's *Der neunundzwanzigste Februar* (1812; "February 29") and *Die Schuld* (1813; "The Debt") and Zacharias Werner's *Der vierundzwanzigste Februar* (1806; "February 24") are among the best-known examples.

Federal Theatre Project *See* WPA FEDERAL THEATRE PROJECT.

Federal Writers' Project *See* WPA FEDERAL WRITERS' PROJECT.

Félibre \fā-ˈlē-brə, *French* -ˈlēbr *with* r *as a uvular trill*\ *plural* Felibres *same or* -brəz\ [French, from Provençal *felibre*] A member or supporter of the Félibrige.

Félibrige \fā-lē-ˈbrēzh\ [French, from Provençal *Felibrige,* a derivative of *felibre* Félibre] Association organized in the 19th century for the maintenance of the Provençal customs and language that stimulated the renaissance of the literature, language, and customs of the whole of southern France. The Félibrige was founded in 1854 by seven poets—Joseph Roumanille, Frédéric Mistral, Théodore Aubanel, Anselme Mathieu, Jean Brunet, Alphonse Tavan, and Paul Giéra—who took their name from a Provençal tale in which Jesus is discovered in the Temple disputing with "Seven Doctors of the Law" ("li sét felibre de la léi"). The group met near Avignon under the guidance of Roumanille, who, from the mid-1840s, had produced secular verse and delightfully humorous prose works in his native Provençal dialect. In 1852 he had also collected and published *Li Prouvençalo,* an anthology of writing in Provençal; he also made the first attempt at regulating the orthography of Provençal in the introduction to his play, *La Part dou bon Dieu* (1853). Mistral was inspired by Roumanille to devote his energy to restoring the glory of the Provençal language, and he became the most powerful personality of its renaissance. He worked with Roumanille on standardizing the Provençal grammar and in 1855 he cofounded with Roumanille the *Armana Prouvençau* ("Provençal Almanac"), an annual periodical that for 80 years published the best contemporary Provençal writing. Later, Mistral compiled a huge Provençal dictionary, *Lou Tresor dóu Félibrige,* 2 vol. (1878). In 1905 he established a museum of Provençal culture in Arles, which is still in existence. Of the other members of the original Félibrige, only Aubanel proved himself worthy to rank with Mistral and Roumanille.

The Félibrige grew considerably in the period after Mistral, attracting followers not only from Provence but also from other southern provinces, such as Gascony, Languedoc, Limousin, and Aquitaine, as well as from Catalonia in Spain. The vigorous regional movement that resulted exerted a strong influence well into the 20th century.

fellow traveler [translation of Russian *poputchik*] Originally, a writer in the Soviet Union who was not against the Bolshevik Revolution of 1917 but did not actively support it as a propagandist. The term was used in this sense by Leon Trotsky in *Literature and the Revolution* (1925) and was not meant to be pejorative. Implicit in the designation was the recognition of the artist's need for intellectual freedom and his dependence on links with the cultural traditions of the past. Fellow travelers were given official sanction in the early Soviet regime; they were regarded somewhat like experts who were filling the literary gap until a true proletarian art emerged. In the 1920s some of the most gifted and popular Soviet writers, such as Osip Mandelshtam, Leonid Leonov, Boris Pilnyak, Isaak Babel, Ilya Ehrenburg, and members of the Serapion Brothers, were fellow travelers. The period during which they dominated the literary scene is now regarded as the brilliant flowering of Soviet literature. They were opposed bitterly by champions of a new proletarian art, and by the end of the decade the term came to be practically synonymous with a counterrevolutionary.

Outside the Soviet Union the term was widely used in the Cold War era of the 1950s, especially in the U.S., as a political label to refer to any person who, while not thought to be an actual "card-carrying" member of the Communist Party, was in sympathy with its aims and supported its doctrines.

Femina Prize *See* PRIX FÉMINA.

feminine caesura In verse, a caesura that follows an unstressed or short syllable. *See* CAESURA.

feminine ending In prosody, having an unstressed and usually extrametrical syllable at the end of a line of verse. In the opening lines from Robert Frost's poem "Directive," the fourth line has a feminine ending while the rest are masculine:

> Back out of all this now too much for us,
> Back in a time made simple by the loss
> Of detail, burned, dissolved, and broken off
> Like graveyard marble sculpture in the weather,
> There is a house that is no more a house
> Upon a farm that is no more a farm
> And in a town that is no more a town.

feminine rhyme *also called* double rhyme. In poetry, a rhyme involving two syllables (as in *motion* and *ocean* or *willow* and *billow*). The term feminine rhyme is also sometimes applied to triple rhymes, or rhymes involving three syllables (such as *exciting* and *inviting*). *Compare* MASCULINE RHYME. Robert

Browning alternates feminine and masculine rhymes in his "Soliloquy of the Spanish Cloister":

> Gr-r-r—there go, my heart's abhorrence!
>   Water your damned flower-pots, do!
> If hate killed men, Brother Lawrence,
>   God's blood, would not mine kill you!
> What? your myrtle-bush wants trimming?
>   Oh, that rose has prior claims—
> Needs its leaden vase filled brimming?
>   Hell dry you up with flames!

feminist criticism Any of a variety of approaches to literary criticism that attempt to examine the ways in which literature has been shaped according to issues of gender.

Feminist literary theory originated largely in the women's movement that followed World War II. Two of the earliest documents of feminist theory are Simone de Beauvoir's book *Le Deuxième Sexe* (1949; *The Second Sex*) and Kate Millett's *Sexual Politics* (1970). Feminist criticism established several aims: to critique the established canon of Western literature and to expose the standards on which it is based as patriarchal; to recover forgotten and neglected texts by women in order to reevaluate them; to establish "gynocriticism," the study of woman-centered writing, and to establish a women's canon; and to explore the cultural construction of gender and identity.

Feminist critics are extremely varied in their approaches. Among the writers who have had a great impact on feminist critical discourse are Ellen Moers, Carolyn Heilbrun, Sandra Gilbert, Susan Gubar, Annette Kolodny, Adrienne Rich, Elaine Showalter, Nina Baym, Alice Jardine, Catherine Stimpson, Gayatri Spivak, Hélène Cixous, Luce Irigaray, and Julia Kristeva.

Fenian cycle \'fē-nē-ən\, *also called* Fionn cycle \'fin\ *or* Ossianic cycle \ˌäsh-ē-'an-ik, ˌäs-\ [*Fenian* member of a legendary warrior band, from Irish & Scottish Gaelic *féinnidh,* derivative of *fian(n)* warrior band] In Irish literature, tales and ballads centering on the deeds of the legendary Finn MacCumhaill (MacCool) and his war band, the Fianna Éireann. An elite volunteer corps of warriors and huntsmen, skilled in poetry, Fianna flourished under the reign of Cormac mac Airt in the 3rd century AD. Fenian lore attained its greatest popularity about 1200, when the cycle's outstanding story, *The Colloquy of the Old Men,* was written down. Other earlier tales were recorded in manuscripts such as *The Book of the Dun Cow* (*c.* 1100) and *The Book of Leinster* (*c.* 1160). The Fenian cycle remains a vital part of Irish folklore and contains many of the best-loved folktales of the country.

An early tale, *The Boyish Exploits of Finn* (*Macgnímartha Finn*), tells how, after Cumhaill (Cool), chief of the Fianna, is killed, his posthumous son is reared secretly in a forest and earns the name Finn ("The Fair") by his exploits. He grows up to triumph over his father's slayer, Goll MacMorna, to become head of the Fianna, which later includes his son Oisín (Ossian), the poet, his grandson Oscar, the handsome Diarmaid (Dermot), and his former clan enemy Goll MacMorna. Finn was reputedly a descendant from the druids. According to legend, he was wise and sensitive to nature.

The other tales of the cycle deal with the Fianna's rise and fall. Its disintegration begins when Diarmaid elopes with Gráinne (Grace), a king's daughter whom Finn, as an old man, wishes to marry. Later, when Diarmaid is wounded, Finn lets him die for lack of water. The king and people finally turn against the overbearing Fianna, a conflict that culminates in the Battle of Gabhra, in which the Fianna is destroyed. Oscar is killed in battle; Oisín survives but is lured away by a fairy princess to Tír na nÓg ("The Land of Youth"). Related to the Fenian sagas is a series of tales concerning Cormac mac Airt, his grandfather Conn of the Hundred Battles, and his son Cairbré of the Liffey.

Fescennine verse \'fes-ə-ˌnīn, -nin\, *Latin* Fescennini versus \ˌfes-ə-'nī-nē-'vər-səs\, *also called* carmina Fescennina \'kär-mə-nə-ˌfes-ə-'nī-nə\. Early native Italic jocular dialogues in Latin verse. At vintage and harvest, and probably at other rustic festivals, they were sung by masked dancers. They were similar to the often ribald wedding songs called epithalamia. (*Compare* EPITHALAMIUM.) It is clear from the literary imitations by Catullus (*c.* 84–*c.* 54 BC) that Fescennine verses were very free, even obscene, in language. Horace (65–8 BC) states that they became so abusive that a law that forbade a malum carmen ("evil song"—i.e., charm intended to hurt) was invoked against them.

It was believed that the verses averted the evil eye; hence, some early authors connected the name with *fascinum* ("charm, bewitchment"). The true derivation may be from Fescennia, an Etruscan city. In their origin they may have had a magico-religious intent—abuse, buffoonery, and obscenity being well-known fertility or luck charms. Whether they developed into the dramatic *satura* (medley, or hodgepodge) that was the forerunner of Roman drama has been debated by modern scholars.

Festschrift \'fest-ˌshrift\ *plural* Festschriften \-ˌshrif-tən\ *or* Festschrifts [German, from *Fest* festival + *Schrift* writings] A usually miscellaneous volume of writings by different authors presented as a tribute or memorial; especially, a volume of learned essays contributed by students, colleagues, and admirers to honor a scholar on a special anniversary.

feuilleton \fœy-'tōⁿ, *Angl* ˌfə-yə-'tōn, ˌfər-\ [French, literally, lower part of a newspaper page reserved for feature articles, third of a paper sheet printed in duodecimo format, a diminutive of *feuillet* leaf, folio sheet] **1.** A part of a European newspaper or magazine devoted to material designed to entertain the general reader. It is presented as a supplement or a feature section. **2.** A piece of writing (such as an installment of a serialized novel) printed in a feuilleton. **3.** A novel printed in installments, also called a *serial.* **4.** A work of fiction that caters to popular taste. **5.** A short literary composition often having a familiar tone and reminiscent content, also called a *sketch.*

fiction \'fik-shən\ **1.** Literature created from the imagination, not presented as fact, though it may be based on a true story or situation. **2.** A work of fiction; especially a NOVEL, SHORT STORY, or NOVELLA.

fictionalize \'fik-shə-nə-ˌlīz\ or **fictionize** \'fik-shə-ˌnīz\ To make into or treat in the manner of fiction.

fictioneer \ˌfik-shə-'nir\ One who writes fiction, especially in quantity.

fictionize *See* FICTIONALIZE.

fifteener *See* INCUNABULUM.

figurative \'fig-yər-ə-tiv, 'fig-ər-\ Of language or writing, characterized by figures of speech (such as metaphor and simile) or elaborate expression, as opposed to literal language.

figure of speech A form of expression used to convey meaning or heighten effect, often by comparing or identifying one thing with another that has a meaning or connotation familiar to the reader or listener. An integral part of language, figures of speech are found in oral literatures, as well as in polished poetry and prose and in everyday speech. Greeting-card rhymes, advertising slogans, newspaper headlines, the captions of cartoons, and the mottos of families and institutions often use figures of speech, generally for humorous, mnemonic, or eye-catching purposes. The argots of sports, jazz, business, politics, or any specialized groups abound in figurative language.

Most figures in everyday speech are formed by extending the vocabulary of what is already familiar and better known to what is less well known. Thus metaphors (implied resemblances) derived from human anatomy are commonly extended to nature or inanimate objects as in the expressions "the mouth of a river," "the bowels of the earth," or "the eye of a needle." Conversely, resemblances to natural phenomena are frequently applied to other areas, as in the expressions "a wave of enthusiasm," "a ripple of excitement," or "a storm of abuse." Use of simile (a comparison, usually indicated by "like" or "as") is exemplified in "We were packed in the room like sardines." Personification (speaking of an abstract quality or inanimate object as if it were a person) is exemplified in "Money talks"; metonymy (using the name of one thing for another closely related to it) in "How would the Pentagon react?"; and synecdoche (use of a part to imply the whole) in expressions such as "brass" for high-ranking military officers or "hard hats" for construction workers. Other common forms of figurative speech are hyperbole (deliberate exaggeration for the sake of effect), as in "I'm so mad I could chew nails"; the rhetorical question (asked for effect, with no answer expected), as in "How can I express my thanks to you?"; litotes (an emphasis by negation), as in "It's no fun to be sick"; and onomatopoeia (imitation of natural sounds by words), in such words as "crunch," "gurgle," "plunk," and "splash."

Almost all the figures of speech that appear in everyday speech may also be found in literature. In serious poetry and prose, however, their use is more fully conscious, more artistic, and much more subtle; it thus has a stronger intellectual and emotional impact, is more memorable, and sometimes contributes a range and depth of association and suggestion far beyond the scope of the casual colloquial use of imagery.

In European languages figures of speech are generally classified in five major categories: (1) figures of resemblance or relationship (e.g., simile, metaphor, kenning, conceit, parallelism, personification, metonymy, synecdoche, and euphemism); (2) figures of emphasis or understatement (e.g., hyperbole, litotes, rhetorical question, antithesis, climax, bathos, paradox, oxymoron, and irony); (3) figures of sound (e.g., alliteration, repetition, anaphora, and onomatopoeia); (4) verbal games and gymnastics (e.g., pun and anagram); and (5) errors (e.g., malapropism, periphrasis, and spoonerism). Figures involving a change in sense, such as metaphor, simile, and irony, are called tropes.

All languages use figures of speech. but differences of language dictate different stylistic criteria. In a culture not influenced by classical Greece and Rome, some figures may be absent. Japanese poetry is based on delicate structures of implication and an entire vocabulary of aesthetic values almost untranslatable to the West. Arabic literature is rich in simile and metaphor, but the constructions used are so different from those familiar in the West that translation requires much adaptation. This condition is also true of oral traditions and of the written literatures deriving from them.

One powerful literary influence upon world cultures has been the Bible. Both the Old Testament and the New Testament are rich in simile, metaphor, and personification and in the special figure of Hebrew poetry, parallelism.

figure poem *See* PATTERN POETRY.

fili \'fē-lē, *Modern Irish* 'fē-lə\ *plural* filid \fē-'lē, *Old Irish* 'fē-ləth\ [Old Irish, seer, diviner, poet] A professional poet in ancient Ireland whose official duties were to know and preserve the tales and genealogies and to compose poems recalling the past and present glory of the ruling class. The filid constituted a large aristocratic class that was expensive to support, and they were severely censured for their extravagant demands on patrons as early as the assembly of Druim Cetta in 575. Their power was not checked, however, since they could enforce their demands by the feared lampoon (*áer*), or poet's curse, which not only could take away a person's reputation but, according to a widely held belief, could cause physical damage or even death. Although by law a fili could be penalized for abuse of the áer, belief in its powers was strong and continued to modern times. After the Christianization of Ireland in the 5th century, filid assumed the poetic function of the outlawed druids, the powerful priesthood of the pagan Celts. They were often associated with monasteries, which were the centers of learning.

Filid were divided into seven grades. One of the lower and less learned grades was bard. The highest grade was the ollam, achieved after at least 12 years of study, during which the poet mastered more than 300 difficult meters and 250 primary stories and 100 secondary stories and was then entitled to wear a cloak of crimson bird feathers and carry a wand of office. Although at first the filid wrote in a verse form similar to the poetry of Germanic languages (two half-lines linked by alliteration), they later developed intricate rules of prosody and rigid and complicated verse forms the most popular of which was the deibide (derived from deibe, "difference, disagreement"), a quatrain composed of two couplets, linked by the rhyme of a stressed syllable with an unstressed one. After the 6th century, filid were granted parcels of land. In return they were required not only to write official poetry but also to instruct the residents of the area in law, literature, and national history. These seats of learning formed the basis for the later great bardic colleges. By the 12th century filid were composing lyrical nature poetry and personal poems that praised the human qualities (especially the generosity) of their patrons, rather than the patrons' heroic exploits or ancestors, and they no longer strictly adhered to set rules of prosody. The distinction between the fili and the bard gradually broke down; the filid gave way to the supremacy of the bards by the 13th century. *See also* BARD.

fin de siècle \fa^{n}-də-'syekl, *Angl* ˌfan-də-sē-'ek-əl, -lə\ [French *fin de siècle* end of the century] Of, relating to, characteristic of, or resembling the late 19th-century literary and artistic climate of sophistication, escapism, extreme aestheticism, world-weariness, and fashionable despair. When used in reference to literature, the term essentially describes the movement inaugurated by the Decadent poets of France and the movement called Aestheticism in England during this period.

Fionn cycle *See* FENIAN CYCLE.

Fire!! Magazine that exerted a marked impact on the Harlem Renaissance of the 1920s and early '30s despite its demise after the first issue (November 1926).

The idea for the experimental, apolitical Negro literary journal was conceived in Washington, D.C., by poet Langston Hughes and writer and graphic artist Richard Nugent. The two, along with an editorial board comprising Zora Neale Hurston, Gwendolyn Bennett, John Davis, and Aaron Douglas, selected the brilliant young critic and novelist Wallace Henry Thurman to edit the publication. Thurman solicited art, poetry, fiction, drama, and essays from his editorial advisers, including a play by Hurston, as well as from such leading figures of the New Negro movement as Countee Cullen and Arna Bontemps. Responses to the magazine ranged from minimal notice in the white press to heated contention among African-American critics. Among the latter, the senior rank of intellectuals (such as W.E.B. Du Bois) tended to dismiss it as self-indulgent, while younger figures reacted with enthusiasm. Financial viability quickly proved unattainable. and several hundred undistributed copies met with an ironic fate when the building they were stored in burned to the ground. *See also* HARLEM RENAISSANCE.

first edition **1.** All of the copies of a literary work printed from the first setting of type for that work and issued at the same time. **2.** A single copy from a first edition.

first person *See* POINT OF VIEW.

fit \'fit\ [Old English *fitt*] *archaic* A division of a poem or song; a canto or a similar division. The word is of Old English date and has an exact correspondent in Old Saxon *fittea,* which occurs in the Latin preface of the *Heliand.* It probably represents figurative use of a common Germanic noun referring to the unraveled edge of a fabric.

fixed form In poetry, any form that has set rules governing most elements of its composition, including length, meter, and rhyme scheme. Such forms include the sonnet, the ballade, the chant royal, and the limerick.

flam \'flam\ [probably short for *flimflam*] *obsolete* A fanciful bit of writing.

flashback \'flash-ˌbak\ **1.** A literary or theatrical technique used also in motion pictures and television that involves interruption of the chronological sequence of events by interjection of events or scenes of earlier occurrence, often in the form of reminiscence. **2.** An instance of flashback—called also *backflash* \'bak-ˌflash\.

flash-forward \'flash-'fȯr-wərd\ [*flash*back + *forward*] A literary or theatrical technique used also in motion pictures and television that involves interruption of the chronological sequence of events by interjection of events or scenes of future occurrence.

flat and round characters Characters as described by the course of their development in a work of literature. Flat characters, as it were, are two-dimensional in that they are relatively uncomplicated and do not change throughout the course of a work. By contrast, round characters are complex and undergo development, sometimes sufficiently to surprise the reader.

The two types were described by E.M. Forster in his book *Aspects of the Novel.* The example he gives of a flat character is Charles Dickens' Mrs. Micawber; of a round character, William Thackeray's Becky Sharp.

fleshly school of poetry Epithet applied to a group of late 19th-century English poets associated with Dante Gabriel Rossetti. The term was invented by Robert Williams Buchanan and appeared as the title of an article in the *Contemporary Review* (October 1871) in which he castigated the poetry of Rossetti and his colleagues, notably Algernon Swinburne, for its "morbid deviation from the healthy forms of life." In Buchanan's view, these poets exhibited "weary wasting, yet exquisite sensuality; nothing virile, nothing tender, nothing completely sane; a superfluity of extreme sensibility." He reviled their decadence, their "amatory forms" and "carnal images." He even went so far as to call Swinburne unclean, among other things. Rossetti replied with "The Stealthy

School of Criticism" in *The Athenaeum,* in December 1871, and Swinburne with a pamphlet, "Under the Microscope," in 1872. The controversy was prolonged and distressed Rossetti, but it had ended before Rossetti's death in 1882, when Buchanan dedicated his novel *God and the Man* to him.

fleur du mal \flœr-dūē-'mál\ *plural* fleurs du mal *same*\ [French, literally, flower of evil] A morbid or scandalous creation in literature or art. The phrase alludes to *Les Fleurs du mal* (1857), a volume of Decadent poetry by French poet Charles Baudelaire.

flourish \'flər-ish\ A florid bit of writing or speech, such as a complicated figure of speech or an ornate metaphor.

flower \'flaù-ər\ A florid insertion or interpolation in a text; a figure of speech or other ornament of literary style.

fluid \'flü-id\ Characterized by or employing a smooth, easy style or producing such an effect, especially in literature or art.

flyting \'flī-tiŋ\ [Scots, literally, quarreling, contention] A dispute or exchange of personal abuse or ridicule in verse form between two characters in a poem (as an early epic) or between two of the Scottish makaris (plural of MAKAR—i.e., poet) of the 15th and 16th centuries.

In the Scottish poetic competition two highly skilled rivals engaged in a contest of verbal abuse, remarkable for its fierceness and extravagance. Although contestants attacked each other spiritedly, they actually had a professional respect for their rival's vocabulary of invective. The tradition seems to be derived from the Gaelic filid (a class of professional poets), who composed savage tirades against persons who slighted them. A Scandinavian counterpart is the *Lokasenna* ("Flyting of Loki"), a poem in the *Poetic Edda* in which the trickster-god Loki bandies words with the other gods, taunting them with coarse jests. Although the flyting became obsolete in Scottish literature after the European Middle Ages, the tradition itself never died out among writers of Celtic background. The style and language of Robert Burns' "To a Louse" ("Ye ugly, creepin, blastit wonner/Detested, shunn'd by saunt an' sinner") parodies earlier Scots flyting, and James Joyce's poem "The Holy Office" is a bard's curse on the society that spurns him.

Examples of Scottish flyting are *The Flyting of Dunbar and Kennedie* (the poets William Dunbar and Walter Kennedy) and *Flytting betwixt Montgomerie and Polwart* (the poet Alexander Montgomerie and Sir Patrick Hume of Polwarth).

foil \'fȯil\ In literature, a character who is presented as a contrast to a second character so as to point to or show to advantage some aspect of the second character. An obvious example is the character of Dr. Watson in Sir Arthur Conan Doyle's Sherlock Holmes stories. Watson is a perfect foil for Holmes because his relative obtuseness makes Holmes' deductions seem more brilliant.

folio \ˈfō-lē-ō\ [Latin, ablative of *folium* leaf] In printing, a sheet of paper folded in half. The term also refers to a book made up of folio sheets, which is the largest regular book size. The collected works of William Shakespeare were first published in a folio edition in 1623, and several other such editions followed so that his works are often referred to in terms of a specific folio edition.

folk drama *also called* folk theater. A form of theater blending performance art and oral literature that is characterized by dances, many of them elaborate, with masks portraying animal or human characters. Folk drama is common in many parts of the preliterate world. Though the action and the dramatic imitation are always the most prominent parts of such performances, they may be part of a ritual and involve speaking or chanting of sacred texts learned and passed on by word of mouth.

Folk drama has long been used as a method of transmitting traditions, teachings, and commentary, as in the ancient Greek mysteries and in secret societies down to the present time. Some ancient folk dramas, however, were part of a public cult. Thus, in ancient Greece the feast of Dionysus led eventually to classical Greek drama, and in medieval Europe the dramatic celebrations of the Christian church developed into folk dramas and at length into the literary drama of the Renaissance and later.

folk literature *also called* oral tradition *or* folklore. The traditional knowledge and beliefs of cultures that are transmitted by word of mouth. It consists of both prose and verse narratives, poems and songs, myths, dramas, rituals, fables, proverbs, riddles, and the like. Folk literature exists side by side with the growing written record.

The individuals who led societies in a variety of ways—shamans, priests and priestesses, rulers, and warriors—provided the greatest stimulus for folk literature, for the telling of and listening to myths, tales, and songs. The medieval romances, especially the Breton lays, drew freely and sometimes directly on these folk sources as did many epics, such as the Anglo-Saxon *Beowulf* and the Finnish *Kalevala*. In literary forms such as the *fabliaux* the tales were often reworked by writers, but in the 16th and 17th centuries, writers such as Gianfrancesco Straparòla and Giambattista Basile went directly to folk literature for much of their material.

Folk literature is characterized by the presence of devices to aid memory, such as repetition, formulaic expressions ("once upon a time," "married and lived happily ever after"), and a variety of conventional motifs and episodes that constitute a formula of structure in the form of familiar plots. It also typically contains enough realism to support the marvelous in tale or song, violent actions, and simple, strong emotions. Its manifestations may vary greatly from region to region; for example, some ethnic groups may favor folk songs while others excel in storytelling.

folklore \ˈfōk-ˌlȯr\ The sum total of traditionally derived and orally transmitted literature, material culture, and custom of subcultures within predominantly literate and technologically advanced societies; comparable study among wholly or mainly nonliterate societies belongs to the disciplines of ethnology and anthropology. The word folklore is sometimes restricted to the tradition of oral literature.

Folklore studies began in the early 19th century. The first folklorists concentrated exclusively upon rural peasants, preferably uneducated, and the few other groups relatively untouched by modern ways (e.g., Gypsies). Their aim was to trace preserved archaic customs and beliefs to their remote origins in order to trace the history of human thought. In Germany, Jacob Grimm used folklore to illuminate Germanic religion of the Dark Ages. In Britain, Sir Edward Tylor, Andrew Lang, and others combined data from anthropology and folklore to "reconstruct" the beliefs and rituals of prehistoric peoples. The best-known work of this type is Sir James Frazer's *The Golden Bough* (1890).

Large collections of material—fairy tales and other types of folktales, ballads and songs, oral epics, folk plays, riddles, proverbs—were amassed in the course of these efforts. Inspired by the Brothers Grimm, whose first collection of fairy tales appeared in 1812, scholars throughout Europe began recording and publishing oral literature of many genres. Similar work was undertaken for music, dance, and traditional arts and crafts; many archives and museums were founded. The underlying impulse often was nationalistic; since the folklore of a group reinforced its sense of ethnic identity, it figured prominently in many struggles for political independence and national unity.

As the scholarship of folklore developed, an important advance was the classification of material for comparative analysis. Standards of identification were devised, notably for ballads (by Francis J. Child) and for the plots and component motifs of folktales and myths (by Antti Aarne and Stith Thompson). Using these, Finnish scholars, led by Kaarle Krohn, developed the "historical-geographical" method of research, in which every known variant of a particular tale, ballad, riddle, or other item was classified as to place and date of collection in order to study distribution patterns and reconstruct "original" forms. This method, more statistical and less speculative than that of the anthropological folklorists, dominated the field throughout the first half of the 20th century.

After World War II new trends emerged, particularly in the United States. Interest was no longer confined to rural communities, since it was recognized that cities too contained definable groups whose characteristic arts, customs, and values marked their identity. Although some Marxist scholars continued to regard folklore as belonging solely to the working classes, in other circles the study of folklore lost its restrictions of class and even of educational level; any group that expressed its inner cohesion by maintaining shared traditions qualified as a "folk," whether the linking factor was occupation, language, place of residence, age, religion, or ethnic origin. Emphasis also shifted from the past to the present, from the search for origins to the investigation of present meaning and function and change and adaptation within tradition were no longer necessarily regarded as corruptive.

folk song A traditional or composed song typically characterized by stanzaic form, refrain, and simplicity of melody. A form of folk literature, folk songs are essentially expressions of commonly shared ideas or feelings. Narrative folk songs are found chiefly in major Western and Asian civilizations, where they have long been cultivated by the most skillful singers. In the course of time these songs of warfare, of adventure, or of domestic life have formed local cycles, with characteristic metrical forms and formulas of plot and verbal expression.

folktale \'fōk-ˌtāl\ A characteristically anonymous, timeless, and placeless tale circulated orally among a people.

The existence of such tales is practically universal both in time and place. Certain peoples tell very simple stories and others tales of great complexity, but the basic elements of storyteller and audience are universal in history. A folktale travels with great ease even through language boundaries because it is characterized by a simple formula and by narrative motifs rather than by its verbal form. In many preliterate cultures folktales are hardly to be distinguished from myths, since, especially in tales of tricksters and heroes, they presuppose a background of belief about tribal origins and the relation of mortals and gods. Conscious fictions, however, enter into such stories. Animals abound, whether in their natural form or anthropomorphized so that they seem sometimes human and sometimes beast. Adventure stories, exaggerations, marvels of all kinds, such as otherworld journeys, and narratives of marriage or sexual adventure, usually between human beings and animals, are common. Much rarer, contrary to the views of earlier students, are explanatory stories. Tales of this description are especially characteristic of Africa, Oceania, and the South American Indians.

folk theater *See* FOLK DRAMA.

fool's literature Allegorical satires popular throughout Europe from the 15th to the 17th century, featuring the fool, or jester, who represented the weaknesses, vices, and grotesqueries of contemporary society. The first outstanding example of fool's literature was Sebastian Brant's *Das Narrenschiff* (1494; *The Ship of Fools*), which inspired such biting moral satires as Thomas Murner's poem *Narrenbeschwörung* (1512; "Exorcism of Fools") and Erasmus' *Encomium moriae* (1509; *The Praise of Folly*).

foot \'fu̇t\ *plural* feet \'fēt\ [translation of Latin *pes* or Greek *poús*] In poetry, the basic unit of verse meter consisting of any of various fixed combinations or groups of stressed and unstressed or long and short syllables. *Compare* CADENCE; METER.

The prevailing kind and number of feet, revealed by SCANSION, determines the meter of a poem. In classical (or quantitative) verse, a foot, or metron, is a combination of two or more long (written –) and short (◡) syllables. There are 28 different feet in classical verse, ranging from the pyrrhic (two short syllables) to the dispondee (four long syllables). The adaptation of classical metrics to the strongly accented Germanic languages, such as English, is in some ways problematic. The terminology persists, however, a foot usually being defined as a group of one stressed (ˊ) and one or two unstressed (˘) syllables. An exception is the spondee, which consists of two stressed syllables; in English verse, this is usually two monosyllables, such as the phrase "he who." The most common feet in English verse are the iamb, an unstressed followed by a stressed syllable, as in:

re̮ | pórt;

the trochee, a stressed followed by an unstressed syllable, as in:

dái | ly̆;

the anapest, two unstressed syllables followed by a stressed syllable, as in:

se̮r | ĕ | náde;

and the dactyl, a stressed syllable followed by two unstressed syllables, as in:

mér | rĭ | ly̆.

If a single line of a poem contains only one foot, it is called monometer; two feet, dimeter; three feet, trimeter; four feet, tetrameter; five feet, pentameter; six feet, hexameter; seven feet, heptameter; eight feet, octameter. More than six, however, is rare.

forensic oratory \fȯr-ˈen-sik\, *also called* legal oratory. Type of suasive speech most often used in the defense of individual freedom and resistance to prosecution. It was the most characteristic type of oratory in ancient Athens, where laws stipulated that litigants should defend their own causes. In the so-called Golden Age of Athens, the 4th century BC, great speakers in both the law courts and the assembly included Lycurgus, Demosthenes, Hyperides, Aeschines, and Dinarchus.

In the 1st century BC of ancient Rome, Cicero became the foremost forensic orator and exerted a lasting influence on later Western oratory and prose style. He successfully prosecuted Gaius Verres, notorious for his mismanagement while governor of Sicily, and he dramatically presented arguments against Lucius Sergius Catiline that showed a command of analysis and logic and great skill in motivating his audience. Cicero also delivered 14 bitter indictments against Mark Antony, who was to him the embodiment of despotism.

Among the great forensic orators of later times was the 18th- and 19th-century English advocate Thomas Erskine, who contributed to the cause of English liberties and the humane application of the legal system. *Compare* DELIBERATIVE ORATORY, EPIDEICTIC ORATORY.

foreshadowing \ˌfȯr-ˈshad-ō-iŋ\ The organization and presentation of events and scenes in a work of fiction or drama so that the reader or observer is prepared to some degree for what occurs later in the work. This can be part of the general atmosphere of the work, or it can be a specific scene or object that gives a clue or hint as to a later development of the plot. The disastrous flood that occurs at the end of George Eliot's *The Mill on the Floss,* for example, is foreshadowed by many references to the river and to water in general throughout the book.

foreshortening \fȯr-ˈshȯrt-ən-iŋ\ Representation in art or literature that is compact, abridged, or shortened.

foreword \ˈfȯr-wərd\ Prefatory comments (as for a book), especially when written by someone other than the author.

formalism \ˈfȯr-mə-ˌliz-əm\ Marked attention to arrangement, style, or artistic means (as in art or literature), usually with corresponding de-emphasis of content. The word is used to refer to the approach taken by literary critics who emphasize the formal aspects of a literary work, in particular the Russian school of literary criticism that flourished from 1914 to 1928.

Formalism \ˈfȯr-mə-ˌliz-əm\, *also called* Russian Formalism. Twentieth-century Russian school of literary criticism that flourished from 1914 to 1928. It began in two groups: OPOYAZ (an acronym for Russian words meaning "Society for the Study of Poetic Language"), founded in 1914 at St. Petersburg and led by the literary critic Viktor Shklovsky; and the Moscow Linguistic Circle, founded in 1915. Both groups made use of the linguistic techniques of Ferdinand de Saussure. Although they based their approach largely on Symbolist notions concerning the autonomy of the text and the discontinuity between literary and other uses of language, the Formalists sought to make their analyses more objective and scientific than those of Symbolist criticism. Closely allied to the Russian Futurists and opposed to sociological criticism, the Formalists analyzed the text itself, apart from its psychological, sociological, biographical, and historical elements.

Although always anathema to the Marxist critics, Formalism was a powerful influence in the Soviet Union until 1929, when it was condemned for its lack of political perspective. Later, largely through the work of the structuralist linguist Roman Jakobson, it became highly influential in the West, notably in Anglo-American New Criticism, which is sometimes called formalism, and in structuralism.

form criticism A method of biblical criticism that seeks to classify units of scripture into literary patterns (such as love poems, parables, sayings, elegies, legends) and that attempts to trace each type to its period of oral transmission in an effort to determine the original form and the relationship of the life and thought of the period to the development of the literary tradition.

fornaldarsǫgur \ˈfȯr-näl-ˌdär-ˈsœ-guer\ [Old Norse, sagas of old times] Icelandic sagas dealing with the ancient myths and hero legends of Germania, with the adventures of Vikings, or with other exotic adventures in foreign lands. The stories take place on the European continent before the settlement of Iceland. Though the existing *fornaldarsǫgur* were written between 1250 and 1350, after the Icelanders' sagas (written between 1200 and 1220), they are thought to be of earlier oral composition. Despite their fantastic content, they are written in a terse, objective style.

The *fornaldarsǫgur* do not have the same literary value as the Icelanders' sagas, but, because they are based on lost heroic poetry, they are of great antiquarian interest. The most important of these is the *Vǫlsunga Saga. Compare* ICELANDERS' SAGAS.

Fortune Theatre \ˈfȯr-chən, ˈfȯr-ˌtyün\ Elizabethan public playhouse in northern London, built in 1600 by Philip Henslowe to compete with Cuthbert Burbage's new Globe Theatre. It was named after the goddess of fortune, whose statue stood over the front doorway. The Fortune resembled the Globe except that it was square and its timbers remained unpainted.

The Fortune opened in 1600 with a performance by the theatrical company known as the Admiral's Men, who continued to use it for many years. After the Puritans closed the public theaters in 1642, the Fortune was used occasionally for clandestine performances. The theater was torn down in 1661.

Forverts \ˈfȯr-ˌverts\, *also called* Jewish Daily Forward. Yiddish-language newspaper founded in 1897 and published in New York City.

The newspaper was established by Abraham Cahan and the Jewish Socialist Press Federation as a civic aid and a unifying device for Jewish immigrants from Europe. From its early days the Forverts strove for variety. It carried socialist-oriented columns on government and politics and covered subjects such as education and etiquette that were intended to familiarize readers with American culture. It included cartoons, letters to the editor, and reports from foreign correspondents. It also published short stories and novels in serial form, most notably those of Isaac Bashevis Singer, as well as current news items. Its reporting occasionally verged on the sensational, and from time to time it carried articles in English.

At the height of its influence, the *Forverts* had a daily circulation of some 200,000 in several regional editions, but by the late 20th century readership was greatly reduced. In 1984 the paper changed from a daily to a weekly, and in 1990 the editors began publishing an English-language version entitled *Forward*.

found poem A poem consisting of words found in a nonpoetic context (such as a product label) and usually broken into lines that convey a verse rhythm. Both the term and the concept are modeled on the *objet trouvé* (French: "found object"), an artifact not created as art or a natural object that is held to have aesthetic value when taken out of its context.

fourteener \ˌfȯr-ˈtē-nər\ A poetic line of 14 syllables; especially, such a line consisting of seven iambic feet. The form is also called a heptameter or septenary. It was used in Greek and Latin prosody and flourished in Elizabethan

English narrative verse but since then has been used only rarely. When each fourteener is written as two lines of eight and six syllables, it becomes the standard ballad meter, as in Samuel Taylor Coleridge's "The Rime of the Ancient Mariner."

fragmentist \'frag-mən-tist\ A writer of a literary fragment.

frame \'frām\ **1.** An event or set of events or circumstances that form the background for the action of a novel or dramatic work. **2.** A literary device used in a story or dramatic work to unite the matter of the story or drama or to provide a plausible excuse for relating or presenting it; especially, such a device that is not essential to the story or dramatic action itself. A work that uses such a device is called a *frame story.*

frame story *also called* frame tale [translation of German *Rahmenerzählung*] Overall unifying story within which one or more tales are related. In the single story, the opening and closing constitutes a frame. In the cyclical frame story—that is, a story in which several tales are related—some frames are externally imposed and only loosely bind the diversified stories. *The Thousand and One Nights,* in which Scheherazade (Shahrazad) avoids death by telling her royal husband a story every night and leaving it incomplete, is an example of a frame story. Other frames are an integral part of the tales, as in Giovanni Boccaccio's *Decameron,* in which a group of 10 people fleeing the Black Death gather in the countryside and as an amusement relate 10 stories each, with a common theme. Another famous example is Geoffrey Chaucer's *The Canterbury Tales,* in which the pilgrimage frame brings together the varied tellers of the tales.

Francien \frä^{n}-'sya^{n}\ [French] The dialect of French used in the Middle Ages in the region of Île-de-France that furnishes the basis for the literary and official form of the modern French language. The French word *francien* was coined in the later 19th century by Romance scholars, there having been no contemporary term in Old French to refer to this dialect.

Frankfurt School \'fräŋk-ˌfürt, *Angl* 'fraŋk-fərt\ Group of German Neo-Marxists associated from the mid-1920s with the Institute of Social Research, which was founded at the University of Frankfurt in 1923. The Frankfurt School's members helped develop western Marxism, which was critical of both moderate socialism and of dogmatic communism. By the 1930s, their initial focus on economics broadened to include such disciplines as literary theory. They viewed literature under capitalism as part of the industry of culture dominated by the existing social order. They searched for revolutionary elements in literature, describing them as reflections of sociopolitical realities.

Notable members of the Frankfurt School included Max Horkheimer, Theodor Adorno, Walter Benjamin, Erich Fromm, Leo Lowenthal, and Herbert Marcuse. The school published the periodical *Zeitschrift für Sozialforschung* ("Journal of Social Research"). With the rise of Nazism in Germany, the Institute of Social Research briefly relocated to Geneva before settling at Columbia

University in New York City by 1934. Although its members began publishing books and journals in English, the institute retained its distance from American Marxists and, in 1951, returned to Frankfurt.

Free Stage *See* FREIE BÜHNE.

free verse Poetry organized to the cadences of speech and image patterns rather than according to a regular metrical scheme. It is "free" only in a relative sense. It does not have the steady, abstract rhythm of traditional poetry, and its rhythms are based on patterned elements such as sounds, words, phrases, sentences, and paragraphs, rather than on the traditional prosodic units of metrical feet per line. Free verse, therefore, eliminates much of the artificiality and some of the aesthetic distance of poetic expression and substitutes a flexible formal organization suited to the modern idiom and more casual tonality of the language.

Although the term is loosely applied to the poetry of Walt Whitman and even earlier experiments with irregular meters, it was originally a literal translation of VERS LIBRE, the name of a movement that originated in France in the 1880s. Free verse became current in English poetics in the early 20th century. The first English-language poets to be influenced by vers libre, notably T.E. Hulme, F.S. Flint, Richard Aldington, Ezra Pound, and T.S. Eliot, were students of French poetry. IMAGISM, a movement started in England in 1912 by Aldington, Pound, Flint, and Hilda Doolittle (H.D.), was concerned with more than versification, but one of its principles was "to compose in sequence of the musical phrase, not in sequence of the metronome." Eliot's early experimentations with free verse (encouraged by Pound) influenced the loosening of formal metrical structures in English poetry. Carl Sandburg, William Carlos Williams, Marianne Moore, and Wallace Stevens all wrote some variety of free verse; the versification of Williams and Moore most closely resembles that of the vers libre poets of France.

Freie Bühne \'frī-ə-'bue̅-nə\ ("Free Stage") Independent theater founded by the critic and director Otto Brahm in 1889 in Berlin for the purpose of staging new, naturalistic plays. The Freie Bühne's first production was of Henrik Ibsen's *Gengangere* (1881"Ghosts") in September 1889. A month later, Brahm staged Gerhart Hauptmann's first play, *Vor Sonnenaufgang* (1889 "Before Daybreak"), a tragedy of working-class people. During the following seasons, Brahm's presentations included an important naturalist drama dealing with a degenerate family, *Die Familie selicke* (1890) by Arno Holz, as well as plays by Leo Tolstoy, Émile Zola, and August Strindberg. Although the Freie Bühne was a success, it lasted for only three seasons, largely because Berlin's commercial theater had by then embraced the new theatrical movement of naturalism. But it inspired the creation of other private theaters and amateur groups in Berlin, Munich, and Vienna.

French Academy *See* ACADÉMIE FRANÇAISE.

Freudian criticism \'frȯi-dē-ən\ Literary criticism that uses the psychoanalytic theory of Sigmund Freud to interpret a work in terms of the known psychological conflicts of its author or, conversely, to construct the author's psychic life from unconscious revelations in his work.

Freud himself examined several literary characters in psychoanalytic terms, for example, Oedipus and Hamlet (in *The Interpretation of Dreams*). The Freudian critics who followed departed from the traditional scope of criticism in reconstructing an author's psychic life on the basis of his or her writings. Edmund Wilson explored this realm in his *The Wound and the Bow* (1941), and Frederick Crews did the same in several works, including *The Sins of the Fathers: Hawthorne's Psychological Themes* (1966). This approach as applied to biography is known as psychobiography, e.g., Van Wyck Brooks' *The Ordeal of Mark Twain* (1920). In addition to literary critics, professional analysts have applied these techniques to literature, notably Ernest Jones in *Hamlet and Oedipus* (1910 and 1949), which traces the famous problem of Hamlet's irresolution back to William Shakespeare's own Oedipal guilt. *See also* PSYCHOANALYTIC CRITICISM.

Freytag's pyramid \'frī-ˌtäks\ A device created by the German writer and critic Gustav Freytag in his book *Die Technik des Dramas* (1863) to illustrate the structure of a typical five-act play. According to Freytag, the typical plot consists of an introduction, rising action that leads to a climax followed by falling action, and finally a catastrophe (or denouement). The climax is positioned at the apex of the pyramid.

frontier humor Vital and exuberant literature that was generated by the westward expansion of the United States in the late 18th and the 19th centuries. The spontaneity, sense of fun, exaggeration, fierce individuality, and irreverence for traditional Eastern values in frontier humor reflected the optimistic spirit of pre-Civil War America. Frontier humor appears mainly in tall tales of exaggerated feats of strength, rough practical jokes (especially on citified Easterners and greenhorns), and tales of encounters with panthers, bears, and snakes. These tales are filled with rough, homely wisdom.

Classic characters of frontier humor include Mike Fink, the semilegendary king of the Mississippi River keelboatmen, Paul Bunyan, hero of the northwestern loggers, and Davy Crockett, an actual historical figure whose *Narrative* (1834) is a combination of tall tales, comic self-portraiture, and humorous proverbs. Representative writers of Southern frontier humor were A.B. Longstreet, Thomas B. Thorpe, Johnson Jones Hooper, and George Washington Harris. Mark Twain represents a culmination of the tradition. *See also* LOCAL COLOR.

fu \'fü\ [Chinese (Beijing dialect) *fù*] Chinese literary form combining elements of poetry and prose. The form developed during the Han dynasty (206 BC–AD 220) from its origins in the long poem *Li sao* ("On Encountering Sorrow") by Qu Yuan (*c.* 343–*c.* 289 BC). It was particularly suitable for description and exposition, in contrast to the more subjective, lyrical *sao*. Its prosody was freer than that of the sao, the rhyme pattern being less restrictive. The elements of the *fu* form include a long line, caesura, and the use of balanced parallel phrases. The use of rhyme removes the fu from the area of pure prose and places it somewhere between poetry and prose.

While some Han writers used the form quite skillfully, it was often abused for purposes of trivial and hackneyed description and was generally characterized by an endless piling up of words. Hundreds of years later, during the Song dynasty (960–1279), the *fu* was enriched by the skill of Ouyang Xiu (1007–72) and Su Dongpo (1036–1101), who made it more prose than poetry and used it to express philosophical concerns.

Fugitive \'fyü-jə-tiv\ Any of a group of young poets and critics formed shortly after World War I at Vanderbilt University in Nashville, Tenn., some of whom later became distinguished men of letters. The group, led by the poet and critic John Crowe Ransom, devoted itself to the writing and discussion of poetry and published a bimonthly magazine, *The Fugitive* (1922–25), edited by poet Allen Tate. Other important members of the group were the poet, essayist, and critic Donald Davidson and the novelist and poet Robert Penn Warren. Outstanding selections from the magazine were collected in the *Fugitive Anthology* (1928).

Acutely aware of their Southern heritage, the Fugitives advocated a form of literary regionalism, concentrating largely on the history and customs of the South in their work. Many of the Fugitives went on to become leaders in the Agrarian movement of the 1930s, which sought to resist the inroads of industrialism by a return to the agricultural economy of the Old South. Their views were published as a symposium in *I'll Take My Stand: The South and the Agrarian Tradition* (1930).

futhark *See* RUNIC WRITING.

Futurism \'fyü-chə-ˌriz əm\, *Italian* Futurismo \ˌfü-tü-'rēz-mō\, *Russian* Futurizm \fü-tü-'rʸēzm\ An artistic movement begun in Italy about 1909 and marked especially by violent rejection of tradition and an effort to give formal expression to the dynamic energy and movement of mechanical processes.

Futurism was first announced on Feb. 20, 1909, when the Paris newspaper *Le Figaro* published a manifesto by Filippo Tommaso Marinetti. The name Futurism, coined by Marinetti, reflected his celebration of change, originality, and innovation in culture and society. The manifesto's rhetoric was passionately bombastic, and its tone was aggressive and inflammatory.

Marinetti also wrote or had a hand in creating a whole series of later manifestos dealing with poetry, the theater, architecture, and other arts. He had founded the journal *Poesia* in Paris in 1905, and he later founded a press with the same name to publish Futurist works. Marinetti traveled to England, France, Germany, and Russia to advance the cause of Futurism. Among those who were influenced by him were Wyndham Lewis, the English founder of Vorticism, and the French poet Guillaume Apollinaire.

Russian Futurism went beyond its Italian model in its revolutionary social and political outlook. Marinetti influenced the two Russian writers considered the founders of Russian Futurism, Velimir Khlebnikov, who remained a poet and a mystic, and the younger Vladimir Mayakovsky, who became "the poet of the Revolution" and the popular spokesman of his generation. The Russians published their own manifesto in December 1912, entitled *Poshchochina obshchestvennomu vkusu* ("A Slap in the Face of Public Taste"). The Russian Futurists repudiated Aleksandr Pushkin, Fyodor Dostoyevsky, and Leo Tolstoy and then-current Russian Symbolist verse and called for the creation of new techniques for writing poetry.

Both the Russian and the Italian Futurist poets discarded logical sentence construction and traditional grammar and syntax; they frequently presented an incoherent string and anarchic blend of words stripped of their meaning and used for their sound alone. As the first group of artists to identify wholeheartedly with the Bolshevik Revolution of 1917, the Russian Futurists were given several important cultural posts. But their challenging literary techniques and their theoretical premises of revolt and innovation proved too unstable a foundation upon which to build a broader literary movement, and their influence was negligible by the time of Mayakovsky's death in 1930.

G

Romantic and gothic elements cannot survive in the sunlit world of sanity.
—Joyce Carol Oates

Gaelic revival \'gāl-ik, 'gal-, 'gäl-\ Resurgence of interest in Irish language, literature, history, and folklore inspired by the growing Irish nationalism of the early 19th century.

With the English military conquest and settlement of Ireland early in the 17th century, Irish became the language of an oppressed people. Schools did not teach the literary language, and no native nobility existed to support Irish writing. By the mid-19th century there was little literary activity, and almost all speakers of Irish were illiterate.

About the same time, translations of heroic tales from ancient Irish manuscripts (e.g., *The Annals of the Four Masters* caught the imagination of the educated classes. Anglo-Irish poets began to write verses with Gaelic patterns and rhythms that echoed the passion and rich imagery of ancient bardic verse. In 1842 the patriotic organization known as Young Ireland founded *The Nation,* a paper that published the works of Thomas Osborne Davis, a master of prose and verse, and of such poets as Thomas D'Arcy McGee, Richard D'Alton Williams, and Speranza (the pseudonym of Lady Wilde, mother of Oscar Wilde). The *Dublin University Magazine* (1833–80), another important literary publication, often included the work of James Clarence Mangan, who translated Gaelic poems into English and also wrote original verse in the Gaelic style. Other poets involved in some aspect of the Gaelic revival were Jeremiah John Callanan and Sir Samuel Ferguson. Thomas Moore, Charles Maturin, and Maria Edgeworth also incorporated Irish themes from earlier Gaelic works into their writings.

The Gaelic revival laid the scholarly and nationalistic groundwork for the IRISH LITERARY RENAISSANCE, the great flowering of Irish literary talent at the end of the 19th and beginning of the 20th century.

gai saber \'gī-sȧ-'ber\ or **gay science** The art of composing love poetry; especially the art of the Provençal troubadours as set forth in a 14th-century work called the *Leys d'amors*. The Old Provençal phrase *gai saber* ("gay knowledge" or "gay science") is associated with the *Consistòri del Gai Saber,* originally the *Sobregaya compannia dels VII Trobadors de Tolosa* ("Very Gay Company of the Seven Troubadours of Toulouse"), a group of seven citizens of Toulouse who in 1323 organized yearly competitions to encourage troubadour poetry, by then in serious decline.

galliambic \\ˌgal-ē-ˈam-bik\\ [Latin *galliambus* galliambic meter, from *gallus* priest of Cybele + *iambus* iamb] In classical prosody, consisting of four Ionic feet, each consisting of two accented and two unaccented syllables. The last of the feet is catalectic (incomplete or truncated). The galliambic meter is scanned as ∪ ∪ ∪̲ – | ∪̲ ∪̲ – – ‖ ∪ ∪ – ∪̲ | ∪̲ ∪ –, with a diaeresis after the second foot. Some of the feet may be varied by resolution (substitution of one long syllable for two short ones) and contraction (the substitution of two short for one long syllable). The meter was named for the priests known as the *galli* because it reproduced the rhythm of their chants during the worship of Cybele, Great Mother of the Gods. It was used occasionally by Hellenistic Greek poets and, in Latin, by the Roman poet Catullus, who usually altered it to scan as ∪ ∪ – ∪ | – ∪ – – ‖ ∪ ∪ – – | ∪ ∪ –.

gasal *See* GHAZEL.

gathering \\ˈgath-ə-riŋ *also* ˈgeth- *or* ˈgäth-\\ **1.** A collection (as of money for charity) or compilation (as of literary fragments). **2.** In printing, the process of collecting together signatures (groups of pages created by folding a single printer's sheet a certain number of times) to be bound into a book. The term is sometimes used in reference to the signature itself.

gaucho literature \\ˈgau̇-chō\\ Latin-American poetic genre that imitates the *payadas* ("ballads") traditionally sung to guitar accompaniment by the wandering gaucho minstrels of Argentina and Uruguay. By extension, the term includes the body of Latin-American literature that treats the gaucho way of life and philosophy. Long a part of Latin-American folk literature, gaucho lore became the subject of some of the best verse of the 19th-century Romantic period. The gaucho's story found its highest poetic expression in Rafael Obligado's poems (1887) on the legendary gaucho minstrel Santos Vega. The gaucho was humorously portrayed in the mock epic *Fausto* (1866) by Estanislao del Campo. Later the gaucho aroused the national conscience and received epic treatment in the classic poem *El gaucho Martín Fierro* (1872) by José Hernández.

In prose the first serious use of gaucho lore was made by Domingo Faustino Sarmiento in *Civilización y barbarie: vida de Juan Facundo Quiroga, y aspecto físico, costumbres, y hábitos de la República Argentina* (1845; *Life in the Argentine Republic in the Days of the Tyrants; or, Civilization and Barbarism*), a classic account of the cultural clash between the Pampas and the civilizing forces of the city. This theme of conflict between old and new informs a rich literature that ranges from the somber descriptive short stories of Uruguay's Javier de Viana and the keen psychological portrayal of rural types in Carlos Reyles' *El terruño* (1916; "The Native Soil") to the simple humorous narrative of *El inglés de los güesos* (1924; "The Englishman of the Bones") by Argentina's Benito Lynch, and the image-studded, evocative prose epic of the gaucho *Don Segundo Sombra* (1926) by the Argentine Ricardo Güiraldes. In *Doña Bárbara* (1929),

Rómulo Gallegos, one of Latin America's masters of plot technique, gave a dramatic and poetic depiction of similar forces at work on the Venezuelan Llanos.

gayatri \ˈgä-yə-ˌtrē\ [Sanskrit *gāyatrī,* a derivative of *gāyatra* song, hymn] **1.** An ancient Vedic meter of 24 syllables generally arranged in a triplet, or three-line verse. **2.** A composition in this meter (such as the noted Hindu Gayatri mantra used daily by the devout).

gay science *See* GAI SABER.

gazel *See* GHAZEL.

Gelosi \jā-ˈlō-sē\ (*in full* Compagnia dei Gelosi \kȯm-ˈpä-nyä-ˌdā-\). One of the earliest and most famous of the commedia dell'arte companies of 16th-century Italy. The name was derived from the troupe's motto, *Virtù, fama ed honor ne fèr gelosi* ("Virtue, fame, and honor make us jealous").

gender studies A field of criticism that studies the influence, conscious or unconscious, of gender upon works of art. It emerged in the mid-1980s as a development of feminist criticism. The principal influence upon gender studies was the publication in 1976 of the first volume of Michel Foucault's *Histoire de la sexualité* (*The History of Sexuality*), which delineates the differences between sex and gender. Although an individual's sex in itself may have little relevance in a work of art, gender—that person's socialization or experience as male or female—may determine his or her responses and choices. Gender studies is a heterogenous field, including advances in feminist criticism, men's studies that use the innovations of women's studies, and certain gay and lesbian studies.

Generación del 1898 or **Generación del '98** or **Generation of 1898** *See* GENERATION OF '98.

Generation of 1927 *Spanish* Generación del 1927. Group of Spanish writers, chiefly poets, who rose to prominence in the late 1920s and who derived their collective name from the year in which several of them produced important commemorative editions of the poetry of Luis de Góngora on the tercentenary of his death.

Chief among the members of the Generation of 1927 were Federico García Lorca, Rafael Alberti, Jorge Guillén, Vicente Aleixandre, Luis Cernuda, Pedro Salinas, Gerardo Diego, and Dámaso Alonso. Generally speaking, they were influenced by Symbolism, Futurism, and Surrealism, and they helped introduce the tenets of these movements into Spanish literature. They rejected the use of traditional meter and rhyme and discarded anecdotal treatment and strictly logical descriptions in their poems. Instead, they made frequent and audacious use of metaphor, coined new words, and introduced highly symbolic or suggestive images into their poems in an effort to convey aspects of inner personal experience. They also drew on ballads, traditional songs and lyrics, and on Góngora's poetry itself for subject matter.

Although they differed in individual style and concerns, the poets of the Generation of 1927 formed what can be considered the dominant trend in

Spanish poetry during the 1920s, '30s, and early '40s. After the Spanish Civil War (1936–39), Spanish poetry turned away from their highly cultivated and abstruse aestheticism.

Generation of '98 *also called* Generation of 1898, *Spanish* Generación del '98 *or* Generación del 1898. In Spain, the novelists, poets, essayists, and thinkers active at the time of the Spanish-American War (1898) who reinvigorated Spanish letters and restored Spain to a position of intellectual and literary prominence that it had not held for centuries.

The shock of Spain's defeat in the war provided an impetus for many writers and thinkers to embark on a period of self-searching. The term Generation of '98 was used loosely at the turn of the century but was elaborated on by the literary critic Azorín in critical essays that appeared in various periodicals and were collected in his *Clásicos y modernos* (1913). It was soon generally applied to the writers who concerned themselves with Spain's heritage and its position in the modern world. Never an organized movement or school, the Generation of '98 had no representative form or style, but all associated with it desired to restore a sense of national pride.

Joaquín Costa, Ángel Ganivet, and Miguel de Unamuno are generally considered precursors of the Generation of '98, but many literary historians consider Ganivet and, usually, Unamuno as members of the group proper. Other outstanding figures were Azorín himself, the philosopher and critic José Ortega y Gasset, the novelists Pío Baroja, Vicente Blasco Ibáñez, and Ramón María del Valle-Inclán, and the poets Antonio Machado and Manuel Machado. In their revitalization of Spanish letters, they brought a new seriousness of purpose to the Spanish novel and elevated the essay—critical, psychological, and philosophical—to a position of literary importance.

género chico \'k̲ā-nā-rō-'chē-kō\ [Spanish, literally, little genre] Spanish literary genre of light dramatic or operatic one-act playlets, as contrasted with the *género grande* of serious drama or opera. Developed primarily in the theaters of Madrid during the late 19th century, *género chico* works usually dealt with Madrid's lower classes, whose way of life was regarded with mingled sentimentality and satiric humor. Carlos Arniches, Ricardo de la Vega, and Tomás Luceño were the chief writers in the genre.

Geneva school \jə-'nē-və\, *French* École de Genève \ā-kȯl-də-zhə-'nev\ A group of critics whose response to literature and approaches to criticism began to be defined in the 1930s. Emphasizing the individual consciousness of the writer, the various members of the Geneva school examined an author's entire body of work as a means of getting at the person's vision of his own self and the world. Their philosophy was in direct opposition to the strictly textual examination that was popular in such objectivist schools as New Criticism.

The first critics to use this phenomenological approach were Marcel Raymond, Albert Béguin, and Georges Poulet, who were friends and correspondents. The second generation of Geneva school critics included Jean Starobinski,

Jean Rousset, and Jean-Pierre Richard. Although they addressed the objects of their critical study in quite different ways and often used language differently, members of the Geneva school shared a belief in the text as experienced from the inside.

genre \'zhän-rə, 'zhä^{n}r, 'jän-rə\ [French, kind, sort] A distinctive type or category of literary composition, such as the epic, tragedy, comedy, novel, and short story.

Despite critics' attempts to systematize the art of literature, such categories must retain a degree of flexibility, for they can break down on closer scrutiny. For example, hybrid forms such as the tragicomedy and prose poem are possible. Newly created forms, such as Vikram Seth's *The Golden Gate* (a novel written in rhyming verse form) and John Fuller's *Flying to Nowhere* (a novel written in highly poetic prose), and numerous prose works of intermediate or very specific length (such as the novella and the short-short) are a clear indication of the difficulty of too close a reliance on genre as a category.

genteel comedy Early 18th-century subgenre of the comedy of manners that reflected the behavior of the British upper class. Contrasted with Restoration comedy, the genteel comedy was somewhat artificial and sentimental. Colley Cibber's play *The Careless Husband* is an example of the type.

Gentleman's Magazine, The Popular English periodical that was published for nearly two centuries (1731–1907). It gave the name *magazine* to its genre. The first general periodical in England, it was founded by Edward Cave as a storehouse, or magazine, of essays and articles culled from other publications, often from books and pamphlets; the magazine's motto—"E pluribus unum"—took note of the numerous sources scoured to assemble one monthly issue. Samuel Johnson joined *The Gentleman's Magazine* in 1738, and a short time later it began to publish parliamentary reports and original writing.

gentry \'jen-trē\ In parts of Ireland, a collective name for the fairies, comparable to "good folk" or "good people" denoting the fairies elsewhere in the British Isles.

Georgian poetry Any of a number of lyrical poems produced in the early 20th century by an assortment of British poets, including Lascelles Abercrombie, Hilaire Belloc, Edmund Charles Blunden, Rupert Brooke, William Henry Davies, John Drinkwater, James Elroy Flecker, Ralph Hodgson, Wilfred Wilson Gibson, Robert Graves, Walter de la Mare, Harold Monro (editor of *The Poetry Review*), Siegfried Sassoon, Sir J.C. Squire, and Edward Thomas.

Brooke and Sir Edward Marsh felt a need to make new poetry more accessible to the public, and with Monro, Drinkwater, and Gibson they planned a series of anthologies, applying the name "Georgian" to suggest the opening of a new poetic age with the accession (1910) of George V. Five volumes of *Georgian Poetry,* edited by Marsh, were published between 1912 and 1922.

The real gifts of Brooke, Davies, de la Mare, Blunden, and Hodgson should not be overlooked, but, taken as a whole, much of the Georgians' work was lifeless. It took inspiration from the countryside and nature, and in the hands of less gifted poets, the resulting poetry was diluted and middlebrow conventional verse of late Romantic character. "Georgian" came to be a pejorative term, used in a sense not intended by its progenitors: rooted in its period and looking backward rather than forward.

georgic \ˈjȯr-jik\ A poem dealing with practical aspects of agriculture and rural affairs. The model for such verse in postclassical literature was Virgil's *Georgica,* itself modeled on a now lost *Geōrgika* (Greek: "agricultural things") by the 2nd-century-BC Greek poet Nicander of Colophon.

gesaku \gā-ˈsä-kü\ [Japanese] Popular Japanese fiction written between approximately the 1770s to about the late 19th century. It was characterized by a flippant tone and a certain erudition. Initially the writers of *gesaku* (called *gesakusha*) were typically sophisticated, educated men who were familiar with popular Chinese literature. They engaged in wordplay and wrote light, rather gossipy stories of events in entertainment quarters. They usually kept their *gesaku* separate from their serious (i.e., nonfiction) writing. Hiraga Gennai is generally acknowledged as the founder of the movement.

Later *gesakusha* were largely motivated by profit. They aimed at as wide a public as possible and followed a successful book with as many sequels as the public would accept. Among the distinct genres within *gesaku* are the humorous books called *sharebon* ("witty books") and *kokkeibon* ("funny books"); the love stories, or *ninjōbon;* the nonillustrated volumes, or *yomihon* ("reading books"); and the illustrated books, or *kibyōshi* ("yellow covers").

Shunshoku umegoyomi (1832–33; "Spring Colors: The Plum Calendar") by Tamenaga Shunsui is the story of Tanjirō, a peerlessly handsome but ineffectual young man who is pursued by a variety of women. The author at one point defended himself against charges of immorality: "Even though the women I portray may seem immoral, they are all imbued with deep sentiments of chastity and fidelity."

gest or **geste** \ˈjest\ [Old French *geste, jeste* narrative, tale, deed, exploit, from Latin *gesta* (plural) deeds, exploits] A story of achievements or adventures. Among several famous medieval collections of gests are Fulcher of Chartres' *Gesta Francorum,* Saxo Grammaticus' *Gesta Danorum,* and the compilation known as the *Gesta Romanorum*. The term was also used to refer to a romance in verse.

ghazel *also spelled* ghazal, gazel, gasal, *or* ghasel \ˈgaz-al, -el; ˈgäz-əl; ˈg̅ȧ-zȧl\ [Arabic *ghazal*] In Islāmic literature, a lyric poem, generally short and graceful in form and typically dealing with themes of love.

As a genre the ghazel developed in Arabia in the late 7th century from the *nasib,* which itself was an often amorous prelude to the qasida (ode). The poems begin with a rhymed couplet whose rhyme is repeated in all subsequent even lines. The odd lines are unrhymed. The two main types of ghazel are native to Hejaz and Iraq.

The ghazels by ʿUmar ibn Abī Rabīʿah (died 712/719) of the Quraysh tribe of Mecca are some of the oldest. ʿUmar's poems, based largely on his own life and experiences, are realistic, lively, and urbane in character. They continue to be popular with modern readers.

What became a classic theme of the ghazel was introduced by Jamīl (died 701), a member of the ʿUdhrah tribe from Hejaz. Jamīl's lyrics tell of hopeless, idealistic lovers pining for each other unto death. These enormously popular works were imitated not only in Arabic but also in Persian, Turkish, and Urdu poetry until the 18th century.

Of additional note is the work of Ḥāfeẓ (also spelled Ḥāfiz; died 1389/90), considered among the finest lyric poets of Persia, whose depth of imagery and multilayered metaphors revitalized and perfected the genre. The form was introduced to Western literature by German Romantics, notably Friedrich von Schlegel and J.W. von Goethe.

ghost story A tale about ghosts. More generally, the phrase may refer to a tale based on imagination rather than fact. Ghost stories exist in all kinds of literature, from folktales to religious works to modern horror stories, and in most cultures. They can be used as isolated episodes or interpolated stories within a larger narrative, as in Lucius Apuleius' *The Golden Ass,* Geoffrey Chaucer's "The Nun's Priest's Tale," William Shakespeare's *Hamlet,* and many Renaissance plays and gothic novels, or they can be the main focus of a work, such as the stories of Sheridan Le Fanu's *In a Glass Darkly,* Henry James' novella *The Turn of the Screw* and Kingsley Amis' novel *The Green Man.*

ghostwriter \ˈgōst-ˌrī-tər\ One who writes for and in the name of another.

Gids, De \də-ˈk̲its\ ("The Guide") Dutch literary journal, published from 1837, that encouraged an emerging national consciousness in The Netherlands. It flourished under the early leadership of Everhardus Johannes Potgieter, whose sharp criticism was often moralistic. Potgieter was coeditor with R.C. Bakhuizen van den Brink in 1838–43 and with Conrad Busken Huet in 1863–65. Printed with a blue cover, *De Gids* was known as *de blauwe beul* ("the blue butcher") for its merciless treatment of complacency, but by the late 19th century it was regarded as a traditionalist magazine. Among the contemporary writers published in *De Gids* were Martinus Nijhoff, Herman Teirlinck, and Karel van de Woestijne.

giftbook \ˈgift-ˌbu̇k\, *also called* annual *or* keepsake. An illustrated literary miscellany, or collection of verse, tales, and sketches. The giftbook was popular in England and the United States during the second quarter of the 19th century and was published annually in ornamental format.

Gilded Age Period of gross materialism and blatant political corruption in American history during the 1870s that gave rise to important novels of social and political criticism. The period takes its name from the earliest of these, *The Gilded Age* (1873), written by Mark Twain in collaboration with

Charles Dudley Warner. The novel gives a vivid and accurate description of Washington, D.C., and is peopled with caricatures of many leading figures of the day, including greedy industrialists and corrupt politicians. Twain's satire was followed in 1880 by *Democracy,* a political novel published anonymously by the historian Henry Adams. Adams' book deals with a dishonest Midwestern senator and suggests that the real source of corruption lies in the unprincipled attitudes of the wild and lawless West. *An American Politician,* by F. Marion Crawford (1884), another product of the period, focuses upon the disputed election of President Rutherford B. Hayes in 1876, but its significance as a political novel was diluted by an overdose of popular romance.

The political novels of the Gilded Age represent the beginnings of a new strain in American literature, the novel as a vehicle of social protest. The trend grew in the late 19th and early 20th centuries with the works of the muckrakers and culminated in the proletarian novelists.

gleeman \'glē-ˌman\ [Old English *glēoman,* from *glēo* entertainment, music + *man* man] In Anglo-Saxon times, a professional traveling entertainer who recited poetry to the accompaniment of musical instruments such as the harp. The gleemen sometimes wrote their own poetry, but often the poetry they recited had been written by a scop (a poet attached to a particular court).

Globe Theatre \'glōb\ Famous London theater in which the plays of William Shakespeare were performed after 1599. It was built by two brothers, Richard and Cuthbert Burbage, who owned its predecessor, The Theatre. Half the shares in the new theater were kept by the Burbages. The rest were assigned equally to Shakespeare and other members of the CHAMBERLAIN'S MEN (the company of players who acted there), of which Richard Burbage was principal actor and of which Shakespeare had been a leading member since late 1594. The theater was destroyed by fire in 1613, rebuilt in 1614, and finally pulled down in 1644. Information about the physical arrangement of the Globe is largely a matter of conjecture. It is thought to have been cylindrical in shape, with a thatched gallery roof. It is known that the Fortune Theatre, built in 1600 for a rival company, the Admiral's Men, was modeled on the Globe.

In 1613, during a performance of Henry VIII, the thatch of the Globe was accidentally set alight by a cannon, set off to mark Henry's entrance onstage in a scene at Cardinal Wolsey's palace. The entire theater was destroyed within the hour. By June 1614 it had been rebuilt, this time with a tiled gallery roof and a circular shape. It was pulled down in 1644, two years after the Puritans had closed all theaters, in order to make way for tenement dwellings.

glosa \'glō-sə\ [Spanish, literally, gloss] Spanish verse form in which an introductory stanza called a *cabeza* is followed by one stanza for each line of the *cabeza,* in which the line is explained or glossed. The form was instituted by court poets of the 14th or 15th century.

gloss \'glȯs\ [Greek *glôssa* difficult word requiring explanation, language, tongue] **1.** A translation or a brief explanation or definition of a textual word or expression felt to be difficult or obscure. Glosses can appear in the margin or between the lines of a text or in a separate vocabulary book based on the text. For example, ancient Greek manuscripts were often published with Latin translations of difficult words provided by the Latin copyists, and medieval manuscripts often included vernacular translations of Latin words that were added by the scribes copying the manuscripts. **2.** An expanded interpretation of or commentary on a textual word, expression, or passage.

glyconic \glī-'kän-ik\ [Greek *Glykṓneus,* a derivative of *Glykṓn,* Greek poet of unknown date] The most common Aeolic verse form used for Greek and Latin lyric poetry and named for the Greek poet Glycon, about whom little is known. The glyconic is usually scanned as ⏓ ⏓ | – ⏑ ⏑ – | ⏓ –. The catalectic form (⏓ ⏓ | – ⏑ ⏑ – | –) is known as a pherecratic. The glyconic was sometimes extended by adding a dactyl (– ⏑ ⏑), a cretic (– ⏑ –), or a choriamb (– ⏑ ⏑ –) at the beginning, middle, or end. The result, used, for example, by Sappho and Alcaeus, was called *Asclepiadean* and was scanned ⏓ ⏓ | – ⏑ ⏑ – – ⏑ ⏑ – | ⏓ – or ⏓ ⏓ | – ⏑ ⏑ – – ⏑ ⏑ – – ⏑ ⏑ – | ⏓ –.

gnome \'nōm, 'nō-ˌmē\ *plural* gnomes *or* gnomae \'nō-ˌmē, -ˌmī\ [Greek *gnṓmē* thought, opinion, maxim] A brief reflection or maxim such as an APHORISM or PROVERB.

The form of such statements may be either imperative, as in the famous command "know thyself," or indicative, as in the English adage "Too many cooks spoil the broth." Gnomes are found in the literature of many cultures; among the best-known examples are those contained in the biblical book of Proverbs. They are found in early Greek literature, both poetry and prose, from the time of Homer and Hesiod onward.

Gnomes appear frequently in Old English epic and lyric poetry. In *Beowulf* they are often interjected into the narrative, drawing a moral from the hero's actions with such phrases as "Thus a man ought to act." The main collections of Old English gnomes are to be found in the Exeter Book and the 11th-century Cotton Psalter.

gnomic \'nō-mik\ [Greek *gnōmikós,* a derivative of *gnṓmē* maxim] **1.** Characterized by or expressive of aphorism or sententious wisdom, especially concerning the human condition or human conduct. **2.** Of a poet, given to the composition of gnomic poetry.

gnomic poetry Aphoristic verse containing short, memorable statements of traditional wisdom and morality. Gnomic poetry is most commonly associated with the 6th-century-BC poets Solon and Simonides and with the elegiac couplets of Theognis and Phocylides. Their aphorisms were collected into anthologies, called *gnomologia* (or gnomologies), and used in instructing the young. One of the best-known *gnomologia* was compiled by Stobaeus in the 5th century AD, and such collections remained popular in the Middle Ages.

Alexander Pope's *An Essay on Man* (1733–34) offers a more modern example of the use of couplets of distilled wisdom interspersed throughout a long poem.

gobbet \'gäb-ət\ A fragment or extract of literature or music.

Godey's Lady's Book \'gō-dē\ A magazine that was one of the most successful and influential periodicals in the United States for much of the 19th century. Founded by Louis Antoine Godey in Philadelphia in 1830, *Godey's Lady's Book* was an important arbiter of fashion and etiquette, the result in great measure of its articles on fashions and its hand-colored fashion plates and copper engravings. The magazine also published works by such American authors as Ralph Waldo Emerson, Henry Wadsworth Longfellow, Edgar Allan Poe, Nathaniel Hawthorne, and Harriet Beecher Stowe as well as stories and verses by less well-known writers who more closely appealed to didactic Victorian sensibilities.

Edited by Godey until 1836, the magazine was then edited by Sarah Josepha Hale until 1877. In its heyday, *Godey's Lady's Book* was said to have been read by 40,000 households. *Peterson's Magazine,* a rival Philadelphia publication, eventually eclipsed *Godey's* in popularity. In 1892, *Godey's* was moved to New York City and renamed *Godey's Magazine*. It published fiction by popular writers of the period until it ceased publication in 1898.

Golden Age In Latin literature, the period, from approximately 70 BC to AD 18, that was a time of literary achievement during which the Latin language was brought to perfection as a literary medium and many classical Latin masterpieces were composed. The Golden Age can be subdivided into the CICERONIAN PERIOD (70–43 BC), dominated by Marcus Tullius Cicero, and the AUGUSTAN AGE (43 BC–AD 18), a period of mature literary achievements by such writers as Virgil, Horace, and Livy. *See also* SILVER AGE.

Golden Age ("Siglo de Oro") The period from the early 16th century to the late 17th century, generally considered the high point in Spain's literary history. The Golden Age began with the political unification of Spain about 1500, and its literature is characterized by patriotic and religious fervor, heightened realism, and a new interest in earlier epics and ballads.

During the Golden Age such forms as the chivalric and pastoral novels underwent their final flowering. They were replaced by the PICARESQUE NOVEL, which usually described the comic adventures of low-born rogues, and which was exemplified by the anonymous *Lazarillo de Tormes* (1554) and by the works of Mateo Alemán and Francisco Gómez de Quevedo. The monumental novel *Don Quixote* (Part I, 1605; Part II, 1615) by Miguel de Cervantes is a satirical treatment of anachronistic chivalric ideals, combining pastoral, picaresque, and romantic elements in its narrative; it remains the single most important literary work produced during the Golden Age. Poetry during the period was initially marked by the adoption of Italian meters and verse forms such as those used by Garcilaso de la Vega. Eventually it was characterized by the elaborate conceits and wordplay of the Baroque movements known as CULTERANISMO and CONCEPTISMO, whose chief practitioners were Luis de Góngora and Quevedo, respectively. The Golden Age also witnessed the almost single-handed creation of the Spanish national theater by the prolific playwright Lope de Vega. The Spanish dramatic tradition he established using characteristically Spanish themes, values, and subject matter was further developed by Tirso de Molina and by Pedro Calderón. The end of the Golden Age is marked by Calderón's death in 1681.

goliard \ˈgōl-yərd, -ˌyärd\ [Medieval Latin *goliardus,* from Old French *golias, gouliart* gourmand, glutton, riotous liver, perhaps ultimately from a Germanic verb akin to Middle High German *goln* to shout, jest, behave unrestrainedly, Gothic *goljan* to greet; influenced in sense by association with Old French *gole* throat, gluttony] Any of the wandering students and clerics in medieval England, France, and Germany, remembered for their satirical verses and poems in praise of debauchery. The goliards described themselves as followers of the legendary Bishop Golias; they were renegade clerics of no fixed abode who were chiefly interested in riotous living. Of the identifiable poets, Hugh Primas of Orléans, Pierre of Blois, Gautier of Châtillon, and Phillipe the Chancellor all became important establishment figures and to some extent outgrew their student high spirits. Only the goliard known as the Archpoet seems to have lived what he preached to the end of his life.

Goliard satires were almost uniformly directed against the church and the pope. In 1227 the Council of Trier forbade priests to permit goliards to take part in chanting the service. In 1229 they played a conspicuous part in disturbances at the University of Paris in connection with the intrigues of the papal legate; in 1289 it was ordered that no cleric should be a goliard, and in 1300 (at Cologne) they were forbidden to preach or to grant indulgences. Finally after several further decrees the privileges of clergy were finally withdrawn from the goliards.

The word *goliard* eventually lost its clerical association, passing into French and English literature of the 14th century in the general meaning of jongleur, or minstrel (its meaning in *Piers Plowman* and in Geoffrey Chaucer's works).

A remarkable collection of the goliards' Latin poems and songs in praise of wine and riotous living was published in the late 19th century under the title *Carmina Burana,* taken from the 13th-century manuscript of that title at Munich. Many of the works were translated by John Addington Symonds as *Wine, Women, and Song* (1884). The collection also includes the only two complete surviving texts of medieval Passion dramas—one with and one without music. In 1937 the German composer Carl Orff based his scenic oratorio *Carmina Burana* on these poems and songs. Many of them are also to be found in the important *Cambridge Songbook* written in England some 200 years earlier.

The subject matter of the goliard poems includes political and religious satire, love songs of an unusual directness, and songs of drinking and carousing. The last category involves the most characteristically goliardic elements: the plaints of unfrocked clergy, a homeless scholar's learned cries of self-pity, the unashamed panegyrics of hedonism, and the dauntless denials of Christian ethics.

It is this last category for which a small trace of written music survives. Present knowledge of medieval poetry and music suggests that all the poems were intended for singing, even though only a few are provided with music in the manuscripts. In musical style the amorous songs are similar to those of the trouvères; in several cases the same melody appears in both repertories. The more goliardic songs have a simpler metrical form, more syllabic melodies, and an unsophisticated repetitive style. *Compare* JONGLEUR; TROUVÈRE.

gongorismo \ˌgōŋ-gō-ˈrēz-mō\ or **Gongorism** \ˈgȯŋ-gə-ˌriz-əm\ Spanish literary style named for Luis de Góngora, whose poetry exhibited the characteristic features of *culteranismo*—the re-Latinizing of poetic language and themes and the use of classical allusion, syntax, and vocabulary—to their limits. His highly ornate rhetorical style was imitated by lesser poets, and *gongorismo* came to mean obscurant poetry chiefly notable for its literary affectation.

good-night \ˈgu̇d-ˈnīt\ Sensational type of BROADSIDE BALLAD, popular in England from the 16th through the 19th century, purporting to be the farewell statement of a criminal made shortly before his execution. Good-nights are usually repentant in tone, containing a sketchy account of how the criminal first went astray, a detailed account of his grisly crime, his sentence by the judge, the grief of his aged parents, and a warning to others not to follow his example. An exception is "Sam Hall," in which the remorseless criminal boasts, "I hate you one and all," to the bitter end. Enterprising hack writers and broadside publishers often had the good-night printed in advance of the execution, ready for sale on the street (or at the scaffold if the execution were public) at the moment it was accomplished. Many good-nights, originating in broadsides, have been incorporated into the folk tradition.

gothic \ˈgäth-ik\ **1.** Of or relating to a late 18th- and early 19th-century style of fiction characterized by the use of medieval settings, a murky atmosphere of horror and gloom, and macabre, mysterious, and violent incidents. **2.** Of or relating to a literary style or an example of such style characterized by grotesque, macabre, or fantastic incidents or by an atmosphere of irrational violence, desolation, and decay. In the mid-20th century, the term SOUTHERN GOTHIC was used to describe such a style as it was adapted by several writers of the American

South to portray their vision of the South at that time. The word is sometimes capitalized.

gothic novel European Romantic, pseudomedieval fiction having a prevailing atmosphere of mystery and terror. Its heyday was the 1790s, but it was frequently revived thereafter. Called gothic because its imaginative impulse was drawn from the rough and primitive grandeur of medieval buildings and ruins, such novels were expected to be dark and tempestuous and full of ghosts, madness, outrage, superstition, and revenge. The settings were often castles or monasteries equipped with subterranean passages, dark battlements, hidden panels, and trapdoors. The vogue was initiated in England by Horace Walpole's immensely successful *Castle of Otranto* (1765). His most respectable follower was Ann Radcliffe, whose *The Mysteries of Udolpho* (1794) and *The Italian* (1797) are among the best examples of the genre. A more sensational type of gothic romance exploiting horror and violence flourished in Germany and was introduced to England by Matthew Gregory Lewis with *The Monk* (1796). Other landmarks of gothic fiction are William Beckford's Oriental romance *Vathek* (1786) and Charles Robert Maturin's story of an Irish Faust, *Melmoth the Wanderer* (1820). The classic horror stories *Frankenstein* (1818), by Mary Wollstonecraft Shelley, and *Dracula* (1897), by Bram Stoker, are written in the gothic tradition but without the specifically gothic trappings.

Easy targets for satire, the early gothic romances died of their own extravagances of plot, but gothic elements continued to haunt the fiction of such major writers as the Brontë sisters, Edgar Allan Poe, and Nathaniel Hawthorne, as well as many modern horror stories. A good deal of early science fiction, like H.G. Wells' *The Island of Doctor Moreau* (1896), also seems to spring out of the gothic movement, and the gothic atmosphere was seriously cultivated in England in the later novels of Dame Iris Murdoch and beginning in 1946 in the Gormenghast sequence of Mervyn Peake. In the second half of the 20th century, the term was applied to paperback romances having themes and trappings similar to the original gothic novels; perhaps the paperback romance's formulaic approach to plot and effect more nearly matches the originals than any of the genres that were more subtly influenced.

Göttinger Hain \'gœt-iŋ-ər-'hīn\ ("Göttingen Grove"), *also called* Göttinger Hainbund \'hīn-ˌbünt\ ("Göttingen Grove Group") A literary association of the era of German "sentimentality" (about 1740 to 1780) that is credited with the reawakening of homely, folk, and nature themes in German lyric and popular national poetry. Members were the young poets—mostly students at the university at Göttingen—H.C. Boie, J.H. Voss, Ludwig Hölty, J.F. Hahn, K.F. Cramer, Friedrich and Christian Stolberg, and J.A. Leisewitz.

Founded in 1772, the group took its name from Friedrich Gottlieb Klopstock's ode *Der Hügel und der Hain* ("The Hill and the Grove"), in which the grove is metaphorically the abode of the German bards, in contrast to the hill as home of the Greek Parnassians, an opposition the Hain felt aptly symbolized their poetic goals. The *Göttinger Musenalmanach* ("Göttingen Muses

Journal"), published from 1770, became the literary organ for the circle and the archetype for many similar German literary journals.

The poets of the Göttinger Hain had in common a desire to free poetry from the confines of the rationalism of the Enlightenment and from social convention; they attempted to make poetry free from foreign, especially French, examples. They idealized Klopstock and attempted to embody in their work a dynamic enthusiasm for the spirit in his poetry. Their ideals were nationalistic, religious, and ethical. The group disbanded after 1774.

gracioso \ˌgrä-thē-ˈō-sō, -sē-\ [Spanish, from *gracioso* (adjective) amusing, comical] A buffoon in Spanish comedy.

gradus \ˈgrād-əs, ˈgrad-\ A dictionary of Greek or Latin prosody and poetic phrases used as an aid in the writing of verse in Greek or Latin. The term is derived from the *Gradus ad Parnassum* ("A Step to Parnassus"), a 17th-century prosody dictionary long used in British schools.

graffito \grə-ˈfē-tō\ *plural* graffiti \-tē\ [Italian, incised inscription, a derivative of *graffiare* to scratch] Any casual writing, rude drawing, or marking on the walls of buildings, as distinguished from a deliberate writing known as an inscription. Centuries-old graffiti, either scratched on stone or plaster by a sharp instrument or, more rarely, written in red chalk or black charcoal, have been found in great abundance, e.g., on the monuments of ancient Egypt. The subject matter of the scribblings includes scrawls, rude caricatures, election addresses, and lines of poetry. Apparently, private owners of property felt the nuisance of the defacement of their walls, for in Rome near the Porta Portese (formerly Porta Portuensis) was found an inscription begging persons not to scribble (*scariphare*) on the walls.

Graffiti are important to the paleographer because they illustrate the forms and corruptions of the various alphabets used by the people and thus may guide the archaeologist to the date of a building. Their chief value, however, is twofold. First, they are important to the linguist since the language of graffiti is closer to the spoken language of the period and place than usual written language. The linguist also learns about other languages, as in the case of the ancient Greek mercenaries who scribbled their names in the Cypriote dialect and syllabary, on an Egyptian sphinx, or the Greek "tourist" from Pamphylia who carved his name on the great pyramid at Giza. Second, graffiti are invaluable to the historian for the light they throw on the everyday life of the period and on intimate details of customs and institutions. The graffiti dealing with the gladiatorial shows at Pompeii are in this respect particularly noteworthy.

The most famous graffito is that generally accepted as representing a caricature of Christ upon the cross found on the walls of the Domus Gelotiana on the Palatine in Rome in 1857 (now in the Luigi Pigorini Museum of Prehistoric Ethnography of the Roman College).

In some ways graffiti may be thought of as a form of folk art. Twentieth-century preoccupation with the accidental and other manifestations of the unconscious has stimulated an interest in this form of self-expression, and the techniques and content of graffiti have influenced several contemporary artists. Graffiti achieved a notorious prominence in New York City in the late 20th century. Large, elaborate, and multicoloured graffiti created with spray paint on building walls and subway cars were both hailed as an innovative art form by aesthetes and condemned as a nuisance by the general public.

Grand Guignol \grän-gē-ˈnyōl\ Short plays emphasizing violence, horror, and sadism, popular in Parisian cabarets in the 19th century, especially at the Théâtre du Grand Guignol. Although Grand Guignol was introduced into England in about 1908, it remained essentially a Parisian theatrical form.

grand rhétoriqueur *See* RHÉTORIQUEUR.

grand style A literary style marked by a sustained and lofty dignity, sublimity, and eloquence (as often attributed to such epic poets as Homer, Virgil, or John Milton).

grand tour A tour of Europe (including The Netherlands, France, Germany, Austria, Switzerland, and Italy especially) that was considered an essential part of a gentleman's education from about the 16th through the 19th century. The tour was considered especially fashionable in the 18th century when it became easier to travel. Many writers, including Henry Fielding, Tobias Smollett, Laurence Sterne, James Boswell, and J.W. von Goethe, toured the European continent and later wrote about their travels, and there are many references in literature to people taking the Grand Tour.

graphic \ˈgraf-ik\ [Greek *graphikós,* literally, of or for writing, a derivative of *gráphein* to write] **1.** Marked by clear, lifelike, or vividly realistic description or striking imaginative power. **2.** Vividly or plainly shown or described.

graveyard school Genre of 18th-century British poetry that focused on death and bereavement. The graveyard school consisted largely of imitations of Robert Blair's popular long poem of morbid appeal, *The Grave* (1743), and of Edward Young's celebrated blank-verse dramatic rhapsody *Night Thoughts* (1742–45). These poems express the sorrow and pain of bereavement, evoke the horror of death's physical manifestations, and suggest the transitory nature of human life. The meditative, philosophical tendencies of graveyard poetry found their fullest expression in Thomas Gray's *An Elegy Written in a Country Church Yard* (1751), a dignified, gently melancholy elegy celebrating the graves of humble and unknown villagers and suggesting that the lives of rich and poor alike "lead but to the grave." The works of the graveyard school were significant as early precursors of the Romantic movement.

great books Certain classics of literature, philosophy, history, and science that are believed to contain the basic ideas of Western culture. These include works by Homer, Plato, Aristotle, Thucydides, Herodotus, Thomas Aquinas, William

Shakespeare, Blaise Pascal, Immanuel Kant, J.S. Mill, and Charles Darwin, among many others. *See also* CANON.

great chain of being *also called* chain of being. The conception of the nature of the universe that had a pervasive influence on Western thought, particularly through the ancient Greek Neoplatonists and derivative philosophies during the European Renaissance and the 17th and early 18th centuries. The term denotes three general features of the universe: plenitude, continuity, and gradation. The principle of plenitude states that the universe is "full," exhibiting the maximal diversity of kinds of existences. The principle of continuity asserts that the universe is composed of an infinite series of forms, each of which shares with its neighbor at least one attribute. According to the principle of linear gradation, this series ranges in hierarchical order from the barest type of existence to the *ens perfectissimum,* or God.

This model of the universe died out in the 19th century but was given renewed currency in the 20th by Arthur O. Lovejoy in *The Great Chain of Being: A Study of the History of an Idea* (1936). A summary of the concept of the great chain of being can be found in the first epistle of Alexander Pope's *An Essay on Man.*

Great Dionysia \ˌdī-ə-ˈnish-ə\, *also called* City Dionysia. Ancient drama festival in which tragedy, comedy, and satyric drama originated. It was held in Athens in March in honor of Dionysus, the god of wine. Tragedy of some form, probably chiefly the chanting of choral lyrics, was introduced by the tyrant Peisistratus when he refounded the festival (534/531 BC), but the earliest tragedy that survives, Aeschylus' *Persians,* dates from 472 BC.

The festivals were attended by all Athenian citizens and visitors from throughout Greece. In the competition for tragedy, three poets wrote, produced, and probably acted in three tragedies on a single theme. Each poet also presented a satyr play, which treated a heroic subject in burlesque fashion. Judges, chosen by lot, awarded a prize to the best poet. In comedy, introduced in 486 BC, five poets competed for the prize, each with one play. The satyr play was always the work of a tragic poet, and the same poet never wrote both tragedies and comedies.

Grecism \ˈgrē-ˌsiz-əm\ Imitation of Greek art, literature, sculpture, or architecture.

Greek mythology The body of myths and stories developed by the ancient Greeks concerning their gods and heroes, the nature of the cosmos, and their own religious practices.

The Greek myths are known today primarily from Greek literature. The oldest known literary sources, the *Iliad* and the *Odyssey* (9th or 8th century BC), focus on events surrounding the Trojan War and the activities of the gods' society on Mt. Olympus. Two poems by Homer's near-contemporary Hesiod, the *Theogony* and the *Works and Days,* contain accounts of the genesis of the cosmos, the succession of divine rulers, the succession of human ages, the origin of human woes, and the origin of sacrificial practices. Myths are also preserved in the Homeric hymns and in fragments of epic poems on the Trojan War; in lyric poems, especially those composed by Pindar; in the works of the tragedians of the 5th century BC, Aeschylus, Sophocles, and Euripides; in writings of scholars and poets of the Hellenistic Age (330–23 BC), such as Callimachus, Euhemerus, and Apollonius of Rhodes; and in writers of the time of the Roman Empire, for example, Ovid, Plutarch, and Pausanias.

Greek religious myths are concerned with gods or heroes in their more serious aspects or are connected with ritual. They include cosmogonical tales of the genesis of the gods and the world out of Chaos and the internecine struggles among immortal beings that culminated in the supremacy of Zeus. Myths about the gods describe their births, victories over monsters or rivals, love affairs, special powers, or connections with a cultic site or ritual. Many myths of the gods, on the other hand, are trivial and lighthearted. Typical of such are the amusing descriptions of conjugal friction between Zeus and his wife, Hera, in the *Iliad*.

Myths were viewed by the Greeks as embodying divine or timeless truths, whereas legends (or sagas) were quasi-historical. Hence, famous events in epics, such as the Trojan War, were generally regarded as having really happened, and the heroes and heroines of the Homeric poems were believed to have actually lived. In another class of legends, the heinous offenses of mortals—such as attempting to make love to a goddess against her will, deceiving the gods grossly by inculpating them in crime or assuming their prerogatives—were punished by everlasting torture in the underworld.

Folktales, consisting of popular recurring themes and told for amusement, inevitably found their way into Greek myth. One such theme is that of lost persons (e.g., Odysseus, Paris, Helen of Troy) found or recovered after long and exciting adventures. Another is the journeys to the land of the dead (such as those undertaken by Orpheus, Heracles, Odysseus, and Theseus).

Greek mythology formed the staple of most Greek poetry and epic, as well as of many dramatic works. It also influenced philosophers and historians to a marked degree. The Romans adopted Greek mythology virtually wholesale into their own literature. Through the medium of Latin and, above all, the works of Ovid, Greek myth was stamped indelibly on the medieval imagination. With subsequent revivals and reinterpretations, its influence has permeated Western culture to an unparalleled extent, from the themes of art and literature to the vocabulary of science and technology.

Greek tragedy The form of drama produced in ancient Greece by the authors Aeschylus, Euripides, and Sophocles. The dramas had a fairly rigid structure consisting of an introductory prologos; a parodos, which marks the entrance of the chorus; several episodes constituting the main action of the play; and the exodus, or conclusion, which follows the last song of the chorus. *See also* TRAGEDY.

grotesque \grō-ˈtesk\ A decorative style in which animal, human, and vegetative forms are interwoven and deformed to the point of absurdity. This nonliterary sense of the word first entered the English language as a noun. The word comes ultimately from 16th-century Italian *grottesea,* explained by contemporary Italian writers as deriving from *grotta* ("cave"), in allusion to certain caves under Rome in which paintings in such a style were found. It came to be used as an adjective describing something in this style and hence to mean bizarre, incongruous, or unnatural, or anything outside the normal.

The term was first used regularly in reference to literature in the 18th century. In literature the style is often used for comedy or satire to show the contradictions and inconsistencies of life. Sometimes writers present the grotesque in the form of a character that is somehow deformed or impaired (physically or psychologically) who acts in a manner that is not considered normal. Examples of the grotesque can be found in the characters and situations in the works of Edgar Allan Poe, Evelyn Waugh, Flannery O'Connor, Eugène Ionesco, Mervyn Peake, and Joseph Heller, among many others.

Group Theatre Company of stage craftsmen founded in 1931 in New York City by Harold Clurman, Cheryl Crawford, and Lee Strasberg, for the purpose of presenting American plays of social significance. The characteristic Group production was a social protest play with a leftist viewpoint. After its first trial production of Sergey Tretyakov's *Roar China,* the Group staged Paul Green's *House of Connelly,* a play of the decadent Old South as reflected by the disintegrating gentry class. The play ran for 91 performances. The Group then followed with two anticapitalist plays, *1931* and *Success Story;* the former closed after only nine days, but the latter ran for more than 100 performances. Financial and artistic success came two years later with the production of Sidney Kingsley's *Men in White,* which was awarded a Pulitzer Prize.

In 1935 the Group Theatre staged *Waiting for Lefty* by one of its actors, Clifford Odets. The play, suggested by a taxicab drivers' strike of the previous year, used flashback techniques and "plants" in the audience to create the illusion that the strikers' meeting was occurring spontaneously. The Group also staged Odets' *Awake and Sing!, Till the Day I Die, Paradise Lost,* and *Golden Boy;* other productions included Paul Green's *Johnny Johnson,* Irwin Shaw's *Bury the Dead,* Robert Ardrey's *Thunder Rock,* and William Saroyan's *My Heart's in the Highlands.* The Group influenced American theater by stimulating the writing talent of such playwrights as Odets and Saroyan. It was disbanded in 1941.

Grub Street \'grəb\ The world of literary hacks, or usually mediocre, needy writers who write for hire.

The term originated during the 18th century. According to Samuel Johnson's *Dictionary,* Grub Street was "originally the name of a street in Moorfields in London, much inhabited by writers of small histories, dictionaries, and temporary poems; whence any mean production is called grubstreet." The street was renamed Milton Street in 1830. The novelist Tobias Smollett, himself engaged much of his life in Grub Street hackwork, provided a memorable scene of a

Grub Street dinner party in *Humphry Clinker* (1771). George Gissing's novel *New Grub Street* (1891) also deals with London literary life.

Gruppe 47 \'grüp-ə-ˌzē-bən-ünt-'firt-sig\ ("Group 47") Informal association of German-speaking writers that was founded in 1947 (hence its name). Gruppe 47 originated with a group of war prisoners in the United States who were concerned with reestablishing the broken traditions of German literature. Feeling that Nazi propaganda had corrupted their language, they advocated a style of sparse, even cold, descriptive realism devoid of pompous or poetic verbiage.

Returning to Germany, they founded the weekly *Der Ruf* ("The Call"), which was suppressed in 1947 by the U.S. military government for political radicalism. As the group's political aims diminished, its literary prestige rose, and its yearly prize conferred high distinction. Both Günter Grass and Heinrich Böll were prizewinners. The last full conference of the group was in 1967.

guslar \'güs-ˌlär\ *plural* guslari \-ˌlär-ē\ [Serbo-Croatian *guslar,* a derivative of *gusle* single-stringed fiddle] Any of a group of popular narrative singers of the Balkans who inherit a tradition that dates from the 17th century. Among the few performers continuing the oral tradition of epic poetry in the West, the *guslari* serve as transmitters and interpreters of a repertory of song and epic. Most of their songs are about the era of Turkish rule and were handed down by teachers or older singers. Because the narratives are orally transmitted, variation in content is inevitable. The *guslari* accompany themselves on the gusla, or gusle (a one-stringed instrument), and intone their musical stories.

guwen or **ku-wen** \'gūē-'wən\ [Chinese *gŭwén,* from *gŭ* ancient + *wén* writing], *also called* wenyan \'wən-'yan\ In Chinese literature, classical or literary prose that aims at the standards and styles set by ancient writers and their distinguished followers of subsequent ages, with the Confucian Classics and the early philosophers as supreme models. While the styles may vary with individual writers, the language is always far removed from their spoken tongues. Sanctioned by official requirement for the competitive examinations and dignified by traditional respect for the cultural accomplishments of past ages, this medium became the linguistic tool of practically all Chinese prose writers. *Compare* BAIHUA.

H

Show me a hero and I will write you a tragedy.
—F. Scott Fitzgerald

Habima or **Habimah** \hä-ˈbē-mä\ ("Stage") Hebrew theater company originally organized as Habima ha-ʿIvrit ("The Hebrew Stage") in Białystok, Poland, in 1912 by Nahum Zemach. In 1913 the troupe traveled to Vienna, where it staged Osip Dymov's *Hear O Israel* before the 11th Zionist Congress. In 1917, after World War I caused the ensemble to dissolve, Zemach reestablished the group in Moscow, calling it Habima.

Encouraged by Konstantin Stanislavsky, the director of the Moscow Art Theater, and inspired by a fervent desire to transcend the tawdry and superficial Yiddish operettas and melodramas then in vogue, Habima opened in 1918 with a production staged by Yevgeny Vakhtangov, a student of Stanislavsky, who remained Habima's chief director until his death in 1922. Vakhtangov's production in 1922 of S. Ansky's *The Dybbuk,* was an immediate success and established Habima as a theater of the highest artistic excellence. It became one of four studios of the Moscow Art Theater. In 1926, after touring Europe, Habima went to the United States. After a division in its membership, the major part of the group left for Palestine without Zemach and in 1931 permanently established itself in Tel Aviv. In 1958 Habima was designated the National Theater of Israel and awarded an annual state subsidy.

Haggada or **Haggadah** \hä-ˈgäd-ə, -ˈgȯd-\ *plural* Haggadoth *or* Haggadot \-ˌdōth, -ˌdōt\ [Hebrew *haggādhāh*] **1.** Explanatory matter occurring in rabbinical literature, often taking the form of story, anecdote, legend, or parable, and treating such varied subjects as astronomy, astrology, magic, medicine, and mysticism. **2.** Explanatory matter in the Talmud interpreting the Scriptures as distinguished from that regulating religious practice. **3.** The prayer book containing the seder ritual.

hagiography \ˌhā-gē-ˈäg-rə-fē, ˌhā-jē-\ or **hagiology** \-ˈäl-ə-jē\ [Greek *hágios* sacred] The writings about or study of the lives of the saints. Elements of hagiography include acts of the martyrs; biographies of saintly monks, bishops, princes, or virgins; and accounts of miracles connected with their tombs, relics, icons, or statues. The genre was developed and became popular during the Middle Ages, and many examples survive from that period. Among the noted early hagiographers are Eusebius of Caesarea in the 4th century, Gregory I the Great in the 6th, the Venerable Bede in the 8th, and Aelfric, an Anglo-Saxon prose writer, in the 10th. Modern critical hagiography began with the 17th-century Belgian historian Jean Bolland and his followers, who compiled the *Acta Sanctorum,* a collection of the lives of the saints arranged in order of their feast days in the ecclesiastical year. *The Lives of the Fathers, Martyrs, and Other Principal Saints* by Alban Butler, a priest and educator, is a well-known collection from the 18th century.

haikai \'hī-ˌkī\ *plural* haikai [Japanese, short for *haikai no renga* humorous linked verse] A comic *renga,* or Japanese linked-verse form. The haikai was developed as early as the 16th century as a diversion from the composition of the more serious *renga* form. *See* RENGA.

haiku \'hī-ˌkü\ *plural* haiku [Japanese] An unrhymed Japanese poetic form consisting of 17 syllables arranged in three lines containing five, seven, and five syllables, respectively. Also, a poem written in the haiku form or a modification of it but in a language other than Japanese.

The term *haiku* is derived from the first element of the word *haikai* (a humorous form of *renga* [linked-verse poem]) and the second of *hokku* (the initial stanza of a *renga*). The hokku, which set the tone of the poem, had to contain in its three lines mention of such subjects as the season, the time of day, and the dominant features of the landscape, making it almost an independent poem. The hokku (often interchangeably called haikai) became known as the haiku late in the 19th century, when it was entirely divested of its original function of opening a sequence of verse; today, even the earlier hokku are usually called haiku. The form gained distinction in the 17th century, when the great master Bashō elevated haiku to a highly refined and conscious art. The subject range of the haiku was eventually broadened, but it remained an art of expressing much and suggesting more in the fewest possible words. Other outstanding haiku masters were Buson in the 18th century, Kobayashi Issa in the 18th and 19th centuries, and Masaoka Shiki in the late 19th century. It has remained Japan's most popular poetic form.

In English, the Imagist poets and others wrote haiku or imitated the form. Reginald H. Blyth's *History of Haiku,* 2 vol. (1963–64), is both a history and an anthology of haiku in English translation; his *Haiku,* 4 vol. (1976–77), expands the anthology.

half rhyme *also called* near rhyme, slant rhyme, *or* oblique rhyme. In prosody, two words that have only their final consonant sounds and no preceding vowel or consonant sounds in common (such as *stopped* and *wept,* or *parable* and *shell*). The device was common in Welsh, Irish, and Icelandic verse years before it was first used in English by Henry Vaughan. It was not used regularly in English until Gerard Manley Hopkins and William Butler Yeats began to do so.

hamartia \ˌhä-ˌmär-'tē-ə\ [Greek *hamartía* error, fault, a derivative of *hamartánein* to miss the mark, err], *also called* tragic flaw. An inherent defect of character, or the error, guilt, or sin of the tragic hero in a literary work.

Aristotle introduced the term casually in the *Poetics* in describing the tragic hero as one of noble rank and nature whose misfortune is not brought about by villainy but by some "error of judgment" (hamartia). This imperfection later came to be interpreted as a moral flaw, such as Othello's jealousy or Hamlet's irresolution, although most great tragedies defy such a simple interpretation. The hero's suffering and its far-reaching reverberations are disproportionate to the flaw. An element of cosmic collusion among the hero's flaw, chance, necessity, and other external forces is essential to bring about the tragic catastrophe.

In Greek tragedy the nature of the hero's flaw is even more elusive. Often the tragic deeds are committed unwittingly, as when Oedipus unknowingly kills his father and marries his own mother. If the deeds are committed knowingly, they often are not committed by choice; Orestes is under obligation to Apollo to avenge his father's murder by killing his mother. Also, an apparent weakness is often only an excess of virtue, such as an extreme probity or zeal for perfection which, in turn, may suggest that the hero is guilty of hubris—i.e., presumption of being godlike and attempting to overstep human limitations.

hapax legomenon \ˌhap-ˌaks-li-ˈgäm-ə-ˌnän, ˌhäp-ˌäks-, -nən\ *plural* hapax legomena \-nə, -ˌnä\ [Greek *hápax legómenon* something said only once] A word or form occurring only once in a document or corpus.

hard-boiled fiction Of or relating to a tough, unsentimental style of American crime writing characterized by impersonal, matter-of-fact presentation of naturalistic or violent themes or incidents, by a generally unemotional or stoic tone, and often by a total absence of explicit or implied moral judgments. Hard-boiled fiction uses graphic sex and violence, vivid but often sordid urban backgrounds, and fast-paced, slangy dialogue.

The genre was popularized by Dashiell Hammett, whose first truly hard-boiled story, "Fly Paper," appeared in the pulp magazine *Black Mask* in 1929. Combining his own experiences with the realistic influence of writers such as Ernest Hemingway and John Dos Passos, Hammett developed a distinctly American type of detective fiction that differed considerably from the more genteel English mystery story, which was usually set in a country house populated by servants and extended families, a pattern that had been followed by American writers.

Hammett's innovations were incorporated in the hard-boiled melodramas of James M. Cain, particularly in such early works as *The Postman Always Rings Twice* (1934) and *Double Indemnity* (1936). Successors included Raymond Chandler, with novels such as *The Big Sleep* (1939), *Farewell, My Lovely* (1940), and *The Little Sister* (1949). Less well known, but also significant are the novels of Jim Thompson. His first-person narratives—in such works as *The Killer Inside Me* (1952), *Savage Night* (1953), and *Pop. 1280* (1964)—reveal protagonists who seem "normal" but prove to be both unreliable narrators and psychopaths. Other important writers of the hard-boiled school were George Harmon Coxe (1901–84), author of such thrillers as *Murder with Pictures* (1935) and *Eye Witness* (1950), and W.R. Burnett (1899–1982), who wrote *Little Caesar* (1929) and *The Asphalt Jungle* (1949). Hard-boiled fiction ultimately degenerated into the extreme sensationalism and undisguised sadism of what *Ellery Queen's Mystery Magazine* called the "guts-gore-and-gals-school," as found in the works of Mickey Spillane, writer of such phenomenal best-sellers as *I, the Jury* (1947).

The works of the hard-boiled school have been extensively translated into films, often through successive versions tailored to different generations of moviegoers. *See also* DETECTIVE STORY.

Harlem Renaissance \'här-ləm\, *also called* New Negro Movement. Period of outstanding literary vigor and creativity that took place in the United States during the 1920s. The Harlem Renaissance altered the character of literature created by many black American writers, moving from quaint dialect works and conventional imitations of white writers to sophisticated explorations of black life and culture that revealed and stimulated a new confidence and racial pride. The movement was centered in the vast black ghetto of Harlem, in New York City, where aspiring black artists, writers, and musicians gathered, sharing their experiences and providing mutual encouragement.

One of the leading figures and chief interpreters of the period was Alain Locke, a teacher, writer, and philosopher. Another leading figure was James Weldon Johnson, author of the pioneering novel *Autobiography of an Ex-Coloured Man* (1912), and perhaps best known for *God's Trombones* (1927), a collection of seven sermons in free verse, expressing the characteristic style and themes of the black preacher in pure and eloquent English. Johnson acted as mentor to many of the young black writers who formed the core of the Harlem group. Claude McKay, an immigrant from Jamaica, produced an impressive volume of verse, *Harlem Shadows* (1922), and a best-selling novel, *Home to Harlem* (1928), about a young black man's return from World War I. Countee Cullen helped bring more Harlem poets to public notice by editing *Caroling Dusk: An Anthology of Verse by Negro Poets* in 1927. Langston Hughes published his first collection of verse, *The Weary Blues,* in 1926, and his novel *Not Without Laughter* appeared in 1930. He also collaborated on a play (*Mule Bone,* 1931) with Zora Neale Hurston, another writer associated with the movement. Wallace Thurman and William Jourden Rapp collaborated on a popular play, *Harlem,* in 1929. Thurman, one of the most individualistic talents of the period, also wrote a satirical novel, *The Blacker the Berry* (1929), that ridiculed elements of the movement. Another notable writer was Arna Bontemps, whose novel *God Sends Sunday* (1931) is considered the final work of the Harlem Renaissance. The movement was accelerated by philanthropic grants and scholarships and was supported by white writers such as Carl Van Vechten.

The Great Depression caused the Harlem group of writers to scatter; many were forced to leave New York or to take other jobs to tide them over the hard times.

harlequinade \ˌhär-lə-kwi-'nād, -ki-\ Play or scene, usually in pantomime, in which Harlequin, a male character, has the principal role. Derived from the Italian commedia dell'arte, harlequinades came into vogue in early 18th-century

England, with a standard plot consisting of a pursuit of the lovers Harlequin and Columbine by the latter's father or guardian, Pantaloon, and his bumpkin servant Pierrot. In the Victorian era the harlequinade was reduced to a plotless epilogue to the main pantomime, which was often a dramatized fairy tale.

harmony \'här-mə-nē\ A systematic arrangement of parallel literary passages (such as those of the Gospels) for the purpose of showing agreement.

Harper's Magazine \'här-pərz\ Monthly magazine published in New York City, one of the oldest and most prestigious literary and opinion journals in the United States. It was founded in 1850 as *Harper's New Monthly,* a literary journal, by the printing and publishing firm of the Harper brothers. Noted in its early years for its serialization of great English novels and for the fine quality of its own essays and other literature of the period, *Harper's* was the first American magazine extensively to use woodcut illustrations. It was a leader in publishing the writings of the most illustrious British and American authors, and before 1865 it had become the most successful periodical in the United States. In the late 1920s the periodical changed its editorial format to that of a forum on public affairs, but the magazine balanced its primary concern for social and political issues with short stories by Aldous Huxley and other contemporary writers. Expenses exceeded revenues in the late 1960s, and the magazine's economic problems worsened. Its certain closing in 1980 was averted by grants by a philanthropic organization, the MacArthur Foundation.

Hartford wit \'härt-fərd\, *also called* Connecticut wit \kə-'net-i-kət\ Any of a group of federalist poets centered in Hartford, Conn., who collaborated to produce a considerable body of political satire just after the American Revolution. Employing burlesque verse modeled upon Samuel Butler's *Hudibras* and Alexander Pope' *The Dunciad,* the wits advocated strong, conservative central government and attacked such proponents of democratic liberalism as Thomas Jefferson. Leaders of the group, all graduates of Yale College, were John Trumbull, Timothy Dwight, and Joel Barlow. Barlow, who was probably the most creative member of the group, later turned apostate and espoused Jeffersonian democracy.

Although the wits sought to demonstrate the possibility of a genuinely American literature based on American subjects, they conventionalized styles of early 18th-century British verse. The works that the wits produced are generally more notable for patriotic fervor than for literary excellence. Their most important effort was a satirical mock epic entitled *The Anarchiad: A Poem on the Restoration of Chaos and Substantial Night* (1786–87), which attacks states slow to ratify the American Constitution.

Hawthornden Prize \'hoth-orn-dən\ The oldest British literary prize, established in 1919 by Alice Warrender. The Hawthornden, which includes a financial award of £2,000, is awarded annually to recognize the best work of imaginative literature published during the previous year and is intended to encourage young authors. British authors under the age of 41 are eligible for the prize and books need not be submitted to be considered. A panel of judges chooses the winner.

headless \'hed-ləs\, *also called* acephalous. In prosody, a line of verse that is lacking the normal first syllable. An iambic line with only one syllable in the first foot is a headless line, as in the third line of the following stanza of A.E. Housman's poem "To An Athlete Dying Young":

> The time you won your town the race
> We chaired you through the market-place;
> Man and boy stood cheering by,
> And home we brought you shoulder-high.

head rhyme *See* ALLITERATION.

heavy \'hev-ē\ In prosody, having stress or conspicuous sonority—used especially of syllables in accentual verse; contrasted with *light.*

Heidelberg Romantics \'hī-dəl-ˌberk, *Angl* -bərg\ Poets of the second phase of Romanticism in Germany, who were centered in Heidelberg about 1806. Their leaders were Clemens Brentano, Achim von Arnim, and Joseph von Görres; their short-lived organ was the *Zeitung für Einsiedler* ("Journal for Hermits"). The most characteristic production of this school was the collection of folk songs entitled *Des Knaben Wunderhorn* (1805–08; "The Boy's Magic Horn"). Compared with the Jena Romantics, who represented the first school of Romanticism in Germany, the Heidelberg writers were more practical, and their immediate influence on German intellectual life was greater. The group stimulated their compatriots' interest in German history and founded the study of German philology and medieval literature. They also strengthened the national and patriotic spirit and helped prepare the way for the rising against Napoleon.

Heimkehrerliteratur \'hīm-ˌkār-ər-lit-er-ä-ˌtür\ [German, literally, literature of those who have returned home] In German literature, body of works written after World War II that portray the efforts of soldiers to come to terms with civilian life. An example is Wolfgang Borchert's *Draussen vor der Tür* (1947; *The Man Outside*).

Hellenistic romance \ˌhel-ə-'nis-tik\ Adventure tale, usually with a quasi-historical setting, in which a virtuous heroine and her valiant lover are separated by innumerable obstacles of human wickedness and natural catastrophe but are finally reunited. A precursor of the modern novel, the Hellenistic romance is the source for such classic love stories as those of Hero and Leander, Pyramus and Thisbe, Sappho and Phaon, and Daphnis and Chloe.

Introduced in the 1st century BC, the form reached its height in the 2nd and 3rd centuries AD in the works of writers such as Chariton, Xenophon, Longus, and Heliodorus. It combined elements of the imaginative rhetorical exercise, popular Alexandrian poems and tales of love and adventure, the erotic Milesian adventure tale, utopian stories, and travel narratives. An example of the Hellenistic romance is Chariton's *Chaereas and Callirhoë* (2nd century), a tale of lovers who marry, quarrel, and are finally reunited.

hemiepes \ˌhem-ē-ˈep-ēz\ *plural* hemiepe \-pē\ [Late Greek *hēmiepés,* from Greek *hēmi-* half + *épē* lines, verses] In classical prosody, a meter of three dactylic feet, the last of which is catalectic, or missing the two final short syllables. It is the first part of a line of dactylic hexameter or pentameter. The meter was used chiefly in Greek epic and lyric verse and is scanned as – ∪ ∪ | – ∪ ∪ | –.

hemistich \ˈhem-i-ˌstik\ [Greek *hēmistíchion,* from *hēmi-* half + *stíchos* line, verse] Half a poetic line, usually determined by the placement of a caesura. It often forms a metrically independent colon or group of feet of less than regular length. The hemistich is used in drama to build up tension through an exchange of half lines of dialogue between at least two characters. The device, which creates the effect of an argument, is called hemistichomythia.

This was used to great effect by William Shakespeare in the following passage from *Richard III:*

> *K. Rich.* Now, by the world—
> *Q. Eliz.* 'Tis full of thy foul wrongs.
> *K. Rich.* My father's death—
> *Q. Eliz.* Thy life hath that dishonour'd.
> *K. Rich.* Then, by myself—
> *Q. Eliz.* Thyself thyself misusest.
> *K. Rich.* Why then, by God—
> *Q. Eliz.* God's wrong is most of all.

hendecacolic \ˌhen-ˌdek-ə-ˈkōl-ik, -ˈkäl-\ [Greek *héndeka* eleven + *kôlon* colon] In classical prosody, made up of eleven colons, or rhythmic phrases.

hendecasemic \ˌhen-ˌdek-ə-ˈsē-mik\ [Greek *héndeka* eleven + *sêma* mark, sign] In classical prosody, containing or equivalent to eleven morae, or short syllables.

hendecasyllable \ˌhen-ˈdek-ə-ˌsil-ə-bəl, -ˌdek-ə-ˈsil-\ [Greek *hendekasýllabos* having eleven syllables, from *héndeka* eleven + *syllabḗ* syllable] In poetry, a line of eleven syllables usually arranged as ∪ ∪ – ∪ ∪ – ∪ – ∪ – – or ∪ – – ∪ ∪ – ∪ – ∪ – – . Hendecasyllables were used often by Greek and Latin poets, and Dante and Petrarch used them in such forms as ottava rima and terza rima. It is not a common form in English, although there are examples of such verses by Alfred, Lord Tennyson, Algernon Charles Swinburne, and Walter Savage Landor.

hendiadys \hen-ˈdī-ə-dis\ [Medieval Latin *endiadis,* modification of Greek (in Latin sources) *hén dià dyoîn,* literally, one through two] The expression of an idea by the use of usually two independent words connected by *and* (as in *nice* *and warm*) instead of the usual combination of an independent word and its modifier (as in *nicely warm*).

hephthemimeral caesura \ˌhef-thə-ˈmim-ər-əl\ [Greek *hephthēmimerḗs* containing seven halves, containing three and a half feet, from *heptá* seven + *hēmi-* half + *méros* part] *See* CAESURA.

heptameter \hep-ˈtam-ə-tər\ In poetry, a line of seven feet. *See* FOURTEENER.

heptastich \ˈhep-tə-ˌstik\ In poetry, a group, stanza, or poem of seven lines.

heptasyllable \ˌhep-tə-ˈsil-ə-bəl\ In poetry, a line of seven syllables.

hermeneutics \ˌhər-mə-ˈnü-tiks, -ˈnyü-\ [Greek *hermeneutikós* interpretative, a derivative of *hermeneúein* to translate, interpret, explain] The study of the general principles of biblical interpretation. For both Jews and Christians throughout their histories, the primary purpose of hermeneutics, and of the exegetical methods employed in interpretation, has been to discover the truths and values of the Bible.

The sacred status of the Bible in Judaism and Christianity rests upon the conviction that it is a receptacle of divine revelation. In the history of biblical interpretation, four major types of hermeneutics have emerged: the literal, moral, allegorical, and anagogical.

Literal interpretation asserts that a biblical text is to be interpreted according to the "plain meaning" conveyed by its grammatical construction and historical context. The literal meaning is held to correspond to the intention of the authors. This type of hermeneutics is often, but not necessarily, associated with belief in the verbal inspiration of the Bible, according to which the individual words of the divine message were divinely chosen. Jerome, an influential 4th-century biblical scholar, championed the literal interpretation of the Bible in opposition to what he regarded as the excesses of allegorical interpretation. The primacy of the literal sense was later advocated by such diverse figures as Thomas Aquinas, Nicholas of Lyra, John Colet, Martin Luther, and John Calvin.

Moral interpretation seeks to establish exegetical principles by which ethical lessons may be drawn from the various parts of the Bible. Allegorization was often employed in this endeavor. *The Letter of Barnabas* (*c.* 100 AD), for example, interprets the food laws prescribed in the Book of Leviticus as forbidding not the flesh of certain animals but rather the vices imaginatively associated with those animals.

Allegorical interpretation interprets the biblical narratives as having a level of reference beyond those persons, things, and events explicitly mentioned in the text. A particular form of allegorical interpretation is the typological, according to which the key figures, main events, and principal institutions of the Old Testament are seen as "types" or foreshadowings of persons, events, and objects in the New Testament. According to this theory, interpretations such as that of Noah's ark as a "type" of the Christian church have been intended by God from the beginning.

The anagogical or mystical interpretation seeks to explain biblical events as they relate to or prefigure the life to come. Such an approach to the Bible is exemplified by the Jewish Kabbala, which sought to disclose the mystical significance of the numerical values of Hebrew letters and words. A chief example of such mystical interpretation in Judaism is the medieval *Zohar*. In Christianity, many of the interpretations associated with Mariology fall into the anagogical category.

Shifts in hermeneutical emphases tend to reflect broader academic and philosophical trends; historical-critical, existential, and structural interpretation figured prominently in the 20th century. On the nonacademic level, the interpretation of prophetic and apocalyptic biblical material in terms of present-day events remains a vigorous pursuit in some circles.

Hermeticism \hər-ˈmet-ə-ˌsiz-əm\ or **Hermetism** \ˈhər-mə-ˌtiz-əm\, *also called* Ermetismo \ˌer-me-ˈtēs-ˌmō\ Modernist poetic movement originating in Italy in the early 20th century. The works produced within the movement are characterized by unorthodox structure, illogical sequences, and highly subjective language. The name was derived from that of Hermes Trismegistos, the reputed author of occult symbolic works. It was used in reference to this particular movement by the critic Francesco Flora in a series of essays collected as *La poesia ermetica* (1936). Although Hermeticism influenced a wide circle of poets, even outside Italy, it remained inaccessible to the larger public.

Hermeticism was rooted in the poetry and poetic theory of the 18th-century German Romantic poet Novalis and of the 19th-century American writer Edgar Allan Poe, as filtered through the French Symbolist poets, particularly Charles Baudelaire, Stéphane Mallarmé, Paul Valéry, and Arthur Rimbaud. The term was particularly applied to the group of 20th-century Italian poets whose forerunner was Arturo Onofri and whose primary exponent and leader was Giuseppe Ungaretti. The formalistic devices of Hermeticism were partly an outgrowth of Futurism, a short-lived but influential movement that encouraged innovation in literary language and content. The cryptic brevity, obscurity, and involution of the Hermetics were forced upon them, however, by fascist censors.

Although two other poets who were to gain international repute, Salvatore Quasimodo and Eugenio Montale, were associated with the movement, its initial leader was Ungaretti, whose education in Paris had introduced him to French Symbolism. In his first volume of poems, *Il porto sepolto* (1916; "The Buried Port"), Ungaretti introduced an intense, purified short lyric, from which punctuation, syntax, and structure had been eliminated to stress the evocative power of individual words. Montale (with *Ossi di seppia,* 1925; "Cuttlefish Bones") and later Quasimodo (with *Acque e terre,* 1930; "Waters and Land") became his disciples.

After World War II all three of Hermeticism's major poets developed their own individual styles. Ungaretti incorporated more structure and a more straightforward tone, Montale moved in the direction of greater human warmth and simplicity, and Quasimodo wrote powerful, socially committed works. In

1959 Quasimodo won the Nobel Prize for Literature, and Montale received the Nobel in 1975. Some Italian poets, such as Leonardo Sinisgalli, Alfonso Gatto, and Mario Luzi, persisted in the introverted, formalized Hermetic manner, but the movement's greatest poets moved on to develop more accessible and universal styles.

hero \'hir-ō, 'hē-rō\ [Greek *hḗrōs*] A mythological or legendary figure often of divine descent who is endowed with great strength or ability, figures such as those found in early heroic epics like *Gilgamesh,* the *Iliad, Beowulf,* or *La Chanson de Roland.* The word is often broadly applied to the principal male character in a literary or dramatic work.

The legendary heroes belong to a princely class existing in an early stage of the history of a people, and they transcend ordinary men in skill, strength, and courage. They are usually born to their role. Some, like the Greek Achilles and the Irish Cú Chulainn (Cuchulain), are of semidivine origin, unusual beauty, and extraordinary precocity. A few, like the Anglo-Saxon Beowulf and the Russian Ilya of Murom, are dark horses, slow to develop.

War or dangerous adventure is the hero's normal occupation. He is surrounded by noble peers and is magnanimous to his followers and ruthless to his enemies. In addition to his prowess in battle, he is resourceful and skillful in many crafts. If shipwrecked, he is an expert swimmer. He is sometimes, like Odysseus, cunning and wise in counsel, but a hero is not usually given to much subtlety. He is a man of action rather than thought and lives by a personal code of honor that admits of no qualification. His responses are usually instinctive, predictable, and inevitable. He accepts challenges and sometimes even courts disaster. Thus baldly stated, the hero's ethos seems oversimple by the standards of a later age. He is childlike in his boasting and rivalry, in his love of reward, and in his concern for his reputation. He is sometimes foolhardy and wrong-headed, risking his life—and the lives of others—for trifles. Roland, for instance, dies because he is too proud to sound his horn for help when he is overwhelmed in battle. Yet the hero still exerts an attraction for sophisticated readers and remains a seminal influence in literature.

The appearance of heroes in literature marks a revolution in thought that occurred when poets and their audiences turned their attention away from gods to mortal men, who suffer pain and death but in defiance of this live gallantly and fully, and create, through their own efforts, a moment's glory that survives in the memory of their descendants. They are the first human beings in literature, and the novelty of their experiences has a perennial freshness.

heroic couplet A couplet of rhyming iambic pentameters often forming a distinct rhetorical as well as metrical unit. The origin of the form in English poetry is unknown, but Geoffrey Chaucer in the 14th century was the first to make extensive use of it. The heroic couplet became the principal meter used in drama in about the mid-17th century, and the form was perfected by John Dryden and

Alexander Pope in the late 17th and early 18th centuries. An example, from Pope's "Eloisa to Abelard," is:

> Then share thy pain, allow that sad relief;
> Ah, more than share it, give me all thy grief.

heroic drama Type of tragic play common in England during the Restoration period of the late 17th century. Heroic drama portrayed epic characters and themes of love and honor and was for the most part written in heroic couplets with overblown dialogue and exotic settings. The plays were staged with spectacular scenery and were influenced by the development of opera at that time in England and by French classical drama. John Dryden wrote some of the best-known examples of heroic drama, such as his *Conquest of Granada*. The genre was satirized by George Villiers, Duke of Buckingham, in *The Rehearsal* (1671), and the popularity of the form soon declined.

heroic line or **heroic meter** *See* HEROIC VERSE.

heroicomic \hir-ˌō-i-ˈkäm-ik\ or **heroicomical** \-ˈkäm-i-kəl\ Comic by being ludicrously noble, bold, or elevated.

heroic poetry Narrative verse that is elevated in mood and uses a dignified, dramatic, and formal style to describe the deeds of aristocratic warriors and rulers. It is usually composed without the aid of writing and is chanted or recited to the accompaniment of a stringed instrument. It is transmitted orally from bard to bard over generations.

The extant body of heroic poetry ranges from quite ancient to modern works, produced over a widespread geographic area. It includes what are probably the earliest forms of the verse—panegyrics praising a hero's lineage and deeds, and laments on a hero's death. Another type of heroic poem is the short, dramatic lay devoted to a single event, such as the Old English *Battle of Maldon* or the Old High German *Hildebrandslied* ("Song of Hildebrand"). The mature form of heroic poetry is the full-scale epic, such as the *Iliad* or *Odyssey*.

Most heroic poetry looks back to a dimly defined "heroic age" when a generation of superior beings performed extraordinary feats of skill and courage. The heroic age varies in different native literatures. The epics of Homer created in the 8th century BC center on the Trojan War, which supposedly occurred about 1200 BC. The heroic poetry of the German, Scandinavian, and English peoples deals chiefly with a period from the 4th to 6th century AD, the time of the great migrations of the Germanic people. Though some of the heroes portrayed are historical personages, their actions are often combined and related for artistic purposes, with no regard for actual historical chronology.

Nevertheless, a heroic tale is assumed by the poet and his listeners to be somehow true. Its style is impersonal and objective, and the graphic realism of its detail gives it an air of probability that outweighs the occasional intrusion of marvelous elements.

Much ancient heroic poetry has been wholly lost, but the tradition is still alive among certain preliterate and semiliterate peoples living in remote communities. In the late 19th and 20th centuries a wealth of new heroic literature was collected from native storytellers in Russia, Estonia, Yugoslavia, Bulgaria, Albania, and Greece. In Central Asia heroic poems have been collected from peoples speaking Turkic languages; some particularly fine examples come from the Kara-Kirgiz of the Tien Shan mountains. The Yakut of northern Siberia, the Ainu of northern Japan, and some of the tribes of Arabia have also composed heroic poetry in modern times.

heroic prose Narrative prose tales that are the counterpart of heroic poetry in subject, outlook, and dramatic style. Whether composed orally or written down, the stories were meant to be recited, and they employ many of the formulaic expressions of oral tradition. A remarkable body of this prose is the early Irish Ulster cycle of stories, recorded between the 8th and 11th centuries, featuring the hero Cú Chulainn (Cuchulain) and his associates. A 12th-century group of Irish stories is the Fenian cycle, focusing on the hero Finn MacCumhaill (MacCool), his son (the poet Oisín), and his elite corps of warriors and hunters, the Fianna Éireann. Interspersed in the narratives are passages of verse, usually speeches, that are often older than the prose. Because of the verse sections, it is thought that these stories may have derived from a lost body of heroic poetry. The formulaic and poetic language of the Irish cycles is admirably preserved in Lady Gregory's retelling of the stories *Cuchulain of Muirthemne* (1902) and *Gods and Fighting Men* (1904).

Other examples of heroic prose are the 13th-century Icelandic sagas. The "heroic sagas," such as the *Völsunga saga* (*c.* 1270) and the *Thidriks saga* (*c.* 1250), are based on ancient Germanic oral tradition of the 4th to 6th century and contain many lines from lost heroic lays. Of higher artistic quality are the "Icelanders' sagas," such as the 13th-century *Grettis saga* and *Njáls saga,* dealing with native Icelandic families.

heroic stanza or **heroic quatrain** In poetry, a rhymed quatrain in heroic verse with rhyme scheme *abab*. The form was used by William Shakespeare and John Dryden among others and was also called an ELEGIAC STANZA after the publication in the mid-18th century of Thomas Gray's poem *An Elegy Written in a Country Church Yard.*

heroic verse or **heroic meter** or **heroic line** The verse form in which the heroic poetry of a particular language is, or according to critical opinion should be, composed. In classical poetry this was dactylic hexameter; in French, the alexandrine; in Italian, the hendecasyllabic line; and in English, iambic pentameter.

heroine \'her-ə-win, 'hir-\ [Greek *hēr¯oínē,* feminine derivative of *hḗrōs* hero] A mythological or legendary woman having the qualities of a HERO. The word is also more broadly applied to the principal female character in a literary or dramatic work.

hexameter \hek-ˈsam-ə-tər\ In classical prosody, a line of six metrical feet (Greek) or of six metra (Latin), usually dactyls (– ∪ ∪). Dactylic hexameter is the oldest known form of Greek poetry and is the preeminent meter of narrative and didactic poetry in Greek and Latin, in which its position is comparable to that of iambic pentameter in English versification. The epics of Homer and of Virgil are composed in dactylic hexameter, as are the didactic poems of Hesiod and Lucretius. A dactylic hexameter line is scanned as: – ∪̲∪̲ | – ∪̲∪̲ | – ∪̲∪̲ | – ∪̲∪̲ | – ∪̲∪̲ | – ∪̲.

Although the hexameter has been used in English verse by such 19th-century poets as Arthur Hugh Clough and Henry Wadsworth Longfellow (notably in the latter's *Evangeline*), its rhythms are not readily adapted to the language, and it has never been a popular form.

Hexapla \ˈhek-sə-plə\ [Late Latin, from Greek *Hexaplâ,* from neuter plural of *hexaplóos* sixfold, having six parts] An edition or work in six texts or versions in parallel columns. The term is derived from the title of a version of the Old Testament compiled about the 2nd century AD by Origen, a theologian and biblical scholar of the early Greek church.

Origen's *Hexapla* was a synopsis of six Old Testament versions: the Hebrew text, a transliteration of the Hebrew in Greek letters, the Septuagint (an authoritative Greek version of the Old Testament), and the versions of Aquila, Symmachus, and Theodotion. In the case of some books, Psalms for instance, as many as three more versions were added.

hexapody \hek-ˈsap-ə-dē\ [Greek *hexapod-, hexápous* (of a line of verse) having six feet] In classical prosody, a prosodic line or group consisting of six feet, often a line of trochaic or iambic verse measured by single feet instead of the more usual dipodies, or a line of dactylic hexameter in which foot and metron coincide.

hexastich \ˈhek-sə-ˌstik\ or **hexastichon** \hek-ˈsas-tə-ˌkän\ *plural* hexastichs *or* hexasticha \hek-ˈsas-tik-ə\ [New Latin *hexastichon,* ultimately from Greek *hexástichos* having six lines], *also called* sextet. A group, stanza, or poem of six lines. *See also* SESTET; SESTINA.

hiatus \hī-ˈā-təs\ [Latin, literally, opening, chasm] In prosody, a break in sound between two vowels that occur together without an intervening consonant, both vowels being clearly enunciated. The two vowels may be either within one word, as in the words V*ie*nna and n*ai*ve, or the final and initial vowels of two successive words, as in the phrases "s*ee i*t" and "g*o i*n." Hiatus is the opposite of elision, the dropping or blurring of the second vowel; it is also distinct from diphthongization, in which the vowels blend to form one sound.

The word also refers to a gap in a sentence or verse that destroys the sense or meaning of the sentence, or, in logic, to a missing step in a proof. *See also* LACUNA.

hierography \ˌhī-ə-ˈräg-rə-fē\ [Greek *hierós* sacred] Descriptive writing on sacred subjects, or a treatise on religion.

hierology \ˌhī-ə-ˈräl-ə-jē\ [Greek *hierós* sacred] A body of knowledge of sacred things, specifically the literary or traditional embodiment of the religious beliefs of a people, such as the Bible or the Qurʿān.

higgledy-piggledy *See* DOUBLE DACTYLS.

high \ˈhī\ **1.** Of an artistic style or movement, advanced toward its acme or fullest extent; specifically, constituting the late, fully developed, or most creative stage or period. **2.** Intensely moving, or characterized by sublime, heroic, or stirring events or subject matter, as in the phrase "high drama."

high comedy Comedy characterized by grace and wit and an appeal to the intellect, as in a comedy of manners. It often takes the form of satirizing human folly and inconsistencies, e.g., the plays of George Bernard Shaw and the novels of George Meredith. The latter helped define the concept of high comedy when he wrote in his lecture later published as *An Essay on Comedy and the Uses of the Comic Spirit* that true comedy should "awaken thoughtful laughter." *Compare* LOW COMEDY.

hipponactean \ˌhip-ə-ˌnak-ˈtē-ən\ Of or relating to the 6th-century-BC Greek poet Hipponax, who is said to have invented the metrical form known as the choliamb (or *scazon*), the "limping" iambic or trochaic trimeter in which the last three syllables are long.

Hisperic \his-ˈper-ik\ [Medieval Latin *Hispericus,* alteration of *Hespericus* western, Italian, hence probably (in reference to Latin style) urbane, elegant] Belonging to or constituting a style of Latin writing that probably originated in the British Isles in the 7th century. It is characterized by extreme obscurity intentionally produced by periphrasis (preference for a longer phrase over a shorter, equally adequate phrase), coinage of new words, and very liberal use of loanwords to express quite ordinary meanings. The style takes its name from the *Hisperica famina* ("Hisperic Sayings"), a work probably composed in Ireland in the mid-7th century.

historical criticism Criticism in the light of historical evidence, or criticism based on the context in which a work was written, including facts about the author's life and the historical and social circumstances of the time. This is in contrast to other types of criticism, such as textual and formal, in which emphasis is placed on examining the text itself while outside influences on the text are disregarded. New historicism is a particular form of historical criticism. *See also* LITERARY CRITICISM.

historical novel A novel that has as its setting a period of history and that attempts to convey the spirit, manners, and social conditions of a past age with realistic detail and fidelity to historical fact.

The work may deal with actual historical personages, as does Robert Graves' *I, Claudius* (1934), or it may contain a mixture of fictional and historical characters. It may focus on a single historic event, as does Franz Werfel's *The Forty Days of Musa Dagh* (1933), which dramatizes the defense of an Armenian stronghold. More often it attempts to portray a broader view of a past society in which great events are reflected by their impact on the private lives of fictional individuals. Since the appearance of the first historical novel, Sir Walter Scott's *Waverley* (1814), this type of fiction has remained popular. Though some historical novels, such as Leo Tolstoy's *War and Peace* (1865–69), are of the highest artistic quality, many are mediocre—the purely escapist costume romance makes no pretense to historicity but uses a setting in the past to lend credibility to improbable characters and adventures.

historical rhyme A form of eye rhyme, in which two words appear to rhyme but in fact are now pronounced differently, where the two words were formerly pronounced the same, as *flood* and *brood* or *far* and *war*.

historiette \ˌhis-ˌtȯr-ē-ˈet\ [French, a derivative of *histoire* history, influenced in form by Latin *historia*] A short history or story.

history play *See* CHRONICLE PLAY.

hokku \ˈhȯk-ˌkü\ [Japanese, from *hok-* opening, first + *ku* stanza] Originally, the opening stanza of a *renga* (linked-verse poem), which developed into an independent poem later called a HAIKU.

holograph \ˈhäl-ə-ˌgraf, ˈhōl-\ [Late Greek *hológraphos* written entirely in the same hand, from Greek *hólos* whole + *-graphos* written] A manuscript or document wholly handwritten by the person in whose name it appears.

Home Journal One of the earliest general-circulation magazines in the United States, founded in 1846 by former newspaper editors Nathaniel Parker Willis and George P. Morris. Intended for readers in high society, the magazine was an attempt to provide both society news and intellectual stimulation in the form of literary pieces. In its early years it published works by such American authors as Edgar Allan Poe, James Fenimore Cooper, and Washington Irving; among the transatlantic authors it introduced to American readers were Honoré de Balzac, Victor Hugo, Thomas Carlyle, and Thomas De Quincey. In 1901 the journal's name was changed to *Town and Country,* and its emphasis became largely the lifestyle of the wealthy.

Homeric simile *See* EPIC SIMILE.

homoeomeral \ˌhōm-ē-ˈäm-ə-rəl, ˌhäm-\ [Greek *homoiomerḗs* consisting of equal parts] In prosody, having parts that are metrically similar, as in the repetition of a stanza form.

homoeoteleuton \ˌhōm-ē-ō-tə-ˈlü-ˌtän, ˌhäm-, -tel-ˈyü-\ [Greek *homoiotéleuton,* from neuter of *homoiotéleutos* having the same ending] An occurrence in writing of the same or similar endings close together (as in the phrase *fairly commonly*). Homoeoteleutons may occur either by chance or by intention (e.g., for rhythmic effect). They may occur in neighboring words, clauses, or lines.

homometrical \ˌhōm-ō-ˈmet-ri-kəl, ˌhäm-\ In prosody, having the same meter throughout.

Horatian ode \hə-ˈrā-shən\ Short lyric poem written in stanzas of two or four lines in the manner of the 1st-century-BC Latin poet Horace. In contrast to the lofty, heroic epinicion odes of the Greek poet Pindar, most of Horace's odes are intimate and reflective; they are often addressed to a friend and deal with friendship, love, and the practice of poetry.

Horace introduced early Greek lyrics into Latin by adapting Greek meters, regularizing them, and writing his romanized versions with a discipline that caused some loss of spontaneity and a sense of detachment but that also produced elegance and dignity. He cautioned Latin writers not to attempt to emulate Pindar, a task that he likened to Icarus' attempt to fly, only to fall into the sea and drown when his wings melted because he flew too close to the sun. His *carmina,* written in stanzas of two or four lines, are now universally called odes, but they have nothing in common with the passionate brilliance of Pindaric odes. Horace's tone is generally serious and serene, often touched with irony and melancholy but sometimes with gentle humor. In later periods, when technical felicity was more highly regarded than imagination and spontaneity, Horace's odes were prized and imitated. Among the preservers of the Horatian tradition were Pierre de Ronsard, Nicolas Boileau, Jean de La Fontaine, and Michael Drayton. Andrew Marvell produced one of the finest English Horatian odes in 1650 on Cromwell's return from Ireland. In the early 18th century, Matthew Prior, Jonathan Swift, and Samuel Johnson revived the Horatian spirit, as did Giacomo Leopardi and Giosuè Carducci in Italy in the 19th century. The influence of the Horatian ode continued into the 20th century in such works as W.H. Auden's "In Memory of W.B. Yeats" and Allen Tate's "Ode to the Confederate Dead." *See also* ODE; PINDARIC ODE.

Horatian satire \hə-ˈrā-shən\ Urbane and amusing satire of contemporary society that seeks to correct by gentle laughter rather than by bitter condemnation. Horatian satire takes its name from its originator, Horace, the Latin lyricist and satirist of the 1st century BC, whose verse satires on Roman society were suffused with charm and warm humanity. In three of his *Satires,* Horace discusses the tone appropriate to the satirist who out of a moral concern attacks the vice and folly he sees around him. As opposed to the harshness of earlier satirists such as Gaius Lucilius, Horace opts for mild mockery and playful wit as the means most effective for his ends. This type of satire has been used in poetry, by Nicolas Boileau, John Dryden, and Alexander Pope, among others; in drama, in such forms as the comedy of manners; and in prose fiction, in the novels of such authors as Miguel de Cervantes and Jane Austen. *Compare* JUVENALIAN SATIRE.

Horizon Magazine first issued in 1940 in England as a medium for literature during World War II. Founded in 1939 by Cyril Connolly, Stephen Spender, and Peter Watson, it was published until 1950. Among the contributors to *Horizon* were some of the foremost writers of the 20th century, including Evelyn Waugh, W.H. Auden, and George Orwell.

hornbook \ˈhȯrn-ˌbu̇k\ Children's primer common in England from the mid-15th to the 18th century and in the colonial United States. It consisted of a paddle-shaped wooden board on which was mounted a printed sheet of vellum or paper. The printed page was protected with thin, transparent sheets of horn. The frame had a pierced handle and was usually hung at the child's belt.

The printed material usually included such information as the alphabet, numerals, simple words, the blessing "In the name of the Father and of the Son and of the Holy Ghost, Amen," and the Lord's Prayer. Thomas Dekker satirized the hornbook in "The Guls Horne-booke" (1609), a spoof primer for young dandies of the time.

horror story A story in which the focus is on creating a feeling of fear. Such tales are of ancient origin and form a substantial part of the body of folk literature. They can feature supernatural elements such as ghosts, witches, or vampires, or they can address more realistic psychological fears. In Western literature, the literary cultivation of fear and curiosity for its own sake began to emerge in the 18th-century pre-Romantic era with the gothic novel. The genre was invented by Horace Walpole, whose *Castle of Otranto* (1765) may be said to have founded the horror story as a legitimate form. Mary Wollstonecraft Shelley introduced the pseudoscientific note in her famous novel *Frankenstein* (1818), about the creation of a monster that ultimately destroys its creator, Dr. Frankenstein.

In the Romantic era the German storyteller E.T.A. Hoffmann and the American Edgar Allan Poe raised the horror story to a level far above mere entertainment through their skillful intermingling of reason and madness, eerie atmosphere and everyday reality. They invested their specters, doubles, and haunted houses with a psychological symbolism that gave their tales a haunting credibility.

The gothic influence persisted throughout the 19th century in such works as Sheridan Le Fanu's *The House by the Churchyard* and "Green Tea," Wilkie Collins' *The Moonstone,* and Bram Stoker's vampire tale *Dracula*. The influence was revived in the 20th century by science-fiction and fantasy writers such as Mervyn Peake in his Gormenghast series. Other masters of the horror tale were Ambrose Bierce, Arthur Machen, Algernon Blackwood, H.P. Lovecraft, and Stephen King. Isolated masterpieces have been produced by writers not usually associated with the genre, for example, Guy de Maupassant's "Le Horla," A.E. Coppard's "Adam and Eve and Pinch Me," Saki's "Sredni Vashtar" and "The Open Window," and W.F. Harvey's "August Heat." Some of the best-known horror stories owe their power to their development of full-bodied characters in a realistic social environment and the very absence of mysterious atmosphere. In this category are Aleksandr Pushkin's "The Queen of Spades" and W.W. Jacobs' "The Monkey's Paw."

Hound and Horn American quarterly of the arts cofounded and edited by Lincoln Kirstein. It was published from 1927 to 1934. The journal's name was taken from a passage in the poem "White Stag" by Ezra Pound: " 'Tis the white stag, Fame, we're a-hunting/ Bid the world's hounds come to horn."

Initially published at Harvard University, *Hound and Horn* became a widely inclusive American arts review by its third issue (1928), and it moved to New York in 1930. The philosophical perspective of the *Hound and Horn* fluctuated drastically, from humanism to Southern agrarianism to Marxism, but it continued to publish works by leading modern poets, writers, and critics, including poetry by Pound, William Carlos Williams, and Wallace Stevens; fiction by Katherine Anne Porter, Kay Boyle, and Sean O'Faolain; and criticism and commentary by T.S. Eliot, Allen Tate, Granville Hicks, and staff editors R.P. Blackmur and Yvor Winters. Apart from literature, it reviewed new developments in film, theater, music, dance, art, and architecture in its columns. It was abandoned when Kirstein, its principal force, began devoting his energies and financial resources to the ballet.

house dramatist A writer of plays for a particular theater.

Household Words Weekly periodical published in London by Charles Dickens from March 30, 1850 to May 28, 1859. Priced at twopence and occasionally reaching a circulation of 300,000, the popular magazine addressed a broad readership with weekly miscellanies of fiction, poetry, and essays. Although Dickens was a co-owner with William Bradbury and Frederick Evans, he exerted total editorial control and eventually bought out his partners in order to shut down *Household Words* and replace it with *All the Year Round,* which he edited and published until his death in 1870 (*All the Year Round* continued publication until 1888).

Dickens himself wrote a great deal for *Household Words,* contributing serialized books, including *Hard Times* (1854) and *Great Expectations* (1860–61), essays, and other miscellaneous pieces, some of which were collected in *Reprinted Pieces* (1858) and *The Uncommercial Traveller* (1861; later amplified). He also contributed many items on current political and social affairs and wrote what he called process articles, explanatory stories about the production methods of various industries. Other distinguished novelists who contributed serials included Mrs. Gaskell, Wilkie Collins, Charles Reade, and Edward Bulwer-Lytton.

Dickens took responsibility for all the opinions expressed (articles were anonymous) and selected and amended contributions accordingly. The poetry in *Household Words* was uniformly feeble, but the reportage was often solid and perceptive. The magazine's success was due not only to Dickens' illustrious name but also to his practical sagacity and unremitting editorial work.

hovering accent *also called* hovering stress. A distribution of energy, pitch, or duration in two adjacent syllables when a heavy syllable occurs next to a syllable bearing the metrical ictus so that the stress seems to be divided or diffused nearly equally over both syllables, as *cornfield* in the line

> “that o’ér / the gréen / cornfield / did páss.”

Hovering accents are common in English verse.

huaju or **hua-chü** \'hwä-'ju̅e̅\ [Chinese *huàjù,* from *huà* word, talk + *jù* drama] Form of Chinese drama featuring realistic spoken dialogue rather than the sung poetic dialogue of the traditional Chinese dramatic forms. *Huaju* was developed in the early 20th century by intellectuals who wanted to replace the traditional Chinese forms with Western-style drama. The first full-length play of this kind was an adaptation of Lin Shu’s *Heinu yu tian lu* (1901; “The Black Slave Cries Out to Heaven”), itself a version of *Uncle Tom’s Cabin;* it was produced by a group of Chinese students in Japan in 1907. At first the *huaju* plays consisted exclusively of translations or adaptations of Western works intended for the appreciation of Western-educated intellectuals, but the appeal of *huaju* was later broadened through the efforts of the China Traveling Dramatic Troupe. In 1936 the troupe performed *Leiyu* (*Thunderstorm*), an original four-act tragedy by Cao Yu, one of the most successful *huaju* writers. The form was created during a period of political instability, and it often featured some element of social commentary.

hubris \'hyü-bris\ or **hybris** \'hī-\ [Greek *hýbris*] In classical Greek ethical and religious thought, overweening presumption suggesting impious disregard of the limits governing human action in an orderly universe. It is the sin to which the great and gifted are most susceptible, and in Greek tragedy it is usually the hero’s tragic flaw. Perhaps the simplest example occurs in the *Persians* of Aeschylus, in which the arrogance of Xerxes in building a bridge of ships across the Hellespont flouts nature by turning sea into land. He is punished by the crushing defeat of the Persians at Salamis. In most other Greek tragedies the hero’s hubris is more subtle, and sometimes he appears wholly blameless.

Hudibrastic \ˌhyü-də-'bras-tik\ Written in humorous octosyllabic couplets. The term is derived from Samuel Butler’s *Hudibras,* a mock-heroic satirical poem in octosyllabic couplets. *See also* MOCK-EPIC.

Hugo Award \'hyü-gō, 'yü-\, *byname of* Science Fiction Achievement Award. Any of several trophies awarded annually by a professional organization for notable achievement in science fiction or science fantasy. The award is given in five writing categories—novel, novella, novelette, short story, and nonfiction. An award for best new writer and special awards are also occasionally presented. The award was established in 1953 in honor of Hugo Gernsback, who founded the first magazine exclusively for science fiction, which he called “scientifiction.”

huitain \w^{y}ē-'te^n\ [French, from Middle French, a derivative of *huit* eight] French verse form consisting of an eight-line stanza with 8 or 10 syllables in each line. The form was written on three rhymes, one of which appeared four times. Typical rhyme schemes were *ababbcbc* and *abbaacac*. The huitain was popular in France in the 15th and early 16th centuries with such poets as François Villon and Clément Marot.

humanism \'hyü-mə-ˌniz-əm, 'yü-\ The learning or cultural impulse that is characterized by a revival of classical letters, an individualistic and critical spirit, and a shift of emphasis from religious to secular concerns that flowered during the Renaissance.

Renaissance humanism is traceable to the 14th-century Italian poet Petrarch, whose scholarship and enthusiasm for classic Latin writings ("the humanities") gave great impetus to a movement that eventually spread from Italy to all of western Europe. The diffusion of humanism was facilitated by the universal use of Latin and by the invention of movable type. Although humanism gradually became identified with classroom studies of the classics, it more properly embraced any attitude that exalted man's relationship to God, free will, and human superiority over nature.

Excitement over Latin sources touched off a widespread search for ancient documents that led in time to Greek and Hebrew studies. Textual criticism and philology were born, and with them renewed interest in Aristotle and the Scriptures. In its return to antiquity, humanism found inspiration in man's personal quest for truth and goodness. Confining systems of philosophy, religious dogmas, and abstract reasoning were shunned in favor of human values. Though ceaseless efforts were made to relate Christian thought to the philosophies of the ancient world, seeds were likewise sown for the flowering of Reformation thought.

In recent years the term humanism has often been used to refer to value systems that emphasize the personal worth of each individual but that do not include a belief in God. In addition to these nontheistic humanisms, there is some tendency among Christian theologians to refer to Christianity as humanistic.

humanities \hyü-'man-i-tēz, yü-\ The branches of learning (such as philosophy or languages) that investigate human constructs and concerns as opposed to natural processes (such as physics or chemistry).

humors \'hyü-mərz, 'yü-\ [Latin *umor, humor* moisture, bodily fluid] The four main fluids present in the human body according to the theory of physiology during the Middle Ages and the Renaissance. The humors were blood, phlegm, yellow bile, and black bile. A person's temperament, disposition, and morality were thought to be determined by the relative proportions of the humors in the body as they released vapors that affected the brain. The four main temperaments, depending on which humor was dominant, were sanguine, phlegmatic, choleric, and melancholic. The theory was carried over to literature in the creation of characters based on the relative balance of the humors and in the development of the COMEDY OF HUMORS.

Hybris *See* HUBRIS.

hymnal stanza *See* COMMON METER.

hymenaic meter \ˌhī-mə-ˈnā-ik\ [Late Latin *hymenaicum metrum,* from Greek *hyménaios* marriage song] In classical prosody, a dactylic dimeter (scanned as – ∪ ∪ – ∪ ∪).

hyperbaton \hī-ˈpər-bə-ˌtän\ [Greek *hyperbatón,* from neuter of *hyperbatós* transposed, inverted, a derivative of *hyperbaínein* to step over, overstep, transgress] A transposition or inversion of usual word order. The device is often used in poetry, as in line 13 from Canto II of Alexander Pope's *The Rape of the Lock:* "Bright as the sun, her eyes the gazers strike."

hyperbole \hī-ˈpər-bə-lē\ [Greek *hyperbolḗ* excess, hyperbole, a derivative of *hyperbállein* to exceed] A figure of speech that is an intentional exaggeration for emphasis or comic effect. Hyperbole is common in love poetry— in which it is used to convey the lover's intense admiration for the beloved. An example is the following passage from William Shakespeare's *The Merchant of Venice:*

> Why, if two gods should play some heavenly match
> And on the wager lay two earthly women,
> And Portia one, there must be something else
> Pawned with the other, for the poor rude world
> Hath not her fellow.

When hyperbole fails to create the desired dramatic effect, the exaggeration may seem ridiculous. Examples of hyperbole occur in sagas recounting the heroic deeds of legendary kings and warriors, tall tales, Greek and Roman mythology, and, in a broader sense, modern political rhetoric and advertising slogans.

hypercatalexis \ˌhī-pər-ˌkat-ə-ˈlek-sis\ In prosody, the occurrence of an additional syllable at the end of a line of verse after the line is metrically complete; especially (in verse measured by dipodies), the occurrence of a syllable after the last complete dipody. A feminine ending is a form of hypercatalexis. *See* FEMININE ENDING.

hypermeter \hī-ˈpər-mi-tər\ or **hypermetron** \-ˌträn\ **1.** A hypercatalectic verse. **2.** In classical prosody, a period comprising more than two or three colons (rhythmical units of an utterance).

hypermetric Having one or more syllables beyond the required measure at the end of a line or other metrical unit. In classical prosody, having metrical continuity from one line to the next, usually as the result of the elision of a final vowel of one line with the opening line of the next, producing synapheia, the fastening of two lines into one period by avoiding a pause between them.

hypermetron *See* HYPERMETER.

hyporrhythmic \ˌhī-pō-ˈrith-mik, ˌhip-ō-\ In Greek and Latin prosody, deficient as to rhythm. The term is used of a hexameter in which the end of a word coincides with the end of each foot and which accordingly has no true caesura.

hypotaxis \ˌhī-pō-ˈtak-sis, ˌhip-ō-\ [Greek *hypótaxis* postposing, subjection, a derivative of *hypotássein* to place under, subjoin] The arrangement of clauses and phrases in a pattern of syntactic subordination (as by the use of conjunctions or relative pronouns). *Compare* PARATAXIS.

hysteron proteron \ˌhis-tə-rän-ˈprä-tə-ˌrän, -tə-rən-ˈprä-tə-rən, ˈprȯ-\ [Greek *hýsteron próteron* (the) later (put before the) earlier] A figure of speech consisting of the reversal of a natural or rational order (as in "then came the thunder and the lightning").

I

Arbuthnot is no more my Friend,
Who dares to Irony pretend;
Which I was born to introduce,
Refin'd it first, and shew'd its Use.
—Jonathan Swift

iamb \'ī-ˌam, -ˌamb\ or **iambus** \ī-'am-bəs\ [Greek *íambos*] In prosody, a metrical foot consisting of one short syllable (as in classical or quantitative verse) or one unstressed syllable (as in modern or accentual verse) followed by one long or stressed syllable, as in the word

∪ ´
be | cause.

Considered by the ancient Greeks to approximate the natural rhythm of speech, iambic meters were used extensively for dramatic dialogue, invective, satire, and fables. Also suited to the cadence of the English language, iambic rhythms, especially iambic tetrameter and pentameter, are the preeminent meters of English verse. Substitution of other types of feet to add variety is common in what's basically iambic verse. An example of iambic meter is the English ballad, composed of quatrains written in alternating lines of iambic tetrameter and iambic trimeter:

∪ ´ ∪ ´ ∪ ´ ∪ ´
There lived | a wife | at Ush | er's Well,
∪ ∪ ´ ∪ ´ ∪ ´
And a weal | thy wife | was she:
∪ ´ ∪ ´ ∪ ´ ∪ ´
She had | three stout | and stal | wart sons,
∪ ´ ∪ ´ ∪ ´
And sent | them o'er | the sea.

The iamb is scanned ∪ – in classical verse and ∪ ´ in modern prosody. *Compare* TROCHEE.

iambe \'yä^{n}b\ [French, literally, iamb] French satiric verse form consisting of alternating lines of 8 and 12 syllables. The total number of lines is variable. Greek writers, especially Archilochus, had used iambics as a vehicle for satire, but the name came into use as a French form in the late 18th and early 19th centuries when André Chénier's *Ïambes* and Auguste Barbier's *Les Ïambes* were published.

iambelegus \ˌī-ˌam-'bel-ə-gəs\ [Greek *iambélegos,* from *íambos* iamb + *élegos* song accompanied by the flute] In classical prosody, a line of verse that consists of an iambic dimeter and half an elegiac pentameter, which is made up of dactylic elements – ⏑ ⏑ – ⏑ ⏑ –. In Greek lyric, an iambelegus is usually ⏓ – ⏑ – ⏓ | – ⏑ ⏑ – ⏑ ⏑ – and is most often found in dactylo-epitrites as used especially by Pindar, where the iambic elements vary in length. In Latin verse, Horace used a longer version in his 13th epode: ⏑ – ⏑ – ⏑ – ⏑ ⏓ | – ⏑ ⏑ – ⏑ ⏑ –.

iambic \ī-ˈam-bik\ A lampoon or piece of usually satiric verse written in iambs (such as that developed by the Ionian Greeks in the period succeeding the epic).

Icelanders' sagas *also called* family sagas. The class of heroic prose narratives written during the 13th century about the great families who lived in Iceland from 930 to 1030. They are a unique contribution to Western literature and are far in advance of any medieval literature in their realism, their controlled, objective style, their powers of character delineation, and their overwhelming tragic dignity. The family sagas represent the highest development of the classical age of Icelandic saga writing. Their artistic unity, length, and complexity have convinced most modern scholars that they are written works by individual authors, although the theory that they were composed orally still has adherents. Whoever they were, the authors constantly aimed at geographic, social, and cultural verisimilitude; they made it their business to depict life in Iceland. The historicity of these sagas has also been the subject of long debate; but, whether they are true to history, they are true to the grim ethos of a vanished way of life, which they portray with dramatic power and laconic eloquence. An important aim of this literature was to encourage people to attain a better understanding of their social environment and a truer knowledge of themselves through studying the real and imagined fates of their forebears. A spirit of humanism, sometimes colored by a fatalistic heroic outlook, pervades the narrative; nevertheless, pleasing storytelling remained the chief aim of the saga writers.

The Icelanders' sagas can be subdivided into several categories according to the social and ethical status of the principal heroes. In some, the hero is a poet and a lover who sets out from the rural society of his native land in search of fame and adventure to become the retainer of some foreign ruler. To this group belong some of the early 13th-century sagas, including *Kormáks saga, Hallfredar saga,* and *Bjarnar saga Hítdaelakappa.* In *Gunnlaugs saga ormstungu,* which may have been written after the middle of the 13th century, the love theme is treated more romantically than in the others. *Fostbraeda saga* ("The Blood-Brothers' Saga") describes two contrasting heroes: one a poet and lover, the other a ruthless killer. *Egils saga* offers a brilliant study of a complex personality—a ruthless Viking who is also a sensitive poet, a rebel against authority from early childhood who ends his life as a defenseless, blind old man. In several sagas the hero becomes an outlaw fighting a hopeless battle against the social forces that have rejected him. To this group belong *Hardar saga ok Hólmverja* and *Droplaugarsona saga,* but the greatest of the outlaw sagas are *Gísla saga,* describing a man who murders his own brother-in-law and whose sister reveals his dark secret, and *Grettis saga,* which deals with a hero of great talents and courage who is constantly fighting against heavy odds and is treacherously slain by an unscrupulous enemy.

Most of the Icelanders' sagas, however, are concerned with fully integrated members of society, either as ordinary farmers or as farmers who also act as chieftains. *Hrafnkels saga* describes a chieftain who murders his shepherd, is then tortured and humiliated for his crime, and finally takes cruel revenge on one of his tormentors. The hero who gives his name to *Hœnsa-Thoris saga* is a man of humble background who makes money as a peddler and becomes a wealthy but unpopular landowner. His egotism creates trouble in the neighborhood, and after he has set fire to one of the farmsteads, killing the farmer and the entire household, he is prosecuted and put to death. *Ölkofra tháttr* (the term "tháttr" is often used for a short story) and *Bandamanna saga* ("The Confederates' Saga") satirize chieftains who fail in their duty to guard the integrity of the law and try to turn other people's mistakes into profit for themselves. The central plot in *Laxdœla saga* is a love triangle, in which the jealous heroine forces her husband to kill his best friend. *Eyrbyggja saga* describes a complex series of feuds between several related families, and *Hávardar saga* is about an old farmer who takes revenge on his son's killer, the local chieftain. *Víga-Glúms saga* tells of a ruthless chieftain who commits several killings and swears an ambiguous oath in order to cover his guilt, while *Vatnsdœla saga* is the story of a noble chieftain whose last act is to help his killer escape.

In the Icelanders' sagas, justice, rather than courage, is often the primary virtue, as might be expected in a literature that places the success of an individual below the welfare of society at large. This theme is an underlying one in *Njáls saga,* the greatest of all the sagas. It is a story of great complexity and richness, with a host of brilliantly executed character portrayals and a profound understanding of human strengths and weaknesses. Its structure is highly complex, but at its core is the tragedy of an influential farmer and sage who devotes his life to a hopeless struggle against the destructive forces of society. In the end his enemies set fire to his house, killing his wife and sons with him.

icon \ˈī-ˌkän, -kən\ A sign (such as a word or graphic symbol) whose form suggests its meaning. The word was brought into common academic use by those who study semiotics (the study of signs). Some literary critics, especially those associated with New Criticism, referred to poems as verbal icons in the sense that the meaning of a poem is contained in or expressed by the structure and mechanics of its language, including the arrangement of images, the meter, and the use of figures of speech such as metaphor. W.K. Wimsatt expressed this view in the essay collection *The Verbal Icon: Studies in the Meaning of Poetry* (1954).

ictus \ˈik-təs\ [Latin, literally, stroke, blow] **1.** The recurring stress or beat in a rhythmic or metrical series of sounds. Metrical accent. **2.** The place of the stress or beat in a metrical foot. *Compare* ARSIS; THESIS.

idealism \ī-ˈdē-ə-ˌliz-əm\ Literary or artistic theory or practice that values ideal or subjective types or aspects of beauty more than formal or sensible qualities. It may also affirm the preeminent value of imagination as compared with the faithful copying of nature. *Compare* REALISM.

idée reçue \ē-ˌdā-rə-ˈsue̅\ [French, received idea] An idea that is unexamined, a phrase particularly associated with Gustave Flaubert, who in his *Le Dictionnaire des idées reçues* (published posthumously in 1913; *Flaubert's Dictionary of Accepted Ideas*) mocked the use of clichés and platitudes and the uncritical reliance on accepted ideas. Initially begun for his own amusement, the so-called dictionary was compiled with the help of the young philosopher Alfred Le Poittevin. Together they invented a grotesque imaginary character called "le Garçon" ("the Boy"), to whom they attributed whatever sort of remark seemed to them most debased. The work reflects Flaubert's disdain for the "bourgeois," by which he meant anyone who "has a low way of thinking."

identical rhyme *See* RIME RICHE.

idiom \ˈid-ē-əm\ [Greek *idíōma* peculiarity, peculiarity of style, idiom, a derivative of *idioûsthai* to make one's own, a derivative of *ídios* one's own, peculiar] A style or form of artistic expression that is characteristic of an individual, a period or movement, or a medium or instrument.

idunit \ˌī-ˈdən-it, ˈī-\ [alteration of *I done it*] An autobiographical or confessional account usually of a sensational character. The word, apparently modeled on the more widely used "whodunit," had little vogue after the 1950s.

idyll or **idyl** \ˈīd-əl, ˈid-\ [Latin *idyllium,* from Greek *eidýllion,* diminutive of *eîdos* shape, form, literary form] **1.** A short descriptive poem usually dealing with pastoral or rural life. *See also* ECLOGUE. **2.** A simple descriptive work either in poetry or prose that deals with rustic life or pastoral scenes or suggests a mood of peace and contentment. **3.** A narrative poem (such as Alfred, Lord Tennyson's *Idylls of the King*) that treats more or less fully an epic, romantic, or tragic theme.

The term idyll was used in Greco-Roman antiquity to designate a variety of brief poems on simple subjects in which the description of natural objects was introduced. The conventions of the pastoral were developed by the Alexandrian school of poetry, particularly by Theocritus, Bion, and Moschus, in the 3rd–2nd century BC.

The word was revived during the Renaissance, when some poets employed it to distinguish narrative pastorals from those in dialogue. The general use, or misuse, of the word arose in the 19th century, from the popularity of two works, the *Idylles héroïques* (1858) of Victor-Richard de Laprade and Tennyson's *Idylls of the King* (1859), neither of which was related to the pastoral tradition. Thereafter, the word was used indiscriminately to refer to works on a variety of subjects.

illuminati \i-ˌlü-mi-ˈnä-tē\ [New Latin, plural of *illuminatus,* from Latin, past participle of *illuminare* to illuminate, reveal] Any of various groups of persons who are or claim to be unusually enlightened. One such group was formed in Bavaria in 1776 by Adam Weishaupt and included writers and philosophers such as J.G. von Herder, Johann Pestalozzi, and J.W. von Goethe.

imagery \ˈim-ij-rē, -ə-rē\ Representation of objects, feelings, or ideas, either literally or through the use of figurative language; specifically, the often peculiarly individual concrete or figurative diction used by a writer in those portions of text where a particular effect (such as a special emotional appeal or a train of intellectual associations) is desired.

The power of incidental images can be seen, for example, in the plays of William Shakespeare. In *Twelfth Night,* barren mountains, salt sea, and the smoke of war, storms, imprisonment, death, and madness are all invoked. When the king and queen of fairies quarrel in *A Midsummer Night's Dream,* Titania's speech evokes a world of chaos:

> The ox hath therefore stretch'd his yoke in vain,
> The plowman lost his sweat, and the green corn
> Hath rotted ere his youth attain'd a beard;
> The fold stands empty in the drowned field,
> And crows are fatted with the murrion flock . . .

In "The Second Coming," William Butler Yeats invokes a powerful image of encroaching anarchy:

> Turning and turning in the widening gyre
> The falcon cannot hear the falconer;
> Things fall apart . . .

imagination [Latin *imaginatio,* a derivative of *imaginari* to imagine, form a mental image of, a derivative of *imago* representation, image] *See* FANCY.

Imaginism \i-ˈmaj-ə-ˌniz-əm\ [Russian *imazhinizm,* probably from French *imaginer* to imagine] Russian poetic movement of the postrevolutionary period that advocated poetry based on a series of arresting and unusual images. It is sometimes called Imagism but is unrelated to the 20th-century Anglo-American movement of that name. The Imaginist movement was founded in 1919 by its leading poet, Sergey Aleksandrovich Yesenin, who rivaled the leading Futurist poet, Vladimir Mayakovsky, in popularity. Like the Futurists, the Imaginists read poetry in cafés during a time of social upheaval when few books were published, but, unlike the Futurists, they were unable to adapt to the demands of Soviet life. Instead they expressed their alienation in acts of irresponsible bohemianism. The Imaginists dissolved at the time of Yesenin's suicide in 1925, and their techniques had little lasting effect on Soviet poetry, although Yesenin himself remained a popular poet and cultural hero.

Imagism \'im-i-ˌjiz-əm\ A movement of American and English poets whose verse was characterized by concrete language and figures of speech, modern subject matter, freedom in the use of meter, and avoidance of romantic or mystical themes.

Imagism was a successor to the French Symbolist movement. The Imagist credo was formulated about 1912 by Ezra Pound—in conjunction with fellow poets Hilda Doolittle (H.D.), Richard Aldington, and F.S. Flint—and was inspired by the critical views of T.E. Hulme, in revolt against the careless thinking and Romantic optimism he saw prevailing.

The Imagists wrote succinct verse of dry clarity and hard outline in which an exact visual image made a total poetic statement but, whereas Symbolism had an affinity with music, Imagism sought analogy with sculpture. In 1914 Pound turned to Vorticism, and Amy Lowell largely took over the spiritual leadership of the group. Among others who wrote Imagist poetry were John Gould Fletcher and Harriet Monroe. The movement influenced the poetry of Conrad Aiken, Marianne Moore, Wallace Stevens, D.H. Lawrence, and T.S. Eliot.

The four anthologies (*Des Imagistes,* 1914; *Some Imagists,* 1915, 1916, 1917), and the magazines *Poetry* (from 1912) and *The Egoist* (from 1914), in the United States and England, respectively, published the work of a dozen Imagist poets. *Compare* SYMBOLIST MOVEMENT.

imitation \ˌim-ə-'tā-shən\ A literary work designed to reproduce the style of another author. *See also* MIMESIS.

immetrical \im-'met-ri-kəl\ Lacking meter; unmetrical.

immram *See* IMRAM.

impressionism \im-'presh-ə-ˌniz-əm\ **1.** The depiction (as in literature) of a scene, emotion, or character by details intended to achieve a vividness or effectiveness more by evoking subjective and sensory impressions than by re-creating or representing an objective reality. The term is sometimes applied to writers—such as Dorothy Richardson, Virginia Woolf, and James Joyce—who employ stream-of-consciousness techniques. **2.** In literary criticism, the practice of presenting and elaborating one's subjective reactions to a work of art. Also, a critical theory that advocates or defends such a practice as the only valid one in criticism.

imram or **immram** \'im-ˌräv\ *plural* immrama \-ˌräv-ä\ [Old Irish *imram* sea voyage, literally, act of rowing, verbal noun of *imm-rá* rows around, navigates] In early Irish literature, a story about an adventurous voyage. This type of story includes tales of Irish saints traveling to Iceland or Greenland, as well as fabulous tales of pagan heroes journeying to the otherworld (*eachtra* or *echtra*). An outstanding example of an *imram* is *Immram Brain Maic Febail* (*The Voyage of Bran, Son of Febal*), which describes a trip to the enchanted Land of Women. After what seems to be a year Bran and his colleagues return home to discover that their voyage lasted longer than any memories and is recorded only in ancient sources.

incantation \ˌin-ˌkan-ˈtā-shən\ [Late Latin *incantatio* spell, enchantment, a derivative of Latin *incantare* to put a spell on, enchant] **1.** A formula of words chanted or recited in a magic ritual and designed to produce a particular effect. An example of this is the recipe recited by the witches in William Shakespeare's *Macbeth.* **2.** An expression (as of music or poetry) designed to move rather than amuse or convince.

incident \ˈin-sə-dənt\ An occurrence or related group of occurrences that are subordinate to a main narrative plot. *See also* EPISODE.

incipit \ˈin-sə-pit, ˈiŋ-ki-\ The introductory words or part of a medieval Western manuscript or early printed book. In the absence of a title page, the text may be recognized, referred to, and recorded by its incipit. As in the title pages or main divisions of later printed books, incipits (Latin for "here begins") provide an occasion for display letters and much calligraphic ornament.

The end of the text in a medieval manuscript was announced by the word *explicit,* probably a reshaping (after *incipit*) of an earlier Latin phrase such as *explicitum est volumen* ("the book has been completely unrolled"), a reminder of the scroll form of the book used in the West before the codex format was adopted in about AD 300.

incremental repetition A device used in poetry of the oral tradition, especially English and Scottish ballads, in which a line is repeated in a changed context or with minor changes in the repeated part. The device is illustrated in the following stanzas from the ballad "Lord Randal":

> "O where ha' you been, Lord Randal, my son?
> And where ha' you been, my handsome young man?"
> "I ha' been at the greenwood; mother, mak my bed soon,
> For I'm wearied wi' huntin', and fain wad lie down."
>
> "And wha met ye there, Lord Randal, my son?
> And wha met you there, my handsome young man?"
> O I met wi' my true-love; mother, mak my bed soon,
> For I'm wearied wi' huntin', and fain wad lie down."

incult \in-ˈkəlt\ [Latin *incultus,* literally, not tilled, untended] Lacking finish or polish; uncultivated, crude, or disordered. The term is used especially of literary style or its products or producers.

incunabulum \ˌin-kyə-ˈnab-yə-ləm\ or **incunable** \in-ˈkyü-nə-bəl\ *plural* incunabula \ˌin-kyə-ˈnab-yə-lə\ *or* incunables [Latin *incunabula* a person's earliest years, literally, bands used to hold a baby in a cradle], *also called* cradle book *or* fifteener. A book printed before 1501. The date, though convenient, is arbitrary, unconnected as it is to any development in the printing art; the initial period of printing, a restless, highly competitive free-for-all, ran well into the 16th century. Printing began to become regulated from within and controlled from without only after about 1550. Use of the word incunabula for early printing in general seems to have first appeared about 1650.

The total number of editions produced by the 15th-century European presses is generally put at about 35,000 or upward, to which must be added a considerable percentage for ephemeral literature (e.g., single sheets, cheap romances, ballads, and devotional tracts), which has either perished completely or exists only in fragments of waste lining bindings and in other unexpected places.

indeterminacy \\ˌin-də-ˈtər-min-ə-sē\\ The quality or state of being not definitely or precisely determined or fixed. Deconstruction theorists in the 1970s gave the word a specifically literary application, using it to refer to the multiplicity of possible interpretations of given textual elements. Indeterminacy is similar to ambiguity as described by the New Critics, but it is applied not only to literature but also to interpretation of texts.

index \\ˈin-ˌdeks\\ A usually alphabetical list that includes all or nearly all items (such as authors, subjects, or keywords) that are considered pertinent and are discussed or mentioned in a printed or written work (such as a book, catalog, or dissertation) or an electronic database. An index gives with each item the location of its mention in the work. The index is usually at or near the end of a printed work.

Index librorum prohibitorum \\ˈin-deks-lī-ˈbrō-rəm-prō-ˌhib-i-ˈtō-rəm\\ ("Index of Forbidden Books") List of books once forbidden by Roman Catholic church authority as dangerous to the faith or morals of Roman Catholics. Publication of the list ceased in 1966, and it was relegated to the status of a historical document.

The origin of the church's legislation concerning the censorship of books is unclear, but books were a source of concern as early as the scriptural account of the burning of superstitious books at Ephesus by the new converts of St. Paul (Acts of the Apostles 19:19). The decree of Pope Gelasius I about 496, which contained lists of recommended as well as banned books, has been described as the first Roman *Index*. The first catalog of forbidden books to include in its title the word *index,* however, was published in 1559 by the Sacred Congregation of the Roman Inquisition (a precursor to the Congregation for the Doctrine of the Faith). The last and 20th edition of the *Index* appeared in 1948.

Indianista novel \\ēn-jä-ˈnēsh-tə\\ [Portuguese *indianista,* literally, advocate of Indians or specialist in Indian cultures] Brazilian literary genre of the 19th century that idealizes the simple life of the South American Indian. The tone of the *Indianista* novel is one of languid nostalgia and *saudade,* a brooding melancholy and reverence for nature characteristic of Portuguese and Brazilian literature. South American Indians had appeared as fictional characters in Brazilian literature from the late 18th century. It was not until the following century, however, that José de Alencar initiated the vogue of the Brazilian *Indianista* novel by contributing two of the most popular works to the genre, *O Guarani* (1857) and *Iracema* (1865), romantic tales of love between Indians and whites and of the conflict between the Indians and their Portuguese conquerors.

indite \in-ˈdīt\ [Middle English *enditen,* from Old French *enditer* to write down, compose, tell] **1.** To make up or compose (a work such as a poem or story). **2.** To give literary or formal expression to. **3.** To put down in writing. **4.** *obsolete* To dictate.

induction \in-ˈdək-shən\ A preface, prologue, or introductory scene, especially of an early English play.

inedita \in-ˈed-i-tə\ [Latin, neuter plural of *ineditus* not published] Unpublished literary material.

initial rhyme *See* ALLITERATION; BEGINNING RHYME.

in medias res \in-ˈmed-ē-ˌäs-ˈrās, -ˈmē-dē-əs-ˈrāz\ [Latin, into the midst of things] In or into the middle of a narrative or plot without the formality of an introduction or other preliminary. In narrative technique, to begin an epic or other fictional form by plunging into a crucial situation is recommended practice; the situation is an extension of previous events and will be developed in later action. The narrative then goes directly forward, and exposition of earlier events is supplied by flashbacks. The principle of opening a narrative *in medias res* is based on the practice of Homer, who in the *Iliad,* for example, begins dramatically with the quarrel between Achilles and Agamemnon. The Latin poet and critic Horace has pointed out the immediate interest created by this opening in contrast to beginning the story *ab ovo* ("from the egg"). *Compare* AB OVO.

In Memoriam stanza A quatrain in iambic tetrameter with a rhyme scheme of *abba.* The form was named for the pattern used by Alfred, Lord Tennyson in his poem *In Memoriam,* which, following an 11-stanza introduction, begins

> I held it truth, with him who sings
>   To one clear harp in divers tones,
>   That men may rise on stepping-stones
> Of their dead selves to higher things.

I novel \ˈī\, *Japanese* watakushi shōsetsu \wä-ˈtä-kə̇-shē-ˈshō-ˌse-tsu̇\ *or* shishōsetsu \shə̇-ˈshō-ˌse-tsu̇\ Form or genre of 20th-century Japanese literature that is characterized by self-revealing narration, with the author usually as the central character.

The I novel grew out of the naturalistic movement that dominated Japanese literature during the early decades of the 20th century. The term is used to describe two different types of novel, the confessional novel (characterized by prolonged, often self-abasing, revelation) and the "mental attitude" novel (in which the writer probes innermost thoughts or attitudes toward everyday events in life). Notable I novelists include Shiga Naoya, Kasai Zenzō, Uno Kōji, Kamura Isota, Amino Kiku, Takii Kōsaku, and Ozaki Kazuo.

inscape \ˈin-ˌskāp\ The essential character or quality belonging to objects or events in nature and human experience, especially as perceived by the blended observation and introspection of the poet and in turn embodied in patterns of such specific poetic elements as imagery, rhythm, rhyme, assonance, sound symbolism, and allusion. The term was coined by the poet Gerard Manley Hopkins; the formative *-scape* suggests both the second element of *landscape* and the word *shape*.

Isopet *See* YSOPET.

installment or **instalment** \in-ˈstȯl-mənt\ One part of a serial.

intentional fallacy The fallacy that the value or meaning of a work of art (such as a poem) may be judged or defined in terms of the artist's intention. The term originated in a 1946 essay by New Critics W.K. Wimsatt and Monroe Beardsley. The fallacy originates in the attempt "to derive the standard of criticism from the psychological *causes* of the poem and ends in biography and relativism."

intentionality \in-ˌten-chə-ˈnal-ə-tē\ In modern literary theory, the study of authorial intention in a literary work and its corresponding relevance to textual interpretation. With the ascendancy of New Criticism after World War I, much of the debate on intentionality addressed whether or not information external to the text could help determine the writer's purpose, and whether or not it was even possible or desirable to determine that purpose.

Modernist critics, such as T.S. Eliot, T.E. Hulme, and John Crowe Ransom, rejected the subjectivity of Romantic critics, whose criteria emphasized originality and individual experience. With the publication of their influential essay "The Intentional Fallacy" in *The Sewanee Review* (1946), authors W.K. Wimsatt and Monroe Beardsley questioned further the value of searching for authorial intention. Other critics as E.D. Hirsch, Jr., stressed that knowledge of the intention of the author is a necessary criterion by which to judge a work; without that knowledge, it is not possible to determine to what extent the work satisfies the original intention and to what extent, therefore, it is successful.

intercalation \in-ˌtər-kə-ˈlā-shən\ The insertion or introduction of something among other existing or original things; also, that which is so inserted.

interchapter \ˈin-tər-ˌchap-tər\ An intervening or inserted chapter.

interior monologue A usually extended representation in monologue of a fictional character's sequence of thought and feeling. These ideas may be either loosely related impressions that approach free association or more rationally ordered sequences of thought and emotion.

Interior monologues encompass several forms, including dramatized inner conflicts, self-analysis, imagined dialogue (as in T.S. Eliot's "The Love Song of J. Alfred Prufrock"), and rationalization. An interior monologue may be a direct first-person expression, apparently devoid of the author's selection and control, as in Molly Bloom's monologue concluding James Joyce's *Ulysses,* or a third-person treatment that begins with a phrase such as "he thought" or "his thoughts turned to."

The term interior monologue is often used interchangeably with "stream of consciousness." But while an interior monologue may mirror all the half thoughts, impressions, and associations that impinge upon the character's consciousness, it may also be restricted to an organized presentation of his rational thoughts. Closely related to the soliloquy and dramatic monologue, the interior monologue was first used extensively by Édouard Dujardin in *Les Lauriers sont coupés* (1888; *We'll to the Woods No More*) and later became a characteristic device of 20th-century psychological novels. *See also* STREAM OF CONSCIOUSNESS.

interlude \ˈin-tər-ˌlüd\ [Medieval Latin *interludium,* from Latin *inter-* between + *ludus* play] Early form of English dramatic entertainment, sometimes considered as the transition between medieval morality plays and Tudor dramas. Interludes were performed at court or at "great houses" by professional minstrels or amateurs. They were performed at intervals between some other form of entertainment, such as a banquet, or preceding or following a play, or between acts. Although most interludes were sketches of a nonreligious nature, some plays were called interludes that are today classed as morality plays. John Heywood, one of the most famous writers of interludes, brought the genre to its peak in his *The Play of the Wether* (1533) and *The Playe Called the Foure P.P.* (*c.* 1544).

internal rhyme Rhyme between a word within a line and another word either at the end of the same line or within another line. An example of internal rhyme is the following quatrain from the last stanza of Percy Bysshe Shelley's "The Cloud":

> I am the daughter of Earth and Water,
> And the nursling of the Sky;
> I pass through the pores of the ocean and shores;
> I change, but I cannot die.

interpretation \in-ˌtər-prə-ˈtā-shən\ **1.** The act or the result of interpreting, such as translation from one language into another (used of oral translation by interpreters). Also, the explanation of actions, events, or statements by the examination of inner relationships or motives or by relating particulars to general principles. **2.** Representation in performance, delivery, or criticism of the thought and mood in a work of art or its producer, especially as filtered through the personality of the interpreter.

intertextuality \ˌin-tər-ˌteks-chü-ˈwal-ə-tē\ [translation of French *intertextualité*] In literary theory, a text's quality of interdependence with all previous and future discourse. Literary critic Julia Kristeva in the 1960s introduced the term to express the idea that every new literary text is an intersection of texts—that it has absorbed and transformed previous works and that it will be absorbed and transformed by future texts. The term has been applied differently by other literary theorists.

intimist \'in-tim-ist\ [French *intimiste,* a derivative of *intime* intimate] Of fiction, dealing chiefly with intimate and private, especially psychological, experiences.

intrigue \'in-ˌtrēg, in-'trēg\ [French, crafty scheme, plot, love affair, from Italian *intrigo*] The plot of a literary or dramatic work that is especially marked by an intricacy of design or action or by a complex interrelation of events.

introverted \'in-trə-ˌvər-təd\ Of a quatrain, having an enclosed rhyme. An example of an introverted quatrain is the *In Memoriam* stanza (named for the poem by Alfred, Lord Tennyson), which has an *abba* rhyme scheme. An introverted stanza may also be called an *envelope.*

intrusive narrator *See* NARRATOR.

inversion \in-'vər-zhən\, *also called* anastrophe. In literary style and rhetoric, the syntactical reversal of the normal order of the words and phrases in a sentence. In English, for example, inversion is evident in the placing of an adjective after the noun it modifies ("the form divine"); a verb before its subject ("Came the dawn"); or a noun preceding its preposition ("worlds between"). Inversion is most commonly used in poetry in which it may both satisfy the demands of the meter and achieve emphasis, as in Samuel Coleridge's "Kubla Khan":

> In Xanadu did Kubla Khan
> A stately pleasure dome decree:

Inversion used only for the sake of maintaining a rhyme scheme is considered a literary defect.

Inversion is a common convention in such anonymous folk ballads as "The Mermaid":

> Then up spoke the captain of our gallant ship,
> And a well-spoken man was he;
> "I have married a wife in Salem town,
> And tonight she a widow will be"

The word *inversion* is also used in a metrical sense to describe a change in cadence from rising to falling or from falling to rising rhythm. *See also* COUNTERPOINT RHYTHM.

invocation \ˌin-vō-'kā-shən\ [Latin *invocatio,* a derivative of *invocare* to summon, call upon] A convention of classical literature and of epics in particular, in which an appeal for aid (especially for inspiration) is made to a muse or deity, usually at or near the beginning of the work. Homer's *Odyssey,* for instance, begins:

> Tell me, Muse, of the man of many ways, who was driven
> far journeys, after he had sacked Troy's sacred citadel.
> Many were they whose cities he saw, whose minds he learned of,
> many the pains he suffered in his spirit on the wide sea,
> struggling for his own life and the homecoming of his
> companions.

involuted novel *See* REFLEXIVE NOVEL.

ionic \ī-ˈän-ik\ **1.** *capitalized* A dialect of ancient Greece used especially in Ionia and the Cyclades that was the vehicle of an important body of literature. **2.** A foot of verse that consists of either two long and two short syllables (also called *major ionic* or *a maiore*) or two short and two long syllables (also called *minor ionic* or *a minore*).

Irish Literary Renaissance The flowering of Irish literary talent at the end of the 19th and the beginning of the 20th century that was closely allied with a strong political nationalism and a revival of interest in Ireland's Gaelic literary heritage. The renaissance was inspired by the nationalistic pride of the GAELIC REVIVAL; by the retelling of ancient heroic legends in books such as the two-volume *History of Ireland* (1878, 1880) by Standish O'Grady and *A Literary History of Ireland* (1899) by Douglas Hyde; and by the Gaelic League, which was formed in 1893 to revive the Irish language and culture. The early leaders of the renaissance, most of whom were members of the privileged class, wrote rich and passionate verse, filled with the grandeur of Ireland's past and the music and mysticism of Gaelic poetry and were adept at English verse forms and familiar with lyric poetry that extolled the simple dignity of the Irish peasant and the natural beauty of Ireland.

The movement developed into a vigorous literary force centered on William Butler Yeats. Though he contributed to the foundation of the Irish Literary Theatre (which later developed into the Abbey Theatre, the first Irish national theater), he wrote only a few plays, which were beautiful but difficult to stage. His chief colleague at the Abbey was Isabella Augusta, Lady Gregory, who took a leading part in the Abbey's management and wrote many plays, mostly peasant comedies. The greatest dramatist of the movement was John Millington Synge, who wrote plays of great beauty and power in a stylized peasant dialect. Lennox Robinson, best known for his political play, *The Lost Leader* (1918), and his comedy, *The Whiteheaded Boy* (1916), and T.C. Murray, author of *The Briary Gap* (1917), were among the early realists. In reaction to peasant realism, Sean O'Casey wrote three great dramas of the Dublin slums: *The Shadow of a Gunman* (1923), *Juno and the Paycock* (1924), and *The Plough and the Stars* (1926).

The two major poets associated with the movement were Yeats and Æ (George Russell), a mystic, patriot, and agricultural reformer. Notable among their younger contemporaries were Padraic Colum, Austin Clarke, Seumas O'Sullivan (James Sullivan Starkey), F.R. Higgins, and Oliver St. John Gogarty. The Irish Republican movement had its poets in Patrick Henry Pearse, Thomas MacDonagh, and Joseph Plunkett, all executed in 1916 for their part in the Easter Rising.

The noteworthy prose fiction of the renaissance includes the historical tales of Emily Lawless and O'Grady. James Stephens also wrote stories and poetry.

irony \'ī-rə-nē\ [Latin *ironia,* from Greek *eirōneía* feigned ignorance, irony, a derivative of *eírōn* dissembler], *also called* verbal irony. The use of words to express something other than and especially the opposite of the literal meaning (as when expressions of praise are used where blame is meant). Also, this mode of expression as a literary style or form. Verbal irony arises from a sophisticated or resigned awareness of contrast between what is and what ought to be and expresses a controlled pathos without sentimentality. It is a form of indirection that avoids overt praise or censure. The term *irony* has its roots in the Greek comic character Eiron, a clever underdog who by his wit repeatedly triumphs over the boastful character Alazon. The Socratic irony of the Platonic dialogues derives from this comic origin. Feigning ignorance and humility, Socrates goes about asking silly and obvious questions of all sorts of people on all sorts of subjects, only to expose their ignorance as more profound than his own.

In drama, irony is produced when the audience has information unknown to the characters. *See also* DRAMATIC IRONY.

irrational \ir-'rash-ə-nəl\ In classical prosody, of or relating to a syllable having a quantity other than that required by the meter, such as a long syllable that takes the place of a short one.

irregular ode A rhymed ode that follows neither the three-part form of the Pindaric ode nor the two- or four-line stanza that typifies the Horatian ode. It is also called *pseudo-Pindaric ode* or *Cowleyan ode* (after Abraham Cowley). *See also* HORATIAN ODE; ODE; PINDARIC ODE.

isochronism \ī-'säk-rə-ˌniz-əm\ or **isochrony** \ī-'säk-rə-nē\ [Greek *isóchronos* consisting of units equal in duration] Equal duration of prosodic units (such as metrical feet). The term is generally used to describe quantitative (usually classical) verse rather than accentual or syllabic poetry. Some theorists have maintained that isochronism is a natural feature of the English language and thus that two-syllable and three-syllable feet occupy approximately the same amount of time in English.

isocolon \'ī-sə-ˌkō-lən\ [Greek *isókōlon,* from neuter of *isókōlos* having equal members] **1.** In Greek prosody, a rhythmical unit (period) consisting of single metrical phrases (colons) of equal length. **2.** The use of equal colons in immediate succession.

isometric \ˌī-sə-ˈmet-rik\ Of a stanza or a strophe, having lines of equal metrical measure. *Compare* ANISOMETRIC.

Italian sonnet *See* PETRARCHAN SONNET.

ithyphallic \ˌith-i-ˈfal-ik\ [Greek *ithyphallikós,* a derivative of *ithýphallos* ode performed at festivals of Bacchus, literally, the erect phallus carried in these festivals] Having a meter typically used in hymns sung at ancient festivals honoring Bacchus; specifically, having the meter of a trochaic dimeter brachycatalectic (– ∪ – ∪ – –).

J

. . . a single night's dream, composed in a Jabberwocky language of sleep.
—Edmund Wilson

jabberwocky \ˈjab-ər-ˌwäk-ē\ Nonsensical or unintelligible speech or writing. The term is derived from the poem "Jabberwocky" in Lewis Carroll's *Through the Looking-Glass,* which begins:

'Twas brillig, and the slithy toves
  Did gyre and gimble in the wabe;
All mimsy were the borogroves,
  And the mome raths outgrabe.

Jacobean \ˌjak-ə-ˈbē-ən\ [New Latin *Jacobus* James] Of or relating to the reign of James I of England (1603–25), or to the writers or literature of his time.

Many of the themes and patterns of Jacobean literature were carried over from the preceding Elizabethan era. Though rich, Jacobean literature is often darkly questioning. William Shakespeare's greatest tragedies were written between about 1600 and 1607. Other Jacobean dramatic writers became preoccupied with the problem of evil; the plays of John Webster, Cyril Tourneur, Thomas Middleton, and William Rowley induce all the terror of tragedy but little of its pity. Comedy was best represented by the acid satire of Ben Jonson and by the varied works of Francis Beaumont and John Fletcher. Another feature of drama at this time, however, was the development of the extravagant courtly entertainment known as the masque. This form reached its literary peak in the works written by Jonson and designed by Inigo Jones. Jonson's comparatively lucid and graceful verse and the writings of his Cavalier successors constituted one of the two main streams of Jacobean poetry. The other poetic stream lay in the intellectual complexity of John Donne and the Metaphysical poets. In prose, Francis Bacon and Robert Burton were among the writers who displayed a new toughness and flexibility of style. The monumental prose achievement of the era was the great King James Version of the Bible, which first appeared in 1611.

Janeite or **Janite** \ˈjā-ˌnīt\ An enthusiastic admirer of the writings of Jane Austen.

jazz poetry \ˈjaz\ Poetry that is read to the accompaniment of jazz music. Authors of such poetry attempt to emulate the rhythms and freedom of the music in the poetry. Forerunners of the style included Vachel Lindsay, who read his poetry in a syncopated and rhythmic style for audiences, and Langston Hughes, who collaborated with musicians. Later poets known for their interest in combining the two forms included Kenneth Patchen, Kenneth Rexroth, Amiri Baraka, and Christopher Logue as well as many of the poets of the Beat movement.

Jena Romanticism \'yā-nə\, *German* Jenaer Romantik \'yā-nä-ər-rō-'män-tik\ The first phase of Romanticism in German literature, centered in Jena from about 1798 to 1804. The Jena Romantics were led by the versatile writer Ludwig Tieck. Two members of the group, the brothers August Wilhelm and Friedrich von Schlegel, laid down the theoretical basis for Romanticism in the circle's organ, the *Athenaeum*. That theory maintained that the first duty of criticism was to understand and appreciate the right of genius to follow its natural bent.

The greatest imaginative achievement of the circle is to be found in the lyrics and fragmentary novels of Novalis. The works of Johann Gottlieb Fichte and Friedrich von Schelling expounded the Romantic doctrine in philosophy, while the theologian Friedrich Schleiermacher demonstrated the necessity of individualism in religious thought. By 1804 the circle at Jena had dispersed. The second phase of Romanticism was initiated two years later in Heidelberg.

Jesuit drama \'jez-ü-ət, 'jezh-, -yü-\ Program of theater developed for educational and propagandist purposes in the colleges of the Society of Jesus during the 16th, 17th, and 18th centuries. Cultivated as a medium for disseminating Roman Catholic doctrine, drama flourished in the Jesuit schools for more than 200 years, evolving from modest student exercises to elaborate productions that often rivaled the contemporary public stage in polish and technical skill.

The earliest recorded performance of a Jesuit play was in 1551, at the newly founded Collegio Mamertino at Messina, in Sicily. In less than 20 years, plays were being performed at Jesuit colleges across the European continent. By the mid-17th century there were nearly 300 Jesuit colleges in Europe, and in almost every one at least one play was given each year.

Originally the plays were to be pious in nature, expressing true religious and moral doctrines; they were to be acted in Latin, decorously, and with little elaboration; and no female characters or costumes were to appear. All these rules were relaxed or revised as Jesuit drama evolved. Favorite subjects came from biblical histories, the lives of saints and martyrs, and incidents in the life of Christ, but Jesuit playwrights also reinterpreted material from pagan mythology, ancient history, and contemporary events. The plays became increasingly elaborate, and their stagecraft kept pace with all the newest technical developments of European theater.

Music was an important element in most of the plays, ranging from simple songs to works that called for a large orchestra and chorus. The colleges of France even included ballet in their performances.

The extravagance and luxury of many of the Jesuit productions came under heavy attack. Opponents of the Jesuit order made these objections part of the wave of anti-Jesuit feeling that grew in the mid-18th century. Dramatic performances ceased altogether in 1773, when the Society of Jesus was temporarily suppressed.

Jeune Belgique, La \lä-zhœ̄n-bel-'zhēk\("Young Belgium") Influential review (1881–97), edited by poet Max Waller; it gave its name to a literary movement (though never a formal "school") that aimed to express a genuinely Belgian consciousness and to free the literature of Belgium from outworn Romanticism. Among writers associated with the movement were Maurice Maeterlinck, Émile Verhaeren, and Max Elskamp—all poets of international stature.

Jewish Daily Forward *See* FORVERTS.

jiggery-pokery *See* DOUBLE DACTYLS.

Jindyworobak movement \ˌjin-dē-'wȯr-ə-ˌbak\ Brief nationalistic Australian literary movement of the 1930s to mid-1940s that sought to promote native ideas and traditions, especially in literature.

The movement was swelled by several circumstances: the Australian depression years focused attention on comparable hardships of an earlier era (the early 1890s); the influx of "alien" culture threatened to overwhelm the young literature then in the making; and travelers described with wonder the little known Australian outback. Among the discoveries of the period was a romantic notion of the spirit of place and the literary importance of what could still be discerned of Aboriginal culture. Xavier Herbert's *Capricornia* (1938) typifies the goals of the Jindyworobak movement.

The poet and novelist James Devaney (1890–1976) took the name Jindyworobak from a 19th-century vocabulary of Wuywurung (an Aboriginal language formerly spoken in the Melbourne region), in which *jindi woraback* is said to mean "to annex."

jingle \'jiŋ-gəl\ A short verse or song marked by catchy repetition of such elements as rhyme, alliterative sounds, and cadences. This is often the form of nursery rhymes, such as "Hickory, Dickory, Dock":

> Hickory, dickory, dock,
> The mouse ran up the clock;
>   The clock struck one,
>   The mouse ran down,
> Hickory, dickory, dock.

jingxi or **ching-hsi** \'jiŋ-'shē\ [Chinese *jīngxì,* from *jīng* capital, Beijing + *xì* play, drama], *also called* Peking opera \'pē-'kiŋ, 'pā-\ Popular Chinese theatrical form that developed during the mid-17th to the mid-19th centuries and is still performed today. It gradually replaced KUNQU, a traditional drama form that had previously dominated the Chinese theater. Performed in the dialect of Beijing and of the traditional elite, the *jingxi* plays came to be produced throughout China, although most provinces and many major cities developed their own operatic variants using local dialect.

Essentially, *jingxi* came into being as a mixture of southern dramatic traditions and clapper opera (an opera form in which clappers provide an essential musical feature), and it is characterized by elaborate and stylized costumes and makeup, spectacular dance and acrobatic routines, a limited melodic range, lyrics in more colloquial language, and musical accompaniment that emphasizes percussion instruments. Highly theatrical and vigorous, *jingxi* is more a medium of the performer than of the dramatist.

Johnsonese \ˌjän-sə-ˈnēz, -ˈnēs\ A literary style that bears characteristics of the writings of 18th-century English lexicographer and writer Samuel Johnson, having balanced phraseology and Latinate diction.

joint author A person who collaborates with one or more persons in the production of a literary work.

jongleur \zhȯ^{n}-ˈglœ̄r, *Angl* -ˈglər, ˈjäŋ-glər\ [French, from Old French, alteration (influenced by *jangleor* chatterer, braggart) of *juglere* buffoon, minstrel, from Latin *joculator* buffoon] Professional storyteller or public entertainer in medieval France. The role of the jongleur included that of musician, juggler, and acrobat, as well as reciter of such literary works as fabliaux, chansons de geste, lays, and other metrical romances that were sometimes of his own composition. Jongleurs performed in marketplaces on public holidays, in abbeys, and in castles of nobles, who sometimes retained them in permanent employment. In such a case the jongleur became known as a *ménestrel* and devoted more of his time to literary creation than to entertainment. Fraternities of jongleurs became known as *puys,* groups that held competitions for lyric poets. The jongleur reached the height of his importance in the 13th century but lapsed into decline in the 14th, when various facets of his complex role were disseminated among other performers—e.g., musicians, actors, and acrobats. *Compare* GOLIARD.

jōruri \ˈjō-ˌrü-rē\ In Japanese literature and music, a type of chanted recitative; often the script for a bunraku puppet drama. Its name derives from the *Jōrurihime monogatari,* a 15th-century romantic ballad, the leading character of which is Lady Jōruri. At first it was chanted to the accompaniment of the four-string biwa (Japanese lute); with the introduction of the three-stringed, plucked samisen (or *shamisen*) from the Ryukyu Islands in the 16th century, both the music and the scripts developed. When puppets were added at the end of the 16th century, the *jōruri* expanded to add a dramatic quality not present in the first simple recitatives. Themes of loyalty, vengeance, filial piety, love, and religious miracles were included; dialogue and descriptive commentary took an increasingly large role. The chanter was at first more important than the writer of the script, until the appearance of one of Japan's greatest playwrights, Chikamatsu Monzaemon, in the late 17th and early 18th centuries. A 30-year collaboration between Chikamatsu and the chanter Takemoto Gidayū (1651–1714) raised the puppet theater to a high art. Gidayū himself became so famous that his style, gidayūbushi ("Gidayū music"), became nearly synonymous with *jōruri*.

Most jōruri are performed by a chanter (*tayū*) and samisen player. One of the world's most highly developed forms of narrative music, jōruri still enjoys a popularity, even when separated from the actual drama.

journal \ˈjərn-əl\ **1.** An account of day-to-day events or a record of experiences, ideas, or reflections kept regularly for private use that is similar to, but sometimes less personal than, a DIARY. **2.** A daily newspaper or a periodical publication especially dealing with matters of current interest. The word is often used of official or semiofficial publications of special groups.

journalism \ˈjər-nə-ˌliz-əm\ Writing designed for publication in a newspaper or magazine. Such writing is sometimes characterized by a direct presentation of facts or description of events without an attempt at interpretation.

The earliest known journalistic product was a newssheet circulated in ancient Rome called the *Acta Diurna*. Published daily from 59 BC, it was hung in prominent places and recorded important social and political events. In China during the T'ang dynasty a court circular called a *pao,* or "report," was issued to government officials. This gazette appeared in various forms and under various names more or less continually to the end of the Ch'ing dynasty in 1911. The first regularly published newspapers appeared in German cities and in Antwerp around 1609. The first English newspaper, the *Weekly Newes,* was published in 1622. One of the first daily newspapers, *The Daily Courant,* appeared in 1702.

At first hindered by government-imposed censorship, restrictions, and taxes, newspapers in the 18th century came to enjoy the reportorial freedom and indispensable function that they have retained to the present day. The growing demand for newspapers owing to the spread of literacy and the introduction of steam- and then electric-driven presses caused the daily circulation of newspapers to rise from the thousands to the hundreds of thousands and eventually to millions.

Magazines, which had started in the 17th century as learned journals, began to feature opinion-forming articles on current affairs, such as those in the *Tatler* (1709–11) and the *Spectator* (1711–12). In the 1830s cheap, mass-circulation magazines aimed at a wider and less well-educated public appeared, as well as illustrated and women's magazines. The cost of large-scale news gathering led to the formation of news agencies, organizations that sold their international journalistic reporting to many different individual newspapers and magazines. The invention of the telegraph and then the radio and television brought about a great increase in the speed and timeliness of journalistic activity and at the same time provided massive new outlets and audiences for their electronically distributed products. In the late 20th century satellites were being used for the long-distance transmission of journalistic information.

Although the core of journalism has always been the news, the latter word has acquired so many secondary meanings that the term "hard news" has gained currency to distinguish items of definite news value from others of marginal significance. This is largely a consequence of the advent of radio and television reporting, which bring news bulletins to the public with speed that the press cannot hope to match. To hold their audience, newspapers have provided increasing quantities of interpretive material—articles on the background of the news, personality sketches, and columns of timely comment by writers skilled in presenting opinion in readable form. By the mid-1960s most newspapers, particularly evening and Sunday editions, were relying heavily on magazine techniques, except for their content of "hard news," where the traditional rule of objectivity still applied. News magazines in much of their reporting were blending news with editorial comment.

judgment tale *See* DILEMMA TALE.

jueju or **chüeh-chü** \ˈjwe-ˈju̅e̅\ [Chinese *juéjù,* from *juè* to cut off, sever + *jù* sentence] A Chinese verse form that was popular during the T'ang dynasty (618–907). An outgrowth of the LÜSHI, it was a four-line poem, each line of which consisted of five or seven words; it omitted either the first four lines, the last four lines, the first two and the last two lines, or the middle four lines of the *lüshi.* Thus it retained the tonal quality of the *lüshi,* but the antithetical structure was made optional. Much like the Persian ROBĀʿI and the Japanese HAIKU, *jueju* depended for their artistry on suggestiveness and economy.

Junges Deutschland *See* YOUNG GERMANY.

Juvenalian satire \ˌjü-və-ˈnāl-yən\ In literature, any bitter and ironic criticism of contemporary persons and institutions that is filled with personal invective, angry moral indignation, and pessimism. The name alludes to the Latin satirist Juvenal, who, in the 1st century AD, brilliantly denounced Roman society, the rich and powerful, and the discomforts and dangers of city life. The 18th-century English man of letters Samuel Johnson modeled his poem *London* on Juvenal's third satire and *The Vanity of Human Wishes* on the 10th. *Gulliver's Travels* established Jonathan Swift as the master of Juvenalian satire. In the 20th century, Karl Kraus' indictments of the prevailing corruption in post-World War I Austria were in the Juvenalian tradition. *Compare* HORATIAN SATIRE.

juvenilia \ˌjü-və-ˈnil-ē-ə\ [Latin, neuter plural of *juvenilis* of a young man, derivative of *juvenis* young man, youth] **1.** Artistic or literary compositions produced in the author's youth and typically marked by immaturity of style, treatment, or thought. An example is Lord Byron's *Hours of Idleness,* written when he was 18 and Charlotte Brontë's large volume of juvenilia portraying the imaginary kingdom of Angria that she created with her brother Branwell. **2.** Artistic or literary compositions suited to or designed for the young.

K

. . . the real vulgarity of Kitsch *can be blamed more on the intellectuals who produce it than on the consumers . . .*

—Alfred Kazin

kabuki \kä-ˈbü-kē\ [Japanese, from earlier *kabuki* (verb) to act dissolutely] Popular Japanese form of theater that is a rich blending of realism and formalism, of music, dance, mime, and spectacular staging and costuming. In modern Japanese, the word is written with three characters: *ka,* signifying "song"; *bu,* "dance"; and *ki,* "skill."

The kabuki form dates from the early 17th century, and its strongest ties are to the Nō and to the bunraku puppet theater. Nō, the prevailing and established form of theater, had long been the exclusive domain of the nobility and the warrior-aristocrats known as samurai; kabuki therefore became the theater of the townspeople and the farmers. Kabuki derived much of its material from the Nō, and when kabuki was banned in 1652, it reestablished itself by adapting and parodying *kyōgen* (plays that provided comic interludes during Nō performances).

Although the basic purposes of kabuki are to entertain and to allow the actors to demonstrate their skills, there is a didactic element, an ideal represented by the notion of *kanzen-chōaku* ("reward the virtuous and punish the wicked"). Thus the plays often present conflicts involving such religious ideas as the transitory nature of the world (from Buddhism), and the importance of duty (from Confucianism), as well as more general moral sentiments.

Kabuki, which is performed by all-male casts, finds its material in domestic stories and in popular history. The actors, without masks, move and speak freely, yet without attempting to be realistic. The highly lyrical plays are regarded less as literature than as vehicles for its actors to demonstrate their enormous range of skills in visual and vocal performance. Notable exceptions include the Chūshingura cycle and the works of Chikamatsu Monzaemon, Tsuruya Namboku IV, Kawatake Mokuami, and Okamoto Kidō.

kafkaesque \ˌkäf-kə-ˈesk, ˌkaf-\ Of, relating to, or suggestive of Franz Kafka or his writings—especially, having a nightmarishly complex, bizarre, or illogical quality.

Kailyard school \ˈkāl-ˌyärd\ Late 19th-century movement in Scottish fiction characterized by a sentimental idealization of humble village life. Its name derives from Scots *kailyaird,* a kitchen garden usually adjacent to a cottage. The Kailyard novels of prominent writers such as Sir James Barrie, author of *Auld*

Licht Idylls (1888) and *A Window in Thrums* (1889), Ian Maclaren (pseudonym of John Watson), and S.R. Crockett were widely read throughout Scotland, England, and the United States and inspired hundreds of imitators. The natural and unsophisticated style and parochial viewpoint quickly degenerated into mawkish sentimentality, which provoked a hostile reaction among contemporary Scottish realists and later writers of the 20th century.

Kanze school \ˈkän-zā\, *Japanese* Kanze-ryū \-ˈryü\ School of Nō drama known for its emphasis on beauty and elegance. The school was founded in the 14th century by Kan'ami, who founded the Yūzaki Theatrical Company, the precursor of the Kanze school. Zeami, the second master and Kan'ami's son, completed the basic form of the art.

Since the Muromachi period (1338–1573), the Kanze school has been the largest Nō group in Japan—registering several hundred Nō musicians and more than half the dues-paying Nō enthusiasts of Japan.

Karagöz \kä-rä-ˈgœz\ ("Black Eyes" or "Gypsy") Type of Turkish shadow play, named for its stock hero, Karagöz. The comically risqué plays are improvised from scenarios for local audiences in private homes, coffee shops, public squares, and inn yards. The Karagöz play apparently was highly developed in Turkey by the 16th century and was adapted in Greece and North Africa. In the 20th century, however, Karagöz plays have lost some popularity to cinema and other forms of entertainment. Their performance in Turkey has been mostly confined to the Muslim holy month of Ramaḍān.

The character of Karagöz is a good-natured underdog who usually gets his turban knocked off in fights. He exchanges satiric and vulgar repartee with his friend Hacivot, a pompous Turk with an affected accent, and with other stock characters, such as a newly rich peasant, a conniving dervish, and a Jewish merchant.

katauta \ˌkä-tä-ˈü-tä\ [Japanese] A Japanese poetic form that consists of 17 or 19 syllables arranged in three lines of either 5, 7, and 5 or 5, 7, and 7 syllables. The form was used for poems addressed to a lover, and a single *katauta* was considered incomplete or a half poem. A pair of *katauta*s of the 5,7,7 type were called a *sedōka;* the 5,7,5 *katauta* may have been the top part of the early tanka. Exchanges of such poems made up a longer question-and-answer poem. The form was rarely used after about the 8th century AD.

kavya \ˈkäv-yə\ [Sanskrit *kāvyaṃ* poetic composition, a noun derivative of *kāvyaḥ* (adjective) of a sage or poet, poetic, a derivative of *kaviḥ* seer, sage, poet] Highly artificial Sanskrit literary style employed chiefly in the court epic of India from the early centuries AD. It evolved an elaborate poetics of figures of speech, among which the metaphor and simile predominated. Other characteristics were the careful use of language, a tendency to use compound nouns, a sometimes ostentatious display of erudition in the arts and sciences, and an adroitness in the use of varied and complicated meters—all applied to traditional themes (such as the epic had provided) and to the rendering of emotions, most often the love between men and women.

The style finds its classical expression in the so-called *mahākāvya* ("great poem"), which is most akin to the epyllion (short epic) art form, the strophic lyric (a lyric based on a rhythmic system of two or more lines repeated as a unit), and the Sanskrit theater. The great masters of the kavya form (which was also exported to Java) were Aśvaghoṣa, Kālidāsa, Bāṇa, Daṇḍin, Māgha, Bhavabhūti, and Bhāravi.

The earliest surviving kavya literature was written by Aśvaghoṣa, a Buddhist. Two works by Aśvaghoṣa, both in the style of *mahākāvya,* are extant: the *Buddhacarita* ("Life of the Buddha") and the *Saundarānanda* ("Of Sundarī and Nanda"). Compared with later examples, they are fairly simple in style but reveal typical propensities of writers in this genre: a great predilection for descriptions of nature scenes, grand spectacles, amorous episodes, and aphoristic observations. The resources of the Sanskrit language are fully exploited, and stylistic embellishments (*alaṅkāra*) such as simile and metaphor, alliteration, assonance, and the like are employed. In his mastery of the intricacies of prosody and the subtleties of grammar and vocabulary, Aśvaghoṣa anticipated the style of the Hindu *mahākāvya* authors. *See also* MAHĀKĀVYA.

kayak American literary magazine founded in San Francisco in 1964 by poet George Hitchcock as a forum for surrealist, imagist, and political poems. The magazine, which eventually published short fiction and essays as well, was known for its irreverence and its openness to experimentation, including found poems (verses made from other printed matter such as flyers or discarded letters). Attention was directed especially to the nature of poetry itself, which was addressed in a number of poems and essays throughout the magazine's history. The magazine moved its headquarters to Santa Cruz, Calif., in 1970. The last issue was produced in 1984. Regular contributors included W.S. Merwin, Wendell Berry, Robert Bly, David Ignatow, James Tate, Margaret Atwood, Raymond Carver, Carolyn Kizer, Charles Simic, and Sharon Olds.

keepsake \'kēp-ˌsāk\ A GIFTBOOK, or more specifically, a giftbook made up for a particular group or occasion and serving as a specimen of fine printing.

kenning \'ken-iŋ\ [Old Norse, a derivative of *kenna* to perceive, know, name] A metaphoric compound word or phrase replacing a common noun, used especially in Old English and other Germanic poetry.

A kenning is commonly a simple stock compound such as "whale-path" or "swan road" for "sea"; "God's beacon" for "sun"; or "ring-giver" for "king." Many kennings are allusions that become unintelligible to later generations. Sometimes kennings are extremely indirect; for example, "the blue land of Haki" (a sea king) refers not to land but to the sea and requires a knowledge of Norse mythology to be understood. *See also* SKALDIC POETRY.

Kenyon Review, The \'ken-yən\ American intellectual serial founded in 1939 as a quarterly magazine of literary criticism by faculty members of Kenyon

College, Gambier, Ohio. John Crowe Ransom was its first editor. Until 1958, *The Kenyon Review* was closely identified with New Criticism, and as such it soon became one of the most influential magazines of its kind in the country. It attracted writers of international literary reputation, including Allen Tate, Robert Penn Warren, and Mark Van Doren. The *Review* published criticism by Ransom, William Empson, Yvor Winters, I.A. Richards, and Cleanth Brooks and poetry by Marianne Moore, Stephen Spender, Wallace Stevens, John Berryman, and Dylan Thomas, among others.

In 1960, when Robie Macauley assumed the editorship, the *Review* began to publish more fiction, including works by such writers as V.S. Naipaul and Nadine Gordimer, though the emphasis remained on criticism. The magazine ceased publication in 1970 but was revived in 1979.

khamseh or **khamsa** \'käm-sə, 'k̲äm-\ [Arabic *khamsa* five, group of five] In Persian and Turkish literature, a set of five long epic poems composed in rhyming couplet, or *mas̄nawī,* form. *Khamseh* takes its name from the five great epic poems written by Neẓāmī and entitled *Khamseh* ("The Quintuplet"). The first of these five poems is the didactic work *Makhzan al-asrār* (*The Treasury of Mysteries*); the next three are traditional love stories; and the fifth, the *Eskandar-nāmeh,* records the adventures of Alexander the Great. Inspired by Neẓāmī's influential model, several other notable poets, including Amīr Khosrow (1253–1325) and ʾAlī Shīr Navaʿī (1441–1501), wrote *khamsehs* in Persian and in Turkish.

kinah meter \kē-'nä\ [Hebrew *qīnāh* dirge, lamentation] A Hebrew poetic meter typically having the line divided into two parts, with three stresses in the first part and two stresses in the second.

King's Men An English theater company known by that name after it came under royal patronage in 1603. It had previously been known as the Lord Chamberlain's Men. William Shakespeare was its leading dramatist and Richard Burbage its principal actor. *See* CHAMBERLAIN'S MEN.

kasida *See* QASIDA.

Kit-Cat Club \'kit-ˌkat\ Club founded by leading members of the Whig Party in London in the early 18th century. Its members included such literary figures as Joseph Addison, Sir Richard Steele, William Congreve, and Sir John Vanbrugh. The club met at a pastry shop owned by Christopher Cat (or Kat), who served pastries known as Kit-Cats.

kitchen-sink \ˌkich-ən-'siŋk\ *chiefly British* Portraying or emphasizing the squalid aspects of modern life. In literature the term has somewhat negative connotations and has been applied mainly to the dramas of the so-called Angry Young Men, who wrote realistically of working-class life in the mid-1950s.

kitsch \'kich\ [German] Artistic or literary material held to be of low quality, often produced to appeal to popular taste, and marked especially by sentimentalism, sensationalism, and slickness.

Klephtic ballad \'klef-tik\ Any of the songs and poems extolling the adventures of the Klephts, Greek nationalists living as outlaws in the mountains during the period of Turkish domination over Greece from 1453 to 1828. Containing some of the most beautiful and vivid verse in Modern Greek, the songs, mainly from the 18th century, are an entirely spontaneous poetry, composed in popular language and in 15-syllable verse, rhymed and unrhymed. They are pervaded with the spirit of the forests and the mountains and, like so much of Greek popular poetry, personify trees, rocks, and rivers. Klephtic ballads have been a constant source of inspiration and rejuvenation to Modern Greek poetry and to Greek nationalism.

knack *obsolete* An ingenious literary device or CONCEIT.

Knickerbocker school \'nik-ər-ˌbäk-ər\ Group of writers active in and around New York City during the first half of the 19th century. Taking its name from Washington Irving's *A History of New York* "by Diedrich Knickerbocker" (1809), the group, whose affiliation was more a regional than an aesthetic matter, sought to promote a genuinely American national culture and establish New York City as its literary center. The most important members of the group were Irving, his friend the novelist J.K. Paulding, James Fenimore Cooper, and William Cullen Bryant. Other writers associated with the group were the abolitionist and woman-suffrage crusader Lydia M. Child, editor and politician G.C. Verplanck, Clement Moore, scholar and author of " 'Twas the Night Before Christmas" (1823), and the poet and travel writer Bayard Taylor. *The Knickerbocker Magazine* (1833–65), a literary monthly edited by Lewis G. and Willis G. Clark, though not an official organ of the group, published members' work.

kommos or **commos** \'käm-əs, 'kȯm-\ [Greek *kommós,* literally, beating of the head and breast in grief, a derivative of *kóptein* to beat] In Greek tragedy, a lament sung in parts alternating between chief actor and chorus.

Krokodil \krə-ˌkə-'dʸēl\ ("Crocodile") Humor magazine published in Moscow, noted for its satire and cartoons.

From 1922 to 1932 the periodical was published as a weekly supplement to the Soviet newspaper *Rabochaya gazeta* ("The Worker's Press"; published for its first three months as *Rabochy* ["The Worker"]). From 1932 until 1992 the magazine was published three times a month but thereafter it was forced by economic hardship to cut back to monthly publication.

Krokodil's humor was chiefly directed against what it termed Western imperialism and bourgeois ideology, but it also assailed "undesirable elements" in Soviet society. Vitaly Goryayev, one of its best-known cartoonists, became known for his comic portrayal of the "capitalist warmongers." *Krokodil* was published by *Pravda,* which until 1991 was the official newspaper of the Communist Party.

Kulchur \'kəl-chər\ A review of contemporary arts, important for the vital nature of its writing and for its role as the representative of the avant-garde arts community in New York City. It was published in New York from spring 1960 to winter 1965–66 and was named for Ezra Pound's *Guide to Kulchur*. Unlike other avant-garde "little" magazines of its time, *Kulchur* concentrated on presenting criticism rather than fiction. Poetry, painting and sculpture, experimental film and theater, dance, jazz and contemporary classical music, sex, and politics were among the subjects that fell within its scope, and the 12th issue was devoted to writings on the subject of civil rights. Essayist Donald Phelps, jazz critic Martin Williams, and authors Frank O'Hara, Amiri Baraka (then LeRoi Jones), Gilbert Sorrentino, and Diane Di Prima were among its contributing editors; poets Charles Olson, Robert Duncan, and Louis Zukovsky, composer Morton Feldman, and Living Theatre cofounder Julian Beck were among its most noted essayists.

kunqu or **k'un-ch'ü** \'kün-'chue̅\ [Chinese *kūnqŭ,* from *kūn* Kunshan + *qŭ* song, tune] Form of Chinese drama that was developed in the 16th century. *Kunqu* was essentially the *chuanqi* form set to a new type of music. The word was originally given to the style of music which was created by Wei Liangfu of Kunshan (near Suzhou), but it was soon applied to the dramatic form as well. Important *kunqu* dramatists were Tang Xianzu, who was noted for the delicate sensitivity of his poetry; Shen Jing, who excelled in versification; and Li Yu, known for his effective theatrical pieces.

Kunqu had begun as a genuinely popular opera form; it was welcomed by audiences in Beijing in the 1600s, and it became the predominant *chuanqi* form through the end of the 18th century. It had, however, turned into a theater of the literati, its poetic forms too esoteric and its music too refined for the common audience. It was gradually replaced in popularity by the form known as *jingxi,* or Peking opera.

Künstlerroman \'kuenst-lər-rō-ˌmän\ [German, literally, artist novel] Class of BILDUNGSROMAN, or apprenticeship novel, that deals with the youth and development of an individual who becomes—or is on the threshold of becoming—a painter, musician, or poet. The classic example is James Joyce's *Portrait of the Artist as a Young Man* (1916). The type originated in the period of German Romanticism with Ludwig Tieck's *Franz Sternbalds Wanderungen* (1798; "Franz Sternbald's Travels"). Later examples are Knut Hamsun's *Hunger* (1890) and Thomas Wolfe's *Look Homeward, Angel* (1929). Unlike the bildungsroman, in which the hero often dreams of becoming a great artist but settles for being a mere useful citizen, the Künstlerroman usually ends on a note of arrogant rejection of the commonplace life.

ku-wen *See* GUWEN.

kyōgen \'kyō-ˌgen\ [Japanese] Brief farce or comic interlude played during a Japanese Nō (lyric drama) cycle, expressed in the vernacular of the second half of the 16th century. Its effect is to relieve the tension of the drama. It is performed in ordinary dress and without masks (unless these are used in parody). There are normally four *kyōgen* interspersed among the usual five Nō pieces.

kyōka \'kyō-ˌkä\ [Japanese] Form of Japanese poetry, a comic or satirical version of the TANKA.

kyrielle \kēr-'yel\ *plural* kyrielle [French, literally, repeated series of words or phrases, litany, from Old French *kiriele,* a derivative of *kyrie* kyrie (a Christian liturgical prayer)] A French verse form in short, usually octosyllabic, rhyming couplets. The couplets are often paired in quatrains and are characterized by a refrain that is sometimes a single word and sometimes the full second line of thc couplet or the full fourth line of the quatrain.

L

More and more I detest poets and literati . . .
—Conrad Aiken

lacuna \lə-ˈkü-nə, -ˈkyü-\ *plural* lacunae \-ˌnē, -ˌnī\ *or* lacunas [Latin, gap, deficiency, literally, depression, pit] In a text or manuscript, a blank or missing section.

Ladies' Home Journal American monthly magazine, one of the oldest in the country and long the trendsetter among women's magazines. It was founded in 1883 as a women's supplement to the *Tribune and Farmer* (1879–85) of Cyrus H.K. Curtis and was edited by Curtis' wife, Louisa Knapp. The *Journal* began independent publication in 1884 with a pious and demure editorial posture and a sentimental literary diet and had a circulation of 20,000. Curtis boosted circulation to more than 100,000 with an innovative subscription "club" and a large advertising campaign. Edward W. Bok became editor in 1889, and under him the *Journal* attracted great writers from Europe and the United States—including W.D. Howells, Hamlin Garland, Mark Twain, Bret Harte, Rudyard Kipling, Sarah Orne Jewett, and Arthur Conan Doyle, becoming an exciting monthly that offered quality fiction and nonfiction articles. By the turn of the century, its circulation surpassed all other U.S. publications. It later went on to publish fiction by John Galsworthy, H.G. Wells, and Willa Cather and nonfiction by Eleanor Roosevelt, Margaret Mead, John Gunther, and Pearl Buck. Its features on domestic architecture, fine arts, and "How America Lives" won renown.

lai *See* LAY.

lai Breton *See* BRETON LAY.

laisse \ˈles, ˈlās\ [French, from Old French, part of a poem spoken or sung without interruption, a derivative of *laissier* to let, leave] The irregular strophe of Old French poetry; especially, a strophe of the chansons de geste.

Lake poets Group of English poets—William Wordsworth, Samuel Taylor Coleridge, and Robert Southey—who lived in the English Lake District of Cumberland and Westmorland (now Cumbria) at the beginning of the 19th century. They were first described derogatorily as the "Lake school" by Francis (afterward Lord) Jeffrey in a series of articles that appeared in *The Edinburgh Review* beginning in August 1817, and the description "Lakers" was also used in a similar spirit by the poet Lord Byron. In reality, however, this grouping of poets is artificial, because Southey did not subscribe in his views or work to the theories of poetry expressed by Wordsworth and Coleridge.

lament \lə-'ment\ A nonnarrative poem expressing deep grief or sorrow over a personal loss. The form developed as part of the oral tradition along with heroic poetry and exists in most languages. Examples include *Deor's Lament,* an early Anglo-Saxon poem, in which a minstrel regrets his change of status in relation to his patron, and the ancient Sumerian "Lament for the Destruction of Ur." *Compare* COMPLAINT; DIRGE; ELEGY.

lampoon \lam-'pün\ [French *lampon,* probably from *lampons!* let us gulp down! (a frequent refrain in 17th-century French satirical poems)] A virulent satire in prose or verse that is a gratuitous and sometimes unjust and malicious attack on an individual. Although the term came into use in the 17th century from the French, examples of the lampoon are found as early as the 3rd century BC in the plays of Aristophanes, who lampooned Euripides in *Frogs* and Socrates in *Clouds.* In English literature the form was particularly popular during the Restoration and the 18th century, as exemplified in the lampoons of John Dryden, Thomas Brown, and John Wilkes.

language \'laŋ-gwij\ Form or manner of verbal expression; more specifically, the style or characteristic mode of expression of an individual speaker or writer.

langue \'läŋ, *French* 'läⁿg\ Language viewed abstractly as a system of forms and conventions used for communication in a community. It is contrasted with *parole,* meaning a language used as a specific individual usage, or a linguistic act. The use of the French word *langue* in this sense was introduced by the linguist Ferdinand de Saussure.

lauda \'laü-də\ or **laude** \-dā\ *plural* laude *or* laudi \-dē\ [Italian, from Latin *laudes* praises, eulogy, plural of *laus* praise] A nonliturgical devotional song in praise of the Virgin Mary, Christ, or the saints that constituted an early Italian poetic genre.

The poetic *lauda* was of liturgical origin, and it was popular from about the mid-13th to the 16th century in Italy, where it was used particularly in confraternal groups and for religious celebrations. The first *lauda* in Italian was St. Francis' moving canticle in praise of "Sir Brother Sun," "Sister Moon," "Brother Wind," "Sister Water," "Brother Fire," and "Mother Earth"—a work that has sometimes been called *Laudes creaturarum o Cantico del Sole* ("Praises of God's Creatures or the Canticle of the Sun"). Another outstanding early master of the *lauda* was the gifted 13th-century Franciscan poet Jacopone da Todi, who wrote many highly emotional and mystical *laudi spirituali* ("spiritual canticles") in the vernacular. Jacopone is also the reputed author of a famous Latin *lauda,* the *Stabat mater dolorosa.* Another famous 13th-century *lauda* in Latin is the *Dies irae* ("Day of Wrath"), a funeral hymn.

Laude were frequently written in *ballata* form for recitation by religious confraternities, the *lauda* usually consisting of exhortations to a moral life or of events in the lives of Christ and the saints. These recitations evolved into dialogues and eventually became part of the Italian version of the miracle play, the *sacra rappresentazione,* a form of religiously inspired drama that became secularized during the Renaissance. Later in the Renaissance some laude were written for musical settings. The *lauda* remained important in Italian devotional life until the 19th century.

lay or **lai** \'lā\ [Old French *lai*] **1.** In medieval French literature, a short romance, usually written in octosyllabic verse, that dealt with subjects thought to be of Celtic origin. The earliest lay narratives were written in the 12th century by Marie de France; her works were largely based on earlier Breton versions thought to have been derived from Celtic legend. The BRETON LAY, a 14th-century English poetic form based on these lays, is exemplified by "The Franklin's Tale" in Geoffrey Chaucer's *The Canterbury Tales.* **2.** A medieval lyric poem. The earliest extant examples are those composed by Gautier de Dargies in the 13th century. These lays had nonuniform stanzas of about 6 to 16 or more lines of 4 to 8 syllables. One or two rhymes were maintained throughout each stanza. **3.** A simple narrative poem or a ballad, such as those written in the early 19th century by Sir Walter Scott and Thomas Macaulay. **4.** A song or melody.

lazzo \'lät-sō\ *plural* lazzi \-sē\ Improvised comic dialogue or action in Italian commedia dell'arte. The word, which means in more general contexts "jest" or "quip" and first appears in Italian in 1660, is of obscure and much debated origin. Lazzi were one of the prime resources of the commedia actors, consisting of verbal asides on current political and literary topics, manifestations of terror, and pratfalls and other acrobatics. The ability to improvise ingenious and engaging lazzi contributed to the reputations of many actors; many lazzi were frequently performed with slight variations and became part of the commedia repertoire. Lazzi were implicit in many of the comedies of Molière and those of William Shakespeare, in which they came to be called jigs.

lection \'lek-shən\ [Latin *lectio* act of reading, reading matter] A variant reading of a text.

legal oratory *See* FORENSIC ORATORY.

legend \'lej-ənd\ [Medieval Latin *legenda* reading, divine lesson, saint's life, from feminine of Latin *legendus,* gerundive of *legere* to read] **1.** The story or account of the life of a saint, or a collection of such stories. **2.** A story coming down from the past; especially, one handed down from early times by tradition and popularly regarded as historical although not entirely verifiable. Also, the total body of such stories and traditions; especially, the collective stories and traditions of a particular group (such as a people or clan). **3.** A popular myth usually of current or recent origin. **4.** The subject of a legend, or a person around whom such stories and traditions have grown up; specifically, one held to possess extraordinary qualities that are usually partly real and partly mythical.

Some legends are the unique property of the place or person to whom they are attached, such as the story of young George Washington chopping down the cherry tree. But many local legends are actually well-known folktales that have become attached to a particular person or place. For example, a widely distributed folktale of an excellent marksman who is forced to shoot an apple, hazelnut, or some other object from his son's head has become associated with the Swiss hero William Tell. Another popular tale, of a younger son whose only inheritance is a cat, which he sells for a fortune in a land overrun with mice, has become associated with Richard Whittington, thrice lord mayor of London in the early 15th century. The story told about King Lear is essentially the folktale "Love Like Salt." Local legends sometimes travel; although the Pied Piper of Hamelin has become famous through literary treatment, many other European towns have a similar legend of a piper who lured their children away. *See also* FOLKTALE.

Lehrstück \'lār-ˌstuek\ [German, literally, lesson play] A form of drama that is specifically didactic in purpose and that is meant to be performed outside of the orthodox theater. Such plays were associated particularly with the epic theater of the German dramatist Bertolt Brecht. In Brecht's *Lehrstücke* the didactic element was political and was based on his studies of Karl Marx.

leitmotiv or **leitmotif** \'līt-mō-ˌtēf\ In literature, a dominant recurring phrase, sentence, or theme within a work, such as the repetition of the phrase "only connect" in E.M. Forster's novel *Howards End.* The word (*German* "leading motif") was originally applied to repeated musical phrases associated with a particular character, situation, or idea in Richard Wagner's music dramas. *Compare* MOTIF.

leonine verse \'lē-ə-ˌnīn\ **1.** Latin or French verse in which the last word in the line rhymes with the word just before the caesura (as in "gloria factorum temere conceditus horum"). Such rhymes were already referred to as *rime leonine* in the anonymous 12th-century romance *Guillaume d'Angleterre.* A later tradition imputes their invention to a 12th-century Parisian canon and Latin poet named Leonius or Leoninus, but "leonine" may simply refer to their supposed preeminence over other verse forms. **2.** English verse in which the end of the line rhymes with a sound occurring near the middle of the line (as in Alfred, Lord Tennyson's "the long light shakes across the lakes"). *See also* INTERNAL RHYME.

letter \'let-ər\, *also called* epistolary literature. A personal written message to another person. The first notable collection of letters was gathered by Atticus and Tiro, who published nearly 1,000 of Cicero's letters. This gave rise to letter writing as a literary genre. Catullus wrote in verse, and Horace established the verse letter with striking examples in his *Epistles.* The popularity of the letter as a genre has continued down to the present day.

libretto \li-'bret-ō\ *plural* librettos *or* libretti \-'bret-ē\ [Italian, literally, booklet, diminutive of *libro* book] Text of an opera or other kind of musical theater. The term is also used, less commonly, of a musical work not intended for the stage. A libretto may be in verse or in prose; it may be specially designed for a particular composer, or it may provide raw material for several; it may be wholly original or an adaptation of an existing play or novel.

The earliest operas, beginning in 1597 with Ottavio Rinuccini's *Dafne,* set to music by Jacopo Peri, were court entertainments, and as a commemoration the words were printed in a small book, or "libretto." In the 1630s Venetian opera became a public spectacle, and audiences used printed librettos to follow the drama. The early French and Italian librettists regarded their works as poetic dramas, with the composer expected to pay faithful regard to the accents of the words. A tendency to more lyrical treatment of the text developed in Venice, however, and purely musical demands began to outweigh strict subservience to the poetry. Despite the enhancement of the composer's role, full operatic scores were rarely printed. It was usually only the librettist who saw his name in print.

The subject matter of librettos developed from the mythology and pastoral dramas of the 17th century through historical figures to lofty poetic drama and later real life subjects in the 18th century. Nineteenth-century Romanticism encouraged texts dealing with medieval history and legends of the supernatural, and exotic subjects and themes drawn from folklore and regional culture found their way into 19th- and 20th-century librettos. Demand for librettos of high literary quality also rose; Richard Wagner wrote his own, as did Hector Berlioz and such later composers as Alban Berg, Leoš Janáček, Arnold Schoenberg, and Gian Carlo Menotti.

Close collaboration between librettist and composer provided another solution to the question of textual quality. Perhaps the best example of successful partnership between librettist and composer is that of Hugo von Hofmannsthal and Richard Strauss, who collaborated on *Elektra* (1909), *Der Rosenkavalier* (1911), two versions of *Ariadne auf Naxos* (1912 and 1916; *Ariadne on Naxos*), *Die Frau ohne Schatten* (1919; *The Woman Without a Shadow*), *Die ägyptische Helena* (1928; *The Egyptian Helen*), and *Arabella* (produced—after von Hofmannsthal's death—in 1933).

Among the rare successful uses of spoken-drama texts are Claude Debussy's setting of Maurice Maeterlinck's *Pelléas et Mélisande* (1902) and Richard Strauss' setting of Oscar Wilde's *Salomé* (1905). Other well-known librettists were Emanuel Schikaneder, who wrote the text for W.A. Mozart's *Die Zauberflöte* (1791; *The Magic Flute*); Arrigo Boito, who wrote his own operas and collaborated with other composers to write the text for theirs; and W.S. Gilbert, who wrote a series of light operas with the composer Arthur Sullivan. Composer Virgil Thomson collaborated with avant-garde writer Gertrude Stein in *Four Saints in Three Acts* (1928) and *The Mother of Us All* (1947).

light comedy Comedy characterized by delicacy and wit. Also, comedy that is lighthearted and amusing and that makes few demands intellectually.

light stress In prosody, an accent or stress on a word that is not accented in everyday speech. The word *if* in the third line of the following stanza from Samuel Taylor Coleridge's poem "The Rime of the Ancient Mariner" exhibits this kind of stress:

> And every tongue, through utter drought,
> Was withered at the root;
> We could not speak, no more than if
> We had been choked with soot.

light verse Verse on trivial or playful themes that is written mainly to amuse and entertain and that often involves nonsense and wordplay. Frequently distinguished by considerable technical competence, wit, sophistication, and elegance, light poetry constitutes a considerable body of verse in all Western languages. The term is a general one that can be applied to such forms as NONSENSE VERSE, LIMERICK, CLERIHEW, EPIGRAM, and MOCK-EPIC.

The Greeks were among the first to practice light verse, examples of which may be found in the Greek Anthology. Roman poets, such as Catullus, singing of his love's sparrow, and Horace, inviting friends to share his wine, set patterns in light poetry that were followed to the end of the 19th century.

Medieval light verse, mainly narrative in form, was often satirical, bawdy, and irreverent but nonetheless sensible and essentially moral, as can be seen in the 12th-century Latin songs of wandering students (goliards), the often indecent French fabliaux, and mock-epics such as the *Roman de Renart.*

French light poetry of the 14th and 15th centuries was written largely in ballades and rondeaux, challenging such poets as Clément Marot and Pierre de Ronsard to great displays of virtuosity. A vein of light melancholy runs through the witty verse of many English Renaissance poets, from Sir Thomas Wyatt to Richard Lovelace. The more cheerful poetry of Ben Jonson and Robert Herrick sometimes celebrated food and simple pleasures.

Late 17th-century examples include Samuel Butler's *Hudibras,* which satirizes the English Puritans, and the *Fables* of Jean de La Fontaine, which offers a comprehensive picture of society and minutely scrutinizes its behavior.

The great English light poem of the 18th century is Alexander Pope's *The Rape of the Lock* (1712–14), a mock-epic in which the polite society of his day is shown by innuendo to be a mere shadow of the heroic days of old. Lord Byron's verse novel *Don Juan* (1819–24), sardonic and casual, combined the colloquialism of medieval light verse with a sophistication that inspired a number of imitations.

Light verse proliferated in the later 19th century, when the rise of humorous periodicals supplied a large market. Among the best-known light works of the period are the limericks of Edward Lear's *Book of Nonsense* (1846), W.S. Gilbert's *Bab Ballads* (1869), and the inspired nonsense of Lewis Carroll's *The*

Hunting of the Snark (1876). The American poet Charles G. Leland exploited the humorous possibilities of immigrant jargon in *The Breitmann Ballads* (first published under that title in 1871).

In the 20th century the distinction between light and serious verse has been obscured by the flippant, irreverent tone used by many modern poets, the nonsense verse of the Dadaists, Futurists, and Surrealists, and the primitivistic techniques of such writers as the Beat poets and E.E. Cummings. In spite of their seeming lightness, the works of such poets as Vladimir Mayakovsky, W.H. Auden, Louis MacNeice, Theodore Roethke, and Kenneth Fearing are usually seriously intended; they may begin by being amusing but often end in terror or bitterness. Though light verse in the traditional manner was occasionally produced by major poets—for example, Ezra Pound's delightful Middle English parody "Ancient Music" ("Winter is icummen in") and T.S. Eliot's *Old Possum's Book of Practical Cats* (1939)—it has come to be associated with exclusive or frequent practitioners of the genre: in the United States, Ogden Nash, Dorothy Parker, and Phyllis McGinley; in England, Sir John Betjeman and Hilaire Belloc; and in Germany, Christian Morgenstern and Erich Kästner.

limerick \\'lim-ə-rik\\ A popular form of short, humorous verse, often nonsensical and frequently ribald. It consists of five lines, rhyming *aabba,* and the dominant meter is anapestic, with two feet in the third and fourth lines and three feet in the others. The origin of the word *limerick,* which is not attested before the 1890s is obscure, but a group of poets in County Limerick, Ireland, wrote limericks in Irish in the 18th century.

The first collections of limericks in English date from about 1820. Edward Lear, who composed and illustrated the limericks in his *Book of Nonsense* (1846), claimed to have gotten the idea from a nursery rhyme beginning "There was an old man of Tobago." An example from Lear's collection is this verse:

> There was an Old Man who supposed
> That the street door was partially closed;
>   But some very large rats
>   Ate his coats and his hats,
> While that futile Old Gentleman dozed.

Toward the end of the 19th century, W.S. Gilbert displayed his skill in a sequence of limericks that Sir Arthur Sullivan set as the familiar song in *The Sorcerer* (1877):

> My name is John Wellington Wells,
> I'm a dealer in magic and spells,
>   In blessings and curses,
>   And ever-fill'd purses,
> In prophecies, witches, and knells.

Gilbert also wrote one of the first offbeat limericks, which were to become nearly as popular as the true kind. Their charm lay in the unexpected jolt caused by failure to find the expected rhyme.

> There was an old man of St. Bees,
> Who was stung in the arm by a wasp,
>   When asked, "Does it hurt?"
>   He replied, "No, it doesn't,
> I'm so glad it wasn't a hornet."

Limericks acquired widespread popularity in the early years of the 20th century, and limerick contests were often held by magazines and business houses. The true limerick addict, however, turned to more complicated verse, such as this anonymous tongue twister:

> A tutor who taught on the flute
> Tried to teach two tooters to toot.
>   Said the two to the tutor,
>   "Is it harder to toot, or
> To tutor two tooters to toot?"

liminary \'lim-ə-ˌner-ē\ [Late Latin *liminaris* initial, preliminary, a derivative of Latin *limen* threshold] Placed at the beginning of a book.

limited edition An issue of something collectible (such as books, prints, or medals) that is advertised to be limited to a relatively small number of copies.

line \'līn\ A unit in the rhythmic structure of verse that is formed by the grouping together of a number of the smallest units of the rhythm (such as syllables, stress groups, metrical feet) according to some principle or norm supplied by the nature or conventions of that type of verse. For instance, if a poem is written in iambic pentameter the rules of the form dictate that a standard line in the poem will consist of 10 syllables arranged in five iambic feet. Lines in turn are composed or combined into larger structural units (such as strophes or stanzas), either by continuous repetition in series or by arrangement in systematic patterns.

lineation \ˌlin-ē-'ā-shən\ An arrangement of lines (as of verse).

linguistic form *also called* speech form. A meaningful unit of speech, as a morpheme, word, or sentence.

linguistics The study of human speech in its various aspects, as the units, nature, structure, and modification of language including such factors as phonetics, phonology, morphology, accent, syntax, semantics, grammar, and the relation between writing and speech.

lipogram \'lip-ə-ˌgram, 'līp-\ [Middle Greek *lipográmmatos* lacking a letter, from Greek *leípein* to leave, be lacking + *grámma* letter] A written text deliberately composed of words not having a certain letter (such as the *Odyssey* of Tryphiodorus, which had no alpha in the first book, no beta in the second, and so on).

lit crit *See* LITERARY CRITICISM.

literary \'lit-ə-ˌrer-ē\ [French *littéraire,* from Latin *litterarius* of reading and writing, a derivative of *litterae* written matter, literary works, plural of *littera* letter of the alphabet] **1.** Of, relating to, or having the characteristics of literature. Of or relating to books. **2.** Having a firsthand knowledge of literature, or being well-read. **3.** Of, relating to, or concerned with men and women of letters or with writing as a profession.

Literary Association *See* LITERARY RESEARCH ASSOCIATION.

Literary Club, The A dining club founded by Samuel Johnson in 1764 as THE CLUB.

literary criticism *also called* (jocularly, and chiefly in academic contexts) lit crit \'lit-'krit\ A discipline concerned with a range of inquiries about literature that have tended to fall into three broad categories: philosophical, descriptive, and evaluative. In other words, criticism that asks what literature is, what it does, and what it is worth.

The Western critical tradition began with Plato in the 4th century BC. In the *Republic* he attacked the poets on two fronts: their art is merely imitative, and it appeals to the worst rather than to the best in human nature. A generation later Aristotle, in his *Poetics,* countered these charges by claiming for literature a level of imaginative truth that transcends that of imitation and by arguing that it excites the emotions simply in order to allay them. In addition to defending literature, Aristotle developed a set of principles of composition that were of lasting importance to European literature. As late as 1674 Nicolas Boileau was still, in *L'Art poétique,* recommending observance of the Aristotelian rules—or unities—of time, action, and place.

European literary criticism from the Renaissance onward has for the most part focused on the same two issues that underlay the debate between Plato and Aristotle: the moral worth of literature and the nature of its relationship to reality. At the end of the 16th century Sir Philip Sidney argued in *The Defence of Poesie* that it is the special property of literature to express moral and philosophical truths in a way that rescues them from abstraction and makes them immediately graspable. A century later, John Dryden, in *Of Dramatick Poesie, An Essay* (1668), put forward the less idealistic view that the business of literature is primarily to offer an accurate representation of the world "for the delight and instruction of mankind." This remains the assumption of the great critical works of 18th-century England, underlying both Alexander Pope's *An Essay on Criticism* (1711) and the extensive work of Samuel Johnson.

In the late 18th century, literary criticism began to reflect the influence of the growing Romantic movements in England and Germany. William Wordsworth's assertion in his "Preface" to the second edition of the *Lyrical Ballads* (1800) that the object of poetry is "truth . . . carried alive into the heart by passion" marks a significant change from the ideas of the mid-18th century. Other important statements of critical theory in the Romantic period were Samuel Taylor Coleridge's *Biographia Literaria* (1817), which drew heavily on the work of such German theorists as F.W.J. von Schelling and A.W. von Schlegel, and Percy Bysshe Shelley's *A Defence of Poetry* (written 1821). The later 19th century saw a development in one direction toward an aesthetic theory of art for art's sake, and in another direction toward the view, expressed by Matthew Arnold, that the cultural role of literature should be to take over the sort of moral and philosophical functions that had previously been fulfilled by religion.

For the future of literary criticism, however, the most important change during the final years of the century was the gradual establishment of literature as an academic discipline. The volume of literary criticism increased greatly in the 20th century. An early example of this in the English-speaking world was I.A. Richards' *Principles of Literary Criticism* (1924), which became influential as the basis of Practical Criticism. From this developed the New Criticism of the 1940s and '50s, which was associated with such American critics as John Crowe Ransom and Cleanth Brooks. The premise of the New Critics, that a work of literature should be studied as a separate and self-contained entity, set them in opposition both to biographical criticism and to those schools of criticism—Marxist, psychoanalytical, historical, and the like—that had their roots in the 19th century and that set out to examine literature from perspectives external to the text.

The late 20th century witnessed a radical reappraisal of traditional modes of literary criticism. Building on the work of the Russian Formalist critics of the 1920s and the examinations of linguistic structure carried out by the Swiss philologist Ferdinand de Saussure, literary theorists began to call into question the overriding importance of the concept of "the author" as the source of the text's meaning. Structuralist and poststructuralist critics, such as Roland Barthes and Jacques Derrida of France, instead directed attention toward the ways in which meaning is created by the determining structures of language and culture. *See also* CHICAGO CRITICS; DECONSTRUCTION; FEMINIST CRITICISM; FORMALISM; FREUDIAN CRITICISM; GENEVA SCHOOL OF CRITICISM; MARXIST CRITICISM; NEW CRITICISM; NEW HISTORICISM; POSTSTRUCTURALISM; PRACTICAL CRITICISM; READER-RESPONSE CRITICISM; STRUCTURALISM.

literaryism \ˈlit-ə-ˌrer-ē-ˌiz-əm\ An instance of or tendency to use excessive refinement of expression in written compositions.

Literary Research Association *also called* Literary Association, *Chinese* Wenxue yanjiu hui. Chinese literary society founded in Beijing in November 1920 by a group of professors, writers, students, and translators. The Literary

Research Association, generally referred to as the realist or "art-for-life's-sake" school, assumed the editorship of the established literary magazine *Xiaoshuo yuebao* ("Fiction Monthly"), in which most major fiction writers—including Mao Dun, Ye Shengtao, Wang Tongzhao, and Xu Dishan, as well as the pioneering women writers Bing Xin and Ding Ling—published their works throughout the 1920s, until the magazine's headquarters was destroyed by Japanese bombs in 1932. The socially reflective writing that characterized this group held sway in China well into the 1940s, when it was gradually eclipsed by more didactic, propagandistic literature. *See also* CREATION SOCIETY.

literary sketch Short prose narrative, often an entertaining account of some aspect of a culture written by someone within that culture for readers outside of it—e.g., anecdotes of a traveler in India published in an English magazine. Relaxed and informal in style, the sketch is less dramatic but more analytic and descriptive than the tale and the short story. A writer of a sketch maintains a chatty and familiar tone, understating his major points and suggesting, rather than stating, conclusions. One common variation of the sketch is the character sketch, a form of casual biography usually consisting of a series of anecdotes about a real or imaginary person.

The sketch was introduced after the 16th century in response to the growing middle-class interest in social realism and in exotic and foreign lands. The form reached its height of popularity in the 18th and 19th centuries and is represented by such famous sketches as those of Joseph Addison and Richard Steele in *The Spectator* (1711–12). *The Sketch Book of Geoffrey Crayon, Gent.* (1819–20) is Washington Irving's account of the English landscape and customs for readers in the United States.

literate \ˈlit-ə-rət\ [Latin *litteratus* versed in literature, cultured, a derivative of *litterae* writing, literary works] **1.** Educated, cultured. **2.** Able to read and write—opposed to *illiterate*. **3.** Versed in literature or creative writing. **4.** Dealing with literature or belles lettres.

literati \ˌlit-ə-ˈrät-ē\ [Latin, plural of *literatus* a person of culture, from *literatus* (adjective) versed in literature, cultured] The educated class or intelligentsia; specifically, persons interested in literature or the arts. The term was originally used in the 17th century to describe the literate class in China. It later meant members of literary clubs of 18th-century Edinburgh and professional men who were supporters of a particular party within the Church of Scotland, and from there it took on its broader meaning.

literator \ˈlit-ə-ˌrā-tər\ [in part from Latin *litterator* schoolmaster, in part from French *littérateur*] *See* LITTERATEUR.

literature \ˈlit-ə-rə-ˌchu̇r, -chər, -ˌtyu̇r\ [Latin *litteratura* writing, elements of elementary education, literature, a derivative of *litteratus* versed in literature, cultured] **1.** *archaic* Knowledge of books; literary culture. **2.** The production of literary work especially as an occupation. **3.** Writings in prose or verse; especially, writings having excellence of form or expression and presenting ideas of permanent or universal interest. **4.** The body of written works produced in a particular language, country, or age. **5.** The body of writings on a particular subject. **6.** Printed matter (as leaflets, handbills, or circulars).

litotes \ˈlīt-ə-ˌtēz, ˈlit-; lī-ˈtō-tēz\ [Greek *litótēs,* literally, plainness, a derivative of *litós* plain, simple] A figure of speech by which conscious understatement is used to create emphasis by negation; examples are the common expressions "not bad!" and "no mean feat." Litotes is responsible for much of the characteristic stoicism of Old English poetry and the Icelanders' sagas.

litterateur \ˌlit-ə-rə-ˈtər, -ˈtu̇r\ or **literator** \ˈlit-ə-ˌrā-tər, ˌlit-ə-ˈrä-ˌtȯr\ [French *littérateur,* a derivative of *littérature* literature] A literary person; especially, a professional writer.

Littérature \lē-tā-rȧ-ˈtue̅r\ The most notable of the French periodicals issued by members of the Dada movement. The review, founded by André Breton, Louis Aragon, and Philippe Soupault, was published in Paris from 1919 to 1924.

littérature engagée \lē-tā-rȧ-tue̅r-ä^{n}-gȧ-ˈzhā\ ("engaged literature") The literature of commitment, popularized in the immediate post-World War II era, when the French existentialists, particularly Jean-Paul Sartre, revived the idea of the artist's serious responsibility to society. Engagement was understood as an individual moral challenge that involved the responsibility of adapting freely made choices to socially useful ends, rather than as "taking a position" on particular issues. The idea is an application to art of a basic existentialist tenet: that a person defines himself by consciously engaging in willed action. The existentialist position was a reaction against the creed of "art for art's sake" and against the "bourgeois" writer, whose obligation was to his craft rather than his audience. Sartre defined such terms in his introductory statement to *Les Temps modernes* (1945), a review devoted to *littérature engagée.*

little magazine Any of various small periodicals devoted to serious literary writings, usually avant-garde and noncommercial. They were published from about 1880 through much of the 20th century and flourished in the United States and England, though French authors (especially the Symbolis poets and critics who wrote about 1880–1900) often had access to a similar type of publication and German literature of the 1920s was also indebted to them. The name signifies most of all a noncommercial manner of editing, managing, and financing. A little magazine usually begins with the object of publishing literary work of some artistic merit that is unacceptable to commercial magazines for any one or all of three reasons—that the writer is unknown and therefore not a good risk; that the work itself is unconventional or experimental in form; or that it violates one of several popular notions of moral, social, or aesthetic behavior.

Foremost in the ranks of such magazines were two American periodicals, *Poetry: a Magazine of Verse* (founded 1912), especially in its early years under the vigorous guidance of Harriet Monroe, and the more erratic and often more sensational *Little Review* (1914–29) of Margaret Anderson; a group of English magazines in the second decade of the 20th century, of which the *Egoist* (1914–19) and *Blast* (1914–15) were most conspicuous; and *transition* (1927–38). In all but the last of these, a major guiding spirit was the American-born poet and critic Ezra Pound, who served as "foreign correspondent" of both *Poetry* and the *Little Review,* maneuvered the *Egoist* from its earlier beginnings as a feminist magazine (*The New Freewoman,* 1913) to the status of an avant-garde literary review, and, with Wyndham Lewis, jointly sponsored the two issues of *Blast*. In this case, the little magazines showed the stamp of a single vigorous personality; similar strong and dedicated figures in little magazine history were the American poet William Carlos Williams, (whose name appears in scores of little magazines, in one capacity or another); the British critic and novelist Ford Madox Ford, editor of the *Transatlantic Review* (January 1924–January 1925) and contributor to many others; and Gustave Kahn, a minor French poet but a very active editor associated with several French Symbolist periodicals.

There were four principal periods in the general history of little magazines. In the first, from 1890 to about 1915, French magazines served mainly to establish and explain a literary movement; British and American magazines served to disseminate information about and encourage acceptance of continental European literature and culture. In the second stage, 1915–30, when other magazines, especially in the United States, were in the vanguard of almost every variation of modern literature, a conspicuous feature was the expatriate magazine, published usually in France but occasionally elsewhere in Europe by young American and British critics and writers. The major emphasis in this period was upon literary and aesthetic form and theory and the publication of fresh and original work, such as that of Ernest Hemingway (in *Little Review, Poetry, This Quarter,* and other publications), T.S. Eliot (in *Poetry, Egoist, Blast*), James Joyce (in *Egoist, Little Review, transition*), and many others. The third stage, the 1930s, saw the beginnings of many leftist magazines, started with specific doctrinal commitments that were often subjected to considerable editorial change in the career of the magazine. *Partisan Review* (1934) was perhaps the best-known example of these in the United States, as was the *Left Review* (1934–38) in England.

The fourth period of little magazine history began about 1940. One of the conspicuous features of this period was the critical review supported and sustained by a group of critics, who were in most cases attached to a university or college. Examples of this kind of periodical were, in the United States, *The Kenyon Review* (1939–70), founded by John Crowe Ransom, and in Great Britain, *Scrutiny,* edited (1932–53) by F.R. Leavis. This and related kinds of support, such as that of publishers maintaining their own reviews or miscellanies, represented a form of institutionalism which was radically different from the more spontaneous and erratic nature of the little magazines of earlier years.

Little Review, The Avant-garde American literary magazine founded in Chicago by Margaret Anderson, published from 1914 to 1929. Despite minimal financial support and numerous fights with censors, *The Little Review* managed to be the most influential arts magazine of its time. Its contributors included William Butler Yeats, T.S. Eliot, Wyndham Lewis, Gertrude Stein, William Carlos Williams, Emma Goldman, Ezra Pound, Ernest Hemingway, and Wallace Stevens, but the magazine is probably best known for its serialization of James Joyce's novel *Ulysses*.

Anderson founded *The Little Review* in Chicago in 1914 as a journal of "the best conversation the world has to offer." The first issue, published in March of 1914, featured work by Chicago poet Vachel Lindsay and essays on feminism, Friedrich Nietzsche, and psychoanalysis. In the May 1914 issue Anderson extolled the ideas of anarchist Emma Goldman and called for the abolition of private property; her few financial backers then abandoned her. In 1916 Anderson's companion, artist Jane Heap, joined her as associate editor. Anderson and Heap moved to New York's Greenwich Village in 1917. It was Pound, who was the European editor, who contributed his own work and brought other works, including Joyce's *Ulysses* to the magazine. The serialization of *Ulysses* began in the March 1918 issue; over the next three years the U.S. Post Office burned entire press runs of four issues for alleged obscenity.

Financially strapped and demoralized by the tepid response to *Ulysses,* in 1921 Anderson and Heap began to publish *The Little Review* as a quarterly rather than a monthly. In 1922 Anderson turned over the editorship to Heap, who in 1927 relocated the then irregularly published magazine to Paris. With Anderson, she drafted a questionnaire mailed to dozens of artists and writers, including questions such as "What is your attitude toward art today?" More than 50 responded, including Sherwood Anderson, Edith Sitwell, Jean Cocteau, Marianne Moore, and Bernard Russell, and their replies made up the last issue of *The Little Review*.

little theater Movement in American theater to free dramatic forms and methods of production from the limitations of large commercial theaters by establishing small experimental centers of drama. The movement was initiated at the beginning of the 20th century by young dramatists, stage designers, and actors who were influenced by the vital European theater of the late 19th century. They were especially impressed by the revolutionary theories of the German director Max Reinhardt, the designing concepts of Adolphe Appia and Edward Gordon Craig, and the staging experiments at such theaters as the Théâtre-Libre of Paris, the Freie Bühne in Berlin, and the Moscow Art Theater. Community playhouses such as the Toy Theatre in Boston, the Little Theatre in Chicago, and the Little Theatre, New York City, all founded in 1912, were centers of the experimental activity. Some groups owned or leased their own theaters; a few, such as the Washington Square Players (1914), the predecessor of the Theatre Guild (1918), became important commercial producers. By encouraging freedom of expression, staging the works of talented young writers, and choosing plays solely on the basis of artistic merit, the little theaters provided a valuable early opportunity for such playwrights as Eugene O'Neill, George S. Kaufman, Elmer Rice, Maxwell Anderson, and Robert E. Sherwood.

liturgical drama In the Middle Ages, type of play acted within or near a church and relating stories from the Bible and of the saints. Although they had their roots in the Christian liturgy, such plays were not performed as essential parts of a standard church service. The language of the liturgical drama was Latin, and the dialogue was frequently chanted to simple monophonic melodies. Music was also used incidentally.

The earliest traces of the liturgical drama are found in manuscripts dating from the 10th century. Its genesis may perhaps be found in the chant "Quem quaeritis" ("Whom do you seek"), a trope to the Introit of the Easter mass. In *Regularis concordia* (mid-10th century), Aethelwold, bishop of Winchester, described in some detail the manner in which the "Quem quaeritis" trope was performed as a small scene during the Matins service on Easter morning. The dialogue represents the well-known story of the three Marys approaching the tomb of Christ:

> "Whom do you seek?"
> "Jesus of Nazareth."
> "He is not here. He has arisen as was prophesied. Go.
> Announce that he has arisen from the dead."

The liturgical drama gradually increased in both length and sophistication and flourished particularly during the 12th and 13th centuries. The most popular themes were derived from colorful biblical tales (Daniel in the lion's den, the foolish virgins, the story of the Passion and death of Jesus, etc.) as well as from the stories of the saints (such as the Virgin Mary and St. Nicholas). Eventually, the connection between the liturgical drama and the church was severed completely as the plays came under secular sponsorship and adopted the vernacular. *See also* MIRACLE PLAY; MORALITY PLAY; MYSTERY PLAY.

Living Newspaper Theatrical production consisting of dramatizations of current events, social problems, and controversial issues, with appropriate suggestions for improvement. The technique was used for propaganda in the U.S.S.R. after the Bolshevik Revolution of 1917. It became part of the EPIC THEATER tradition initiated by Erwin Piscator and Bertolt Brecht in Germany in the 1920s.

The Living Newspaper was initiated in the United States in 1935 as part of the WPA FEDERAL THEATRE PROJECT. One of its major supporters was Elmer Rice, a dramatist and producer who believed in the value of drama as an instrument of social change. It became the most effective new theater form developed by the Project, vividly dealing, in flashing cinematic techniques, with the realities of agriculture, housing, and economics. Outstanding productions included

Triple-A Plowed Under, dealing with the Supreme Court's invalidation of the Agricultural Adjustment Administration (AAA), and *One-Third of a Nation,* dramatizing the plight of the poor. Criticism of the Living Newspaper for alleged communist leanings contributed to the cancellation of the Federal Theatre Project in 1939.

Living Theatre, The Theatrical repertory company known for its innovative production of experimental drama, often on radical themes, and for its confrontations with tradition, authority, and audiences. It was formed in New York City in 1951 by Julian Beck and Judith Malina. The group struggled during the 1950s, producing little-known, new, and experimental plays by Gertrude Stein, Luigi Pirandello, Alfred Jarry, T.S. Eliot, Jean Cocteau, August Strindberg, and others. Its first big success came with its 1959 production of *The Connection,* Jack Gelber's drama about drug addiction.

After touring Europe and returning to the United States, members of the troupe tangled with the federal government over their political (nonviolent and anarchial) views and failure to pay income taxes. Beck and Malina were jailed briefly, and The Living Theatre was closed.

In 1964 the company took up "voluntary exile" in Europe. Influenced by Oriental mysticism, Gestalt psychology, and an Artaudian desire to abolish the distinction between art and life, The Living Theatre moved toward deliberately shocking and confronting its audiences. In such works as *Paradise Now,* the actors performed rituals, provoked arguments, and carried on until members of the audience left. In 1970 the troupe split into several groups and dispersed.

loan word A word taken from another language and at least partially naturalized. *Anadiplosis* is a loan word in English, as is *karaoke.*

local color Style of writing marked by the presentation of the features and peculiarities of a particular locality and its inhabitants. The name is given especially to a type of American literature that in its most characteristic form made its appearance just after the Civil War. For nearly three decades it was the single most popular form of American literature, fulfilling a newly awakened public interest in distant parts of the country and, for some, providing a nostalgic memory of times gone by. Writers of this genre—sometimes known as local colorists—sought to depict the character of a region, concentrating especially upon matters such as dialect, manners, folklore, and landscape that distinguish the area.

The frontier novels of James Fenimore Cooper have been cited as precursors of the local-color story, as have the New York Dutch tales of Washington Irving. The California gold rush provided a vivid and exciting background for the stories of Bret Harte, whose "The Luck of Roaring Camp" (1868), with its use of miners' dialect, colorful characters, and western background, is among the early local-color stories. Mark Twain, who once worked for Harte in California, adapted the methods of the local-color story in writing of his native Missouri and of Mississippi River life. Many authors first achieved success with vivid descriptions of their own localities: Harriet Beecher Stowe, Rose Terry Cooke, and Sarah Orne Jewett wrote of New England; George Washington Cable, Joel Chandler Harris, and Kate Chopin described the Deep South; T.N. Page did the same for Virginia; Edward Eggleston wrote of Indiana frontier days; Mary Noailles Murfree, under the pseudonym of Charles E. Craddock told stories of the Tennessee mountaineers; and O. Henry chronicled both the Texas frontier and the streets of New York City.

locus classicus \ˈlō-kəs-ˈklas-i-kəs\ *plural* loci classici \ˈlō-ˌsī-ˈklas-i-ˌsī\ [New Latin, literally, classical passage] A passage that has become a standard for the elucidation of a word or subject. The term is also used to refer generally to a classic case or example.

logaoedic \ˌläg-ə-ˈē-dik\ [Late Greek *logaoidikós,* from *lógos* utterance, prose + *aoidḗ* music, poetry] In prosody, having a metrical rhythm marked by the mixture of several meters; specifically, having a rhythm that uses both dactyls and trochees or anapests and iambs.

logographer \lō-ˈgäg-rə-fər\ [Greek *logógraphos* prose writer, from *lógos* utterance, prose + *gráphein* to write] A prose writer in ancient Greece whose purpose was the systematic recording of factual material. As such, logographers are the precursors of historians proper who are said to have started with Herodotus.

London Magazine, The \ˈlən-dən\ An English periodical that was dedicated to an adventurous exploration of various subjects, particularly literature and literary criticism. The magazine was published monthly from January 1820 to June 1829.

It initially was edited by John Scott, assisted by William Hazlitt, Thomas Hood, and Mary Russell Mitford. Thomas De Quincey's *Confessions of an English Opium-Eater* and a series of essays by Charles Lamb that were eventually collected as *Essays of Elia,* as well as the work of other important young English writers such as Thomas Carlyle, Leigh Hunt, John Keats, and William Wordsworth, were published there. In addition, the magazine published a wide range of foreign literature, including works from Denmark, Serbia, Russia, and Iceland. It competed fiercely with *Blackwood's Edinburgh Magazine,* which harshly insulted Scott's writers; after Scott revealed some of his rival's libels, he was mortally wounded in a duel with one of its representatives. More than a few writers considered Scott's successor, John Taylor, to be a meddling editor, and several noted contributors withdrew their work from the magazine.

A later monthly literary review, founded in 1954 by John Lehmann, was also named *The London Magazine*. It was geared toward the common reader who was interested in serious literature, and its scope was later expanded to include coverage of other arts, as well. The journal published international authors as well as English ones, and its contributors included W.H. Auden, Louis MacNeice, Evelyn Waugh, Derek Walcott, and Jaroslav Seifert.

long meter or **long measure** *abbreviated* L.M. In poetry, a quatrain in iambic tetrameter lines with the second and fourth lines rhyming and often the first and third lines rhyming. An example is the following stanza from the poem "When I Survey the Wondrous Cross" by Isaac Watts:

> See, from his head, his hands, his feet,
> Sorrow and love flow mingled down;
> Did e'er such love and sorrow meet,
> Or thorns compose so rich a crown?

Compare BALLAD METER; COMMON METER.

long particular meter *abbreviated* L.P.M. In verse, a hymn meter of six iambic tetrameter lines to the stanza.

loose sentence A sentence in which the principal clause comes first and subordinate modifiers or trailing elements follow. *Compare* PERIODIC SENTENCE.

Lope de Vega Prize \ˈlō-pā-t͟hā-ˈb̲ā-gä\ Literary prize awarded annually to the Spanish or Latin-American playwright of the year's finest play not yet published or performed. The winner of the first prize receives 600,000 pesetas and production of the play at the Teatro Español in Madrid. A second prize is also awarded. The prize was established in 1932 by the Ayuntamiento de Madrid in memory of dramatist Lope de Vega, the celebrated and prolific playwright of Spain's Golden Age.

Lord Chamberlain's Men *See* CHAMBERLAIN'S MEN.

Lost Generation In general, the post-World War I generation, but specifically a group of American writers who came of age during the war and established their literary reputations in the 1920s. The term stems from a remark made by Gertrude Stein to Ernest Hemingway, "You are all a lost generation." Hemingway used the comment as an epigraph to *The Sun Also Rises* (1926), a novel that captures the attitudes of a hard-drinking, fast-living set of disillusioned young expatriates in postwar Paris and Spain. The generation was "lost" in the sense that its inherited values could no longer operate in the postwar world and because of its spiritual alienation from a country that, basking under President Harding's "return to normalcy" policy, seemed to its members to be hopelessly provincial, materialistic, and emotionally barren. The term embraces Hemingway, F. Scott Fitzgerald, John Dos Passos, E.E. Cummings, Archibald MacLeish, Hart Crane, and many other writers who made Paris the center of their literary activities in the 1920s. They were never a literary school. In the 1930s, as these writers turned in different directions, their works lost the distinctive stamp of the postwar period. The last representative works of the era were Fitzgerald's *Tender Is the Night* (1934) and Dos Passos' *The Big Money* (1936).

low comedy Dramatic or literary entertainment with no underlying purpose except to provoke laughter by boasting, boisterous jokes, drunkenness, scolding, fighting, buffoonery, and other riotous activity. Used either alone or added as comic relief to more serious forms, low comedy has its origins in the comic improvisations of actors in ancient Greek and Roman comedy. Written forms of low comedy can also be found in medieval religious drama, in the works of William Shakespeare, and in farce and vaudeville.

lüshi or **lü-shih** \ˈlw̄ē-ˈshə̇\ [Chinese *lǜshī,* from *lǜ* rule, constraint + *shī* poetry, verse] A form of Chinese poetry introduced in the T'ang dynasty (618–907). It consists of eight lines of five or seven syllables—each line set down in accordance with strict tonal patterns. Exposition (*qi*) was called for in the first two lines; the development of the theme (*cheng*), in parallel verse structure, in the middle, or second and third, couplets; and the conclusion (*he*) in the final couplet. *Lüshi* provided a new, formal alternative to the long-popular free *gushi* ("ancient style"). The poet Du Fu was particularly associated with *lüshi,* and Bo Juyi also frequently used the form.

The symmetry and lyricism of *lüshi* inspired JUEJU, a condensed form of *lüshi* consisting of quatrains and depending for its artistry on suggestiveness and economy. Another variation, *pailü,* followed most of the rules of *lüshi,* but also allowed the poet to alter the rhyme and elongate the poem.

lyric \ˈlir-ik\ [Latin *lyrica* lyric poetry, from neuter plural of *lyricus* of lyric poetry, literally, of the lyre, from Greek *lyrikós,* a derivative of *lýra* lyre] A verse or poem that can, or supposedly can, be sung to the accompaniment of a musical instrument (in ancient times, usually a lyre) or that expresses intense personal emotion in a manner suggestive of a song. Lyric poetry expresses the thoughts and feelings of the poet and is sometimes contrasted with narrative poetry and verse drama, which relate events in the form of a story. Elegies, odes, and sonnets are important types of lyric poetry.

In ancient Greece an early distinction was made between the poetry chanted by a choir of singers (choral lyrics) and the song that expressed the sentiments of a single poet. The latter, the melos, or song proper, had reached a height of technical perfection in "the Isles of Greece, where burning Sappho loved and sung," as early as the 7th century BC. Sappho and her contemporary Alcaeus and the later Anacreon were the chief Doric lyric poets. A later group of poets, including Alcman, Arion, Stesichorus, Simonides, and Ibycus, wrote choral lyric poetry. At the close of the 5th century Bacchylides and Pindar developed the tradition of the dithyrambic odes to its highest point. Latin lyrics were written by Catullus and Horace in the 1st century BC.

In medieval Europe the lyric form can be found in the songs of the troubadours, in Christian hymns, and in various ballads. In the Renaissance the most finished form of lyric, the sonnet, was brilliantly developed by Petrarch, William Shakespeare, Edmund Spenser, and John Milton. Especially identified with the lyrical forms of poetry in the late 18th and 19th centuries were the Romantic poets, including such diverse figures as Robert Burns, William Blake, William

Wordsworth, John Keats, Percy Bysshe Shelley, Alphonse de Lamartine, Victor Hugo, J.W. von Goethe, and Heinrich Heine. With the exception of some dramatic verse, most Western poetry in the late 19th and the 20th centuries may be classified as lyrical. *See also* ELEGY; ODE; SONNET.

lyric caesura A type of feminine caesura. *See* CAESURA.

M

All slang is metaphor, and all metaphor is poetry
—G.K. Chesterton

macaronic \ˌmak-ə-ˈrän-ik\ [New Latin *macaronicus* or Old Italian *maccaronico* in the style of a macaronic, a derivative of Italian dialect *maccaroni* dumpling, macaroni] Originally, a comic Latin verse form that is characterized by the introduction of vernacular words with appropriate but absurd Latin endings; later variants apply Latinate formations to modern languages. The form was first written by Tisi degli Odassi in the late 15th century and was popularized in the early 16th century by Teofilo Folengo, a dissolute Benedictine monk who applied Latin rules of form and syntax to an Italian vocabulary in his burlesque epic of chivalry, *Baldus* (1517; modern edition, *Le maccheronee,* 1927–28; "The Macaronic Works"). Folengo described the macaronic as the literary equivalent of the Italian dish, which, in its 16th-century form, was a rustic mixture of flour, butter, and cheese. His work soon found imitators in Italy and France, and some macaronics were even written in mock Greek.

The outstanding English-language poem in this form is the *Polemo-Medinia inter Vitarvam et Nebernam* (1645?), an account of a battle between two Scottish villages, in which William Drummond subjected Scots dialect to Latin grammatical rules. A modern English derivative of the macaronic pokes fun at the grammatical complexities of ancient languages taught at school, as in A.D. Godley's illustration of declension in "Motor Bus":

Domine defende nos
Contra hos Motores Bos

("Lord protect us
from these motor buses")

In a broader sense, *macaronic* may simply describe a mixture of two languages, with or without comic intent.

The form has survived in comic combinations of modern languages. The German-American medleys of Charles G. Leland in *The Breitmann Ballads* (complete edition, 1895) are examples of the modern macaronic, in particular his warning "To a Friend Studying German":

Vill'st dou learn die Deutsche Sprache?
Den set it on your card

Dat all de nouns have shenders,
Und de shenders all are hard.

MacDowell Colony \mək-ˈdau̇-əl\ Permanent summer school for composers, painters, and writers founded in 1907 by pianist Marian Nevins MacDowell (1857–1956), wife of the composer Edward MacDowell (1860–1908), at their summer home in Peterborough, N.H. They had found inspiration in the wooded setting and envisaged a sanctuary for other creative artists.

After Edward's death Marian devoted her remaining 48 years to expanding the acreage and guiding the colony. During her lifetime more than 750 artists used the colony as a working retreat.

machine \mə-ˈshēn\ A literary device or contrivance (such as a supernatural agency) introduced for dramatic effect; also, an agency so introduced. *See also* DEUS EX MACHINA.

madrigal \ˈmad-ri-gəl\ [Italian *madriale, madrigale,* perhaps from Medieval Latin *matricale,* from neuter of **matricalis* simple, natural, native, presumed sense development of Late Latin *matricalis* of the womb, original, a derivative of Latin *matric-, matrix* womb] A medieval short lyrical poem especially of love.

The 14th-century madrigal is based on a relatively constant poetic form of two or three stanzas of three lines each, with 7 or 11 syllables per line. Musically, it is most often set polyphonically (i.e., having more than one voice part) in two parts, with the musical form reflecting the structure of the poem. A typical two-stanza madrigal has an *aab* form with both stanzas (*aa*) being sung to the same music, followed by a one- or two-line coda (*b*), or concluding phrase, the text of which sums up the sense of the poem.

The 16th century madrigal is based on a different poetic form from its precursor and was characteristically of higher literary quality. Not only madrigals but also other poems of fixed form (e.g., canzones, sonnets, sestinas, and ballatas) were set to music. The poetic form of the madrigal proper is generally free but quite similar to that of a one-stanza canzone: typically, it consists of a 5- to 14-line stanza of 7 or 11 syllables per line, with the last two lines forming a rhyming couplet. The favorite poets of the madrigal composers were Petrarch, Giovanni Boccaccio, Jacopo Sannazzaro, Pietro Bembo, Ludovico Ariosto, Torquato Tasso, and Battista Guarini.

magazine \ˌmag-ə-ˈzēn\, *also called* periodical \ˌpir-ē-ˈäd-ə-kəl\ A printed collection of texts (essays, articles, stories, poems), often illustrated, that is produced at regular intervals. The original sense of the English word was "storehouse"; from its use in periodical titles in the figurative sense to mean "storehouse of information" (as in the *Gentleman's Magazine,* first published in 1731), it became the general word for such publications.

The modern magazine has its roots in early printed pamphlets, broadsides, chapbooks, and almanacs, a few of which gradually began appearing at regular intervals. The earliest magazines collected a variety of material designed to appeal to particular interests. One of the earliest magazines was a German publication, *Erbauliche Monaths-Unterredungen* ("Edifying Monthly Discussions"), issued periodically from 1663 to 1668. Other learned journals soon appeared in France, England, and Italy, and in the early 1670s lighter and more entertaining magazines began to appear, beginning with *Le Mercure galant* (1672; later renamed *Le Mercure de France*) in France. In the early 18th century, Joseph Addison and Richard Steele brought out *The Tatler* (1709–11; published three times weekly) and *The Spectator* (1711–12, 1714; published daily). These influential periodicals contained essays on matters political and topical that continue to be regarded as examples of some of the finest English prose written. Other critical reviews treating literary and political issues also started up in the mid-1700s throughout western Europe, and at the end of the century specialized periodicals began appearing, devoted to particular fields of intellectual interest, such as archaeology, botany, or philosophy.

By the early 19th century a different, less learned audience had been identified, and new types of magazines for entertainment and family enjoyment began to appear, among them the popular weekly, the women's weekly, the religious and missionary review, the illustrated magazine, and the children's weekly. Their growth was stimulated by the general public's broader interest in social and political affairs and by the middle and lower classes' growing demand for reading matter. Woodcuts and engravings were first extensively used by the weekly *Illustrated London News* (1842) and by the end of the 19th century many magazines were illustrated.

Magazine publishing benefited in the late 19th and in the 20th centuries from a number of technical improvements, including the production of inexpensive paper, the invention of the rotary press and the halftone block, and, especially, the use of advertisements as a means of financial support. Other developments since then have included a greater specialization of topics; more illustrations, especially those reproducing color photographs; a decline in power and popularity of the critical review and a rise in that of the mass-market magazine; and an increase in magazines for women. *See also* LITTLE MAGAZINE.

Magazine Club *See* SATURDAY CLUB.

magic realism Latin-American literary phenomenon characterized by the incorporation of fantastic or mythical elements matter-of-factly into otherwise realistic fiction. The term was applied to literature in the late 1940s by Cuban novelist Alejo Carpentier, who recognized the tendency of his region's traditional storytellers as well as contemporary authors to illumine the mundane by means of the fabulous. Proponents of this narrative technique assert that it faithfully represents the subjective reality of a culture blended from European, Indian, and African sensibilities. Prominent among the magic realists, in addition to Carpentier, were the Brazilian Jorge Amado, the Argentines Jorge Luis Borges and Julio Cortázar, the Colombian Gabriel García Márquez, and the Chilean Isabel Allende.

magnum opus \'mag-nəm-'ō-pəs\ [Latin, great work] A literary or artistic work of importance; more specifically, the greatest achievement of an artist.

mahākāvya \mə-'hä-ˌkäv-yə\ [Sanskrit *mahākāvyaṃ,* literally, great kāvya] Form of the Sanskrit literary style known as KAVYA. It is a short epic similar to the epyllion and is characterized by elaborate figures of speech.

In its classical form, a *mahākāvya* consists of a variable number of comparatively short cantos, each composed in a meter appropriate to its particular subject matter. The subject matter of the *mahākāvya* is taken from the epic. Most *mahākāvyas* display such set pieces as descriptions of cities, oceans, mountains, the seasons, the rising of the Sun and Moon, games, festivals, weddings, embassies, councils, wars, and triumphs. It is typical of the genre that, while each strophe, or stanza, is intended to be part of a narrative sequence, it more often stands by itself and is a discrete unit conveying one idea or developing one image that is suggested by double meaning and inference rather than explicitly conveyed. Traditionally there are several model *mahākāvyas*, including two by Kālidāsa and one each by Bhāravi, Māgha, and Śrīharṣa. The *Bhaṭṭikāvya,* a poem by Bhaṭṭi (probably 6th or 7th century), is sometimes added to the list of model *mahākāvyas*. It illustrates in stanza after stanza the principal rules of Sanskrit grammar and poetics. The *mahākāvya* has been used by modern poets to commemorate such noteworthy individuals as Mahatma Gandhi and Jawaharlal Nehru.

Maison de Molière, La *See* COMÉDIE-FRANÇAISE.

Máj circle \'mī\ Group of young Czech writers of the mid-19th century whose aim was to create a new Czech literature that would reflect their liberalism and practical nationalism. They published in an almanac called *Máj* (1858; "May") after the lyrical epic poem of the same name by Karel Hynek Mácha, whom the group regarded as the forerunner of their literary revolution. Prominent members of the group were Vitězslav Hálek, Jan Neruda, and Karolina Světlá (Johanna Mužáková).

makar or **maker** \'mäk-ər, 'māk-\ [Middle English (Scots), author, poet, literally, maker] *plural* makaris *or* makeris \-ə-riz\, *also called* Scottish Chaucerian \chȯ-'sir-ē-ən\ *or* courtly makar. Any of the Scottish courtly poets who flourished from about 1425 to 1550. The best known are Robert Henryson, William Dunbar, Gawin Douglas, and Sir David Lyndsay; the group is sometimes expanded to include James I of Scotland and Harry the Minstrel (Blind Harry). Because Geoffrey Chaucer was their acknowledged master and they often employed his verse forms and themes, they are usually called "Scottish Chaucerians," but they actually are a product of more than one tradition. Chaucerian influence is apparent in their courtly romances and dream allegories, yet even these display a distinctive "aureate" style, a language richly ornamented by polysyllabic Latinate words.

In addition, the makaris used different styles for different types of poems. The language they used in their poems ranges from courtly aureate English, to mixtures of English and Scots, to the broadest Scots vernacular. The poetry itself might take the form of moral allegory, everyday realism, flyting (a dispute in verse between two characters), or grotesquely comic Celtic fantasy.

Spelled *maker,* the word has also been used more generally as a synonym of *poet,* but it is now archaic in this sense.

malapropism \ˈmal-ə-ˌpräp-ˌiz-əm\ Verbal blunder in which one word is replaced by another similar in sound but different in meaning. Although William Shakespeare had used the device for comic effect, the term derives from Richard Brinsley Sheridan's character Mrs. Malaprop, in his play *The Rivals* (1775). Her name is taken from the term *malapropos* (French: "inappropriate") and is typical of Sheridan's practice of concocting names to indicate the essence of a character. Thinking of the geography of contiguous countries, she spoke of the "geometry" of "contagious countries," and she hoped that her daughter might "reprehend" the true meaning of what she was saying. She regretted that her "affluence" over her niece was very small.

mandarin \ˈman-də-rin\ A person of position and influence, especially in intellectual or literary circles. The term is often used to refer to an elder and often traditionalist or reactionary member of such a circle.

manifesto \ˌman-i-ˈfes-tō\ [Italian, poster, announcement, manifesto] A written statement declaring publicly the intentions, motives, or views of its issuer. Among many notable literary manifestos are André Breton's *Manifeste du surréalisme* (1924; "Manifesto of Surrealism") and Antonin Artaud's *Manifeste du théâtre de la cruauté* (1932; "Manifesto of the Theater of Cruelty").

man of letters **1.** A learned man or scholar. **2.** A literary man. Also, an author or a litterateur.

Maple Tree school *See* CONFEDERATION GROUP.

maqāmah \mȧ-ˈkä-mə\ *plural* maqāmat \-mət\ [Arabic, literally, assembly, session] Arabic literary genre in which entertaining anecdotes, often about rogues, mountebanks, and beggars, written in an elegant, rhymed prose (*sajʿ*), are presented in a dramatic or narrative context most suitable for the display of the author's eloquence, wit, and erudition. The *maqāmah* is the most typical prose expression of the Arabic—and Islāmic—spirit. It tells a basically simple story in an extremely and marvelously complicated style abounding in wordplay, logographs, double entendres, and the like. It is the Arabic genre closest in style to the Western short story.

The first collection of such writings was the *Maqāmāt* of al-Hamadhānī. It consists mainly of picaresque stories in both rhymed prose and verse woven round two imaginary characters, the narrator and the protagonist. The genre was revived and finally established in the 11th century by al-Ḥarīrī of Basra (Iraq), whose *Maqāmāt,* closely imitating al-Hamadhānī's, is regarded as a masterpiece of literary style and learning.

The chief characteristics of the original maqāmah are its anecdotal and fictional nature, its episodic structure, and its emphasis on sajʿ style. Often the rhymed and rhythmical prose form was interspersed with straightforward prose and verse. The episodic structure freed the author to use many different genres, such as the sermon and the travelogue.

Märchen \'mer-k̲ən\ *plural* Märchen [German, news, report, story, fantastic tale, a diminutive of *Märe* news] Folktale characterized by elements of magic or the supernatural such as the endowment of a mortal character with magical powers or special knowledge. Variations expose the hero to supernatural beings or objects. The German term *Märchen,* used universally by folklorists, also embraces tall tales and humorous anecdotes; although it is often translated as "fairy tale," the fairy is not a requisite motif.

Märchen usually begin with a formula such as "once upon a time," setting the story in an indefinite time and place. Their usual theme is the triumph over difficulty, with or without supernatural aid, of the one least likely to succeed. The characters are stylized—wicked stepmothers, stupid ogres, or handsome princes. The situations are familiar and often reflect the economic and domestic arrangements of peasants and simple workers, such as millers, tailors, or smiths. Those of ancient origin may reflect archaic social conditions, such as matriarchy, primitive birth and marriage customs, or old forms of inheritance. The hero, however poor or friendless, has easy access to the king and may, through luck, cleverness, or magical intervention, win the king's daughter in marriage and inherit the kingdom.

Versions of these stories, sometimes almost identical, have been found all over the world. The first systematic attempt to transcribe and record *Märchen* verbatim from oral tradition was the collection *Kinder- und Hausmärchen* (1812–15) of the Brothers Grimm, popularly known as *Grimm's Fairy Tales. See also* FAIRY TALE.

marginalia \ˌmär-jə-'nāl-yə\ Notes in the form of commentary or annotation written in the margin of a work by a reader.

Marinism \'mar-i-ˌniz-əm\ or **marinismo** \ˌmä-rē-'nēz-mō\, *also called* secentismo \ˌsā-chen-'tēz-mō\ A florid, bombastic literary style fashionable in 17th-century Italy marked by extravagant metaphors, far-fetched conceits, hyperbole, fantastic wordplay, original myths, and forced antitheses. A reaction against classicism, it was named for the 17th-century poet Giambattista Marino and inspired by his collection of lyrical verse, *La lira* (1608–14; "The Lyre").

The style was used in sonnets, madrigals, and narrative poems. Marino's imitators carried his stylistic conceits to excess, and by the end of the 18th century the word was used pejoratively. By then, however, the movement was dying out along with the Baroque period of which it was a part. Parallel movements were *gongorismo* in Spain, preciosity in France, and Metaphysical poetry in England. A general revival of interest in the Baroque after World War II led to both a resurgence in interest and a reassessment of Marino and

Marinism. *Compare* EUPHUISM; GONGORISMO; METAPHYSICAL POETRY; PRECIOSITY. *See also* Academy of ARCADIA.

marwysgafn \mär-ˈwəs-ˌgävn\ [Welsh, deathbed, deathbed poem, from *marw* dead + *ysgafn* couch, bed] Welsh religious ode in which the poet, sensing the approach of death, confesses his sins and prays for forgiveness. The *marwysgafn* was popular during the period of the Welsh court poets, called *gogynfeirdd* in the 12th to 14th century.

Marxist criticism \ˈmärk-sist\ A method of literary analysis based on the writings of Karl Marx and Friedrich Engels. Rather than viewing a text as the product of an individual consciousness, Marxist critics examine a work as the product of an ideology particular to a specific historical period. Such critics judge a text on the basis of its portrayal of social actions and institutions and on its representation of class struggle.

The more rigid Marxists have insisted on works that reflected Marxist ideology (*See* SOCIALIST REALISM). Other, more flexible, critics were able to appreciate the great 19th-century realists, despite the distinctly literary nature of their work. Still other Marxist theorists, such as Bertolt Brecht, embraced modernism and shunned realism as lulling the audience into passive acceptance of capitalist ascendency.

Those who are counted among Marxist critics include György Lukács, Walter Benjamin, and Fredric Jameson.

masculine caesura In verse, a caesura that follows a stressed or long syllable. *See* CAESURA.

masculine ending In poetry, a stressed final syllable at the end of a line of verse. *Compare* FEMININE ENDING.

masculine rhyme In verse, a monosyllabic rhyme, or a rhyme that occurs only in stressed final syllables (such as *claims, flames* or *rare, despair*). *Compare* FEMININE RHYME. Emily Dickinson used the masculine rhyme to great effect in the last stanza of "After great pain, a formal feeling comes—":

> This is the Hour of Lead—
> Remembered, if outlived,
> As Freezing persons, recollect the Snow—
> First—Chill—then Stupor—then the letting go—

mask *See* MASQUE.

mas̄nawī \ˈmäs-nä-ˌwē\ or **mas̄navī** \-ˌvē\ or **mathnavī** \ˈmäth-nä-ˌvē\ [Persian *masnavī* (spelled *mathnawī*), probably a derivative of Arabic *mathnā* two by two] A series of distichs (couplets) in rhymed pairs (*aa, bb, cc,* and so on) that makes up a characteristic type of Persian verse, used chiefly for heroic, historical, and romantic epic and didactic poetry.

The form originated in the Middle Persian period (roughly from the 3rd century BC to the 9th century AD). It became a favorite poetic form of the Persians and those cultures they influenced. Only a restricted number of meters was employed, and no meter allowed more than 11 syllables in a hemistich (half-line). Meter and diction were prescribed in accordance with the topic; a didactic mas̄nawī required a style and meter different from a heroic or a romantic one. Most mas̄nawīs, however, begin with a praise of God, and this strikes the keynote of the poem. Epic poetry was unknown to the Arabs, who were averse to fiction, whether it was expressed in poetry or in prose. Eventually, however, the *mas̄nawī* also took root in Arabic literature, where it bore the Arabic name *muzdawij*.

masque or **mask** \'mask\ [Middle French, mask, masquerade] A short, allegorical dramatic entertainment of the 16th and 17th centuries performed by masked actors. Most likely originating in pre-Christian religious rites and folk ceremonies known as disguising, or mummery, masques evolved into elaborate court spectacles that, under various names, entertained royalty throughout Europe.

During the 16th century the continental European masque traveled to Tudor England, where it became a court entertainment played before the king. Gorgeous costumes, spectacular scenery with elaborate machinery to move it on- and offstage, and rich allegorical verse marked the English masque. The masque reached its zenith when Ben Jonson became court poet. He endowed the form with great literary as well as social force. In 1605 Jonson and the scene designer and architect Inigo Jones produced the first of many excellent masques, which they continued to collaborate on until 1634.

Jonson invented the antimasque—also known as the antemasque, the false masque, and the antic masque—and produced the first one in 1609. It took place before the main masque and concentrated on grotesque elements, in direct contrast to the elegance of the masque that followed. In later years the masque developed into opera, and the antimasque became primarily a farce or pantomime. After Jonson's retirement, masques became mainly vehicles for spectacle.

masterpiece \'mas-tər-ˌpēs\ A work of art of notable excellence or brilliance. A supreme intellectual or artistic achievement; specifically, an artist's most accomplished or climactic work marking the high point of his or her creativity.

mathnavī *See* MAS̄NAWĪ

matra \'mä-trə\ [Sanskrit *mātrā,* literally, measure, quantity] A unit of metrical quantity equal to a short vowel in Sanskrit and other Indian languages.

Matter of Britain *See* ARTHURIAN LEGEND.

maxim \'mak-sim\ [Medieval Latin *maxima,* short for *maxima propositio* axiom, literally, greatest proposition] A saying of proverbial nature.

Mbari Mbayo Club \m-'bä-rē-m-'bä-yō\ Meeting place for African writers, artists, and musicians, founded in Ibadan, Nigeria, in 1961. The first club, known as Mbari Club (*mbari* being the Igbo [Ibo] word for "creation"), was established by a group of young writers with the help of Ulli Beier, a teacher at the University of Ibadan. *Mbari* refers to the traditional painted mud houses of the area, which must be renewed periodically. The club operated an art gallery and theater and published *Black Orpheus,* a journal of African and African-American literature.

Duro Ladipo, a Yoruba playwright, established a similar club in Oshogbo, about 50 miles (80 km) northeast of Ibadan. With Beier's help, Ladipo converted his father's house into an art gallery and a theater, where he produced his plays. The Oshogbo club became a vital part of the community. To engage his local audience, Ladipo drew upon Yoruba mythology, drumming, dance, and poetry and soon developed a type of Yoruba opera. The name of the club (Mbari Club, like its model) was inadvertently altered when the Igbo word *mbari* was mistaken for a Yoruba phrase, *mbari mbayo,* meaning "when we see it we shall be happy."

Beier organized art workshops in Ibadan in 1961 and 1962 and at Oshogbo in 1962 to help the artists develop a committed, critical audience. Drawing on their traditions and their contemporary environment, the young artists rapidly created a fresh, sophisticated art and were further protected from the easy tourist market by social acceptance of the Mbari Mbayo Club, which provided a lively, local, outspoken audience.

measure Poetic rhythm measured by temporal quantity or accent, specifically, meter.

medieval drama Any of several types of performance popular during the European Middle Ages. *See* INTERLUDE; MIRACLE PLAY; MORALITY PLAY.

medievalism \mē-'dē-və-ˌliz-əm, mi-, me-, -dē-'ē-və-\ In literature, a spirit of devotion to the institutions, arts, and practices of the Middle Ages; sometimes the devotion is rather to a later age's images of the Middle Ages. This quality can be seen in the works of such authors as Edmund Spenser, John Keats and other Romantic poets, and the Pre-Raphaelite poets.

medieval romance *See* ROMANCE.

meditation \ˌmed-ə-'tā-shən\ A spoken or written discourse treated in a contemplative manner and intended to express its author's reflections or (especially when religious) to guide others in contemplation. A well-known literary example is Alphonse de Lamartine's *Méditations poétiques.*

meiosis \mī-'ō-sis\ [Greek *meíōsis* lessening, diminution] Deliberate understatement, used in literature for emphasis or comic effect.

meistersinger \'mīs-tər-ˌsiŋ-ər\, *German* Meistersinger \'mīs-tər-ˌziŋ-ər\ *plural* meistersingers, *German plural* Meistersinger [German, from Middle

High German, literally, master singer] A member of any of various German guilds, especially of the 15th and 16th centuries, composed chiefly of workingmen and craftsmen and formed for the cultivation of poetry and music.

The meistersingers claimed to be heirs of 12 old masters, accomplished poets skilled in the medieval *artes* and in musical theory; the 13th-century poet Frauenlob was said to be their founder. Their true predecessors, however, probably were fraternities of laymen trained to sing in church and elsewhere. Later, these fraternities became *Singschulen* ("song schools"), organized like craft guilds. Their main activity became the holding—still in church— of singing competitions. Composition was restricted to fitting new words to tunes ascribed to the old masters; subject matter, meter, language, and performance were governed by an increasingly strict code of rules (*Tablatur*). These restrictions led Hans Folz, a barber-surgeon from Worms (d. *c.* 1515), to persuade the Nürnberg Singschule to permit a wider range of subjects and the composition of new tunes. These reforms, adopted elsewhere, restored some life to the *Singschulen;* thenceforth, a member, having passed through the grades of *Schüler, Schulfreund, Singer,* and *Dichter,* became a "master" by having a tune of his own approved by the *Merkern,* or adjudicators.

Despite the changes, music, form, and subject matter remained remarkably constant through the centuries. The music, derived from Gregorian chant, folk song, and other sources, determined the meter. Verses were based on syllable counting regardless of stress or quantity; rhyme schemes were often elaborate. Three stanzas or a multiple of three constituted a song, or Bar (the musical Bar form provided music for one stanza). Songs were unaccompanied solos. For the Singschulen in church, a wide range of religious subjects were versified. From the 15th century, secular subjects also were used. At the *Zechsingen,* held afterward at a tavern (perhaps not an official part of the Singschule), subjects were humorous, sometimes obscene.

From the earliest centers, Mainz, Worms, and Strassburg, the movement spread throughout southern Germany and to Silesia and Bohemia; northern Germany had individual meistersingers but no Singschulen. The best-documented center is Nürnberg. The meistersingers were not the popular figures depicted in Richard Wagner's opera, *Die Meistersinger von Nürnberg* (1868); they were largely ignored by the general populace, and their songs were not published. After the year 1600, the Singschulen slowly declined and disappeared, although the last one, at Memmingen, was not disbanded until 1875.

melic \'mel-ik\ [Greek *melikós* of lyric poetry, a derivative of *mélē* lyric poetry, choral songs, plural of *mélos* song, musical phrase, literally, limb] Of or relating to lyric Greek poetry of the 7th and 6th centuries BC.

melodrama \'mel-ə-ˌdräm-ə. -ˌdram-\ [French *mélodrame* drama accompanied by instrumental music, from Greek *mélos* song, musical phrase + French *drame* drama] A play characterized by extravagant theatricality, subordination of characterization to plot, and predominance of physical action. Also, the genre of dramatic literature constituted by such plays.

In Western literature melodramas usually have an improbable plot that generally concerns the vicissitudes suffered by the virtuous at the hands of the villainous but ends happily with virtue triumphant. Featuring stock characters such as the noble hero, the long-suffering heroine, and the cold-blooded, hard-hearted villain, the melodrama emphasizes sensational incident and spectacular staging at the expense of character development.

The pioneer and prime exponent of the 18th-century French melodrama with its music, singing, and spectacular effects was Guilbert de Pixérécourt. His *Coelina, ou l'enfant de mystère* (1800; "Coelina, or The Child of Mystery") was translated as *A Tale of Mystery* (1802) by Thomas Holcroft, who thereby helped establish the genre in England. (The form was not entirely unknown in England, however; the restrictions of the Licensing Act of 1737 had been habitually evaded by combining drama with music, singing, and dancing.)

Another prominent dramatist whose melodrama influenced that of other countries was the German August von Kotzebue. His *Menschenhass und Reue* (1789) became tremendously popular in England as *The Stranger* (1798); he also provided the original of Richard Brinsley Sheridan's *Pizarro* (1799).

In the early 19th century, melodrama spread throughout the European theater; in Russia the authorities welcomed it, because it diverted popular attention from more serious issues. Among the best known and most representative of the melodramas popular in England and the United States are *The Octoroon* (1859) and *The Colleen Bawn* (1860), both by Dion Boucicault. More sensational were Boucicault's *The Poor of New York* (1857) and Augustin Daly's *Under the Gaslight* (1867). The realistic staging and the social evils touched upon, however perfunctorily and sentimentally, anticipated the later theater of the naturalists.

By the early 20th century motion pictures had become the most popular vehicle for melodramas; later, television also became a popular medium for the form.

melofarce \ˈmel-ō-ˌfärs\ Melodrama of farcically exaggerated character.

memoir \ˈmem-ˌwär, -ˌwȯr\ [French *mémoire,* from Old French *memoire* written account, narrative, masculine derivative of *memoire* (feminine) memory] **1.** *usually plural* A history or narrative composed from or stressing personal experience and acquaintance with the events, scenes, or persons described. The French have excelled at the genre; the Duke de Saint-Simon's *Mémoires* (covering the early 1690s through 1723), with their penetrating character sketches, provide an invaluable source of information about the court of Louis XIV. Another of the great French memoirists was Viscount de Chateaubriand famous for his *Mémoires d'outre-tombe* (published posthumously, 1849–50; *The Memoirs of Chateaubriand*). In the 20th century, many distinguished statesmen and military men have described their experiences in memoirs. Notable reminiscences of World War II include the memoirs of Dwight Eisenhower, Viscount Montgomery, and Charles de Gaulle. **2.** *usually plural* An autobiographical account, often anecdotal or intimate in tone, whose focus of attention is usually on the persons, events, or times known to the writer. Contemporary examples of this type of writing include Eudora Welty's *One Writer's Beginnings* (1984) and Malcolm Cowley's *Exile's Return* (1934; rev. ed., 1951). **3.** A biography or biographical sketch, usually based on personal acquaintance with the subject and sometimes having the character of a memorial.

Closely related to, and often confused with, autobiography, a memoir usually differs chiefly in the degree of emphasis placed on external events; whereas writers of autobiography are concerned primarily with themselves as subject matter, writers of memoir are usually persons who have played roles in, or have been close observers of, historical events and whose main purpose is to describe or interpret those events.

memorialist \mə-ˈmȯr-ē-ə-list\ A writer of memorials or memoirs.

Menckenese \ˌmeŋ-kə-ˈnēz, ˌmen-, -ˈnēs\ The peculiarly vigorous, racy, flamboyant, and often caustic style that is characteristic of the work of American journalist and satirist H.L. Mencken.

Menippean satire \mə-ˈnip-ē-ən\, *also called* Varronian satire \və-ˈrō-nē-ən\ Form of satire named for the 3rd-century-BC Greek philosopher Menippus of Gadara, who produced the prototype in his criticism by mixing elements of prose and verse to mock institutions, ideas, and conventions. This type of satire was introduced to Rome by Marcus Terentius Varro in his *Saturae Menippeae* and was further developed by Lucian, who created his own harmonious blend of Platonic dialogue and comic fantasy and raised Menippean satire to the level of art by his broad, fluent, and seemingly effortless command of the Attic Greek language and literary style. The 1st-century-AD *Satyricon* of Petronius Arbiter, a picaresque tale in verse and prose containing long digressions in which the author airs his views on topics having nothing to do with the plot, is in the Menippean tradition. A later example is the *Satire Ménippée* (1593; enlarged edition, 1594) a French prose and verse satire on the Holy League, the political party of the Roman Catholics, written by several royalists. Another instance of Menippean influence can be seen in Jonathan Swift's *Tale of a Tub,* which contains a relatively simple allegory of Reformation history (the *Tale* proper) that is interrupted by a series of editorial digressions.

Mercure de France, Le \lə-mer-kue̅r-də-ˈfrä^{n}s\ French literary journal published (with some interruptions) for almost 300 years. Founded by Jean Donneau de Visé as *Le Mercure galant* in 1672, the magazine was renamed *Le Mercure de France* in 1724. It printed poetry, literary criticism, and political commentary in a light, humorous fashion. Napoleon suppressed the publication in 1811; it flourished briefly after his fall in 1815, but it ceased publication in the early 1820s.

Le Mercure de France was revived in 1890 by Alfred Vallette and his friends, who turned it into a strictly literary journal. Vallette became the patron of Symbolism, publishing the most eminent names in French literature, from Stéphane Mallarmé to the absurdist Alfred Jarry. After 1935, despite a brief flourish under the editorship of Georges Duhamel, the *Mercure* fell into decline, and it finally ceased publication in 1965.

Mermaid Tavern Famous London meeting place of the Friday Street Club, of which William Shakespeare, Sir Walter Raleigh, John Donne, and Ben Jonson were notable members. It stood to the east of St. Paul's Cathedral, with entrances in Bread Street and Friday Street.

The Mermaid Tavern has intrigued scholars interested in Shakespeare's personality and in those of other great men of Elizabethan and Jacobean letters, mainly because of a passage in a poem by the playwright Francis Beaumont (also a member of the club):

What things have we seen
Done at the Mermaid! heard words that have been
So nimble, and so full of subtle flame,
As if that every one from whence they came
Had meant to put his whole wit in a jest,
And had resolved to live a fool the rest
Of his dull life.

mesode \ˈmes-ˌōd\ [Greek *mesōidós,* from *mésos* middle + *ōidḗ* song] In poetry, a stanza different in form from the rest of the poem that is inserted between the strophe and the antistrophe of an ode. *Compare* MESYMNION.

mesymnion \me-ˈsim-nē-än\ [Greek *mesýmnion,* from *mésos* middle + *hýmnos* hymn, ode] In classical prosody, a short colon or rhythmic sequence interpolated in a stanza. A mesode is an entire stanza thus composed and occurring within an ode (between the strophe and antistrophe).

metafiction Fiction which refers to or takes as its subject fictional writing and its conventions.

metalepsis A figure of speech consisting in the substitution by metonymy of one figurative sense for another.

metaphor \ˈmet-ə-ˌfór\ [Greek *metaphorá* change of a word to a new sense, metaphor, a derivative of *metaphérein* to transfer, change, from *metá* after, beyond + *phérein* to carry] A figure of speech in which a word or phrase denoting one kind of object or action is used in place of another to suggest a likeness or analogy between them (as in *the ship plows the seas* or in *a volley of oaths*). A metaphor is an implied comparison (as in *a marble brow*) in contrast to the explicit comparison of the simile (as in *a brow white as marble*). *Compare* SIMILE.

The metaphor makes a qualitative leap from a reasonable, perhaps prosaic, comparison to an identification or fusion of two objects to make a new entity partaking of the characteristics of both. Many critics regard the making of metaphors as a system of thought antedating or bypassing logic. Metaphor is the fundamental language of poetry, although it is common on all levels and in all kinds of language. Many words were originally vivid images, although they exist now as dead metaphors whose original aptness has been lost—for example, "daisy" (day's eye). In addition to single words, everyday language abounds in phrases and expressions that once were metaphors. For example, "time flies" is an ancient metaphorical expression. When the poet says, "The Bird of Time has but a little way/To flutter—and the Bird is on the Wing" (*The Rubáiyát of Omar Khayyám*), he is constructing a new metaphor on the foundations of an older, stock metaphor. Likewise, when Tennessee Williams entitles his play *Sweet Bird of Youth,* he, too, is referring to the bird of time that flies.

In poetry a metaphor may perform varied functions, from the mere noting of a likeness to the evocation of a swarm of associations; it may exist as a minor beauty, or it may be the central concept and controlling image of the poem. The familiar metaphor "Iron Horse" for train, for example, is the elaborate central concept of one of Emily Dickinson's poems:

> I like to see it lap the Miles—
> And lick the Valleys up—
> And stop to feed itself at Tanks—
> And then—prodigious step
>
> Around a Pile of Mountains—
> And supercilious peer
> In Shanties—by the sides of Roads—
> And then a Quarry pare
>
> To fit its sides
> And crawl between
> Complaining all the while
> In horrid—hooting stanza—
> Then chase itself down Hill—
>
> And neigh like Boanerges—
> Then—prompter than a Star
> Stop—docile and omnipotent
> At its own stable door—

A *mixed metaphor* is the linking of two or more disparate elements, which often results in an unintentionally comic effect produced by the writer's insensitivity to the literal meaning of the words or by the falseness of the comparison. A mixed metaphor may also be used with great effectiveness, however, as in Hamlet's speech:

> Whether 'tis nobler in the mind to suffer
> The slings and arrows of outrageous fortune
> Or to take arms against a sea of troubles . . .

For strictly correct completion of the metaphor, "sea" should be replaced by "host."

metaphrast \'met-ə-ˌfrast\ [Middle Greek *metaphrastḗs,* a derivative of Greek *metaphrázein* to translate, from *metá* after, beyond + *phrázein* to point out, show, tell] A translator; specifically, one who turns verse into a different meter or prose into verse.

Metaphysical poetry \ˌmet-ə-'fiz-i-kəl\ Highly intellectualized poetry written chiefly in 17th-century England. It is marked by bold and ingenious conceits, complexity and subtlety of thought, frequent use of paradox, and often deliberate harshness or rigidity of expression. Metaphysical poetry is chiefly concerned with analyzing feeling. The most notable of the Metaphysical poets is John Donne. Others include George Herbert, Henry Vaughan, Richard Crashaw, Andrew Marvell, John Cleveland, and Abraham Cowley.

Metaphysical poetry is a blend of emotion and intellectual ingenuity, characterized by CONCEIT, or "wit"—that is, by the sometimes forced juxtaposition of apparently unconnected ideas and things so that the reader is startled out of complacency and forced to think through the argument of the poem. The boldness of the literary devices used—especially obliquity, irony, and paradox—is always reinforced by a dramatic directness of language, the rhythm of which is derived from that of living speech.

Metaphysical poetry was especially esteemed in the 1930s and '40s, largely because of T.S. Eliot's influential essay "The Metaphysical Poets" (1921). In this essay Eliot pointed out that the works of these poets embody a fusion of thought and feeling that later poets were unable to achieve because of a "dissociation of sensibility," which resulted in works that were either intellectual or emotional but not both at once. In their own time, however, the epithet "metaphysical" was used pejoratively: in 1630 the Scottish poet William Drummond of Hawthornden objected to those of his contemporaries who attempted to "abstract poetry to metaphysical ideas and scholastic quiddities." At the end of the century, John Dryden censured Donne for affecting "the metaphysics" and for perplexing "the minds of the fair sex with nice speculations of philosophy when he should engage their hearts . . . with the softnesses of love." Samuel Johnson, in referring to the learning their poetry displays, dubbed them "the metaphysical poets," and the term has continued in use ever since.

meter \'mē-tər\ [Greek *métron* meter, measure] **1.** Systematically arranged and measured rhythm in verse, such as rhythm that continuously repeats a single basic pattern (as in iambic meter) or rhythm characterized by regular recurrence of a systematic arrangement of basic patterns in a larger figure (as in ballad meter). **2.** A fixed metrical pattern, or a verse form.

Various principles, based on the natural rhythms of language, have been devised to organize poetic lines into rhythmic units. These have produced distinct kinds of versification, among which the most common are quantitative, syllabic, accentual, and accentual-syllabic.

Quantitative verse, the meter of classical Greek and Latin poetry, measures the length of time required to pronounce syllables, regardless of their stress. Various combinations of long and short syllables (the long syllables being roughly equivalent to twice the duration of the short syllables) constitute the basic rhythmic units. Quantitative verse has been adapted to modern languages but with limited success.

Syllabic verse is most common in languages that are not strongly accented, such as French and Japanese. It is based on a fixed number of syllables within a line, although the number of accents or stresses may be varied. Thus, the classic meter of French poetry is the alexandrine, a line of 12 syllables with a medial caesura (a pause occurring after the 6th syllable). The Japanese haiku is a poem of 17 syllables, composed in three lines of 5, 7, and 5 syllables.

Accentual verse occurs in strongly stressed languages such as the Germanic. It counts only the number of stresses or accented syllables within a line and allows a variable number of unaccented syllables. Old Norse and Old English poetry are based on lines having a fixed number of strongly stressed syllables reinforced by alliteration. Accentual meters are evident in much popular English verse and in nursery rhymes, as in

> “Óne, twó, Búck | lĕ my̆ shóe”

In the late 19th century, the English poet Gerard Manley Hopkins used such meters as the basis for his poetic innovation “sprung rhythm.”

Accentual-syllabic verse is the usual form of English poetry. It combines Romance syllable counting and Germanic stress counting to produce lines of fixed numbers of alternating stressed and unstressed syllables. Thus, the most common English meter, iambic pentameter, is a line of 10 syllables, or five iambic feet. Each iambic foot is composed of an unstressed syllable followed by a stressed syllable.

Variations within any of these regular meters are not only permissible but also inevitable and desirable. For instance, the words

> ă | gáin and fŏr | lórn

each constitute an iambic foot, but they are vastly different in quality. Even in the most formal metrical designs, the quality, pitch, and force of certain sounds, along with the interplay of other poetic devices such as assonance, consonance, alliteration, or rhyme, may act to reinforce or obscure the basic metrical pattern.

The function of regular meter in poetry is complex. In its most primitive aspects, as in nursery rhymes or folk ballads, it creates the physical pleasure that all simple rhythmic acts such as rocking, swaying, trotting, or foot tapping provide. Used mimetically, it may be lulling, galloping, staccato, heavy and slow, or quick and light to match the content and emotional tone of the poem. In more sophisticated poetry, regular meter is a subtle and flexible device, organically integrated into the total poem through its sensitive interaction with the natural rhythms of speech and the meaning of words. Although the late 19th century and early 20th century witnessed a widespread rebellion against the restrictions of metrically regular poetry, the challenge of condensing an imaginative impulse into a formal framework still appeals to poets. *See also* SCANSION.

metonymy \me-ˈtän-i-mē\ [Greek *metōnymía* use of one word for another, metonymy, from *metá* after, beyond + *ónyma* name] Figure of speech that consists of using the name of one thing for something else with which it is associated (as in "I spent the evening reading Shakespeare" or "lands belonging to the crown" or "demanding action by city hall"). Richard Brinsley Sheridan in his speech on the impeachment of Warren Hastings (the first governor-general of India) alludes to Mr. Middleton, who "extended his iron sceptre without resistance." In this sentence the sceptre is an attribute of government; an iron sceptre implies harsh government.

Metonymy is closely related to SYNECDOCHE, the naming of a part for the whole or a whole for the part and is a common poetic device. The use of synecdoche enables the writer to replace generalities and abstractions with concrete and vivid images. It is also a standard journalistic device, as in the use of "city hall" for "municipal government" or "the White House" for "the President of the United States."

metreme \ˈmet-ˌrēm\ [probably from French *métrème,* from *mètre* meter + *-ème* (as in *phonème* phoneme)] The minimal unit of metrical structure. *See also* FOOT.

metric \ˈmet-rik\ The part of prosody that deals with metrical structure. The term, now seldom used, is often found in the plural but may be either singular or plural in construction.

metrical romance A medieval verse tale based on legend, chivalric love and adventure, or the supernatural. It was eventually superseded by the prose romance. *See* ROMANCE.

metrification \ˌmet-rə-fi-ˈkā-shən\ Composition in metrical form.

metrist \ˈmet-rist, ˈmēt-\ **1.** A maker of verses. **2.** One skillful in handling meter. **3.** A student of meter or metrics.

metron \ˈmet-ˌrän\ *plural* metra \-rə\ [Greek *métron* measure, meter] In classical prosody, the minimal unit of measure. In some meters (the choriamb, epitrite, cretic, ionic, bacchius [bacchiac], and dochmiac) there is no difference between a foot and a metron, but in more complex meters—such as the iambic metron (⏓ – ∪ –), the trochaic metron (– ∪ – ⏓), and the anapestic metron (∪ ∪ – ∪ ∪ –)— a metron can consist of two feet, in which one of the feet is always varied in the same way (such as iambic trimeter, in which the basic unit is two iambs: ⏓ – ∪ –). *See also* FOOT.

Middle \ˈmid-əl\ Constituting a period of a language or literature that is between one called *Old* and one called *New* or *Modern*.

middle article *British* A popular or light literary essay or article of less immediate current significance than an editorial printed in or suitable for printing in a newspaper or weekly.

Middle Comedy Style of drama that prevailed in Athens from about 400 BC to about 320 BC. Preoccupied with social themes, Middle Comedy represented a transition from Old Comedy, which presented literary, political, and philosophical commentary interspersed with scurrilous personal invective, to New Comedy, with its gently satiric observation of contemporary Athenian society, especially domestic life. Aristophanes' last play, *Wealth,* is an extant work that reflects this transition. Antiphanes and Alexis were preeminent Middle Comedy dramatists, but none of their plays has survived complete.

Midwestern Regionalism American literary movement of the late 19th century that is characterized by the realistic depiction of Midwestern small-town and rural life. The movement was an early stage in the development of American realistic writing. E.W. Howe's *The Story of a Country Town* (1883) and Joseph Kirkland's *Zury* (1887) and *The McVeys* (1888) foreshadowed the stories and novels of Hamlin Garland, the foremost representative of Midwestern Regionalism. Garland's *Main-Travelled Roads* (1891) and *A Son of the Middle Border* (1917) are works that deal with the poverty and hardship of Midwestern rural life and that explode the myth of the pioneer idyll. Chicago was the focal point of Midwestern realist activity; Garland lived in the city for a time, as did such others as Theodore Dreiser, Edgar Lee Masters, and Sherwood Anderson. These latter figures were writers from small towns in the Midwest who were deeply influenced by the regional movement of the 1890s and became the leading exponents of 20th-century realism and naturalism.

Milesian tale \mī-ˈlē-zhən, -shən\ [translation of Latin *Milesia fabula,* literally, tale of Miletus (alluding to Aristides of Miletus)] One of a class of short salacious tales of Greek and Roman antiquity. Characteristically, a Milesian tale is an erotic or picaresque story of romantic adventure. This type of tale was first written or collected by Aristides of Miletus (*c.* 2nd century BC). In the 1st century BC, Aristides' collection was translated into Latin by Lucius Cornelius Sisenna as *Milesiae fabulae;* this volume served as a model for episodes in Petronius' *Satyricon* (1st century AD) and for *The Golden Ass* (2nd century AD) by Lucius Apuleius, an account of the ribald advertures of a hero who is changed into an ass. The Greek and Latin Milesian tales later provided prototypes for many tales included in Giovanni Boccaccio's *Decameron* (1353) and the *Heptaméron* (1558–59) of Margaret of Angoulême.

mimesis \mi-ˈmē-sis, mī-\ [Greek *mímēsis* imitation, representation, a derivative of *mimeîsthai* to imitate, a derivative of *mîmos* mime] Imitation, or mimicry. It has long been held to be a basic theoretical principle in the creation of art.

Plato and Aristotle spoke of mimesis as the representation of nature. According to Plato, all artistic creation is a form of imitation: that which truly exists (in the "world of Ideas") is a type created by God; the concrete things humans perceive in daily life are shadowy representations of this ideal type. To Plato artists were imitators of imitations and were therefore twice removed from the truth. Aristotle wrote that tragedy is an "imitation of an action"—that of falling from a higher to a lower estate. William Shakespeare, in Hamlet's speech to the actors, referred to the purpose of acting as being ". . . to hold, as 'twere, the mirror up to nature." Perhaps the best-known modern work on the subject is Erich Auerbach's *Mimesis: Dargestellte Wirklichkeit in der abendländischen Literatur* (1946; *Mimesis: The Representation of Reality in Western Literature*).

minimalism \ˈmin-ə-məl-ˌiz-əm\ A style or technique in music, literature, or design that is characterized by extreme spareness and simplicity.

minnesinger \ˈmin-ə-ˌziŋ-ər\, *German* Minnesänger \-ˌzeŋ-ər\ Any of certain German poet-musicians of the 12th and 13th centuries. In the usage of these poets themselves, the term *Minnesang* denoted only songs dealing with courtly love (*Minne*). The term has since come to be applied to the entire poetic-musical body, *Sprüche* (political, moral, and religious song) as well as *Minnesang*.

The songs of courtly love, like the concept, came to Germany either directly from Provence or through northern France. The minnesingers, like their Romance counterparts, the troubadours and trouvères, usually composed both words and music and performed their songs in open court, so that their art stood in an immediate relationship to their public. Some were of humble birth; at the other end of the social scale were men such as the emperor Henry VI, son of Frederick I Barbarossa. Most, however, were *ministeriales,* or members of the lower nobility, who depended on court patronage for their livelihood. From the vicissitudes of such an existence come many of the motifs in their poetry.

In general the music follows the tripartite form taken over from the Provençal *canso:* two identical sections, called individually *Stollen* and collectively *Aufgesang,* and a third section, or *Abgesang* (the terms were applied by the later Meistersingers); the formal ratio between *Aufgesang* and *Abgesang* is variable, since the basic *aab* pattern was subject to much variation.

On a larger scale was the *Leich,* analogous to the French lay. It was an aggregation of short stanzas (versicles), typically couplets, each line of which was sung to the same music and each versicle having its own music. The *Leiche* were often several hundred lines long, and many incorporated religious motifs (such as the veneration of the Virgin Mary), which are also found in the shorter lyrics. Musical unity in both the *Leich* and the shorter forms was often achieved by the recurrence and variation of brief motifs or even entire phrases.

Some of the early songs were probably sung to troubadour melodies, because their texts closely resemble Provençal models. Yet the German songs usually differ in general musical character from the Romance songs. For example, the melodies are more often basically pentatonic (based on a five-tone scale). Popular song and Gregorian chant are other musical roots of the style.

The poems of the earliest minnesinger known by name, Der Kürenberger (fl. 1160), are not much influenced by troubadour style, for his realistic verses show a proud, imperious knight with a woman pining for his love. But by the end of the century the courtly love themes of the troubadours and trouvères had taken control. In the 12th century the poetry of the Thuringian Heinrich von Morungen is marked by intensity of feeling and moral involvement, and the Alsatian Reinmar von Hagenau gives the courtly love lyric such an expression of social ideals that he was taken by his contemporaries as the most representative poet of "pure" *Minnesang.*

Walther von der Vogelweide, one of the greatest lyric poets of the European Middle Ages, absorbed much of his teacher Reinmar's craftsmanship, but he went far beyond the artificial conventions by which the *Minnesang* had been governed by introducing an element of practical realism, both in his love poetry and in his Sprüche. By the time of Neidhart von Reuenthal, a Bavarian squire (d. *c.* 1250), the knight had turned his attention from the ladies of the castle to the wenches of the villages; Neidhart's melodies likewise have a certain affinity with folk song.

Whereas poets like Ulrich von Lichtenstein strove to keep the conceits of chivalry alive, others—among them Reinmar von Zweter, the Marner, and Konrad von Würzburg (mid-13th century)—cultivated didactic poetry, which Walther von der Vogelweide, building on the work of earlier poets, had already raised to a high level. At the end of the 13th century stands Frauenlob (Heinrich von Meissen), who, by his versatility, his power of rhetoric, and his technical refinement, points to the stylized art of the meistersingers. *Compare* MEISTERSINGER; TROUBADOUR; TROUVÈRE.

minstrel \'min-strəl\ [Old French *menestrel* servant, worker, craftsman, minstrel, from Medieval Latin *ministerialis* servant, official, a derivative of Latin *ministerium* condition or duties of a servant, a derivative of *minister* servant] One of a class of medieval musical entertainers; especially, a singer of verses to the accompaniment of a harp. The word originally referred to a professional entertainer of any kind, including juggler, acrobat, and storyteller, but it began to be used in the more specific sense of a musician about the beginning of the 17th century. The word *ménestrel* replaced the earlier *jongleur* (from Provençal *joglar*) about the 14th century.

The minstrel profession antedates its name. In earlier centuries the gleeman (from Old English *gléoman*) is heard of among the Angles and the Germanic scop is referred to. The Old English poem "Widsith" describes the role of a fictitious scop in Germanic society. Many minstrels were attached to courts, some as musicians. Others, the great majority, traveled widely, staying for short times at places of potential patronage. They performed traditional ballads and epics. Most were unable to write their music down, and consequently little of their music survives.

With the introduction of printing and more simplified musical notation in the late 15th century, the profession began to decline. Though the guilds, town bands, and wandering musicians continued to exist, the importance of the minstrel as a separate part of the musical profession faded after the 16th century. *Compare* MEISTERSINGER, MINNESINGER, SCOP; TROUBADOUR, TROUVÈRE.

miracle play *also called* saint's play. One of three principal kinds of vernacular drama of the European Middle Ages (along with the MYSTERY PLAY and the MORALITY PLAY). A miracle play presents a real or fictitious account of the life, miracles, or martyrdom of a saint. The genre evolved from liturgical offices developed during the 10th and 11th centuries to enhance calendar festivals. By the 13th century they had become vernacularized and filled with unecclesiastical elements. They had been divorced from church services and were performed at public festivals. Almost all surviving miracle plays concern either the Virgin Mary or St. Nicholas, the 4th-century bishop of Myra in Asia Minor, both of whom had active cults during the Middle Ages when belief in the healing powers of saintly relics was widespread. In this climate, miracle plays flourished.

The Mary plays consistently involve her in the role of deus ex machina, coming to the aid of all who invoke her, be they worthy or wanton. She saves, for example, a priest who has sold his soul to the devil, a woman falsely accused of murdering her own child, and a pregnant abbess. Typical of these is a play called *St. John the Hairy*. At the outset the title character seduces and murders a princess. Upon capture, he is proclaimed a saint by an infant. He confesses his crime, whereupon God and Mary appear and aid John in reviving the princess, which done, the murderous saint is made a bishop.

The Nicholas plays are similar, an example being Jehan Bodel's *Le Jeu de Saint Nicolas* (*c.* 1200), which details the deliverance of a crusader and the conversion of a Saracen king. Few English miracle plays are extant, for they were banned by Henry VIII in the mid-16th century and most were subsequently destroyed or lost.

miscellany \\'mis-ə-ˌlā-nē, mi-'sel-ə-nē\\ A collection of writings on various subjects. One of the first and best-known miscellanies in English was the collection of poems by various authors published by Richard Tottel in 1557. Thereafter the miscellany became a popular form of publication, and many more appeared in the next 50 years, including *The Paradise of Dainty Devices* (1576), *The Phoenix Nest* (1593), *England's Parnassus* (1600), and *England's Helicon* (1600).

mise-en-scène *plural* mise-en-scènes **1.** The arrangement of actor and scenery on a stage for a theatrical production. **2.** stage setting.

misline \mis-ˈlīn\ To incorrectly arrange or divide lines (as of poetry) in the process of copying or printing.

mistery *See* MYSTERY PLAY.

mixed metaphor A figure of speech that combines two or more inconsistent or incongruous metaphors. *See* METAPHOR.

Młoda Polska *See* YOUNG POLAND MOVEMENT.

mock-epic or **mock-heroic** Form of satire that applies the elevated heroic style of the classical epic to a trivial subject. The tradition, which originated in classical times with an anonymous burlesque of Homer, the *Batrachomyomachia* (*Battle of the Frogs and the Mice*), was honed to a fine art in the late 17th- and early 18th-century Neoclassical period. A double-edged satirical weapon, the mock-epic was sometimes used by the "moderns" of this period to ridicule contemporary "ancients" (classicists). More often it was used by the ancients to point up the unheroic character of the age by subjecting thinly disguised contemporary events to a heroic treatment. The classic example of this use is Nicolas Boileau's *Le Lutrin* (1674, 1683; "The Lectern"), which begins with a quarrel between two ecclesiastical dignitaries about where to place a lectern in a chapel and ends with a battle in a bookstore in which champions of either side hurl their favorite ancient or modern authors at each other. Jonathan Swift's "Battle of the Books" (1704) is a variation on the theme in prose. The outstanding English mock-epic is Alexander Pope's tour de force *The Rape of the Lock* (final version, 1714), which concerns a society beau's theft of a lock of hair from a society belle.

Most mock-epics begin with an invocation of the Muse and use the familiar epic devices of set speeches, supernatural interventions, and descents to the underworld, as well as infinitely detailed descriptions of the protagonist's activities. Thus, they provide much scope for display of the author's ingenuity and inventiveness. An American mock-epic, Joel Barlow's *The Hasty Pudding* (1796), celebrates his favorite New England dish, cornmeal mush, in three 400-line cantos.

model \ˈmäd-əl\ *archaic* An abstract or summary of a written work. *See also* EPITOME.

Modern \ˈmäd-ərn\, *also called* New \ˈnü\ Of, relating to, or having the characteristics of the present or most recent period of development of a language or literature. *Modern* is often applied in distinction to *Old* and *Middle,* as in "Early Modern English," a term used to describe the language and literature of the period immediately following that of Middle English.

moderne gennembrud, det \dā-mō-'der-nə-'gen-nem-ˌbrü\ [Danish, literally, the modern breakthrough] Danish literary movement that began about 1870 and introduced naturalism and realism to Scandinavia.

The movement was dominated by the Danish critic Georg Brandes, who felt that his mission as a critic was to bring Denmark out of its cultural isolation. Brandes himself was influenced by Hippolyte Taine, Charles-Augustin Sainte-Beuve, and John Stuart Mill. Brandes' *Hovedstrømninger i det 19de aarhundredes litteratur* (1872–90; *Main Currents in 19th Century Literature*) caused a great sensation not only in Denmark but throughout the rest of Scandinavia. His demands that literature should concern itself with life and reality, not with fantasy, and that it should work in the service of progress rather than reaction, provoked much discussion. He influenced both Henrik Ibsen and August Strindberg. Jens Peter Jacobsen was among the first Danish writers to exhibit the influence of Brandes' theories; his novel *Niels Lyhne* and his short stories deal with the problem of dreams versus reality. Holger Drachmann, the greatest lyrical poet of the period, began his career as a staunch supporter of Brandes but later reacted strongly against him. Henrik Pontoppidan emerged as one of Denmark's great novelists. His early stories examined social injustices, and in several of his short novels he discussed the political, moral, and religious problems of his day. Herman Bang was another novelist who cultivated a determined realism. His works deal with insignificant people, the gray and lonely and miserable men and women who are normally overlooked because their lives are undramatic.

Also associated with the movement are novelists Sophus Schandorph, Vilhelm Topsøe, Edvard Brandes, and Karl Gjellerup and playwrights Sven Lange, Einar Christiansen, and Henri Nathansen.

modernism \'mä-dər-ˌniz-əm\ In literature, a chiefly European movement of the early-to-mid-20th century that represented a self-conscious break with traditional forms and subject matter and a search for a distinctly contemporary mode of expression.

Initially modernism had a radical and utopian spirit stimulated by new ideas in anthropology, psychology, philosophy, political theory, and psychoanalysis. This exuberance can be seen in the works of such writers as Ezra Pound and the other poets of the Imagist movement. The outbreak of World War I had a sobering effect, however, and postwar modernism, as seen in such works as T.S. Eliot's *The Wasteland,* reflected the prevailing sense of fragmentation and disillusion. Other characteristics of later modernism are increasing self-awareness, introspection, and openness to the unconscious and to humanity's darker fears and instincts.

Modernismo \ˌmō-t̲h̲er-ˈnēz-mō\ or **Modernism** \ˈmäd-ər-ˌniz-əm\ Late 19th- and early 20th-century Spanish-language literary movement begun in the late 1880s by the Nicaraguan poet Rubén Darío.

Modernismo began as a reaction against the sentimental romantic writers then holding sway in Latin America. Young writers across the Americas immersed themselves in the world literary community. Somewhat disparagingly labeled *modernistas* by the older generation, they wrote on exotic themes, often shutting themselves off from their immediate environment in artificial worlds of their own making—the ancient past, the distant Orient, and the lands of childhood fancy and sheer creation. Beauty was their goddess and "art for art's sake" their creed. Influenced by French movements, they followed no regular path; Symbolism, Parnassianism, Decadentism, and other influences coexisted or held sway successively in any given writer.

Foremost among the early *modernistas* were the Mexican Manuel Gutiérrez Nájera, whose elegiac verse and restrained rhythmic prose sketches and tales best represented the transition from the excesses of Romanticism to the more filigreed Modernismo; the Colombian José Asunción Silva, who wrote a small but influential body of savagely ironic and elegiac poems; the Cuban Julián del Casal, cultivator of the Parnassian sonnet; and his compatriot José Martí, martyr and symbol of Cuba's struggle for freedom from Spain, whose inspired prose style and deceptively simple, sincere verse set his work above and apart from all schools and movements.

The full flowering of Modernismo came under the leadership of Darío, one of the greatest poets in Spanish. His *Azul* (1888; "Blue"), a collection of verse and prose, pointed the way, but *Prosas profanas* (1896; "Profane Hymns") represented the high point of the escapist, cosmopolitan phase of the movement. Darío blended the best of modernist formal experimentation with an expression of inner despair or an almost metaphysical joy in *Cantos de vida y esperanza* (1905; "Songs of Life and Hope"). When Spain's empire crumbled in 1898 and mutual sympathy allayed the old distrust between Spain and its former colonies, Darío turned to Hispanic traditions as he had always turned to Hispanic forms, and in the face of U.S. imperialism, he spoke for Hispanic solidarity. Darío's imitators, particularly of his early experimental, escapist phase, were often slavish copiers, but Darío and his fellow modernists brought about the greatest revitalization of language and poetic technique in Spanish since the 17th century. Many of his contemporaries were writers of considerable merit: Mexico's Amado Nervo, whose Orientally influenced mysticism was reflected in *Serenidad* (1914) and *Elevación* (1917); Peru's José Santos Chocano, whose exalted Americanism gave birth to *Alma América* (1906; "American Soul"); Bolivia's Ricardo Jaimes Freyre, who drew upon Scandinavian mythology for *Castalia bárbara* (1899; "The Barbarous Castalia"); Colombia's Guillermo Valencia, whose classic bent was manifest in *Ritos* (1898; "Rites"); and Uruguay's José Enrique Rodó whose *Ariel* (1900) distinguished him as the leading theoretician and exponent of modernist ideals. In Spain the principal members of the movement were the poets Antonio Machado and Juan Ramón

Jiménez and the novelist Ramón María del Valle-Inclán. Although the movement had run its course by 1920, its influence on both prose and poetry continued well into the 20th century.

Modernismo \mō-ˌder-ˈnēz-mü\ In Brazil, a post-World War I aesthetic movement that attempted to bring national life and thought abreast of modern times by creating new and authentically Brazilian methods of expression in the arts. Rebelling against the academicism and European influence they felt dominated the arts in Brazil, the *modernistas* attempted in their works to reflect colloquial Brazilian speech (rather than "correct" Portuguese) and often treated distinctively Brazilian themes based on native folklore and legend. They experimented with literary form and language, using free verse and unconventional syntax. Their concern with literary reform was often matched by a desire for social reform.

The Modernismo movement first gained wide recognition with its Semana de Arte Moderna ("Week of Modern Art"), held in São Paulo in 1922; the event provoked controversy, with lectures on the aims of Modernismo and readings from works by such poets as Mário de Andrade. The movement soon splintered into several groups with differing goals—some *modernistas,* among them Oswald de Andrade, focused on the nationalistic aims of the movement and agitated for radical social reform; others, such as Manuel Bandeira, who is generally considered the greatest of the *modernista* poets, sympathized with its aesthetic principles but lost interest in its political activism. By 1930 Modernismo had lost its coherence as a movement, although its organizers continued to write in the *modernista* idiom. Its influence on the development of contemporary Brazilian literature, however, has been profound, both through its stylistic innovations and through its emphasis on folklore and native themes.

modernize \ˈmäd-ər-ˌnīz\ **1.** To change a text to make it conform to modern usage in spelling and language. Among the authors who have been modernized are Geoffrey Chaucer, whose use of Middle English often makes his meaning unclear to the nonscholar. Sometimes modernization can help the reader surmount the difficulties produced by early printing practices. Early printed books, for example, often used *u* and *v* interchangeably, spelled the same words inconsistently, and (in the very earliest stages) used slashes, colons, and periods more or less interchangeably to indicate pauses. **2.** To act, write, or speak in a modern manner. The plays of William Shakespeare, for example, are sometimes acted in modern dress, and the actors sometimes substitute elements of modern speech for ease of comprehension.

molossus \mō-ˈläs-əs\ [Greek *molossós,* from *Molossós* of the Molossians (tribal group of northwestern Greece)] In classical prosody, a foot of three long syllables that occurs as a variant of an iambic metron, as a substitution for a cretic, or as a contracted ionic metron.

Monk's Tale stanza A stanza of eight five-stress lines with the rhyme scheme *ababbcbc*. The type was established in "The Monk's Tale" from Geoffrey Chaucer's *The Canterbury Tales*. It bears some similarity to the French ballade form and is one of the forms thought to have influenced the Spenserian stanza.

monodrama \'män-ə-ˌdräm-ə, -ˌdram-\ **1.** A drama acted or designed to be acted by a single person. A number of plays by Samuel Beckett, including *Krapp's Last Tape* and *Happy Days,* are monodramas. **2.** A dramatic representation of what passes in an individual mind. **3.** A musical drama for a solo performer.

monody \'män-ə-dē\ [Greek *monōidía,* from *mónos* single, alone + *ōidḗ* song] An ode sung by one voice (as by one of the actors in a Greek tragedy).

monogatari \'mō-nō-gä-tä-rē\ [Japanese *mono-gatari* tale, narrative, from *mono* thing + *katari* talk, narration] Japanese works of fiction, especially those written from the Heian to the Muromachi periods (794–1573).

Monogatari developed from the storytelling of women at court. During the Heian period (794–1185), men wrote in Chinese, and it was women who developed this form of Japanese prose. Some early *monogatari,* however, are believed to have been written by men under women's names. Records describe 11th-century literary competitions where women prepared short *monogatari* for an audience.

The form has many subgenres. *Uta monogatari* (poem tales) are exemplified by the *Ise monogatari* (*c.* 980), consisting of 143 episodes, each containing one or more poems and a prose description of the circumstances of composition. *Tsukuri monogatari* (courtly romance) is exemplified by Murasaki Shikibu's incomparable masterpiece, *Genji monogatari* (*c.* 1010). Perhaps the finest work in all of Japanese literature, and the first important novel in the world, it tells of Prince Genji, remarkable not for his martial or political talents but for his amorous ones. The story is related in terms of the successive women Genji loves. Like other works of the genre, it incorporates poems and verse fragments.

As the militaristic samurai came to power at the end of the 12th century, women lost favor, and *gunki monogatari* (military tales) developed as a subgenre. The most famous of the military tales is *Heike monogatari,* which describes the warfare between two families; its lengthy, varied text reflects its origins as an improvised story told by priest-entertainers. Later works told of medieval warlords and clan vendettas.

Other types of *monogatari* include *rekishi monogatari* (historical tales), exemplified by the *Ōkagami,* and *setsuwa monogatari* (didactic tales) originating in Buddhist legends but in their secular form often humorous and earthy.

monograph \'män-ə-ˌgraf\ [Greek *mónos* single + *gráphein* to write] A learned treatise on a small area of learning. Also, a written account of a single subject.

monologue or **monolog** \'män-ə-ˌlȯg, -ˌläg\ [French *monologue,* from Greek *mónos* single, alone + French *-logue* (as in *dialogue* dialogue)] An extended speech by one person. The term has several synonyms and distinctive literary uses. A DRAMATIC MONOLOGUE is any speech of some duration addressed by a character to a second person. A SOLILOQUY is a type of monologue in which a character directly addresses an audience or speaks thoughts aloud while alone or while the other actors remain silent. In fiction, an INTERIOR MONOLOGUE is a type of monologue that exhibits the thoughts and feelings passing through a character's mind. *See also* APOSTROPHE.

monometer \mə-'näm-ə-tər\ A rare form of verse in which each line consists of a single metrical unit (a foot or dipody). The best-known example of an entire poem in monometer is Robert Herrick's "Upon His Departure Hence":

> Thus I
> Passe by,
> And die:
> As One,
> Unknown,
> And gon:
> I'm made
> A shade,
> And laid
> I'th grave,
> There have
> My Cave.
> Where tell
> I dwell,
> *Farewell.*

Another example in light verse is Desmond Skirrow's "Ode on a Grecian Urn Summarized":

> Gods chase
> Round vase.
> What say?
> What play?
> Don't know
> Nice, though.

monopody \mə-'näp-ə-dē\ [Late Greek *monopodía* measurement by single feet, from Greek *mónos* single + *pod-, poús* foot] In prosody, a measure consisting of a single metrical foot.

monorhyme or **monorime** \'män-ō-ˌrīm\ A strophe or poem in which all the lines have the same end rhyme. Monorhymes are rare in English but are a common feature in Latin, Welsh, and Arabic poetry.

monostich \'män-ə-ˌstik\ [Greek *monóstichon,* from neuter of *monóstichos* consisting of one verse, from *mónos* single + *stíchos* row, line, verse] A single verse; also, a poem of one verse.

monostrophe \mə-'näs-trə-fē, 'män-ō-ˌstrōf\ **1.** A poem of one stanza. **2.** A poem in which all the stanzas are of the same metric form.

montage \män-'täzh, mōⁿ-'tȧzh\ A literary technique, taking its name from cinematic montage, in which heterogeneous images, themes, or fragments of ideas are juxtaposed to produce a single total effect. Also, a literary composite made by means of such technique.

Montreal group \ˌmän-trē-'ȯl, ˌmən-\ Coterie of poets who precipitated a renaissance of Canadian poetry during the 1920s and '30s and advocated a break with the traditional picturesque landscape poetry that had dominated Canadian poetry since the late 19th century. They encouraged an emulation of the realistic themes, metaphysical complexity, and techniques of the American and British poets Ezra Pound, T.S. Eliot, and W.H. Auden that resulted in an Expressionist poetry reflective of the values of an urban civilization. Based in Montreal, then Canada's most cosmopolitan city, the group included A.M. Klein and A.J.M. Smith, whose *The Book of Canadian Poetry* (1943) and other anthologies contributed greatly to the raising of literary standards in Canada. Leo Kennedy, and Francis Reginald Scott, as well as two kindred spirits from Toronto, E.J. Pratt and Robert Finch were also members. First brought together at McGill University in Montreal, the poets founded the *Canadian Mercury* (1928–29), a literary organ for young writers, and subsequently founded, edited, and wrote for a number of other influential journals, including the *McGill Fortnightly Review* and *Canadian Forum.*

monument \'män-yə-mənt\ A written tribute or a testimonial.

mora \'mȯr-ə\ *plural* morae \'mȯr-ˌē, -ˌī\ *or* moras [Latin, lapse of time, delay] **1.** The minimal unit of quantitative measure in temporal prosodic systems. The mora is equivalent in time value to an average short syllable. **2.** A unit used in linguistic analysis, especially with reference to vowel length or syllable weight. A syllable ending in a short vowel has the value of one mora, whereas a syllable ending in a long vowel, a diphthong, or a consonant has the value of two morae.

morality play *also called* morality. An allegorical play popular in Europe especially during the 15th and 16th centuries, in which the characters personify moral qualities (such as charity or vice) or abstractions (as death or youth) and in which moral lessons are taught.

With the MYSTERY PLAY and the MIRACLE PLAY, the morality play is one of three main kinds of vernacular drama of the European Middle Ages. The action of the morality play centers on a hero, such as Mankind, whose inherent weaknesses are assaulted by such personified diabolic forces as the Seven

Deadly Sins but who may choose redemption and enlist the aid of such figures as the Four Daughters of God (Mercy, Justice, Temperance, and Truth).

Morality plays were a step in the transition from liturgical to professional secular drama and combine elements of each. They were performed by quasi-professional groups of actors who relied on public support; thus the plays were usually short, their serious themes tempered by elements of farce. In the Dutch play *Het esbatement den appelboom* ("The Miraculous Apple Tree"), for example, a pious couple, Staunch Goodfellow and Steadfast Faith, are rewarded when God creates for them an everbearing apple tree that makes whomever touches it without permission stick fast. This leads to predictable and humorous consequences.

The most famous of the French morality plays is Nicolas de la Chesnaye's *Condemnation des banquets* (1507), which argues for moderation by showing the bad end that awaits a company of unrepentant revelers, including Gluttony and Watering Mouth. Among the oldest of morality plays surviving in English is *The Castle of Perseverance* (*c.* 1425), about the battle for the soul of Humanum Genus. Of all morality plays, *Everyman* is considered the greatest and is still performed.

morceau \mȯr-ˈsō\ *plural* morceaux *same*\ *or* morceaus \-ˈsōz\ [French, piece, morsel] A short literary or musical piece.

mosaic rhyme A type of multiple rhyme in which one word is made to rhyme with two or more words, as in the rhymes at the ends of the following two lines from W.S. Gilbert's song "The Modern Major-General":

> About binomial theorem I'm teeming with a lot o' news,
> With interesting facts about the square of the hypotenuse.

Moscow Art Academic Theater \ˈmäs-ˌkau̇, -ˌkō\, *also called* (until 1920) Moscow Art Theater, *Russian* Moskovsky Khudozhestvenny Akademichesky Teatr *or* Moskovsky Khudozhestvenny Teatr, abbreviation MKHAT. Outstanding Russian theater specializing in naturalism, the Moscow Art Academic Theater was founded in 1898 by two teachers of dramatic art, Konstantin Stanislavsky and Vladimir Nemirovich-Danchenko. Its purpose was to establish a theater of new art forms. In 1932 Maksim Gorky's name was added to that of the theater.

The Moscow Art Theater opened with Aleksey Tolstoy's *Tsar Fyodor Ioannovich* in October 1898. For its fifth production it staged Anton Chekhov's *Chayka* (*The Seagull*), its first major success, and thus began a long artistic association with one of Russia's most celebrated playwrights. In Chekhov's artistic realism, the Art Theater discovered a style well-suited to its aesthetic sensibilities. In *The Seagull,* as in all of Chekhov's plays, the Art Theater emphasized the subtext, the underlying meaning of the playwright's thought.

The Art Theater accepted many challenges. Its repertoire included works of Maksim Gorky, L.N. Andreyev, Leo Tolstoy, Maurice Maeterlinck, and

Gerhart Hauptmann, among others, and it staged works of political and social significance as well as satires, fantasies, and comedies.

After the Russian Revolution it received crucial support from V.I. Lenin and A.V. Lunacharsky, first commissar of education in the Soviet Union. In 1922 the Art Theater toured Europe and the United States, garnering critical acclaim wherever it performed. Returning to Moscow in 1924, the theater continued to produce new Soviet plays and Russian classics until its evacuation in 1941. Two successful tours of London in the late 1950s and early 1960s reestablished its preeminence in world theater.

motif \mō-ˈtēf\ [French, from Italian *motivo* musical motif, subject of a painting, reason, cause, from Medieval Latin *motivum* motive, impulse, reason] A usually recurring salient thematic element, especially a dominant idea or central theme. *Compare* LEITMOTIV.

motto \ˈmät-ō\ *plural* mottoes *or* mottos [Italian, saying, word] A short, usually quoted, passage placed at the beginning of a literary work (such as a novel, essay, or poem) or one of its divisions (such as a chapter or canto) and intended to suggest the subject matter that follows. *Compare* EPIGRAPH.

muckraker \ˈmək-ˌrā-kər\ Any of a group of American writers identified with pre-World War I reform and exposé literature. The name was pejorative when used by President Theodore Roosevelt in his speech of April 14, 1906; he borrowed a passage from John Bunyan's *Pilgrim's Progress,* which referred to the man with the muckrake who "could look no way but downwards." But "muckraker" also came to take on favorable connotations of social concern and courageous exposure of injustice.

The muckrakers' work grew out of the yellow journalism of the 1890s, which whetted the public appetite for news arrestingly presented, and out of popular magazines, especially those established by S.S. McClure, Frank A. Munsey, and Peter F. Collier. The emergence of muckraking was heralded in the January 1903 issue of *McClure's Magazine* by articles on municipal government, labor, and trusts, written by Lincoln Steffens, Ray Stannard Baker, and Ida M. Tarbell. The movement as such largely disappeared between 1910 and 1912. Among the novels produced by muckrakers were Upton Sinclair's *The Jungle* (1906), about the meatpacking industry in Chicago, and Brand Whitlock's *The Turn of the Balance* (1907), which opposed capital punishment.

mumming play \ˈməm-iŋ\, *also called* mummers' play \ˈməm-ərz\ [Middle English *mommen* to speak incoherently, be silent, perform (a mumming play), probably in part a derivative of *mom* an inarticulate sound (of imitative origin), in part from Old French *mommer* to perform wearing masks] Traditional dramatic entertainment, still performed in a few villages of England and Northern Ireland, in which a champion is killed in a fight and is then brought to life by a doctor. It is thought likely that the play has links with primitive ceremonies held to mark important stages in the agricultural year.

Mummers were originally bands of masked persons who during winter festivals in Europe paraded through the streets and entered houses to dance or play dice in silence. "Momerie" was a popular amusement between the 13th and 16th centuries. In the 16th century it was absorbed by Italian carnival masquerading (and hence was a forerunner of the courtly entertainment known as the masque).

It is not known how old the mumming play is. Although contemporary references to it do not begin to appear until the late 18th century, the basic narrative framework is the story of St. George and the Seven Champions of Christendom, which was first popularized in England toward the end of the 16th century. It is possible that there was a common (lost) original play, which widely separated communities in England, Ireland, and Scotland modified to their own use. The plot remained essentially the same: St. George, introduced as a gallant Christian hero, fights an infidel knight, and one of them is slain. A doctor is then presented, who restores the dead warrior to life. Other characters include a presenter, a fool in cap and bells, and a man dressed in woman's clothes. Father Christmas also appears. It is likely that the basic story of death and resurrection was grafted onto an older game that stemmed from primitive ritual.

muwashshaḥ \mü-ˈwȧsh-shȧk̲\ [Arabic, probably a derivative of *wishāʿ* embroidered or painted fabric] An Arabic poetic genre in strophic form developed in Andalusia (part of Muslim Spain) from roughly the 9th to the 12th century. From the 12th century onward, its use spread to North Africa and the Muslim Middle East.

Especially adapted to singing, the *muwashshaḥ* is written in classical Arabic, and its subjects are those of classical Arabic poetry—love, wine, court figures. It sharply differs in form, however, from classical poetry, in which each verse is divided into two metric halves and a single rhyme recurs at the end of each verse. The *muwashshaḥ* is usually divided into five strophes, or stanzas, each numbering four, five, or six lines. A master rhyme appears at the beginning of the poem and at the end of the strophes, somewhat like a refrain; it is interrupted by subordinate rhymes. A possible scheme is *ABcdcdABefefABghghABijijABklklAB*. The last *AB,* called *kharjah,* or *markaz,* is usually written in vernacular Arabic or in the Spanish Mozarabic dialect; it is normally rendered in the voice of a girl and expresses her longing for her absent lover. Jewish poets of Spain also wrote *muwashshaḥ*s in Hebrew, with *kharjah*s in Arabic and Spanish. Beginning about the 13th century, Ṣūfī (Muslim mystic) poets began to adapt the form to mystical themes.

mystery play or **mistery** \ˈmis-tə-rē\ One of three principal kinds of vernacular drama of the European Middle Ages (with the MORALITY PLAY and the MIRACLE PLAY).

The mystery plays, usually representing biblical subjects, developed from plays presented in Latin by churchmen on church premises. The plays depicted such subjects as the Creation, Adam and Eve, the murder of Abel, and the Last

Judgment. During the 13th century, various guilds began producing the plays in the vernacular at sites removed from the churches. Under these conditions, the strictly religious nature of the plays declined, and they became filled with irrelevancies and apocryphal elements. Furthermore, satirical elements were introduced to mock physicians, soldiers, judges, and even monks and priests. In England, over the course of decades, groups of 25 to 50 plays were organized into lengthy cycles. In France a single play, *The Acts of the Apostles* by Arnoul and Simon Gréban, contained 494 speaking parts and 61,908 lines of rhymed verse; it was performed over the course of 40 days.

The form in which the mystery plays developed contributed to their demise at the end of the 16th century. The Roman Catholic church no longer supported them because of their dubious religious value, Renaissance scholars found little of interest in their great rambling texts, and the general public preferred professional traveling companies that were beginning to arrive from Italy.

At their height, the mystery plays were quite elaborate in their production. In England they were generally performed on pageant wagons, which provided both scaffold stage and dressing room and could be moved about readily. In France and Italy, however, a production might take place on a stage 100 feet wide, with paradise represented above the stage, hell represented below it, and earthly scenes represented on the stage itself. They did not attempt to achieve unity of time, place, and action, and therefore they could represent any number of different geographic locations and climates in juxtaposition. Mechanical devices, trapdoors, and other artifices were employed to portray flying angels, fire-spouting monsters, miraculous transformations, and graphic martyrdoms.

mystery story Work of fiction in which the evidence related to a crime or to a mysterious event is so presented that the reader has an opportunity to solve the problem, the author's solution being the final phase of the piece.

The mystery story is an age-old popular genre and is related to several other forms. Elements of mystery may be present in narratives of horror or terror, pseudoscientific fantasies, crime stories, accounts of diplomatic intrigue, affairs of codes and ciphers and secret societies, or any situation involving an enigma. By and large, however, the true mystery story is one specifically concerned with a riddle of some kind.

Riddle stories have an ancient heritage. The riddle of Samson, propounded in the Bible (Judges 14:12–18), is a famous early example, but puzzles were also popular among the ancient Egyptians and the Greeks. The distinguishing feature of the riddle story is that the reader be confronted with a number of mysterious facts and situations, explanation of which is reserved until the end of the story.

Edgar Allan Poe's short story "The Gold Bug" is a classic example of one perennially popular type of mystery, the story of a search for lost treasure. Murder mysteries, which are generally among the more sinister mystery stories, also contain elements of riddle-solving. Two notable riddle stories of modern times—"The Lady or the Tiger?" by Frank R. Stockton and "The Mysterious

Card" by Cleveland Moffett—offered no solution to the riddle posed and gained wide attention by their novelty.

See also DETECTIVE STORY; HARD-BOILED FICTION; GOTHIC NOVEL; SPY STORY.

myth \'mith\ [Greek *mŷthos* thing said, speech, tale] **1.** A usually traditional story of ostensibly historical events that serves to unfold part of a worldview of a people or a practice, belief, or natural phenomenon. *Compare* EUHEMERISM; FABLE; FOLKTALE. Also, the theme or plot of a mythical tale occurring in forms differing only in detail. **2.** The whole body of myths.

Myths relate the paradigmatic events, conditions, and deeds of gods or superhuman beings that are outside ordinary human life and yet basic to it. These extraordinary events are set in a time altogether different from historical time, often at the beginning of creation or at an early stage of prehistory.

Features of myth are shared by other kinds of literature. Etiological tales explain the origins or causes of various aspects of nature or human society and life. Fairy tales deal with extraordinary beings and events but lack the authority of myth. Sagas and epics claim authority and truth but reflect specific historical settings.

The modern study of myth arose with the Romantic movement of the early 19th century, but interpretations of myth were offered much earlier. The influence of philosophy in ancient Greece led to allegorical views of myth or to the historical reductionism of Euhemerus (fl. 300 BC), who believed that the gods of myth were originally simply great people. The development of comparative philology in the 19th century, together with ethnological discoveries in the 20th, established the main contours of MYTHOLOGY, the science of myth. Since the Romantics, all study of myth has been comparative. Wilhelm Mannhardt, Sir James Frazer, and Stith Thompson employed the comparative approach to collect and classify the themes of folklore and mythology. Bronisław Malinowski emphasized the ways in which myth fulfills common social functions. Claude Lévi-Strauss and other structuralists have compared the formal relations and patterns in myths throughout the world.

Sigmund Freud put forward the idea that symbolic communication does not depend on cultural history alone but also on the workings of the psyche. Thus Freud introduced a transhistorical and biological approach and a view of myth as an expression of repressed ideas. Carl Jung extended Freud's approach with his theory of the "collective unconscious" and the archetypes, often encoded in myth, that arise out of it.

Some scholars, such as Mircea Eliade (a historian of religion) and the German theologian Rudolf Otto, hold that myth is to be understood solely as a religious phenomenon, irreducible to nonreligious categories. Scholars of the so-called Myth and Ritual School contend that any myth functions, or at one time functioned, as the "explanation" of a corresponding ritual.

Because myths are thought to be the repository of truth and knowledge, they are supposed to help control the universe or to make human activities efficacious. Cosmogonic myths, which relate the origins of the cosmos, are recited in many cultures in conjunction with the enthronement of kings or other events on which depend the well-being of the world. Closely connected to accounts of the origin of the cosmos are myths relating human origins or the institutions of society. Eschatological myths deal with the end of the world, while other myths explain the relation between eternity and time. Myths sometimes revolve around cultural heroes, who made the earth habitable for humanity, or around great beings who made salvation from earthly existence possible. Myths explain how evil and death were introduced into life, or they may tell how fundamental knowledge was "forgotten" and "remembered." *See also* MYTHOS.

mythicist \ˈmith-i-sist\ **1.** A student or interpreter of myths. **2.** An adherent of the view that apparently supernatural persons or events have their origin in human imagination, especially as it is revealed in myth.

mythoclast \ˈmith-ə-ˌklast\ [*myth* + *-clast* (as in *iconoclast*)] A decrier of myths.

mythography \mi-ˈthäg-rə-fē\ **1.** The representation of mythical subjects in art. **2.** A critical compilation of myths.

mythologem \mi-ˈthäl-ə-jem\ [Greek *mythológēma* mythical narrative] A basic or recurrent theme of myth.

mythology **1.** An allegorical narrative. **2.** A body of myths dealing with the gods, demigods, and legendary heroes of a particular people. **3.** A branch of knowledge that deals with myth. *See also* MYTH; MYTHOS.

mythopoeia \ˌmith-ə-ˈpē-ə\ [Greek *mythopoiía* the making of tales, a derivative of *mythopoieîn* to relate or invent tales] A creating of myth or a giving rise to myths.

mythopoem \ˌmith-ə-ˈpō-əm, -ˈpōm\ A mythological poem.

mythos \ˈmī-ˌthäs\ *plural* mythoi \-ˌthȯi\ **1.** A myth. **2.** Mythology. **3.** The underlying theme or symbolic meaning of a creative work. *See also* MYTH; MYTHOLOGY.

N

The only obligation to which in advance we may hold a novel is that it be interesting.
—Henry James

naive narrator *See* NARRATOR.

nanxi or **nan-hsi** \ˈnän-ˈshē\ [Chinese *nánxì*] One of the first fully developed forms of Chinese drama. *Nanxi* ("southern drama") emerged in the area around Wenzhou in southern China during the Song dynasty (960–1279). Originally the creation of folk authors, the earliest *nanxi* were a combination of Song plays and local folk songs and ballads. They were characterized by their colloquial language and large numbers of scenes; flexible verses (*qu*) set to popular local music, which made both poetry and music accessible to the ordinary spectator, alternated with vernacular spoken passages. Professional playwrights belonging to Hangzhou's book guilds (*shuhui*) wrote large numbers of *nanxi* for local troupes. Of these, however, only 283 titles and 20 play texts remain. *Zhang Xie zhuangyuan* ("Top Graduate Zhang Xie") is one of the best-known of the extant texts. The form was the precursor of the *chuanqi* style.

Naoki Prize \nä-ˈō-kē\ Japanese literary prize awarded twice yearly to an outstanding Japanese novelist of popular literature. The Naoki Prize is one of the most prestigious Japanese literary awards. It confers on the winner 1,000,000 yen and a watch.

Kikuchi Kan established the Naoki Prize in 1935 in memory of his friend Naoki Sanjūgo, an eccentric writer who had turned from writing a gossip column to writing historical and popular fiction, in the hope of elevating the prestige of popular literature.

narodnost \nə-ˈrȯd-nəsʸt\ [Russian *narodnost',* a derivative of *narodnyĭ* national, folk, a derivative of *narod* people] (literally "folkness" or "national quality") Doctrine or national principle, the meaning of which has changed over the course of Russian literary criticism. Originally denoting simply literary fidelity to Russia's distinct cultural heritage, *narodnost,* in the hands of radical critics such as Nikolay Dobrolyubov, came to be the measure of an author's social responsibility, both in portraying the aspirations of the common people and in making literature accessible to the masses. These complementary values of *narodnost*—reflection of the people's interest and accessibility—became prescribed elements of Socialist Realism, the officially approved style of writing in the Soviet Union from the early 1930s to the mid-1980s.

narration The act or process of telling a story in detail.

narrative verse A verse or poem that tells a story. It is often contrasted with lyric verse and verse drama. The main forms of narrative verse are the epic and the ballad, both of which are products of the oral tradition.

The earliest versions of narrative poetry took the form of the chanting of ritual myth. The gods of the myths were eventually replaced by human heroes, which led to the development of epic heroic poetry, and when the elements of adventure and the love interest were stressed, to the romance. Among the earliest recorded narratives are various versions of the creation myth and of the story of Gilgamesh, which dates from about 2000 BC.

The next phase of oral literature to be recorded was in Palestine and Greece, where parts of the Hebrew scripture and the stories of Homer and Hesiod appeared. It was also in Greece that the first written narrative texts were produced beginning in about the 4th century BC. One of the first written epics was the *Argonautica* of Apollonius of Rhodes. At the same time there developed a shorter form of the epic called the EPYLLION. Since then narrative verse has been produced by writers throughout the world, in all times, and on subjects ranging from the classical and biblical stories of the early writers to the folk themes and songs of the people that were the focus of the Romantic writers of the 18th and 19th centuries. Examples include the Roman author Virgil's *Aeneid,* the lives of the saints by the 8th-century English author known as the Venerable Bede, the 13th-century collection of Old Norse poems known as the *Poetic Edda,* the Anglo-Saxon *Beowulf,* the French chansons de geste, the German *Nibelungenlied,* and works by the Italians Torquato Tasso and Ludovico Ariosto, the Spanish Alonso de Ercilla y Zúñiga, the Portuguese Luís de Camões, Marko Marulić and Ivan Gundulić in Croatia, and such English authors as John Milton, Samuel Taylor Coleridge, and John Keats.

narratology \ˌnar-ə-ˈtäl-ə-jē\ In literary theory, the study of narrative structure. Like structuralism, from which it derived, narratology is based on the idea of a common literary language, or a universal pattern of codes that operates within the text of a work. The development of this body of theory, and its corresponding terminology, accelerated in the mid-20th century.

The foundations of narratology were laid in such books as Vladimir Propp's *Morfologiya skazki* (1928; *Morphology of the Folk Tale*), which created a model for folktales based on seven "spheres of action" and 31 "functions" of narrative; Claude Lévi-Strauss' *Anthropologie structurale* (1958; *Structural Anthropology*), which outlined a grammar of mythology; A.J. Greimas' *Sémantique structurale* (1966; *Structural Semantics*), which proposed a system of six structural units called "actants"; and Tzvetan Todorov's *Grammaire du Décaméron* (1969; "The Grammar of the Decameron"), which introduced the term *narratologie*. In *Figures III* (1972; partial translation, *Narrative Discourse*) and *Nouveau Discours de récit* (1983; *Narrative Discourse Revisited*), Gérard Genette codified a system of analysis that examined both the actual narration and the act of narrating as they existed apart from the story or the content. Other influential theorists in narratology were Roland Barthes, Claude Bremond, and Northrop Frye. *See also* ARCHETYPAL CRITICISM; STRUCTURALISM.

narrator \'nar-ˌā-tər, -ə-tər; na-'rā-tər\ [Latin, a derivative of *narrare* to tell, relate] One who tells a story. In a work of fiction the narrator determines the story's point of view. If the narrator is a full participant in the story's action, the narrative is said to be in the first person. A story told by a narrator who is not a character in the story is a third-person narrative. *See also* POINT OF VIEW.

A work may have more than one narrator, as in an epistolary novel such as Samuel Richardson's *Clarissa,* which consists of letters by a variety of characters. In Emily Brontë's *Wuthering Heights,* one character tells part of the story and then introduces another who continues it or provides another perspective on events.

Narrators are sometimes categorized by the way in which they present their story. An *intrusive narrator,* a common device in many 18th- and 19th-century works, is one who interrupts the story to provide a commentary to the reader on some aspect of the story or on a more general topic. An *unreliable narrator* is one who does not understand the full import of a situation or one who makes incorrect conclusions and assumptions about events witnessed; this type is exemplified by the narrator of Ford Madox Ford's *The Good Soldier.* A related device is the *naive narrator,* who does not have the sophistication to understand the full import of the story's events, though the reader understands. Such narrators are often children, as in Robert Louis Stevenson's *Treasure Island.* The protagonist of Laurence Sterne's *Tristram Shandy* is the paradigm of the *self-conscious narrator,* who calls attention to the text as fiction.

National Book Awards Annual awards given to books of the highest quality written by Americans and published by American publishers. The awards were founded in 1950 by the American Book Publishers Council, American Booksellers Association, and Book Manufacturers Institute. From 1976 to 1979 they were administered by the National Book Committee, and in 1980 they were replaced by American Book Awards given by the Association of American Booksellers. They were renamed the National Book Awards, administered by the National Book Foundation, in 1987. Publishers submit selected books to be judged, and fiction, nonfiction, and poetry prizes are awarded.

National Institute of Arts and Letters *See* AMERICAN ACADEMY OF ARTS AND LETTERS.

naturalism \'nach-ər-ə-ˌliz-əm\ A theory that art or literature should conform exactly to nature or depict every appearance of the subject that comes to the artist's attention; specifically, a theory in literature emphasizing the role of heredity and environment upon human life and character development.

This theory was the basis of a late 19th- and early 20th-century aesthetic movement that, in literature, was inspired by adaptation of the principles and methods of natural science, especially the Darwinian view of nature, to literature and art. In literature it extended the tradition of realism, aiming at an even more faithful, unselective representation of reality, presented without moral judgment. Naturalism differed from realism in its assumption of scientific determinism, which led naturalistic authors to emphasize the accidental, physiological nature of their characters rather than their moral or rational qualities. Individual characters were seen as helpless products of heredity and environment, motivated by strong instinctual drives from within, and harassed by social and economic pressures from without. As such, they had little will or responsibility for their fates, and the prognosis for their "cases" was pessimistic at the outset.

Naturalism originated in France, and had its direct theoretical basis in the critical approach of Hippolyte Taine, who announced in his introduction to *Histoire de la littérature anglaise* (1863–64; *History of English Literature*), that ". . . there is a cause for ambition, for courage, for truth, as there is for digestion, for muscular movement, for animal heat. Vice and virtue are products, like vitriol and sugar . . ." Though the first "scientific" novel was the Goncourt brothers' case history of a servant girl, *Germinie Lacerteux* (1864), the leading exponent of the movement was Émile Zola, whose essay "Le Roman expérimental" (1880; "The Experimental Novel") became the literary manifesto of the school. According to Zola, the novelist was no longer to be a mere observer, content to record phenomena, but a detached experimenter who subjects his characters and their passions to a series of tests and who works with emotional and social facts as a chemist works with matter. With Zola's example the naturalistic style became widespread and affected to varying degrees most of the major writers of the period. The early works of Joris-Karl Huysmans, of the German dramatist Gerhart Hauptmann, and of the Portuguese novelist José Maria de Eça de Queirós were based on the precepts of naturalism.

The Théâtre Libre was founded in Paris in 1887 by André Antoine and the Freie Bühne of Berlin in 1889 by Otto Brahm to present plays dealing with the new themes of naturalism in a naturalistic style with naturalistic staging.

Despite their claim to complete objectivity, the naturalists were handicapped by certain biases inherent in their deterministic theories. Though they faithfully reflected nature, it was always nature "red in tooth and claw." Their views on heredity gave them a predilection for simple characters dominated by strong, elemental passions. Their views on the overpowering effects of environment led them to select for subjects the most oppressive environments—the slums or the underworld—and they documented these milieus, often in dreary and sordid detail. Finally, they were unable to suppress an element of romantic protest against the social conditions they described.

In American literature, naturalism had a delayed blooming in the work of Hamlin Garland, Stephen Crane, Frank Norris, and Jack London, and it reached its peak in novels of Theodore Dreiser.

natya \'nä-tyə\ [Sanskrit *nāṭyaṃ* dance, acting, drama] The dramatic (narrative) element of Indian classical dance.

Nāyaṉār \ˈnä-yə-ˌnär\ Any of the Tamil poet-musicians of the 7th and 8th centuries AD who composed devotional hymns of great beauty in honor of the Hindu god Shiva (Śiva).

The first of the Nāyaṉārs was the poetess Kāraikkāl Ammaiyār, who called herself a *pēy,* or ghostly minion of Shiva and sang ecstatically of his dances. There were 12 early Nāyaṉār saints. The most important Nāyaṉārs were Appar and Ñānacampantar, in the 7th century, and Cuntaramūrtti, in the 8th. These poets were often known as "the three"; their images are worshiped in South Indian temples as saints. They were approximately contemporary with the Āḻvārs, who worshiped Vishnu.

Appar, who was a self-mortifying Jain ascetic before he became a devotee of Shiva, sings of his conversion to a religion of love, having been surprised by the Lord stealing into his heart. Ñānacampantar, too, wrote these personal, "bone-melting" songs for the common individual. Cuntaramūrtti, however, who sees a vision of 63 Tamil saints—rich, poor, male, female, of every caste and trade, unified even with bird and beast in the love of God—epitomizes *bhakti* (intense personal devotion). To him every act is worship, every word God's name.

The hymns of the Nāyaṉārs were collected in the 10th century by Nambi Āṇḍar Nambi under the title *Tēvāram* and set to Dravidian music for incorporation into the services of South Indian temples. An inscription of the Chola (Cōḻa) king Rājarāja the Great (985–1014) records his introduction of the singing of the hymns in the great temple at Thanjāvūr (Tanjore). Often associated with the Nāyaṉārs, though probably slightly later in date, is the superb devotional poet Māṇikkavācakar, whose hymns are collected under the title *Tiruvācakam* ("Sacred Utterance").

Unlike the ascetics, the Nāyaṉārs bring hope, joy, and beauty into religion and make worship an act of music. Not only did their songs become a part of temple ritual but further, in *bhakti*, erotic love in all its phases became a metaphor for human love for God, the lover.

Nea grammata \ˈnā-ä-ˈḡrä-mä-tä\ ("New Letters") Greek avant-garde magazine, founded in 1935, that served as the prime vehicle for the poetry of the Generation of the '30s, an influential group that included George Seferis and Odysseus Elytis, who in 1979 won the Nobel Prize for Literature.

near rhyme *See* HALF RHYME.

negative capability As defined by John Keats, a writer's ability to accept "uncertainties, mysteries, doubts, without any irritable reaching after fact and reason." Keats first employed the phrase in an 1817 letter. An author possessing negative capability is objective and not driven by intellectual or philosophical didacticism.

negrismo \nā-ˈgrēz-mō\ [Spanish, a derivative of *negro* black, black person] Literary movement of the 1920s that sought to emphasize contributions by black artists to Latin-American culture. Nicolás Guillén is one of the better-known authors associated with the movement.

Negritude \nā-grē-ˈtu̇ēd\ [French *négritude,* a derivative of *nègre* black person] Literary movement of the 1930s, '40s, and '50s that began among French-speaking African and Caribbean writers living in Paris as a protest against French colonial rule and the policy of assimilation. Its leading figure was Léopold Sédar Senghor (elected first president of the Republic of Senegal in 1960), who, along with Aimé Césaire from Martinique and Léon Damas from French Guiana, began to examine Western values critically and to reassess African culture.

The group's quarrel with assimilation was that, although it was theoretically based on a belief in universal equality, it still assumed the superiority of European culture and civilization over that of Africa (or assumed that Africa had no history or culture). They were also disturbed by the world wars, in which they saw their countrymen not only dying for a cause that was not theirs but being treated as inferiors on the battlefield. They became increasingly aware, through their study of history, of the suffering and humiliation of black people first under the bondage of slavery and then under colonial rule. These views inspired many of the basic ideas behind Negritude: that the mystic warmth of African life, gaining strength from its closeness to nature and its constant contact with ancestors, should be continually placed in proper perspective against the soullessness and materialism of Western culture; that Africans must look to their own cultural heritage to determine the values and traditions that are most useful in the modern world; that committed writers should use African subject matter and poetic traditions and should excite a desire for political freedom; that Negritude itself encompasses the whole of African cultural, economic, social, and political values; and that, above all, the value and dignity of African traditions and peoples must be asserted.

Senghor treated all of these themes in his poetry and inspired a number of other writers: Birago Diop from Senegal, whose poems explore the mystique of African life; David Diop, writer of revolutionary protest poetry; Jacques Rabemananjara, whose poems and plays glorify the history and culture of Madagascar; Cameroonians Mongo Beti and Ferdinand Oyono, who wrote anticolonialist novels; and the Congolese poet Tchicaya U Tam'si, whose extremely personal poetry does not neglect the sufferings of the African peoples. Since the early 1960s, however, with the political and cultural objectives of the movement achieved in most African countries, there has been much less work produced with Negritude themes, and the focal point of literary activity in West Africa has moved from Senegal to Nigeria.

Neoclassicism \ˌnē-ō-ˈklas-ə-ˌsiz-əm\ Adherence to or practice of the virtues thought to be characteristic of classical art, literature, and, in modern times, music. These virtues, which include formal elegance and correctness, simplicity, dignity, restraint, order, and proportion, are taken to be universally and enduringly valid. Neoclassicism always refers to the art produced later but inspired by antiquity. Thus the terms classicism and Neoclassicism are often used interchangeably. *Compare* AUGUSTAN AGE.

neologism \nē-ˈäl-ə-ˌjiz-əm\ [Greek *néos* new + *lógos* word] A word, usage, or expression newly introduced into the language.

Neorealism \ˌnē-ō-ˈrē-ə-ˌliz-əm\ or **neorealismo** \ˌnā-ō-rā-ä-ˈlēz-mō\ Italian literary movement that flourished especially after World War II and that sought to deal realistically with the events leading up to the war and with the social problems that were engendered during the period and afterwards.

The movement was rooted in the 1920s and, though suppressed for nearly two decades by fascist control, emerged in great strength after the fascist regime fell at the end of World War II. Neorealism is similar in general aims to the earlier Italian movement *verismo* ("realism"), from which it originated, but it differs in that its upsurge was brought about by the intense feelings, experiences, and convictions that fascist repression, the Resistance, and the war instilled in its many gifted writers. Added impetus was given the movement by the translation of many socially conscious American and English writers during the 1930s and 1940s.

Among the outstanding Neorealist writers are Nobel Prize-winning poet Salvatore Quasimodo and the fiction writers Alberto Moravia, Ignazio Silone, Carlo Levi, Vasco Pratolini, Carlo Bernari, Cesare Pavese, Elio Vittorini, Carlo Cassola, Italo Calvino, and Curzio Malaparte (in postwar writings).

The emergence of Neorealism during the fascist years was sporadic. Alberto Moravia wrote perhaps the first representative work in *Gli indifferenti* (1929; *Time of Indifference*). Silone was internationally known for antifascist works written from Swiss exile, beginning with *Fontamara* (1930); and Vittorini wrote veiled criticism of the fascist regime in a brilliant, Hemingwayesque novel, *Conversazione in Sicilia* (1941; "Conversation in Sicily"). During the fascist years many Neorealist writers were driven into hiding (Moravia), put in prison (Cesare Pavese, Elio Vittorini), or sent into exile (Ignazio Silone, Carlo Levi); some joined the Resistance (Vittorini, Italo Calvino, Carlo Cassola); others took refuge in introspective movements such as Hermeticism (Salvatore Quasimodo) or in translating the works of others (Pavese, Vittorini).

After the war the movement exploded in full strength. Vasco Pratolini left his autobiographical work behind and published such vivid and moving accounts of the Florentine poor as *Il quartiere* (1945; "The Naked Streets") and one of the finest novels of the Neorealist movement, *Cronache di poveri amanti* (1947; *A Tale of Poor Lovers*). Malaparte, who had repudiated his earlier fascist loyalties, produced two powerful novels about the war, *Kaputt* (1944) and *La pelle* (1949; *The Skin*). Vittorini wrote openly about his Resistance experiences in *Uomini e no* (1945; *Men and Not Men*), and Levi earned international fame with his compassionate study of the plight of peasants in southern Italy (where he had been exiled) in *Cristo si è fermato a Eboli* (1945; *Christ Stopped at Eboli*). Other writers also felt the compulsion to communicate life as it then was or as it had been. Quasimodo emerged from Hermeticism and began to publish poetry about the war and social problems, beginning with *Giorno dopo giorno* (1947; "Day After Day"); Moravia resumed his writing and published many outstanding Neorealist novels. Pavese contributed two accounts of his life in a fascist prison and many introspective novels about contemporary despair. Calvino and Cassola left stirring accounts of the Resistance experience, Calvino in *Il sentiero dei nidi di ragno* (1947; *The Path to the Nest of Spiders*) and Cassola in *Il taglio del bosco* (1955; "Timber Cutting") and *La ragazza di Bube* (1960; *Bébo's Girl*). The ideas of the movement were also reflected in the Italian cinema and art of the same period as filmmakers, especially, presented documentary-like views of ordinary people involved in commonplace situations.

neōteros \nā-ˈō-ter-ˌȯs\ *plural* neōteroi \-ter-ˌȯi\ Any of a group of poets who sought to break away from the didactic-patriotic tradition of Latin poetry by consciously emulating the forms and content of Alexandrian Greek models. They were referred to as *hoi neōteroi* (Greek: "the younger men") by the Roman author and orator Cicero. The *neōteroi* deplored the excesses of alliteration and onomatopoeia and the ponderous meters that characterized the epics and didactic works of the Latin tradition of Ennius. They wrote meticulously refined, elegant, and sophisticated epyllia (brief epics), lyrics, epigrams, and elegies. They cultivated a literature of self-expression and a light poetry of entertainment and introduced into Latin literature the aesthetic attitude later known as "art for art's sake."

First arising in the 2nd century BC, the school was essentially non-Roman; it centered on the Milanese poet-teacher Publius Valerius Cato, and most of its adherents came from remote regions of northern Italy. Among them was Gaius Valerius Catullus, who wrote finely wrought love lyrics and epyllia in Latin and Greek during the Ciceronian period (70–43 BC) of the Golden Age. In the Augustan Age (43 BC to AD 18), the influence of the *neōteroi* can be discerned particularly in the pastoral idylls of Virgil and in the elegies of Sextus Propertius and Albius Tibullus and in a general refinement of works of the didactic-patriotic tradition. Two centuries later a group called the novel poets modeled themselves after the neōteroi, writing in Greek and following Greek models.

Neustadt Prize \ˈnü-ˌstat\ (*after 1976* Neustadt International Prize for Literature) Award established in 1969 as the *Books Abroad* International Prize for Literature. It was founded to recognize important achievement in fiction, drama, or poetry. The award is sponsored by the University of Oklahoma and *World Literature Today* (formerly *Books Abroad*), the literary quarterly published by the university, and is conferred every two years. It is funded by an endowment established by the Neustadt family, longtime benefactors of the university. Winners of the prize are chosen by a 12-member international jury that is selected by the editor of *World Literature Today,* in consultation with an editorial board and the president of the university. Any living writer in any language is eligible for the award as long as a representative sampling of his or her work is available in English or French translation. Winners have included Gabriel García Márquez, Elizabeth Bishop, Czesław Miłosz, and Raja Rao.

New *See* MODERN.

New Adelphi, The *See* THE ADELPHI.

New Apocalypse Literary movement in England during the 1940s that was founded by J.F. Hendry and Henry Treece as a reaction against the politically committed poetry of the 1930s. The movement produced three anthologies inspired by Neoromantic anarchism. The first, *The New Apocalypse* (1940), was edited by Hendry, while the other two—*The White Horseman* (1941) and *The Crown and the Sickle* (1944)—were edited by Hendry and Treece. Treece also wrote a collection of essays entitled *How I See Apocalypse* (1946). Other poets of the New Apocalypse were Nicholas Moore and Vernon Watkins.

Newbery Medal \ˈnü-bə-rē, -ˌber-ē\ Award given annually to the author of the most distinguished American children's book of the previous year. It was established in 1922 by Frederic G. Melcher of the R.R. Bowker Publishing Company and named for John Newbery, the 18th-century English publisher who was among the first to publish books specifically for children. The award is presented at the annual conference of the American Library Association along with the Caldecott Medal, an award to an artist for the best illustrations for a children's book. Winners of the award include Hugh Lofting, Madeleine L'Engle, and William Pène Du Bois.

New Comedy Greek drama from about 320 BC to the mid-3rd century BC that offers a mildly satiric view of contemporary Athenian society, especially in its familiar and domestic aspects. Unlike Old Comedy, which parodies public figures and events, New Comedy features fictional average citizens in domestic life. Thus, the chorus, the representative of forces larger than life, recedes in importance and becomes a small band of musicians and dancers who periodically provide light entertainment.

The plays commonly deal with the conventionalized situation of thwarted lovers and contain such stock characters as the cunning slave, the wily merchant, the boastful soldier, and the cruel father. One of the lovers is usually a foundling, the discovery of whose true birth and identity makes marriage possible in the end. Although it does not realistically depict contemporary life, New Comedy accurately reflects the disillusioned spirit and moral ambiguity of the bourgeois class of this period. Menander introduced the New Comedy in his works about 320 BC and became its most famous exponent, writing in a quiet, witty style. Although most of his plays are lost, *Dyscolus* survives, along with large parts of *Perikeiromenē, Epitrepontes,* and *Samia*. Menander's plays are mainly known through the works of the Roman dramatists Plautus and Terence, who translated and adapted them, along with other stock plots and characters of Greek New Comedy, for the Roman stage. Elements of New Comedy influenced European drama down to the 18th century. The commedia erudita, plays from printed texts popular in Italy in the 16th century, and the improvisational commedia dell'arte that flourished in Europe from the 16th to the 18th century used characters and plot conventions that originated in Greek New Comedy. They were also used by William Shakespeare and other Elizabethan and Restoration dramatists. Richard Rodgers and Lorenz Hart's *The Boys from Syracuse*

(1938) is a musical version of Shakespeare's *Comedy of Errors,* which in turn is based on Plautus' *Menaechmi* and *Amphitruo,* which are adaptations of Greek New Comedy.

New Criticism *also called* formalism. A type of literary criticism that developed in England and the United States after World War I. New Criticism focused intensively upon the language, imagery, and emotional or intellectual tensions in particular literary works in an attempt to explain their total formal aesthetic organization. New Critics insisted on the intrinsic value of a work of art and focused attention on the work alone as an independent unit of meaning; they were opposed to the critical practice of bringing historical or biographical data to bear on interpretation. To the New Critics, poetry was a special type of discourse, a means of communicating feeling and thought that could not be expressed in any other kind of language. These critics set out to define and formalize the qualities of poetic thought and language, with special emphasis on the connotative and associative values of words and on the multiple functions of figurative language—symbol, metaphor, and image—in the work.

The primary technique employed in New Criticism was analytic (or "close") reading of the text, a technique that dates to Aristotle's *Poetics*. The New Critics, however, introduced refinements into the method. Early seminal works in the tradition were those of the English critics I.A. Richards (*Principles of Literary Criticism,* 1924) and William Empson (*Seven Types of Ambiguity,* 1930), as well as John Crowe Ransom's *The New Criticism* (1941), a work that loosely organized the principles of this basically linguistic approach to literature. Other figures associated with the movement included Robert Penn Warren, Cleanth Brooks, and Allen Tate.

Newdigate Prize \'nü-di-git, 'nyü-, -ˌgāt\ Poetry prize founded in 1805 by Sir Roger Newdigate and awarded at Oxford University. The award is given annually for the best student poem of up to 300 lines on a given subject. The winner recites the poem at commencement exercises. Famous winners in the past include Matthew Arnold and John Ruskin.

New England Renaissance *See* AMERICAN RENAISSANCE.

new historicism \hi-'stȯr-i-ˌsiz-əm\ Modern school of literary criticism that treats the work of literature not so much as a transcendent document worthy of analysis, but as a representation of historical forces. The new historicist takes the social, cultural, and historical implications of the text and extends the analysis to the economic and the political. New historicism makes history itself an object of interpretation; the critic reads literary works to uncover the ideologies that determine culture and law. Foremost among the practitioners of this method are Stephen Greenblatt, Jerome McGann, Marjorie Levinson, and Marilyn Butler.

New Humanism Critical movement in the United States between 1910 and 1930, based on the literary and social theories of the English Victorian poet and critic Matthew Arnold, who sought to recapture the moral quality of past civilizations in an age of industrialization and materialism. Reacting against the scientifically oriented philosophies of literary realism and naturalism, New Humanists refused to accept deterministic views of human nature. They argued that: (1) human beings are unique among nature's creatures; (2) the essence of experience is fundamentally moral and ethical; and (3) the human will, although subject to genetic laws and shaped by the environment, is essentially free. With these points of contention, the New Humanists—Paul Elmer More, Irving Babbitt, Norman Foerster, and Robert Shafer, to name only a few—outlined an entire program and aesthetic to incorporate their beliefs. By the 1930s the New Humanists had come to be regarded as cultural elitists and advocates of social and aesthetic conservatism, and their influence became negligible.

New Journalism Journalism that features the author's subjective responses to people and events and that often includes fictional elements meant to illuminate and dramatize those responses. Hunter Thompson and Tom Wolfe are among those who have practiced New Journalism.

New Negro Movement *See* HARLEM RENAISSANCE.

New Norse *See* NYNORSK.

newspeak \ˈnü-ˌspēk, ˈnyü-\ Propagandistic language that is characterized by euphemism, circumlocution, and the inversion of customary meanings. The term was coined by George Orwell in his novel *Nineteen Eighty-four* (1949). Newspeak, "designed to diminish the range of thought," was the language preferred by Big Brother's pervasive enforcers.

New Statesman Political and literary weekly magazine published in London, probably the best known of its kind in England, and one of the world's leading journals of opinion. It was founded in 1913 by Sidney and Beatrice Webb. He was a Fabian Socialist and she his political and literary partner. The journal reflected the viewpoint of the Fabian Socialists and became an independent socialist forum for serious intellectual discussion, political commentary, and criticism. It became famous for its aggressive and often satirical analysis of British and world political scenes, and contributors are drawn from among the most distinguished writers in Britain. As a result, its political commentary, cultural articles and critical reviews of the arts, and also its "Letters to the Editor" page, are known for their elegance and wit.

New Worlds British magazine that was a leading innovative force in 1960s science fiction. Founded in 1946 and edited by E.J. Carnell for 18 years, the monthly featured stories by most noted English science-fiction writers, including "The Sentinel" by Arthur C. Clarke, the source of the film *2001: A Space Odyssey,* and avant-garde works by young writers such as Brian Aldiss and J.G. Ballard. Under the editorship of Michael Moorcock, *New Worlds* concentrated on experimental science fiction. Many of the magazine's stories offered severe social criticism and radical interpretations of history, culture, and religion. In addition to such stories, the magazine published nonfiction essays, concrete poetry, and visual collages. Works published by *New Worlds* included *Bug Jack Barron* by Norman Spinrad, sections of *Stand on Zanzibar* by John Brunner, and several of Moorcock's own stories, notably "Behold, the Man." The magazine suspended publication in 1970, although several numbers appeared in the late 1970s. A series of anthologies of original stories, most of which were edited by Moorcock, was published in the 1970s and again in the 1990s.

New Writing International book-periodical that was founded in Vienna and moved to London, where it was edited by John Lehmann. From the spring of 1936, it appeared under a variety of titles: *New Writing* (quarterly; 1936–39), *Folios of New Writing* (1940–41), *Daylight* (1941), *New Writing and Daylight* (annually or semiannually; 1942–46), and *Penguin New Writing* (monthly 1940–42; quarterly 1942–50). The general goal of the magazine was to publish working-class writers. It featured the prose and poetry of mainly young authors from Europe and the United States, though writers from New Zealand, South Africa, India, Russia, and China were also encouraged. The periodical published W.H. Auden, Christopher Isherwood, Jean-Paul Sartre, Stephen Spender, V.S. Pritchett, Saul Bellow, Gore Vidal, Roy Fuller, Laurie Lee, and Paul Bowles, among others.

New Yorker, The \nü-ˈyȯr-kər\ American weekly magazine, famous for its varied literary fare and humor. It was founded in 1925 by Harold Ross, who was its editor until his death in 1951. *The New Yorker*'s initial focus was on New York City's amusements and social and cultural life, but the magazine gradually acquired a broader scope that encompassed literature, current affairs, and other topics. *The New Yorker* became renowned for its short fiction, essays, foreign reportage, and probing biographical studies, as well as its comic drawings and its detailed reviews of cinema, books, theater, and other arts. The magazine offered a blend of reportage and commentary, short stories and poetry, reviews, and humor to a national, well-educated, upper-middle-class audience.

Contributors to the magazine included such well-known literary figures as S.J. Perelman, Robert Benchley, Ogden Nash, E.B. White, John O'Hara, John Hersey, Edmund Wilson, J.D. Salinger, John Updike, Rebecca West, and Dorothy Parker. Among its great cartoonists were Charles Addams, Helen Hokinson, George Price, James Thurber (a writer as well), and Rea Irvin, who was the magazine's first art director and the creator of Eustace Tilley, the early American dandy who is the magazine's trademark.

In 1985 *The New Yorker* was sold to the publisher Samuel I. Newhouse, Jr., this being the first time in its history that the magazine's ownership had changed hands. William Shawn was the magazine's editor from 1952 to 1987 and was succeeded by Robert Gottlieb. Tina Brown succeeded Gottlieb in 1992.

New York Intellectuals \nü-ˈyȯrk\ A group of literary critics who were active from the late 1930s through the 1970s in New York City. Characterized by their rejection of bourgeois culture, their adherence to democratic socialism, and their espousal of modernism in literature, the critics were famous for book reviews and essays published in such journals as *The Nation, Commentary,* and *Dissent*. The moniker "New York Intellectuals" was coined by Irving Howe in his 1968 essay of the same name. Some of the leading figures in the movement were Lionel Trilling, Philip Rahv, and Alfred Kazin.

Nieuwe Gids, De \də-ˈnyü-və-ˈḵits\ ("The New Guide") Dutch journal that heralded a literary revival in the northern Netherlands during the 1880s. It was founded on Oct. 1, 1885, by the poets Willem Kloos and Albert Verwey and the prose writer Frederik Willem van Eeden. Unlike the periodical *De Gids*—published from 1837—it pursued an exclusively aesthetic ideal in regard to literature. It also accepted contributions on politics, science, philosophy, and art. Among the leaders of the literary revival were the poets Herman Gorter, Pieter Cornelis Boutens, and Jan Hendrik Leopold; critic Lodewijk van Deyssel; dramatist Herman Heijermans; and the prose writer Louis Marie Anne Couperus.

Gorter's poem "Mei" ("May"), which was first published in *De Nieuwe Gids* in 1889, was regarded as the seminal work of the movement. By 1890 the editorial staff was fragmented over socialist issues. After much infighting, Kloos disbanded the editorial board and published the magazine under his own name from 1893. It declined gradually in popularity and finally ceased publication in 1943 after Kloos' death.

night piece A work of art (such as a picture, composition, or writing) dealing with night.

nihilism \ˈnī-ə-ˌliz-əm, ˈnē-, -hə-ˌliz\ [Latin *nihil* nothing] Any of various philosophical positions that deny that there are objective foundations for human value systems. In 19th-century Russia, nihilism (Russian *nigilizm*) came to be applied to a philosophy of skepticism that originated during the early years of the reign of Alexander II. Fundamentally, nihilism represented a philosophy of negation of all forms of aestheticism; it advocated utilitarianism and scientific rationalism. The social sciences and classical philosophical systems were rejected entirely. Nihilism represented a crude form of positivism and materialism and a revolt against the established social order; it negated all authority exercised by the state, the church, or the family. It based its belief on nothing but scientific truth. All evils, nihilists believed, derived from a single source—ignorance—which science alone would overcome.

In Russian literature *nigilizm* was probably first used by N.I. Nadezhdin, who applied it to Aleksandr Pushkin in an article in the *Messenger of Europe*. Nadezhdin equated nihilism with skepticism, as did V. Bervi later. Mikhail N. Katkov, a well-known conservative journalist mainly responsible for interpreting nihilism as synonymous with revolution, presented nihilism as constituting a social menace by its negation of all moral principles.

If to the conservative elements the nihilists were the curse of the time, to liberals such as N.G. Chernyshevsky they represented a mere transitory factor in the development of national thought, a stage in the struggle for individual freedom, a true spirit of the rebellious young generation. In his celebrated novel *Fathers and Sons* (1862), Ivan Turgenev popularized the term through the figure of Bazarov the nihilist. The nihilists of the 1860s and '70s eventually came to be regarded as disheveled, unruly, ragged persons who rebelled against tradition and social order. The philosophy of nihilism then began to be associated erroneously with the regicide of Alexander II and the political terror that was employed by those active in clandestine organizations against absolutism. In time, however, nihilism did degenerate into a philosophy of violence. A comparison between Turgenev's hero Bazarov and the hero of Leonid Andreyev's drama *Savva,* written during the early 20th century, reveals the deterioration of nihilist philosophy, which changed from a faith in science into a justification of terror and destruction as a means to attain set goals.

Nobel Prize for Literature \nō-'bel, 'nō-bel\ One of six prizes that are awarded annually by four institutions (three Swedish and one Norwegian) from a fund established under the will of Alfred Bernhard Nobel. The first award was given on Dec. 10, 1901, the fifth anniversary of the death of the founder, whose will specified that the awards should annually be made "to those who, during the preceding year, shall have conferred the greatest benefit on mankind" in the fields of physics, chemistry, physiology or medicine, literature, and peace. The additional award, in economic science, was set up in 1968 by the Bank of Sweden, and the first award was given in 1969. The institution that awards the prize for literature is the Swedish Academy in Stockholm.

The Nobel Foundation, established in pursuance of the provisions of the will, is the legal owner and functional administrator of the funds. The award consists of a gold medal, a diploma bearing a citation, and a sum of money, the amount depending on the income of the foundation.

The selection of the prizewinners begins in the early autumn of the year preceding the award, with the prize-awarding institution sending out invitations to nominate candidates to those qualified under the Nobel statutes to do so. The basis of selection is professional competence and international range; self-nomination automatically disqualifies a person. An individual may not be nominated posthumously, but a prize duly proposed may be so awarded, as was the case with Erik A. Karlfeldt, winner in 1931.

A prize is either given entire to one person, divided equally between at most two works, or shared jointly by two or more (in practice never more than three) persons. Prizes have been declined, and in some instances governments have forbidden their nationals to accept Nobel prizes. Those who win a prize but decline are nevertheless entered into the list of Nobel laureates with the remark "declined the prize," as was Boris Pasternak in 1958.

The general principles governing awards were laid down by Nobel in his will. In 1900 supplementary rules of interpretation and administration were agreed upon; and these rules have on the whole remained unchanged but have been somewhat modified in application. For example, the will's ambiguous words "idealistic tendency," as qualification for the prize for literature, were in the beginning interpreted strictly but have gradually been interpreted more broadly.

noble savage In literature, an idealized concept of an uncivilized individual who symbolizes the innate goodness of one not exposed to the corrupting influences of civilization.

The glorification of the noble savage is a dominant theme in the Romantic writings of the 18th and 19th centuries, especially in the works of Jean-Jacques Rousseau. For example, *Émile,* 4 vol. (1762), is a long treatise on the corrupting influence of traditional education; the autobiographical *Confessions* (1782–89) reaffirms the basic tenet of the innate goodness of humans; and *Rêveries* (1782) contains descriptions of nature and the natural human response to it. The concept of the noble savage, however, can be traced to ancient Greece, where Homer, Pliny, and Xenophon idealized the Arcadians and other primitive groups, both real and imagined. Later Roman writers such as Horace, Virgil, and Ovid gave comparable treatment to the Scythians. From the 15th to the 19th centuries, the noble savage figured prominently in popular travel accounts and appeared occasionally in English plays such as John Dryden's *The Conquest of Granada* (1672), in which the term *noble savage* was first used, and in *Oroonoko* (1695) by Thomas Southerne, based on Aphra Behn's novel of the same title about a dignified African prince enslaved in the British colony of Surinam.

François Chateaubriand sentimentalized the North American Indian in *Atala* (1801), *René* (1805), and *Les Natchez* (1826), as did James Fenimore Cooper in the Leather-Stocking Tales (1823–41), which feature the noble chief Chingachgook and his son Uncas. The three harpooners of the ship *Pequod* in Herman Melville's *Moby-Dick* (1851), Queequeg, Daggoo, and Tashtego, are other examples of the noble savage, as is the character of John the Savage in Aldous Huxley's *Brave New World* (1932).

node \'nōd\ [Latin *nodus,* literally, knot] An entangling complication (such as in drama); a predicament.

Nō drama or **Noh drama** \'nō\ Classic Japanese dance-drama having a heroic theme, a chorus, and highly stylized action, costuming, and scenery. It is one of the oldest extant theatrical forms in the world. Nō, meaning "talent" or "skill," is unlike Western narrative drama in that its performers are simply storytellers who use their visual appearances and their movements to suggest the essence of their tale rather than to enact it. The total effect of a Nō drama is less that of a present action than of a simile or metaphor made visual.

Nō developed from ancient forms of dance-drama and from various types of festival drama at shrines and temples that had emerged by the 12th or 13th century. It became a distinctive form in the 14th century and was continually refined up to the years of the Tokugawa period (1603–1867). Nō gradually became a ceremonial drama performed on auspicious occasions by professional actors for the warrior class as, in a sense, a prayer for peace, longevity, and the prosperity of the social elite. The collapse of the feudal order in 1868 threatened the existence of Nō, but after World War II the form was revived.

The five types of Nō plays are the *kami* ("god") play, which involves a sacred story of a Shintō shrine; the *shura mono* ("fighting play"), which centers on warriors; the *katsura mono* ("wig play"), which has a female protagonist; a fourth type, varied in content, that includes the *gendai mono* ("present-day play")—in which the story is contemporary and "realistic" rather than legendary and supernatural—and the *kyōjo mono* ("madwoman play")—in which the protagonist becomes insane through the loss of a lover or child; and the fifth type, the *kiri,* or *kichiku* ("final," or "demon"), play, in which devils, strange beasts, and supernatural beings are featured. A standard Nō program consists of three plays selected from the five types so as to achieve both an artistic unity and the desired mood. KYŌGEN, humorous sketches, are performed as interludes between plays.

About 2,000 Nō texts survive in full, of which about 230 remain in the modern repertoire. Zeami (1363/64–1443) and his father, Kan'ami (1333–84), wrote many of the most beautiful and exemplary of Nō texts, including Matsukaze ("Wind in the Pines"), which was written by Kan'ami and adapted by Zeami. Nō has been transmitted from generation to generation remaining fairly close to the earlier forms, in part because of the preservation of texts containing detailed descriptions of how they were to be performed. There have been gradual changes made throughout the years; the 20th century saw the production of Nō plays that had new content but adhered to traditional conventions in production and old plays with new twists.

noir \'nwär\ [short for *film noir,* French, literally, black film] Crime fiction featuring hard-boiled cynical characters and bleak sleazy settings.

nom de plume \ˌnäm-də-'plüm, *French* nōⁿd-'plue̅m\ *plural* noms de plume *same or* ˌnämz\ *or* nom de plumes *same or* 'plümz\ [French, pen name; probably coined in English] A pseudonym or pen name assumed by a writer, such as George Orwell for Eric Blair and Mark Twain for Samuel Langhorne Clemens.

nominy \'näm-i-nē\ [perhaps from Latin *in nomine* in the name (in formulas such as *in nomine Patris* in the name of the Father, etc.)] In northern England, a formulaic or conventional piece of folk verse, such as counting-out rhymes; the word can also mean rigmarole, or rambling, unconnected speech.

nonce word \'näns\ A word coined and used apparently to suit one particular occasion. Nonce words are sometimes used independently by different writers and speakers, but they are not adopted into general use. James Joyce employed many such words in *Finnegans Wake,* as did Anthony Burgess in *A Clockwork Orange*. *Compare* NEOLOGISM.

nonfiction \ˌnän-'fik-shən\ Literary works that are based mainly on fact rather than on the imagination, although they may contain fictional elements. Examples are essays and biographies.

nonfiction novel A book-length narrative of actual people and actual events written in the style of a novel. The American writer Truman Capote claimed to have invented the genre with his book *In Cold Blood* (1966). A true story of the brutal murder of a Kansas farm family, the book was based on six years of exacting research and interviews with the two captured murderers and neighbors and friends of the victims. The story is told from the points of view of different "characters," and the author attempts not to insert his own comments or to distort facts. Critics pointed out earlier precedents for this type of journalistic novel, such as John Hersey's *Hiroshima* (1946), an account of the World War II bombing of the Japanese city told through the histories of six survivors. Norman Mailer's *The Executioner's Song* (1979) is a later example of the genre.

nonhero *See* ANTIHERO.

nonsense verse Humorous or whimsical verse that features absurd characters and actions and often contains evocative but meaningless nonce words. Nonsense verse differs from other comic verse in its resistance to any rational or allegorical interpretation. Though it often makes use of coined, meaningless words, it is unlike the ritualistic gibberish of children's counting-out rhymes in that it makes such words sound purposeful. There are various specific forms of nonsense verse, including AMPHIGORY, double dactyl, and LIMERICK.

Skilled literary nonsense verse is rare; most of it has been written for children and is modern, dating from the beginning of the 19th century. The cardinal date could be considered 1846, when *The Book of Nonsense* was published. The work is a collection of limericks composed and illustrated by the artist Edward Lear, who first created them in the 1830s for the children of the Earl of Derby.

Lear also wrote other nonsense verses, including "The Owl and the Pussy-Cat," which begins:

> The Owl and the Pussy-cat went to sea
>   In a beautiful pea-green boat,
> They took some honey and plenty of money,
>   Wrapped up in a five-pound note.

Lear's book was followed by the inspired fantasy of Lewis Carroll, whose *Alice's Adventures in Wonderland* (1865) and *Through the Looking-Glass* (1871) both contain brilliant nonsense rhymes. "Jabberwocky," from *Through the Looking-Glass,* may be the best-known example of nonsense verse.

Hilaire Belloc's volume *The Bad Child's Book of Beasts* (1896) holds an honored place among the classics of English nonsense verse, while, in the United States, Laura E. Richards, a prolific writer of children's books, published verses in *Tirra Lirra* (1932) that have been compared to those of Lear.

North American Review, The American magazine first published in 1815 that became one of the country's leading literary journals of the 19th and 20th centuries. Founded in Boston as *The North American Review and Miscellaneous Journal* (a title it kept until mid-1821), the magazine followed the model of established English and Scottish literary journals. It was established as a regional magazine reflecting the intellectual ideas and tastes of Boston and New

England. The work of J.W. von Goethe and Friedrich von Schiller first became known to American readers in its pages. It later, under the editorship of Allen Thorndike Rice, moved to New York City and became a national periodical, providing an impartial forum in which current public affairs could be discussed. By 1891 it had attained a circulation of 76,000. Noted for its outstanding writing on social and political issues, the magazine featured the work of numerous distinguished authors, including Henry George, David Dudley Field, Wendell Phillips, Walt Whitman, William Gladstone, Oliver Wendell Holmes, and H.G. Wells. In 1935 the magazine was sold to Joseph Hilton Smyth, under whose ignominious editorship it ceased publication in 1940. It was resurrected in 1964.

Northeastern school *Portuguese* Colégio Nordestino. Group of 20th-century Brazilian regional writers whose fiction dealt primarily with the culture and social problems of Brazil's hinterland northeast. Stimulated by the revival of modernist-inspired nationalism of the 1920s, the regionalists examined the diverse ethnic and racial cultures of Brazil.

The remarkably gifted and dedicated group of prose writers of the Northeastern school included Gilberto Freyre, leader of the movement and author of the monumental *Casa-grande e senzala* (1933; *The Masters and the Slaves*); José Lins do Rego, who depicted the clash of the old and new ways of life in his Sugar Cane cycle of novels (1932–36); and Jorge Amado, who gave Brazil some of its best proletarian literature in such novels as *Cacau* (1933; "Cocoa Bean"), *Jubiabá* (1935), and *Terras do sem fim* (1942; *The Violent Land*). Also associated with the school were Graciliano Ramos, who explored the inner struggle of the individual, and Rachel de Queiroz, who wrote of the bandits, religious mystics, and forgotten peoples of the hinterland.

nouveau roman \nü-vō-rō-ˈmä^n\ ("new novel") In French literature, a form of antinovel developed in the mid-1950s in the work of Alain Robbe-Grillet, Claude Simon, Nathalie Sarraute, Michel Butor, and Marguerite Duras. What was new about these novelists, apart from the label applied to them, was their systematic rejection of the traditional framework of fiction—chronology, plot, character—and of the omniscient author. In place of these reassuring conventions, they offer texts that demand more of the reader, who is presented with compressed, repetitive, or only partially explained events from which to derive a meaning that will not, in any case, be definitive. In Robbe-Grillet's *La Jalousie* (1957; *Jealousy*), for example, the narrator's suspicions of his wife's infidelity are never confirmed or denied, but their obsessive quality is conveyed by the replacement of a chronological narrative with the insistent repetition of details or events. In *Le Libéra* (1968) by Robert Pinget there is no single narrator, while in the later novels of Jean Cayrol the narrative emanates from the sea, a field, or the desert.

The *nouveau roman* was open to influence from works being written abroad (notably the work of William Faulkner) and from the cinema (Robbe-Grillet and Duras contributed to the *nouvelle vague,* or New Wave, style of filmmaking). By the time Robbe-Grillet's *Pour un nouveau roman* (*Toward a New Novel*) appeared in 1963, it was clear that the term covered a variety of approaches. In the same year, the Prix Renaudot was awarded to Jean-Marie Le Clézio for *Le Procès-verbal* (*The Interrogation*), a novel welcomed partly because it was both "modern" and accessible. It was also heralded (prematurely) as offering an escape from the *nouveau roman*'s overintellectuality. *See also* ANTINOVEL; NOVEL.

Nouvelle Revue française, La \lä-nü-ˌvel-rā-ˌvue̅-fräⁿ-ˈsez\ ("The New French Review"), *abbreviated* NRF. Leading French review of literature and the other arts. It was founded in February 1909 (after a false start in November 1908) by a group that included André Gide, Jacques Copeau, and Jean Schlumberger. The *NRF*'s founders wished to publish criticism that emphasized aesthetic issues and to remain independent of any political party or intellectual school. During the period between the two world wars, under the editors Jacques Rivière (1919–25) and Jean Paulhan (1925–40), the *NRF* became France's leading literary journal, publishing works by many notable writers. After the German occupation of France in 1940, Pierre Drieu la Rochelle became editor, and the *NRF* became profascist; it ceased publication in 1943. The review was revived in 1953 as *La Nouvelle Nouvelle Revue française,* under the direction of Paulhan and Michel Arland; it resumed its present name in 1959. The publishing house Editions Gallimard was established in 1911 as an offshoot of the *NRF*.

novel \ˈnäv-əl\ [Italian *novella* novella] A fictional prose narrative of considerable length and a certain complexity that deals imaginatively with human experience through a connected sequence of events involving a group of persons in a specific setting. The term also refers to the literary type constituted by such narratives. Within its broad framework, the genre of the novel has encompassed an extensive range of types and styles, including picaresque, epistolary, gothic, romantic, realist, and historical.

Although forerunners of the modern genre are to be found in a number of places, including classical Rome, 10th- and 11th-century Japan, and Elizabethan England, the European novel is usually said to have begun with the *Don Quixote* of Miguel de Cervantes (part I, 1605). In its juxtaposition of impossible idealism and earthy practicality in the figures of the knight and his squire, this work suggests what was to become one of the central concerns of the Western novel, just as its playful exploitation of the authorial persona anticipates many of the technical questions raised by later novelists.

Although some interesting works were produced in 17th-century France, it was in England that the genre first took permanent root. Daniel Defoe, Samuel Richardson, and Henry Fielding were all writing works in the first half of the 18th century that did much to establish the novel as the most popular literary form in England. Their popularity soon became a general phenomenon, leading in the 19th century to an extraordinary surge of fiction writing, particularly in Britain, France, Russia, and the United States.

A partial explanation of the novel's popularity is to be found in the scope it gave writers to explore areas of human experience that had previously lain outside the province of literature. For the first time, the minutiae of daily life became a fit subject for the writer's attention. The heroes and heroines of this new genre were as likely to be servants as courtiers. Their lives might be pedestrian, their destinies mundane. Inevitably, this shift in emphasis was helped or hindered by the social and historical context in any given country.

In essence the Western novel has remained popular because it can provide a more faithful image of everyday reality than can be achieved by any other literary form. Even the extravagant fantasies of the gothic novel or the modern science-fiction novel depend for their impact on the detailed rendering of surface reality. The history of the novel is in part a history of the changes in conventions established to achieve this verisimilitude. Perhaps because of the novel's realistic bias, its greatest period is usually held to be the mid- to late 19th century, a time when improved literacy rates had increased the size of the potential audience and the modern mass media had not yet arrived to diminish it. During this period and just before, Charles Dickens, William Makepeace Thackeray, and George Eliot were writing in England; Honoré de Balzac, Gustave Flaubert, and Émile Zola in France; Ivan Turgenev, Leo Tolstoy, and Fyodor Dostoyevsky in Russia; and Nathaniel Hawthorne and Herman Melville in the United States.

With the coming of the 20th century the novel began to change somewhat in character. The old certainty that experience could be adequately represented by the language and structures of the conventional novel was increasingly called into question. Writers such as James Joyce, Virginia Woolf, and Dorothy Richardson began to examine the ways in which reality eluded the grasp of literature. In trying to capture the complex and fragmentary quality of experience, some of these writers stretched the limits of the conventional novel to a point at which it became more and more remote from the expectations—and sometimes the comprehension or interest—of the average reader, a process that perhaps culminated in the mid-20th century in the so-called antinovel, or *nouveau roman.* These modernist experiments sometimes produced works of outstanding interest, but they also tended to widen the gap between the popular and the "literary" novel.

See also ANTINOVEL; BILDUNGSROMAN; EPISTOLARY NOVEL; GOTHIC NOVEL; HISTORICAL NOVEL; NOVEL OF MANNERS; NOUVEAU ROMAN; PICARESQUE NOVEL; PROLETARIAN NOVEL; PSYCHOLOGICAL NOVEL; ROMAN À CLEF; SENTIMENTAL NOVEL.

novelese \ˌnäv-ə-ˈlēz, -ˈlēs\ A writing style characteristic of bad novels; especially, a style marked by the use of trite expressions.

novelette \ˌnäv-ə-ˈlet\ **1.** A work of fiction intermediate in length or complexity between a short story and a novel. **2.** *British* A light, usually sentimental, romantic novel.

novelization \ˌnäv-ə-lə-ˈzā-shən, -ˌlī-\ The act or process of turning a story into the form of a novel, especially when the story was originally in another form such as a play.

novella \nō-ˈvel-ə\ *plural* novellas *or* novelle \-ˈvel-ā, -ē\ [Italian, from feminine of *novello* new] **1.** *plural* novelle. A story with a compact and pointed plot, often realistic and satiric in tone. Originating in Italy during the European Middle Ages, the novella was based on local events, humorous, political, or amorous in nature; the individual tales often were gathered into collections along with anecdotes, legends, and romantic tales. Writers such as Giovanni Boccaccio, Franco Sacchetti, and Matteo Bandello later developed the novella into a psychologically subtle and highly structured short tale, often using a FRAME STORY to unify the tales around a common theme.

The novella is an enlarged anecdote like those found in Boccaccio's *Decameron,* the 14th-century Italian classic. Geoffrey Chaucer introduced the novella to England with *The Canterbury Tales.* During the Elizabethan period, William Shakespeare and other playwrights extracted dramatic plots from the Italian novella. The realistic content and form of these tales influenced the development of the English novel in the 18th century and the short story in the 19th century.

2. *plural usually* novellas. A work of fiction intermediate in length and complexity between a short story and a novel. Leo Tolstoy's *Smert Ivana Ilicha* (*The Death of Ivan Ilich*), Fyodor Dostoyevsky's *Zapiski iz podpolya* (*Notes from the Underground*), Joseph Conrad's *Heart of Darkness,* and Henry James' "The Aspern Papers" are examples of novellas.

Novelle \nō-ˈvel-ə\ *plural* Novellen \-ən\ [German, from Italian *novella* novella] Genre of German short narrative that flourished in the 18th, 19th, and early 20th centuries in the works of writers such as Heinrich von Kleist, Gerhart Hauptmann, J.W. von Goethe, Thomas Mann, and Franz Kafka. *Novellen* are often encompassed within a FRAME STORY based on a striking news item (plague, war, or flood), either real or imaginary. The individual tales are related by various reporter-narrators as a diversion from the present misfortune. Characterized by brevity, self-contained plots that end on a note of irony, a literate and facile style, restraint of emotion, and objective rather than subjective presentation, these tales were a major stimulant to the development of the modern short story in Germany. The *Novelle* also survived as a unique form, although unity of mood and style often replaced the traditional unity of action, and the importance of the frame was diminished as was the necessity for maintaining absolute objectivity .

novel of manners Work of fiction that re-creates a social world, conveying with finely detailed observation the customs, values, and mores of a highly developed and complex society. The conventions of the society—codified behavior, acceptable forms of speech, and so on—dominate the story, and characters are differentiated by the degree to which they measure up to or fall below the uniform standard, or ideal, of behavior. The range of a novel of manners may be limited, as in the works of Jane Austen, which deal with the domestic affairs of English country gentry families of the early 19th century and ignore elemental human passions and larger social and political determinations, or sweeping, as in the novels of Honoré de Balzac, which mirror the 19th century in all its complexity in stories dealing with Parisian life, provincial life, private life, public life, and military life. Notable writers of the novel of manners from the end of the 19th century into the 20th include Henry James, Evelyn Waugh, Edith Wharton, H.H. Munro ("Saki"), and John Marquand. Waugh's *Handful of Dust* (1934) depends upon the exact notation of the manners of a closed society, and personal tragedies are a mere temporary disturbance of collective order. Even Waugh's trilogy *Sword of Honour* is as much concerned with the minutiae of surface behavior in an army, a very closed society, as with the causes for which that army fights. Munro's *The Unbearable Bassington* (1912), an exquisite novel of manners, says more of the nature of Edwardian society than many a more earnest work.

Novy Mir \ˈnȯ-vē-ˈmʸēr\ ("New World") Literary journal, a highly influential monthly published in Moscow. Founded in 1925, it was an official organ of the writers' union of the U.S.S.R. until the breakup of the Soviet Union. Its pages carried the work of many of the Soviet Union's leading writers, and under the liberal editorship of Aleksandr Tvardovsky (1958–70), *Novy Mir* was the first to publish Aleksandr Solzhenitsyn's novel *One Day In The Life of Ivan Denisovich* (1962). Censorship of the magazine in the 1970s and '80s contributed to the development of a large underground press in the Soviet Union. *Novy Mir* still features literary criticism and commentary concerning the problems of contemporary Russian literature and occasional analysis of domestic and international political issues and it continues to publish new fiction and essays. *See also* SAMIZDAT.

N-Town plays \ˈen-ˌtau̇n\ An English cycle of 42 scriptural plays, or mystery plays, dating from the second half of the 15th century and so called because an opening proclamation refers to performance "in N. town." Since evidence suggests that the cycle was not peculiar to one city or community but traveled from town to town, the abbreviation "N." would indicate that the appropriate name of the town at which the cycle was being presented would have been inserted by the speaker.

The cycle is preserved in the Hegge Manuscript, named for its 17th-century owner, Sir Robert Hegge, and it is therefore sometimes referred to as the Hegge cycle. On the flyleaf of the Hegge Manuscript is written "Ludus Conventriae" ("Play of Coventry") and for nearly two centuries it was believed that the plays represented the Coventry cycle, but that supposition has since proved false. In the 19th century individual plays from Coventry were discovered and found to be totally different from equivalent plays in the N-Town cycle. Some scholars have attempted to show, however, that the N-Town cycle is closely related to the (lost) Coventry cycle, which was performed at Lincoln.

The cycle begins with the creation of the angels and the Fall of Lucifer and ends with the Assumption of the Virgin and the Last Judgment. Among the plays with no equivalent in other cycles are one on the death of Cain and five whose central figure is that of the Virgin, with whom the cycle is generally much preoccupied. Typically, the N-Town plays are grave and dignified; the comic relief distinguishing other surviving cycles (from Chester, York, Wakefield) is markedly absent. A basic difference between the N-Town plays and those of the other cycles is that this cycle, because it was a traveling one, was apparently presented by professional actors. It did not use pageant wagons, whereby plays were presented as a procession, but was given in a single open space, with "mansions" (indicating general scenes) set up about a single acting area. The performances may have taken place over two successive days. *See also* MYSTERY PLAY.

number \ˈnəm-bər\ **1.** In poetry, metrical structure, or meter. **2.** A particular musical, theatrical, or literary selection or production. **3.** A particular issue of a periodical. **4.** Verses or poetry in general, as in Alexander Pope's statement that he "lisp'd in numbers" to indicate that he began writing poetry at an early age. The term has become almost obsolete, but it was used fairly often in older poetry, for example, in the following lines from Edmund Spenser's "The Ruines of Time":

> For deeds do die, however nobly done,
> And thoughts of men do as themselves decay,
> But wise words taught in numbers for to run,
> Recorded by the Muses, live for ay.

nursery rhyme Verse customarily told or sung to small children. The oral tradition of nursery rhymes is ancient, but new verses have steadily entered the stream. A French poem numbering the days of the month, similar to "Thirty days hath September," was recorded in the 13th century, but such latecomers as "Twinkle, Twinkle, Little Star" (1806) by Ann and Jane Taylor and "Mary Had a Little Lamb" (1830) by Sarah Josepha Hale seem to be just as firmly established in the repertoire. The largest number of nursery rhymes date from the 16th, 17th, and, most frequently, the 18th centuries.

Some of the oldest rhymes are probably those accompanying babies' games, such as "Handy, dandy, prickly, pandy, which hand will you have?" (recorded 1598) and its German equivalent, "Windle, wandle, in welchem Handle, oben oder unt?" The existence of numerous European parallels for "Ladybird, ladybird (or, in the United States, "Ladybug, ladybug"), fly away home" and for the singing game "London Bridge is falling down" and for the riddle-rhyme "Humpty-Dumpty" suggests the possibility that these rhymes come down from very ancient sources, since direct translation is unlikely.

Such relics of the past are exceptional. Apparently, most were originally composed for adult entertainment. Many were popular ballads and songs. "The frog who would a-wooing go" first appeared in 1580 as *A Moste Strange weddinge of the ffrogge and the mowse*. "Oh where, oh where, ish mine little dog gone?" was a popular song written in 1864 by the Philadelphia composer Septimus Winner.

Although many ingenious theories have been advanced attributing hidden significance, especially political allusions, to nursery rhymes, there is no reason to suppose they are any more arcane than the popular songs of the day. Some were inspired by personalities of the time, and occasionally these can be identified. In Somerset County, England, "Little Jack Horner" (recorded 1725) is associated with a Thomas Horner of Mells who did well for himself during the dissolution of the monasteries.

The earliest known published collection of nursery rhymes was *Tommy Thumb's (Pretty) Song Book,* 2 vols. (London, 1744). It included "Little Tom Tucker," "Sing a Song of Sixpence," and "Who Killed Cock Robin?" The most influential collection was *Mother Goose's Melody; or, Sonnets for the Cradle,* published by the firm of John Newbery in 1781. Among its 51 rhymes were "Jack and Jill," "Ding Dong Bell," and "Hush-a-bye baby on the tree top." An edition was reprinted in the United States in 1785 by Isaiah Thomas. Its popularity is attested by the fact that these verses are still commonly called "Mother Goose rhymes" in the United States. *See also* ALPHABET RHYME.

Nynorsk \ˈnue-ˌnöshk, *Angl* nü-ˈnörsk, nyü-\, *also called* New Norse *or* Landsmål \ˈläns-ˌmöl\ A literary form of Norwegian based on the spoken dialects of Norway. It dates from a grammar and dictionary produced by Ivar Aasen about 1850 and was designed as a national language distinct from that of Denmark. *Nynorsk* literally means "new Norwegian" and *Landsmål* means "country language." *Compare* BOKMÅL.

Nyugat \ˈnyü-göt\ ("The West") Hungarian literary periodical founded in 1908 to provide a forum for serious young writers. The magazine, which published its last issue in 1941, also helped to modernize Hungarian literature by exposing its readers to European literature and culture. Endre Ady was the spiritual leader of the group of writers associated with *Nyugat.* Other members of the *Nyugat* school included the poets Mihály Babits, an outstanding intellectual and humanist; Dezső Kosztolányi, the best Hungarian Impressionistic poet; Árpád Tóth, an original, melancholy lyric poet; and Gyula Juhász, an Impressionist with deep roots in Hungarian tradition. Of the prose writers of the Nyugat school, the novelist Zsigmond Móricz was the outstanding figure. In his realistic stories and novels, he drew effective characterizations economically and treated a multitude of social themes. Frigyes Karinthy, who wrote effective short stories with a strong satirical and grotesque element, and Margit Kaffka, the first major woman writer in Hungary, were also associated with the magazine.

O

. . . an author whose oeuvre already savors of stringent selection and encyclopedic compression . . .
—John Updike

objective correlative Literary theory first set forth by T.S. Eliot in the essay "Hamlet and His Problems" and published in *The Sacred Wood* (1920). According to the theory,

> The only way of expressing emotion in the form of art is by finding an "objective correlative"; in other words, a set of objects, a situation, a chain of events which shall be the formula of that *particular* emotion; such that when the external facts, which must terminate in sensory experience, are given, the emotion is immediately evoked.

The term was originally used by the painter Washington Allston in his lectures on art to suggest the relation between the mind and the external world. This notion was enlarged upon by George Santayana in *Interpretations of Poetry and Religion.* Santayana suggested that correlative objects could not only express a poet's feeling but also evoke it. More recent critics find that Eliot's idea was influenced, as was much of Eliot's work, by the poetics of Ezra Pound and that the theory dates at least to the criticism of Edgar Allan Poe.

objectivism \əb-ˈjek-tə-ˌviz-əm\ The theory or practice of objective art or literature. The term was used by the poet William Carlos Williams in the 1930s to describe a movement in which emphasis was placed on viewing poems as objects that could be considered and analyzed in terms of mechanical features. According to Williams this meant examining the structural aspects of the poem and considering how it was constructed. Other poets involved in the short-lived movement were Louis Zukofsky, George Oppen, and Charles Reznikoff.

oblique rhyme *See* HALF RHYME.

obscurantism \əb-ˈskyu̇r-ən-ˌtiz-əm, ˌäb-skyu̇-ˈran-\ or **obscuranticism** \ˌäb-skyu̇-ˈran-tə-ˌsiz-əm\ [French *obscurantisme,* a derivative of *obscurant* one practicing obscurantism, from Latin *obscurant-, obscurans,* present participle of *obscurare* to obscure] A style (as in literature or art) characterized by deliberate vagueness or abstruseness. In literature this involves the use of difficult allusions, archaic and foreign words, and unfamiliar imagery.

occasional verse Poetry written to commemorate a specific occasion or event. This can include poetry written by a poet laureate or other writer on an official occasion, such as the poem that Maya Angelou was commissioned to write and deliver for the inauguration of United States president Bill Clinton in 1993, as well as more personal works, such as Edmund Spenser's *Epithalamion,* which he wrote to celebrate his marriage.

occupatio [New Latin, from Latin, preoccupation, prior engagement of a person's interest] *See* PARALIPSIS.

octameter \äk-ˈtam-ə-tər\ A line of verse consisting of eight metrical feet.

octastich \ˈäk-tə-ˌstik\ or **octastichon** \äk-ˈtas-tə-ˌkän\ *plural* octastichs *also* octasticha \äk-ˈtas-tə-kə\ A verse unit of eight lines. *See also* HUITAIN; OCTAVE.

octastrophic \ˌäk-tə-ˈsträf-ik\ Having eight strophes, or stanzas.

octave \ˈäk-tiv, -ˌtāv\ **1.** A stanza of eight lines, called OTTAVA RIMA. **2.** The first two quatrains or first eight lines of an Italian sonnet—also called *octet. Compare* SESTET.

octet \äk-ˈtet\ A stanza or group of eight verse lines; specifically, the first two quatrains or eight lines of an Italian sonnet.

octonarius \ˌäk-tə-ˈnar-ē-əs\ *plural* octonarii \-ēˌī\ Latin, from *octonarius* (adjective) containing eight] In early Roman drama (especially comedy), an eight-foot verse (such as a line of four iambic or trochaic metra), in which in certain situations both short elements of the metron can be lengthened and long syllables and anceps (long or short, scanned ⏓) syllables are commonly resolved (*See* RESOLUTION). The scheme of an iambic metron thus is ⏓/⏑⏑ ⏑̄⏑̄ ⏓/⏑⏑ ⏑⏑, the scheme of a trochaic metron ⏑⏑ ⏓/⏑⏑ ⏑⏑ ⏓/⏑⏑. Both identification and scansion are further complicated by the variety of metra possible, the frequency of elision, and unusual quantities produced by the law of *brevis brevians* (in which a short syllable shortens a following long syllable that is preceded or followed by an accented syllable).

octonary \ˈäk-tə-ˌner-ē\ In poetry, a stanza or group of eight verses; especially, one of the stanzas of the 119th Psalm.

octosyllable \ˈäk-tə-ˌsil-ə-bəl\ A word or line of eight syllables.

ode \ˈōd\ [Greek (Attic) *ōidḗ,* a contraction of Greek *aoidḗ,* a derivative of *aeídein* to sing] A ceremonious lyric poem on an occasion of public or private dignity in which personal emotion and general meditation are united. The form is usually marked by particular exaltation of feeling and style and by varying length of line and complexity of stanza forms.

The Greek word *ōidē* alluded to a choric song, usually accompanied by a dance. Alcman (7th century BC) originated the strophic arrangement of the ode, which is a rhythmic system composed of two or more lines repeated as a unit. Stesichorus (7th–6th century BC) invented the triadic, or three-part, structure (strophic lines followed by antistrophic lines in the same meter, concluding with a summary line, called an epode, in a different meter) that characterizes the odes of Pindar and Bacchylides. Choral odes were also an integral part of the Greek drama. In Latin the word was not used until about the time of Horace, in the 1st century BC. His *carmina* ("songs"), written in stanzas of two or four lines of polished Greek meters, are now universally called odes, although the implication that they were to be sung to the accompaniment of a lyre is probably only a literary convention. Both Pindaric and Horatian ode forms were revived during the European Renaissance and continued to influence Western lyric poetry into the 20th century. The first version of Allen Tate's widely acclaimed "Ode to the Confederate Dead," for example, was published in 1926.

In pre-Islāmic Arabic poetry, the ode flourished in the form of the qasida. Two great collections of these date from the 8th and 9th centuries. The qasida was also used in Persian poetry for panegyric and elegies in the 10th century, gradually being replaced by the shorter ghazel for bacchic odes and love poetry. In the hands of Indian poets from the 14th century onward, Persian forms became increasingly obscure and artificial. *See also* HORATIAN ODE; IRREGULAR ODE; PINDARIC ODE; QASIDA.

oeuvre \'œv-rə, 'ərv- *French* 'œvr *with* r *as a uvular trill*\ *plural* oeuvres *same or* -rəz\ [French, literally, work] A substantial body of work constituting the lifework of a writer, an artist, or a composer.

Off-Broadway \'ȯf-'brȯd-ˌwā, 'äf-\ In the theater of the United States, small professional productions that have served for years as New York City's alternative to the commercially oriented theaters of Broadway. Off-Broadway plays, usually produced on low budgets in small theaters, have tended to be freer in style and more imaginative than those on Broadway, where high production costs often oblige producers to rely on commercially safe attractions to the neglect of the more serious or experimental drama. The designations Broadway and Off-Broadway refer not so much to the location of the theater as to its size and the scale of production.

Off-Broadway theaters enjoyed a surge of growth in quality and importance after 1952, with the success of the director José Quintero's productions at the Circle in the Square Theatre in Greenwich Village. In two decades of remarkable vitality, Off-Broadway introduced many important theatrical talents, such as the director Joseph Papp, whose later productions included free performances of William Shakespeare in Central Park and who formed the Public Theatre, a multitheater complex dedicated to experimental works. The works of such prizewinning American playwrights as Edward Albee, Charles Gordone, Paul Zindel, Sam Shepard, Lanford Wilson, and John Guare were first produced Off-Broadway, along with the unconventional works of such avant-garde dramatists as Eugène Ionesco, Ugo Betti, Jean Genet, Samuel Beckett, and Harold Pinter, and revivals of Bertolt Brecht and Eugene O'Neill.

Like those on Broadway, Off-Broadway theaters eventually began to suffer from soaring costs, which stimulated the emergence of still less expensive and more daring productions, quickly labeled Off-Off-Broadway. Among the most successful of these groups were The Negro Ensemble Company, La Mama Experimental Theatre Company, the Open Theatre, Manhattan Theatre Club, Ensemble Studio Theatre, and Roundabout.

Okyeame \ˌō̆k-yā-ˈä-mā\ Ghanaian literary magazine published irregularly by the University of Ghana from 1961 to 1972. *Okyeame* (which means "spokesman" or "linguist") was published in English and edited by Efua Sutherland, a Ghanaian writer. Each issue centered on poetry, fiction, or drama and included a writers' forum with essays on African art.

Old \ˈōld\ Belonging to an early period in the development of a language or literature.

Old Comedy Initial phase of ancient Greek comedy (*c.* 5th century BC), known through the works of Aristophanes. Old Comedy plays are characterized by an exuberant and high-spirited satire of public persons and affairs. Composed of song, dance, personal invective, and buffoonery, the plays consist of loosely related episodes containing outspoken political criticism and comment on literary and philosophical topics. They were first performed in Athens for the religious festival of Dionysus. The plays gradually took on a six-part structure: a prologos, in which the basic fantasy is explained and developed; the parodos, entry of the chorus; the contest, or agon, a ritualized debate between two parties—either an actor and the chorus or two actors, each supported by half of the chorus; the parabasis, or "coming forward," in which the chorus addresses the audience on the topics of the day and hurls scurrilous criticism at prominent citizens; a series of farcical scenes; and a final banquet or wedding. Members of the chorus often were dressed as animals, while the characters wore street dress and masks with grotesque features.

Old Comedy sometimes is called Aristophanic comedy, for its most famous exponent; 11 of his plays survive intact. They include *Clouds* (423 BC), a satire on the misuse of philosophical argument directed chiefly against Socrates, and *Frogs* (405 BC), a satire on Greek drama directed chiefly against Euripides. The dramatists Cratinus, Phrynichus, and Eupolis also wrote plays of this type.

Old Vic \ˈvik\ London theater company, specializing in productions of William Shakespeare, that eventually became the nucleus of the National Theatre. The company's theater building opened in 1818 as the Royal Coburg and produced mostly popular melodramas. In 1833 it was redecorated and renamed the Royal Victoria and became popularly known as the Old Vic. In 1914, under the management of Lilian Baylis, the Old Vic initiated a regular Shakespeare season. By 1918 it was established as the only permanent Shakespearean theater in London, and by 1923 all of Shakespeare's plays had been performed. The reputation of the Old Vic grew considerably during the 1920s and '30s under directors such as Andrew Leigh, Harcourt Williams, and Tyrone Guthrie. Beginning in the

1940s, under the combined direction of Laurence Olivier, Ralph Richardson, and John Burrell, the Old Vic company presented memorable productions of Shakespeare's plays and other classics, including *Cyrano de Bergerac, Oedipus Rex, Love for Love,* and *Peer Gynt.* In 1946 the Old Vic School and the Young Vic, a company formed to perform for children, were established. In 1963 the company was dissolved, and until 1976 the Old Vic Theatre was the home of the new National Theatre. The Young Vic was reconstituted in 1970, and by 1976 it had become an independent company. The Old Vic was refurbished and reopened in the late 1980s.

Omar stanza *See* RUBAIYAT STANZA.

one-act play A form of drama that is to a full-length play as a short story is to a novel. Originally used as a curtain-raiser, or short play presented before the main show, at the end of the 19th century the form became accepted in its own right. The popularity of one-act plays was spread in part by the little theater movement in the United States, where two or more such plays were often presented together on one program. Playwrights in many countries have written one-act plays, some of the most well known of which are Edward Albee's *The Zoo Story* and *The American Dream,* Samuel Beckett's *Fin de partie* (*Endgame*) and *Krapp's Last Tape,* Eugène Ionesco's *La Cantatrice chauve* (*The Bald Soprano*), Anton Chekhov's *Predlozheniye* (*The Proposal*) and *Svadba* (*The Wedding*), John Millington Synge's *Riders to the Sea,* and Harold Pinter's *The Dumbwaiter.*

Onitsha market literature \ō-ˈnē-chä\ Subliterary genre of sentimental, moralistic novellas and pamphlets produced in the 20th century by a semiliterate school of writers (students, fledgling journalists, and taxi drivers) and sold at the bustling Onitsha market in eastern Nigeria. Among the most prolific of the writers were Felix N. Stephen, Speedy Eric, Thomas O. Iguh, and O. Olisah, the latter two having also written chapbook plays about prominent literary figures.

Characteristic features of the Onitsha writings include a fascination with Westernized urban life and the desire to warn the newly arrived against the corruption and dangers that accompany it. Typical titles are "Rose Only Loved My Money," "Drunkards Believe Bar as Heaven," "Why Some Rich Men Have No Trust in Some Girls," "How to Get a Lady in Love," and "How John Kennedy Suffered in Life and Death Suddenly," all of which have achieved great commercial success. Booksellers hawk these cheap, locally produced pamphlets (which are printed on handpresses) at Onitsha alongside farmers and fishermen, cattlemen from the north, and cocoa merchants from the West. Usually less than 50 pages in length, Onitsha market literature encompasses sentimental novelettes, political tracts, and how-to guides on writing love letters, handling money, and attaining prosperity.

As a literary phenomenon the Onitsha market literature, similar in many ways to the chapbooks of 17th- and 18th-century England, are important for the close relationship of writer and audience without reference to a world outside Africa.

onomatopoeia \ˌän-ə-ˌmät-ə-ˈpē-ə, -ˌmat-\ [Greek *onomatopoiía,* from *onomat-, ónoma* name + *poieîn* to make] **1.** The naming of a thing or action by a vocal imitation of the sound associated with it (such as *buzz* or *hiss*). **2.** The use of words whose sound suggests the sense. This occurs frequently in poetry, where a line of verse can express a characteristic of the thing being portrayed. The following lines from "The Brook" by Alfred, Lord Tennyson are an example:

I chatter over stony ways,
In little sharps and trebles,
I bubble into eddying bays,
I babble on the pebbles.

open couplet or **run-on couplet** In poetry, a couplet the sense of which requires completion by what follows; a dependent couplet, one that by itself does not contain a complete or relatively complete thought. *See also* COUPLET.

Open Theatre Experimental United States theater company founded in 1963 in New York City by Peter Feldman and Joseph Chaikan. The group—made up of actors, playwrights, musicians, and choreographers—sought to explore the possibilities of uniting improvisation, pantomime, music, and dance in new dramatic productions. Playwrights worked closely with the entire troupe, and they generated communal works that usually addressed subjects of current political or social relevance.

The best-known Open Theatre productions were *The Serpent* (1969), written by Jean-Claude Van Itallie, which combined biblical material with contemporary political events, and *Terminal* (1969–70), directed by Chaikan and Roberta Sklar from a text by Susan Yankowitz, which explored the deathlike alienation of modern man. The Open Theatre disbanded in 1973 and most of its members joined other experimental troupes.

opera \ˈäp-rə, ˈäp-ə-rə\ [Italian, short for *opera musicale,* literally, musical work] A drama set to music and made up of vocal pieces with orchestral accompaniment and interludes.

Opera had its origins in the liturgical drama of the Middle Ages, which was combined in 16th-century Florence with contemporary notions of classical Greek tragedy. The subjects chosen by such early operatic composers as Jacopo Peri, Jacopo Corsi, Francesco Cavalli, and Claudio Monteverdi were the ancient myths about figures like Daphne, Ulysses, and Orpheus, though Monteverdi in his *L'incoronazione di Poppea* (1642; *The Coronation of Poppea*) dealt with the Roman historical personages of Nero and Poppaea.

In Paris at the court of Louis XIV the new art was encouraged in the lavish works of Jean-Baptiste Lully, while at the court in Vienna the Italian operas of Pietro Antonio Cesti were performed. In England the development was more sketchy. When opera did become popular in London, in the middle of the 18th century, it was in a form imported from Italy and refined by the German-born composer George Frideric Handel. Meanwhile, the achievements of W.A. Mozart in reconciling music and drama, particularly in comic works like *The Marriage of Figaro* and *The Magic Flute,* set standards that remain unsurpased.

In the 19th century opera developed along national lines. In Italy, Giovanni Bellini's affecting works and Gaetano Donizetti's tragedies and comedies preceded the great achievements of Giuseppi Verdi, whose popular operas include *Rigoletto, La traviata,* and *Falstaff*. The great Italian tradition was continued at the turn of the century by Giacomo Puccini's *Tosca, La Bohème,* and *Madama Butterfly*. In Germany the most important figure was Richard Wagner, whose music dramas revolutionized opera. His major works—*Die Meistersinger, Tristan und Isolde, Parsifal,* and *Der Ring des Nibelungen*—remain among the peaks of operatic achievement.

In France, Russia, and elsewhere nationalism was also prevalent. Opera has remained a vital art in the 20th century, with composers like Richard Strauss and Alban Berg making major contributions to the form.

opera omnia \ˈō-pə-rə-ˈäm-nē-ə, ˈäp-\ [Latin, literally, all works] The complete works of a writer.

Opportunity (*in full* Opportunity: A Journal of Negro Life) African-American magazine associated with the Harlem Renaissance and published from 1923 to 1949. The editor, Charles S. Johnson, aimed to give voice to black culture, hitherto neglected by mainstream American publishing. Johnson sponsored three literary contests to encourage young writers to submit their work. The 1925 winners included Zora Neale Hurston, Langston Hughes, and Countee Cullen. *Ebony and Topaz, A Collectanea* (1927) was an anthology of the best works published in the magazine. *See also* HARLEM RENAISSANCE.

opusculum \ō-ˈpəs-kyə-ləm\ *plural* opuscula \-lə\ [Latin, diminutive of *opus* work] A minor work (as of literature)—normally used in the plural.

oral tradition *See* FOLK LITERATURE.

oration [Latin *oratio* speech, formal address, a derivative of *orare* to pray to, beseech, plead before an assembly] An elaborate discourse delivered in a formal and dignified manner and especially a formal discourse on a special occasion.

oratory \ˈȯr-ə-ˌtȯr-ē\ [Latin *oratoria,* a derivative of *orator* public speaker, orator] The rationale and practice of persuasive public speaking. Oratory is instrumental and practical, as distinguished from poetic or literary composition, which traditionally aims at beauty and pleasure, and it relies on the use of rhetoric for its effectiveness. *See also* RHETORIC. *Compare* DELIBERATIVE ORATORY; EPIDEICTIC ORATORY; FORENSIC ORATORY.

organic form The structure of a work that has grown naturally from the author's subject and materials as opposed to that of a work shaped by and conforming to artificial rules. The concept was developed by Samuel Taylor Coleridge to counter those who claimed that the works of William Shakespeare were formless.

organic unity In literature, a structural principle first discussed by Plato (in *Phaedrus, Gorgias,* and the *Republic*) and later described and defined by Aristotle. The principle calls for internally consistent thematic and dramatic development, analogous to biological growth, which is the recurrent, guiding metaphor throughout Aristotle's writings. To possess organic unity the action of a narrative or drama must be "a complete whole, with its several incidents so closely connected that the transposal or withdrawal of any one of them will disjoin and dislocate the whole." Following this stricture, art was expected to grow naturally from a kernel of thought and to seek its own form. The artist was discouraged from interfering with a work's natural growth by adding ornament, wit, love interest, or some other convention.

Organic form was a preoccupation of the German Romantic poets and was also claimed for the novel by Henry James in *The Art of Fiction* (1884).

Orientalia \ˌȯr-ē-ən-ˈtāl-yə\ Materials (such as literary, artistic, and archaeological products and remains) related to the Orient.

Origin (*in full* Origin: A Quarterly for the Creative) American literary magazine largely devoted to poetry, published and edited by poet Cid Corman as a 64-page quarterly in several intermittent series. The first series, published from 1951 to 1957, probably had the greatest impact. While it included works by such classic modern poets as Wallace Stevens and William Carlos Williams, its primary focus was on such younger postwar poets as Denise Levertov, Robert Duncan, and, especially, Robert Creeley, Charles Olson, and Corman himself. *Origin*'s second series (1961–64) included works by Louis Zukofsky, Gary Snyder, and Michael McClure, and Douglas Woolf's short novel *John-Juan* appeared in the third series (1966–71). In addition to works by English and American authors, the magazine published translations of troubadour poetry, Chinese and Japanese poetry, and works by 20th-century European and Latin-American poets, including César Vallejo. Corman's anthology *The Gist of Origin* (1975) includes selected works from the magazine.

orthometry \ȯr-ˈthäm-ə-trē\ [*ortho-* (as in *orthography*) + Greek *-metria* measurement, meter] The art of correct versification.

Ossianic ballads \ˌäs-ē-ˈan-ik, ˌäsh-\ Irish Gaelic and Scottish lyric and narrative poems dealing with the legends of Finn MacCumhaill (MacCool) and his war band. They are named for Oisín (Ossian), the chief bard of the Fenian cycle, a collection of tales and verses on the same subject. The Ossianic ballads belong to a common Scots-Irish Gaelic tradition: some are found in the Scottish Highlands, others in Ireland, but their subjects are of Irish origin. Consisting of more than 80,000 lines, they were formed from the 11th to the 18th century, although their themes of pursuits and rescues, monster slayings, mutually destructive strife, elopements, and magic visitors go back to about the 3rd century AD. The tone of the Ossianic ballads is strikingly different from that of the earlier Fenian literature, which reflected a mutual respect between pagan and Christian tradition. The Ossianic ballads, usually introduced by a dialogue between Ossian and St. Patrick, are stubbornly pagan and anticlerical, full of lament for past glories and contempt for the Christian present. St. Patrick is often portrayed as a bigoted cleric. The earliest collection of these late ballads, made by Sir James MacGregor between 1512 and 1526, is known as *The Book of the Dean of Lismore*.

Ossianic cycle *See* FENIAN CYCLE.

Others (*in full* Others: A Magazine of New Verse) American literary magazine founded by Alfred Kreymborg and published monthly, with some irregularity, from July 1915 to July 1919. Created in response to the conservatism of *Poetry,* the most notable of the little magazines, *Others* featured experimental poetry and, from December 1918, prose and artwork. Though the mainstream press received the magazine with hostility, its success as an outlet for modernism resulted in three anthologies and a short-lived theater troupe.

Individual issues of *Others* were devoted to such themes as women writers and writers in Chicago and in Latin America. In addition to Kreymborg, William Carlos Williams and Lola Ridge served as editor for various issues of the magazine. Its contributors included T.S. Eliot, Mina Loy, Max Bodenheim, Amy Lowell, Wallace Stevens, Marianne Moore, Ezra Pound, Hilda Doolittle (H.D.), Carl Sandburg, Richard Aldington, Conrad Aiken, and Sherwood Anderson.

ottava rima \ō-ˈtäv-ə-ˈrē-mə, *Italian* ȯt-ˈtä-vä-ˈrē-mä\ *plural* ottava rimas [Italian, stanza of eight lines, literally, eighth stanza] Italian stanza form composed of eight 11-syllable lines, rhyming *abababcc*. It originated in the late 13th and early 14th centuries and was developed by Tuscan poets for religious verse and drama and in troubadour songs. In his romantic epics *Il filostrato* (written *c.* 1338) and *Teseida* (written 1340–41), Giovanni Boccaccio established ottava rima as the standard form for epic and narrative verse in Italian. The form acquired new flexibility and variety in Ludovico Ariosto's *Orlando furioso* (*c.* 1507–32) and Torquato Tasso's *Gerusalemme liberata* (1581).

Ottava rima appeared in Spain and Portugal in the 16th century. It was used in 1600 in England (where the lines were shortened to 10 syllables) by Edward Fairfax in his translation of the work of Tasso. In original English verse ottava rima was written in iambic pentameter and used for heroic poetry in the 17th and 18th centuries, but it achieved its greatest effectiveness in Lord Byron's *Beppo* (1818) and *Don Juan* (1819–24), which combined elements of comedy, seriousness, and mock-heroic irony. Percy Bysshe Shelley employed it for a serious subject in "The Witch of Atlas" (1824). Others who have written poems in the form include Edmund Spenser, John Milton, John Keats, Shelley, Robert Browning, and William Butler Yeats.

OuLiPo \ü-lē-ˈpō\ (*in full* Ouvroir de Littérature Potentielle; "Workshop of Potential Literature") A group of French writers active in the 1970s whose aim was to generate new literary forms and to rejuvenate poetic language through experimentation with linguistic games. They were inspired by Alfred Jarry and Raymond Queneau, whose *Exercices de style* (1947; *Exercises in Style*) consisted of a single anecdote presented in 99 different forms demonstrating different figures of speech, style, and other literary elements. The group's fondness for wordplay and sometimes unbelievably demanding forms can be seen in the work of Georges Perec, whose novel *La Disparition* (1969) was composed entirely without using the letter *e*.

outride \'aůt-ˌrīd\ In Gerard Manley Hopkins' system of prosody, an unstressed syllable or group of syllables added to a foot but not counted in the scansion because of its lack of effect upon the rhythmic movement. *See* SPRUNG RHYTHM.

Ouvroir de Littérature Potentielle *See* OULIPO.

Overland Monthly Literary magazine published in San Francisco from 1868 to 1875 and from 1883 to 1935. This ambitious venture, edited for the first two and a half years by Bret Harte, was begun in an attempt to establish Western literature as a legitimate genre. Harte's local-color parables such as "The Luck of Roaring Camp" and "The Outcasts of Poker Flat" first appeared in its pages and solidified his reputation. The magazine itself gained national respect, publishing such writers as C.W. Stoddard, Ina Coolbrith, Prentice Mulford, and Ambrose Bierce, among others.

Oxfordian \äks-'fȯr-dē-ən\ Of or relating to Edward de Vere, the 17th Earl of Oxford, or to the doctrine that he was the author of the dramatic works usually attributed to William Shakespeare. *Compare* STRATFORDIAN.

oxymoron \ˌäk-sē-'mȯr-ˌän\ [Late Greek *oxýmōron* (in Latin authors), from neuter of *oxýmōros* pointedly foolish, from Greek *oxýs* sharp, keen + *mōrós* dull] *plural* oxymora \-'mȯr-ə\ A word or group of words that is self-contradicting, as in *bittersweet* or *plastic glass*. Oxymorons are similar to such other devices as paradox and antithesis and are often used in poetry and other literature. *Compare* ANTITHESIS; PARADOX.

One of the most famous examples of the use of oxymorons is the following speech by Romeo from William Shakespeare's *Romeo and Juliet:*

> Why, then, O brawling love! O loving hate!
> O any thing, of nothing first create!
> O heavy lightness! serious vanity!
> Mis-shapen chaos of well-seeming forms!
> Feather of lead, bright smoke, cold fire, sick health!
> Still-waking sleep, that is not what it is!
> This love feel I, that feel no love in this.

oxytone \'äk-sē-ˌtōn\ [Greek *oxýtonos,* from *oxýs* sharp + *tónos* pitch, accent] Having or characterized by an acute accent or heavy stress on the last syllable.

P

Parodies and caricatures are the most penetrating of criticisms.
—Aldous Huxley

paean \'pē-ən\ [Greek *paián, paiṓn,* from *Paián, Paiṓn,* epithet of Apollo in such songs] Solemn choral lyric of invocation, joy, or triumph, originating in ancient Greece where it was addressed to Apollo in his guise as Paean, physician to the gods. Paeans were sung at banquets following the boisterous dithyrambs, at the festivals of Apollo, and at public funerals. It was the custom for them to be sung by an army on the march and before going into battle, when a fleet left the harbor, and after a victory. Paeans were later addressed to other gods as well as to mortals, such as the 5th-century-BC Spartan commander Lysander, who were more or less deified for their achievements.

paeon \'pē-ən, -ˌän\ [Greek *paián, paiṓn,* literally, paean] In classical prosody, a metrical foot consisting of one long and three short syllables. The position of the long syllable determines the designation of the foot as a first (– ∪ ∪ ∪) or fourth (∪ ∪ ∪ –) paeon. (Second and third paeons exist in theory only.) They occur in bacchic or cretic verse, and the fourth paeon occurs as a syncopated iambic or trochaic metron.

pageant \'paj-ənt\ [Middle English *pagent* play in a mystery cycle, movable stage (corresponding to Medieval Latin *pagina, pagenda*), of unknown origin] An elaborate, colorful exhibition or spectacle, often with music, that consists of a series of tableaux, of a loosely unified theatrical production, or of a procession, usually with floats. In its earlier use the word denoted the vehicle designed for the presentation of religious plays or cycles as well as the presentations themselves. Because these plays were generally accompanied by great ceremony and showmanship, pageant has come to mean also any lavish production, whether indoors or outdoors, without regard to any specifically religious content.

Pageants are usually used as a means of expressing national, communal, religious, or other kinds of group purpose or identity. In primitive societies processions have always been one of the most basic demonstrations of communal unity. The occasions for such processions varied greatly, ranging from fertility rites to the casting out of evil spirits to displays of military strength. Once such periods of festivity and spectacle have been established, they and the customs and processions connected with them have tended to be passed down from one culture to the next. Thus, for example, the carnival processions that precede Lent in many Roman Catholic countries are probably derived from the ancient

Roman pagan feasts of the Saturnalia, the Lupercalia, and the Bacchanalia, which were occasions for parades, music, sacrifices, and general merrymaking.

An essential feature of pageantry through the ages has been the element of drama, in which the theme of a procession is illustrated with spoken words or simple dramatic action. Pageant dramas were an integral part of the major festivals of the Roman Catholic church, and these religious pageants gradually developed into the MYSTERY PLAY, the MASQUE, and other theatrical precursors of Western secular drama. In some pageants, the staged presentation or dramatic storytelling is preeminent over simple spectacle and display. Two such pageant dramas are especially notable. Among the Shīʿite Muslims, a passion play known as the *taʿziyah* ("consolation") is performed during the first 10 days of the month of Muharram. Recounting, in often highly emotional and graphic detail, the martyrdom of the descendants of ʿAli, the son-in-law of Muḥammad, the pageant retains elements that date back to the 10th century. The *Passionsspiel* (a presentation of Christ's last hours on earth) of the village of Oberammergau in Bavaria is perhaps the best-known religious pageant drama in the West.

The early 20th century saw a revival of a "pure" form of pageant (one that is first and foremost historical drama), most notably in the works of Louis N. Parker. Parker's insistence on accurate retellings of history, use of natural settings with little or no artificial scenery, and reliance on amateur actors served to repopularize the pageant as historical drama. Max Reinhardt also made notable contributions to modern pageant drama with his efforts to stage plays in many different kinds of locales.

pai-hua *See* BAIHUA.

Palais-Royal Theater \pȧ-le-rwȧ-'yȧl\ Paris playhouse most noted for 17th-century productions by Molière.

The Palais-Royal traces its history to a small private theater located in the residence of Cardinal Richelieu and known by the name of the residence, the Palais-Cardinal. Following Richelieu's death, the palace became royal property, and, as the Théâtre du Palais-Royal, it was used for courtly entertainments. In 1660 the theater was given to Molière and his troupe, who occupied it until the dramatist-actor's death in 1673. Thereafter, it was used by the Royal Academy of Music. It burned down in 1763, was rebuilt, and burned again in 1781. The entire area was then redeveloped into an amusement area by its owner, the Duke de Chartres. It contained a number of theaters, many called Palais-Royal at various times.

palilogy or **palillogy** \pə-'lil-ə-jē\ [Greek *palillogía* recapitulation, from *pálin* back, again + *lógos; word, speech*] Repetition of a word for emphasis, as in the Bible, at Isaiah 38:19, "the living, the living, he shall praise thee."

palimpsest \'pal-imp-ˌsest, pə-'limp-səst\ [Greek *palímpsēston,* from neuter of *palímpsēstos* scraped again, from *pálin* again + *-psēstos,* verbal adjective of *psên* to rub, scrape] Writing material such as parchment that has been used one or more times after earlier writing has been erased or partly erased. The underlying text is said to be "in palimpsest," and, even though the parchment or other surface is much abraded, the older text is recoverable in the laboratory by such means as the use of ultraviolet light. The motive for making palimpsests usually seems to have been economic—reusing parchment was cheaper than preparing a new skin. Another motive may have been directed by Christian piety, as in the conversion of a pagan Greek manuscript to receive the text of a Church Father.

palindrome \'pal-in-ˌdrōm\ [Greek *palíndromos* running back, going backwards, from *pálin* back, again + *-dromos,* a derivative of *drameîn* to run] A word, number, sentence, or verse that reads the same backward or forward. Examples of word palindromes include "civic," "madam," "radar," and "deified." Numerical palindromes include sequences that read the same in reverse order (e.g., 1991), as well as those that can be read upside down and backward (e.g., 1961). Examples of such sentences include "Able was I ere I saw Elba" and "Lewd did I live & evil I did dwel." Examples of palindromic verse include (in Latin) "Roma tibi subito motibus ibit amor" and "Signa te, signa temere me tangis et angis." Some writers have refined the palindrome, composing verses in which each word reads the same backward and forward—for instance, that of William Camden:

> Odo tenet mulum, madidam mappam tenet Anna,
> Anna tenet mappam madidam, mulum tenet Odo.

palinode \'pal-ə-ˌnōd\ [Greek *palinōidía,* from *pálin* back, again + *-ōidia,* a derivative of *aeídein* to sing] An ode or song recanting or retracting something in a former one.

pamphlet \'pam-flət\ [Middle English *pamf(i)let* short written text, small book, from Old French *Pamphilet,* vernacular title (originally, the supposed author) of *Pamphilus seu de amore,* a 12th-century Latin love poem] An unbound printed publication with no cover or with a paper cover. Pamphlets were among the first printed materials, and they were widely used in England, France, and Germany, often for purposes of religious or political propaganda.

The first great age of pamphleteering was inspired by the religious controversies of the early 16th century. In France so many pamphlets were issued in support of the Reformed religion that edicts prohibiting them were promulgated in 1523, 1553, and 1566. In Germany the pamphlet was first used by the leaders of the Protestant Reformation to inflame popular opinion against the pope and the Roman Catholic church. Martin Luther was one of the earliest and most effective pamphleteers. The coarseness and violence of the pamphlets on both sides and the public disorder attributed to their distribution led to their prohibition by imperial edict in 1589.

In England the pamphlet was popular in the Elizabethan age, being used not only for religious controversy but also by such men as Thomas Dekker, Thomas Nashe, and Robert Greene for romantic fiction, autobiography, scurrilous personal abuse, and social and literary criticism.

In France didactic and abusive religious pamphleteering gave way to a more flippant and lively writing that satirized the morals of the court and the chief ministers. The pamphlets of Blaise Pascal, known as *Les Provinciales,* raised the form to the level of literature. In England pamphlets gained increasing propagandist influence during the political and religious controversies of the 17th century. They played an important role in the debates between Puritan and Anglican, and king and Parliament in the years before, during, and after the English Civil Wars. At the time of the Restoration in England in 1660, the flow of pamphlets was checked, their range restricted to some extent by newspapers and periodicals. During the Revolution of 1688, however, pamphlets increased in importance as political weapons. The development of party politics gave employment to pamphleteers, including such writers as Joseph Addison, Richard Steele, Matthew Prior, Francis Atterbury, and Jonathan Swift.

The pamphlet continued to have a powerful influence throughout the 18th century. In North America, pre-Revolutionary War political agitation stimulated the beginning of extensive pamphleteering; foremost among the writers of political pamphlets was Thomas Paine, whose *Common Sense* appeared in January 1776. After the United States was founded, another wave of pamphleteering was caused by the proposal of a new constitution in 1787. From this material there emerged *The Federalist Papers,* contributions made to the discussion of government by the revolutionary pamphleteers Alexander Hamilton, John Jay, and James Madison. *The Federalist Papers* may also be regarded as marking the end of the era of the political pamphlet; thereafter political dialogue was largely carried on in newspapers, periodicals, and bound books.

Noted writers of 18th-century France—Voltaire, Jean-Jacques Rousseau, Montesquieu, and Denis Diderot, among others—used pamphlets to express the philosophy of the Enlightenment. Their pamphlets were reasoned discourses, though with the arrival of the French Revolution, pamphlets once again became powerful polemical weapons. The revolution itself produced many popular anonymous pamphlets, slandering the queen and the nobility and commenting on events, and also occasioned one of the outstanding English pamphlets, Edmund Burke's *Reflections on the Revolution in France* (1790). It provoked many replies, the most famous of which is Thomas Paine's *Rights of Man* (1791–92).

In the 19th century pamphlets continued to be used for political propaganda in France and England. In France, Paul-Louis Courier wrote polemic masterpieces. In England the pamphlet played a part in all political movements of the 19th century. Most notable were pamphlets on Chartism, Irish Home Rule, and the Oxford Movement. At the turn of the century, Fabian Society members George Bernard Shaw, Beatrice Webb, and Graham Wallas propagated political doctrine in a series of pamphlets. In the 20th century the pamphlet has more often been used for information than for controversy, chiefly by government departments and learned societies.

panegyric \ˌpan-ə-ˈjir-ik, -ˈjīr-\ [Greek *panēgyrikós,* from *panēgyrikós* (adjective) of or for a festival or assembly, a derivative of *panēgyrís* general or national assembly, from *pan-* all + *ágyris* gathering] Eulogistic oration or laudatory discourse that originally was a speech delivered at an ancient Greek general assembly (panegyris), such as the Olympic and Panathenaic festivals. Speakers frequently took advantage of these occasions, when Greeks of various cities were gathered together, to advocate Hellenic unity. With this end in view and also in order to gratify their audience, they tended to expound on the former glories of Greek cities; hence the elaborate and flowery connotations of the term. The most famous ancient Greek panegyrics to survive intact are the *Panegyricus* (*c.* 380 BC) and the *Panathenaicus* (*c.* 340 BC), both by Isocrates.

Similar to panegyric was the *epitaphion,* or funeral oration, such as Pericles' funeral speech as recorded by Thucydides, which was a panegyric both on war heroes and on Athens itself.

In the 2nd century AD, Aelius Aristides, a Greek rhetorician, combined praise of famous cities with eulogy of the reigning Roman emperor. By his time panegyric had probably become specialized in the latter connection and was, therefore, related to the old Roman custom of celebrating at festivals the glories of famous men of the past and of pronouncing *laudationes funebres* at the funerals of eminent persons.

Another kind of Roman eulogistic speech was the *gratiarum actio* ("thanksgiving"), delivered by a successful candidate for public office. *The XII Panegyrici Latini,* an ancient collection of these speeches, includes the *gratiarum actio* delivered by Pliny the Younger when he was nominated consul by the emperor Trajan in AD 100. Roman writers of the 3rd to the 5th century indiscriminately praised and flattered the emperors in panegyrics that were sometimes written in verse.

Although primarily associated with classical antiquity, panegyrics continued to be written on occasion in the European Middle Ages, often by Christian mystics in praise of God, and in the Renaissance and Baroque periods, especially in Elizabethan England, in Spain during the Golden Age, and in France under the reign of Louis XIV.

pantomime \ˈpan-tə-ˌmīm, -ˌmēm\ [Greek *pantómimos,* from *panto-* all + *mîmos* mime] **1.** An ancient Roman dramatic performance featuring a solo dancer and a narrative chorus. **2.** An 18th century French or English ballet modeled on the Roman pantomime with subjects from classical mythology. **3.** An 18th century English harlequinade originally burlesquing the pantomime ballet, performed by dancing comedians, and serving as an interlude or afterpiece. **4.** A British theatrical entertainment of the Christmas season based on a nursery tale and featuring topical songs, tableaux, and dances. **5.** A dramatic performance using no dialogue. **6.** The art of expressing the action of a story by simplified, exaggerated, and often conventionally symbolic gestures without words. **7.** The genre of theatrical entertainment comprising pantomimes.

pantoum \pan-ˈtüm\ [French, from Malay *pantun*] A Malaysian poetic form in French and English. The pantoum consists of a series of quatrains rhyming *abab* in which the second and fourth lines of a quatrain recur as the first and third lines in the succeeding quatrain; each quatrain introduces a new second rhyme (as *bcbc, cdcd*). The first line of the series recurs as the last line of the closing quatrain, and in some English examples the third line of the poem recurs as the second line of the closing quatrain, rhyming *xaxa*.

Although the pantoum was introduced into Western literature in the 19th century, it bears some resemblance to older French fixed forms, such as the rondeau and the villanelle. French poets who wrote pantoums include Victor Hugo, Théodore de Banville, and Leconte de Lisle, among others. Austin Dobson was one of the more proficient English practitioners of the form.

pantun or **pantoun** \pan-ˈtün\ [Malay *pantun*] Indonesian verse consisting of four lines rhyming *abab;* the first two present a figurative suggestion of what is more directly and clearly stated in the final lines.

pap \ˈpap\ Something (such as reading matter) that serves only to entertain or is not otherwise intellectually stimulating.

paper \ˈpā-pər\ A literary composition, especially of brief, occasional, or fragmentary nature—normally used in the plural.

parabasis \pə-ˈrab-ə-sis\ *plural* parabases \-ˌsēz\ [Greek *parábasis*, a derivative of *parabaínein* to step forward] An important choral ode in Greek Old Comedy delivered by the chorus at an intermission in the action while facing and moving toward the audience. It was used to express the author's views on political or religious topics of the day.

parable \ˈpar-ə-bəl\ [Greek *parabolḗ* juxtaposition, comparison, parable, a derivative of *parabállein* to throw or set alongside, compare] A usually short fictitious story that illustrates a moral attitude, a doctrine, a standard of conduct, or a religious principle.

The term originally referred to a Greek rhetorical figure, a kind of extended simile, involving the use of a literary illustration. The parable differs from the fable in the inherent plausibility of its story and in the exclusion of anthropomorphism, but resembles it in the essential qualities of brevity and simplicity. The storytelling aspect of a parable is usually subordinated to the analogy it draws between a particular instance of human behavior and human conduct at large. The simple narratives of parables give them a mysterious, suggestive tone and make them especially useful for the teaching of moral and spiritual truths. Parables can often be fully understood only by an informed elite, who can discern the meaning within their brief, enigmatic structures.

Some of the most famous Western parables are in the New Testament; in them, Jesus illustrates his message to his followers by telling a fictitious story that is nevertheless true to life.

Throughout Christian history, the parable has been a popular preaching device. The more paradoxical aspects of the parable were revived in the 19th century through treatises written by the Danish philosopher Søren Kierkegaard. His use of the form influenced the works of Franz Kafka and of Albert Camus.

Parables have a considerable role also in Ṣūfism (Islāmic mysticism), rabbinic (Jewish exegetical) literature, Ḥasidism (Jewish pietism), and Zen Buddhism.

paradiplomatic \ˌpar-ə-ˌdip-lə-ˈmat-ik\ Concerned with or based on evidence apart from strict textual authority. *Compare* DIPLOMATIC.

paradox \ˈpar-ə-ˌdäks\ [Greek *parádoxon,* from neuter of *parádoxos* contrary to expectation, from the phrase *parà dóxan* in violation of expectation] **1.** A tenet or proposition contrary to received opinion. **2.** An apparently self-contradictory statement, the underlying meaning of which is revealed only by careful scrutiny. The purpose of a paradox is to arrest attention and provoke fresh thought. The statement "Less is more" is an example. Francis Bacon's comment that "The most corrected copies are commonly the least correct" is an earlier literary example. In George Orwell's anti-utopian satire *Animal Farm* (1945), the first commandment of the animals' commune is revised into a witty paradox: "All animals are equal, but some animals are more equal than others." Paradox has a function in poetry, however, that goes beyond mere wit or attention-getting. Modern critics view it as a device, integral to poetic language, encompassing the tensions of error and truth simultaneously, not necessarily by startling juxtapositions but by subtle and continuous qualifications of the ordinary meaning of words. When a paradox is compressed into two words, as in "loud silence," "lonely crowd," or "living death," it is called an OXYMORON. **3.** Something (such as a person, phenomenon, state of affairs, or action) with seemingly contradictory qualities or phases.

paralipsis \ˌpar-ə-ˈlip-sis\, *also called* occupatio \ˌäk-yu̇-ˈpā-shē-ō, -ˈpä-tē-ō\ *or* preterition \ˌpret-ə-ˈrish-ən\ [Greek *paráleipsis,* a derivative of *paraleípein* to neglect, pass over] Rhetorical device by which a speaker or writer draws attention to a subject while professing to ignore or pass over it, as in the use of the phrases "Needless to say" or "It goes without saying" before a statement.

parallelism \ˈpar-ə-lel-ˌiz-əm\ In rhetoric, a component of literary style in both prose and poetry, in which coordinate ideas are arranged in phrases, sentences, and paragraphs that balance one element with another of equal importance and similar wording. The repetition of sounds, meanings, and structures serves to order, emphasize, and point out relations. In its simplest form, the doublet, parallelism may consist of a pair of single words that are synonymous or have a slight variation in meaning: "ordain and establish" or "overtake and surpass." Another variety contains three or more parallel units as in "Reading maketh a full man, conference a ready man, and writing an exact man" (Francis Bacon, "Of Studies"). Chiasmus is a form of parallelism in which the separate clauses are inverted for stronger emphasis; e.g., "I have changed in many things: in this I have not" (John Henry Newman, *Apologia pro Vita Sua*). Parallelism lends wit and authority to the antithetical aphorism; e.g., "We always love those who admire us, but we do not always love those whom we admire" (La Rochefoucauld, *Maximes*).

Parallelism is a prominent figure in Hebrew poetry as well as in most literatures of the ancient Middle East. The Old Testament and New Testament, reflecting the influence of Hebrew poetry, contain many striking examples of parallelism, as in the following lines from Psalms 78:36: "but they flattered him with their mouths; they lied to him with their tongues."

paraphrase \'par-ə-ˌfrāz\ [Greek *paráphrasis,* a derivative of *paraphrázein* to retell in other words, from *para-* aside, beyond + *phrázein* to point out, show, tell] A restatement of a text, passage, or work giving the meaning in another form, usually for clearer and fuller exposition. A paraphrase is a free rendering as opposed to a direct translation from one language to another.

parataxis \ˌpar-ə-'tak-sis\ [Greek *parátaxis* act of placing side by side, a derivative of *paratássein* to set side by side] The placing of clauses or phrases one after another without coordinating or subordinating connectives.

parchment \'pärch-mənt\ [Middle English *parchemin,* from Old French *parchemin, parcamin,* alteration (influenced by *parche, parge,* kind of red leather, from Late Latin *Parthica (pellis),* literally, Parthian skin) of Gallo-Romance **pergamīnus,* ultimately from Greek *pergamēnḗ,* from feminine of *Pergamēnós* of Pergamum] The processed skins of certain animals—chiefly sheep, goats, and calves—that have been prepared for the purpose of writing on them. Parchment made from the more delicate skins of calf or kid or from stillborn or newly born calf or lamb came to be called vellum, a term that was broadened in its usage to include any especially fine parchment. The production of parchment facilitated the success of the codex. A sheet of parchment could be cut in a size larger than a sheet of papyrus, it was flexible and durable, and it could better receive writing on both sides. In making a parchment or vellum codex, a large sheet was folded to form a folio of two leaves, a quaternion (quarto) of four, or even an octavo of eight. Gatherings were made from a number of these folded sheets, which were then stitched together to form a book. Because papyrus, on the other hand, was more brittle and could not be made in large enough sheets, the folio collected in quires (i.e., loose sheets) was the limit of its usefulness. At the same time, because of the vertical alignment of the fibers on one side, papyrus was not well adapted for writing on both sides in a horizontal script.

For 400 years the book roll and the codex existed side by side. Contemporary references to the codex date from the 1st century BC, but the earliest actual survivals date from the 2nd century AD. In the 4th century AD parchment as a material and the codex as a form became dominant, although there are later examples of rolls, and papyrus was occasionally used for official documents until the 10th century.

In modern usage, the terms *parchment* and *vellum* may be applied to a type of paper of high quality made chiefly from wood pulp and rags and frequently having a special finish.

Paris Review, The \'par-is\ English-language literary quarterly founded in 1953 and edited by George Plimpton. The cofounders, Peter Matthiessen and Harold Humes, modeled the review on the small literary magazines published in Paris in the 1920s. *The Paris Review* presented quality fiction and poetry by new or relatively unknown writers; it introduced Philip Roth, Jack Kerouac, and Raymond Carver among others. It was also the first American journal to publish Samuel Beckett.

The Paris Review was also known for its interviews with such writers as E.M. Forster, Ernest Hemingway, Aldous Huxley, Nadine Gordimer, T.S. Eliot, and many others. Beginning in 1958, these interviews were published in a series known as *Writers at Work.*

Parnassian \pär-'nas-ē-ən\ or **Parnassien** \pȧr-nȧs-'ye^{n}\ [French *parnassien* pertaining to the Parnassian school or to poetry in general, literally, of Parnassus, a mountain in central Greece sacred in antiquity to Apollo and the Muses] Of, having the characteristics of, or constituting a school of French poets of the second half of the 19th century that was headed by Leconte de Lisle. The school stressed restraint, objectivity, technical perfection, and precise description as a reaction against the emotionalism and verbal excess of the Romantics. The poetic movement led by the Parnassians resulted in experimentation with meters and verse forms and the revival of the sonnet, and paralleled a late 19th-century trend toward realism in drama and the novel. Initially taking their themes from contemporary society, the Parnassians later turned to the mythology, epics, and sagas of exotic lands and past civilizations, notably India and ancient Greece, for inspiration. The Parnassians derived their name from the anthology to which they contributed, *Le Parnasse contemporain,* 3 vol. (1866, 1871, 1876), edited by Louis-Xavier de Ricard and Catulle Mendès and published by Alphonse Lemerre; their principles, though, had been formulated earlier in Théophile Gautier's preface to *Mademoiselle de Maupin* (1835), which expounded the theory of art for art's sake, in Leconte de Lisle's preface to his *Poèmes antiques* (1852), and in *La Revue fantaisiste* founded in 1861 by Mendès. Gautier's *Émaux et camées* (1852; "Enamels and Cameos"), a collection of carefully worked, formally perfect poems, pointed to a new conception of poetry and influenced the works of major Parnassians such as Albert Glatigny, Théodore de Banville, François Coppée, Léon Dierx, and José María de Heredia, the most representative of the group, who looked for precise details, double rhymes, sonorous words, and exotic names, and concentrated on making the 14th line of his sonnets the most striking.

The influence of the Parnassians was felt throughout Europe and was particularly evident in the Modernismo movement of Spain and Portugal and in the La Jeune Belgique ("Young Belgium") movement. In the late 19th century a new generation of poets, the Symbolists, followers of Stéphane Mallarmé and

Paul Verlaine, themselves Parnassians in their youth, broke away from precise description in search of an art of nuance and musical suggestion.

parodos or **parodus** \ˈpar-ə-dəs\ *plural* parodoi \-ˌdȯi\ *or* parodi \-dē\ [Greek *párodos,* literally, entrance, first entrance of the chorus] The first choral passage in an ancient Greek drama, recited or sung as the chorus entered the orchestra.

parody \ˈpar-ə-dē\ [Greek *parōidía,* from *para-* alongside, derivative + *ōidḗ* song] A literary work in which the style of an author is closely imitated for comic effect or in ridicule.

Differing from burlesque by the depth of its technical penetration and from travesty, which treats dignified subjects in a trivial manner, true parody mercilessly exposes the tricks of manner and thought of its victim yet cannot be written without a thorough appreciation of the work it ridicules.

An anonymous poet of ancient Greece imitated the epic style of Homer in *Batrachomyomachia* (*The Battle of the Frogs and Mice*), one of the earliest examples of parody; Aristophanes parodied the dramatic styles of Aeschylus and Euripides in *Frogs;* Geoffrey Chaucer parodied the chivalric romance in "The Tale of Sir Thopas" (*c.* 1375), as did Miguel de Cervantes in *Don Quixote* (Part I, 1605); François Rabelais parodied the Scholastics in his series of comic novels *Gargantua and Pantagruel* (1532–64); William Shakespeare mimicked Christopher Marlowe's high dramatic style in the players' scene in *Hamlet* and was himself parodied by John Marston, who wrote a parody of *Venus and Adonis* entitled *The Metamorphosis of Pigmalions Image* (1598).

Later examples of parody also abound. George Villiers, 2nd Duke of Buckingham in *The Rehearsal* (1671) and Richard Brinsley Sheridan in *The Critic* (1779) both parodied the heroic drama, especially John Dryden's *The Conquest of Granada* (1670); John Phillips in *The Splendid Shilling* (1705) caught all the superficial epic mannerisms of John Milton's *Paradise Lost* (1667); Jean Racine parodied Pierre Corneille's lofty dramatic style in *Les Plaideurs* (1668; *The Litigants*); Henry Fielding parodied Samuel Richardson's sentimental novel *Pamela* (1740) in *Shamela* (1741) and *Joseph Andrews* (1742) and mimicked the heroic play in *Tom Thumb* (1730).

In England the first parody to be widely successful was Horace and James Smith's *Rejected Addresses* (1812), a series of dedicatory odes on the reopening of the Drury Lane Theatre in the manner of such contemporary poets as Sir Walter Scott, Lord Byron, Robert Southey, William Wordsworth, and Samuel Taylor Coleridge. Unique among the Victorians is Lewis Carroll, whose parodies preserve verses that would otherwise not have survived—e.g., Southey's "Old Man's Comforts" (the basis for "You are Old, Father William") and the verses of Isaac Watts that gave rise to "How Doth the Little Crocodile" and "The Voice of the Lobster."

In the United States the 19th-century poems of Edgar Allan Poe, Walt Whitman, John Greenleaf Whittier, and Bret Harte were mimicked by their contemporaries, particularly by the poet and translator Bayard Taylor. Because of the variety of accents of 19th-century immigrants, U.S. parody often played on dialect—e.g., Charles G. Leland's *The Breitmann Ballads* (complete edition, 1895), a parody of the German poets Heinrich Heine and Ludwig Uhland in macaronic German American. Among more modern parodists, Samuel Hoffenstein is outstanding for his carefully damaging versions of A.E. Housman and the Georgian poets.

The art of parody has been encouraged in the 20th century by such periodicals as *Punch* and *The New Yorker*. The scope of parody has been widened to take in the far more difficult task of parodying prose. One of the most successful examples is Max Beerbohm's *The Christmas Garland* (1912), a series of Christmas stories in the style and spirit of various contemporary writers, most notably Henry James. Another innovation is double parody, invented by Sir John Squire in the period between the two world wars; it is the rendering of the sense of one poet in the style of another—e.g., Squire's version of Thomas Gray's *An Elegy Written in a Country Church Yard* written in the style of Edgar Lee Masters' *Spoon River Anthology* resulted in "If Gray Had Had to Write his Elegy in the Cemetery of Spoon River Instead of in That of Stoke Poges." Other outstanding parodists are Sir Arthur Quiller-Couch, Stephen Leacock, E.B. White, and Frederick Crews, whose *The Pooh Perplex* is a parody of various styles of literary criticism. *Compare* BURLESQUE; TRAVESTY.

paroemia \pə-ˈrē-mē-ə\ [Greek *paroimía,* from *para-* alongside, past + *oimḗ* song, verse narrative] A rhetorical proverb or adage.

paroemiac \pə-ˈrē-mē-ˌak\ In classical prosody, an anapestic dimeter catalectic. The verse, which may have been used for proverbs (the word *paroimia* means "proverb"), is scanned as ⏑̲⏑̲ – ⏑ ⏑ – ⏑ ⏑ – –.

parole \pə-ˈrōl\ Language viewed as a specific individual usage. The use of the French word *parole* ("speech") in this sense was introduced by the linguist Ferdinand de Saussure. *Compare* LANGUE.

paronomasia [Greek *paronomasía* derivative, byname, play on words, a derivative of *paronomázein* to call by a slight change of name, from *para-* alongside + *onomázein* to name] *See* PUN.

paroxytone \ˌpär-ˈäk-sē-ˌtōn\ [Greek *paroxýtonos,* from *para-* to the side of, beyond + *oxýtonos* oxytone] Having or characterized by an acute accent or a heavy stress on the penultimate syllable.

partimen \ˈpär-ti-men\ [Old Provençal, literally, division, a derivative of *partir* to divide] A lyric poem of dispute composed by Provençal troubadours in which one poet stated a proposition and a second disputed it. The first poet would then defend his position. The debate continued, usually for three rounds, after which the question was presented to an arbiter for resolution. The partimen was characterized by a more limited and less personal range of debate than a tenson, a similar form from which the partimen developed. *Compare* TENSON.

Partisan Review American literary quarterly founded by William Phillips and Philip Rahv in 1933 as a vehicle for the communist John Reed Club. It was published irregularly from 1934 to 1962 and quarterly thereafter. During its first years the magazine sought to represent the fight for intellectual and political freedom and asked for contributions by revolutionary writers. Over the years, however, the magazine became more oriented toward literature and art criticism. Works by W.H. Auden, Saul Bellow, Robert Lowell, Mary McCarthy, Denise Levertov, and Susan Sontag among others have been published in its pages.

pasquinade \ˌpas-kwə-ˈnād\ [Middle French, from Italian *pasquinata,* a derivative of *Pasquino*] A lampoon or satire in prose or verse usually having a political significance. Pasquino was the popular name for the remains of an ancient Roman statue unearthed in Rome in 1501. "Pasquino," supposedly named after a local shopkeeper near whose house or shop the statue was discovered, was the focus for bitingly critical political squibs attached to its torso by anonymous satirists. These pasquinades and their imitations, some ascribed to important 16th-century writers such as Pietro Aretino, were collected and published. After the 16th century the vogue of posting pasquinades died out, and the term acquired its more general meaning.

Passion play Religious drama of medieval origin dealing with the suffering, death, and Resurrection of Christ. Early Passion plays (in Latin) consisted of readings from the Gospel with interpolated poetical sections on the events of Christ's Passion and related subjects, such as Mary Magdalene's life and repentance, the raising of Lazarus, the Last Supper, and the lament of the Virgin Mary. Use of the vernacular in these interpolations led to the development of independent vernacular plays, the earliest surviving examples being in German. Such plays were at first only preludes to dramatic presentations of the Resurrection. The introduction of the character Satan, which became typical of German and Czech plays, led to the further elaboration of the fall of Lucifer and the Fall of Man (as in the early 14th-century Vienna Passion). These and other additions, such as the introduction of scenes from the Old Testament and the Last Judgment, led to development of cyclic plays similar to the Corpus Christi cycles. This type of Passion play is exemplified by the great Celtic Passion cycles of Cornwall and Brittany.

The earliest Passion plays of France and Flanders are thought to have their source in a nondramatic narrative poem of the 13th century, the *Passion des jongleurs*. These plays became highly elaborated in the course of their development, culminating in performances lasting more than a week. Confraternities were founded for performance of Passion plays, the most famous being the Confrérie de la Passion (1402). Passion plays were also performed in Spain, Italy, and elsewhere with local variations.

By the 16th century, many of the Passion plays, debased by secular influences, had degenerated into mere popular entertainments full of crude slapstick and buffoonery. Many were forbidden by ecclesiastical authorities, and many more were suppressed after the Reformation.

pastiche \pas-'tēsh, päs-\ or **pasticcio** \pas-'tē-chō, päs-, -chē-ō\ [French *pastiche,* from Italian *pasticcio* muddle, pastiche, literally, pie] **1.** A literary, artistic, musical, or architectural work that imitates the style of previous work. **2.** A musical, literary, or artistic composition made up of selections from different works, or a usually incongruous medley of different styles and materials. James Joyce's novel *Ulysses* is an organized pastiche of different styles and narrative voices.

pastoral *noun is* ˌpas-tə-'räl, -'ral; *adjective is* 'pas-tə-rəl\ [translation of Latin *Bucolica* (plural) the pastoral poems of Virgil or Theocritus] A literary work (such as a poem or play) dealing with the lives of shepherds or rural life in general and typically drawing a contrast between the innocence and serenity of the simple life and the misery and corruption of city and especially court life. The characters in such works are often used as vehicles for the expression of the author's moral, social, or literary views.

Many pastoral poems are remote from the realities of any life, rustic or urban. Among the writers who have used the pastoral convention with striking success and vitality are the classical poets Theocritus and Virgil and the English poets Edmund Spenser, Robert Herrick, John Milton, Percy Bysshe Shelley, and Matthew Arnold.

The pastoral convention sometimes uses the device of "singing matches" between two or more shepherds, and it often presents the poet and his friends in the (usually thin) disguises of shepherds and shepherdesses. Its themes often include love and death. Both devices and motifs of pastoral poetry were largely established by Theocritus, whose bucolics are the first examples of pastoral poetry. The tradition was passed on from Greece to Rome, where Virgil (who transferred the setting from Sicily to Arcadia, in the Greek Peloponnese, ever since the symbol of a pastoral paradise) alluded to contemporary problems—agrarian, political, and personal—in the rustic society he portrayed. His *Eclogues* exerted a powerful effect on poets of the Renaissance, including Dante, Petrarch, and Giovanni Boccaccio in Italy; Pierre de Ronsard in France; and Garcilaso de la Vega in Spain. These were further influenced by medieval Christian commentators on Virgil and by the pastoral scenes of the Old and New Testaments (Cain and Abel, David, the Bethlehem shepherds, and the figure of Christ the Good Shepherd). The model for prose romances in the Renaissance was the Greek writer Longus' *Daphnis and Chloe,* written in the 2nd–3rd century AD and considered the first pastoral prose romance. During the 16th and 17th centuries pastoral romance novels (by Jacopo Sannazzaro, Jorge de Montemayor, Miguel de Cervantes, and Honoré d'Urfé) appeared, as did the pastoral drama (by Torquato Tasso and Battista Guarini) in the 15th and 16th centuries.

In English poetry there had been some examples of pastoral literature in the earlier 16th century, but the appearance in 1579 of Edmund Spenser's

Shepheardes Calender, which imitated not only classical models but also the Renaissance poets of France and Italy, brought about a vogue for the pastoral. Sir Philip Sidney, Robert Greene, Thomas Nashe, Christopher Marlowe, Michael Drayton, Thomas Dekker, John Donne, Sir Walter Raleigh, Robert Herrick, Andrew Marvell, Thomas Heywood, Thomas Campion, William Browne, William Drummond, and Phineas Fletcher all wrote pastoral poetry. (This vogue was subjected to some satirical comment in William Shakespeare's *As You Like It*—itself a pastoral play.) Robert Greene and Thomas Lodge wrote prose romances in the pastoral mode; apart from Shakespeare, playwrights who attempted pastoral drama included John Lyly, George Peele, John Fletcher, Ben Jonson, John Day, and James Shirley.

The climax of this phase of the pastoral tradition was reached in the freshness and learned imitation of the poetry of Robert Herrick and of Andrew Marvell. Later 17th-century work, apart from that of Milton, was more pedantic. The 18th-century revival of the pastoral mode is chiefly remarkable for its place in a larger quarrel between Neoclassical critics who preferred "ancient" poetry and others who supported the "modern."

In later centuries, a reaction against the artificialities of the genre, combined with new attitudes to the natural man and the natural scene, resulted in a sometimes bitter injection of reality into the rustic scenes of many poets and novelists. Only the pastoral elegy survived, through Percy Bysshe Shelley and Matthew Arnold. *Compare* ECLOGUE; ELEGY; IDYLL.

pastourelle or **pastorelle** \ˌpas-tə-ˈrel, ˌpäs-\ [French *pastourelle,* from Old French *pasturele,* feminine diminutive of *pastour* shepherd] A conventional form of poetic pastoral composed in Europe during the late Middle Ages and consisting of a love debate between a knight and a shepherdess.

patent theaters *British commonly* ˈpāt-ənt, *U.S.* ˈpat-\ Any of several London theaters that, through government licensing, held a monopoly on legitimate dramatic production in London between 1660 and 1843. When he reopened the theaters that had been closed by the Puritans, Charles II issued letters patent to Thomas Killigrew and William Davenant giving them exclusive right to form two acting companies. Killigrew established The King's Servants at Drury Lane, where they stayed. Davenant established The Duke of York's Servants at Lincoln's Inn Fields, from which they moved to Dorset Garden, finally settling at Covent Garden in 1732.

The legality of the patents was confirmed by Parliament with the Licensing Act of 1737, affirming Drury Lane and Covent Garden as the only legitimate theaters in England. Parliament began authorizing theaters outside London in 1768, however, and in 1788 a bill was passed permitting local magistrates to license theaters outside a 20-mile radius of London. In London evasion of the law was common, with unlicensed theaters offering undefined "public entertainments" and pantomime. In 1766 a third London patent was issued to Samuel Foote for operation of the Haymarket Theatre during the summer months, and in 1807 the Earl of Dartmouth, as lord chamberlain, loosely interpreted the Licensing Act and began authorizing other theaters in London. The Theatre Regulation Act of 1843 finally abolished the exclusive rights of the patent theaters to present legitimate drama.

pathetic fallacy Poetic practice of attributing human emotion or responses to nature, inanimate objects, or animals. The practice is a form of personification that is as old as poetry, where it has always been common to find smiling or dancing flowers, angry or cruel winds, brooding mountains, moping owls, or happy larks. The term was coined by John Ruskin in *Modern Painters* (1843–60). In some classical poetic forms such as the pastoral elegy, the pathetic fallacy is actually a required convention. In John Milton's "On The Morning of Christ's Nativity," all aspects of nature react to the event of Christ's birth.

> The Stars with deep amaze
> Stand fixt in steadfast gaze

Ruskin considered the excessive use of the fallacy the mark of an inferior poet. Later poets, however—especially the Imagists of the early 20th century, as well as T.S. Eliot and Ezra Pound—used the pathetic fallacy freely and effectively.

pathos \ˈpā-ˌthäs, -ˌthȯs, -ˌthōs\ [Greek *páthos* incident, experience, emotion, passion] An element in artistic representation evoking pity or compassion. *See also* BATHOS. In rhetoric the term describes a certain kind of emotion and is contrasted with ETHOS.

pattern poetry *also called* altar poem, figure poem, carmen figuratum \ˈkär-mən-ˌfig-yə-ˈrā-təm\, *or* shaped verse. Verse in which the lines or typography are arranged in an unusual configuration, usually to convey or extend the emotional content of the words. Of ancient (probably Eastern) origin, pattern poems are found in the *Greek Anthology,* which includes work composed between the 7th century BC and the late 10th century. In this collection one poem was recorded in the shape of an ax, another as an egg. Notable later examples are the wing-shaped "Easter Wings" of the early 17th-century English Metaphysical poet George Herbert

Lord, who createdst man in wealth and store,
Though foolishly he lost the same,
Decaying more and more
Till he became
Most poor:
With thee
O let me rise
As larks, harmoniously,
And sing this day thy victories;
Then shall the fall further the flight in me.

My tender age in sorrow did begin;
And still with sicknesses and shame
Thou didst so punish sin,
That I became
Most thin.
With thee
Let me combine,
And feel this day thy victory;
For, if I imp my wing on thine,
Affliction shall advance the flight in me.

In the 19th century, the French Symbolist poet Stéphane Mallarmé employed different type sizes in *Un Coup de dés* (1897; "A Throw of Dice"). Representative poets in the 20th century included Guillaume Apollinaire in France and E.E. Cummings in the United States. The works of Apollinaire, whose calligrammes (*Calligrammes* [1918]), inspired by Cubism, are visual evocations as well as poems; in a poem about rain, the words fall in long, slanting lines. Cummings is also notable for his typographical eccentricities and was perhaps most successful in making these visual innovations meaningful elements of his poems. In the 20th century, pattern poetry sometimes crossed paths with CONCRETE POETRY; a basic distinction between the two types is the ability of pattern poetry to hold its meaning apart from its typography—i.e., it can be read aloud and still retain its meaning.

pause \'pȯz\ A break in writing, such as a caesura in verse.

Peking opera *See* JINGXI.

PEN, International \'pen\ Worldwide organization of writers. The original PEN was founded in London in 1921 by the English novelist John Galsworthy, and, though still headquartered there, it has since grown to include writers worldwide. The name PEN is an acronym standing for "poets, playwrights, editors, essayists, and novelists." International PEN promotes intellectual exchanges and goodwill among writers and promotes freedom of expression regardless of their nationality, race, religion, or the political system under which they live. PEN is especially active in defending and supporting writers who are being harassed, persecuted, or oppressed by their government. The organization also bestows literary awards, sponsors translations of works written in obscure or neglected languages, holds conferences on current political-literary topics and publishes pamphlets and newsletters. To become a member of PEN an author normally must have published at least two books, one of which shows considerable literary distinction. PEN is headquartered in London, and there are more than 80 PEN Centres (branch organizations) situated in a total of about 60 countries worldwide.

pen name An author's PSEUDONYM or nom de plume.

penny dreadful *plural* penny dreadfuls, *also called* bloods. A novel of violent adventure or crime especially popular in mid-to-late Victorian England and originally costing one penny. They were often issued in eight-page installments. The appellation, like *dime novel* and *shilling shocker,* conveyed rather careless and second-rate writing as well as gory themes. Among the notably prolific writers of the penny dreadful were James Malcolm Rymer (pseudonym Malcolm J. Errym) and Thomas Peckett Prest. A collection of penny dreadfuls might include such titles as *Vice and Its Victim, The Death Grasp, or A Father's Curse,* and *Varney, the Vampire or, The Feast of Blood.* Later penny dreadfuls were more associated with adventure than gore and were often written for boys.

Penny dreadful is also now used to denote more generally any story or periodical characterized by sensationalism and violence.

pensée \pä^{n}-'sā\ [French, literally, thought] A thought expressed in literary form. A pensée can be short and in a specific form, such as an aphorism or epigram, or it can be as long as a paragraph or a page. The term was derived from the French mathematician and philosopher Blaise Pascal's *Pensées* (1670), a collection of some 800 to 1,000 notes and manuscript fragments expressing his religious beliefs. Although Pascal's work was in truth an unfinished apologia, the form became popular, particularly among French writers. Another outstanding example is found in Denis Diderot's *Pensées philosophiques* (1746).

pen sketch A literary sketch.

pentalogy \pen-'tal-ə-jē\ A series of five closely related published works.

pentameter \pen-'tam-ə-tər\ In poetry, a line of five metrical feet. In English verse, in which pentameter has been the predominant meter since the 16th century, the preferred foot is the iamb—i.e., an unstressed syllable followed by a stressed one, represented in scansion as ∪ ′.

Geoffrey Chaucer employed iambic pentameter in *The Canterbury Tales* as early as the 14th century, although without the regularity that is found later in the heroic couplets of John Dryden and Alexander Pope. Most English sonnets have been written in iambic pentameter, as in this example from William Shakespeare's 18th sonnet:

> ∪ ′ | ∪ ′ | ∪ ′ | ∪ ′ | ∪ ′
> So long | as men | can breathe | or eyes | can see,
> ∪ ′ | ∪ ′ | ∪ ′ | ∪ ′ | ∪ ′
> So long | lives this | and this | gives life | to thee.

Iambic pentameter is also the meter of heroic verse written in English.

pentapody \pen-'tap-ə-dē\ [*penta-* five + *-pody* (as in *dipody*)] In classical prosody, a metrical unit consisting of five feet.

pentastich \'pen-tə-ˌstik\ In poetry, a unit, stanza, or poem consisting of five lines.

penthemimer \ˌpen-thə-ˈmim-ər\ [Greek *penthēmimerés,* from *penthēmi-* two and a half (from *pénte* five + *hēmi-* half) + *méros* part] In Greek and Latin prosody, a group of two and a half feet comprising a short colon of five syllables scanned ⏓ – ∪ – ⏓ .

penthemimeral caesura \ˌpen-thə-ˈmim-ər-əl\ *See* CAESURA.

pericope \pə-ˈrik-ə-pē\ *plural* pericopes *or* pericopae \-ˌpē, -ˌpī\ [Greek *perikopḗ* section] A selection or extract from a book; especially, a selection from the Bible appointed to be read in church or used as a text for a sermon.

period \ˈpir-ē-əd\ [Greek *períodos* circuit, cycle, period in rhetoric] A complete sentence, or an utterance from one full stop to another; usually, a well-proportioned sentence of several clauses.

periodic \ˌpir-ē-ˈäd-ik\ Of or relating to a form of construction found in some Greek odes in which the second and third in a group of four strophes are alike in structure and the first and fourth differ from these and from each other.

periodical \ˌpir-ē-ˈäd-i-kəl\ A journal or other publication whose issues appear at fixed or regular intervals. *See* MAGAZINE.

periodic sentence A usually complex sentence that has no subordinate or trailing elements following its principal clause, or one in which the main clause comes last, as in "Yesterday, while I was walking down the street, I saw him." *Compare* LOOSE SENTENCE.

period piece A piece (as of fiction, art, furniture, or music) whose special or chief value lies in its characterization or evocation of a historical period. *See also* HISTORICAL NOVEL.

peripeteia \ˌper-i-pə-ˈtē ə, -ˈtī-\ or **peripetia** \-ˈtī-ə\ [Greek *peripéteia* reversal, sudden change, a derivative of *peripetḗs* changing suddenly, literally, falling round, falling into] A sudden or unexpected reversal of circumstances or situation in a literary work. Peripeteia is the turning point in a drama after which the plot moves steadily to its denouement. It is discussed by Aristotle in the *Poetics* as the shift of the tragic protagonist's fortune from good to bad, which is essential to the plot of a tragedy. It is often an ironic twist, as in Sophocles' *Oedipus Rex* when a messenger brings Oedipus news about his parents that he thinks will cheer him; the news, instead, slowly brings about the awful recognition that leads to Oedipus' catastrophe. The term is also used to refer to the protagonist's shift from bad fortune to good in a comedy.

periphrasis \pə-ˈrif-rə-sis\ *plural* periphrases \-ˌsēz\, *also called* circumlocution \ˌsər-kəm-lō-ˈkyü-shən\ [Greek *períphrasis,* a derivative of *periphrázein* to express in a roundabout way, from *perí* around + *phrázein* to point out, show, declare] Use of a longer phrasing in place of a possible shorter form of expression, or a roundabout or indirect way of speaking. In literature it is sometimes used for comic effect, as by Charles Dickens in the speech of the character Wilkins Micawber, who appears in *David Copperfield.*

peroration \ˌper-ə-ˈrā-shən, ˌpər-\ [Latin *peroratio,* a derivative of *perorare* to conclude a plea or speech] The concluding part of a discourse and especially of an oration.

persona \pər-ˈsō-nə\ *plural* personae \-ˌnē, -ˌnī\ [Latin, actor's mask, character in a play, person, probably from Etruscan *phersu* mask, from Greek *prósōpa,* plural of *prósōpon* face, mask] In literature, the person who is understood to be speaking (or thinking or writing) a particular work. The persona is almost invariably distinct from the author; it is the voice chosen by the author for a particular artistic purpose. The persona may be a character in the work in question or merely an unnamed narrator, but, insofar as the manner and style of expression in the work exhibit taste, prejudice, emotion, or other characteristics of a human personality, the work may be said to be in the voice of a persona. *See also* NARRATOR.

personage \ˈpər-sə-nij\ A dramatic, fictional, or historical character; also, a character as assumed or represented, as in an impersonation.

personification \pər-ˌsän-ə-fi-ˈkā-shən\ Figure of speech in which human characteristics are attributed to an abstract quality, animal, or inanimate object. Two examples are "The Moon doth with delight / Look round her when the heavens are bare" (William Wordsworth, "Ode: Intimations of Immortality from Recollections of Early Childhood," 1807) and "Death lays his icy hand on kings" (James Shirley, "The Glories of Our Blood and State," 1659). Personification has been used in European poetry since Homer and is particularly common in allegory; for example, the medieval morality play *Everyman* (*c.* 1500) and the Christian prose allegory *The Pilgrim's Progress* (1678) by John Bunyan contain characters such as Death, Fellowship, Knowledge, Giant Despair, Sloth, Hypocrisy, and Piety. Personification became almost an automatic mannerism in 18th-century Neoclassical poetry, as exemplified by these lines from Thomas Gray's *An Elegy Written in a Country Church Yard:*

> Here rests his head upon the lap of Earth
>   A youth to Fortune and to Fame unknown.
> Fair Science frowned not on his humble birth,
>   And Melancholy marked him for her own.

perspectivism \pər-ˈspek-tə-ˌviz-əm\ Consciousness of or the process of using different points of view (as in literary criticism or artistic representation).

Petrarchan sonnet \pi-ˈträr-kən, pe-, pē-\, *also called* Italian sonnet. A poem of 14 lines divided into an octave rhyming *abbaabba* and a sestet with a variable rhyme scheme—it can be *cdecde, cdcdcd,* or *cdcdce,* or some other variation—that never ends in a final couplet. The octave usually presents the theme or problem of the poem, and the sestet presents a change in thought or a resolution of the problem. The sonnet form, developed in 13th-century Italy, reached its highest expression in the works of Petrarch, for whom the Petrarchan sonnet was named. Later brought to England, the Petrarchan sonnet was adapted to create the form now called a SHAKESPEAREAN SONNET. Many English writers continued to write Petrarchan sonnets, however, including William Wordsworth, John Keats, and Elizabeth Barrett Browning. One of the best-known examples of this kind in English is Wordsworth's "The World Is Too Much with Us."

> The world is too much with us; late and soon,
> Getting and spending, we lay waste our powers;
> Little we see in Nature that is ours;
> We have given our hearts away, a sordid boon!
> This Sea that bares her bosom to the moon,
> The winds that will be howling at all hours,
> And are up-gathered now like sleeping flowers,
> For this, for everything, we are out of tune;
> It moves us not.—Great God! I'd rather be
> A Pagan suckled in a creed outworn;
> So might I, standing on this pleasant lea,
> Have glimpses that would make me less forlorn;
> Have sight of Proteus rising from the sea;
> Or hear old Triton blow his wreathèd horn.

The Petrarchan sonnet exerted a major influence on European poetry. It soon became naturalized in Spain, Portugal, and France and was introduced to Poland, whence it spread to other Slavic literatures. In most cases the form was adapted to the staple meter of the language—e.g., the alexandrine (12-syllable iambic line) in France and iambic pentameter in English.

phantasy *See* FANTASY.

phenomenological criticism \fə-ˌnäm-ə-nə-ˈläj-i-kəl\ School of criticism based on phenomenology, the philosophy that arose at the turn of the 20th century with the work of Edmund Husserl.

The primary objective of phenomenology was to take a fresh approach to concretely experienced phenomena through the direct investigation of the data of consciousness—without theories about their causal explanation and as free as possible from unexamined presuppositions—and to attempt to describe them as faithfully as possible. Adherents argued that, by carefully exploring examples, it was possible to fathom the essential structures and relationships of phenomena.

As applied to literary criticism, phenomenology is most evident in the theory and practice of the GENEVA SCHOOL. *See also* READER-RESPONSE CRITICISM.

pherecratean \ˌfer-ə-ˈkrat-ē-ən\, *also called* pherecratic \-ˈkrat-ik\ **1.** *also called* first pherecratean *or* aristophanic \ə-ˌris-tə-ˈfan-ik\ A classical verse or rhythmic system that scans as – ∪ ∪ – ∪ – ⩊. The pherecratean colon takes its name from the Greek comic poet Pherecrates (5th century BC). **2.** *also called* second pherecratean. A classical verse or rhythmic system that scans as ⩊ ⩊ – ∪ ∪ – ⩊.

philippic \fə-ˈlip-ik\ [Greek *Philippikoì lógoi,* speeches of Demosthenes against Philip II of Macedon, literally, speeches relating to Philip] A discourse or declamation full of acrimonious invective; a tirade.

philology \fi-ˈläl-ə-jē\ [Greek *philología* love of learning and literature, a derivative of *philólogos* fond of learning, literary, from *phílos* dear + *lógos* word, speech] Study of literature that includes or may include grammar, criticism, literary history, language history, systems of writing, and anything else that is relevant to literature or to language as used in literature. This sense of the term is now rarely used because a distinction is made between literary and linguistic scholarship. When it is used, it is generally a synonym for *linguistics.* It survives in the titles of a few learned journals that date to the 19th century. Comparative philology was a former name for what is now called comparative linguistics.

philosophe \ˌfē-lə-ˈzȯf\ [French, literally, philosopher] Any of the writers, scientists, and thinkers of 18th-century France who were united, in spite of divergent personal views, in their conviction of the supremacy and efficacy of human reason.

The philosophes were inspired by the philosophic thought of René Descartes, the skepticism of the libertines, or freethinkers, and the popularization of science by Bernard de Fontenelle. They expressed support for social, economic, and political reforms that were brought about by sectarian dissensions within the church, the weakening of the absolute monarchy, and the ruinous wars that had occurred toward the end of Louis XIV's reign. In the early part of the 18th century, the movement was dominated by Voltaire and Montesquieu, but this restrained phase gave way to a more volatile one in the second half of the century.

Denis Diderot, Jean-Jacques Rousseau, Georges-Louis Leclerc de Buffon, Étienne Bonnot de Condillac, Anne-Robert-Jacques Turgot, and the Marquis de Condorcet were among the philosophes who compiled *L'Encyclopédie,* one of the great intellectual achievements of the century.

physical poetry Poetry (such as Imagist poetry) that is primarily concerned with the projection of a descriptive image of material things, as in the poem "Sea Poppies" by Hilda Doolittle (H.D.):

> Amber husk
> fluted with gold
> fruit on the sand
> marked with a rich grain

treasure
spilled near the shrub-pines
to bleach on the boulders:

your stalk has caught root
among wet pebbles
and drift flung by the sea
and grated shells
and split conch-shells.

Beautiful, wide-spread,
fire upon leaf,
what meadow yields
so fragrant a leaf
as your bright leaf?

pianwen or **p'ien-wen** \'pyen-'wən\ [Chinese *piánwén,* from *pián* parallel, antithetical + *wén* language, literary composition] Genre of Chinese literature characterized by antithetic construction and balanced tonal patterns without the use of rhyme; the term is suggestive of "a team of paired horses," as is implied in the Chinese word *pian*. Despite the polyphonic effect thus produced, which approximates that of poetry, it has often been made the vehicle of proselike exposition and argumentation.

By the early ninth century, *pianwen* had been cultivated for almost 1,000 years and had become so burdened with restrictive rules as to make forthright expression virtually impossible. Han Yu and his ally Liu Zongyuan advocated the use of Zhou philosophers and early Han writers as models for prose writing. This seemingly conservative reform had, in fact, a liberalizing effect, for the sentence unit in prose writing was freed to seek its own length and structural pattern as logic and content might dictate.

picaresque novel \ˌpik-ə-'resk, ˌpēk-\ An early form of the novel, usually a first-person narrative, relating the adventures of a rogue or lowborn adventurer (Spanish: *pícaro*) who drifts from place to place and from one social milieu to another in an effort to survive.

In its episodic structure the picaresque novel resembles the long, rambling romances of medieval chivalry, to which it provided the first realistic counterpart. Unlike the idealistic knight-errant hero, however, the picaro is a cynical and amoral rascal who would rather live by his wits than by honorable work. The picaro wanders about and has adventures among people from all social classes and professions, often just barely escaping punishment for lying, cheating, and stealing. He is an outsider who feels unrestrained by social codes and mores and conforms to them outwardly only when it serves his own ends. The picaro's narrative becomes in effect an ironic or satirical survey of the hypocrisies and corruptions of society, while also offering astute observations about people in low or humble walks of life.

The picaresque novel originated in Spain with *Lazarillo de Tormes* (1554; of unknown authorship), in which the poor boy Lázaro describes his services under seven successive lay and clerical masters, each of whom hides his dubious character under a mask of hypocrisy. The irreverent wit of *Lazarillo* helped make it one of the most widely read books of its time. The next picaresque novel to be published, Mateo Alemán's *Guzmán de Alfarache* (1599), the supposed autobiography of the son of a ruined Genoese moneylender, became the true prototype of the genre and helped establish realism as the dominant trend in the Spanish novel.

Among Guzmán's numerous successors were several short novels by Miguel de Cervantes in the picaresque manner, notably *Rinconete y Cortadillo* (1613) and *El coloquio de los perros* (1613; "Colloquy of the Dogs"). Francisco López de Úbeda's *La pícara Justina* (1605; "Naughty Justina") tells the story of a woman picaro who deceives her lovers just as the picaro does his masters. Francisco Gómez de Quevedo's *La vida del buscón* (1626; "The Life of a Scoundrel") is a masterpiece of the genre, in which the profound psychological depiction of a petty thief and swindler is underlain by a deep concern for moral values. After about 1625 the picaresque novel in Spain evolved gradually into the novel of adventure.

In the meantime, however, late 16th-century translations of *Lazarillo de Tormes* introduced the picaro into other European literatures. The first picaresque novel in England was Thomas Nashe's *The Unfortunate Traveller; or, The Life of Jacke Wilton* (1594). In Germany the type was represented by H.J. von Grimmelshausen's *Simplicissimus* (1669). In England the female picaro was revived in Daniel Defoe's *Moll Flanders* (1722), and many picaresque elements can be found in Henry Fielding's *Joseph Andrews* (1742), *Jonathan Wild* (1743), and *Tom Jones* (1749), and Tobias Smollett's *Roderick Random* (1748), *Peregrine Pickle* (1751), and *Ferdinand, Count Fathom* (1753). The outstanding French example is Alain-René Lesage's *Gil Blas* (1715–35) which preserves a Spanish setting and borrows incidents from forgotten Spanish novels but portrays a gentler, more humanized picaro.

In the mid-18th century the growth of the realistic novel with its tighter, more elaborate plot and its greater development of character led to the final decline of the picaresque novel, which came to be considered somewhat inferior in artistry. But the opportunities for satire provided by the picaresque novel's mingling of characters from all walks of life, its vivid descriptions of industries and professions, its realistic language and detail, and above all its ironic and detached survey of manners and morals helped to enrich the realistic novel and contributed to that form's development in the 18th and 19th centuries. Elements of the picaresque novel proper reappeared in such mature realistic novels as Nikolay Gogol's *Myortvye dushi* (1842–52; "Dead Souls"), Mark Twain's *Huckleberry Finn* (1884), and Thomas Mann's *Felix Krull* (1954).

pièce bien faite *See* WELL-MADE PLAY.

p'ien-wen *See* PIANWEN.

Pindaric ode \pin-'dar-ik\ Ceremonious poem by or in the manner of Pindar, a Greek professional lyric poet of the 5th century BC. Pindar employed the triadic structure of Stesichorus (7th and 6th centuries BC), consisting of a strophe (two or more lines repeated as a unit) followed by a metrically harmonious antistrophe, concluding with a summary line (called an epode) in a different meter. These three parts corresponded to the movement of the chorus to one side of the stage and then to the other and their return to deliver the epode.

Although fragments of Pindar's poems in all of the classical choral forms are extant, it is the collection of four books of epinicion odes that has influenced poets of the Western world since their publication by Aldus Manutius the Elder in 1513. Each of the books is devoted to one of the great series of Greek classical games: the Olympian, Pythian, Isthmian, and Nemean. Celebrating the victory of a winner with a performance of choral chant and dance, these epinicion odes are elaborately complex, rich in metaphor and intensely emotive language. They reveal Pindar's sense of vocation as a poet dedicated to preserving and interpreting great deeds and their divine values. The metaphors, myths, and gnomic sayings that ornament the odes are often difficult to grasp because of the rapid shifts of thought and the sacrifice of syntax to achieving uniform poetic color.

With the publication of Pierre de Ronsard's four books of French *Odes* (1550), the Pindaric ode began to be adapted to the vernacular languages. Some English poets, notably Ben Jonson, wrote imitation Pindaric odes, while Abraham Cowley's *Pindarique Odes* (1656) introduced a looser version known as Pindarics. These irregular rhymed odes suggest, but do not reproduce, the style and manner of Pindar. The odes, in which the length of line and stanza is capriciously varied, are among the greatest in the English language; they include John Dryden's "Alexander's Feast," William Wordsworth's "Ode: Intimations of Immortality," Percy Bysshe Shelley's "Ode to the West Wind," Alfred, Lord Tennyson's "Ode on the Death of the Duke of Wellington," and John Keats' "Ode on a Grecian Urn." *See also* EPINICION; ODE.

pirated edition An edition of a work reproduced without authorization, especially in infringement of copyright. Pirated editions are often copied and distributed in a country other than that of the work's origin.

plagiarism \'plā-jə-ˌriz-əm\ An act or instance of plagiarizing (i.e., taking the writings of another person and passing them off as one's own). The fraudulence is closely related to forgery and piracy—practices generally in violation of copyright laws. There is no breach of copyright laws if it can be proved that duplicated wordage was arrived at independently.

plaint A verse lament. *See* COMPLAINT.

play \'plā\ The stage representation of an action or story, or a dramatic composition. *See also* COMEDY; TRAGEDY.

playwright \'plā-ˌrīt\, *also called* dramatist \'dram-ə-tist, 'dräm-\ A person who writes plays.

Pléiade, La \lä-plā-'yȧd\ Group of seven French writers of the 16th century, led by Pierre de Ronsard, whose aim was to elevate the French language to the level of the classical tongues as a medium for literary expression. La Pléiade, whose name was taken from that given by the ancient Alexandrian critics to seven tragic poets of the reign of Ptolemy II Philadelphus (285–246 BC), also included Joachim du Bellay, Jean Dorat, Jean-Antoine de Baïf, Rémy Belleau, Pontus de Tyard, and Étienne Jodelle.

The principles of La Pléiade were authoritatively set forth by du Bellay in *La Défense et illustration de la langue française* (1549; *The Defence and Illustration of the French Language*), a document that advocated the enrichment of the French language by discreet imitation and borrowing from the language and literary forms of the classics and the works of the Italian Renaissance—including such forms as the Pindaric and Horatian ode, the Virgilian epic, and the Petrarchan sonnet. Du Bellay also encouraged the revival of archaic and provincial French words, the incorporation of words and expressions from provincial dialects, the use of technical terms in literary contexts, the coining of new words, and the development of verse forms new to French literature. The writers of La Pléiade are considered the first representatives of French Renaissance poetry, in part because they revived the alexandrine verse form (12-syllable lines rhyming in alternate masculine and feminine couplets), the dominant poetic form of the French Renaissance. The members of La Pléiade are sometimes charged with attempting to Latinize the French language and are criticized for inspiring the slavish imitation of the classics that occasionally occurred among their followers.

pleonasm \'plē-ə-ˌnaz-əm\ [Greek *pleonasmós,* literally, excess, a derivative of *pleonázein* to be in excess, be redundant] **1.** The use of more words than those necessary to denote mere sense (such as *the man he said, saw with his own eyes, true fact*). Pleonasm especially refers to the coincident use of a word and its substitute for the same grammatical function and is similar in meaning to *redundancy* and *tautology*. **2.** An instance or example of such iteration.

ploce \'plō-sē, 'plȯs-\ [Greek *plokḗ* complication, literally, something twisted] **1.** Emphatic repetition of a word with particular reference to its special significance (as in "a wife who was a wife indeed"). **2.** In rhetoric, the repetition of a word in an altered grammatical function, as in the line "Why wilt thou sleep the sleep of death?" from William Blake's poem *Jerusalem,* in which the word *sleep* is used as both a verb and a noun. The term also refers to such repetition in general, as in the phrases "pin the pin on" or "dance the dance." *Compare* ANADIPLOSIS.

plot \'plät\ The plan or the main story of a literary work (such as a novel, play, short story, or poem); also known as narrative structure. Plot involves a considerably higher level of narrative organization than normally occurs in a story or fable. According to E.M. Forster in *Aspects of the Novel* (1927), a story is a "narrative of events arranged in their time-sequence," whereas a plot organizes the events according to a "sense of causality."

In the history of literary criticism, plot has undergone a variety of interpretations. In the *Poetics,* Aristotle assigned primary importance to plot (*mythos*) and considered it the very "soul" of a tragedy. Later critics tended to reduce plot to a more mechanical function, until, in the Romantic era, it was theoretically degraded to an outline on which the content of fiction was hung. The publication of books of "basic plots" brought plot to its lowest esteem.

In the 20th century there have been many attempts to redefine plot, and some critics have even reverted to the position of Aristotle in giving it primary importance in fiction. These neo-Aristotelians, following the leadership of the critic Ronald S. Crane, have described plot as the author's control of the reader's emotional responses—the arousal of the reader's interest and anxiety and the careful control of that anxiety over a duration of time. This approach is only one of many attempts to restore plot to its former place of priority in fiction.

poem \\'pō-əm, -im; 'pōm\\ [Latin *poema,* from Greek *poíēma* work, product, poem, a derivative of *poieîn* to make] A composition in verse. *See also* POETRY.

poesy or **poesie** \\'pō-ə-zē, -sē\\ *plural* poesies [Middle English *poesie,* from Middle French, from Latin *poesis,* from Greek *poíēsis* literally, fabrication, making, a derivative of *poieîn* to make] **1.** A poem or body of poems. **2.** A synonym for POETRY. **3.** Artificial or sentimentalized poetic writing. **4.** Poetic inspiration.

poet \\'pō-ət, -it\\ [Greek *poiētḗs* maker, composer, poet, a derivative of *poieîn* to make] **1.** One who writes poetry; a maker of verses. **2.** One (such as a writer) having great imaginative and expressive capabilities and possessing a special sensitivity to the medium.

poetaster \\'pō-ə-ˌtas-tər\\ An inferior poet.

poète maudit \\pō-et-mō-'dē\\ [French, literally, accursed poet] In literary criticism, the poet as an outcast of modern society, despised by its rulers who fear the artist's penetrating insights into their spiritual emptiness. The phrase was first applied by Paul Verlaine in *Les Poètes maudits* (1883). This work, published in book form in 1884, included critical and biographical studies that focused on the tragedy of the lives of the then little-known Symbolist poets Tristan Corbière, Stéphane Mallarmé, and Arthur Rimbaud. A revised edition, published in 1888, added material on Marceline Desbordes-Valmore, Auguste Villiers de L'Isle-Adam, and Verlaine himself. Verlaine may have taken *les poètes maudits* from Charles Baudelaire's "Bénédiction," in which a poet is described as untouched by the suffering and contempt he experiences. The term carries the implication of the low estate into which the poet has fallen from the ancient position as seer and prophet.

poeticism \pō-ˈet-ə-ˌsiz-əm\ An archaic, trite, or strained expression in poetry.

poetic justice An outcome in which vice is punished and virtue rewarded, usually in a manner peculiarly or ironically appropriate. The term was coined by the English literary critic Thomas Rymer in the 17th century, when it was believed that a work of literature should uphold moral principles and instruct the reader in correct moral behavior.

poetic license Deviation from fact, form, or rule by an artist or writer for the sake of the effect gained.

poetics \pō-ˈet-iks\ **1.** A treatise on poetry or aesthetics. **2.** *also* poetic \pō-ˈet-ik\ Poetic theory or practice. **3.** Poetic feelings or utterances.

poet laureate \ˈlȯr-ē-ət, ˈlär-\ *plural* poets laureate *or* poet laureates. **1.** A person honored for achievement in the art of poetry. **2.** One regarded by a country or region as its most eminent or representative poet. **3.** A poet appointed for life by an English sovereign as a member of the royal household and formerly expected to compose poems for court and national occasions. The title stems from traditions concerning the laurel and dating to the earliest Greek and Roman times.

In England the office of poet laureate is remarkable for its continuity. It began in 1616 with a pension granted to Ben Jonson by James I. Jonson's pension specifically recognized his services to the crown as a poet and envisaged their continuance, but not until sixteen months after Jonson's death in 1637 was a similar pension for similar services granted to Sir William Davenant. It was with John Dryden's appointment in 1668, within a week of Davenant's death, that the laureateship was recognized as an established royal office to be filled automatically when vacant.

During the Revolution of 1688, Dryden was dismissed for refusing the oath of allegiance, and this gave the appointment a political flavor which it retained for more than 200 years. Dryden's successor, Thomas Shadwell, inaugurated the custom of producing New Year and birthday odes; this hardened into a tradition between 1690 and about 1820, becoming the principal task of the office. The odes were set to music and performed in the sovereign's presence. On his appointment in 1813, Robert Southey sought unsuccessfully to end this custom, but it was allowed tacitly to lapse and was finally abolished by Queen Victoria. Her appointment of William Wordsworth in 1843 signified that the laureateship had become the reward for eminence in poetry, and the office since then has carried no specific duties. The laureates from Alfred, Lord Tennyson onward have written poems for royal and national occasions as the spirit has moved them.

The list of poets laureate (with dates of tenure) follows: John Dryden (1668–89), Thomas Shadwell (1689–92), Nahum Tate (1692–1715), Nicholas Rowe (1715–18), Laurence Eusden (1718–30), Colley Cibber (1730–57), William Whitehead (1757–85), Thomas Warton (1785–90), Henry James Pye (1790–1813), Robert Southey (1813–43), William Wordsworth (1843–50), Alfred, Lord Tennyson (1850–92), Alfred Austin (1896–1913), Robert Bridges

(1913–30), John Masefield (1930–67), C. Day-Lewis (1968–72), Sir John Betjeman (1972–84), and Ted Hughes (from 1984).

In 1985 the United States government created the title of poet laureate, to be held by the same person who holds the post of consultant in poetry to the Library of Congress. Both appointments are annual ones. The American poet laureate receives a modest stipend and is expected to present one major poetic work and to be present at certain national ceremonies.

poetomachia \pō-ˌet-ə-ˈmāk-ē-ə, -ˈmak-\ [Greek *poiētḗs* poet + *máchē* battle, fight] A contest of poets; specifically, the literary quarrel known as the WAR OF THE THEATERS involving a number of Elizabethan dramatists, notably Ben Jonson, John Marston, and Thomas Dekker.

poetry \ˈpō-ə-trē\ [Middle English *poetrie,* from Old French, from Medieval Latin *poetria*] **1.** Metrical writing. **2.** The productions of a poet; poems. **3.** Writing that formulates a concentrated imaginative awareness of experience in language chosen and arranged to create a specific emotional response through its meaning, sound, and rhythm.

Poetry may be distinguished from prose literature in terms of form by its compression, by its frequent (though not prescribed) employment of the conventions of meter and rhyme, by its reliance upon the line as a formal unit, by its heightened vocabulary, and by its freedom of syntax. The characteristic emotional content of poetry finds expression through a variety of techniques, from direct description to highly personalized symbolism. One of the most ancient and universal of these techniques is the use of metaphor and simile to alter and expand the reader's imaginative apprehension through implicit or explicit comparison. This may involve an appeal to sense experience, especially visual sensation, or to emotional experience or cultural and historical awareness. Thus, by conjuring up pictures or images and by invoking different kinds of imaginative associations, the poet elicits in others something of his or her own feeling and consciousness.

Poetry encompasses many modes: narrative, dramatic, aphoristic, celebratory, satiric, descriptive, didactic, erotic, and personal. Within a single work the poet may move from one mode to another, preserving overall unity through the consistency of the formal pattern. The formal patterns available to the poet vary considerably: in English poetry the formal unit may be the single unrhymed line (as in blank verse), the rhymed couplet, the rhymed stanza of four lines or more, or more complex rhyming patterns such as the 14-line sonnet.

Poetry is an ancient mode of expression; it was often used by nonliterate societies who formulated poetic expressions of religious, historical, and cultural significance and transmitted these to the next generation in hymns, incantations, and narrative poems. Something of this early association with the cultural traditions of the tribe has persisted in later theories of poetic inspiration and poetic privilege, though from the time of the Romantics the autonomous creative imagination has been regarded as the source of poetic energy and the guarantee of poetic authenticity. Some modern poets, such as the Surrealists, would claim that the poetic faculty is a mode of access to individual and collective unconscious experience.

In the 19th and 20th centuries Western poetry has responded more to the expressive possibilities of poetic idiom and convention in different traditions. Some poets have experimented with reviving or adapting the subject matter and the verse forms of other times and places. For other poets it has been important to break with tradition and convention and attempt a studied informality of manner, an approximation of the relaxed rhythms and colloquial vocabulary of ordinary speech, and a self-consciously "prosaic" imagery. *Compare* PROSE. *See also* LINE; METER; RHYME.

Poetry (*in full* Poetry: A Magazine of Verse) American poetry magazine founded in Chicago in 1912 by Harriet Monroe who also served for many years as the magazine's editor.

The first issue of *Poetry: A Magazine of Verse* appeared in October 1912. Because its inception coincided with the Midwestern cultural ferment later known as the CHICAGO LITERARY RENAISSANCE, it is often thought of particularly as the vehicle for the raw, original, local-color poetry of Carl Sandburg, Edgar Lee Masters, Vachel Lindsay, and Sherwood Anderson, but it also championed new formalistic movements in verse. The poet and critic Ezra Pound was European correspondent. Imagism, impressionism, and vers libre were expounded in its pages. "The Love Song of J. Alfred Prufrock" by the then-unknown T.S. Eliot appeared in *Poetry* (1915), as did the experimental poems of Wallace Stevens, Marianne Moore, D.H. Lawrence, and William Carlos Williams. *Poetry* survived the withering of the Chicago literary renaissance and World Wars I and II. It remained a highly respected journal even after Monroe's sudden death in 1936. Its later editors included George Dillon, John Frederick Nims, Hayden Carruth, and Karl Shapiro.

Poet's Corner A section of London's Westminster Abbey that contains the tombs of many notable authors and monuments to many others. Among those buried or memorialized there are Geoffrey Chaucer, Edmund Spenser, John Dryden, Samuel Johnson, Alfred, Lord Tennyson, the Brontë sisters, Robert Browning, Henry James, T.S. Eliot, W.H. Auden, and Sir Noël Coward.

point of view The perspective from which a story is presented to the reader. The three main points of view are first person, third person singular, and third person omniscient. In a first person narrative, the story is told by "I," one of the characters involved in the story, as in Charlotte Brontë's *Jane Eyre* and Herman Melville's *Moby-Dick*. Third person is the voice in which a story is presented when the narrator is not a character in the story. The term actually refers to either of two narrative voices. A story told in the third person singular is one in which the narrator writes from the point of view of a single character, describing or noticing only what that character has the opportunity to see and hear and know, but not in the voice of that character, as in Henry James' *What Maisie Knew*. A third person omniscient narrator is not limited in viewpoint to any one character and thus can comment on every aspect of the story. George Eliot's *Middlemarch* uses such a narrator. *See also* NARRATOR.

polemic \pə-ˈlem-ik\ [French *polémique,* from *polémique* (adjective) disputatious, from Greek *polemikós* pertaining to war, a derivative of *pólemos* war] An aggressive attack on or refutation of the opinions or principles of another. One of the best-known examples in literature is John Milton's *Areopagitica.*

police procedural *plural* police procedurals. A mystery story written from the point of view of the officer or detective investigating the crime.

political verse Byzantine or Modern Greek accentual verse; especially, verse of 15-syllable iambic lines.

polygraph \ˈpäl-ē-ˌgraf\ [French *polygraphe,* from Greek *polýgraphos* writing much or on many topics] A voluminous or versatile writer.

polyphonic prose A freely rhythmical form of prose employing characteristic devices of verse other than strict meter (such as alliteration, assonance, rhyme). The form was developed in the early 20th century by Amy Lowell, who demonstrated its techniques in her book *Can Grande's Castle.*

polyptoton \pä-ˈlip-tə-ˌtän\ [Late Latin, from Greek *polýptōton,* neuter of *polýptōtos* using many inflected forms (of the same word), from *poly-* many + *-ptōtos,* a derivative of *ptôsis* accidence, inflection, literally, the act of falling] The rhetorical repetition within the same sentence of a word in a different case, inflection, or voice or of etymologically related words in different parts of speech. The device is exemplified in the following lines from T.S. Eliot's poem "The Dry Salvages":

> There is no end of it, the voiceless wailing,
> No end to the withering of withered flowers,
> To the movement of pain that is painless and motionless,
> To the drift of the sea and the drifting wreckage,
> The bone's prayer to Death its God. Only the hardly, barely prayable
> Prayer of the one Annunciation.

polyschematist \ˌpäl-ē-ˈskē-mə-tist\ [Greek *polyschēmátistos* multiform, composed of various meters, from *poly-* many + *schēma* form, shape] In classical prosody, a unit of five to usually eight syllables whose last four syllables form a choriamb (– ∪ ∪ –), with the other syllables being indeterminate (either long or short) and diverse as to quantity. It is considered by many to be the basic figure of all the Greek lyric meters known as aeolic meters, which were used for poetry that was sung rather than recited. A common form was

⏕ ⏖ ⏑̲ ⏑̄ | – ∪ ∪ –.

This base may be expanded by the addition of more choriambs and following syllables. *See also* AEOLIC.

polysyndeton \ˌpäl-ē-ˈsin-də-ˌtän\ [Late Greek *polysýndeton,* neuter of *polysýndetos* using many conjunctions, from Greek *poly-* many + *sýndetos* bound together, conjunctive] Repetition of conjunctions in close succession, as in the sentence "We have ships and men and money and stores."

pony *See* TROT.

pornography \pȯr-ˈnäg-rə-fē\ [Greek *pornográphos* (adjective) writing about prostitutes, from *pórnē* prostitute + *gráphein* to write] The depiction of erotic behavior intended to cause sexual excitement. *Compare* EROTICA.

Little is known of the origins and earliest forms of pornography. One of the first clear examples of pornography in Western culture can be found in the salacious songs performed in ancient Greece at festivals honoring the god Dionysius. Indisputable evidence of graphic pornography in Roman culture is found at Pompeii, where erotic paintings dating from the 1st century AD cover walls depicting bacchanalian orgies. A classic of written pornography is the Roman poet Ovid's *Ars Amatoria* (*The Art of Love*), a treatise on the art of seduction, intrigue, and sensual arousal.

During the Middle Ages pornography was widespread but held in low repute, finding expression mostly in riddles, common jokes, doggerel, and satirical verses. A notable exception is Giovanni Boccaccio's *Decameron,* which contains several licentious stories. A principal theme of medieval pornography was the sexual license of monks and other clerics, along with their attendant displays of hypocrisy.

The invention of printing led to the rebirth of ambitious pornographic written works. They frequently contained elements of humor and romance and were written to entertain as well as to arouse. Many such works harked back to classical writings in their treatment of the joys and sorrows of marital deception and infidelity. The *Heptaméron* of Margaret of Angoulême is similar to the *Decameron* in that it uses the device of a group of people telling stories, some of which are salacious.

In 18th-century Europe there appeared the first modern works that were both devoid of literary value and designed solely to arouse sexual excitement. A small underground traffic in such works became the basis of a separate publishing and bookselling business in England. A classic of this period was John Cleland's widely read *Fanny Hill.* At about this time erotic graphic art began to be widely produced in Paris, eventually coming to be known as French postcards.

Pornography flourished in the Victorian era despite, or perhaps because of, the prevailing taboos on sexual topics. A notable work of Victorian pornography is the massive and anonymous autobiography *My Secret Life* (1890), which is both a social chronicle of the underside of a puritanical society and a minutely detailed recounting of an English gentleman's lifelong pursuit of sexual gratification.

The development of photography and later of motion pictures contributed greatly to the proliferation of pornographic materials. Since World War II, written pornography has been largely superseded by explicit visual representations of erotic behavior.

Pornography has long been the target of moral and legal sanction in the belief that it may tend to deprave and corrupt minors and adults and cause the commission of sexual crimes. Occasionally, important works of art or even of religious significance may be banned by a state or other jurisdiction because they are considered pornographic under such assumptions.

portmanteau word \pȯrt-'man-tō, ˌpȯrt-man-'tō\ A word composed of parts of two or more words (such as *chortle* from *chuckle* and *snort* and *motel* from *motor* and *hotel*). The term was first used by Lewis Carroll to describe many of the unusual words in his *Through the Looking-Glass,* particularly in the poem "Jabberwocky." Other authors who have experimented with such words are James Joyce and Gerard Manley Hopkins. *Compare* NONCE WORD.

position \pə-'zish-ən\ In Greek or Latin prosody, the condition of having a short vowel followed by two consonants or a double consonant (such as *-pp-* in Greek *hippos*), which makes its syllable long. Such a syllable is said to be long by position, in contrast to a syllable having a long vowel or a diphthong, which is said to be long by nature.

postmodern \ˌpōst-'mäd-ərn\ Of or relating to any of several artistic movements that have challenged the philosophy and practices of modern arts or literature since about the 1940s. In literature this has amounted to a reaction against an ordered view of the world and therefore against fixed ideas about the form and meaning of texts. This reaction is reflected in eclectic styles of writing through the use of such devices as pastiche and parody as well as in the development of such concepts as the absurd, the antihero and the antinovel, and magic realism. The perception of the relativity of meaning has also led to a proliferation of critical theories, most notably deconstruction and its offshoots.

poststructuralism \ˌpōst-'strek-chə-rə-ˌliz-əm\ Movement in literary criticism conceived in France in the late 1960s. Based on the linguistic theories of Ferdinand de Saussure and the deconstructionist theories of Jacques Derrida, poststructuralism is centered around the idea that language is inherently unreliable and thus cannot possess absolute meaning in itself. Poststructuralists believe that all meaning resides in intertextuality, or the relationship of the text to past and future texts.

Like the practitioners of reader-response, feminist, Marxist, and psychoanalytic criticism, poststructuralists do not support the traditional Western insistence on a single correct reading of a text. Writers associated with the movement include Roland Barthes, Jacques Lacan, Julia Kristeva, and Michel Foucault. *Compare* DECONSTRUCTION; STRUCTURALISM. *See also* INTERTEXTUALITY.

poulter's measure \'pōl-tərz\ A meter in which lines of 12 and 14 syllables alternate. *Poulter* is a now-obsolete variant of *poulterer* (poultry dealer); poulterers would traditionally give one or two extra eggs when counting by the dozen.

practical criticism *also called* applied criticism. Form of literary criticism with a largely implicit theoretical approach that addresses a particular work or writer. It differs from theoretical criticism in both its methodology and its goal. Early practitioners of this type of criticism included Longinus, Aristotle, and Plato. Other notable practical critics were Samuel Johnson, William Hazlitt, William Coleridge, Matthew Arnold, and Virginia Woolf.

pragmatic criticism Critical method that judges a work by its success in achieving its intended goal. It concerns the judgment of intention as well as the analysis of an author's strategies.

Prague school \'präg, 'prāg\, *also called* Prague Linguistic Circle. School of structuralist linguistic thought and analysis established in Prague during the early 20th century. Among its most prominent members were the linguists Nikolay Trubetskoy and Roman Jakobson. The school was most active during the 1920s and '30s.

The Prague school is renowned for its interest in the application of functionalism—the study of how elements of a language accomplish cognition and expression—to syntax and the structure of literary texts. The members designed the first systematic formulation of linguistic structuralism based on the work of Ferdinand de Saussure and constructed a theory of poetic language that was expressed in several significant essays on literature and aesthetics, including one that Jakobson cowrote with Claude Lévi-Strauss on a poem by Charles Baudelaire.

Prairie Schooner, The *also called* (after 1956) Prairie Schooner. Quarterly literary magazine founded in 1927 by Lowry Charles Wimberly and associated with the University of Nebraska. At first the journal published only literature and criticism relevant to the Midwest, but it later adopted a broader, more national perspective, publishing authors such as Randall Jarrell, Robert Penn Warren, and Tillie Olsen. The magazine was responsible for establishing Willa Cather's reputation as a serious writer.

praise song One of the most widely used African poetic forms; a series of laudatory epithets applied to gods, people, animals, plants, and towns that capture the essence of the object being praised. Professional bards, who may be both praise singers to a chief and court historians of their tribe, chant praise songs such as these concerning the great Zulu chieftain Shaka that were translated by Es'kia Mphahlele:

> He is Shaka the unshakeable,
> Thunderer-while-sitting, son of Menzi.
> He is the bird that preys on other birds,
> The battle-axe that excels over other
> battle-axes.
> He is the long-strided pursuer, son of Ndaba,
> Who pursued the sun and the moon.

He is the great hubbub like the rocks of Nkandla
Where elephants take shelter
When the heavens frown.

Although expected to know all of the traditional phrases handed down by word of mouth in his tribe, the bard is also free to make additions to existing poems. Thus the praise songs of Shango, the Yoruba god of thunder and lightning, may contain a modern comparison of the god to the power and noise of a railway.

Among some Bantu-speaking peoples, the praise song is an important form of oral literature. The Sotho of Lesotho traditionally required all boys undergoing initiation to compose praises for themselves that set forth the ideals of action or manhood. Sotho bards also composed traditional praises of chiefs and warriors, and even a very young man was allowed to create praises of himself if he had performed feats of great courage. Sotho praises are telegraphic, leaving much to the listener's imagination; their language is poetic, and the sequence of events not necessarily logical. Metaphor is a key device for suggesting worth (for example, a reciter might call himself a ferocious animal), and poetic license is granted for coining new words.

To the subjects used by the Sotho, the Tswana of Botswana add women, tribal groups, domestic (especially cattle) and wild animals, trees, crops, various features of the landscape, and divining bones. Their praise songs consist of a succession of loose stanzas with an irregular number of lines and a balanced metrical form. Experiences such as going abroad to work for Europeans have become a subject of recent praise poems, and recitation has been extended from tribal meetings and ritual occasions such as weddings to the beer hall and labor camp.

In West Africa praise songs also have been adapted to the times, and a modern praise singer often serves as an entertainer hired to flatter the rich and socially prominent or to act as a master of ceremonies for paramount chiefs at state functions—e.g., among the Hausa people (of Nigeria and Niger) and Malinke people (of Guinea, Côte d'Ivoire, Mali, Senegal, The Gambia, and Guinea-Bissau). Thus praise-song poems, though still embodying and preserving a tribe's history, have also been adapted to an increasingly urbanized and Westernized African society.

preciosity \ˌpresh-ē-ˈäs-ə-tē, ˌpres-\ [French *préciosité,* literally, preciousness] Fastidious or excessive refinement (as in language); specifically, the affected purism characteristic of the style of thought and expression that was prevalent in the 17th-century French salons. Initially a reaction against the coarse behavior and speech of the aristocracy, this spirit of refinement and bon ton was first instituted by the Marquise de Rambouillet in her salon and gradually extended into literature. The wit and elegance of the *honnête homme* ("cultivated man") became a social ideal, which was expressed in the vivid, polished style of Vincent Voiture's poems and letters and in the eloquent prose works of Jean-Louis Guez de Balzac. The ideal revived the medieval tradition of courtly love, as expressed in the novels of Honoré d'Urfé. The success of his *L'Astrée*

(1607–27; *Astrea*), a vast pastoral set in the 5th century, was attributable as much to its charming analysis of the phases of love and the corresponding adventures and complications as to its portraits of members of contemporary society.

While the conceits and circumlocutions of the précieux, or "precious," writers were greatly admired by many, others—such as Molière in his comedy *Les Précieuses ridicules* (1659; *The Affected Young Ladies*)—mocked them for their pedantry and affectation. Preciosity in France was eventually carried to excess and led to exaggeration and affectation (particularly as reflected in burlesque writers), as it did in other countries—seen, for example, in such movements as *gongorismo* in Spain, Marinism in Italy, and euphuism in England.

précis \prā-ˈsē, ˈprā-ˌsē\ [French, from *précis* cut short, precise] A concise epitome or abstract of a book, or a brief summary of essential points, statements, or facts.

preface \ˈpref-əs\ [Middle English, from Old French *prefaice,* from Latin *praefatio,* a derivative of *praefari* to say beforehand] The author's introduction to a work, usually explaining the object and scope of what follows. For works of literature, prefaces can sometimes be extended essays, such as those of Henry James and George Bernard Shaw.

Premio de Literatura en Lengua Castellana Miguel de Cervantes *See* CERVANTES PRIZE.

prequel \ˈprē-kwəl\ [*pre-* + *-quel* (as in *sequel*)] A literary or dramatic work whose story precedes that of an earlier work. For example, Lillian Hellman's play *Another Part of the Forest* (1946) portrays the earlier lives of the characters she first wrote about in *The Little Foxes* (1939) since the action of the later play takes place 20 years before that of *The Little Foxes*.

Pre-Raphaelites \ˌprē-ˈräf-ē-ə-ˌlīts, -ˈrāf-\ Group of young British painters, led by Dante Gabriel Rossetti, William Holman Hunt, and John Everett Millais, who banded together in 1848 in reaction against what they conceived to be the unimaginative and artificial historical painting of the Royal Academy and who sought to express a new moral seriousness and sincerity in their works. Their adoption of the name Pre-Raphaelite Brotherhood expressed their admiration for what they saw as the direct and uncomplicated depiction of nature typical of Italian painting before the High Renaissance and, particularly, before the time of Raphael. Although the group's active life lasted less than 10 years, its influence on painting in Britain, and ultimately on the decorative arts and literature, was profound.

Despite its emphasis on painting, the Pre-Raphaelite Brotherhood also functioned as a school of writers who linked the incipient Aestheticism of John Keats and Thomas De Quincey to the Decadent movement of the fin de siècle. Rossetti in particular expanded the Brotherhood's aims by linking poetry, painting, and social idealism and by interpreting the term Pre-Raphaelite as synonymous with a romanticized medieval past. Rossetti was also attracted for aesthetic reasons by the ritual and ornament of the High Church movement, calling himself an "art-catholic." The "art-catholic" appears, though not with any specifically religious intent, in the rich word-painting and emotional force of his poem "The Blessed Damozel," published in 1850 in the first issue of *The Germ,* the Pre-Raphaelite magazine. He later collected his early writing in *Poems* (1870), a volume that led the critic Robert Buchanan to attack him as the leader of "The Fleshly School of Poetry."

Rossetti combined subtle treatments of contemporary life with a new kind of medievalism, seen also in *The Defence of Guenevere* (1858) by William Morris. These writers also used medieval settings as a context that made possible an uninhibited treatment of sex and violence. The shocking subject matter and vivid imagery of Morris' first volume were further developed by Algernon Charles Swinburne in *Atalanta in Calydon* (1865) and *Poems and Ballads* (1866), where he combined them with an intoxicating metrical power.

The exquisitely wrought religious poetry of Christina Rossetti is perhaps truer to the original, pious purposes of the Pre-Raphaelite Brotherhood.

pre-Romanticism \ˌprē-rō-ˈman-ti-ˌsiz-əm\ Cultural movement in Europe from roughly the 1740s to the 1780s that preceded and presaged the artistic movement known as Romanticism. Chief among the trends of this movement was a shift in public taste away from the grandeur, austerity, nobility, idealization, and elevated sentiments of Neoclassicism toward simpler, more sincere, and more natural forms of expression. This new emphasis partly reflected the tastes of the growing middle class, who found the refined and elegant art forms patronized by aristocratic society to be artificial.

A major intellectual precursor of Romanticism was the French philosopher and writer Jean-Jacques Rousseau. He emphasized the free expression of emotion, repudiated aristocratic elegance and recognized the virtues of middle-class domestic life, helped reveal the beauties of nature, and introduced the idea that the expression of the creative spirit is more important than strict adherence to formal rules and traditional procedures.

The new emphasis on genuine emotion can be seen in the graveyard school of English poetry; Samuel Richardson's *Pamela* (1740) and other sentimental novels that exploited the reader's capacity for tenderness and compassion; the "novel of sensibility" of the 1760s, with its emphasis on emotional sensitivity and deeply felt personal responses to art and nature; the Sturm und Drang movement in Germany; the English gothic novel of terror, fantasy, and mystery; and, finally, the ambitious efforts to collect and preserve folktales and ballads of all types. By the 1790s pre-Romanticism had been supplanted by Romanticism proper.

preterition [Late Latin *praeteritio,* literally, act of passing by, omission, a derivative of Latin *praeterire* to pass by, omit] *See* PARALIPSIS.

Priapea or **Priapeia** \ˌprī-ə-ˈpē-ə\ Poems in honor of the god of fertility, Priapus. Although there are ancient Greek poems addressed to him, the name *Priapea* is mainly applied to a collection of 85 or 86 short Latin poems composed in various meters. They deal with the fertility god, who, with his sickle, protected gardens and vineyards against thieves and from whose ax-hewn image of fig wood or willow there protruded an erect, red-painted phallus. The majority of the poems, marked by occasional flashes of wit and humor, are remarkable only for their obscenity. An example is *Tibullus,* an elegy of 84 lines in which Priapus assumes the role of a professor of love (*magister amoris*) and instructs the poet Albius Tibullus on how best to secure the affection of the boy Marathus. Most appear to belong to the Augustan Age (*c.* 43 BC–AD 18) or to a date not much later and show evidence of indebtedness to the poet Ovid. They in turn influenced the poet Martial. Some may originally have been the leisure products of aristocratic voluptuaries; others, genuine inscriptions on shrines of Priapus.

priapean \ˌprī-ə-ˈpē-ən\ In Roman poetry, an Aeolic verse composed of a glyconic followed by a pherecrean (also known as a catalectic glyconic). A priapean is scanned ⏑̲ ⏑̄ | – ⏑ ⏑ – | ⏑ – | ⏑̲ ⏑̄ | – ⏑ ⏑ – | –. The meter is so called from its use in Latin poems honoring the fertility god Priapus.

Prix Fémina \ˌprē-fā-mē-ˈnȧ\ French literary prize for the best novel published in France each year by a man or woman. The monetary award is 5,000 French francs, and the jury consists of women of letters.

The prize was established in 1904 by the reviews *Fémina* and *Vie Heureuse* as an alternate to the Prix Goncourt, which was then unlikely to be given to works written by women. The Prix Fémina-Vacaresco for nonfiction was established in 1937, and foreign works are awarded the Prix Fémina Étranger. Laureates include Pierre Fleutiaux in 1990 for *Nous sommes éternals,* Sylvie Germain in 1989 for *Jours de colère,* and Louise Bellocq in 1960 for *La Porte retombée.*

Prix Goncourt \ˌprē-gȯ^{n}-ˈkür\ One of the most important literary prizes awarded in France. It was first conceived in 1867 by the brothers Edmond and Jules de Goncourt, authors of *Journals,* and created in 1903 by a bequest of Edmond that established the Académie Goncourt, a literary society of 10 members whose chief duty it is to select the winner of the award. Along with a now-inconsiderable 50 francs, the prize confers recognition on the author of an outstanding work of imaginative prose each year; novels are preferred. The prize is awarded each November. Among the writers who have won the Prix Goncourt are Marcel Proust, André Malraux, Elsa Triolet, Simone de Beauvoir, Romain Gary, André Schwarz-Bart, Michel Tournier, and Marguerite Duras.

Prix Renaudot \ˌprē-rā-nȯ-ˈdō\ French literary prize awarded to the author of an outstanding original novel published during the previous year. Named for Théophraste Renaudot (1586?–1653), who founded *La Gazette* (later *La Gazette de France*), an influential weekly newspaper, the prize was established in 1925 and first awarded in 1926. Like the Prix Goncourt, with which it competes, the Prix Renaudot is awarded annually at a ceremony in a Parisian restaurant. Its winners have included Michel del Castillo, Jean-Marie Le Clézio, Édouard Glissant, Michel Butor, Jean Cayrol, Louis Aragon, Louis-Ferdinand Céline, and Marcel Aymé.

problem play *also called* thesis play. Type of drama that developed in the 19th century to deal with controversial social issues in a realistic manner, to expose social ills, and to stimulate thought and discussion on the part of the audience.

The genre had its beginnings in the work of the French dramatists Alexandre Dumas *fils* and Émile Augier, who adapted the then-popular formula of Eugène Scribe's "well-made" play to serious subjects, creating somewhat simplistic and didactic thesis plays on subjects such as prostitution, business ethics, illegitimacy, and female emancipation. The problem play reached its maturity in the works of the Norwegian playwright Henrik Ibsen, whose works had artistic merit as well as topical relevance. His first experiment in the genre was *Love's Comedy,* a critical study of contemporary marriage. He exposed the hypocrisy, greed, and hidden corruption of society in a number of masterly plays, including *A Doll's House,* which portrays a woman's escape from her dependent, subservient role as a bourgeois wife, *Ghosts,* which attacks the convention that even loveless and unhappy marriages are sacred, *The Wild Duck,* which shows the consequences of an egotistical idealism, and *An Enemy of the People,* which reveals the expedient morality of respectable provincial townspeople.

Ibsen's influence helped encourage the writing of problem plays throughout Europe. Other Scandinavian playwrights, among them August Strindberg, discussed sexual roles and the emancipation of women from both liberal and conservative viewpoints. Eugène Brieux attacked the French judicial system in *The Red Robe*. In England, George Bernard Shaw brought the problem play to its intellectual peak. More recent examples of problem plays are those of the Irish playwright Sean O'Casey, the South African Athol Fugard, the Americans Arthur Miller and August Wilson, and the English dramatists David Hare and Caryl Churchill.

When problem plays advocate a specific response to the problem being discussed, as in Clifford Odets' *Waiting for Lefty,* which is a plea for unionism, they are sometimes called propaganda plays.

The term problem play has also been used in a different sense to describe the plays of William Shakespeare that do not fit neatly into a category such as drama or comedy. These include *All's Well That Ends Well* and *Measure for Measure*.

proceleusmatic \ˌpräs-ə-lüs-ˈmat-ik, ˌprō-sə-\ [Greek *prokeleusmatikós,* a derivative of *prokeleúein* to give orders beforehand, from *pro-* before + *keleúein* to urge, drive on, command; probably from the use of proceleusmatics in ancient Greek rowing songs] In classical prosody, a metrical foot consisting of four short syllables.

procephalic \ˌprō-sə-ˈfal-ik\ [Greek *proképhalos* procephalous] In classical prosody, of a dactylic hexameter (usually scanned as:

– ∪ ∪ | – ∪ ∪ | – ∪ ∪ | – ∪ ∪ | – ∪ ∪ | – ⏓),

having an extra short syllable at the beginning and scanned:

∪ | – ∪ ∪ | – ∪ ∪ | – ∪ ∪ | – ∪ ∪ | – ∪ ∪ | – ⏓.

prodelision \ˌprō-di-ˈlizh-ən\ [Latin *prod-*, variant, before vowels, of *pro-* before, in front of + English *elision*] In classical prosody, the suppression of a short vowel at the beginning of a word when the preceding word ends with a long vowel.

proem \ˈprō-ˌem, -əm\ [Latin *prooemium,* from Greek *prooímion,* from *pro-* before, in front of + *oimḗ* song] A preliminary discourse to a longer piece of writing or a speech; a preface or a preamble.

programma \prō-ˈgram-ə\ *plural* programmata \-mə-tə\ [Greek *prógramma* public notice, a derivative of *prográphein* to set forth, give written notice of] A preface, especially to a learned literary work.

prolegomenon \ˌprō-li-ˈgäm-ə-ˌnän, -nən\ *plural* prolegomena \-nə\ [Greek *prolegómenon,* neuter present passive participle of *prolégein* to say beforehand, from *pro-* before, in advance + *légein* to say] Prefatory remarks; specifically, a formal essay or critical discussion serving to introduce and interpret an extended work.

prolepsis \prō-ˈlep-sis\ [Greek *prólēpsis* anticipation (in rhetoric), a derivative of *prolambánein* to take in advance, anticipate] A figure of speech in which a future act or development is represented as if already accomplished or presently existing. The following lines from John Keats' "Isabella," for example, proleptically anticipate the assassination of a living character:

> So the two brothers and their murdered man
> Rode past fair Florence

The word may also refer to the anticipation of objections to an argument, a tactic aimed at weakening the force of such objections.

proletarian novel Novel that presents the lives of the working class and that springs out of direct experience of proletarian life. Early examples such as William Godwin's *Caleb Williams* (1794) or Robert Bage's *Hermsprong* (1796)—though, like Charles Dickens' *Hard Times* (1854), sympathetic to the lot of the oppressed worker—are more concerned with the imposition of reform from above than with revolution from within. The proletarian novel is essentially an intended device of revolution.

The Russian Maksim Gorky, in works such as *Foma Gordeyev* (1899) and *Mat* (1906; *Mother*), as well as many short stories portraying poverty and unemployment, may be taken as an exemplary proletarian writer. The United States has produced a rich crop of working-class fiction, including that of such socialist writers as Jack London, Upton Sinclair, John Dos Passos, and Edward Dahlberg. England, too, has produced its share of working-class novelists, such as Alan Sillitoe and John Braine.

Proletkult \prə-lʸit-ˈkülʸt\, *abbreviation of* Proletarskaya Kultura ("Proletarian Culture") Organization established in the Soviet Union in 1917 to provide the foundations for a truly proletarian art—i.e., one that would be created by proletarians for proletarians and would be free of all vestiges of bourgeois culture. Its leading theoretician was Aleksandr Bogdanov. Subsidized by the state, but independent of Communist Party control, the Proletkult established workshops throughout the country where workers were taught to read and encouraged to write plays, novels, and poems. Although the workshops produced a few poets, their styles and techniques were invariably imitative of writers of the past. Vladimir Lenin soon realized the inadvisability of trying to force a new culture and withdrew his support. By 1923 Proletkult was abolished.

prolog *See* PROLOGUE.

prologos \prō-ˈlō-ˌgäs\ or **prologus** \-gəs\ *plural* prologoi \-ˌgȯi\ *or* prologi \-ˌjī\ [Greek *prólogos,* a derivative of *prolégein* to say beforehand, from *pro-* before + *légein* to speak] In ancient Greek drama, the first part of the play, in which exposition or character development is presented through a monologue or dialogue. The prologos precedes the parodos, the first choral passage in the drama.

prologue or **prolog** \ˈprō-ˌlȯg, -läg\ [Greek *prólogos* prologos] **1.** The preface or introduction to a literary work. **2.** A speech, often in verse, addressed to the audience by one or more of the actors at the opening of a play. *Compare* EPILOGUE. Also, the actor speaking such a prologue.

The ancient Greek prologos was of wider significance than the modern prologue, effectually taking the place of an explanatory first act. A character, often a deity, appeared on the empty stage to explain events prior to the action of the drama, which consisted mainly of a catastrophe. On the Latin stage, the prologue was generally more elaborately written, as in the case of Plautus' *Rudens,* which contains some of his finest poetry.

In England the mystery and miracle plays began with a homily. In the 16th century Thomas Sackville used a dumb show (pantomime) as a prologue to the first English tragedy, *Gorboduc;* William Shakespeare began *Henry IV, Part 2* with the character of Rumour to set the scene, and *Henry V* began with a chorus. The Plautine prologue was revived by Molière in France during the 17th century.

Though epilogues were rarely written after the 18th century, prologues have been used effectively in such 20th-century plays as Hugo von Hofmannsthal's

Jedermann (*Everyman*), Thornton Wilder's *Our Town,* Tennessee Williams' *Glass Menagerie,* and Jean Anouilh's *Antigone*.

prologus *See* PROLOGOS.

proode \ˈprō-ˌōd\ [Greek *proōidós,* from *pro-* before, in front of + *ōidḗ* ode] **1.** A distich with the first line shorter than the second—opposed to *epode.* **2.** A strophic unit in an ancient ode preceding the strophe and antistrophe and differing from them in structure.

propaganda novel *also called* thesis novel. A sometimes didactic work that addresses a specific social problem.

propaganda play A type of PROBLEM PLAY that advocates a specific solution to the conflict dramatized.

proparoxytone \ˌprō-ˌpär-ˈäk-si-ˌtōn\ [Greek *proparoxýtonos,* from *pro-* before + *paroxýtonos* paroxytone] Having or characterized by an acute accent or a heavy stress on the antepenultimate syllable.

prosaic \prō-ˈzā-ik\ **1.** Characteristic of prose as distinguished from poetry, i.e., factual or literal. **2.** Having a dull, flat, unimaginative quality of style or expression.

prose \ˈprōz\ [Latin *prosa,* short for *prosa oratio,* literally, straightforward speech] A literary medium distinguished from poetry especially by its greater irregularity and variety of rhythm and its closer correspondence to the patterns of everyday speech. Although prose is readily distinguishable from poetry in that it does not treat a line as a formal unit, the significant differences between prose and poetry are of tone, pace, and object of attention. *Compare* POETRY.

prose poem A work in prose that has some of the technical or literary qualities of a poem (such as regular rhythm, definitely patterned structure, or emotional or imaginative heightening) but that is set on a page as prose.

The form was introduced into French literature by Louis Bertrand, with his *Gaspard de la nuit* (1842; "Gaspard of the Night"). His poetry attracted little interest at the time, but his influence on the Symbolists at the end of the century was acknowledged by Charles Baudelaire in his *Petits Poèmes en prose* (1869; later titled, as Baudelaire intended, *Le Spleen de Paris*). It was this work that gave the form its name, and the *Divagations* (1897) of Stéphane Mallarmé and *Illuminations* (1886) of Arthur Rimbaud firmly established prose poetry in France. Other turn-of-the-century poets who wrote prose poetry were Paul Valéry, Paul Fort, and Paul Claudel.

Prose poems were written in the early 19th century by the German poets Friedrich Hölderlin and Novalis and at the end of the century by Rainer Maria Rilke. The 20th century saw a renewed interest in the form in such works as Pierre Reverdy's *Poèmes en prose* (1915) and in the works of the French poet Saint-John Perse. Amy Lowell's polyphonic prose is a type of prose poetry.

prosodiac \prō-ˈsō-dē-ˌak\ [Greek *prosodiakós* of a prosodion] *See* ENOPLION.

prosodion \prə-ˈsō-dē-ən\ [Greek *prosódion,* from neuter of *prosódios* processional, a derivative of *prósodos* approach, procession] A procession song that was a form of ancient Greek choral lyric.

prosodist \ˈpräs-ə-dist, ˈpräz-\ A specialist in prosody.

prosody \ˈpräs-ə-dē, ˈpräz-\ [Medieval Latin *prosodia* observance of the correct accent and quantity of words in reading and writing, from Latin, accent of a syllable, from Greek *prosōidía* variation in pitch, pronunciation of a syllable on a given pitch, from *pros-* toward, in addition to + *ōidḗ* song] The metrical structure of poetry and the study of such structure.

This study has led to the classification of verse according to metrical structure. The four most common forms of versification are QUANTITATIVE VERSE, which is the system of classical Greek and Latin poetry; SYLLABIC VERSE, used in Romance languages and Japanese; ACCENTUAL VERSE, which is used mainly in Germanic poetry, including Old English and Old Norse; and ACCENTUAL-SYLLABIC VERSE, which is considered the traditional prosody of English literature as it dominated that poetry from the 16th to the 19th century and is still commonly used.

The terminology of "traditional" English prosody was established by Renaissance theorists who sought to impose the rules of classical prosody on vernacular English forms. They merely succeeded in redefining, in classical terms, the elements of an already existing syllable-stress meter.

Nonmetrical prosody is a feature of modern poetry, although many critics deny that it is possible to write poetry without employing some kind of meter. Visual prosodies have been fostered by movements such as Imagism and by such experimenters as E.E. Cummings, who revived the practice of some Metaphysical poets in "shaping" the verse by typographical arrangement.

Prosody entails several important elements other than meter. Rhyme scheme, for example, is one of a variety of effects, including alliteration and assonance, that influence the total "sound meaning" of a poem. Very often, prosodic study involves examining the subtleties of a poem's rhythm, its "flow," a quality rooted in such elements as accent, meter, and tempo but not synonymous with them.

Prosody also takes into account a consideration of the historical period to which a poem belongs, the poetic genre, and the poet's individual style. Finally, the term prosody encompasses the theories that have been developed through the ages about the value of structure: from the emphasis on decorum in the classical age, which identified certain meters as suitable only for particular subjects; to Renaissance formulations of laws restricting modern verse to classical meters; to the 18th-century insistence on the notion that the movement of sound and meter should represent the actions they carry; to Gerard Manley Hopkins' controversial theories of sprung rhythm based on the natural stress of words. Since the publication in 1906–10 of George Saintsbury's *A History of English*

Prosody, the subject has been a respected part of literary study. *See also* METER; SCANSION.

prosopopoeia \ˌprä-sə-ˈpō-pē-ə, ˌprō-\ [Greek *prosōpopoiía,* from *prósōpon* face, person, character + *poieîn* to make] A figure of speech in which an imaginary or absent person is represented as speaking or acting. The word is also sometimes used as a synonym for PERSONIFICATION.

prospect poem Subcategory of TOPOGRAPHICAL POETRY that considers a particular landscape as viewed from an elevated vantage point.

protagonist \prō-ˈtag-ə-nist\ [Greek *prōtagōnistḗs,* from *prôtos* first + *agōnistḗs* actor, contestant] In ancient Greek drama, the first or leading actor. The poet Thespis is credited with having invented tragedy when he introduced this first actor into Greek drama, which formerly consisted only of choric dancing and recitation. The protagonist stood opposite the chorus and engaged in an interchange of questions and answers. According to Aristotle in his *Poetics,* Aeschylus brought in a second actor, or deuteragonist, and presented the first dialogue between two characters. Sophocles then added a third actor, the tritagonist, and was able to write more complex dialogue. That there were only three actors did not limit the number of characters because each actor would play more than one character. The term protagonist has since come to be used for the principal character in a novel, story, drama, or poem.

protasis \ˈprät-ə-sis\ *plural* protases \-ˌsēz\ [Late Greek *prótasis,* from Greek, something put forward, proposition, problem] **1.** The introductory part of a play or narrative poem; specifically, in a drama, the introduction or part that precedes the EPITASIS. *Compare* CATASTASIS. **2.** The subordinate clause of a conditional statement.

proverb \ˈpräv-ərb\ [Latin *proverbium,* from *pro-* before, in front of + *verbum* word] Succinct and pithy saying that is in general use and that expresses commonly held ideas and beliefs. Proverbs are part of every spoken language and are related to other forms of folk literature that have originated in oral tradition. Often, the same proverb may be found in many variants in different parts of the world. In Europe this may result from the currency of Latin proverbs in the Middle Ages. The proverb known in English as "A bird in the hand is worth two in the bush" originated in medieval Latin, and variants of it are found in Romanian, Italian, Portuguese, Spanish, German, and Icelandic. Many biblical proverbs have parallels in ancient Greece. "A soft answer turneth away wrath" was known to Aeschylus as well as to Solomon, and "Physician, heal thyself" (Luke 4:23) was also known to the Greeks. Certain stylistic similarities have been found in proverbs from the same part of the world. Middle Eastern proverbs, for instance, make use of hyperbole and colorful forms of expression. Typical is the proverbial Egyptian description of a lucky man: "Fling him in the Nile and he will come up with a fish in his mouth." Classical Latin proverbs are typically pithy and terse (e.g., Praemonitus, praemunitis; "forewarned is forearmed"). Many languages use rhyme, alliteration, and wordplay in their proverbs, as in the Scots "Many a mickle makes a muckle" ("Many small things make one big thing"). Folk proverbs are commonly illustrated with homely imagery—household objects, domesticated animals, and the events of daily life.

Proverbs come from many sources, most of them anonymous. Their first appearance in literary form is often an adaptation of an oral saying. Abraham Lincoln is said to have invented the saying about not swapping horses in the middle of the river, but he may only have used a proverb already current.

Most literate societies have valued their proverbs and collected them for posterity. There are ancient Egyptian collections dating from as early as 2500 BC. Sumerian inscriptions give grammatical rules in proverbial form. Proverbs were used in ancient China for ethical instruction, and the Vedic writings of India used them to expound philosophical ideas. The biblical Book of Proverbs, traditionally associated with Solomon, actually includes sayings from earlier compilations.

One of the earliest English proverb collections, *The Proverbs of Alfred* (*c.* 1150–80), contains religious and moral precepts. The use of proverbs in monasteries to teach novices Latin, in schools of rhetoric, and in sermons, homilies, and didactic works led to their preservation in manuscripts. Proverbs in literature and oratory were at their height in England in the 16th and 17th centuries, used by such practitioners as John Heywood, who wrote a dialogue in proverbs (1549; later enlarged) and Michael Drayton, who wrote a sonnet. In North America the best-known collection of proverbs is probably that of *Poor Richard's,* an almanac published annually between 1732 and 1757 by Benjamin Franklin. Many of Poor Richard's sayings were traditional European proverbs reworked by Franklin and given an American context when appropriate.

Provincetown Players \'präv-ins-ˌtau̇n\ Theatrical organization that began performing in 1915 in Provincetown, Mass., U.S. It was founded by a nontheatrical group of writers and artists whose common aim was the production of new and experimental plays. Among the original Provincetowners who staged the first plays in members' homes were Mary Heaton Vorse, George Cram Cook, Susan Glaspell, Hutchins Hapgood, Wilbur Steele, and Robert Edmond Jones.

The group, which took up residence in New York City's Greenwich Village in 1916, discovered and developed the work of such noted writers as Eugene O'Neill, Floyd Dell, Edna St. Vincent Millay, and Paul Green. The Provincetown Players flourished as a noncommercial theater group until its demise in 1929.

pseudepigraphy \ˌsü-də-'pig-rə-fē\ [Greek *pseudepígraphos* spuriously titled, not genuine, from *pseudḗs* false + *epigráphein* to entitle, ascribe] The ascription of false names of authors to works, a practice intended to lend to the writings an authority that they would otherwise lack.

pseudonym \'sü-də-ˌnim\ [Greek *pseudṓnymos* under a false name, from *pseudḗs* false + *ónyma, ónoma* name] A fictitious name, especially a pen name or such a name used by an author. The practice of publishing under an assumed name has been known since classical times. The reasons for the use of a pseudonym are various. In political and religious controversy it may be unsafe or unwise to publish the writer's name. When it was not considered respectable for women to be writers, some women adopted masculine pseudonyms, such as George Eliot (Mary Ann Evans) and George Sand (Amandine-Aurore-Lucile Dudevant). Some authors writing in more than one kind of literature prefer to keep their literary careers separate by using pseudonyms: the detective-story writers Nicholas Blake and Amanda Cross are the poet C. Day-Lewis and scholar Carolyn Heilbrun, respectively. *See* NOM DE PLUME; PEN NAME.

pseudo-Pindaric ode *See* IRREGULAR ODE.

psychoanalytic criticism Literary criticism that uses psychoanalytic theory to analyze readers' responses to literature, to interpret literary works in terms of their authors' psychological conflicts, or to recreate authors' psychic lives from unconscious revelations in their work.

Psychoanalytic criticism originated with the theories of Sigmund Freud. Freud himself was the first to employ this approach in the analysis of literature; other Freudian critics included Ernest Jones, Otto Rank, and Marie Bonaparte. Developments in psychoanalytic theory were reflected in the different approaches to criticism that evolved. Carl Jung's concept of the collective unconscious, which assumes universally similar responses to archetypal human situations, influenced such works as *Archetypal Patterns in Poetry* (1934) by Maud Bodkin and *A Jungian Approach to Literature* (1984) by Bettina L. Knapp. Norman O. Brown used classical literature to drastically reinterpret Sigmund Freud in *Life Against Death* (1959) and *Love's Body* (1966). "Ego-psychology," as developed by Norman N. Holland in *The Dynamics of Literary Response* (1968) and *5 Readers Reading* (1975), is an aspect of psychoanalytic criticism that studies how readers respond to texts. In the later 20th century French psychoanalyst Jacques Lacan reinterpreted Freud in terms of structural linguistics and stressed the importance of the relationship between language and the unconscious. Lacan's work influenced many later critics, including feminist critics Julia Kristeva, Hélène Cixous, and Luce Irigaray, who added a feminist perspective to psychoanalytic criticism by exploring the patriarchal nature of language and the way notions of gender are determined by language.

psychobiography \ˌsī-kō-bī-ˈäg-rə-fē, -bē-\ A biography written from a psychodynamic or psychoanalytic point of view. Examples include the psychoanalyst Erik Erikson's biographies of Martin Luther and Mohandas Gandhi, Marie Bonaparte's work on Edgar Allan Poe, and Phyllis Greenacre's *Swift and Carroll* (1955), on Jonathan Swift and Lewis Carroll.

psychological novel Work of fiction in which the thoughts, feelings, and motivations of the characters are of equal or greater interest than is the external action of the narrative. In a psychological novel the emotional reactions and internal states of the characters are influenced by and in turn trigger external events. Events may not be presented in chronological order, but rather as they occur in the character's thought associations, memories, fantasies, reveries, contemplations, and dreams. This emphasis on the inner life of characters is a fundamental element of a vast body of fiction: William Shakespeare's *Hamlet* is perhaps the prime early example of it in dramatic form.

An overtly psychological approach is found among many novels written from the 18th century on, including Samuel Richardson's *Pamela* (1740), which is told from the heroine's point of view; Laurence Sterne's introspective first-person narrative *Tristram Shandy* (1759–67); the works of Fyodor Dostoyevsky and Leo Tolstoy, which display a penetrating insight into psychological complexities and unconscious motivations; and the works of George Eliot and George Meredith. It was not until the 20th century that the psychological novel reached its full potential. Its development coincided with, though it was not necessarily caused by, the growth of interest in psychology and the theories of Sigmund Freud. The detailed recording of the impingement of external events on individual consciousness as practiced by Henry James, the associative memories called up by Marcel Proust, the stream-of-consciousness technique of James Joyce and William Faulkner, and the continuous flow of experience as presented by Virginia Woolf were arrived at relatively independently.

In the psychological novel, plot is dependent upon the probing delineation of character. For instance, the action of James Joyce's *Ulysses* (1922) takes place in Dublin in a 24-hour period, but the events of the day evoke associations that interweave past and present. In the complex works of Franz Kafka, the subjective world is externalized, and events in reality are governed by the subjective logic of dreams.

Pulitzer Prize \'pu̇l-it-sər, 'pyül-\ Any of a series of annual prizes awarded by Columbia University, New York City, for outstanding public service and achievement in American journalism, letters, and music. Fellowships are also awarded. The prizes, originally endowed with a gift of $500,000 from the newspaper magnate Joseph Pulitzer, are highly esteemed and have been awarded each May since 1917. The awards are made on the recommendation of The Pulitzer Prize Board, appointed by Columbia University. The prizes have varied in number and category over the years but in the 1990s number 14 prizes in the field of journalism, 6 prizes in letters, 1 prize in music, and 4 fellowships. The awards in letters are for fiction, drama, U.S. history, biography or autobiography, verse, and nonfiction not covered by another category.

pulp magazine A publication printed on cheap paper (originally, paper made from wood pulp) and often dealing with sensational material.

pun \'pən\ [perhaps from Italian *puntiglio* quibble, fine point], *also called* paronomasia \ˌpar-ə-nō-'mā-zhə, ˌpar-ˌän-ə-, -zhē-ə\ A humorous use of a word in such a way as to suggest different meanings or applications, or a play on words, as in the use of the word *rings* in the following nursery rhyme:

> Ride a cock-horse to Banbury Cross,
> To see a fine lady upon a white horse;
> Rings on her fingers and bells on her toes,
> She shall have music wherever she goes.

Common as jokes and in riddles, puns may be used seriously, as in John Donne's "A Hymne to God the Father":

> Sweare by thy selfe, that at my death thy sonne
>   Shall shine as he shines now, and heretofore;
> And, having done that, Thou haste done;
>   I fear no more.

This quatrain contains two puns, *son/sun* and *done/Donne*.

Authors as diverse as William Shakespeare, Lewis Carroll, James Joyce, and Tom Stoppard have made extensive use of puns in their works.

Punch \'pənch\ (*in full* Punch, or the London Charivari \ˌshär-ē-'vär-ē, shə-'riv-ə-rē\) English illustrated periodical published from 1841 to 1992, famous for its satiric humor, caricatures, and cartoons. The first editors of what was then a weekly radical paper were Henry Mayhew and Mark Lemon. Among the most famous early members of the staff were the authors William Makepeace Thackeray and Thomas Hood and the illustrator-cartoonists John Leech and Sir John Tenniel. The cover drawing of Punch and his dog Toby by Richard Doyle was used until the mid-20th century, when each issue's cover was made different and printed in color, although the traditional figures usually appeared somewhere.

puppetry \'pəp-i-trē\ The making and manipulation of puppets for use in a theatrical show. A puppet is a figure—human, animal, or abstract in form—that is moved by human, and not mechanical, aid.

The origins of puppetry may lie with ritual magic, and, undoubtedly, predate the invention of writing. From its beginnings in tribal society, puppetry has been part of every subsequent civilization. In 17th century Europe, the strutting puppet character, then as ever a type rather than an individual, appeared as Pulcinella in Naples, Polichinelle in France, Petrushka in Russia, and Punch in London.

Despite a similar foundation in folklore and heroic drama, Eastern puppetry developed along somewhat different lines. The shadow puppets of Java, Bali, and Thailand are manipulated by rods against a transparent screen lit from behind. In early 19th-century Japan the puppet master Uemura Bunrakuken gave his name to the most stylized puppetry yet devised. Bunraku puppets are less than life size but are operated by the puppet master who controls the head, eyes, and right arm of the puppet, while one assistant moves the left arm and another the legs.

Purāṇa \pü-ˈrä-nə\ In Hindu sacred literature, any of a number of popular encyclopedic collections of myth, legend, and genealogy, varying greatly as to date and origin. *Purāṇa* is the nominalized form of a Sanskrit adjective meaning "old, ancient."

A *Purāṇa* traditionally treats five subjects: primary creation of the universe, secondary creation after periodic annihilation, genealogy of gods and saints, grand epochs, and history of the royal dynasties. *Purāṇa*s are connected in subject with the *Mahābhārata* ("Great Epic of the Bharata Dynasty") and have some relationship to the lawbooks (*Dharma-śāstra*s). Around this central core are many other works of religious concern dating from the period AD 400 to 1000. These describe customs, ceremonies, sacrifices, festivals, caste duties, donations, construction of temples and images, and places of pilgrimage. *Purāṇa*s are written almost entirely in narrative couplets in much the same easy, flowing style as epic poems.

The 18 principal surviving *Purāṇa*s are often grouped loosely according to whether they exalt Vishnu, Śiva (Shiva), or Brahmā. The main *Purāṇa*s are usually regarded as (1) the *Viṣṇu-*, *Nāradīya-*, *Bhāgavata-*, *Garuḍa-*, *Pādma-*, and *Vārāha-Purāṇa*s; (2) the *Mātsya-*, *Kūrma-*, *Liṅga-*, *Śiva-*, *Skanda-*, and *Agni-Purāṇa*s; and (3) the *Brāhmāṇḍa-*, *Brahmavaivarta-*, *Mārkandeya-*, *Bhaviṣya-*, *Vāmana-*, and *Brāhma-Purāṇa*s. By far the most popular is the Bhāgavata-Purāṇa, which in its treatment of the early life of Krishna had profound influence on the religious beliefs of India. There are also 18 "lesser" *Purāṇa*s, or *Upapurāṇa*s, that treat similar material and a large number of *sthala-Purāṇa*s (or *māhātmyas*) glorifying temples or sacred places.

pure poetry Message-free verse that is concerned with exploring the essential musical nature of the language rather than with conveying a narrative or didactic purpose. The term has been associated particularly with the poems of Edgar Allan Poe and by such other writers as George Moore (who published *An Anthology of Pure Poetry* in 1924), Charles Baudelaire, and T.S. Eliot. Others who have experimented with the form include Stéphane Mallarmé, Paul Verlaine, Paul Valéry, Juan Ramón Jiménez, and Jorge Guillén.

purism \ˈpyu̇r-ˌiz-əm\ [French *purisme,* a derivative of *pur* pure] Rigid adherence to or insistence on purity or nicety (as in literary style or use of words). This can refer to an insistence on following fine points of grammar, diction, or style, or it can apply to an effort to purify a language in terms of excluding foreign terms.

purple passage or **purple patch** **1.** A passage conspicuous for brilliance or effectiveness in a work that is dull, commonplace, or uninspired. **2.** *chiefly British* A piece of obtrusively ornate writing.

The phrase "purple patch" is a translation from a metaphor in Horace's *Ars poetica:* "Inceptis gravibus plerumque et magna professis / purpureus, late qui splendeat, unus et alter / adsuitur pannus" ("One or two purple patches, which gleam far and wide, are often sewn onto works that were begun seriously and promise many things."). Horace had in mind ornate descriptive passages that violated the stylistic unity of a long narrative poem. The splendor of purple cloth, associated with wealth and power, was proverbial.

Pushkin Prize \'püsh-kʸin, *Angl* 'pu̇sh-kən\ Russian literary prize established in 1881 in honor of Aleksandr Pushkin, one of Russia's greatest writers. The prize was awarded to Russian (later Soviet) authors who achieved the highest standard of literary excellence, as exemplified by the prize's namesake. Winners have included Anton Chekhov and Ivan A. Bunin.

putative author The author of a work as defined in the work rather than the actual author, or the person or character said to be the author of the work when this is different from the actual author. For example, in William Makepeace Thackeray's *The Newcomes* the character Arthur Pendennis is the narrator and supposed author of the work. *The Moonstone* by Wilkie Collins has several putative authors as the narrative is supposedly a collection of documents and letters written by various characters involved in the story.

pyŏlgok \'pyȯl-'gu̇k\, *also called* changga \'chäŋ-gä\ [Korean] Korean poetic form that flourished during the Koryŏ period (935–1392). Of folk origin, the *pyŏlgok* was sung chiefly by women, and it was intended for performance on festive occasions. The theme of most of these anonymous poems is love, and its joys and torments are expressed in frank and powerful language. The *pyŏlgok* is characterized by the presence of a refrain either in the middle or at the end of each stanza. The refrain not only establishes a mood or tone that carries the melody and spirit of the poem but also serves to link the discrete parts and contents of the poem. The *pyŏlgok* entitled "Tongdong" ("Ode on the Seasons") and "Isanggok" ("Winter Night") are among the most moving love lyrics in the Korean language.

pyrrhic \'pir-ik\ [Greek (*poùs*) *pyrrhíchios,* a derivative of *pyrríchē,* a type of dance performed by armed men] In prosody, a foot consisting of two short or unaccented syllables.

pythiambic \ˌpith-ē-'am-bik, pith-ˌī-\ In classical Latin prosody, a distich, or pair of lines, composed of a pythian, or dactylic hexameter line followed by an iambic dimeter or trimeter. This distich was used in the *Epodes* of Horace following such Greeks as Archilochus. As Archilochus used it, the iambic line was usually catalectic, or missing the final syllable. In its acatalectic form it scans as:

> – ∪ ∪ | – ∪ ∪ | – ∪ ∪ | – ∪ ∪ | – ∪ ∪ | – ⏓
> ⏓ – ∪ – | ⏓ – ∪ – (dimeter)

or

> – ∪ ∪ | – ∪ ∪ | – ∪ ∪ | – ∪ ∪ | – ∪ ∪ | – ⏓
> ∪ – ∪ – | ∪ – ∪ – | ∪ – ∪ – (trimeter).

Pythian verse \'pith-ē-ən\ In classical prosody, name formerly given to dactylic hexameter verse because that was the meter used in the Pythian, or Delphic, oracles. It scans as:

– ⏑̲ ⏑̲ | – ⏑̲ ⏑̲ | – ⏑̲ ⏑̲ | – ⏑̲ ⏑̲ | – ⏑̲ ⏑̲ | – –,

where one long can always substitute for two short syllables and the last foot is invariably a spondee. *See* PYTHIAMBIC.

Q

You shall see them on a beautiful quarto page,
where a neat rivulet of text shall meander.
—Richard Brinsley Sheridan

qasida or **kasida** \kä-ˈsē-də\ *plural* qasida *or* kasida [Arabic *qaṣīda*] A poetic form developed in pre-Islāmic Arabia and perpetuated throughout Islāmic literary history. It is a laudatory, elegiac, or satiric poem that is found in Arabic, Persian, and many related Oriental literatures.

The classic qasida is an elaborately structured ode of between 60 and 100 lines (though lengths vary considerably), maintaining a single end rhyme that runs through the entire piece; the same rhyme also occurs at the end of the first hemistich (half line) of the first verse. Virtually any meter is acceptable for the qasida.

The qasida opens with a short prelude (the *nasīb*), which is elegiac in mood. The nasīb depicts the poet stopping at an old tribal encampment to reminisce about the happiness he shared there with his beloved and about his sorrow when they parted; Imruʿ al-Qays is said to have been the first to use this device, and nearly all subsequent authors imitate him. After this follows the *raḥīl,* which consists of similes and descriptions of the poet's horse or camel, of desert animals, scenes of desert events, Bedouin life, and warfare; it may conclude with a piece on *fakhr,* or self-praise. The main theme, the *madīḥ,* or panegyric, often coupled with a *hijaʿ* (satire of enemies), is last and is the poet's tribute to himself, his tribe, or his patron.

The qasida has always been respected as the highest form of the poetic art and as the special forte of the pre-Islāmic poets. By the end of the 8th century the qasida began to decline. It was successfully restored for a brief period in the 10th century by al-Mutanabbī and has continued to be cultivated by the Bedouin. Qasida were also written in Turkish and Urdu until the 19th century.

quantitative verse In prosody, a metrical system based on the duration of the syllables that make up the feet, without regard for accents or stresses. Quantitative verse is made up of long and short syllables, whose duration is determined by the amount of time needed for their pronunciation. This system has only rarely been used successfully in English poetry because of the strongly accentual nature of the English language. It was used mainly by classical Greek and Roman poets. *See also* METER.

quantity \'kwän-tə-tē\ In classical prosody, the relative length or duration of a syllable in a verse based on the length of time it took to pronounce the syllable. Syllables were classified as long, short, or anceps (either long or short at the poet's discretion), and in scansion they were designated by a macron for long (–), a breve for short (∪), and a combination of the two or an × for anceps (⊻ or ×). Whereas the meter of modern accentual prosody is based on the pattern of stressed and unstressed syllables in a verse, the meter of classical, or quantitative, verse was determined by the pattern of long and short syllables.

Quarterly Review, The British literary journal, published from 1809 to 1967, that became a major cultural force, especially in its influence on the development of Romanticism in England. Founded by the London publisher John Murray, the magazine was first edited by William Gifford and subsequently by John Gibson Lockhart from 1825 to 1853. It was established as a Tory organ to rival the Whig-dominated *Edinburgh Review*. The competition between the two journals lasted throughout the 19th century, although the ground eventually shifted from politics to literature. Sir Walter Scott and Robert Southey were both major contributors. The journal developed a reputation for savagery because of its sometimes vicious literary reviews, many of which attacked writers who were currently being championed by *The Edinburgh Review. The Quarterly* held to the standards of Samuel Johnson and Alexander Pope in their estimation of good writing, espousing formalism as one of the highest virtues. During the Romantic era *The Quarterly Review* supported William Wordsworth, Washington Irving, and Jane Austen but damned John Keats, William Hazlitt, Percy Bysshe Shelley, Alfred, Lord Tennyson, and Charles Dickens.

quartet \kwȯr-'tet\ In poetry, any group of four lines taken as a unit. The lines may or may not be printed as a separate stanza or QUATRAIN.

quarto \'kwȯr-tō\ [Latin, ablative of *quartus* fourth (of a leaf)] In printing, a sheet of paper folded into quarters. The term also refers to a book made up of quarto signatures. Many of William Shakespeare's plays were originally published as quartos and are sometimes referred to in terms of a specific quarto edition. *Compare* FOLIO.

quatorzain \kə-'tȯr-ˌzān, 'kat-ər-ˌzān\ [Middle French *quatorzaine* group of fourteen] A poem of 14 lines; specifically, a poem resembling a sonnet but lacking strict sonnet structure.

quatrain \'kwä-ˌtrān, kwä-'trān\ [French, a derivative of *quatre* four] A verse unit of four lines.

quattrocento \ˌkwät-trō-'chen-tō\ [Italian, literally, four hundred, short for *mille quattrocento* the year 1400] The 15th century; specifically, the 15th-century period in Italian literature and art.

quindecasyllabic \ˌkwin-ˌdek-ə-sə-ˈlab-ik\ [Latin *quindecim* fifteen] Having 15 syllables.

quintain \ˈkwin-ˌtān, kwin-ˈtān\ [Latin *quintus* fifth + English *-ain* (as in *quatrain*)] *obsolete* A five-line stanza.

R

Keeping time, time, time
In a sort of Runic rhyme
—Edgar Allan Poe

rabbinical literature \ra-'bin-i-kəl\ The literature of Hebrew theology and philosophy, including the Talmud and its exegesis.

race, milieu, and moment According to the French critic Hippolyte Taine, the three principal motives or conditioning factors behind any work of art. Taine sought to establish a scientific approach to literature through the investigation of what created the individual who created the work of art.

By "race" he meant the inherited disposition or temperament that persists stubbornly over thousands of years. By "milieu" he meant the circumstances or environment that modify the inherited racial disposition. By "moment" Taine meant the momentum of past and present cultural traditions.

The literature of a culture, according to Taine, shows the most sensitive and unguarded displays of motive and the psychology of a people.

Rambler, The A twopenny sheet issued twice weekly in London by the publisher John Payne between 1750 and 1752, each issue containing a single anonymous essay. All but five of the 208 periodical essays were written by Samuel Johnson. A majority of the essays deal with the disappointments inherent in life and with setbacks to ambition. Many of the titles reflect this: "Happiness not Local," "The Frequent Contemplation of Death Necessary to Moderate the Passions," "The Luxury of Vain Imagination." *The Rambler,* in short, is of fundamental importance in any estimate of Johnson's approach to literature itself: it was intended to instruct, not to entertain. The essays make little mention of current events or current literature, even though they do contain much acute literary criticism and reflect the social and literary conditions of the time. *The Rambler* did not sell well as a periodical, though it was an immense success when it was reissued, with the essays revised, in book form in 1753. It also inspired other periodicals, notably John Hawkesworth's *The Adventurer* (1752–54), Edward Moore's lively *The World* (1753–56), George Colman's and Bonnell Thornton's *The Connoisseur* (1754–56), and Henry Mackenzie's Scottish periodical *The Mirror* (1779–80).

RAPP \'räp\, *abbreviation of* Rossiyskaya Assotsiatsiya Proletarskikh Pisateley("Russian Association of Proletarian Writers") Soviet association formed

(1928) out of various groups of proletarian writers (among them former members of Proletkult). RAPP was dedicated to defining a truly proletarian literature and to eliminating writers whose works were not thoroughly imbued with communist ideology. Under the leadership of Leopold Leonardovich Averbakh, the association managed to seize control of literary activity in 1929, when it received official sanction for its program of establishing the Soviet First Five-Year Plan as the sole theme of Soviet literature. The mechanical literature that was written on assignment and that resulted from RAPP's dictatorship led to an official about-face in 1932, when RAPP was liquidated and the all-inclusive Union of Soviet Writers was founded to promote the doctrine of Socialist Realism.

rasa \'rəs-ə\ [Sanskrit *rasaḥ* essence, taste, flavor, literally, sap, juice] In Sanskrit literature, the concept of aesthetic flavor, or an essential element of any work of art that can only be suggested, not described. It is a kind of contemplative abstraction in which the inwardness of human feelings suffuses the surrounding world of embodied forms.

The theory of *rasa* is attributed to Bharata, a sage-priest who may have lived about AD 500. It was developed by the rhetorician and philosopher Abhinavagupta (*c.* AD 1000), who applied it to all varieties of theater and poetry. The principal human feelings, according to Bharata, are delight, laughter, sorrow, anger, energy, fear, disgust, heroism, and astonishment, all of which may be recast in contemplative form as the various *rasa*s: erotic, comic, pathetic, furious, heroic, terrible, odious, marvelous, and quietistic. These rasas comprise the components of aesthetic experience. The power to taste rasa is a reward for merit in some previous existence.

rat rhyme *chiefly Scottish* A scrap of nonsense or doggerel verse.

rāwī \'rä-ˌwē\ [Arabic, reciter] In Arabic literature, a professional reciter of poetry. The *rāwī*s preserved pre-Islāmic poetry in oral tradition until it was written down in the 8th century.

One or more *rāwī*s attached themselves to a particular poet and learned his works by heart. They then recited and explained the poet's verse before a wider audience. Such an attachment often became an apprenticeship, and, after mastering the poetic technique, some rāwīs became poets in their own right. When the great philological schools of Basra and Kūfah in Iraq were formed in the 8th century, the rāwīs were sought out by scholars as preservers of an ancient language and poetic style that was falling into disuse.

The method of preserving poetry through rāwīs, relying as it did on memory, however, was imperfect, and the poetry of the pre-Islāmic period was subject to mutations, omissions, unauthorized additions, and the transposition of lines and verses.

Some of the most famous rāwīs, especially two who first wrote down poems, Ḥammād ar-Rāwiyah and Khalaf al-Aḥmar, are thought to have dealt freely with their originals and have even been called clever forgers. It is thus necessary to consider carefully the evidence for authenticity of any verse attributed to a particular pre-Islāmic poet.

readerly \'rē-dər-lē\ [translation of French *lisible*] Of or relating to a text that is straightforward and demands no special effort to understand. Such texts were contrasted with so-called writerly texts by the French critic Roland Barthes in his book *S/Z* (1970). According to Barthes, a readerly text is one that presents a world of easily identifiable characters and events and in which the characters and their actions are understandable. Realistic novels such as those of George Eliot are readerly texts. *Compare* WRITERLY.

reader-response criticism Critical method that examines the reader and the act of reading rather than the text being read. The reader-response approach evolved out of phenomenological (experiential) and interpretive analyses and is closely related to reception theory; it analyzes the reader's role in the production of meaning when engaged with a written text. Reader-response critics examine, for example, the inferences the reader must supply, the set of assumptions the reader must make, the gaps the reader must fill, the set of schemata the reader must actualize in order to make sense of the text, and the ideologies that determine all of the above.

The major figures of this analytical school initially included I.A. Richards, Louise Rosenblatt, and Walker Gibson and, later, Gerald Prince, Michael Riffaterre, and Georges Poulet. Among other contributors to reader-response theory were Wolfgang Iser, Jonathan Culler, Norman Holland, and David Bleich.

realism \'rē-ə-ˌliz-əm\ The theory or practice in art and literature of fidelity to nature or to real life and to accurate representation without idealization of the most typical views, details, and surroundings of the subject. Realism rejects imaginative idealization in favor of a close observation of outward appearances. The word has also been used critically to denote excessive minuteness of detail or preoccupation with trivial, sordid, or squalid subjects in art and literature.

The works of the 18th-century English novelists Daniel Defoe, Henry Fielding, and Tobias Smollett are among the earliest examples in English literature of writings considered to be realistic.

Realism was stimulated by several intellectual developments in the first half of the 19th century, including the anti-Romantic movement in Germany, with its emphasis on the commoner as an artistic subject; Auguste Comte's positivist philosophy, in which the importance of the scientific study of society was emphasized; the rise of professional journalism, with its ideal of accurate and dispassionate recording of current events; and the development of photography, with its capability of mechanically reproducing visual appearances with extreme accuracy.

Realism was a major trend in French novels and paintings between 1850 and 1880. The French proponents of realism uniformly rejected the artificiality of both classicism and Romanticism and insisted that, to be effective, a work must be contemporaneous. They attempted to portray the lives, appearances, problems, customs, and mores of people of the middle and lower classes, and they conscientiously set themselves to reproducing all the hitherto-ignored aspects of contemporary life and society—its attitudes, physical settings, and material conditions.

The novelist Honoré de Balzac was the chief precursor of French realism, notably in his attempt to create a detailed, encyclopedic portrait of the whole range of society in his *La Comédie humaine*. Inspired by the painter Courbet, the French journalist Champfleury wrote a manifesto for writers, *Le Réalisme* (1857), in which he asserted that the hero of a novel should be an ordinary rather than exceptional figure. In 1857 Gustave Flaubert published *Madame Bovary,* with an unrelentingly objective portrait of the bourgeois mentality that became both the principal masterpiece of realism and the work that established the movement in European literature. Flaubert's *L'Éducation sentimentale* (1870, *A Sentimental Education*), with its presentation of a vast panorama of France under Louis-Philippe, was another principal realist work. The brothers Jules and Edmond de Goncourt, in their masterpiece, *Germinie Lacerteux* (1864), and in other works covered a variety of social and occupational milieus and frankly described social relations among both the upper and the lower classes.

Realist tenets—an emphasis on detachment, objectivity, and accurate observation; on lucid but restrained criticism of social environment and mores; and on humane understanding—entered the mainstream of European literature during the 1860s and '70s and became an integral part of the fabric of the modern novel during the height of the genre's development. Charles Dickens, Anthony Trollope, and George Eliot in England, Ivan Turgenev, Leo Tolstoy, and Fyodor Dostoyevsky in Russia, William Dean Howells in the United States, and Gottfried Keller and the early Thomas Mann in Germany all incorporated realist elements in their novels. A significant offshoot of literary realism was naturalism, a late 19th- and early 20th-century movement that aimed at an unselective representation of reality. The French novelist Émile Zola was the leading exponent of naturalism.

Realism in the theater was a general movement in the later 19th century that steered theatrical texts and performances toward greater fidelity to real life. The leaders of this movement included Henrik Ibsen and August Strindberg in Scandinavia and Anton Chekhov and Maksim Gorky in Russia. These and other playwrights rejected the complex and artificial plotting of the so-called well-made play, instead treating the themes and conflicts of contemporary society. They dispensed with poetic language and extravagant diction, using instead action and dialogue that looked and sounded like everyday behavior and speech.

recension \rē-'sen-shən\ [French *récension* or German *Rezension,* both ultimately from Latin *recensere* to make a review of, enumerate] **1.** A revision of a text (as of an ancient author) by an editor; especially, a critical revision with intent to establish a definitive text. **2.** A version of a text established by critical revision.

récit \rā-'sē\ [French, narrative, account] A brief novel usually with a simple narrative line.

One of the writers who consciously used the form was André Gide. Both *L'Immoraliste* (*The Immoralist*) and *La Porte étroite* (*Strait is the Gate*) are examples of the *récit*. Both are studiedly simple but deeply ironic tales in which the first-person narrator reveals the inherent moral ambiguities of life by means of seemingly innocuous reminiscences.

recognition \ˌrek-əg-'nish-ən\ An incident or solution of plot in tragedy in which the main character recognizes his own or another character's true identity or discovers the true nature of his own situation. *See* ANAGNORISIS.

recto \'rek-tō\ [New Latin *recto (folio)* on the right-hand leaf] **1.** The side of a leaf (as of a manuscript) that is to be read first. **2.** A right-hand page. *Compare* VERSO.

redaction \ri-'dak-shən\ [French *rédaction* act of editing, edited work, ultimately from Latin *redigere* (past participle *redactus*) to drive back, convert, reduce to] An edition or version. A work that has been edited or revised for publication. The word also denotes the act or an instance of editing a work for publication.

rederijkerskamer \'rā-də-ˌreik-ərs-ˌkäm-ər\ [Dutch, literally, rhetorician's chamber] Medieval Dutch dramatic society. Modeled after contemporary French dramatic societies (*puys*), such chambers spread rapidly across the French border into Flanders and Holland in the 15th century. At first they were organized democratically; they later acquired sponsorship by the nobility and had a designated leader, assistants, a paid manager, and a jester. Like guilds, they had their own names, slogans, and emblems and were commissioned by the towns that supported them to provide the ceremonial at local festivals.

Drama by this time had largely passed from the hands of the clergy into the hands of the laity; the introduction of secular themes had necessitated the use of stages or carts outside religious buildings. The *rederijkerskamers* organized national festivals (*landjuwelen*) during which poetry and drama competitions were held. One of the finest plays of this period, *Elckerlyc,* a morality play written about 1485 and attributed to Pieter Doorlant, became well known in England as *Everyman.* In addition to morality plays, the *rederijkerskamers* sponsored miracle plays, farces, and romantic plays. The miracle play (a type of play based on the life of a saint) *Mariken van Nieumeghen* (*c.* 1500) is remarkably modern both in its psychological insight and in its technique. The "miracle" of the renegade's conversion is achieved through the simple and realistic device of her confrontation with a topical "pageant" street play, a theme within a theme. It was also within the rederijkerskamers that the farce thrived in the 15th century; the romantic play, too, was a popular genre, although only one example is extant.

The poetic style sanctioned by the *rederijkers* (members of the dramatic society), with its emphasis on complex forms and meters, laid the foundation for later Dutch dramatic and heroic verse by perfecting the rhymed alexandrine couplet. The rederijkers also developed a new poetic form, the *referein,* seen at its best in the poetry of Anna Bijns.

By the end of the 16th century many of the societies had degenerated into mutual admiration societies for poetasters; this, coupled with the new laws against public assemblies and the religious upheavals of the era, led to their decline. The Egelantier ("Wild Briar") and the Wit Lavendel ("White Lavender") rederijkerskamers, however, remained popular into the 17th century because of their association with leading Renaissance poets.

redondilla \rā-dōn-'dēl-yä, -'dē-yä\ [Spanish, a derivative of *redondo* round] A Spanish stanza form consisting of four trochaic lines, usually of eight syllables each, with a rhyme scheme of *abba.* Quatrains in this form with a rhyme scheme of *abab,* sometimes also called redondillas, are more commonly known as *serventesios.* Redondillas have been common in Castilian poetry since the 16th century.

refacimento *See* RIFACIMENTO.

reflexive novel *also called* involuted novel *or* self-reflexive novel. A novel that calls attention to the fact that it is a novel and is not meant to be a straightforward reflection of reality. Examples include the works of Samuel Beckett and James Joyce.

refrain \ri-'frān\ [Middle French, alteration of *refrait* melody, liturgical response, repeated subject, a derivative of *refraindre* to break, moderate, echo] A phrase, line, or verse that recurs regularly at intervals throughout a poem or song, especially at the end of each stanza or division. Refrains are found in the ancient Egyptian Book of the Dead and are common in preliterate tribal chants. They appear in literature as varied as ancient Hebrew, Greek, and Latin verse, popular ballads, and Renaissance and Romantic lyrics. Three common refrains are the chorus, recited by more than one person; the burden, in which a whole stanza is repeated; and the repetend, in which the words are repeated erratically throughout the poem. A refrain may be an exact repetition, or it may exhibit slight variations in meaning or form as in the following excerpt from the folk ballad "Jesse James":

> Jesse had a wife to mourn him all her life,
> The children they are brave.
> 'Twas a dirty little coward shot
> Mister Howard,
> And laid Jesse James in his grave.
>
> . . .
>
> It was Robert Ford, the dirty little coward,
> I wonder how he does feel,
> For he ate of Jesse's bread and he slept in
> Jesse's bed,
> Then he laid Jesse James in his grave.

regionalism \ˈrē-jə-nə-ˌliz-əm\ Emphasis on regional locale and characteristics in art or literature. Regionalism was a significant movement in Canadian literature early in the 20th century. Other national literatures also had periods in which regionalism was emphasized. *See also* MIDWESTERN REGIONALISM.

reification \ˌrā-ə-fi-ˈkā-shən, ˌrē-\ [Latin *res* thing + *-ification* (as in *personification*)] The treatment of something abstract as a material or concrete thing, as in the following lines from Matthew Arnold's poem "Dover Beach":

> The Sea of Faith
> Was once, too, at the full, and round earth's shore
> Lay like the folds of a bright girdle furled.

reizianum \ˌrīt-sē-ˈan-əm, -ˈän-, -ˈān-\ In Greek prosody, usually the aeolic pattern ⏔ | – ∪ ∪ – | –, but occasionally the anapestic ⏔. In Latin prosody, *reizianum* refers to any variant of the scheme ⏔ ⏕ ⏔ ⏕ –, usually found in comic verse in an iambic context.

The word *reizianum* is derived from the surname of Friedrich Wilhelm Reiz, an 18th-century German philologist.

Renaissance \ˌren-ə-ˈsäns, -ˈzäns; ri-ˈnā-səns\ [French, literally, rebirth] The transitional period in Europe between medieval and modern times beginning in the 14th century in Italy, lasting into the 17th century, and marked by a humanistic revival of classical influence expressed in a flowering of the arts and literature and by the beginnings of modern science.

In literature, medieval forms continued to dominate the artistic imagination throughout the 15th century. Besides the vast devotional literature of the period—the *ars moriendi,* or books on the art of dying well, the lives of the saints, and manuals of methodical prayer and spiritual consolation—the most popular reading of noble and burgher alike was a 13th-century love allegory, the *Roman de la Rose*. In spite of a promising fecundity in the late Middle Ages—when, for example, England produced William Langland, the *Gawain* poet, John Gower, and, most notably, Geoffrey Chaucer—literary creativity suffered from the domination of Latin as the language of "serious" expression. The result of this circumstance was that, if the vernacular attracted writers, they tended to overload it with Latinisms and artificially applied rhetorical forms. This was the case with the so-called *rhétoriqueurs* of Burgundy and France. A highlight of 15th-century English literature, however, was Sir Thomas Malory's *Le Morte Darthur*. In France there was a vigorous tradition of chronicle writing, which was distinguished by such eminently readable works as the *Chronicles* of Jean Froissart and the *Mémoires* of Philippe de Commynes. Mid-15th-century France also produced the vagabond and great poet François Villon. In Germany *Das Narrenschiff* (*The Ship of Fools*) by Sebastian Brant was a lone masterpiece.

The 16th century saw a true renaissance of national literatures. In Protestant countries, the Reformation had an enormous impact upon the quantity and quality of literary output. If Martin Luther's rebellion destroyed the chances of unifying the nation politically, his translation of the Bible into German created a national language. Biblical translations, vernacular liturgies, hymns, and sacred drama had analogous effects elsewhere. For Roman Catholics, especially in Spain, the Counter-Reformation was a time of deep religious emotion expressed in art and literature. On all sides of the religious controversy, chroniclers and historians writing in the vernacular were recording their versions for posterity.

While the Reformation was providing a subject matter, the Italian Renaissance was providing literary methods and models. The Petrarchan sonnet inspired French, English, and Spanish poets, while the Renaissance Neoclassical drama finally began to end the reign of the medieval mystery play. Ultimately, of course, the works of true genius were the result of a crossing of native traditions and new forms. The Frenchman François Rabelais assimilated all the themes of his day—and mocked them all—in his story of the giants Gargantua and Pantagruel. The Spaniard Miguel de Cervantes, in *Don Quixote,* drew a composite portrait of the Spanish that caught their exact mixture of idealism and realism. In England, Christopher Marlowe and William Shakespeare used Renaissance drama to probe the deeper levels of English character and experiences.

Renaissance man *also called* Universal man, *Italian* Uomo universale. An ideal that developed in Renaissance Italy from the notion expressed by one of its most accomplished representatives, Leon Battista Alberti, that "a man can do all things if he will." The ideal embodied the basic tenets of Renaissance humanism, which considered humans the center of the universe, limitless in their capacities for development, and led to the notion that all knowledge should be embraced and natural capacities developed as fully as possible.

Thus the gifted individuals of the Renaissance sought to develop skills exemplified in Alberti—who was an accomplished architect, painter, classicist, poet, scientist, and mathematician and who also boasted of his skill as a horseman and in physical feats—and in Leonardo da Vinci, whose gifts were manifest in the fields of art, science, music, invention, and writing.

In the 20th century, the term is still used to refer to an accomplished, well-rounded individual, although contemporary society admits of the occasional Renaissance woman, as well. (It may also be noted that well-educated, even philosophical, women who were skilled in a variety of arts also existed in Renaissance times, but their lives were rarely recorded.)

Renaixensa, La \lə-ˌren-ī-ˈshen-zə\ Literary and linguistic renascence in Catalan letters that had its origins in 1814, when *Gramática y apologia de la llengua cathalana* ("Grammar and Defense of the Catalan Language") of Josep Pau Ballot i Torres was published. The pioneers of the movement, while promoting the revitalization of the language, did recognize its inability to express more modern spiritual and intellectual ideas. The Institute of Catalan Studies, founded in Barcelona in 1907, played a large part in the enrichment and purifying of the Catalan language.

Among the movement's poetic contributions, Buenaventura Carles Aribau's patriotic *Oda a la patria* (1832; "Ode to the Fatherland") and the verse of Joaquim Rubió i Ors and Victor Balaguer prepared the way for the mysticism of Jacintó Verdaguer Santaló, a great epic poet who wrote *L'Atlántida* (1877) and *Canigó* (1886). Miguel Costa i Llobera cultivated a classical perfection of form. In Joan Maragall i Gorina, Catalonia found its first great modern poet who, in spiritual quality, exerted a powerful influence on later poets.

The foundations of modern Catalan prose were laid by the critical writings of Rubió i Ors, Francisco Pi i Margall, one of the four presidents of the Spanish Republic of 1873, and Josep Torras i Bages, author of *La tradició catalana* (1892; "The Catalan Tradition"). One of the best and most influential writers in prose was the essayist Eugeni d'Ors (pseudonym "Xenius"), whose philosophical novel *La ben plantada* (1911; "Firmly Rooted") was one of the most notable works in modern Catalan literature.

Catalan dramatists produced plays of considerable originality. Àngel Guimerà achieved a European reputation with *Terra baixa* (1896; *Marta of the Lowlands*), which inspired a German and a French opera and was widely translated. The many social dramas of Ignasi Iglésias, inspired by the early works of Gerhart Hauptmann, included one near-masterpiece, *Els Vells* (1903). Adrià Gual, author of several works of fantasy, directed a Catalan-language theater that helped acquaint the public with the great drama of all countries and ages.

renga \ˈreŋ-ˌgä\ [Japanese] Genre of Japanese linked-verse poetry in which two or more poets supplied alternating sections of a poem. The *renga* form began as the composition of a single tanka (a traditional five-line poem) by two people and was a popular pastime from ancient times, even in remote rural areas.

The *Kin'yō-shū* (*c.* 1125) was the first Imperial anthology to include *renga,* which was at the time simply tanka composed by two poets, one supplying the first three lines of five, seven, and five syllables, and the other the last two of seven syllables each. The first poet often gave obscure or even contradictory details to make it harder for the second to complete the poem intelligibly and, if possible, inventively. These early examples were *tan renga* (short *renga*) and were generally light in tone.

The form developed fully in the 15th century, when a distinction came to be drawn between *ushin renga* (serious *renga*), which followed the conventions of court poetry, and *mushin renga,* or haikai (comic *renga*), which deliberately broke the conventions in vocabulary and diction. Gradually, the composition of *renga* spread to the court poets, who saw the artistic possibilities of this diversion and drew up "codes" intended to establish *renga* as an art. The codes made possible the masterpieces of the 15th century, but their insistence on formalities (e.g., how often a "link" on the moon might appear, and which links must end with a noun and which with a verb) inevitably diluted the vigor and freshness of the early *renga,* itself a reaction against the excessively formal tanka.

The standard length of a *renga* was 100 verses, although there were variations. Verses were linked by verbal and thematic associations, while the mood of the poem drifted subtly as successive poets took up one another's thoughts. An outstanding example of the form is the melancholy *Minase sangin hyakuin* (1488; *Minase Sangin Hyakuin: A Poem of One Hundred Links Composed by Three Poets at Minase*), composed by Sōgi, Shōhaku, and Sōchō. Later the initial verse (hokku) of a *renga* developed into the independent haiku form.

repetend \ˈrep-i-ˌtend, ˌrep-i-ˈtend\ [Latin *repetendum* something to be repeated] A repeated sound, word, or phrase. In poetry a repetend is a type of refrain, but it differs from the more common variety in that it usually refers to only part of a line and can appear at unexpected points in the poem, unlike the regular placement of the refrain at the end of a stanza. T.S. Eliot used repetends frequently in "Ash Wednesday," as can be seen in the first two stanzas:

> Because I do not hope to turn again
> Because I do not hope
> Because I do not hope to turn
> Desiring this man's gift and that man's scope
> I no longer strive to strive towards such things
> (Why should the aged eagle stretch its wings?)
> Why should I mourn
> The vanished power of the usual reign?
>
> Because I do not hope to know again
> The infirm glory of the positive hour
> Because I do not think
> Because I know I shall not know
> The one veritable transitory power
> Because I cannot drink
> There, where trees flower, and springs flow, for there is
> nothing again

reportage \ˌrep-ȯr-ˈtäzh, ri-ˈpȯr-tij\ [French, reporting] Writing intended to give a factual account of directly observed or carefully documented events.

resolution \ˌrez-ə-ˈlü-shən\ **1.** The division of a prosodic element into its component parts (such as the division of the components of a long syllable in ancient Greek and Latin verse into two short syllables). Also, the substitution in Greek or Latin prosody of two short syllables for a long syllable. *Compare* CONTRACTION. **2.** A product of prosodic resolution. **3.** The point in a play or other work of literature at which the chief dramatic complication is worked out.

Restoration literature English literature written after the Restoration of the monarchy in 1660 following the period of the Commonwealth. Some literary historians speak of the era as bounded by the reign of Charles II (1660–85), while others prefer to include within its scope the writings produced during the reign of James II (1685–88). The period led into England's "classical" Augustan Age under Queen Anne (1702–14). Many typical literary forms of the modern world—including the novel, biography, history, travel writing, and journalism—began to develop with sureness during the Restoration period, when new scientific discoveries and philosophic concepts as well as new social and economic conditions came into play. There also was a great outpouring of pamphlet literature, much of it political and religious, while John Bunyan's great allegory, *The Pilgrim's Progress,* also belongs to the period. Much of the best poetry, notably that of John Dryden (the great literary figure of his time, in both poetry and prose), the Earl of Rochester, Samuel Butler, and John Oldham, was satirical and led directly to the later achievements of Alexander Pope, Jonathan Swift, and John Gay in the Augustan Age. The Restoration period excelled, above all, in drama. Heroic plays influenced by principles of French Neoclassicism enjoyed a vogue, but the age is chiefly remembered for its glittering, critical comedies of manners by such playwrights as George Etherege, William Wycherley, Sir John Vanbrugh, and William Congreve.

revenge tragedy Drama in which the dominant motive is revenge for a real or imagined injury; it was a favorite form of English tragedy in the Elizabethan and Jacobean eras and found its highest expression in William Shakespeare's *Hamlet.*

The revenge drama derived originally from the Roman tragedies of Seneca but was established on the English stage by Thomas Kyd with *The Spanish Tragedie* (*c.* 1592). This work, which opens with the Ghost of Don Andrea and the Spirit of Revenge, deals with the predicament of Hieronimo, a Spanish gentleman who is driven to melancholy by the murder of his son. Between spells of madness, he discovers who the murderers are and plans his ingenious revenge. He stages a play in which the murderers take part, and, while enacting his role, Hieronimo actually kills them and then kills himself. The influence of the play, apparent in *Hamlet* (1600–01), is also evident in other plays of the period, such as John Marston's *Antonio's Revenge* (*c.* 1602), where the ghost of Antonio's slain father urges Antonio to avenge his murder, which he does during a court masque. In George Chapman's *The Revenge of Bussy d'Ambois* (*c.* 1610), Bussy's ghost begs his introspective brother Clermont to avenge his murder. Clermont hesitates and vacillates but at last complies, then kills himself. Most revenge tragedies end with a scene of carnage that disposes of the avenger as well as the victims. Other examples are Shakespeare's *Titus Andronicus* (1594), Cyril Tourneur's *The Revenger's Tragedie* (1607), and Henry Chettle's *The Tragedy of Hoffman* (published posthumously, 1631).

reversal *See* PERIPETEIA.

reversed foot A foot in which the prevailing cadence of a metrical series or of an adjacent foot is reversed or inverted by exchanging the positions of stressed and unstressed or long and short elements. *Compare* INVERSION.

review \ri-ˈvyü\ **1.** A critical evaluation (as of a book or play). **2.** A magazine devoted chiefly to reviews and essays.

revised edition An edition (as of a book) that incorporates major revisions by the author or an editor and often includes supplementary matter designed to bring it up to date.

Revue des Deux Mondes \rə-vue̅-dā-dœ̄-'mȯ^{n}d\ Fortnightly journal of criticism of and commentary on literature and other arts, published in Paris in 1829 and from 1831 to 1944. It was one of a number of journals set up in France following the suspension of censorship in 1828, and it attained a critical influence in that country comparable to the great Scottish and English journals of the day. *Revue des Deux Mondes,* however, limited its concerns to the arts. François Buloz was its editor from 1831 to 1877 and established a tradition of excellence that attracted contributions from such literary eminences as Charles-Augustin Sainte-Beuve, Honoré de Balzac, Victor Hugo, Hippolyte Taine, and Ernest Renan. The journal suspended publication in 1944 but was brought out again from 1948 under the title *La Revue de Littérature, Histoire, Arts et Sciences des Deux Mondes.*

rhapsoder \'rap-sō-dər\ *obsolete* A collector of literary pieces.

rhapsodist \'rap-sə-dist\ [Greek *rhapsōidós,* from *rháptein* to sew, stitch together + *ōidḗ* song] Any of the dramatic reciters of ancient Greece active from the 6th century BC. In the oral epic tradition, rhapsodists were preceded by Homeric singers (*aoidoi*) of their own epic songs and, like them, were musically accompanied on the lyre and aulos. To heighten dramatic effect, rhapsodists used a staff for symbolic gesturing. Their intonation of poetry probably involved a simple chant rather than a recognizable tune.

Rhapsodists recited Homeric poems, but Plato implies in the *Ion* that their repertory may have included works by Hesiod and Archilochus. Rhapsodists became a chief feature of the annual Panathenaea festival in Athens. By the 3rd century BC they were incorporated with actors in the union of the Dionysiac artists. The Homerids, who perpetuated Homer's works, were originally rhapsodists.

rhapsody \'rap-sə-dē\ [Greek *rhapsōidía* activity of a rhapsodist, portion of an epic poem, a derivative of *rhapsōidós* rhapsodist] **1.** A portion of an epic poem adapted for recitation. **2.** *archaic* A miscellaneous collection. **3.** A highly emotional literary work.

rhetoric \'ret-ə-rik\ [Greek *rhētorikḗ,* from feminine of *rhētorikós* rhetorical, oratorical, a derivative of *rhḗtōr* public speaker] The art of speaking or writing effectively. This may entail the study of principles and rules of composition formulated by critics of ancient time. It can also involve the study of writing or speaking as a means of communication or persuasion.

Classical rhetoric was a dual matter of practical application and philosophy. Most historians of rhetoric attribute its invention to the development of democracy in Syracuse in the 5th century BC, when dispossessed landowners were given a chance under the new egalitarian government to argue their claims before a group of fellow citizens. So important was the ability to speak well and persuasively that shrewd speakers sought help from teachers of oratory, called rhetors, who in turn developed theories for successful speechmaking, or rhetoric.

This use of language was also of interest to philosophers because the oratorical arguments called into question the relationships among language, truth, and morality. Plato and Aristotle shared the belief that language was basically decoration for fixed ideas, and rhetoric was the method of arranging these ideas in appealing ways and elaborating on them.

According to Aristotle, the uses of rhetoric were divided into deliberative speeches, made to advise political assemblies; forensic speeches, made in law courts; and epideictic speeches, made during ceremonies to praise and sometimes blame. In each of these areas there was a suasive element, an attempt to persuade listeners of something or to produce an intended effect.

Rome adopted most of this theory in its public life, and the educated class was trained in rhetoric to produce effective legislators and statesmen. The two most prominent rhetoricians of the empire were Cicero, of the 1st century BC, and Quintilian, of a century later. By elaborating Greek practices, Roman rhetoric developed a process of speech composition broken into five categories: invention, or analyzing and researching the speech topic; disposition, or arranging the material into an oration; elocution, fitting words to the situation; pronunciation, or action, delivering the speech orally; and memory, lodging ideas within the mind.

This compartmentalizing of process gave rhetoric a mechanical quality that became more pronounced as the times changed. By the 16th century rhetoric was being applied to letter writing. Through the influence of the French rhetorician Petrus Ramus, rhetoric was reduced to matters of style mainly and became a collection of tropes, or figures of speech, like metaphor, simile, and personification. At this point it gained a reputation for being flowery ornamentation without substance.

Post-Renaissance changes in the theories of knowledge wrought changes in the principles of rhetoric. Beginning with René Descartes and John Locke through Friedrich Nietzsche to such contemporary philosophers as Thomas Kuhn, views of the relationship of language to reality have changed. The classical idea that language reflects an absolute truth or reality has given way to the idea that language largely determines what reality means. In the late 20th century, the notion that words convey some recognizable and agreed-upon meaning has been challenged by such literary-critical schools as deconstruction.

Philosophers of the poststructuralist school see language as a cultural structure which preexists and conditions the individual. They would have rhetoric examine not only language but other forms of discourse in culture related to language, such as motion pictures, television, advertising, financial markets, political parties, educational systems, and so forth, which are rhetorical by nature, that is, instituted to persuade and to effect particular results. Other modern rhetoricians feel that all linguistic communication is argumentation, and they advocate the analysis and interpretation of such discourse based on an understanding of audience response and social situations.

rhetorical criticism \ri-ˈtȯr-i-kəl\ Critical method that studies a text (or other form of discourse) in the light of the effects it achieves; rhetorical critics examine the structure, forms, devices, and organization of a text and attempt to correlate these elements with the effects produced. Criticism based on rhetoric is a form of reader-response study, and it is one of the oldest methods of examining meaning. *Compare* HERMENEUTICS; READER-RESPONSE CRITICISM.

rhetorical question A question not intended to elicit an answer to but asked for rhetorical effect often with an assumption that only one answer is possible. The much used "What's the difference?" or "Who cares?" are rhetorical questions.

rhetorician \ˌret-ə-ˈrish-ən\ **1.** A master or teacher of rhetoric. **2.** An eloquent or grandiloquent writer or speaker.

rhétoriqueur or **grand rhétoriqueur** \grä^{n}-rā-tō-rē-ˈkœr\ [Middle French, literally, rhetorician] Any of the principal poets of the school that flourished in 15th- and early 16th-century France (particularly in Burgundy), whose poetry, based on historical and moral themes, employed allegory, dreams, symbols, and mythology for didactic effect.

Guillaume de Machaut, who popularized the new lyric genres such as the rondeau, ballade, lay, and virelay in the 14th century, is considered to have been the leader of the new *rhétorique,* or poetic art. The tradition was continued by Eustache Deschamps, Christine de Pisan, and Charles, Duke d'Orléans, as well as by Jean Froissart, the historian, and the political orator Alain Chartier. In his role as chronicler, Froissart was followed by Georges Chastellain, Olivier de La Marche, and Jean Molinet, historiographers of the Burgundian court who became known as the *grands rhétoriqueurs*. Like Chartier, they favored a didactic, elegant, and Latinate style in prose and verse, and they brought the long didactic poem of Deschamps and Christine de Pisan to new prominence. Their short poems exhibited astonishing verbal ingenuity, often relying on the pun, riddle, or acrostic for effects. Pretentious and erudite, they enhanced their poetry through mythological inventions and attempted to enrich the French language by multiplying compound words, derivatives, and scholarly diminutives.

Other *rhétoriqueur*s were Jean Bouchet, Jean Marot, Guillaume Crétin, and Pierre Gringore. Crétin composed patriotic poems on current events, as did Gringore, whose sotie-moralité (satirical play) entitled *Le Jeu du prince des sots* ("Play of the Prince of Fools") supported the policy of Louis XII through a forceful attack on Pope Julius II.

The last and one of the best rhétoriqueurs was Jean Lemaire de Belges, whose works reveal the influence of Dante and Petrarch. Inspired by his travels through Italy, he attempted new meters, such as the terza rima, and expressed some of his views in the *Concorde des deux langages* ("Harmony Between Two Languages"), an allegory encouraging a spiritual harmony between French and Italian.

rhopalic or **ropalic** \rō-ˈpal-ik\ [Greek *rhopalikós,* literally, like a club (i.e., thicker toward the end), a derivative of *rhópalon* club, cudgel], *also called* wedge verse. Having each succeeding unit in a prosodic series larger or longer than the preceding one. For example, a rhopalic may have each successive word in a line or verse longer by one syllable than its predecessor. Each successive line of a stanza may be made longer by the addition of one element (such as a syllable or metrical foot).

rhupunt or **rhupynt** \ˈhrē-ˌpint\ [Welsh] One of the 24 meters of the Welsh bardic tradition. A rhupunt is a verse composed of three, four, or five four-syllable sections linked by cynghanedd (an intricate system of accentuation, alliteration, and internal rhyme) and rhyme. The first three of the four-syllable sections are made to rhyme with one another and the fourth section to rhyme with the fourth of the next verse. The whole is written as a single line or is divided into as many lines as it has rhyming sections.

rhyme or **rime** \ˈrīm\ [Middle English *rime,* from Old French, of unknown origin] A type of echoing produced by the close placement of two or more words with similarly sounding final syllables. Rhyme is used by poets (and occasionally by prose writers) to produce sounds that appeal to the ear and to unify and establish a poem's stanzaic form. End rhyme (i.e., rhyme used at the end of a line to echo the end of another line) is most common, but internal, interior, or leonine rhyme is frequently used as an occasional embellishment in a poem; two familiar examples are William Shakespeare's "Hark; hark! the lark at heaven's gate sings " and Edgar Allan Poe's "The Raven":

> And the silken, sad, uncertain rustling of each purple curtain
> Thrilled me—filled me with fantastic terrors never felt before;
> So that now, to still the beating of my heart, I stood repeating:
> " 'Tis some visitor entreating entrance at my chamber door—"

Three rhymes are recognized by purists as "true rhymes": *masculine rhyme,* in which the two words end with the same vowel-consonant combination (stand/land); *feminine rhyme* (sometimes called *double rhyme*), in which two syllables rhyme (profession/discretion); and *trisyllabic rhyme,* in which three syllables rhyme (patinate/latinate). The too-regular effect of masculine rhyme is sometimes softened by using *trailing rhyme,* or *semirhyme,* in which one of the two words trails an additional unstressed syllable behind it (trail/failure).

Other types of rhyme include *eye rhyme,* in which syllables are identical in spelling but are pronounced differently (cough/slough), and *pararhyme,* first used systematically by the 20th-century poet Wilfred Owen, in which the two syllables have different vowel sounds but identical penultimate and final consonantal groupings (grand/grind). *Feminine pararhyme* has two forms, one in which both vowel sounds differ (ran in/run on) and one in which only one does (blindness/blandness). *Weakened,* or *unaccented, rhyme* occurs when the relevant syllable of the rhyming word is unstressed (bend/frightened). Because of the way in which lack of stress affects the sound, a rhyme of this kind may often be regarded as consonance, which occurs when the two words are similar only in having identical final consonants (best/least). Another form of near rhyme is assonance, in which only the vowel sounds are identical (grow/home). Assonance was regularly used in French poetry until the 12th century, when end rhyme was introduced. It continues to be important in the poetic technique of Romance languages but performs only a subsidiary function in English verse.

Many traditional poetic forms use set rhyme patterns; for example, the sonnet, villanelle, rondeau, ballade, chant royal, triolet, canzone, and sestina. Rhyme seems to have developed in Western poetry as a combination of earlier techniques of end consonance, end assonance, and alliteration. It is found only occasionally in classical Greek and Latin poetry but more frequently in medieval religious Latin verse and in songs from the 4th century (especially those of the Roman Catholic liturgy). Although it has been periodically opposed by devotees of classical verse, it has never fallen into complete disuse. Shakespeare interspersed rhymed couplets into the blank verse of his dramas; John Milton disapproved of rhyme, but Samuel Johnson favored it. In the 20th century, although many advocates of free verse ignore rhyme, other poets have continued to introduce new and complicated rhyme schemes. *See also* ALLITERATION; ASSONANCE; CONSONANCE; POETRY.

rhymer or **rimer** \\'rī-mər\\ One who makes rhymes, a versifier; specifically, a mediocre poet.

rhyme royal or **rime royal** \\'rīm-'rȯi-əl\\ *plural* rhyme royals. A stanza of seven lines in iambic pentameter, rhyming *ababbcc*.

The rhyme royal was first used in English verse in the 14th century by Geoffrey Chaucer in *Troilus and Criseyde* and *The Parlement of Foules*. Traditionally, the name rhyme royal is said to derive from *The Kingis Quair,* attributed to James I of Scotland (1394–1437), but some critics trace the name to the French chant royal. Chaucer probably borrowed it from the French poet and musician Guillaume de Machaut (*c.* 1300–77).

Rhyme royal became the favorite form for long narrative poems during the 15th and early 16th centuries, concluding with William Shakespeare's *The Rape of Lucrece* (1594). John Milton later experimented with the form in the 17th century, as did William Morris in the 19th and John Masefield in the 20th. *Compare* BALLADE ROYAL; CHANT ROYAL.

rhyme scheme The formal arrangement of rhymes in a stanza or a poem. If it is one of a number of set rhyme patterns, it may be identified by the name of the pattern (for example, Spenserian stanza). The rhyme scheme is usually notated with lowercase letters of the alphabet (as *ababbcbcc,* in the case of the Spenserian stanza), each different letter representing a different rhyme.

rhymester or **rimester** \\'rīm-stər\\ An inferior poet.

rhyme-tag \'rīm-ˌtag\ A word or phrase used primarily to produce a rhyme. Rhyme-tags are used to comic effect in much light verse, as in W.S. Gilbert's "The Modern Major General," which reads in part

> I am the very pattern of a modern Major General,
> I've information vegetable, animal, and mineral;
> I know the kings of England, and I quote the fights historical,
> From Marathon to Waterloo, in order categorical;
> I'm very well acquainted, too, with matters mathematical,
> I understand equations, both the simple and quadratical;
> About binomial theorem I'm teeming with a lot o' news,
> With interesting facts about the square of the hypotenuse.
> I'm very good at integral and differential calculus,
> I know the scientific names of beings animalculous.
> In short, in matters vegetable, animal, and mineral,
> I am the very model of a modern Major General.

rhythm \'rith-əm\ [Greek *rhythmós* recurrent motion, rhythm] **1.** An ordered, recurrent alternation of strong and weak elements in the flow of sound and silence in speech.

Although rhythm in poetry is difficult to define, it is readily discriminated by the ear and the mind, having as it does a physiological basis. It is universally agreed to involve qualities of movement, repetition, and pattern and to arise from the poem's nature as a temporal structure. Rhythm, by any definition, is essential to poetry; prose may be said to exhibit rhythm but in a much less highly organized sense. The presence of rhythmic patterns heightens emotional response and often affords the reader a sense of balance.

Although it is often equated with rhythm, METER is perhaps more accurately described as one method of organizing a poem's rhythm. Unlike rhythm, meter is not a requisite of poetry; it is, rather, an abstract organization of elements of stress, duration, or number of syllables per line into a specific formal pattern. The interaction of a given metrical pattern with any other aspect of sound in a poem produces a tension, or counterpoint, that creates the rhythm of metrically based poetry.

Compared with the wide variety of metrical schemes, the types of metrically related rhythms are few. *Duple rhythm* occurs in lines composed in two-syllable feet, as in William Shakespeare's line:

> ´ ∪ | ∪ ∪ | ∪ ´ | ∪ ´ | ∪ ´
> Tired with | all these, | for rest | ful death | I cry

In metrical schemes based on three-syllable feet, the rhythm is known as *triple rhythm,* as in Rudyard Kipling's lines:

For the strength | of the Pack | is the Wolf, |
and the strength | of the Wolf | is the Pack

Rising rhythm results when the stress falls on the last syllable of each foot in a line, as in John Milton's line:

When I | consid | er how | my light | is spent

The reverse of this is *falling rhythm,* as in John Dryden's line:

Bacchus' | blessings | are a | treasure

Running, or *common, rhythm* occurs in meters in which stressed and unstressed syllables alternate (duple rhythm, rising or falling). Gerard Manley Hopkins, in reaction against traditional meters, coined the term SPRUNG RHYTHM to apply to verse in which the line is measured by the number of speech-stressed syllables, the number of unstressed syllables being indeterminate.

In free verse, rhythm most commonly arises from the arrangement of linguistic elements into patterns that more nearly approximate the natural cadence of speech and that give symmetry to the verse. The rhythmical resources available to free verse include syntactical patterning; systematic repetition of sound, words, phrases, and lines; the relative value of temporal junctures occasioned by caesura (a marked pause in the middle of a line); line length; and other determinants of pace. Some authorities recognize in the highly organized patterning of imagery a further source of poetic rhythm.

The following lines from Walt Whitman's "Song of Myself" illustrate many of these rhythmical devices:

Twenty-eight young men bathe by the shore,
Twenty-eight young men and all so friendly;
Twenty-eight years of womanly life and all so lonesome.
She owns the fine house by the rise of the bank,
She hides, handsome and richly drest aft the blinds of the window.

The rhythms that are characteristic of particular poets are sometimes ascribed to units of breath, as in the essay *Projective Verse* (1950) by the poet and critic Charles Olson: "And the line comes (I swear it) from the breath, from the breathing of the man who writes, at the moment that he writes. . . ." **2.** The repetition in a literary work at varying intervals and in an altered form or under changed circumstances of phrase, incident, character type, or symbol. **3.** The effect created by the elements in a play, motion picture, or novel that are related to the temporal development of the action (such as the length and diversity of scenes and language).

riddle \ˈrid-əl\ [Old English *rǣdelse* opinion, conjecture, riddle] A deliberately enigmatic or ambiguous question requiring a thoughtful and often witty answer. The riddle is a form of guessing game that has been a part of the folklore of most cultures from ancient times. Western scholars generally recognize two main kinds of riddle: the descriptive riddle and the shrewd or witty question.

The descriptive riddle usually describes an animal, person, plant, or object in an intentionally enigmatic manner, to suggest something different from the correct answer. "What runs about all day and lies under the bed at night?" suggests "A dog," but the answer is "A shoe." The description usually consists of one general and one specific element. The general element stands first and is to be understood metaphorically. The second element is to be understood literally and sometimes appears to contradict the first. An apparently late development is the use of puns: "What's black and white and red all over?"—"A newspaper." Descriptive riddles deal with appearance, not function. Thus, an egg is "A little white house without door or window," not something to eat or something from which a chicken hatches. Paradoxical riddles provide descriptions in terms of action, for example, "What grows bigger the more you take from it?"—"A hole," and "The man who made it did not want it; the man who bought it did not use it; the man who used it did not know it"—"A coffin."

Descriptive riddles rarely occur in folktales or ballads. An unusual example of one in a folktale is that asked by the Sphinx, the monster that terrorized the Thebans of ancient Greece: "What has one voice, and walks on four legs in the morning, two at noon, and three in the evening?" The answer was given by Oedipus: "A man, who crawls on all fours in infancy, walks on two feet when grown, and leans on a staff when aged."

Lacking a generic name in English, shrewd or witty questions are classed with riddles. They, too, are of ancient origin. A classical Greek example that has been widely translated is "What is the strongest of all things?"—"Love: iron is strong, but the blacksmith is stronger, and love can subdue the blacksmith." Shrewd questions may be classified by subject and form. Those dealing with letters of the alphabet, words, and symbols are generally statements calling for interpretation: "ICUR YY 4 me" ("I see you are too wise for me"); "What is in the middle of Paris?"—"R"; "Spell 'dry grass' with three letters"—"Hay." The influence of the classroom in such riddles (sometimes called "catch riddles") is clear.

riding rhyme A rhymed couplet in iambic pentameter, such as those used by Geoffrey Chaucer and John Lydgate. It is an early form of HEROIC COUPLET.

rifacimento \rē-ˌfäch-ē-ˈmen-tō\ or **refacimento** \rā-\ *plural* rifacimenti \-tē\, rifacimentos, refacimenti, *or* refacimentos [Italian *rifacimento* remaking, revision, a derivative of *rifare* to remake] A recasting or adaptation especially of a literary work or musical composition.

Riksmål or **Riksmaal** *See* BOKMÅL.

rime *See* RHYME.

rime riche \ˌrēm-ˈrēsh\ *plural* rimes riches \ˈrēsh\ [French, literally, rich rhyme] In French and English prosody, a rhyme produced by agreement in sound not only of the last accented vowel and any succeeding sounds but also of the consonant preceding this rhyming vowel—*also called* identical rhyme. A rime riche may consist of homographs (fair/fair) or homophones (write/right). It is distinguished from *rime suffisante.*

rime royal *See* RHYME ROYAL.

rimester *See* RHYMESTER.

rime suffisante \ˌrēm-ˌsü-fē-ˈzäⁿt\ *plural* rimes suffisantes \-ˈzäⁿt\ [French, literally, sufficient rhyme] In French and English prosody, end rhyme produced by agreement in sound of an accented final vowel and following final consonant or consonants, if any. Examples of rimes suffisantes in English include the rhymes ship/dip and flee/see. It is distinguished from *rime riche.*

rimur or **rímur** \ˈrē-mər\ [Old Norse *rīmur,* plural of *rīma* rhyme, ballad, a derivative of *rīm* rhyme, from Middle Low German, from Old French *rime*] *singular* ríma. Versified sagas, or episodes from the sagas, a form of adaptation that was popular in Iceland from the 15th century.

One of three genres of popular early Icelandic poetry (the other two being dances and ballads), rimur were produced from the 14th to the 19th century. Originally used for dancing, they combine an end-rhymed metrical form derived from Latin hymns with the techniques of syllable counting, alliteration, and internal rhyme used by the earlier Norse court poets, the skalds. Rimur also preserve the skald's elaborate diction but in a stereotyped fashion as though the original meaning of complex epithets had been lost. Most rimur are long narratives based on native tradition or foreign romances. Often a long prose saga was converted into a rimur cycle. Though not high in literary quality, rimur were important for preserving the skaldic diction and the content of lost sagas.

rising action In drama and other literature, the events leading up to the climax of the plot. It is in contrast to *falling action,* the events that follow the climax and lead to the denouement.

rising rhythm *also called* ascending rhythm. In prosody, a rhythm in which the stresses regularly fall on the last syllable of each foot (as in iambic or anapestic lines). Its opposite is falling, or descending, rhythm. *See also* CADENCE.

rispetto \rē-ˈspet-tō\ *plural* rispetti \-tē\ [Italian, literally, respect] A Tuscan folk verse form, a version of STRAMBOTTO. The rispetto lyric is generally composed of eight hendecasyllabic (11-syllable) lines. In its earliest form the rhyme scheme was usually *abababcc;* later, the scheme *ababccdd* became more prominent, and other variations can also be found.

The form reached its pinnacle of both artistic achievement and popularity in the 14th and 15th centuries, particularly in the work of Politian, to whom some 200 rispetti are ascribed. Lorenzo de' Medici also wrote rispetti.

robāʿī *See* RUBAʿI.

Robinsonade \ˌräb-in-sə-ˈnād, ˌrō-bin-zō-ˈnäd-ə\ *plural* Robinsonades \-ˈnādz\ *or* Robinsonaden \-ˈnäd-ən\ A fictitious narrative of often fantastic adventures in real or imaginary distant places; especially, a story of the adventures of a person marooned on a desert island. The word, originally coined in German, is derived from the fictional prose narrative *Robinson Crusoe* by the English journalist and novelist Daniel Defoe.

Rococo \rə-ˈkō-kō, ˌrō-kō-ˈkō\ [French, irregular derivative of *rocaille,* 18th-century style of ornament characterized by sinuous foliate forms] Of or relating to an artistic style widespread in 18th-century Europe that was characterized by fanciful, curved asymmetrical forms and elaborate ornamentation. In literature, the term describes a style marked by lightheartedness, grace, and often wit. Examples include Alexander Pope's *The Rape of the Lock* and Voltaire's *Candide.*

rodomontade \ˌräd-ō-ˌmän-ˈtād, -ˈtäd\ **1.** A bragging speech. **2.** Vain boasting or bluster. The word, originally coined in French, derives from the name of the character Rodomonte in Matteo Boiardo's *Orlando innamorato* and is used in literature in reference to boasting speech or behavior by a character such as William Shakespeare's Falstaff.

roman à clef \rō-män-ȧ-ˈklā\ *plural* romans à clef \rō-mänz\ [French, literally, novel with a key] A novel that has the extraliterary interest of portraying identifiable, sometimes real people more or less thinly disguised as fictional characters.

The tradition dates to 17th-century France, when fashionable members of the aristocratic literary coteries, such as Mlle de Scudéry, enlivened their historical romances by including in them fictional representations of well-known figures in the court of Louis XIV. In the 20th century, W. Somerset Maugham's *Cakes and Ale* is widely held to contain portraits of the novelists Thomas Hardy and Hugh Walpole. A more common type of roman à clef is Simone de Beauvoir's *Les Mandarins,* in which the disguised characters are immediately recognizable only to a small circle of insiders.

In a general sense, every work of literary art offers a key or clue to the artist's preoccupations (for example, the jail in Charles Dickens or the mysterious tyrants in Franz Kafka, each leading back to the author's own father), but the true roman à clef is more specific in its disguised references. Jonathan Swift's *A Tale of a Tub,* John Dryden's *Absalom and Achitophel,* and George Orwell's

Animal Farm make complete sense only when their disguised historical content is disclosed. These examples illustrate that the literary purpose is not primarily aesthetic. In understanding D.H. Lawrence's *Aaron's Rod* it helps to have a knowledge of the author's personal enmities, and to understand Aldous Huxley's *Point Counter Point* fully one should know, for instance, that the character of Mark Rampion represents D.H. Lawrence himself and that of Denis Burlap represents the critic John Middleton Murry. Marcel Proust's *À la recherche du temps perdu* becomes a richer literary experience when the author's social milieu is explored, and James Joyce's *Finnegans Wake* has so many personal references that it may be called the most massive roman à clef ever written. The more important the key becomes to full understanding, the closer the work comes to being didactic. That is, when it is dangerous to expose the truth directly, the novel or narrative poem may present it obliquely. Nonetheless, the ultimate vitality of the work depends on those elements in it that require no key.

romance \rō-ˈmans, ˈrō-ˌmans\ [Old French *romans, romanz* French, something composed in French, tale in verse, from Medieval Latin *Romanice* in a vernacular language (as opposed to Latin), a derivative of Late Latin *Romanus* Gallo-Romance (as opposed to Frankish), from Latin, of Rome, Roman] **1.** A medieval tale based on legend, chivalric love and adventure, or the supernatural. *Compare* EPIC. **2.** A prose narrative treating imaginary characters involved in events remote in time or space and usually heroic, adventurous, or mysterious. *Compare* FANTASY; HISTORICAL NOVEL. **3.** A love story. **4.** A class or division of literature comprising romance or romantic fiction.

The romance literary form, usually characterized by its treatment of chivalry, came into being in France in the mid-12th century. It had antecedents in many prose works from classical antiquity (the so-called Greek romances), but as a distinctive genre it was developed in the context of the aristocratic courts of such patrons as Eleanor of Aquitaine.

The romance had its heyday in France and Germany between the mid-12th and mid-13th century in the works of such masters as Chrétien de Troyes, Benoît de Sainte-Maure, and Gottfried von Strassburg. By the time it reached England (about 1250), it was already beginning to show signs of a decline from its original form.

The staple subject matter of romance is chivalric adventure. Love stories and religious allegories can often be found interwoven with this material, but they are not essential to it. The majority of romances drew their plots from three basic areas: classical history and legend, the adventures of King Arthur and the knights of the Round Table (certainly the most significant group), and the doings of Charlemagne and his knights. To these must be added a number of romances concerned specifically with the deeds of English heroes, such as Havelock the Dane and Richard Coeur de Lion (Richard the Lion-hearted), and a number of other romances, such as *Sir Orfeo* and *Floire et Blancheflor,* that belong to no particular cycle.

Among the earlier romances were those that took their subjects from classical antiquity. These include the *Roman de Thèbes* and the *Roman d'Enéas,* both adapted from the work of Latin poets. Benoît de Sainte-Maure's *Roman de Troie,* which tells the story of Troy, is notable in this group for containing the first literary treatment of the narrative of Troilus and Cressida, later developed by Giovanni Boccaccio, Geoffrey Chaucer, and William Shakespeare. Also popular were stories based on the life of Alexander the Great, among them the *Roman d'Alexandre* and the later *King Alisaunder.*

The most celebrated romances of the Arthurian cycle were those written in the second half of the 12th century by Chrétien de Troyes. It was he who in *Perceval, ou Le Conte du Graal* introduced the theme of the Holy Grail into European literature. The French Arthurian romances were of particular importance for English literature, since they provided the material that Sir Thomas Malory later adapted in *Le Morte Darthur* (first printed 1485). *Sir Gawayne and the Grene Knight,* written in the mid-14th century and regarded as one of the most beautiful English poems of the Middle Ages, also belongs in this group. Into the third category fall a number of lesser romances about such figures as Roland (Orlando) and Sir Ferumbras, who fought in the campaigns of Charlemagne.

As the etymology of the word *romance* indicates, the romance was written in the vernacular rather than in Latin. There are examples of the genre in both verse and prose, though in general prose romances tend to belong to the later period. From the start, these works share a taste for the exotic, the remote, and the miraculous. Descriptive detail is lavish, and love stories on the whole end happily—*Tristan und Isolde,* written by Gottfried von Strassburg in the early 13th century, being a notable exception. Overall, it can be said that by comparison with the epic form of the chanson de geste ("song of deeds"), which it superseded, the romance shows a general sophistication of narrative method and psychological insight.

In later centuries the romance underwent various transformations. The continued popularity of one form of it, the prose romance of 15th- and 16th-century Spain, is attested by Miguel de Cervantes' satire of the romance in *Don Quixote.* Although the chivalric ideal of the perfect knight was essentially medieval, lingering echoes of romance can be found in the changing connotations of the word itself. Thus, at the end of the 18th century the Romantic movements beginning in England and Germany were in some respects an attempt to turn back to the spirit of medieval romance in reaction against the prevailing philosophies of the time. Even today, in the popular romantic novel, there can be detected within the formulaic plots a debased survival of some of the original values.

See also ALEXANDER ROMANCE; ARTHURIAN LEGEND; CHANSON DE GESTE.

romancero \ˌrō-män-ˈthā-rō\ [Spanish *el Romancero,* from *romancero* collection of ballads, a derivative of *romance* ballad] Collective body of Spanish folk ballads (*romances*) constituting a unique tradition of European balladry. They resemble epic poetry in their heroic, aristocratic tone, their themes of battle and honor, and their pretense to historicity; but they are, nevertheless, ballads, compressed dramatic narratives sung to a tune.

Once thought to be the source of such 12th-century Spanish epics as *Cantar de mio Cid* ("Song of My Cid"), the genre is now believed to be a development of the epic tradition. The earliest known *romances* date from the late 14th and early 15th centuries.

Some ballads are brief dramatizations of episodes from known epics. They frequently deal with the conflicts between or the amours of Spaniards and Moors. Other popular subjects are the Arthurian and Charlemagne legends. Traditional ballads were collected in the Antwerp *Cancionero de romances* ("Ballad Songbook") and in the *Silva de varios romances* ("Miscellany of Various Ballads"), both first published about 1550 and thereafter repeatedly. The form (octosyllabic, alternate lines having a single assonance throughout) was soon exploited for lyrical purposes by the most famous poets of the age. Unlike the folk poetry of England, Scandinavia, or Germany, which followed a tradition independent of the national literatures, the ballads formed a continuous link in the chain of tradition from the earliest Spanish vernacular literature to the literature of the 20th century. As the sourcebook of history and of the character of Spaniards of all classes, they lie at the heart of the national consciousness. They inspired many of the poems, dramas, and novels by the masters of Spanish literature and remain the chosen medium for popular narrative verse.

romance stanza *also called* romance-six. A six-line verse stanza common in metrical romances in which lines 1, 2, 4, and 5 have four accents each and lines 3 and 6 have three accents each and in which the rhyme scheme is *aabaab*. It is a type of tail rhyme.

roman-fleuve \rō-mäⁿ-ˈflœ̄v\ *plural* romans-fleuves *same*\ [French, literally, river novel] A novel having the form of a long, multivolume, and usually loosely structured chronicle of persons comprising a family, community, or other social group.

Inspired by Honoré de Balzac's *Comédie humaine* and Émile Zola's Rougon-Macquart cycle, the *roman-fleuve* was a popular literary genre in France during the first half of the 20th century. Examples include *Jean-Christophe* (1904–12) by Romain Rolland, *À la recherche du temps perdu* (1913–27; *Remembrance of Things Past*) by Marcel Proust, *Les Thibault* (1922–40) by Roger Martin du Gard, and *Les Hommes de bonne volonté* (1932–46; *Men of Good Will*) by Jules Romains. Comparable to the French roman-fleuve is the English-language saga novel, represented by such works as John Galsworthy's *The Forsyte Saga* (1906–21) and the "Jalna" series of Canadian writer Mazo de la Roche. Proust's work is usually considered to be the masterpiece of the genre.

Romanticism \rō-ˈman-tə-ˌsiz-əm\ A literary, artistic, and philosophical movement originating in Europe in the 18th century and lasting roughly until the mid-19th century. Romanticism is characterized chiefly by a reaction against the Enlightenment and Neoclassicism with their stress on reason, order, balance, harmony, rationality, and intellect. Romanticism emphasized the individual, the subjective, the irrational, the imaginative, the personal, the spontaneous, the emotional, the visionary, and the transcendental. *Compare* CLASSICISM.

Among the characteristic attitudes of Romanticism were a deepened appreciation of the beauties of nature; a general exaltation of emotion over reason and of the senses over intellect; a turning in upon the self and a heightened examination of human personality; a preoccupation with the genius, the hero, and the exceptional figure; a new view of the artist as a supremely individual creator, whose creative spirit is more important than strict adherence to formal rules and traditional procedures; an emphasis upon imagination as a gateway to transcendent experience and spiritual truth; a consuming interest in folk culture, national and ethnic cultural origins, and the medieval era; and a predilection for the exotic, the remote, the mysterious, the weird, the occult, the monstrous, the diseased, and even the satanic.

In literature, Romanticism proper was preceded by several related developments from the mid-18th century on that can be termed pre-Romanticism. Among such trends was a new appreciation of the medieval romance, from which the Romantic movement derives its name. The romance, with its emphasis on individual heroism and on the exotic and the mysterious, was in clear contrast to the elegant formality and artificiality of prevailing classical forms of literature, such as the French Neoclassical tragedy or the English heroic couplet in poetry. This new interest in relatively unsophisticated but overtly emotional literary expressions of the past was to be a dominant note in Romanticism.

Romanticism in English literature began in the late 1790s with the publication of *Lyrical Ballads* of William Wordsworth and Samuel Taylor Coleridge. Wordsworth's "Preface" to the second edition (1800) of *Lyrical Ballads,* in which he described poetry as "the spontaneous overflow of powerful feelings," became the manifesto of the English Romantic movement in poetry. William Blake was the third principal poet of the movement's early phase in England. The first phase of the Romantic movement in Germany—an outgrowth of the *Sturm und Drang* period—was marked by innovations in both content and literary style and by a preoccupation with the mystical, the subconscious, and the supernatural. A number of writers, including Friedrich Hölderlin, the early J.W. von Goethe, Jean Paul, Novalis, Ludwig Tieck, A.W. and Friedrich von Schlegel, Wilhelm Heinrich Wackenroder, and Friedrich Schelling belonged to this first phase. In Revolutionary France, the Viscount de Chateaubriand and Mme de Staël were the chief initiators of Romanticism by virtue of their influential historical and theoretical writings.

The second phase of Romanticism, comprising the period from about 1805 to the 1830s, was marked by a quickening of cultural nationalism and a new attention to national origins, as attested by the collection and imitation of native folklore, folk ballads and poetry, folk dance and music, and previously ignored medieval and Renaissance works. This revived appreciation of history was translated into imaginative writing by Sir Walter Scott, often considered the inventor of the historical novel. About the same time English Romantic poetry reached its zenith in the works of John Keats, Lord Byron, and Percy Bysshe Shelley.

A notable by-product of the Romantic interest in the emotional were works dealing with the supernatural, the weird, and the horrible, as in Mary Shelley's *Frankenstein* and works by C.R. Maturin, the Marquis de Sade, and E.T.A. Hoffmann. The second phase of Romanticism in Germany was dominated by Achim von Arnim, Clemens Brentano, J.J. von Görres, and Joseph von Eichendorff.

By the 1820s Romanticism had broadened to embrace the literatures of almost all of Europe. In this later phase, the movement also examined the passions and struggles of exceptional individuals. Romantic or Romantic-influenced writers across the European continent included Thomas De Quincey, William Hazlitt, and the Brontë sisters in England; Victor Hugo, Alfred de Vigny, Alphonse de Lamartine, Alfred de Musset, Stendhal, Prosper Mérimée, Alexandre Dumas (*père*), and Théophile Gautier in France; Alessandro Manzoni and Giacomo Leopardi in Italy; Aleksandr Pushkin and Mikhail Lermontov in Russia; José de Espronceda and Ángel de Saavedra in Spain; and Adam Mickiewicz in Poland. Almost all of the important writers in pre-Civil War America were influenced by Romanticism. *See also* TRANSCENDENTALISM.

romp \'rämp\ A high-spirited, carefree, and boisterous play. Also something suggestive of such a play, as a light, fast-paced narrative, dramatic, or musical work, usually in a comic mood.

rondeau \'rän-dō, *French* rȯ^{n}-'dō\ *plural* rondeaux \'rän-dōz, *French* rȯ^{n}-'dō\ [French, from Old French *rondel* rondel] One of several fixed forms in French lyric poetry and song of the 14th and 15th centuries. The rondeau has only two rhymes (allowing no repetition of rhyme words) and consists of 13 or 15 lines of 8 or 10 syllables divided into three stanzas. The beginning of the first line of the first stanza serves as the refrain of the second and third stanzas. (This form is sometimes called rondel. *Compare* RONDEL.)

The full form of a rondeau consists of three stanzas of five, four, and six lines. If *c* stands for the refrain, the rhyme scheme of a rondeau is *aabba aabc aabbac*.

The earliest rondeaux had stanzas of two or three lines; later, especially in the 15th century, stanzas of four, five, or even six lines were common. Because of the unwieldy length of the refrains in such cases, the literary rondeau, which in the 15th century began to be distinct from the sung rondeau, often curtailed the refrains in the second and fourth stanzas, leaving only a *rentrement* ("reentry") of the opening words. This proved to be a pleasing development, because it often produced unexpected changes of meaning as a result of the new context.

rondeau redoublé \ròn-'dō-rə-dü-'blā, 'rän-dō\ *plural* rondeaux redoublés *same*\ [French, literally, double rondeau] A fixed form of verse, a variant of the rondeau, that runs on two rhymes. The rondeau redoublé usually consists of five quatrains and one quintet. The lines of the first quatrain are used consecutively to end each of the remaining four quatrains; the quintet, which follows the rhyme scheme established in the five quatrains, terminates with the opening words of the poem.

rondel \'rän-ˌdel, -dəl, *French* rō^{n}-'del\ or **rondelle** \rän-'del, *French* rō^{n}-'del\ [Old French *rondel,* a derivative of *ruunt, reont* round] A fixed form of verse, a variant of the rondeau, that runs on two rhymes. Also, a poem in this form.

The rondel often consists of 14 lines of 8 or 10 syllables divided into three stanzas (two quatrains and a sextet), with the first two lines of the first stanza serving as the refrain of the second and third stanzas. In some instances rondels are 13 lines long, with only the first line of the poem repeated at the end. The designation rondel is sometimes used interchangeably with rondeau. The form, which originated in 13th-century France, was later used by such poets as Edmund Gosse, Robert Louis Stevenson, and W.E. Henley. *Compare* RONDEAU.

rondelet \ˌrän-də-'let, *French* rō^{n}d-'lā\ [Middle French, a diminutive of *rondel* rondel] A modified rondeau running on two rhymes and consisting usually of one stanza of seven lines in which the first line of four syllables is repeated as the third line and as the final line (or refrain). The remaining lines are made up of eight syllables each.

rondelle *See* RONDEL.

ropalic *See* RHOPALIC.

round character *See* FLAT AND ROUND CHARACTERS.

rounded \'raùn-dəd\ Conceived, drawn, or presented in full form or in all aspects; shown perceptively or penetratingly; or comprehensively realized.

roundel or **roundle** \'raùn-dəl\ [Old French *rondel* rondel] An English modified rondeau, an 11-line poem in three stanzas. The 4th and 11th lines constitute a refrain taken from the first part of the first line of the poem.

Used by its earliest practitioners as a synonym for rondel or rondeau, the term was appropriated by Algernon Swinburne, who in 1883 published a work entitled *A Century of Roundels.*

roundelay \'raùn-də-ˌlā, 'rän-\ [modification of Middle French *rondelet* rondelet] A poem with a refrain that recurs frequently or at fixed intervals, as in a rondel. The term is also loosely used to refer to any of the fixed forms of poetry (such as the rondeau, the rondel, and the roundel) that use refrains extensively.

roundle *See* ROUNDEL.

Round Table, The *See* ALGONQUIN ROUND TABLE.

rove-over \'rōv-ˌō-vər\ Having an extrametrical syllable at the end of one line that forms a foot with the first syllable of the next line. The term is used of a type of verse in sprung rhythm, Gerard Manley Hopkins' method of counting only the stressed syllables of a line. Thus, the meter of a verse is determined by feet of varying length but always having the accent on the first syllable. The third and fourth lines of Hopkins' "Spring and Fall" (here shown for the sake of clarity without Hopkins' own accent marks) are an example of rove-over:

> Leaves, like the things of man, you
> With your fresh thoughts care for, can you?

row \'rō\ *obsolete* A written line, especially a metrical written line.

Royal Shakespeare Company *former name* (until 1961) Shakespeare Memorial Company. Important English theatrical company, established in 1879 and currently based in Stratford-upon-Avon and in London. The repertoire of the original Stratford-based part of the company consists of works by William Shakespeare and other Elizabethan and Jacobean playwrights, while the newer London-based unit performs modern plays and non-Shakespearean classics.

The company was originally attached to the Shakespeare Memorial Theatre in Stratford-upon-Avon, which opened in 1879 as the site of an annual festival of Shakespeare's plays, and its resident company came to be called the Shakespeare Memorial Company. The director Peter Hall reorganized the company in 1961: it was renamed the Royal Shakespeare Company and divided into twin units, one to play at Stratford and the other to be based in London.

rubaʿi \rü-'bä-ˌē, 'rü-ˌbī, 'rü-bä-ˌē\, *plural* rubaiyat \'rü-bī-ˌyät, -bē-; rü-ˌbä-ē-'yät\ *or* rubais, *Persian* robāʿī, *Persian plural* robāīyāt [Persian *robāʿī* quatrain, from Arabic *rubāʿī*] In Persian literature, a genre of poetry; specifically, a quatrain with a rhyme scheme *aaba*. With the *mas̄nawī* (the rhymed couplet), it is a purely Persian poetic genre and not a borrowing from the Arabic, as were the formal ode (qasida) and the love lyric (ghazel). It was adopted and used in other countries under Persian influence.

The most famous example of the genre known in the Western world is the rubaiyat of ʿOmar Khayyām, in the version *The Rubáiyát of Omar Khayyám* (1859), translated by Edward FitzGerald.

Rubaiyat stanza \'rü-bē-ˌät, -bī-, -ˌat\, *also called* Omar stanza \'ō-mär\ From *The Rubáiyát of Omar Khayyám,* an iambic pentameter quatrain (*rubaʿi*) with a rhyme scheme *aaba*. *See* RUBAʿI.

run \'rən\ [translation of Scottish Gaelic *ruith* or Irish *rith*] A stereotyped passage of narrative or description introduced into Gaelic popular tales.

rune \'rün\ [Finnish *runo* poem, canto, of Germanic origin; akin to Old Norse *rūn* secret, character of the runic alphabet, writing] A Finnish poem of folkloric origin, such as the *Kalevala* or one of its divisions. The word has also been applied in a technically incorrect way to medieval Scandinavian poems.

rune \ˈrün\ [Old Norse and Old English *rūn* mystery, runic character, writing] Any of the characters of several scripts used by the Germanic peoples from about the 3rd to the 13th century.

runic writing \ˈrü-nik\, *also called* futhark \ˈfü-ˌthärk\ Writing system of uncertain origin used by Germanic peoples of northern Europe, Britain, Scandinavia, and Iceland from roughly the 3rd century to the 16th or 17th century AD.

There are at least three main varieties of runic script: Early, or Common Germanic (Teutonic), used in northern Europe before about 800 AD; Anglo-Saxon, or Anglian, used in Britain from the 5th or 6th century to about the 12th century AD; and Nordic, or Scandinavian, used from the 8th to about the 12th or 13th century AD in Scandinavia and Iceland. After the 12th century, runes were still used occasionally for charms and memorial inscriptions until the 16th or 17th century, chiefly in Scandinavia. The Common Germanic script had 24 letters, divided into three groups, called *ættir,* of 8 letters each. The sounds of the first six letters were *f, u, th, a, r,* and *k* (thus, futhark). The Anglo-Saxon script added letters to the futhark to represent sounds of Old English that did not occur in the languages that had used the Common Teutonic script. Anglo-Saxon had 28 letters, and after about 900 AD it had 33. There were also slight differences in letter shape. The Scandinavian languages were even richer in sounds than Old English; instead of adding letters to the futhark to represent the new sounds, however, the users of the Nordic script compounded the letter values, using the same letter to stand for more than one sound—e.g., one letter for *k* and *g,* one letter for *a, æ,* and *o.* This compounding eventually resulted in the reduction of the futhark to 16 letters.

Other varieties of runes included the Hälsinge Runes, the Manx Runes, and the *stungnar runir,* or "dotted runes," all of which were variants of the Nordic script. More than 4,000 runic inscriptions and several runic manuscripts are extant. Approximately 2,500 of these come from Sweden, the remainder being from Norway, Denmark and Schleswig, Britain, Iceland, various islands off the coast of Britain and Scandinavia, and other countries of Europe, including France, Germany, and Russia.

run-on \ˈrən-ˌän, -ˌȯn\ *See* ENJAMBMENT.

run-on couplet *See* OPEN COUPLET.

Russian Formalism *See* FORMALISM.

S

Satire should, like a polished razor keen,
Wound with a touch that's scarcely felt or seen.
—Lady Mary Wortley Montague

sacra rappresentazione \ˈsäk-rä-ˌräp-prā-ˌzen-tä-ˈtsyō-nā\ [Italian, literally, sacred performance] In theater, 15th-century Italian ecclesiastical drama similar to the mystery play of France and England and the *auto sacramental* of Spain. Originating and flourishing in Florence, these religious dramas represented scenes from the Old and New Testaments, from pious legends, and from the lives of the saints. The plays were didactic, using dialogues drawn from the sacred Scriptures to instruct the audience in lessons of good conduct by dramatizing the punishment of vice and the reward of virtue.

saga \ˈsäg-ə\ [Old Norse, story, legend, history, saga] A literary genre consisting of a prose narrative sometimes of legendary content but typically dealing with prominent figures and events of the heroic age in Norway and Iceland, especially as recorded in Icelandic manuscripts of the late 12th and 13th centuries.

Modern scholars recognize several subdivisions of the genre, including the kings' sagas, recounting the lives of Scandinavian rulers; the legendary sagas, treating themes from myth and legend; and the Icelanders' sagas, sometimes called family sagas. The last group, the best known and most important in terms of literary merit, are fictionalized accounts of life in Iceland during the so-called saga age (about 930 to 1030) and were written down during the 13th century.

The term *saga* is also used to refer to any of various historical or fictional narratives, such as a modern retelling usually in verse or highly stylized prose of the events of the Icelanders' sagas or of similar subjects; an episodic story centering on a usually heroic figure of earlier ages with factual or fictional details drawn from various sources; a series of legends that embodies in detail the oral history of a people; or a long, detailed narrative usually without psychological or historical depth (for example, of a particular occupation, area, historical event, period, or person).

In Icelandic, *saga* (related to *segja,* "to say") has the etymological sense "what is said, or told," a derivation that indicates the importance of oral tradition in the development of the form. Indeed, it used to be thought that the sagas of Icelanders were little more than collections of oral traditions, concerning real individuals, that had finally been given written form after generations of circulation among the people. This view has now been largely discredited, and contemporary scholars are increasingly inclined to regard these works as much closer to the modern conception of a historical novel, in which characters and situations may be real or imaginary but in which artistic rather than historical considerations are paramount. Although this view tends to decrease their value as historical record, it does not undermine the importance of the Icelanders' sagas in helping modern readers to understand the ethos of a past civilization.

Human tragedy is dominant in the Icelanders' sagas. Ideals of heroism and loyalty are important, and revenge—in particular, the blood feud—often plays a significant part in the unfolding of the narrative. Action is preferred to reflection, with the result that the inner motivation of the protagonists and the point of view of the author intrude far less than in most modern novels. Characterizations of surprising depth and subtlety are often achieved by this technique, and parallels have been drawn between this feature of saga writing and the works of some modern writers.

The kings' sagas tell of the kings of Norway and reflect the continued interest of Icelanders in their old homeland. The earliest collections of these sagas, the anonymous *Morkinskinna* and *Fagrskinna* and the monumental *Heimskringla* ("Orb of the World") by Snorri Sturluson, appeared in the period from 1200 to 1235.

As the 13th century progressed, legendary sagas became increasingly popular. These latter works make no pretentions to historical truth and express a delight in the bizarre and the supernatural. They are concerned with the Scandinavian and Germanic past, before the settlement of Iceland, and their heroes are usually legendary or semilegendary figures. They are of considerable antiquarian interest. A well-known example of this type of work is *Vǫlsunga saga* (*c.* 1270), a retelling of the legends of the German epic Nibelungenlied. *See also* ICELANDERS' SAGAS.

saga novel A long, multivolume, and usually easygoing chronicle of persons comprising a family, community, or other social group. *See* ROMAN-FLEUVE.

sagaman \'säg-ə-ˌman\ *plural* sagamen \-ˌmen\ [translation of Old Norse *sǫgumathr*] A narrator of a saga.

saint's play *See* MIRACLE PLAY.

Salmagundi \ˌsal-mə-'gən-dē\ (*in full* Salmagundi; or, The Whim-Whams and Opinions of Launcelot Langstaff, Esq., and Others) Popular American periodical consisting of pamphlets containing humorous and satiric essays and poems, published from 1807 to 1808 and from 1819 to 1820.

Salmagundi was originally published by William Irving, James Kirke Paulding, and Washington Irving, all writing under such pseudonyms as Anthony Evergreen, Jeremy Cockloft the Younger, Will Wizard, Pindar Cockloft, Esq., and Mustapha Rub-a-Dub Keli Khan (a Tripolitan prisoner of war observing American society from his cell in New York). The 20 pamphlets (Jan. 24, 1807, to Jan. 25, 1808) were collected and published in book form in 1808. The periodical consisted of light verse and droll commentary, and caricatures of New York City tastemakers and society were included, along with essays on such topics as "the conduct of the world," politics, public mores and women's fashions, music, and theater. The best of the satirical magazines yet published in the United States, *Salmagundi* was an immediate success.

Paulding published a second series (May 1819 to September 1820) by himself, but it did not contain the heterogeneous mixture that constitutes an authentic salmagundi, and it was unsuccessful.

salon \sə-ˈlän, ˈsal-ˌän, sa-ˈlō^{n}\ A social gathering place for nobles and intellectuals, including writers and artists. Salons were held in private homes and were especially popular in France in the 17th and 18th centuries. One of the first to be established was that of Madame de Rambouillet in about 1610 as a reaction against the coarseness of the French court at the time. Other well-known salons were those of Mme de Staël, Mme de Récamier, and Madeleine de Scudéry.

samizdat \ˈsä-mēz-ˌdät\ In the Soviet Union, the system by which government-suppressed literature was clandestinely written, printed, and distributed. The word was also applied to the literature itself.

Samizdat began appearing in the 1950s, largely as a revolt against official restrictions on artistic freedom of expression. After the ouster of Nikita Khrushchev in 1964, samizdat publications expanded their focus beyond freedom of expression to a critique of many aspects of official Soviet policies and activities. The Russian word *samizdat,* coined from *sam-* ("self") and *izdat,* short for *izdatelstvo* ("publishing house"), humorously imitated the compound names of state publishing monopolies, such as Goslitizdat. Because of the government's strict monopoly on presses, photocopiers, and other such devices, samizdat publications typically took the form of carbon copies of typewritten sheets that were passed by hand from reader to reader. The major genres of samizdat included reports of dissident activities and other news suppressed by official media, protests addressed to the regime, transcripts of political trials, analyses of socioeconomic and cultural themes, and even pornography.

In its earliest days, samizdat was largely a product of the intelligentsia of Moscow and Leningrad. Similar underground literatures later spread throughout the constituent republics of the Soviet Union and among its many ethnic minorities.

From its inception, the samizdat movement and its contributors were subjected to surveillance and harassment by the KGB (the secret police). The suppression worsened in the early 1970s at the height of samizdat activity. Culminating in a show trial of Pyotr Yakir and Viktor Krasin in August 1973, the government's assault wounded the movement. It survived, nonetheless, though reduced in numbers and deprived of many of its leaders.

Samizdat began to flourish again in the mid-1980s, but because of Soviet leader Mikhail Gorbachev's policy of glasnost ("openness"), KGB harassment virtually ceased. Samizdat had almost disappeared by the early 1990s following the emergence of publishing and other media outlets that were independent of government control.

śaṅgam literature *See* CAṄKAM LITERATURE.

sapphic \'saf-ik\ Of, relating to, or consisting of an aeolic meter associated with the Greek lyric poet Sappho that scans as – ⏑ – ⏓ | – ⏑ ⏑ – | ⏑ – – (a sapphic hendecasyllable) or a four-line strophe that is characteristic of her verse. The first three lines of the strophe are sapphic hendecasyllables, and the fourth is an adonean (scanned as – ⏑ ⏑ – –). The strophe therefore scanned as follows:

– ⏑ – ⏓ | – ⏑ ⏑ – | ⏑ – –
– ⏑ – ⏓ | – ⏑ ⏑ – | ⏑ – –
– ⏑ – ⏓ | – ⏑ ⏑ – | ⏑ – –
– ⏑ ⏑ | – –

In Latin, Catullus first adapted the sapphic stanza or strophe, and Horace used it extensively in his *Odes*. In Horace's sapphics, the fourth syllable is always long, not variable, and there is always a caesura after the fifth or sixth syllable:

– ⏑ – – – ¦ ⏑ ¦ ⏑ – ⏑ – – .

Satanic school Pejorative designation for the poets John Keats, Percy Bysshe Shelley, Leigh Hunt, and Lord Byron, used of them by Robert Southey in the preface to his *A Vision of Judgement* (1821). The term expressed Southey's disapproval of the unorthodox views and lifestyles of the poets.

satire \'sa-ˌtīr\ [Latin *satura, satira,* perhaps from (*lanx*) *satura* dish of mixed ingredients] A usually topical literary composition holding up human or individual vices, folly, abuses, or shortcomings to censure by means of ridicule, derision, burlesque, irony, or other methods, sometimes with an intent to bring about improvement.

Though there are examples of satire in Greek literature, notably the works of Aristophanes, the great Roman poets Horace and Juvenal established the genre known as the formal verse satire and, in so doing, exerted pervasive, if often indirect, influence on all subsequent literary satire. The two Romans approached the form from radically different perspectives. The character of the satirist as projected by Horace is that of an urbane man of the world, concerned about folly, which he sees everywhere, but moved to laughter rather than rage. Juvenal, more than a century later, conceives the satirist's role differently. His most characteristic posture is that of the upright man who looks with horror on the corruptions of his time, his heart consumed with anger and frustration. Juvenal's declamatory manner, the amplification and luxuriousness of his invective, are wholly out of keeping with the stylistic prescriptions set by Horace. Satiric writing after Horace and Juvenal traditionally followed the example of one of the two writers. This resulted in the formation of two subgenres identified by John Dryden as comic satire and tragic satire. These denominations have come to mark the boundaries of the satiric spectrum, whether reference is to poetry or prose or to some form of satiric expression in another medium.

Satire is found embodied in an indefinite number of literary forms. Its targets range from one of Alexander Pope's dunces to the entire race of man, as in *Satyr Against Mankind* (1679) by John Wilmot, the Earl of Rochester, and from Erasmus' attack on corruptions in the church to Jonathan Swift's excoriation of all civilized institutions in *Gulliver's Travels*. Its forms are as varied as its victims: from an anonymous medieval invective against social injustice to the superb wit of Geoffrey Chaucer and the laughter of Rabelais; from the burlesque of Luigi Pulci to the scurrilities of Pietro Aretino and the "black humor" of Lenny Bruce; from the flailings of John Marston and the mordancies of Francisco Gómez de Quevedo to the bite of Jean de La Fontaine and the great dramatic structures of Ben Jonson and Molière; from an epigram of Martial to the fictions of Nikolay Gogol and of Günter Grass and the satirical utopias of Yevgeny Zamyatin, Aldous Huxley, and George Orwell.

Saturday Club *also called* Magazine Club *or* Atlantic Club. American social club of New England literati that was founded in 1855 and that met monthly at the Parker House, a Boston hotel. It was closely associated with the literary periodical *The Atlantic Monthly* as most of its members were contributors to the magazine. Notable members included Oliver Wendell Holmes, Ralph Waldo Emerson, Henry Wadsworth Longfellow, James Russell Lowell, Richard Henry Dana, John Greenleaf Whittier, William Dean Howells, Nathaniel Hawthorne, Henry James, and Charles Sumner.

Club meetings were described in the poem "At the Saturday Club" (1884) by Holmes, as well as in the books *The Early Years of the Saturday Club, 1855–1879* (1918) by Edward W. Emerson and *The Later Years of the Saturday Club* (1927) by M.A. DeWolfe Howe.

Saturday Review, The *also called* (until 1952) The Saturday Review of Literature. Literary periodical founded in New York by Henry Seidel Canby in 1924. It was originally devoted to the work of new writers, including many foreign writers in translation, as well as to that of earlier writers such as Walt Whitman and Ralph Waldo Emerson. Among the early contributors to the periodical were Mary Austin, Edgar Lee Masters, and G.K. Chesterton. The scope of the review was expanded by Norman Cousins, who edited the magazine for more than 30 years. Cousins established a separate book-review department and hired the critic John Mason Brown to write on a wide range of issues. Other contributors wrote on political, technical, and scientific topics. The Review also featured regular columns, including one on travel; one about publishers, edited for a time by Bennett Cerf; and one by William Rose Benét, the original poetry editor and brother of Stephen Vincent Benét. The magazine was published as four separate reviews of the arts, society, education, and the sciences in 1973, after which it was published with several interrruptions as *The Saturday Review/World* and *The Saturday Review* until it folded in 1986.

Saturnian verse or **Saturnian meter** \sa-ˈtər-nē-ən\ [Latin *Saturnius* of Saturnian meter, literally, of Saturn] The ancient Latin verse used mainly by Livius

Andronicus and Gnaeus Naevius before the adoption of Greek verse forms by later Latin writers. Little is known about its origins or whether its rhythm was accentual or quantitative.

satyr play Burlesque comedy performed as comic relief after a classical Greek tragic trilogy. Satyr plays are believed to have developed from the dithyramb, a hymn to Dionysus, concurrently with tragedy. They were evidently introduced at the Great Dionysia drama festival at Athens in the late 6th century BC. Written by the competing authors of the three tragedies, these plays featured a legendary hero, frequently the protagonist of the preceding trilogy. This character was joined by a cowardly, lecherous, and wine-loving chorus of 11 satyrs led by Silenus, the foster father of Dionysus, in a farcical plot or a parody of a myth. Euripides' *Cyclops* is the only complete satyr play extant.

saudade \saů-'däj-ē\ [Portuguese, literally, longing, yearning] Overtone of melancholy and brooding loneliness and an almost mystical reverence for nature that permeates Portuguese and Brazilian lyric poetry. *Saudade* was a characteristic of the earliest Portuguese folk poetry and has been cultivated by sophisticated writers of later generations. In the late 19th century António Nobre and Teixeira de Pascoais were the foremost of a growing cult of *saudosismo,* a combination of *saudade* and pantheism that was a reflection of a type of mystical nationalism. Especially in the poems collected in *Só* (1892), Nobre was intensely Portuguese in his themes, his mood (an all-pervading *saudade*), and his rhythms, whereas Teixeira de Pascoais typified the pantheist tendencies of Portuguese poetry. They inspired the movement known as the Renascença Portuguesa (*c.* 1910), centered on Porto. The poets of the Portuguese Renaissance, particularly Mário Beirão, Augusto Casimiro, and João de Barros, adopted *saudosismo* as the key to the nation's greatness.

scald *See* SKALD.

scaldic poetry *See* SKALDIC POETRY.

scan \'skan\ [Middle English *scanden, scannen,* from Late Latin *scandere,* from Latin, to climb] To read or mark so as to show metrical structure.

scansion \'skan-shən\ [Late Latin *scansio,* from Latin, act of climbing, a derivative of *scandere* to climb] The analysis of a rhythmic structure (such as a verse) so as to show its meter. Also, the product or result of scansion, such as a description or visual representation of a given metrical structure.

Scansion in English prosody employs a system of symbols to reveal the mechanics of a poem—i.e., the predominant type of foot (the smallest metrical unit of stressed and unstressed syllables); the number of feet per line; and the rhyme scheme. The purpose of scansion is to enhance the reader's sensitivity to the ways in which rhythmic elements in a poem convey meaning. Variations in a poem's metrical pattern sometimes serve to emphasize its ideas.

English has three major types of scansion: the graphic, the musical, and the acoustic. The primary symbols used in graphic scansion, the most common type of scansion, are (ˊ) to represent a syllable that is stressed in context; (∪) to represent a syllable that is unstressed in context; a vertical line (|) to indicate a division between feet; and a double vertical line (‖) to show a caesura, a pause within a line of verse. Using these symbols, graphic scansion begins by marking the accented, then the unaccented, syllables according to the natural rhythm of speech. Following are the last two lines from Alfred, Lord Tennyson's "Ulysses," which are written in iambic pentameter, with the lines scanned in the graphic method:

> ∪ ˊ | ∪ ˊ | ∪ ˊ | ∪ ˊ | ∪ ˊ
> Made weak | by time | and fate, | but strong | in will
>
> ∪ ˊ | ∪ ˊ | ∪ ˊ | ∪ ˊ | ∪ ˊ
> To strive, | to seek, | to find, | and not | to yield.

Both musical and acoustic scansion, which are highly complex systems, afford greater sensitivity than graphic scansion to the tonal and accentual variety of speech. Musical symbols (e.g., eighth notes for unstressed syllables, quarter or half notes for stressed syllables, and musical rests for pauses) record accentual differences. Machines such as the oscillograph are used by modern acoustic linguists to catch even slightly varying degrees of stress.

Modern scansion was adapted from the classical method of analyzing ancient Greek and Roman quantitative verse. The graphic scansion used for English poetry can still be used for classical verse with some modification to account for the differences between modern accentual-syllabic and the classical quantitative types of versification. The symbols used for classical prosody are (–) for long syllables, (∪) for short syllables, and (⏓) for syllables of indeterminate length. Further distinctions include the symbol ⏔, termed contraction, which indicates that two short syllables may be contracted into a single long syllable, and ⏕, termed resolution, which indicates that one long syllable may be resolved into two short syllables.

scapigliatura \ˌskä-pēl-yä-ˈtü-rä\ [Italian, literally, a disheveled state, dissoluteness, loose living, a derivative of *scapigliare* to dishevel] A mid-19th-century Italian avant-garde movement centered in Milan. Influenced by Charles Baudelaire, the French Symbolist poets, Edgar Allan Poe, and German Romantic writers, it sought to replace the classical, Arcadian, and moralistic traditions of Italian literature with works that featured bizarre and pathological elements and direct, realistic narrative description. One of the founding members, Cletto Arrighi (pseudonym for Carlo Righetti), coined the name for the group in his novel *Scapigliatura e il 6 febbraio* (1862; "Scapigliatura and February 6"). The chief spokesmen were the novelists Giuseppe Rovani and Emilio Praga. Other members included the poet and musician Arrigo Boito (chiefly remembered today as Giuseppe Verdi's librettist), the poet and literary professor Arturo Graf, and Iginio Ugo Tarchetti.

Although some members of the group produced important literary work, they were more important as catalysts, inspiring the major writers of verismo ("realism"), Luigi Capuana and Giovanni Verga, both of whom drew part of their inspiration from the scapigliati. As iconoclasts, the group also served as an example to such 20th-century groups as the Futurists, and the Hermetic poets.

scazon \'skāz-ən\ [Greek *skázōn,* literally, one that limps, from present participle of *skázein* to limp], *also called* choliamb. In classical poetry, a verse with a limping or halting movement; an iambic or trochaic verse in which the last foot consists of a spondee.

scél \'shkāl\ *plural* scéla \'shkā-lə\ [Old Irish, news, narration, tale] In the Gaelic literature of Ireland, early prose and verse legends of gods and folk heroes, most of which originated during or before the 11th century. Scéla were divided into primary and secondary types. The primary, or most important, types were classified according to the actions they celebrated: destructions, cattle raids, navigations, elopements, violent deaths, conflagrations, and other events. In modern times these tales have been grouped into cycles comprising (1) the mythological cycle, dealing with immortal beings; (2) the Ulster (Ulaid) cycle, dealing with the Ulster heroes during the reign of the semihistorical King Conor (Conchobar mac Nessa) in the 1st century BC; and (3) the Fenian cycle, dealing mainly with the deeds of Finn MacCumhaill's war band during the reign of Cormac mac Airt in the 3rd century AD. *See also* FENIAN CYCLE; ULSTER CYCLE.

scenario \sə-'nar-ē-ˌō, -'när-\ [French, from Italian, callboy's list of actors' entrances, stage scenery, flats, a derivative of *scena* stage, scene, from Latin *scena, scaena*] An outline or synopsis of a play; specifically, a plot outline used by actors of the commedia dell'arte.

scene \'sēn\ [Middle French, stage, division of an act, from Latin *scena, scaena* stage, scene, ultimately from Greek *skēnḗ* booth, tent, structure serving as backdrop for plays, stage] **1.** One of the subdivisions of a play, such as a division of an act presenting continuous action in one place or a single situation or unit of dialogue. **2.** The place in which represented action (as in a play or story) occurs.

Schauspiel \'shau̇-ˌshpēl\ [German, from *Schau* show, sight + *Spiel* play] Any spectacle or public performance. In late 18th-century German literature the word took on the more specific meaning of a play that has characteristics of both a tragedy and a comedy in that it is a serious play with a happy ending.

scheme \'skēm\ In prosody, a diagram or table showing metrical structure or rhyme arrangement (such as of a stanza).

Schicksalstragödie *See* FATE TRAGEDY.

Schlüsselroman \'shlues-əl-rō-ˌmän\ [German, literally, key novel] A novel in which real people or actual events figure though they are portrayed as fictional. This type of novel is more commonly known by the French phrase ROMAN À CLEF.

school \'skül\ A group of writers or other artists under a common influence or that have certain common ideas or assumptions about their work. Such a group can have an influence of its own on other writers or artists. The term can also apply to the artists or art of a particular country or region. Examples include the graveyard school of 18th-century British poets, the Kailyard school of late 19th-century Scotland, and the mid-20th-century group of literary critics known as New Critics.

school drama Any play performed by students in schools and colleges throughout Europe during the Renaissance. At first these plays were written by scholars in Latin as educational works, especially in Jesuit schools, but they later were viewed as entertainment as well and were performed in the vernacular. The works included translations and imitations of Latin authors such as Terence and Plautus as well as original plays written in the vernacular. The first known English comedy, *Ralph Roister Doister,* was a school drama written by Nicholas Udall, a playwright and schoolmaster, to be performed at Westminster school.

Schüttelreim \'shuet-əl-ˌrīm\ [German, from *schütteln* to shake, jolt, churn + *Reim* rhyme] German equivalent of a spoonerism, in which the intial letters or syllables of two or more words are transposed. *See also* SPOONERISM.

science fiction Fiction dealing principally with the impact of actual or imagined science upon society or individuals, or more generally, literary fantasy including a scientific factor as an essential orienting component.

Such literature may consist of a careful and informed extrapolation of scientific facts and principles, or it may range into far-fetched areas flatly contradictory of such facts and principles. In either case, plausibility based on science is a requisite, so that such a precursor of the genre as Mary Shelley's gothic novel *Frankenstein* (1818) and Robert Louis Stevenson's *Dr. Jekyll and Mr. Hyde* (1886) are science fiction, whereas Bram Stoker's *Dracula* (1897), based as it is purely on the supernatural, is not. Other notable precursors of the genre included imaginary voyages to the moon or to other planets in the 18th century and space travel in Voltaire's *Micromégas* (1752); alien cultures in Jonathan Swift's *Gulliver's Travels* (1726); and science-fiction elements in the 19th-century stories of Edgar Allan Poe, Nathaniel Hawthorne, and Fitz-James O'Brien.

Science fiction proper began, however, toward the end of the 19th century with the scientific romances of Jules Verne, whose science was rather on the level of invention, as well as the science-oriented novels of social criticism by H.G. Wells.

The development of science fiction as a self-conscious genre dates from 1926 when Hugo Gernsback, who coined the portmanteau word scientifiction, founded *Amazing Stories* magazine, which was devoted exclusively to science-fiction stories. Published in this and other pulp magazines with growing success, such stories were viewed as sensationalist. With John W. Campbell's editorship (from 1937) of *Astounding Science Fiction* and with the publication of stories and novels by such writers as Isaac Asimov, Arthur C. Clarke, and Robert A. Heinlein, science fiction emerged as a mode of serious fiction. Ventures into the genre by writers not devoted exclusively to science fiction, such as Aldous Huxley, C.S. Lewis, and Kurt Vonnegut, also added respectability.

A great boom in the popularity of science fiction followed World War II. The increasing sophistication of the genre and the emphasis on broader issues significantly increased its appeal to the reading public. Serious criticism of the genre became common, and, in the United States particularly, science fiction was studied as literature in colleges and universities.

Besides such acknowledged masters of the genre as Clarke, Heinlein, and Asimov, science-fiction writers of notable merit in the postwar period included A.E. Van Vogt, J.G. Ballard, Ray Bradbury, Frank Herbert, Harlan Ellison, Poul Anderson, Samuel R. Delany, Ursula K. Le Guin, Frederik Pohl, Octavia E. Butler, and Brian Aldiss. These writers' approaches included predictions of future societies on Earth, analyses of the consequences of interstellar travel, and imaginative explorations of forms of intelligent life and their societies in other worlds. Radio, television, and, notably in the 1970s and 1980s, film reinforced the popularity of the genre. Useful histories of science fiction include Brian W. Aldiss, *Billion Year Spree* (1973); James Gunn, *Alternate Worlds* (1975), with illustrations; and Robert Scholes and Eric S. Rabkin, *Science Fiction: History, Science, Vision* (1977). Neil Barron, *Anatomy of Wonder,* 3rd ed. (1987); and Marilyn P. Fletcher (comp. and ed.), *Reader's Guide to Twentieth-Century Science Fiction* (1989), are annotated critical bibliographies.

Science Fiction Achievement Award *See* HUGO AWARD.

scop \'skäp, 'skōp\ [Old English] An Anglo-Saxon minstrel, usually attached to a particular royal court, although scops also traveled to various courts to recite their poetry. In addition to being an entertainer who composed and performed his own works the scop served as a kind of historian and preserver of the oral tradition of the Germanic peoples. The Old English poem "Widsith," a fictional biography of a scop, gives an idea of the status and role of the scop in society. *Compare* MINSTREL.

Scottish Chaucerian *See* MAKAR.

Scottish Enlightenment An intellectual movement that began in Glasgow, Scot., in the early 18th century and by the second half of that century was largely centered in the Old Town district of Edinburgh. Its leading figures included the philosophers Adam Ferguson, Francis Hutcheson, Adam Smith, John Millar, Dugald Stewart, Thomas Reid, and David Hume and the historian William Robertson. Perhaps the best-known publication to emerge from the Scottish Enlightenment was the *Encyclopædia Britannica,* first published in 1768–71. The movement qualified Edinburgh as one of the world's great cultural capitals.

Scottish Renaissance A movement in 20th-century Scottish literature, particularly vital between World Wars I and II. Its members sought to preserve regional dialects in their writings, and the poets among them modeled their verse on Scottish poetry of four and five centuries past. Politically they were inclined to Scottish nationalism, and they aimed to generate a Scottish national literature and to revive Lowland Scots (Lallans) as a literary language. The leading figure of the Scottish Renaissance was poet-critic Hugh MacDiarmid, who founded several small literary periodicals.

The book of essays *Scottish Literature, Character & Influence* (1919) by G. Gregory Smith was an important influence on the movement, as was the quarterly *Saltire Review,* published by the Saltire Society (1936–60) to stimulate research and writing in Scottish Gaelic. Other prominent Scottish Renaissance figures included poets Sorley Maclean and William Soutar and novelist Lewis Grassic Gibbon.

scrapiana \ˌskrap-ē-ˈan-ə\ Miscellaneous literary scraps.

screed \ˈskrēd\ **1.** A lengthy discourse. **2.** An informal piece of writing.

screeve \ˈskrēv\ *chiefly British* A piece of writing; especially, a begging letter. *Screeve* was originally an argot word that probably ultimately derives from Italian *scrivere* ("to write").

scribe \ˈskrīb\ [Latin *scriba* official in charge of public records, a derivative of *scribere* to mark, write, put down in writing, make a record of] **1.** A copier of manuscripts. **2.** A writer; specifically, a journalist.

Scriblerus Club \skri-ˈblē-rəs\ Eighteenth-century British literary club whose founding members were the brilliant Tory wits Alexander Pope, Jonathan Swift, John Gay, Thomas Parnell, and John Arbuthnot. Its purpose was to ridicule pretentious erudition and scholarly jargon through the person of a fictitious literary hack, Martinus Scriblerus (whose surname was a pseudo-Latin coinage signifying "a writer"). The collaboration of the five writers on the *Memoirs of Martinus Scriblerus* began as early as 1713 and led to frequent, spirited meetings when they were in London; when they were separated, they pursued their project through correspondence. The zest, energy, and time that these five highly individualistic talents put into their joint enterprise may be gauged by Pope's statement in a letter to Swift, "The top of my own ambition is to contribute to that great work [the *Memoirs*], and I shall translate Homer by the by."

Of the five, only Pope and Swift lived to see the publication of the *Memoirs* in 1741, although miscellaneous minor pieces written in collaboration or individually had appeared earlier under the Scriblerus name. Although Pope is credited with originating the character of Scriblerus, most of the ideas were Arbuthnot's, and he was the most industrious of the collaborators. The stimulation the members derived from one another had far-reaching effects. Gay's *The Beggar's Opera* grew out of a suggestion made by Swift to the club, and the imprint of Scriblerus on *Gulliver's Travels,* especially Book III, describing the voyage to Laputa, is unmistakable. Other prominent Tories such as the Earl of Oxford and Viscount Bolingbroke were members of the club, but there is no evidence that they contributed to the writing.

scriptory \ˈskrip-tə-rē\ [Latin *scriptorius,* a derivative of *scribere* to mark, write] Of, relating to, expressed in, or used in writing.

scripture \ˈskrip-chər, -shər\ [Late Latin *scripturae* the Bible (translation of Greek *hai graphaí*), from Latin, plural of *scriptura* act of writing, text] **1.** *usually capitalized* The sacred writings of a religion; specifically, the books of the Bible—often used in the plural. **2.** A body of writings considered sacred or authoritative—often used in the plural. **3.** Something written.

scrivener \ˈskriv-ən-ər\ [Middle English *scriveiner,* an extension of *scrivein* copyist, scribe, from Old French *escrivein*] **1.** *also called* scribe. A professional or public copyist or writer. One of the most anthologized stories by Herman Melville, "Bartleby the Scrivener," concerns a man of this profession. **2.** A usually minor author.

sdrucciola \ˈstrüt-chō-lä\ [Italian (*rima*) *sdrucciola,* literally, slippery rhyme] In poetry, a triple rhyme in which the accent falls on the first syllable (as in *femina, semina*).

secentismo *See* MARINISM.

seguidilla \ˌsā-gē-ˈth̲ēl-yä, -ˈth̲ē-yä\ [Spanish, probably a derivative of *seguida,* a name for the criminal underworld about 1600] In Spanish poetry, a stanza of seven short lines divided into two sections of alternating lines of five and seven syllables (arranged as 7, 5, 7, 5; 5, 7, 5). There is a pause in thought between lines 4 and 5, and there is one assonance, or a kind of rhyme, in lines 2 and 4 and another in lines 5 and 7. The seguidilla form probably began as a dance song about the 17th century and gradually evolved from a four-line strophe of alternating long and short lines into its present form, which is sometimes used as a concluding section for another piece.

seicento \sā-ˈchen-tō\ [Italian, literally, six hundred, short for *mille seicento* the year 1600] The 17th century; specifically, the 17th-century period in Italian literature and art.

self-conscious narrator *See* NARRATOR.

self-referential Referring to itself; especially, concerned with the mental attitudes and creative processes that brought it into existence.

self-reflexive novel *See* REFLEXIVE NOVEL.

semiotics \ˌsēm-ē-ˈä-tiks, ˌsem-, -ī-ˈä-\, *also called* semiology \-ˈäl-ə-jē\ The study of signs and sign-using behavior; both words are ultimately based on the Greek *sēmeion* ("sign"). Semiology was defined by one of its founders, the Swiss linguist Ferdinand de Saussure, as the study of "the life of signs within society." Although the English philosopher John Locke applied the Greek word *sēmiōtikē* to "the doctrine of signs" in the 17th century, the idea of semiotics as an interdisciplinary mode for examining phenomena in different fields emerged in the late 19th and early 20th centuries with the independent work of Saussure and of the American philosopher Charles Sanders Peirce.

Peirce's seminal work in the field was anchored in pragmatism and logic. He defined a sign as "something which stands to somebody for something," and one of his major contributions to semiotics was the categorization of signs into three main types: (1) an icon, which resembles its referent (such as a road sign for falling rocks); (2) an index, which is associated with its referent (as smoke is a sign of fire); and (3) a symbol, which is related to its referent only by convention (as with words or traffic signals). Peirce also demonstrated that a sign can never have a definite meaning, because the meaning must be continuously qualified.

Saussure's work in linguistics supplied the concepts and methods that semioticians apply to sign systems other than language. One such basic semiotic concept is Saussure's distinction between the two inseparable components of a sign: the signifier, which in language is a set of speech sounds or marks on a page, and the signified, which is the concept or idea behind the sign. Saussure also distinguished *parole,* or actual individual utterances, from *langue,* the underlying system of conventions that makes such utterances understandable; it is this *langue* that most interests semioticians. Interest in the structure behind the use of particular signs links semiotics with the methods of STRUCTURALISM. Indeed, Saussure's theories are considered fundamental to structuralism (especially structural linguistics) and to POSTSTRUCTURALISM.

Modern semioticians have applied Peirce's and Saussure's principles to a variety of fields, including aesthetics, anthropology, communications, psychology, and semantics. Among the most influential of these thinkers are Claude Lévi-Strauss, Jacques Lacan, Michel Foucault, Jacques Derrida, Roland Barthes, and Julia Kristeva.

Senecan tragedy \'sen-i-kən\ Body of nine closet dramas (plays intended to be read rather than performed) written in blank verse by the Roman Stoic philosopher Seneca in the 1st century AD. Rediscovered by Italian humanists in the mid-16th century, they became the models for the revival of tragedy on the Renaissance stage. The two great, but very different, dramatic traditions of the age—French Neoclassical tragedy and Elizabethan tragedy—both drew inspiration from Seneca.

Seneca's plays were reworkings chiefly of Euripides' dramas and also of works of Aeschylus and Sophocles. Probably meant to be recited at elite gatherings, they differ from their originals in their long declamatory, narrative accounts of action, their obtrusive moralizing, and their bombastic rhetoric. They dwell on detailed accounts of horrible deeds and contain long reflective soliloquies. Though the gods rarely appear in these plays, ghosts and witches abound. In an age when the Greek originals were scarcely known, Seneca's plays were mistaken for high classical drama. The Renaissance scholar J.C. Scaliger, who knew both Latin and Greek, preferred Seneca to Euripides.

The French Neoclassical dramatic tradition, which reached its highest expression in the 17th-century tragedies of Pierre Corneille and Jean Racine, drew on Seneca for form and grandeur of style. These Neoclassicists adopted Seneca's innovation of the confidant (usually a servant), his substitution of speech for action, and his moral hairsplitting.

The Elizabethan dramatists found Seneca's themes of bloodthirsty revenge more congenial to English taste than they did his form. The first English Senecan tragedy, *Gorboduc* (1561), by Thomas Sackville and Thomas Norton, is a chain of slaughter and revenge written in direct imitation of Seneca. Senecan tragedy is also evident in William Shakespeare's *Hamlet:* the revenge theme, the corpse-strewn climax, and such points of stage machinery as the ghost can all be traced back to the Senecan model.

senryū \'sen-ˌryü\ *plural* senryū [Japanese] A three-line unrhymed Japanese poem structurally similar to haiku but treating human nature usually in an ironic or satiric vein. It is also unlike haiku in that it usually does not have any references to the seasons. Senryū developed from haiku and became especially popular among the common people about the 18th century. It was named for Karai Hachiemon (pen name Senryū), one of the most popular practitioners of the form.

sensibility \ˌsen-sə-'bil-ə-tē\ **1.** A capacity of emotion or feeling as distinguished from intellect and will. Also, an acuteness of feeling. **2.** Refined sensitiveness in emotion and taste with especial responsiveness to the pathetic. These qualities were especially admired and reflected in the literature of the 18th century as a reaction against the stoicism and emphasis on self-interest of the 17th century. Such authors as Thomas Gray, William Cowper, and Laurence Sterne all displayed an admiration of sensibility to differing degrees. The excesses of this trend were mocked by other authors, including Jane Austen in her *Sense and Sensibility*.

sentiment \'sen-tə-mənt\ [French, feeling] **1.** Refined feeling; keen or delicate sensibility especially as expressed in a work of art or evinced in conduct. **2.** An emotional idea as set forth in literature or art. **3.** The emotional significance of a passage or expression as distinguished from its verbal context.

sentimental comedy A dramatic genre of 18th-century England, denoting plays in which middle-class protagonists triumphantly overcome a series of moral trials. The genre was similar to the French *comédie larmoyante.* Such comedy aimed at producing tears rather than laughter. Sentimental comedies reflected contemporary philosophical conceptions of humans as inherently good but capable of being led astray through bad example; by an appeal to their noble sentiments, men and women could be reformed and set back on the path of virtue. Although the plays contain characters whose natures seem overly virtuous and whose trials are too easily resolved, they were nonetheless accepted by audiences as truthful representations of the human predicament. Sentimental comedy had its roots in early 18th-century tragedy, which had a vein of morality similar to that of sentimental comedy but had loftier characters and subject matter.

Writers of sentimental comedy included Colley Cibber and George Farquhar, with their respective plays *Love's Last Shift* (1696) and *The Constant Couple* (1699). The best-known sentimental comedy is Sir Richard Steele's *The Conscious Lovers* (1723), which deals with the trials and tribulations of its penniless heroine, Indiana. The discovery that she is an heiress affords the necessary happy resolution. Steele, in describing the effect he wished the play to have, said he would like to arouse "a pleasure too exquisite for laughter." Sentimental comedies continued to coexist with such conventional comedies as Oliver Goldsmith's *She Stoops to Conquer* (1773) and Richard Brinsley Sheridan's *The Rivals* (1775) until the sentimental genre waned in the early 19th century.

sentimental novel Broadly, any novel that exploits the reader's capacity for tenderness, compassion, or sympathy to a disproportionate degree by presenting a beclouded or unrealistic view of its subject. In a restricted sense the term refers to a widespread European novelistic development that reflected the trend toward sensibility in the 18th century, which arose partly in reaction to the austerity and rationalism of the Neoclassical period. The sentimental novel exalted feeling above reason and raised the analysis of emotion to a fine art. An early example in France is Antoine-François Prévost d'Exiles' *Manon Lescaut,* the story of a courtesan for whom a young seminary student of noble birth forsakes his career, family, and religion and ends as a card shark and confidence man. His downward progress, if not actually excused, is portrayed as a sacrifice to love.

The assumptions underlying the sentimental novel were Jean-Jacques Rousseau's doctrine of the natural goodness of humans and his belief that moral development was fostered by experiencing powerful sympathies. In England, Samuel Richardson's sentimental novel *Pamela* was recommended by clergymen as a means of educating the heart. In the 1760s the sentimental novel developed into the "novel of sensibility," which presented characters possessing a pronounced susceptibility to delicate sensation. Such characters were not only deeply moved by sympathy for others but also reacted emotionally to the beauty inherent in natural settings and in works of art and music. The prototype was Laurence Sterne's *Tristram Shandy* (1759–67), which devotes several pages to describing Uncle Toby's horror of killing a fly. The literature of Romanticism adopted many elements of the novel of sensibility, including responsiveness to nature and belief in the wisdom of the heart and in the power of sympathy. It did not, however, assimilate the novel of sensibility's characteristic optimism.

septenarius \ˌsep-tə-ˈnar-ē-əs\ *plural* septenarii \-ˈnar-ē-ˌī, -ˌē\ [Latin, from *septenarius* (adjective) consisting of seven (of something), a derivative of *septeni* seven each, a derivative of *septem* seven] In classical Latin prosody, iambic or trochaic lines of seven feet (equal to Greek tetrameter catalectic verse). The septenarius was commonly used for dialogue in comedies.

septenary \'sep-tə-ˌnar-ē; sep-'ten-ə-rē, -'tēn-\ *See* FOURTEENER.

septet or **septette** \sep-'tet\ A stanza or poem having seven lines, such as a RHYME ROYAL.

septisyllable \ˌsep-ti-'sil-ə-bəl\ A word or line of verse having seven syllables.

sequel \'sē-kwəl\ The next installment (as of a speech or story); especially, a literary or cinematic work continuing the course of a story begun in a preceding work.

sequence \'sē-kwəns, -ˌkwens\ A group of similar or related elements; specifically, an extended series of poems united by a single theme. Examples include many sonnet sequences, such as Elizabeth Barrett Browning's *Sonnets from the Portuguese*.

Serapion Brothers \sə-'rä-pē-ən, -'rā-\, *Russian* Serapionovy Bratya \sʸi-rə-pʸi-'ȯn-ə-və̇-'brȧt-yə\ Group of young Russian writers formed in 1921 under the unsettled conditions of the early Soviet regime. Though they had no specific program, they were united in their belief that a work of art must stand on its own intrinsic merits, that all aspects of life or fantasy were suitable subjects, and that experiments in a variety of styles were desirable. The writers were admirers of E.T.A. Hoffmann, the German Romantic storyteller who wrote a series of exotic tales that were supposedly exchanged by a group gathered around a hermit, Serapion. The young Russian writers adopted this name as indicative of their interest in the art of storytelling. Though they retained social themes in their work, the Serapion Brothers introduced a fresh use of intricate plots, surprise endings, and techniques of mystery and suspense. They regarded much of the escapist literature of the West, such as the romantic adventure stories of Alexandre Dumas, Robert Louis Stevenson, and Rider Haggard, as superior in technical artistry to traditional Russian realism.

The Serapion Brothers met in the House of Arts, a cultural institute established in Petrograd (i.e., St. Petersburg) by Maksim Gorky. They learned their craft from the innovative elder writer Yevgeny Zamyatin. The members, most of whom were in their early 20s, included Mikhail Zoshchenko, Vsevolod Ivanov, Veniamin Kaverin, Konstantin Fedin, Lev Lunts, Nikolay Nikitin, Nikolay Tikhonov, Vladimir Pozner, Mikhail Slonimsky, and Viktor Shklovsky, but their influence extended beyond their nuclear group and affected most of the other writers who remained aloof from political orthodoxy and dominated the literary scene in the early Soviet period.

serial \'sir-ē-əl\ A novel or other work appearing (as in a magazine) in parts at intervals. It was a common way of publishing novels in the 19th century. Many works by Charles Dickens, George Eliot, William Makepeace Thackeray, Anthony Trollope, and others first appeared serially in such magazines as Dickens' *Household Words* and Thackeray's *The Cornhill Magazine*.

series \'sir-ēz\ *plural* series **1.** A group of works featuring the same characters or set in the same locations, such as Anthony Powell's 12-volume series *A Dance to the Music of Time*. Trilogies and quartets are specific kinds of series. **2.** A succession of volumes or issues published with related subjects or authors, similar format and price, or continuous numbering.

serpentine verse In poetry, a line of verse beginning and ending with the same word, as in the following line from Matthew Arnold's "Dover Beach":

> Begin, and cease, and then again begin,

The phrase likens such verses to depictions of serpents with their tails in their mouths.

servile \'sər-vəl, -ˌvīl\ Slavishly imitative of a model, especially in literature or art, or more generally, lacking independence or originality.

sestet \ses-'tet\ A stanza or poem of six lines; specifically, the last six lines of a Petrarchan sonnet. *Compare* OCTAVE.

sestina \ses-'tē-nə\ [Italian, a derivative of *sesto* sixth] or **sextain** \'seks-tān\ An elaborate lyrical verse form developed before 1200 by Provençal troubadours and employed by medieval Provençal and Italian, and occasional modern, poets. It consists, in its pure medieval form, of six stanzas of blank verse, each of six lines—hence the name—followed by a three-line stanza. The final words of each line of the first stanza appear in varied order in the next five stanzas, the order used by the Provençals being *abcdef, faebdc, cfdabe, ecbfad, deacfb,* and *bdfeca*. In the final three-line stanza, the six key words are repeated in the middle and at the end of the lines, summarizing the poem or dedicating it to someone.

The sestina was invented by the Provençal troubadour Arnaut Daniel and was used in Italy by Dante and Petrarch, after which it fell into disuse until it was revived by the 16th-century French group of poets known as La Pléiade, particularly Pontus de Tyard. In the 19th century, Ferdinand, Count de Gramont, wrote a large number of sestinas, and Algernon Charles Swinburne's "Complaint of Lisa" is an astonishing tour de force—a double sestina of 12 stanzas of 12 lines each. In the 20th century Ezra Pound, T.S. Eliot, and W.H. Auden wrote noteworthy sestinas.

set piece In literature, a composition executed in a fixed or ideal form, often with studied artistry and brilliant effect. Or, a scene, depiction, speech, or event that is obviously designed to have an imposing effect.

settecento \ˌset-tā-'chen-tō\ The 18th century; specifically, the 18th-century period in Italian literature and art.

setting \'set-iŋ\ The location and time frame in which the action of a narrative takes place.

The makeup and behavior of fictional characters often depend on their environment quite as much as on their personal characteristics. Setting is of great importance for Émile Zola, for example, because he believed that environment determined character. In some cases the entire action of a novel is determined by the locale in which it is set. Gustave Flaubert's *Madame Bovary* could hardly have been placed in Paris, because the tragic life and death of the heroine have a great deal to do with the circumscriptions of her provincial milieu. It sometimes happens that the main locale of a novel assumes an importance in the reader's imagination comparable to that of the characters and yet somehow separable from them. Wessex is a giant, brooding presence in Thomas Hardy's novels. The popularity of Sir Walter Scott's "Waverley" novels is due in part to their evocation of a romanticized Scotland. Setting may be the prime consideration of some readers, who can be drawn to Joseph Conrad because he depicts life at sea or in the East Indies; they may be less interested in the complexity of human relationships that he presents.

The setting of a novel may be an actual city or region made greater than life, as in James Joyce's Dublin. But settings may also be completely the work of an author's imagination: in the Russian expatriate Vladimir Nabokov's *Ada* there is an entirely new space-time continuum, and the English scholar J.R.R. Tolkien in his *Lord of the Rings* created an "alternative world" in his Middle Earth.

seven \'sev-ən\ Something having as an essential feature seven units or members; especially, an English trochaic meter with seven syllables to the line and typically four lines to the stanza—usually used in the plural.

seven deadly sins *also called* cardinal sins. Any of the sins originally identified during the early history of Christian monasticism and grouped together as early as the 6th century by St. Gregory the Great. A sin was classified as deadly not merely because it was a serious offense morally but because, in the words of St. Thomas Aquinas, "it gives rise to others, especially in the manner of a final cause" or motivation. The traditional catalog of the seven deadly sins is: (1) vainglory, or pride; (2) covetousness; (3) lust, understood as inordinate or illicit sexual desire; (4) envy; (5) gluttony, which usually included drunkenness; (6) anger; and (7) sloth. The classical discussion of the subject is in the *Summa theologiae,* by the 13th-century theologian St. Thomas Aquinas. The seven deadly sins were a popular theme in the sermons, morality plays, and art of the European Middle Ages.

Seven Sages of the Bamboo Grove *also called* Seven Worthies of the Bamboo Grove, *Chinese* Zhulin qi xian \'jü-'lin-'chē-'shyan\ Group of Chinese scholars and poets of the mid-3rd century AD who banded together to escape from the hypocrisy and danger of the official world to a life of drinking wine and writing verse in the country. Their poems and essays frequently center on the impossibility of palace life for the scholar (with criticisms of the court sometimes necessarily veiled in allegory) and on the pleasures and hardships of country life.

Their retreat was typical of the Daoist-oriented *qingtan* ("pure conversation") movement that advocated freedom of individual expression and hedonistic escape from the extremely corrupt politics of the short-lived Wei dynasty (AD 220–265/266).

Most prominent among the Seven Sages was the freethinking, eccentric, and highly skilled poet Yuan Ji. Xiang Xiu wrote a famous commentary, the *Zhuangzi zhu,* with Guo Xiang, a neo-Daoist contemporary, on the works of the early Daoist philosopher Zhuangzi (died *c.* 300 BC). Other members of the group included the musician Yuan Xian, the devout Daoist Shan Tao, the poet Liu Ling, and Wang Rong.

The gifted writer and amateur metal worker Xi Kang, whose independent thinking and scorn for court custom led to his execution by the state, was host of the group at his country home in Shanyang, in the south of present-day Shandong province. Strongly protested by his several thousand followers, Xi Kang's execution testifies to the very real dangers that forced the Sages' retirement from palace life.

The tensions of such forced retirement are revealed in the writings of the Seven Sages and other eremitic poets of the time. Their retirement served as a model for that of later Chinese writers living in troubled times.

Sewanee Review, The \sə-'wȯn-ē, 'swȯn-\ Quarterly periodical of general culture with an emphasis on literature, founded at the University of the South in Sewanee, Tennessee, in 1892. Though the original outlook of the journal was essentially regional, under the editorship of Andrew Lytle (1942–44) and later Allen Tate (1944–46), the review developed a national reputation. In the early 1940s the review began publishing fiction, and the emphasis on criticism was also increased. *The Sewanee Review* became associated in particular with the New Criticism, though it published other views as well. Contributors included Cleanth Brooks, Robert Lowell, Wallace Stevens, Robert Penn Warren, Malcolm Cowley, W.H. Auden, Dylan Thomas, Louise Bogan, and George Woodcock.

sextain \'seks-tān\ [modification (influenced by quatr*ain*) of French *sextine* sestina] *See* SESTINA.

sextet or **sextette** \seks-'tet\ A six-line stanza or poem, sometimes used as a synonym for SESTET.

shadow play Type of theatrical entertainment performed with puppets, probably originating in China and on the Indonesian islands of Java and Bali, where the form is called *wayang*. Flat images are manipulated by the puppeteers between a bright light and a translucent screen, on the other side of which sits the audience. Shadow plays are also performed in Turkey and Greece. In the 18th and 19th centuries, European versions of shadow plays, called *ombres chinoises* ("Chinese shadows"), achieved a limited degree of popularity, especially in France. *See also* KARAGÖZ.

shāʿir \'shä-ēr, *Arabic* -ʿēr\ [Arabic, poet] In pre-Islāmic Arabic literature, a poet and tribal dignitary whose poetic utterances were deemed supernaturally inspired by such spirits as jinn and shaitans. As such, his word was believed to be necessary to insure the success of certain tribal activities, particularly war, grazing, and the invocation of the gods. In times of intertribal strife, the satire (*hijāʿ*) was the *shāʿir*'s most potent form of magic and equivalent to warfare itself.

In later times, when the supernatural association diminished, the *shāʿir* became the poetic spokesman for his tribe, praising its accomplishments and abusing its enemies. His art was highly developed and respected, and the more famous poets were surrounded by *rāwīs* (reciters) who memorized their verses.

Muḥammad looked on the pre-Islāmic poets with suspicion, but, with the development of Arabic grammar and philology in the 8th century, it was their language of the desert that, once influenced by the Qurʿān, became the standard of classical Arabic literature.

Shakespeare Memorial Company *See* ROYAL SHAKESPEARE COMPANY.

Shakespearean sonnet \shāk-'spir-ē-ən\ or **English sonnet** Poem of 14 lines grouped into three quatrains and a couplet with the rhyme scheme *abab cdcd efef gg*. It was developed in England by Sir Thomas Wyatt in the 16th century as an adaptation of the Petrarchan sonnet that had been imported from Italy, and it reached its maturest expression in the sonnets of William Shakespeare. An example is Shakespeare's 116th sonnet:

> Let me not to the marriage of true minds
> Admit impediments. Love is not love
> Which alters when it alteration finds,
> Or bends with the remover to remove:
> Oh, no! it is an ever-fixéd mark,
> That looks on tempests and is never shaken;
> It is the star to every wandering bark,
> Whose worth's unknown, although his height be taken.
> Love's not Time's fool, though rosy lips and cheeks
> Within his bending sickle's compass come;
> Love alters not with his brief hours and weeks,
> But bears it out even to the edge of doom.
> If this be error and upon me proved,
> I never writ, nor no man ever loved.

See also PETRARCHAN SONNET; SONNET.

shaped verse *See* PATTERN POETRY.

shilling shocker **1.** A novel of crime or violence especially popular in late Victorian England and originally costing one shilling. *Compare* DIME NOVEL;

PENNY DREADFUL. **2.** A usually short novel that is characterized by sensational incidents and lurid writing.

shisōsetsu *See* I NOVEL.

shocker \'shäk-ər\ A work of fiction or drama designed to shock the moral sensibilities, especially by the use of sordid detail, or to hold interest by the use of a high proportion of suspense, intrigue, or sensational matter (as crime or violence). *Compare* DREADFUL.

short \'shȯrt\ *of a syllable in prosody* **1.** Of relatively brief duration (in Greek and Latin prosody). **2.** Unstressed (in English verse).

short meter *also called* short measure, *abbreviation* S.M. **1.** A quatrain of which the first, second, and fourth lines are in iambic trimeter and the third in iambic tetrameter. **2.** A poulter's measure (alternating lines of 12 and 14 syllables) written as a quatrain.

short-short \'shȯrt-ˌshȯrt\ An extremely brief short story usually seeking an effect of shock or surprise.

short story Brief fictional prose narrative to be distinguished from longer, more expansive narrative forms such as the novel, epic, saga, and romance. The short story is usually concerned with a single effect conveyed in a single significant episode or scene and involving a limited number of characters, sometimes only one. The form encourages economy of setting and concise narration; character is disclosed in action and dramatic encounter but seldom fully developed. A short story may concentrate on the creation of mood rather than the telling of a story.

Despite the precedent of ancient Greek fables and brief romances, the tales of *The Thousand and One Nights,* and the earthy fabliaux that found their way into the collections of Geoffrey Chaucer and Giovanni Boccaccio or were inserted within longer narratives in novels, the short story did not emerge as a distinct literary genre until the 19th century. It was prompted at least in part by literary romanticism, which stimulated interest in the strange and fantastic and in abnormal sensation and heightened experience that was most intensely explored within the compass of a brief prose narrative. Edgar Allan Poe's *Tales of the Grotesque and Arabesque* are of this order and were very influential not only in the United States but also in Europe, particularly in France. In Germany the tales of Heinrich von Kleist and E.T.A. Hoffmann made use of the fabulous as a means of exploring psychological and metaphysical issues. The Puritan-derived fascination with the ordeals of individual experience, particularly the experience of evil, encouraged later American writers such as Nathaniel Hawthorne, Herman Melville, and Henry James to write short stories that emphasize subjective and possibly unreliable perception rather than action; James' *The Turn of the Screw* (1898) is a notable example.

Simultaneously with these developments, realistic fiction was aspiring to the function of investigative journalism, reporting on unfamiliar, unattractive, or neglected aspects of the contemporary situation with scrupulous fidelity. The reports could be effectively terse. In France Prosper Mérimée can be regarded as a pioneer of the short story of detached, dispassionate observation, a technique perfected in the tales of Guy de Maupassant, whose special skill was to capture a particularly illuminating and revealing moment in the unremarkable, perhaps dreary or sordid lives of ordinary citizens. Similar, often painful, revelations flash or flicker in the unhopeful, even paralyzed urban world of James Joyce's *Dubliners* (1914), a highly influential collection of short stories.

Short stories were often published in the first instance in magazines and newspapers, which encouraged the element of journalistic "local color" to be found in the American Bret Harte's stories of mining camps, Rudyard Kipling's early stories of life in India, or Mark Twain's yarns of the Mississippi and elsewhere. But Twain's early humorous sketches were succeeded by more somber short stories, such as "The Man That Corrupted Hadleyburg" (1900), that used realistic narrative techniques to create timeless moral fables. Writers such as Ernest Hemingway combined the particularities of scrupulous realism with hints of more universal significance, as implied in such titles as "The Light of the World." Some of Kipling's stories, such as "The Brushwood Boy" and "They," explore strange psychic phenomena beyond the thresholds of normal experience but within a framework of faithfully realistic description of ordinary life that serves to emphasize the strangeness.

In Russia the stories of Nikolay Gogol combined the realistic emphasis on often ordinary people with a more subjective exploration of states of consciousness conveyed through dream and vision, a pattern subsequently developed in the work of Fyodor Dostoyevsky. In the sketches of Ivan Turgenev and the stories of Anton Chekhov, as well as in many later short stories, atmosphere and isolated moments of special awareness can be more important than anything that actually happens.

The concentration on the special moment, often achieved through ironic coincidence, provides opportunities for a surprise ending, a savage "twist in the tale," particularly in the enormously popular stories of O. Henry. The moment of revelation may also disclose to the reader some underlying pattern or significance drawn from history or myth. This is one of the ways in which the modern short story can explore the nature of fictionality itself, addressing a sophisticated and specialized rather than a popular audience. The erudite Argentinian Jorge Luis Borges has written many intricate and subtle stories to this end.

Other notable writers of short narratives include Saki, Katherine Anne Porter, Eudora Welty, William Trevor, and Alice Munro.

short title An abbreviated form of entry for a book in a list or catalog that usually gives only the author's name, the title in brief, the date and place of publication, and the publisher's or printer's name.

Sicilian octave An Italian stanza or poem having eight lines of 11 syllables (hendecasyllables) rhyming *abababab*. The form may have originated in Tuscany about the 13th century, though little is known about its origins. The Sicilian octave was in use until the 16th century, when the madrigal overtook it in popularity.

Sicilian school A group of Sicilian, southern Italian, and Tuscan poets centered in the courts of Emperor Frederick II (reigned 1197–1250) and his son Manfred (d. 1266); they established the vernacular, as opposed to Provençal, as the standard language for Italian love poetry, and they are also credited with the invention of the canzone and the sonnet, two major Italian poetic forms that show the influence of Provençal, northern French, and possibly Arabic poetic traditions. Among the outstanding poets of the Sicilian school were Giacomo da Lentini, Guido delle Colonne, Giacomino Pugliese, and Rinaldo d'Aquino.

The brilliant Frederick II, a writer himself, a master of six languages, the founder of the University of Naples, and a generous patron of arts, attracted some of the finest minds and talents of his time to his court. His circle included perhaps 30 men, most of them Sicilians, with added groups of Tuscans and southern Italians. Dante's term for the group, "Sicilian," in *De vulgari eloquentia* (*Concerning Vernacular Eloquence*) is not entirely accurate; some of the poets were mainlanders, the court was not always located in Palermo, and their dialect was influenced by Provençal and southern Italian dialects. Acquainted with the poetry of the Provençal troubadours (Frederick had married the sister of the Count of Provence) and the northern French and German minstrels, Frederick's poets produced many poems, of which some 125 are extant, all in Sicilian dialect. About 85 of these are canzone (adapted from a Provençal form called the canso), and most of the rest are sonnets, the invention of which is usually attributed to Giacomo, the author of most of them. The majority of the poems were formalized and lacking in genuine inspiration, but some—particularly those describing the pain, anguish, and uncertainty of love—have singular directness and emotional power.

The importance of the poetic forms bequeathed by the Sicilian school can scarcely be overstressed. The canzone became a standard form for Italian poets for centuries. The Sicilian-school sonnet became, with variations, the dominant poetic form not only in Renaissance Italy—where it was brought to perfection by Guido Cavalcanti, Dante, and Petrarch—but also elsewhere in Europe, and in Elizabethan England, particularly, where, after its introduction in the 16th century, it was modified to form the distinctive English, or Shakespearean, sonnet.

sic passim \'sik-'pas-əm, 'sēk-'päs-im\ Literally, in Latin, "so throughout," a phrase used especially to indicate that something (such as a word or idea) is to be found at various places throughout a book or writer's work.

siècle des Lumières *See* ENLIGHTMENT.

Siglo de Oro *See* GOLDEN AGE.

sigmatism \'sig-mə-ˌtiz-əm\ [*sigma* Greek letter representing a dental or alveolar sibilant] In poetry, the deliberate concentration of sibilant speech sounds, as in the line "Softer be they than slippered sleep" from E.E. Cummings' poem "All in green went my love riding."

sign A fundamental linguistic unit that designates an object or relation or has a purely syntactic function. *See also* SEMIOTICS; STRUCTURALISM.

signature \'sig-nə-ˌchu̇r, -chər\ **1.** A letter or figure placed usually at the bottom of the first page on each sheet of printed pages (as of a book) as a direction to the binder in arranging and gathering the sheets. **2.** A printer's sheet that is folded into four or more pages to form one unit of a book. A book is a collection of signatures that are bound together.

signified \'sig-nə-ˌfīd\ A concept or meaning as distinguished from the sign through which it is communicated. *See also* SEMIOTICS.

signifier \'sig-nə-ˌfī-ər\ A symbol, sound, or image (as a word) that represents an underlying concept or meaning. *See also* SEMIOTICS.

sijo \'shē-jō\ [Korean] A Korean verse form appearing in Korean in three lines of 14 to 16 syllables. In English translation the verse form is divided into six shorter lines.

sillographer \si-'läg-rə-fər\ [Greek *sillógraphos,* from *síllos* invective, satirical poem in hexameters + *gráphein* to write] A writer of satires.

Silver Age In Latin literature, the period from approximately AD 18 to AD 133 that is a time of marked literary achievement second only to the previous Golden Age (70 BC–AD 18). By the 1st century AD political patronage of the arts begun in the Augustan Age (43 BC–AD 18) and a stifling reverence for the literature of the Golden Age, particularly for the poetry of Virgil, had led to a general decline in original literary output. Under such tyrants as Caligula and Nero, speech making was a dangerous art and rhetoricians turned to literature, influencing the development of the elaborate and poetical style characteristic of Silver Age prose. An increased provincial influence in Rome, while leading to an adulteration of the pure classical forms, contributed to the cosmopolitan outlook that was reflected in the psychologically perceptive and humanist tone of much of the best works of the period.

A great variety of literary forms is evident during the Silver Age. Of these, satire is the most vigorous, as exemplified by Juvenal in virulent satires of rich and powerful figures; by Martial in elegant epigrams on contemporary society; by Petronius in the picaresque novel *The Satyricon* (1st century AD); and by Persius in poetic satires supporting the stoic philosophy. History was the particular realm of Tacitus and Suetonius; Pliny the Elder and Pliny the Younger wrote letters on biography, science, natural history, grammar, history, and contemporary affairs. Quintilian excelled in literary criticism, Lucan in the epic form, Statius in poetry, Lucius Annaeus Seneca in rhetoric, and his son of the same name in tragedy.

simile \'sim-ə-lē\ [Latin, comparison, from neuter of *similis* like, similar] Figure of speech involving a comparison between two unlike entities. In the simile, unlike the metaphor, the resemblance is explicitly indicated by the words "like" or "as." The common heritage of similes in everyday speech usually reflects simple comparisons based on the natural world or familiar domestic objects, as in "He eats like a bird," "She is as smart as a whip," or "He is as slow as molasses." In some cases the original aptness of the comparison is lost, as in the expression "dead as a doornail." *Compare* METAPHOR.

A simile in literature may be specific and direct or more lengthy and complex, as in the following speech by Othello from William Shakespeare's *Othello:*

> Never, Iago. Like to the Pontic Sea,
> Whose icy current and compulsive course
> Ne'er feels retiring ebb, but keeps due on
> To the Propontic and the Hellespont;
> Even so my bloody thoughts, with violent pace,
> Shall ne'er look back . . .

The simile does more than merely assert that Othello's urge for vengeance cannot now be turned aside; it also suggests huge natural forces. The proper names also suggest an exotic, remote world, with mythological and historical associations, reminiscent of Othello's foreign culture and adventurous past. *See also* EPIC SIMILE.

situation \ˌsich-ü-'wā-shən\ A particular or striking complex of affairs at a stage in the action of a narrative or drama. *Compare* CRISIS; CLIMAX.

skald or **scald** \'sköld, 'skäld\ [Old Norse *skald*] One of the ancient Scandinavian poets who developed skaldic poetry. One of the greatest skalds was Egil Skallagrímsson, whose life and works are preserved in *Egils saga.*

skaldic poetry or **scaldic poetry** \'sköl-dik, 'skäl-\ Oral court poetry originating in Norway but developed chiefly by Icelandic poets (skalds) from the 9th to the 13th century. Skaldic poetry was contemporary with Eddic poetry but differed from it in meter, diction, and style. Eddic poetry is anonymous, simple, and terse, often taking the form of an objective dramatic dialogue. Skalds, on the other hand, were identified by name. Their poems were descriptive, occasional, and subjective, their meters strictly syllabic instead of free and variable, and their language ornamented with *heiti* and kennings. (*Heiti* ["names"] are uncompounded poetic nouns, fanciful art words rather than everyday terms—e.g., "brand" for "sword" or "steed" for "horse." Kennings are metaphorical circumlocutions such as "sword liquid" for "blood," or "wave-horse" for "ship.")

Of the 100 skaldic verse forms, the drótt-kvaett (court meter), which uses a syllable count and a regular pattern of alliteration, internal rhyme, and assonance, was most popular. The formal subjects of the skalds were shield poems (descriptions of the mythological engravings on shields), praise of kings, epitaphs, and genealogies. There were also less formal occasional poems, dream songs, magic curses, lampoons, flytings (poems of abuse), and (although forbidden by law) many love songs. Because they so often praised current feats of the kings, the poems have high historical value, limited only by their abstruse language.

Skamander \skȧ-'mȧn-der\ Group of young Polish poets who were united in their desire to forge a new poetic language that would accurately reflect the experience of modern life.

Founded in Warsaw about 1918, the group had antecedents in the Young Poland movement. Its monthly publication (first published in January 1920) was named *Skamander,* and the group soon became known by that name. Skamander was cofounded by Jarosław Iwaszkiewicz, known primarily for his novels and short stories, and Julian Tuwim, a lyrical poet. Also associated with the group were Kazimierz Wierzyński, Jan Lechoń (pseudonym of Leszek Serafinowicz), Maria Pawlikowska-Jasnorzewska, and Antoni Słonimski, as well as Władysław Broniewski, a powerful lyrical poet who used traditional meters and forms to express concern with current social and ideological problems.

skaz \'skȧs, *Angl* 'skäz\ [Russian, literally, tale, a derivative of *skazat'* to say] In Russian literature, a device in which the author creates a persona through which he can present a first-person narrative using dialect, slang, and the peculiar idiom of that persona. Among the well-known writers who have used this device are Nikolay Leskov, Aleksey Remizov, Mikhail Zoshchenko, and Yevgeny Zamyatin.

Skeltonics \skel-'tän-iks\ Short verses of an irregular meter much used by John Skelton. The verses have two or three stresses arranged sometimes in falling and sometimes in rising rhythm. They rely on such devices as alliteration, parallelism, and multiple rhymes and are related to doggerel. Skelton wrote his verses as works of satire and protest, and thus the form was considered deliberately unconventional and provocative.

sketch \'skech\ A short literary composition somewhat resembling the short story and the essay but intentionally slight in treatment, discursive in style, and familiar in tone. *See also* LITERARY SKETCH.

slack \'slak\, *also called* unstress \'ən-ˌstres, ˌən-'stres\ In the prosodic theory of Gerard Manley Hopkins, the weak or stressless element in a rhythmic unit or foot.

slant rhyme *See* HALF RHYME.

slave narrative American literary genre consisting of slave memoirs of daily plantation life, including the sufferings and humiliations borne and the eventual escape to freedom. The narratives contain humorous anecdotes of the deception and pretenses that the slave was forced to practice, expressions of religious fervor and superstition, and, above all, a pervasive longing for freedom, dignity, and self-respect.

A Narrative of the Uncommon Sufferings and Surprising Deliverance of Briton Hammon, a Negro Man, which is often considered the first slave narrative, was published in Boston in 1760. (Some scholars cite *Adam Negro's Tryall* [1703] as the first slave narrative, but it is about Adam, not by him.) Other early examples, such as *A Narrative of the Lord's Wonderful Dealings with J. Murrant, a Black, Taken Down from His Own Relation* (1784) and *The Interesting Narrative of Olaudah Equiano, or Gustavus Vassa, the African* (1789), followed.

The major period of slave narratives was 1830–60. Their publication was encouraged by abolitionists, and during this period the narratives, many of them based on oral accounts, multiplied. Although some, such as *Scenes in the Life of Harriet Tubman* (1869), are factual autobiographies, many others were influenced or sensationalized by the writer's desire to arouse sympathy for the abolitionist cause. The reworkings and interpolations in such works are usually obvious. In some cases, such as *The Autobiography of a Female Slave* (1856) by Mattie Griffith and Richard Hildreth's *The Slave, or Memoirs of Archy Moore,* the accounts were entirely fictitious. The slave-narrative genre reached its height with Frederick Douglass' classic autobiography *Narrative of the Life of Frederick Douglass, an American Slave* (1845; revised 1882).

In the first half of the 20th century a number of folklorists and anthropologists compiled documentary narratives based on recorded interviews with former black slaves. Notable compilations of such narratives include the brief accounts in Charles S. Johnson's *Shadow of the Plantation* (1934) and the fuller narratives found in B.A. Botkin's *Lay My Burden Down* (1945), which was an extract from 17 volumes of slave narratives collected by black and white interviewers for the WPA Federal Writers' Project. In the second half of the 20th century the growth of black cultural consciousness stimulated a renewed interest in slave narratives.

slice of life In literature, a straightforward, realistic portrayal of life. The phrase is a translation of the French *tranche de vie,* which was used in reference to the works of naturalistic French writers such as Émile Zola.

śloka \'shlō-kə\ [Sanskrit *ślokaḥ* sound, song of praise, praise, stanza] Chief verse form of the Sanskrit epics. A fluid meter that lends itself well to improvisation, the *śloka* consists of two verse lines (a distich) of 16 syllables each or of four half lines (hemistichs) of eight syllables each.

Smart Set, The American literary magazine founded by William D'Alton Mann and published monthly in New York City from 1900 to 1930. Most notable among its editors were S.S. Van Dine and the team of H.L. Mencken and George Jean Nathan. It was a consciously fashionable magazine that featured novelettes, short stories in English and in French, essays, poems, plays, criticisms, and humorous sketches. Mencken regularly wrote a book review.

Among the American writers whose early work was published in *The Smart Set* were Eugene O'Neill, F. Scott Fitzgerald, and O. Henry; it also introduced the nation to the writings of James Joyce, D.H. Lawrence, Ford Madox Ford, and Gabriele D'Annunzio. Other notable contributors included W. Somerset Maugham, Frank Norris, Sinclair Lewis, Theodore Dreiser, Willa Cather, Sherwood Anderson, Ezra Pound, and James Branch Cabell.

Socialist Realism The officially sanctioned theory and method of artistic, including literary, composition prevalent in the Soviet Union from 1932 to the mid-1980s. For that period of history Socialist Realism, which called for the didactic use of art to develop social consciousness in an evolving socialist state, was the sole criterion for measuring artistic works. Defined and reinterpreted over half a century of polemical criticism, it remained a vague term.

In literature Socialist Realism followed the great tradition of 19th-century Russian realism in that it purported to serve as a faithful and objective mirror of life. It differed from the earlier tradition, however, in several important respects. The realism of Leo Tolstoy and Anton Chekhov inevitably conveyed a critical picture of the society it portrayed (hence the term *critical realism*). On the other hand, the primary theme of Socialist Realism was the struggle to build socialism and a classless society. In portraying this struggle, the writer could note imperfections but was expected to take an essentially positive and optimistic view of socialist society and to keep in mind its larger historical relevance.

One requisite of Socialist Realism was *narodnost,* a doctrine of social responsibility both in portraying the aspirations of the proletariat and in making the work accessible to all. Another requisite was the hero who perseveres against all odds or handicaps. Socialist Realism thus looked back to Romanticism in that it encouraged a certain heightening and idealizing of characters and events to mold the consciousness of the masses. Hundreds of protagonists—usually engineers, inventors, or scientists—created to this specification were strikingly alike in their lack of credibility. In rare cases, when the writer's deeply felt experiences coincided with the official doctrine, the works were successful, as with the Soviet classic *Kak zakalyalas stal* (1932–34; *How the Steel Was Tempered*), written by Nikolay Ostrovsky, an invalid who died at 32. His hero, Pavel Korchagin, wounded in the October Revolution, overcomes the handicaps caused by wounds and disease to become a writer who inspires the workers of the Reconstruction. The young novelist's passionate sincerity and autobiographical involvement lends a poignant conviction to Korchagin that is lacking in most heroes of Socialist Realism.

Socialist Realism remained the official aesthetic of the Soviet Union (and of its eastern European satellites) until the late 1980s, when changes in Soviet society led to the general decline of state socialism and of the rigid commitment to Marxism in the region.

sock \'säk\ [Latin *soccus*] A shoe worn by actors in Greek and Roman comedy. *Compare* BUSKIN.

soft-boiled Of or relating to literary expression that is regarded satirically as given to wholesome sentiment and moralism. The term is used in opposition to *hard-boiled,* a tough, unsentimental style made popular in detective fiction. *See also* HARD-BOILED FICTION.

solar myth **1.** A myth that concerns a sun god. **2.** *also called* solarism \'sō-lə-ˌriz-əm\ A traditional story (such as a folktale or legend) that is interpreted as a primitive explanation of the course, motion, or influence of the sun.

solecism \'säl-ə-ˌsiz-əm, 'sōl-\ [Greek *soloikismós,* a derivative of *soloikízein* to speak incorrectly, probably a derivative (after *attikízein* to speak Attic) of *sóloι,* town in Cilicia where a nonstandard form of Attic was reputedly spoken] An ungrammatical combination of words in a sentence. *You could of been on time* may be considered a solecism.

soliloquy \sə-'lil-ə-kwē\ [Late Latin *soliloquium* monologue, from Latin *solus* alone + *loqui* to speak] In drama, a monologue that gives the illusion of being a series of unspoken reflections. The actor directly addresses the audience or speaks thoughts aloud, either alone upon the stage or with the other actors keeping silent.

The device was long an accepted dramatic convention, especially in the theater of the 16th, 17th, and 18th centuries. Long, ranting monologues were popular in the revenge tragedies of Elizabethan times, such as Thomas Kyd's *The Spanish Tragedy,* and in the works of Christopher Marlowe, who usually substituted the outpouring of one character's thoughts for normal dramatic writing. William Shakespeare used the device more artfully, as a true indicator of the mind of his characters, as in the famous "To be or not to be" soliloquy in *Hamlet.* Among the French playwrights, Pierre Corneille made use of the lyrical quality of the form, often producing soliloquies that are actually odes or cantatas, whereas Jean Racine, like Shakespeare, used the soliloquy more for dramatic effect. The soliloquy fell into disfavor after much exaggeration and overuse in the plays of the late 17th-century English Restoration, but it remains useful for revealing the inner life of characters.

Twentieth-century playwrights have experimented with various substitutes for the set speech of the soliloquy. Eugene O'Neill in *The Great God Brown* (1926) had the characters wear masks when they were presenting themselves to the world, but they were maskless when expressing what they actually felt or thought in soliloquy. In O'Neill's *Strange Interlude* (1928), the characters spoke a double dialogue—one to each other, concealing the truth, and one to the audience, revealing it. In Samuel Beckett's *Krapp's Last Tape* (1958), interior monologue was presented through the device of having an old man replay tape recordings he made in his youth. *Compare* DRAMATIC MONOLOGUE.

song **1.** A poetical composition. **2.** A melody for a lyric poem or ballad. **3.** A poem easily set to music.

sonnet \'sän-ət\ [Italian *sonetto,* from Old Provençal *sonet* song, air, a derivative of *son* tune, sound] A fixed verse form of Italian origin consisting of 14 lines that are typically five-foot iambics rhyming according to a prescribed scheme; also, a poem in this pattern.

The sonnet is unique among poetic forms in Western literature in that it has retained its appeal for major poets for five centuries. The form seems to have originated in the 13th century among the Sicilian school of court poets who were influenced by the love poetry of Provençal troubadours. From there it spread to Tuscany, where it reached its highest expression in the 14th century in the poems of Petrarch. His *Canzoniere,* a sequence of poems that includes 317 sonnets, addressed to his idealized beloved, Laura, established and perfected the Petrarchan (or Italian) sonnet, which remains one of the two principal sonnet forms, as well as the one most widely used. The other major form is the Shakespearean (or English) sonnet.

The Petrarchan sonnet characteristically treats its theme in two parts. The first eight lines, the octave, state a problem, ask a question, or express an emotional tension. The last six lines, the sestet, resolve the problem, answer the question, or relieve the tension. The octave is rhymed *abbaabba.* The rhyme scheme of the sestet varies; it may be *cdecde, cdccdc,* or *cdedce.*

The sonnet was introduced to England, along with other Italian verse forms, by Sir Thomas Wyatt and Henry Howard, Earl of Surrey, in the 16th century. The new forms precipitated the great flowering of Elizabethan lyric poetry, and the period marks the peak of the sonnet's English popularity. In the course of adapting the Italian form to English, the Elizabethans gradually arrived at the distinctive English sonnet, which is composed of three quatrains, each having an independent rhyme scheme, and is ended with a rhymed couplet. The rhyme scheme of the Shakespearean sonnet is *abab cdcd efef gg.* Its greater number of rhymes makes it a less demanding form than the Petrarchan sonnet, but this is offset by the difficulty presented by the couplet, which must summarize the impact of the preceding quatrains with the compressed force of a Greek epigram. Even William Shakespeare sometimes failed at it.

The Elizabethan sonnet typically appeared in a sequence of love poems in the manner of Petrarch. Although each sonnet was an independent poem, partly conventional in content and partly self-revelatory, the sequence had the added interest of providing something of a narrative development. Among the notable Elizabethan sequences are Sir Philip Sidney's *Astrophel and Stella* (1591), Samuel Daniel's *Delia* (1592), Michael Drayton's *Ideas Mirrour* (1594), and Edmund Spenser's *Amoretti* (1595). The latter work uses a common variant of the sonnet (known as Spenserian) that follows the Shakespearean quatrain and couplet pattern, but resembles the Petrarchan in using a linked rhyme scheme: *abab bcbc cdcd ee.* Perhaps the greatest of all sonnet sequences is Shakespeare's, addressed to a young man and a "dark lady." In these sonnets the supposed love story is of less interest than the underlying reflections on time and art, growth and decay, and fame and fortune.

In its subsequent development, the sonnet was to depart even further from themes of love. By the time John Donne wrote his religious sonnets (*c.* 1610) and John Milton wrote sonnets on political and religious subjects or on personal themes such as his blindness (i.e., "When I consider how my light is spent"), the sonnet had been extended to embrace nearly all the subjects of poetry.

It is the virtue of this short form that it can range from "light conceits of lovers" to considerations of the human condition, time, death, and eternity, without doing injustice to any of them. Even during the Romantic era, in spite of the emphasis on freedom and spontaneity, the sonnet forms continued to challenge major poets. The sonnets of William Wordsworth (e.g., "It Is a Beauteous Evening; Calm and Free" and "The World Is Too Much With Us") and those of John Keats (e.g., "When I Have Fears That I May Cease To Be" and "Bright Star, Would I Were Steadfast as Thou Art") are among the finest and best known in English.

In the later 19th century the love sonnet sequence was revived by Elizabeth Barrett Browning in *Sonnets from the Portuguese* (1850) and by Dante Gabriel Rossetti in "The House of Life" (1870 and 1881). The most distinguished 20th-century work of the kind is Rainer Maria Rilke's *Sonette an Orpheus* (1923; *Sonnets to Orpheus*).

Use of the word *sonnet* to mean any short, usually lyric and amatory poem or piece of verse is now rare or obsolete. *Compare* CURTAL SONNET; PETRARCHAN SONNET; SHAKESPEAREAN SONNET; SPENSERIAN SONNET; TAILED SONNET.

sonnet sequence A series of sonnets often having a unifying theme.

Sons of Ben *See* TRIBE OF BEN.

sooterkin \ˈsu̇t-ər-kin, ˈsüt-\ Something that is imperfect or unsuccessful; in this sense the term is used especially to indicate an imperfect literary composition.

sotadean verse \ˌsōt-ə-ˈdē-ən, ˌsät-\ A truncated four-measure line (catalectic tetrameter) of major ionics (two long and two short syllables) having the normal form – – ∪ ∪ | – – ∪ ∪ | – – ∪ ∪ | – ⏓. The meter was allegedly invented by Sotades, a Greek satirist of the 3rd century BC, and it was associated primarily with scurrilous or salacious verse.

sotie or **sottie** \sȯ-ˈtē\ [French *sotie, sottie,* from Middle French *sottie,* a derivative of *sot* fool] Short topical and farcical play popular in France in the 15th and early 16th centuries, in which a company of *sots* ("fools") exchanged badinage on contemporary persons and events. The *sots,* wearing the traditional short jacket, tights, bells, and dunce cap of the fool, also introduced acrobatics and farcical humor into the sketches. At first used as introductory pieces to mystery and morality plays, soties developed into an independent form and were created and staged by both amateur associations and permanent acting companies. Pierre Gringore became the preeminent sotie dramatist. The sotie was openly satirical and was used as a weapon in political battles. It was proscribed in the 16th century and replaced by more general forms of satire.

Southern gothic A style of writing practiced by many writers of the American South whose stories set in that region are characterized by grotesque, macabre, or fantastic incidents. Flannery O'Connor, Tennessee Williams, Truman Capote, William Faulkner, and Carson McCullers are among the best-known writers of Southern gothic. *See also* GOTHIC.

space opera Futuristic melodramatic fantasy involving space travelers and extraterrestrial beings.

Spasmodic school Group of poets that included P.J. Bailey, Sydney Dobell, J.S. Bigg, and Alexander Smith, who were known for the erratic nature of their verse with its formlessness, chaotic imagery, and exaggerations of passion. The descriptive name was first applied to the group by Charles Kingsley in 1853 and was established by the Scottish poet and humorist W.E. Aytoun in his satirical light verse *Firmilian, or The Student of Badajoz: A Spasmodic Tragedy by 'T. Percy Jones'* (1854).

Spectator, The Periodical published in London by the essayists Richard Steele and Joseph Addison from March 1, 1711, to Dec. 6, 1712 (appearing daily), and subsequently revived by Addison in 1714. It succeeded *The Tatler,* which Steele had launched in 1709. In its aim to "enliven morality with wit, and to temper wit with morality," *The Spectator* adopted a fictional method of presentation through a "Spectator Club," whose imaginary members expressed the authors' own ideas about society. These "members" included representatives of commerce, the army, the town (respectively, Sir Andrew Freeport, Captain Sentry, and Will Honeycomb), and the country gentry (Sir Roger de Coverley). The papers were ostensibly written by Mr. Spectator, an "observer" of the London scene. Though Whiggish (a word generally used to refer to the aristocratic, landowning classes, who sought to limit royal authority) in tone and opinion, *The Spectator* usually steered clear of party politics.

Because of its fictional framework, *The Spectator* is sometimes said to have heralded the rise of the English novel in the 18th century. This is perhaps an overstatement, since the fictional framework, once adopted, ceased to be of primary importance and served instead as a social microcosm within which a tone at once grave, good-humored, and flexible could be sounded. The real authors of the essays were free to consider whatever topics they pleased, with reference to the fictional framework (as in Steele's account of Sir Roger's views on marriage, which appeared in issue no. 113) or without it (as in Addison's critical papers on *Paradise Lost,* John Milton's epic poem, which appeared in issues no. 267, 273, and others).

In addition to Addison and Steele themselves, contributors included Alexander Pope, Thomas Tickell, and Ambrose Philips. Addison's reputation as an essayist has surpassed that of Steele, but their individual contributions to the success of *The Spectator* are less to the point than their collaborative efforts: Steele's friendly tone was a perfect balance and support for the more dispassionate style of Addison. Their joint achievement was to make serious discussion a normal pastime of the leisured class. Together they set the pattern and established the vogue for the periodical throughout the rest of the century and helped to create a receptive public for novelists.

More than 3,000 copies of *The Spectator* were published daily, and the 555 numbers were then collected into seven volumes. The revival of the paper from June 18 to Dec. 20, 1714, consisted of 80 additional issues, which were later reprinted as volume eight.

speech, figure of *See* FIGURE OF SPEECH.

speech form *See* LINGUISTIC FORM.

Spelvin, George \ˈjȯrj-ˈspel-vin\ Name used by American theatrical convention in the credits commonly to conceal dual roles or for a corpse or anthropomorphic props. Spelvin first "appeared" on Broadway in the cast list of Charles A. Gardiner's *Karl the Peddler* in 1886. Winchell Smith employed the character in many of his plays, beginning with *Brewster's Millions* in 1906. Spelvin appeared with Maude Adams in *Joan of Arc* (1908), as a Betting Man in *High Button Shoes* (1947), and as Colonel Dent in *Jane Eyre* (1958).

D.W. Griffith cast Spelvin as a Union soldier in his epochal film *The Birth of a Nation* (1915) and as a dancer in *Way Down East* (1920). He also had a small role in the Academy Award-winning *From Here to Eternity* (1953). Spelvin was first listed in television credits in the dramatic series *The Fugitive,* and from time to time he has filled out the cast of such daytime soap operas as *The Guiding Light* and *Edge of Night*.

When a female character is needed, the player is listed as Georgiana, or Georgette, Spelvin. Spelvin's British counterparts are Walter Plinge, Mr. F. Anney, and Mr. Bart.

Spenserian sonnet \spen-ˈsir-ē-ən\ A sonnet in which the lines are grouped into three interlocked quatrains (four-line units) and a couplet, with the rhyme scheme *abab bcbc cdcd ee*. The Spenserian sonnet is a hybrid form, using a linked rhyme scheme, as does the Petrarchan, or Italian, sonnet, but merging that element with the Shakespearean (or English) quatrain and couplet scheme.

Spenserian stanza \spen-ˈsir-ē-ən\ A stanza that consists of eight lines of iambic pentameter (five feet) followed by a ninth line of iambic hexameter (six feet), known as an alexandrine; the rhyme scheme is *ababbcbcc*. The first eight lines produce an effect of formal unity, while the hexameter completes the thought of the stanza. Invented by Edmund Spenser for his poem *The Faerie Queene* (1590–1609), the Spenserian stanza has origins in the Old French ballade (eight-line stanzas, rhyming ababbcbc), the Italian ottava rima (eight 11-syllable lines with a rhyme scheme of abababcc), and the stanza form used by Geoffrey Chaucer in his "Monk's Tale" (eight lines rhyming ababbcbc). While it was a revolutionary innovation in its day, it fell into general disuse during the 17th and 18th centuries. It was revived in the 19th century by the Romantic poets—e.g., by Lord Byron in *Childe Harold's Pilgrimage,* by John Keats in "The Eve of St. Agnes," and by Percy Bysshe Shelley in *Adonais*.

Spielmann \'shpēl-män\ [German, from Old High German *spilman,* from *spil* play, diversion + *man* man, person] *plural* Spielleute. Wandering entertainer who performed at fairs, markets, and castles in medieval Europe. The *Spielleute* included singers, mimics, and sword-swallowers. Also among them were the storytellers credited with keeping alive the native Germanic vernacular legends at a time when nearly all written literature was religious and when the court poets, under foreign influence, were concerned chiefly with love lyrics and Arthurian legends. A number of carefree adventure tales, such as the 12th-century *König Rother,* are evidence of a highly developed underground literature characterized by its humor, amoral tone, and powers of social observation and presumably propagated by the *Spielleute.*

spondee \'spän-ˌdē\ [Greek *spondeîos* (short for *spondeîos poús* spondaic foot), from *spondeîos* of a libation, a derivative of *spondḗ* libation] Metrical foot consisting of two long or stressed syllables occurring together. Verses consisting entirely of spondees were sung or chanted by the ancient Greeks during performance of a libation, and from such hymns the foot took its meaning.

Spondaic meter occurred occasionally in classical verse as two long syllables. It does not, however, form the basis for any English verse, as there are virtually no English words in which syllables receive equal stress. An approximation of a spondaic foot is sometimes achieved with such compounds as "heyday" or "childhood," but even these words can be seen as examples of primary and secondary stress rather than equal stress. In English verse, the spondaic foot is usually composed of two monosyllables. It is frequently used as an introductory variation in a line of iambic meter, such as the following line from Robert Burns:

> ´ ´ | ∪ ´ | ∪ ´
> Green grow | the rush | es, O

spoonerism \'spü-nər-ˌiz-əm\ Reversal of the initial letters or syllables of two or more words, such as "I have a half-warmed fish in my mind" (for "half-formed wish") and "a blushing crow" (for "a crushing blow"). The word is derived from the name of William Archibald Spooner (1844–1930), a distinguished Anglican clergyman and warden of New College, Oxford, who was a nervous man who committed many "spoonerisms." Such transpositions are sometimes made intentionally for their comic effect.

sprung rhythm A poetic rhythm designed to approximate the natural rhythm of speech and characterized by the frequent juxtaposition of single accented syllables and the occurrence of mixed types of feet (such as the accentual trochee, dactyl, and first paeon) whose sequence is broken or interrupted by outrides (unstressed syllables that are not counted in the scansion).

This system of prosody was developed by the 19th-century English poet Gerard Manley Hopkins. In sprung rhythm, a foot may be composed of from one to four syllables. (In regular English meters, a foot consists of two or three syllables.) Because stressed syllables often occur sequentially in this patterning rather than in alternation with unstressed syllables, the rhythm is said to be "sprung." Hopkins claimed to be only the theoretician, not the inventor, of sprung rhythm. He saw it as the rhythm of common English speech and the basis of such early English poems as William Langland's *Piers Plowman* and of nursery rhymes such as the following:

> Ding, dong, bell;
> Pussy's in the well.

Sprung rhythm is a bridge between regular meter and free verse. The first two lines of Hopkins' "Spring and Fall: To a Young Child" are an example:

> Margaret are you grieving
> Over Goldengrove unleaving?

spy story A tale of international intrigue and adventure. Among the best examples of the genre are works written by John Buchan, Len Deighton, Sapper (H. Cyril McNeile), and many others. Two directions taken by the modern spy story were typified by Ian Fleming's enormously popular James Bond thrillers, which emphasized technological marvels much in the manner of science-fiction fantasy, and John Le Carré's bleakly realistic stories such as *The Spy Who Came in from the Cold*.

squib \'skwib\ A short humorous, satiric, or lampooning piece of writing or speech.

stanza \'stan-zə\ [Italian, act or place of staying, abode, room, stanza] A division of a poem consisting of two or more lines arranged together as a unit. More specifically, a stanza usually is a group of lines arranged together in a recurring pattern of metrical lengths and a sequence of rhymes.

The structure of a stanza is determined by the number of lines, the dominant meter, and the rhyme scheme. Thus, a stanza of four lines of iambic pentameter, rhyming *abab,* would be described as a quatrain.

Some of the most common stanzaic forms are designated by the number of lines in each unit—e.g., tercet or terza rima (three lines) and ottava rima (eight lines). Other stanzaic forms are named for poets who used them or poems that exemplify them—e.g., the Spenserian stanza or the *In Memoriam* stanza, popularized by Alfred, Lord Tennyson in the poem by that title. The term *strophe* is often used interchangeably with stanza, although strophe is sometimes used specifically to refer to a unit of a poem that does not have a regular meter and rhyme pattern or to a unit of a Pindaric ode.

stemma \'stem-ə\ *plural* stemmata \-ə-tə\ *or* stemmas. A tree showing the relationships of the manuscripts of a literary work.

stich \'stik\ [Greek *stíchos* row, line, verse] A measured part (such as a line) of something written, especially in verse.

stichic \'stik-ik\ Of, relating to, or consisting of lines of verse, or lines that are rhythmic units; also, arranged or divided by lines rather than by stanzas.

stichomythia \ˌstik-ə-'mith-ē-ə\ or **stichomythy** \sti-'käm-ə-thē\ *plural* stichomythias *or* stichomythies [Greek *stichomythía,* from *stíchos* row, line, verse + *mŷthos* thing said, speech, tale] Dialogue especially of altercation or dispute delivered in alternating lines (as in classical Greek drama).

This device, which is found in such plays as Aeschylus' *Agamemnon* and Sophocles' *Oedipus the King,* is frequently used as a means to show characters in vigorous contention or to heighten the emotional intensity of a scene. Characters may take turns voicing antithetical positions, or they may take up one another's words, suggesting other meanings or punning upon them.

Repartee in the form of polished aphorisms was a stylistic feature of the Roman tragedies of Seneca, which were intended for private readings rather than public performance. Through the influence of Seneca, stichomythia was adapted to the drama of Elizabethan England, most notably by William Shakespeare in comedies such as *Love's Labour's Lost* and in the memorable exchange between Richard and Queen Elizabeth in *Richard III* (Act IV, scene iv). A similar type of "cut-and-thrust" or "cut-and-parry" dialogue figures in the clipped, epigrammatic speech of the prose plays of the 1920s, such as those of Noël Coward.

stock character A character in a drama or fiction that represents a type and that is recognizable as belonging to a certain genre. Most of the characters in the commedia dell'arte are stock characters. In Roman and Renaissance comedy there is the miles gloriosus, or braggart soldier; in Elizabethan drama there is usually a fool; in fairy tales a prince charming; and in melodrama a scheming villain. Although these characters are common types they are not always treated or presented in a stock manner. A skillful author can develop them into more complex individuals. For example, in William Shakespeare's *Henry IV,* Falstaff is an interesting version of the braggart soldier.

stop \'stäp\ A pause or break in a verse that marks the end of a grammatical unit.

storiette \ˌstȯr-ē-'et\ A brief story or tale.

storify \'stȯr-ə-ˌfī\ To narrate or describe in a story.

story \'stȯr-ē\ [Old French *storie, istorie, hystoire,* narrative, especially, of the remote past, from Latin *historia* record of research, history, narrative, from Greek *istoría*] **1.** An account of incidents or events. **2.** A fictional narrative shorter than a novel; specifically, a SHORT STORY. **3.** The intrigue or plot of a narrative or dramatic work.

story line The plot of a story or drama.

stracittà \ˌsträ-chēt-'tä\ An Italian literary movement that developed after World War I. Massimo Bontempelli was the leader of the movement, which was connected with his idea of *novecentismo*. Bontempelli called for a break from traditional styles of writing, and his own writings reflected his interest in such modern forms as Surrealism and magic realism. The name *stracittà,* a type of back-formation from the word *stracittadino* ("ultra-urban"), was meant to emphasize the movement's adherence to general trends in European literature, in opposition to *strapaese* (from *strapaesano* ["ultra-local"]), collectively, those authors who followed nationalist and regionalist trends.

strain \'strān\ A portion of a poem. Also, a passage of verbal or musical expression.

strambotto \stràm-'bȯt-tō\ *plural* strambotti \-'bȯt-tē\ One of the oldest of Italian verse forms, composed of a single stanza of either six or eight hendecasyllabic (11-syllable) lines. *Strambotti* were particularly popular in Renaissance Sicily and Tuscany, and the origin of the form in either of the two regions is still uncertain. Variations of the eight-line *strambotto* include the Sicilian octave (*ottava siciliana*), with the rhyme scheme *abababab;* the OTTAVA RIMA, with the typical rhyme scheme *abababcc;* and the RISPETTO, a Tuscan form usually with the rhyme scheme *ababccdd* or with ottava rima. Six-line variants usually rhyme *ababab, ababcc,* or *aabbcc*. The subject of the *strambotto* was generally love (sometimes satire).

The Italian word *strambotto,* first attested in a Genoese document of the 13th century, is obscurely related to a group of words in other Romance dialects designating medieval poetic compositions, such as Old Provençal *estribot,* Old French *estrabot,* and Spanish *estribote* (later *estrambote*); their ultimate origin is uncertain.

Stratfordian \strat-'fȯr-dē-ən\ [*Stratford*-upon-Avon, Shakespeare's birthplace] One who believes that William Shakespeare was the author of the dramatic works usually attributed to him. *Compare* OXFORDIAN.

stream of consciousness Narrative technique in nondramatic fiction intended to render the flow of myriad impressions—visual, auditory, physical, associative, and subliminal—that together with rational thought impinge on the consciousness of an individual. The term was first used in the 19th century by the philosopher Alexander Bain in *Senses and Intellect* (1855) and by the psychologist William James in *The Principles of Psychology* (1890). As the psychological novel developed in the 20th century, some writers attempted to capture the total flow of their characters' consciousness, rather than limit themselves to rational thoughts. To represent the full richness, speed, and subtlety of the mind at work, the writer may incorporate snatches of incoherent thought, ungrammatical constructions, and free association of ideas and images.

The stream-of-consciousness novel commonly uses the narrative techniques of INTERIOR MONOLOGUE. Probably the most famous example is James Joyce's *Ulysses* (1922) in which there is a complex evocation of the inner states of the characters Leopold and Molly Bloom and Stephen Dedalus. Other notable examples include *Leutnant Gustl* (1901) by Arthur Schnitzler, an early use of stream of consciousness to re-create the atmosphere of pre-World War I Vienna, and William Faulkner's *The Sound and the Fury* (1929), which records the fragmentary and impressionistic responses in the minds of three members of the Compson family to events that are immediately being experienced or events that are being remembered. Another master of stream of consciousness is Virginia Woolf (especially in *The Waves* [1931]). An often overlooked English-language pioneer in the technique is Dorothy M. Richardson, whose multivolume *Pilgrimage* was published from 1915 to 1938.

Strega Prize \'strā-gä\ Italian literary award established in 1947 by writers Goffredo and Maria Bellonci and the manufacturer of Strega liquor, Guido Alberti. It carries an award of one million lire, presented to the author of the outstanding Italian narrative (fiction or nonfiction) published the preceding year. Such writers as Cesare Pavese, Alberto Moravia, Elsa Morante, Carlo Cassola, Natalia Ginzburg, and Primo Levi have been recipients of the award.

stress \'stres\ In prosody, the relative force or prominence of a syllable in a verse. Though stress is often equated with accent, some prosodists make the distinction that accent refers to normal language usage while stress is used in metrics to fit a syllable to a particular metrical pattern. Stress is also sometimes considered one of the constituents of accent along with such things as tone and pitch. In modern accentual or accentual-syllabic prosody, the meter of a verse is determined by the pattern of stressed and unstressed syllables in the verse. In scansion, or analysis of the meter, a stressed syllable is marked with the symbol ˊ and an unstressed syllable with the symbol ᴗ. *Compare* ACCENT.

strophe \'strō-ˌfē\ [Greek *strophḗ* act of turning, turning of the chorus, strophe] In poetry, a group of verses that form a distinct unit within a poem. The term is sometimes used as a synonym for *stanza,* usually in reference to a Pindaric ode or to a poem that does not have a regular meter and rhyme pattern, such as free verse. In ancient Greek drama the strophe was the first part of a choral ode that was performed by the chorus while moving from one side of the stage to the other. The strophe was followed by an antistrophe of the same metrical structure (performed while the chorus reversed its movement) and then by an epode of different structure that was chanted as the chorus stood still. *Compare* STANZA.

structuralism \'strək-chə-rə-ˌliz-əm\ European critical movement of the mid-20th century. It was based on the linguistic theories of Ferdinand de Saussure, which held that language is a self-contained system of signs, and the cultural theories of Claude Lévi-Strauss, which held that cultures, like languages, could be viewed as systems of signs and could be analyzed in terms of the structural relations among their elements. Literary structuralism views literary texts as systems of interlocking signs and seeks to make explicit in a semiscientific way the "grammar" (the rules and codes or system of organization) that governs the form and content of all literature. Michel Foucault, Roman Jakobson, and Roland

Barthes are among the more prominent structuralists. Areas of study that have adopted and developed structuralist premises and procedures are SEMIOTICS and NARRATOLOGY. *Compare* DECONSTRUCTION; POSTSTRUCTURALISM.

study \ˈstəd-ē\ A literary or artistic production intended as a preliminary outline, an experimental interpretation, or an exploratory analysis of specific features (such as those of character or motivation) or characteristics.

Sturm und Drang \ˈshtůrm-ˌůnt-ˈdräŋ\ [German, storm and stress] A German literary movement of the latter half of the 18th century characterized by a revolt against the strictures imposed by the Enlightenment cult of rationalism and the sterile imitation of French literature. It exalted nature, intuition, impulse, instinct, emotion, fancy, and inborn genius as the wellsprings of literature.

Works of the Sturm und Drang movement typically are loosely constructed, written in direct language, and marked by rousing action and high emotionalism. They frequently deal with the individual in revolt against the injustices of society. J.W. von Goethe and Friedrich Schiller began their careers as prominent members of the movement.

The exponents of Sturm und Drang were profoundly influenced by the philosophy of Jean-Jacques Rousseau and Johann Georg Hamann, who held that the basic verities of existence were to be apprehended through faith and the experience of the senses. The young writers also found inspiration in the works of the English poet Edward Young, the pseudo-epic poetry of James Macpherson's "Ossian," and the works of William Shakespeare (which had just been translated into German).

While a student at Strasbourg, Goethe made the acquaintance of Johann Gottfried von Herder, a former pupil of Hamann, who interested him in Gothic architecture, German folk songs, and Shakespeare. Energized by Herder's ideas, Goethe embarked upon a period of extraordinary creativity. In 1773 he published the play *Götz von Berlichingen,* based upon the life of that 16th-century German knight, and he collaborated with Herder and others on the pamphlet "Von deutscher Art und Kunst," which served as a manifesto for the movement. Goethe's novel *Die Leiden des jungen Werthers* (1774; *The Sorrows of Young Werther*), which epitomized the spirit of the movement, made him world famous and inspired a host of imitators.

Dramatic literature was the most characteristic product of Sturm und Drang. Indeed, the very name of the movement was borrowed from the title of a play by Friedrich von Klinger. Inspired by the desire to present on the stage figures of Shakespearean grandeur, Klinger subordinated structural considerations to character and rejected the conventions of French Neoclassicism, which had been imported by the critic Johann Christoph von Gottsched. With the production of *Die Räuber* (1781; *The Robbers*) by Schiller, the drama of Sturm und Drang entered a new phase.

Self-discipline was not a tenet of Sturm und Drang, and the movement soon exhausted itself. Its two most gifted representatives, Goethe and Schiller, went on to produce great works that formed the body and soul of classical German literature.

style \'stīl\ [Latin *stilus* spike, stem, stylus (for writing on wax tablets), style of writing] In literature, a distinctive manner of expression. Since words represent ideas, there cannot be abstract literature unless a collection of nonsense syllables can be admitted as literature. Even the most avantgarde writers associated with the Cubist or nonobjective painters used language, and language is meaning, though the meaning may be incomprehensible. Oscar Wilde and Walter Pater, the great 19th-century exponents of "art for art's sake," were in fact tireless propagandists for their views, which dominate their most flowery prose. The veiled style of Henry James, with its subtleties, equivocations, and qualifications, perfectly reflects his complicated and subtle mind and his abiding awareness of ambiguity in human motives. At the other extreme, the style of the early 20th-century American novelist Theodore Dreiser—bumbling, clumsy, dogged, troubled—perfectly embodies his own attitudes toward life and is, in fact, his constant judgment of his subject matter. Sometimes an author, under the impression that he is simply polishing his style, may completely alter his content. As Gustave Flaubert worked over the drafts of *Madame Bovary,* seeking always the apposite word that would precisely convey his meaning, he lifted his novel from a level of sentimental romance to make it one of the great ironic tragedies of literature. Yet, to judge from his correspondence, he seems never to have been completely aware of what he had done, of the severity of his own irony.

Literature may be an art, but writing is a craft, and a craft must be learned. Talent, special ability in the arts, may appear at an early age; the special personality called genius may indeed be born, not made. But skill in matching intention and expression comes with practice. Naïve writers, "naturals" like the 17th-century English diarist Samuel Pepys, the late 18th-century French naïf Nicolas-Edme Restif, the 20th-century American novelist Henry Miller, are all deservedly called stylists, although their styles are far removed from the deliberate, painstaking practice of a Flaubert or a Ivan Turgenev. They wrote spontaneously whatever came into their heads; but they wrote constantly, voluminously, and were, by their own standards, skilled practitioners.

stylist \'stī-list\ A writer or speaker who is eminent in matters of style.

stylistics \stī-'lis-tiks\ An aspect of literary study that emphasizes the analysis of various elements of style (such as metaphor and diction).

The ancients saw style as the proper adornment of thought. In this view, which prevailed throughout the Renaissance, devices of style can be catalogued. The essayist or orator was expected to frame ideas with the help of model sentences and prescribed types of figures suited to the mode of discourse.

The traditional idea of style as something properly added to thoughts contrasts with the ideas that derive from Charles Bally (1865–1947), the Swiss philologist. According to followers of Bally, style in language arises from the possibility of choice among alternative forms of expression, as, for example, among the synonymous words "children," "kids," "youngsters," and "youths," each of which has a different evocative value. This theory emphasizes the relationship of style to linguistics, as does the theory of Edward Sapir, who talked about literature that is form-based (such as that of Algernon Charles Swinburne, Paul Verlaine, Horace, Catullus, and Virgil, and much of Latin literature) and literature that is content-based (such as that of Homer, Plato, Dante, and William Shakespeare) and the near untranslatability of the former. A linguist, for example, might note the effective placing of dental and palatal spirants in these famous lines from Verlaine:

> Les *s*anglots longs des violons de l'automne
> Ble*ss*ent mon coeur d'une langueur monotone,
> Tout *s*uffocant et blême quand *s*onne l'heure,
> *Je* me *s*ouviens des *j*ours anciens, et *j*e pleure.

The impressionistic "slow, dragging" effect of Edgar Allan Poe's

> On desperate seas long wont to roam

can be made more objective by the linguist's knowledge of the stress contour, or intonation. Here the predominance of the stronger primary and secondary stresses creates the drawn-out interminable effect.

Style is also seen as a mark of character. The Count de Buffon's famous epigram, "Le style est l'homme même" ("Style is the man himself") in his *Discours sur le style* (1753), and Arthur Schopenhauer's definition of style as "the physiognomy of the mind" suggest that, no matter how calculatingly choices may be made, a writer's style will bear the mark of his personality. An experienced writer is able to rely on the power of his habitual choices of sounds, words, and syntactic patterns to convey his personality or fundamental outlook.

stylometry \stī-ˈläm-ə-trē\ [*style* + *-metry* (as in *craniometry*)] The statistical study—based especially on analysis of the recurrence of particular turns of expression or trends of thought—of the literary style of an author or work.

suasoria \swä-ˈsȯr-ē-ə\ *plural* suasoriae \-ē-ˌē, -ˌī\ [Latin, from feminine of *suasorius* persuasive, from *suasus* + *-orius* -ory] An ancient Roman form of oration dealing with a problem of conscience. The writer Seneca (the Elder) was a notable writer of suasoriae.

sublime \sə-ˈblīm\ In literary criticism, grandeur of thought, emotion, and spirit that characterizes great literature. It is the topic of *On The Sublime,* an incomplete treatise dated to the first century AD attributed to Longinus.

The author of *On the Sublime* defines sublimity as "excellence in language," the "expression of a great spirit," and the power to provoke "ecstasy." Departing from traditional classical criticism, which sought to attribute the success of literary works to their balance of certain technical elements—diction, thought, metaphor, music, etc.—he saw the source of the sublime in the moral, emotional, and imaginative depth of the writer and its expression in the flare-up of genius that rules alone could not produce.

The concept had little influence on modern criticism until the late 17th and 18th centuries, when it had its greatest impact in England. Its vogue there coincided with renewed interest in the plays of William Shakespeare, and it served as an important critical basis for Romanticism.

subliterature \ˌsəb-ˈlit-ə-rə-ˌchu̇r, - chər, -ˌtyu̇r\ Popular writing (such as mystery or adventure stories) considered inferior to standard literature.

subplot \ˈsəb-ˌplät\ In fiction or drama, a story line or plot that is subordinate to the main plot.

substitution \ˌsəb-stə-ˈtü-shən, -ˈtyü-\ **1.** In Greek or Latin prosody, the replacement of a prosodic element that is required or expected at a given place in a given meter by another which is more or less equivalent in temporal quantity. **2.** In modern prosody, the use within a metrical series of a foot other than the prevailing foot of the series. A silence may also replace expected sound and occupy the time of a foot or syllable. The early American poet Anne Bradstreet used substitution to great effect in the following lines from "The Author to Her Book":

> I stretched thy joints to make thee even feet,
> Yet still thou run'st more hobbling than is meet;

Compare INVERSION; IONIC.

subtext \ˈsəb-ˌtekst\ [probably translation of Russian *podtekst*] Of a literary text, the implicit or metaphorical meaning.

subtitle \ˈsəb-ˌtīt-əl\ A secondary or explanatory title. Such titles can explain the form of the work, as in Samuel Taylor Coleridge's *Remorse: A Tragedy, in Five Acts;* they can give an idea of the theme or contents of the book, as in George Eliot's *Middlemarch: A Study of Provincial Life;* or they can be an alternate title, which may or may not be a comment on the work, such as *Pamela; or, Virtue Rewarded* by Samuel Richardson and Mary Shelley's *Frankenstein; or, the Modern Prometheus.*

supercommentary \ˌsü-pər-ˈkäm-ən-ˌtar-ē\ A commentary upon a commentary.

superfluous man [translation of Russian *lishniĭ chelovek*] Character type whose frequent recurrence in 19th-century Russian literature is sufficiently striking to make him a national archetype. He is usually an aristocrat, intelligent, well-educated, and informed by idealism and goodwill but incapable, for reasons as complex as Hamlet's, of engaging in effective action. Although he is aware of the stupidity and injustice surrounding him, he remains a bystander.

The term gained wide currency with the publication of Ivan Turgenev's story "The Diary of a Superfluous Man" (1850). Although most of Turgenev's heroes fall into this category, he was not the first to create the type. Aleksandr Pushkin introduced the type in *Eugene Onegin* (1833), the story of a Byronic youth who wastes his life, allows the girl who loves him to marry another, and lets himself be drawn into a duel in which he kills his best friend. The most extreme example of this character is the hero of Ivan Goncharov's *Oblomov* (1859). An idle, daydreaming noble who lives on the income of an estate he never visits, Oblomov spends all his time lying in bed thinking about what he will do when (and if) he gets up.

The radical critic Nikolay A. Dobrolyubov analyzed the superfluous man as an affliction peculiar to Russia and the by-product of serfdom. Throughout the 19th and early 20th century, the type dominated Russian novels and plays. Despite their inability to act, these men include some of the most attractive and sympathetic characters in literature: Pierre Bezukhov (in Leo Tolstoy's *War and Peace,* 1865–69), Prince Myshkin (in Fyodor Dostoyevsky's *The Idiot,* 1868–69), and several protagonists in the works of Anton Chekhov.

superhero \ˈsü-pər-ˌhir-ō, -ˌhē-rō\ A fictional hero (as in a comic book) having extraordinary or supernatural powers.

Surrealism \sər-ˈrē-ə-ˌliz-əm\ [French *surréalisme,* from *sur-* above, over + *réalisme* realism] The principles, ideals, or practice of producing fantastic or incongruous imagery in art or literature by means of unnatural juxtapositions and combinations. A movement in visual art and literature based on these principles flourished between Wars I and II. Although Surrealism grew principally out of the earlier Dada movement, which before World War I produced works of anti-art that deliberately defied reason, Surrealism's emphasis was not on negation but on positive expression. The movement represented a reaction against what its members saw as the destruction wrought by the "rationalism" that had guided European culture and politics in the past and that had culminated in the horrors of World War I. According to the major spokesman of the movement, the poet and critic André Breton, who published "The Surrealist Manifesto" in 1924, Surrealism was a means of reuniting conscious and unconscious realms of experience so completely that the world of dream and fantasy would be joined to the everyday rational world in "an absolute reality, a surreality."

In the poetry of Breton, Paul Éluard, Pierre Reverdy, Louis Aragon, and others, Surrealism manifested itself in a juxtaposition of words that was startling because it was determined not by logical but by psychological—that is, unconscious—thought processes. Automatic writing was a technique favored by Surrealist writers because of its reliance on the power of the subconscious. The influence of Surrealism can be seen in the works of such later authors as Samuel Beckett, Jean Genet, and other writers of the Theater of the Absurd, the French writers of the *nouveau roman* of the 1950s and '60s, and the various practitioners of the stream-of-consciousness technique.

sutra \'sü-trə\, *Pali* sutta [Sanskrit *sūtram,* literally, thread] In Hinduism, a brief, aphoristic composition summarizing a Vedic precept, or a collection of such compositions.

The early Indian philosophers did not work with written texts and later often disdained the use of them, and the sutras filled the need for explanatory works of the utmost brevity that could be committed to memory. The earliest sutras were expositions of ritual procedures, but their use spread. Pāṇini's grammatical sutras (5th–6th century BC) became in many respects a model for later compositions. All of the Indian philosophical systems (except the Saṃkhyā, which had its *kārikā*s, or doctrinal verses) had their own sutras, most of them preserved in writing early in the Christian era.

In Buddhism, the word *sutra* refers to a more extended exposition, the basic form of the scriptures of both the Theravāda ("Way of Elders") and Mahāyāna ("Greater Vehicle") traditions. Buddhist sutras are doctrinal works, sometimes of considerable length. The most important collection of the Theravāda sutras is to be found in the *Sutta* section of the Pali canon, which contains the discourses attributed to the Gautama Buddha.

swashbuckler \'swäsh-ˌbək-lər, 'swȯsh-\ A novel or drama dealing with the adventures of a swashbuckling hero and usually having a setting in a romantic past era or exotic locale. The protagonist is typically a daredevil, a boasting, violent soldier, an adventurer, or a ruffian.

sweetness and light Phrase used by Matthew Arnold in his book *Culture And Anarchy* to describe the elements of perfection. He equates sweetness with beauty and light with intelligence and says that the objective of culture is to bring all people together harmoniously, living in an atmosphere of sweetness and light. Arnold borrowed the phrase from Jonathan Swift, who, in the "Battle of the Books" section of his *A Tale of a Tub,* compared ancient and modern methods of scholarship and praised the ancients for their search for "The two noblest of things, which are Sweetness and Light."

syllabic verse In prosody, a metrical system based solely on the number of syllables in a line of verse. Syllabic verse is used mainly in Romance languages and in Japanese, although such English poets as Dylan Thomas, W.H. Auden, and Marianne Moore have experimented with the form. *See also* METER.

syllepsis \si-'lep-sis\ *plural* syllepses \-ˌsēz\ [Greek *sýllēpsis,* literally, taking together, inclusion, a derivative of *syllambánein* to take together, comprehend] **1.** The use of a word to modify or govern syntactically two or sometimes more words with only one of which it formally agrees in gender, number, or case, as in "the pineapple was eaten and the apples neglected." **2.** The use of a word in the same grammatical relation to two adjacent words but with a different meaning for each, as in the sentence "The tank fired, and the bridge and many hopes sank." *See also* ZEUGMA.

symbol \'sim-bəl\ [Greek *sýmbolon* token of identity verified by comparing its other half, sign, symptom, a derivative of *symbállein* to throw together, compare] Something that stands for or suggests something else by reason of relationship, association, convention, or accidental resemblance; especially, a visible sign of something invisible (for example, the lion is a symbol of courage and the cross is a symbol of Christianity). In this sense all words can be called symbols, but the examples given—the lion and the cross—are really metaphors: that is, symbols that represent a complex of other symbols, and which are generally negotiable in a given society (just as money is a symbol for goods or labor). These are considered public symbols in that they are universally recognized. The symbols used in literature are often of a different sort: they are private or personal in that their significance is only evident in the context of the work in which they appear. For instance, the optician's trade sign of a huge pair of spectacles in F. Scott Fitzgerald's *Great Gatsby* (1925) is acceptable as a piece of scenic detail, but it can also be taken as a symbol of divine myopia. Similarly, a cinema poster in Malcolm Lowry's *Under the Volcano* (1947), advertising a horror film, can be read as naturalistic background, but it is evident that the author expects the illustrated fiend—a concert pianist whose grafted hands are those of a murderer—to be seen also as a symbol of Nazi infamy; the novel is set at the beginning of World War II, and the last desperate day of the hero, Geoffrey Firmin, stands also for the collapse of Western civilization.

Symbol is distinguished from allegory in that the allegorical figure has no meaning apart from the idea it is meant to indicate within the structure of the allegory, whereas a symbol has a meaning independent of the rest of the narrative in which it appears. A symbol can also have more than one meaning while the meaning of an allegorical figure is clear and specific to the rest of the allegory. *Compare* ALLEGORY.

Symbolist movement \'sim-bə-list\ Literary and artistic movement that originated with a group of French poets in the late 19th century, spread to painting and the theater, and influenced Russian, European, and American literature of the 20th century to varying degrees. Symbolist artists sought to express individual emotional experience through the subtle and suggestive use of highly metaphorical language. Because of their interest in the bizarre and the artificial and in themes of decay and ruin, many of the Symbolist poets were identified with the Decadent movement of the same period.

The principal Symbolist poets included Stéphane Mallarmé, Paul Verlaine, Arthur Rimbaud, Jules Laforgue, Henri de Régnier, Gustave Kahn, Émile Verhaeren, Georges Rodenbach, Jean Moréas, and Francis Viélé-Griffin. Rémy de Gourmont was the principal Symbolist critic. Symbolist criteria were applied most successfully to the novel by Joris-Karl Huysmans and to the theater by Maurice Maeterlinck. The French poets Paul Valéry and Paul Claudel are sometimes considered to be direct 20th-century heirs of the Symbolists.

Symbolism originated in the revolt of certain French poets against the rigid conventions governing both technique and theme in traditional French poetry, as seen in the precise description of Parnassian poetry. The Symbolists wished to liberate poetry from its expository functions and its formalized oratory in order to evoke the fleeting, immediate sensations of human experience and the inner life. They sought to communicate the underlying mystery of existence through a free and highly personal use of metaphors and images that, though lacking in precise meaning, would nevertheless convey the state of the poet's mind and hint at the "dark and confused unity" of an inexpressible reality.

Such Symbolist forerunners as Verlaine and Rimbaud were greatly influenced by Charles Baudelaire, particularly by his poems in *Les Fleurs du mal* (1857; *The Flowers of Evil*). They adopted Baudelaire's concept of the correspondences between the senses and combined this with the Wagnerian ideal of a synthesis of the arts to produce an original conception of the musical qualities of poetry. Thus, to the Symbolists, the theme within a poem could be developed and "orchestrated" by the sensitive manipulation of the harmonies, tones, and colors inherent in carefully chosen words. The Symbolists' attempt to emphasize the essential and innate qualities of the poetic medium was based on their conviction of the supremacy of art over all other means of expression or knowledge.

Such works as Verlaine's *Romances sans paroles* (1874; "Songs Without Words") and Mallarmé's *L'Après-midi d'un faune* (1876; "The Afternoon of a Faun") sparked a growing interest in the nascent innovations of progressive French poets. The Symbolist manifesto itself was published by Moréas in *Le Figaro* on Sept. 18, 1886; in it he attacked the descriptive tendencies of realist theater, naturalistic novels, and Parnassian poetry. He also proposed replacing the term *décadent,* which was used to describe Baudelaire and others, with the terms *symboliste* and *symbolisme*. Mallarmé became the leader of the Symbolists, and his *Divagations* (1897) remains the most valuable statement of the movement's aesthetics. In their efforts to escape rigid metrical patterns and to achieve freer poetic rhythms, many Symbolist poets resorted to the composition of prose poems and the use of vers libre ("free verse"), which has now become a fundamental form of contemporary poetry.

The Symbolist movement also spread to Russia, where Valery Bryusov published an anthology of Russian and French Symbolist poems in 1894–95 entitled *Russkie simvolisty* (1894–95; "Russian Symbolists"). The revival of poetry in Russia stemming from this movement had as its leader Vladimir Sergeyevich Solovyov. His poetry expressed a belief that the world was a system of symbols expressing metaphysical realities. The greatest poet of the movement was Aleksandr Blok, who in *Dvenadtsat* (1918; *The Twelve*) united the Russian Revolution and God in an apocalyptic vision in which 12 Red Army men became apostles of the New World, headed by Christ. Other Russian Symbolist poets were Vyacheslav Ivanovich Ivanov, Fyodor Sologub, Andrey Bely, and Nikolay Gumilyov.

The movement reached its peak among French poets around 1890 and began to enter a precipitous decline in popularity around 1900. The atmospheric, unfocused imagery of Symbolist poetry eventually came to be seen as overrefined and affected, and the term *décadent,* which the Symbolists had once proudly flaunted, became with others a term of derision denoting mere fin-de-siècle preciosity. Symbolist works nonetheless had a strong and lasting influence on much British and American literature in the 20th century. Their experimental techniques greatly enriched the technical repertoire of modern poetry, and Symbolist theories bore fruit both in the poetry of William Butler Yeats and T.S. Eliot and in the modern novel as represented by James Joyce and Virginia Woolf, in which word harmonies and patterns of images often are more important than the narrative.

The 20th-century American critic Edmund Wilson's survey of the Symbolist movement, *Axel's Castle* (1931), is considered a classic of modern literary analysis and the authoritative study of the movement.

Noteworthy examples of Symbolist theater include Villiers de L'Isle-Adam's *Axël* (first performed 1884; definitive edition 1890), Maeterlinck's *Pelléas et Mélisande* (1892; *Pelléas and Mélisande*), with its dreamlike atmosphere, and the highly satirical *Ubu roi* (1896; "King Ubu") by Alfred Jarry. In 1890 the French poet Paul Fort founded the Theatre d'Art, where Symbolist dramas were presented along with readings from ancient and modern poetry. When Fort retired in 1892 Aurélien-François-Marie Lugné-Poe continued Symbolist production at his Théâtre de l'Oeuvre well into the 20th century. *Compare* AESTHETICISM; DECADENT.

synaeresis *See* SYNIZESIS.

synaesthesia *See* SYNESTHESIA.

synaesthesis \ˌsin-is-ˈthē-sis\ [Greek *synaísthēsis* joint perception, awareness, a derivative of *synaisthánesthai* to perceive simultaneously, share in perception, from *syn-* together + *aisthánesthai* to perceive] Harmony of different or opposing impulses produced by a work of art. For example, one is said to experience synaesthesis of thought and feeling in philosophical poetry or the synaesthesis of anxiety and calmness in a tragedy. *See also* SYNESTHESIA.

synaloepha or **synalepha** \ˌsin-ə-ˈlē-fə\ [Greek *synaloiphḗ,* a derivative of *synaleíphein* to clog up, coalesce, unite two syllables into one, from *syn-* together + *aleíphein* to anoint] The reduction to one syllable of two vowels of adjacent syllables (as in *th' army* for *the army*). *Compare* ELISION.

synaphea \ˌsin-ə-ˈfē-ə\ [Greek *synápheia,* literally, connection, union] In classical prosody, metrical continuity between lines, in which the quantity of the last syllable of a line is determined by the beginning of the next line.

syncope \ˈsiŋ-kə-ˌpē, ˈsin-\ [Greek *synkopḗ,* literally, the act of cutting up or cutting short] The omission of one or more sounds or letters within a word in the pronunciation of the word (as in *fo'c'sle* for *forecastle*); also, a form resulting from such a loss of sounds or letters. Syncope is a form of elision, and like elision it is a device that is often used in poetry to fit a word to a particular metrical pattern.

In classical prosody, syncope is a suppression or omission of a short syllable within a metrical foot or measure, usually with compensating protraction of an adjacent long. *See also* ELISION.

synecdoche \si-ˈnek-də-ˌkē\ [Greek *synekdochḗ,* from *syn-* together + *ekdochḗ* understanding in a certain way, interpretation, a derivative of *ekdéchesthai* to receive, understand] Figure of speech in which a part represents the whole, as in the expression "hired hands" for workmen or, less commonly, the whole represents a part, as in the use of the word "society" to mean high society. Closely related to metonymy—the replacement of a word by one closely related in meaning to the original—synecdoche is an important poetic device for creating vivid imagery. An example is Samuel Taylor Coleridge's line in "The Rime of the Ancient Mariner," "The western wave was all aflame," in which "wave" substitutes for "sea." *See also* METONYMY.

syneresis *See* SYNIZESIS.

synesthesia or **synaesthesia** \ˌsin-əs-ˈthē-zhə, -zhē-ə; ˌsin-ēs-ˈthē-zē-ə\ [*syn-* together + *-esthesia* (as in *anesthesia*)] The evocation or transposition of one sense (such as sound) by another (such as vision). The device is much used in both poetry and common speech. In one of the poems from *Façade,* for example, Edith Sitwell refers to "The enormous and gold-rayed rustling sun." In stanza one of Rudyard Kipling's "Mandalay" is the phrase "An' the dawn comes up like thunder."

synizesis \ˌsin-i-ˈzē-sis\ [Greek *synízēsis,* literally, collapse], *also called* syneresis *or* synaeresis \si-ˈner-ə-sis, -ˈnē-rə-\ The contraction of two syllables into one by uniting in pronunciation two adjacent vowels (as when the *ee* of *eleemosynary* is pronounced as one syllable).

system \ˈsis-təm\ In classical prosody, a series with fixed limits, such as a group of two or more periods (i.e., rhythmical units of two or more cola) or a group of verses in the same measure.

systole \ˈsis-tə-lē\ [Greek *systolḗ,* literally, contraction, a derivative of *systéllein* to draw together, contract, reduce] In prosody, the shortening of a syllable that is by pronunciation or by position long. Systole is most often used to adjust the rhythm of a line to achieve metrical regularity. It is the opposite of DIASTOLE.

syzygy \'siz-i-jē\ [Greek *syzygía,* literally, the state of being yoked together, a derivative of *sýzygos* yoked together, united] In Greek or Latin prosody, a group of two coupled feet. Syzygy may be a combination of two differing feet or a foot of four syllables (such as the ionic foot).

T

. . . the essence of dramatic tragedy is not unhappiness. It resides in the solemnity of the remorseless working of things.
—A.N. Whitehead

table talk Informal conversation at or as if at a dining table; especially, the social talk of a celebrity recorded for publication. Collections of such conversations exist from as early as the 3rd century AD, and the term has been in use in English since about the 16th century. The practice of recording conversations and sayings of the famous became especially popular in the 17th century. Such material is especially useful for biographers and can be a form of literary biography in itself. One of the best-known examples of this is James Boswell's biography of Samuel Johnson, which consists mostly of Johnson's own words reproduced by Boswell.

tableau \tab-ˈlō, ˈtab-ˌlō\ *plural* tableaux \tab-ˈlōz, ˈtab-ˌlōz\ also tableaus *same as* tableau *or* tableaux\. [short for *tableau vivant,* from French, literally, living picture] A sustained pose of a depiction of a scene usually presented on a stage by silent and motionless costumed participants.

Tabulatur \ˌtäb-ü-lä-ˈtür\ [German (16th century) *Tablatur, Tabulatur* tablature, set of prescriptive rules, probably from Middle French *tabulature* tablature, Latinization of Italian *intavolatura,* a derivative of *intavolare* to tabulate, systematize] The system of rules for poetic and musical composition that were established by the meistersingers, members of 15th- and 16th-century German guilds of poets and singers.

tag \ˈtag\ **1.** A brief quotation used for rhetorical emphasis or sententious effect. **2.** A rhyming end of a line of verse.

Tagelied \ˈtäg-ə-ˌlēt\ *plural* Tagelieder \-ˌlē-dər\ [German, from Middle High German *tageliet,* literally, day song] A medieval German dawn song, or song of lament by lovers parting at dawn. The *Tagelied* is similar to the Provençal alba and may have been derived from it. The most notable composer of *Tagelieder* was the 13th-century poet Wolfram von Eschenbach.

tailed sonnet A sonnet augmented by additional lines that are arranged systematically and are often shorter than the basic line of the sonnet proper.

tail rhyme or **tailed rhyme** A verse form in which rhymed lines such as couplets or triplets are followed by a tail—a line of different (usually shorter) length that does not rhyme with the couplet or triplet. In a tail-rhyme stanza (also called a tail-rhymed stanza), the tails rhyme with each other.

Taiyō \ˈtī-ˌyō\ ("The Sun") Japanese magazine published from 1895 to 1928 and especially known for its literary criticism, contemporary fiction, and translations of Western authors.

Although *Taiyō* treated various practical, intellectual, and aesthetic subjects, its literary editors Takayama Chogyū (1871–1902) and Hasegawa Tenkei (1876–1940) were especially instrumental in popularizing the literature of late Romanticism and naturalism, both from abroad (in translations of such writers as Edgar Allan Poe, Gustave Flaubert, Guy de Maupassant, Mark Twain, Maurice Maeterlinck, and Leo Tolstoy) and at home in such fiction writers as the naturalists Tokuda Shūsei, Tayama Katai, and Shimazaki Tōson. When naturalism faded, the magazine also faded in importance.

tall tale Narrative that depicts the extravagantly exaggerated wild adventures of North American folk heroes.

The tall tale is essentially an oral form of entertainment; the audience appreciates the imaginative invention rather than the literal meaning of the tales. Associated with the lore of the American frontier, tall tales often explain the origins of lakes, mountains, and canyons; they are spun around such legendary heroes as Paul Bunyan, the giant lumberjack of the Pacific Northwest; Mike Fink, the rowdy Mississippi River keelboatman; and Davy Crockett, the backwoods Tennessee marksman. Other tall tales recount the superhuman exploits of Western cowboy heroes such as William F. Cody and Annie Oakley. Native to the New England region are the tales of Captain Stormalong, whose ship was driven by a hurricane across the Isthmus of Panama, digging the Panama Canal, and Johnny Appleseed, who planted apple orchards from the East Coast to the Western frontier. Washington Irving, in the *History of New York* (1809), and later Mark Twain, in *Life on the Mississippi* (1883), made literary use of the tall tale.

One of the few examples of the tall tale not native to the United States is found in the German collection *Baron Munchausen's Narratives of His Marvellous Travels and Campaigns in Russia* (1785) by the German scholar and adventurer R.E. Raspe. It includes such humorous tales as one about the soldier who loaded his rifle with a cherry pit, fired it into the head of a stag, and later found a cherry tree rooted in its head.

tamāshā \tə-ˈmä-ˌshä\ [Hindi or Marathi, spectacle, entertainment, from Persian, literally, a recreational walk, from Arabic *tamāshī*] Erotic form of Indian folk drama begun in the early 18th century in Mahārāshtra. In all other forms of Indian folk theater, men are cast in the major roles. The leading female role in *tamāshā,* however, is played by a woman. *Tamāshā* plays, which are known to be bawdy, originated as entertainments for encamped armies. In the 20th century they became commercially successful.

Tanizaki Prize \ˌtä-nē-ˈzä-kē\ Japanese literary award given annually to a Japanese writer in recognition of an exemplary literary work. The prize consists of a trophy and one million yen. It was established in honor of Japanese novelist Tanizaki Jun'ichirō in 1965, the year of his death. Winners have included Endō Shūsaku for the novel *Chimmoku* (1966; *Silence*) and Ōe Kenzaburō for *Man'en gannen no futtōbōru* (1967; *The Silent Cry*).

tanka \'täŋ-kä\ [Japanese] A Japanese fixed form of verse of five lines, the first and third of which have five syllables and the others seven. It has historically been the basic form of Japanese poetry, and as such the term tanka is synonymous with the term WAKA, which more broadly denotes all traditional Japanese poetry in classical forms.

Tatler, The \'tat-lər\ Periodical launched in London by the essayist Richard Steele on April 12, 1709, appearing three times weekly until January 2, 1711. At first its avowed intention was to present poetry, foreign and domestic news, and accounts of gallantry, pleasure, and entertainment, all reported and "issued" from various London coffee and chocolate houses. In time *The Tatler* began to investigate manners and society, establishing its principles of ideal behavior, its concepts of a perfect gentleman and gentlewoman, and its standards of good taste. Dueling, gambling, rakish behavior, and coquettishness were criticized, and virtuous action was admired. Numerous anecdotes and stories gave point to the moral codes advanced.

The English periodical essay began to flower in the issues of *The Tatler* written by Steele under the pseudonym of Isaac Bickerstaff and reached full bloom in the hands of Joseph Addison. Two months after *The Tatler* ceased publication, Joseph Addison and Steele launched the brilliant periodical *The Spectator*.

tautology \tȯ-'täl-ə-jē\ [Greek *tautología,* from *tautós* same, identical + *lógos* word, speech] Needless or meaningless repetition in close succession of an idea, statement, or word or an instance of such repetition. The phrase "a beginner who has just started" is a tautology.

telestich \tə-'les-tik, 'tel-ə-ˌstik\ [Greek *têle* far off, at a distance (probably confused with *télos* end) + *stíchos* line] A poem in which the consecutive final letters of the lines spell a word or words. *Compare* ACROSTIC.

Tel Quel \ˌtel-'kel\ French avant-garde literary review published from 1960 to 1982 by Éditions du Seuil. Founded by Philippe Sollers and other young writers, this eclectic magazine published works by such practitioners of the *nouveau roman* ("new novel") as Alain Robbe-Grillet and Nathalie Sarraute, as well as works by these writers' acknowledged predecessors, e.g., James Joyce and Francis Ponge.

Much influenced by surrealism, *Tel Quel* had as a goal the evaluation of 20th-century literature; it printed previously unpublished works by Antonin Artaud, Georges Bataille, and Ezra Pound. The review promoted the renewal of French philosophy and literary criticism through contributions by Michel Foucault, Jacques Derrida, Julia Kristeva, Roland Barthes, and Jacques Lacan. From 1966 to 1970 *Tel Quel* represented a Maoist view of Marxism.

From 1974 the review relinquished political involvement, becoming a supporter of such intellectuals as Bernard-Henri Lévy and André Glucksmann and others in the "new philosophers" movement. The critical orientation of *Tel Quel* shifted toward the classical Greco-Hebrew tradition, including discussion of biblical and theological questions. Its new stance included unequivocal support of worldwide human rights and the beginnings of an appreciation of modern culture, particularly that of the United States.

temporal \'tem-pə-rəl\ In classical prosody, of or relating to the quantity of syllables, or the length of time it takes to pronounce them.

temporalist \'tem-pə-rə-list\ In prosody, one who emphasizes the temporal element in analyzing the rhythmic structures of verse.

tendenz \ten-'dents\ *plural* tendenzen \-'dent-sən\ [German *Tendenz* intention, trend, tendency] A dominating point of view or purpose influencing the structure and content of a literary work.

tenor and vehicle \'ten-ər . . . 'vē-i-kəl, 'vē-ˌhi-\ The components of a metaphor, with the tenor referring to the concept, object, or person meant, and the vehicle being the image that carries the weight of the comparison. The words were first used in this sense by the critic I.A. Richards. In the first stanza of Abraham Cowley's poem "The Wish," the tenor is the city and the vehicle is a beehive:

> Well then; I now do plainly see,
> This busy world and I shall ne'er agree;
> The very honey of all earthly joy
> Does of all meats the soonest cloy;
> And they, methinks, deserve my pity
> Who for it can endure the stings,
> The crowd, and buzz, and murmurings
> Of this great hive, the city.

tension \'ten-chən, -shən\ A balance maintained in an artistic work (such as a poem, painting, or musical composition) between opposing forces or elements; a controlled dramatic or dynamic quality.

In literature the term has been variously used and defined. The poet and critic Allen Tate used it to refer to the elements that are necessary for a work to be considered whole or complete. This sense of tension was derived by Tate from two terms used in logic—extension (literal meaning) and intension (metaphorical meaning)—from which he dropped the prefixes, and it refers to a mutually dependent relationship between these different forms of meaning. The existence of both kinds of meaning creates a conflict or tension that gives poetry its meaning. The term can also refer to a balance between other conflicting structures, such as the rhythm and meter of a poem.

tenson \'ten-sȯn\ or **tenso** \-sō\ or **tenzon** \-zȯn\ [*tenson* from French, from Middle French, from Old Provençal, literally, dispute, quarrel; *tenso* from Provençal, from Old Provençal *tenson*; *tenzon* from Italian *tenzone,* from Old Provençal *tenson*] A lyric poem of dispute or personal abuse composed by Provençal troubadours in which two opponents speak alternate stanzas, lines, or groups of lines usually identical in structure. In some cases these debates were imaginary and both sides were composed by the same person. The tenson was a specific form of débat, a kind of medieval poetic contest. The form later spread to Italy, where it became popular among the poets of the *dolce stil nuovo,* including Dante. *Compare* DÉBAT; PARTIMEN.

teratology \ˌter-ə-'täl-ə-jē\ [Greek *teratología,* from *téras* marvel, monster + *lógos* word, speech, account] **1.** Fantastic mythmaking or storytelling in which unusual events and monsters play a large part. **2.** A collection of such stories.

tercet \'tər-sət\ or **tiercet** \'tir-sət\ [French *tercet,* from Middle French *tiercet,* from Italian *terzetto,* a derivative of *terzo* third] A unit or group of three lines of verse, usually containing rhyme, as in William Shakespeare's "The Phoenix and the Turtle":

> Death is now the phoenix' nest;
> And the turtle's loyal breast
> To eternity doth rest, . . .

The term is often used specifically in reference to the three-line stanzas of the terza rima verse form or to one of the two groups of three lines that form the sestet in a Petrarchan sonnet.

terminal rhyme A rhyme that occurs at the end of two or more successive lines of verse. This is the most common form of rhyme in English poetry.

tertulia \ter-'tü-lē-ä\ A type of Spanish literary salon that was popular in Spain from at least the 17th century and that eventually replaced the more formal academies. *Tertulias* were held in private homes at first, but from the early 19th century they met in clubs and cafés. Some well-known *tertulias* were described in novels and memoirs of the participants, including *La fontana de oro* (1870) by Benito Pérez Galdós and *Pombo* (1918) by Ramón Gómez de la Serna. The popularity of tertulias continued well into the 20th century.

The Spanish word *tertulia,* originally referring to a section of a theater, may be a back formation from *tertuliante* or *tertuliano,* a name for a person frequenting this section. Both words appear to allude to the church father Tertullian (Spanish: *Tertuliano*), but the origin of the allusion is uncertain.

terza rima \'tert-sə-'rē-mə\ [Italian, stanza of three lines, literally, third stanza] A verse form consisting of tercets, or three-line stanzas, in which the second line of each rhymes with the first and third lines of the next. The series ends with a separate line that rhymes with the second line of the last stanza, so that the rhyme scheme is *aba, bcb, cdc, . . . , yzy, z.* In English poems of this form, the meter is often iambic pentameter.

The Italian poet Dante, in his *The Divine Comedy* (*c.* 1310–14), was the first to use terza rima for a long poem, though a similar form had previously been used by the troubadours. After Dante, terza rima was favored in 14th-century Italy, especially for allegorical and didactic poetry, by Petrarch and Giovanni Boccaccio, and in the 16th century for satire and burlesque, notably by Ludovico Ariosto. A demanding form, terza rima has not been widely adopted in languages less rich in rhymes than Italian. It was introduced in England by Sir Thomas Wyatt in the 16th century. Many 19th-century Romantic poets such as Percy Bysshe Shelley (in his "Ode to the West Wind"), Lord Byron, Robert and Elizabeth Barrett Browning, and Henry Wadsworth Longfellow experimented with it. In the 20th century, W.H. Auden used terza rima in *The Sea and the Mirror,* and Archibald MacLeish in *Conquistador,* but with many deviations from the strict form.

testament \ˈtes-tə-mənt\ In literature, a tribute or an expression of conviction, as in Thomas Usk's prose allegory *The Testament of Love* (*c.* 1384) and Robert Bridges' poem *The Testament of Beauty* (1929). A literary testament can also be a kind of last will and testament, a form that was popular in France and England during the 15th century. The mock legacies *Le Petit Testament* and *Le Grand Testament* of François Villon are well-known examples, as is Robert Henryson's *The Testament of Cresseid,* which completes the story of Geoffrey Chaucer's *Troilus and Criseyde.*

tetrabrach \ˈtet-rə-ˌbrak\ [Greek *tetrábrachys,* from *tetra-* four + *brachýs* short] In classical prosody, a metrical foot of four short syllables.

tetracolon \ˌtet-rə-ˈkō-lən\ [Greek *tetrákōlon,* neuter of *tetrákōlos* having four members] In classical prosody, a period made up of four colons, or a unit of four metrical sequences that each constitute a single metrical phrase of not more than about 12 syllables. A tetracolon recurs as a unit within a composition.

tetralogy \te-ˈtral-ə-jē\ [Greek *tetralogía,* from *tetra-* four + *lógos* word, speech, account] **1.** In ancient Greek theater, a group of four dramatic pieces including three tragedies and one satyr play or sometimes four tragedies represented consecutively on the Attic stage at the Dionysiac festival. **2.** A series of four connected works, such as Paul Scott's novel series *Raj Quartet.*

tetrameter \te-ˈtram-ə-tər\ In prosody, a line of four metrical units, either four metra (as in classical verse) or four feet (as in modern English verse).

In English versification, the feet are usually iambs, an unstressed syllable followed by a stressed one, as in the word

Be | cause,

trochees, a stressed syllable followed by an unstressed one, as in the word

tí | gĕr,

or a combination of the two. Iambic tetrameter is, next to iambic pentameter, the most common meter in English poetry; it is used in the English and Scottish traditional ballads, which are usually composed of four-line stanzas of alternating iambic tetrameter and trimeter.

tetrapody \te-ˈträp-ə-dē\ [Greek *tetrapodía,* a derivative of *tetrápous* four-footed, from *tetra-* four + *pod-, poús* foot] In classical prosody, a unit of four metrical feet, or two dimeters.

tetrasemic \ˌtet-rə-ˈsē-mik\ or **tetraseme** \ˈtet-rə-ˌsēm\ [Greek *tetrásēmos* having four time units (in music), from *tetra-* four + *sêma* mark, sign] In classical prosody, consisting of or of the length of four morae, or of the equivalent of four short syllables or two long syllables.

tetrastich \ˈtet-rə-ˌstik\ [Greek *tetrástichos* of four lines, from *tetra-* four + *stíchos* row, line, verse] In prosody, a unit or stanza of four lines.

text \ˈtekst\ [Medieval Latin *textus,* from Latin, interlacing, makeup, structure, a derivative of *texere* to weave, construct] **1.** The original words and form of a written or printed work or an edited or emended copy of an original work. **2.** The main body of printed or written matter on a page, or the principal part of a book exclusive of front and back matter. **3.** A verse or passage of scripture chosen especially as the subject of a sermon or for authoritative support, or a passage from an authoritative source providing an introduction or basis (as for a speech). **4.** The word of something (such as a poem) set to music. **5.** Something written or spoken considered as an object to be examined, explicated, deconstructed, or something likened to a text.

textual criticism The study of a literary work for the purpose of establishing the original form or a single definitive form of its text. *Text* refers to any literary forms preserved in autograph or in transmitted form. Transmitted texts are those whose preserved forms were not written out by the author in any manner. When there is mixture, the transmitted and autograph parts are to be distinguished.

Textual criticism encompasses modern as well as historical works. Sometimes the author's intention may be difficult to discern. William Faulkner's novel *Absalom, Absalom!,* for example, is notorious for the many printing errors caused by the author's reliance on complex typography to represent narrative levels. Occasionally a text is studied to undo deliberate correction or censorship, as in the case of novels by Stephen Crane and Theodore Dreiser and the published journals of Nathaniel Hawthorne. Lack of knowledge of language or subject matter and accidental damage or omission are other causes of variation in texts.

Variation occurs any time a text is transmitted, whether in print, in manuscript, or orally. Early printed books exhibit variation because printers did not emphasize textual accuracy. The problems with the study of manuscript transmission lie in establishing the genealogy of what may be a large number of handwritten versions, each of which is textually unique. Variations are not regarded as error; variation describes only a difference between two readings. Factors in the reconstruction of an authoritative original include the amount of time taken to copy, the date of the copy in relation to that of the original, and the existence of an extant original. When a text was originally transmitted orally—as were Homeric texts or the Provençal poets—critics often cannot reconstruct an "original" but must assume a common source.

Textual criticism remains an art of intuition and conjecture. It proceeds in three steps. The first is recension—the reconstruction, from surviving evidence, of the earliest form or forms of the text. The second step is examination, the attempt to determine if any of the transmitted variants are "authentic" (what the author intended). The third step is emendation, the restoration of the established text to a state approximating an authorial fair copy, a step that frequently requires conjecture.

The term textual criticism is also used to denote a critical study of literature emphasizing a close reading and analysis of the text. *See also* DECONSTRUCTION; NEW CRITICISM.

texture \'teks-chər\ The concrete, physical elements of prose or poetry that are separate from the structure or argument of the work. Such elements include metaphor, imagery, meter, and rhyme. The distinction between structure and texture is associated particularly with the New Critics, especially John Crowe Ransom.

textus receptus \'teks-təs-ri-'sep-təs\ [New Latin, literally, received text] The generally accepted text of a literary work (such as the Greek New Testament).

theater-in-the-round *plural* theaters-in-the-round *also called* arena theater. A theater in which the stage is located in the center of the auditorium.

Theater of Cruelty Project for an experimental theater that was proposed by the French poet, actor, and theorist Antonin Artaud and that became a major influence on avant-garde 20th-century theater. Artaud formulated a theory for what he called a Theater of Cruelty in a series of essays published in *La Nouvelle Revue Française* and collected in 1938 as *Le Théâtre et son double* (*The Theatre and Its Double*).

Artaud believed that civilization had turned people into sick and repressed creatures and that the true function of the theater was to rid them of these repressions and liberate their instinctual energy. He proposed removing the barrier of the stage between performers and audience and producing mythic spectacles that would include verbal incantations, groans and screams, pulsating lighting effects, and oversized stage puppets and props. Although only one of Artaud's plays, *Les Cenci* (1935), based on works by Percy Bysshe Shelley and Stendhal, was ever produced to illustrate these theories, his ideas influenced the productions of Jean-Louis Barrault, Jerzy Grotowski, Jean Vilar, and The Living Theatre as well as the work of such playwrights as Arthur Adamov, Jean Genet, and Jacques Audiberti.

Theater of Fact *also called* documentary theater, *German* Dokumentartheater *or* dokumentarisches Theater. German dramatic movement that arose during the early 1960s, associated primarily with Rolf Hochhuth, Peter Weiss, and Heinar Kipphardt. Their political plays examined recent historical events, often through official documents and court records. Their concern that the West, and especially Germany, was forgetting the horrors of the Nazi era led them to explore themes of guilt and responsibility in recent history. Hochhuth's *Der Stellvertreter* (1963; U.K. title, *The Representative;* U.S. title, *The Deputy*) indicts Pope Pius XII for not taking a public stand against the Nazi extermination of the Jews; Weiss' *Die Ermittlung* (1965; *The Investigation*) presents extracts from official hearings on the Auschwitz concentration camp; and Kipphardt's *In der Sache J. Robert Oppenheimer* (1964; *In the Matter of J. Robert Oppenheimer*) re-creates the American inquiry into Oppenheimer's loyalty because of his opposition to the development of the hydrogen bomb.

Theater of Fact playwrights sought to cut through official versions of recent history by using the techniques of advocacy journalism and by a reliance on edited documentary sources. Their work stimulated political drama in Europe and North America, and plays dealing with the Vietnam War, the Chicago Conspiracy Trial, the Pueblo incident, and other such events appeared throughout the 1970s.

Theater of the Absurd The collection of dramatic works of certain European and American dramatists of the 1950s and early '60s who embraced Albert Camus' assessment, in his essay *Le Mythe de Sisyphe* (1942; *The Myth of Sisyphus*), that the human situation is essentially absurd, devoid of purpose. The term is also loosely applied to those dramatists and the production of those works. Though no formal absurdist movement existed as such, dramatists as diverse as Samuel Beckett, Eugène Ionesco, Jean Genet, Arthur Adamov, Harold Pinter, and a few others shared a vision of a hopeless, bewildered, and anxious humanity struggling vainly to find a purpose and to control its fate.

The ideas that informed the plays also dictated their structure. Absurdist playwrights ignored most of the logical structures of traditional theater. Dramatic action as such is negligible; what action occurs only serves to underscore the absence of meaning in the characters' existence. In Beckett's *En attendant Godot* (*Waiting for Godot*), first performed 1953, plot is eliminated, and a timeless, circular quality emerges as two lost creatures spend their days waiting—but without any certainty of whom they are waiting for or of whether that person will ever come. Language in absurdist plays is often dislocated, full of clichés, puns, repetitions, and non sequiturs. The characters in Ionesco's *La Cantatrice chauve* (*The Bald Soprano*), first performed in 1950, sit and talk, repeating the obvious until it sounds like nonsense, thus revealing the inadequacies of verbal communication. The combination of purposeless behavior and ridiculous conversation gives the plays a sometimes dazzling comic surface, but there is an underlying message of metaphysical distress.

Initially shocking in its flouting of theatrical convention while popular for its apt expression of the preoccupations of the mid-20th century, the Theater of the Absurd had lost some of its shock value by the mid-1960s. Many of its innovations were absorbed into mainstream theater; other elements inspired a new avant-garde to further experimentation.

Théâtre de l'Oeuvre \tā-ˈȧtr-də-ˈlœ̄vr, *Angl* tā-ˈät-rə-də-ˈlər-vrə\ French Symbolist theater founded in Paris in 1893 by Aurélien-François-Marie Lugné-Poe and directed by him until 1929. Assisted by the poet and critic Camille Mauclair and the painter Édouard Vuillard, Lugné-Poe dedicated the Théâtre de l'Oeuvre to presenting the work of the young French Symbolist playwrights and introducing major foreign dramas. He produced works by Maurice Maeterlinck, Oscar Wilde, Gerhart Hauptmann, and Gabriele D'Annunzio and was instrumental in introducing Henrik Ibsen's plays to France. Alfred Jarry's nihilistic farce *Ubu roi* ("King Ubu") premiered there in 1896.

Lugné-Poe sought to create a unified nonrealistic theater of poetry and dreams through atmospheric staging and stylized acting. He closed the Théâtre de l'Oeuvre in 1899 but revived it in 1912 and again for a time after World War I. He continued to produce the works of new French playwrights, such as Paul Claudel, and those of Dadaist and Surrealist writers.

Théâtre de Vieux-Colombier \tā-ˈȧtr-də-ˌvyœ̄-kō-lȯ^{n}-ˈbyā\ French experimental theater founded in Paris in 1913 by writer and critic Jacques Copeau to present alternatives to both the realistic "well-made" plays of the time and the star system of actor-celebrities. Copeau sought to renovate French theater by focusing attention on the actor, whom he viewed as the essential element in translating the dramatic text into the "poetry of the theater." Copeau and Louis Jouvet designed a small (400-seat) theater with a permanent stage setting and without the proscenium that separated actors and audience. After Copeau's departure in 1924 the theater was used by various acting companies and for showings of avant-garde cinema. In 1961 it was renamed the Theatre de Vieux-Colombier–Jacques Copeau.

Théâtre-Français, Le *See* COMÉDIE-FRANÇAISE.

Theatre Guild A theatrical society founded in New York City in 1918 for the production of high-quality, noncommercial American and foreign plays. The guild, founded by Lawrence Langner, departed from the usual theater practice in that its board of directors shared the responsibility for choice of plays, management, and production. The first two seasons included plays by Jacinto Benavente y Martínez, Saint John Ervine, John Masefield, and August Strindberg.

Following the world premiere of George Bernard Shaw's *Heartbreak House* in 1920, the guild became Shaw's American agent, producing 15 of his plays, including world premieres of *Back to Methuselah* and *Saint Joan.* Eugene O'Neill's long association with the guild began with its production of *Marco Millions* in 1928. Other American authors whose works were produced by the guild included Sidney Howard, William Saroyan, Maxwell Anderson, and Robert Sherwood—all Pulitzer Prize winners. Many distinguished actors appeared in Theatre Guild productions, including Helen Hayes in *Caesar and Cleopatra* and Alla Nazimova in *Mourning Becomes Electra.* Lynn Fontanne and Alfred Lunt first acted as a team there in Ferenc Molnár's *Guardsman* and went on to act together in many other notable guild productions, such as *Arms and the Man* and *The Taming of the Shrew.*

The Theatre Guild contributed to American musical theater by producing George Gershwin, Ira Gershwin, and DuBose Heyward's *Porgy and Bess* and by bringing Richard Rodgers and Oscar Hammerstein II together for such collaborations as *Oklahoma!* The "Theatre Guild of the Air" (1945–63) successfully produced plays for radio and television.

theatricalism \thē-ˈat-ri-kə-ˌliz-əm\ In 20th-century Western theater, the general movement away from the dominant 19th-century techniques of naturalism in acting, staging, and playwriting; it was especially directed against the illusion of reality that was the highest achievement of the naturalist theater.

The theatricalists accepted the obvious truth that the playgoers were in a theatre and that actors were on a stage, carrying out dramatic action with the help of settings that were obviously scenic constructions illuminated by stage lights. For a stage, they favored a platform projecting into the audience in order to put the actor in direct contact with the spectators and remove the psychological barriers between them. They believed that the abolition of such barriers between actors and audience served to reestablish full dramatic communication between them.

Theatricalism attracted designers such as Gordon Craig in England and Robert Edmond Jones and Norman Bel Geddes in the United States. It appealed to such directors as Max Reinhardt and Leopold Jessner in Germany, Jacques Copeau, Louis Jouvet, A.M. Lugné-Poe, Charles Dullin, Gaston Baty, and Georges Pitoëff in France, and Vsevolod Meyerhold, Aleksandr Tairov, and Yevgeny Vakhtangov in the Soviet Union.

Even after the extreme stylization of acting and staging found in the Expressionist, Dadaist, and Surrealist drama of the early part of the century had subsided, theatricalism's frank acceptance of dramatic artifices remained a permanent part of the modern theater.

theme \ˈthēm\ The dominant idea of a work of literature.

thesis \ˈthē-sis\ *plural* theses \-ˌsēz\ [Greek *thésis* act of placing or laying down, lowering of the foot in keeping time] In prosody, the unaccented or shorter part of a poetic foot. Originally, in Greek poetry, the thesis was the accented part of the foot, but in Latin prosody it came to mean the unaccented part and this meaning has been retained in modern usage. *Compare* ARSIS.

thesis novel *See* PROPAGANDA NOVEL.

thesis play *See* PROBLEM PLAY.

third person *See* POINT OF VIEW.

thread of life The course of individual existence especially as fabled in ancient times to be spun and cut by the Fates.

threnody \'thren-ə-dē\ [Greek *thrēnōidía,* from *thrênos* lamentation, dirge + *ōidḗ* song] A song, poem, composition, or speech of lamentation especially for the dead, similar to a DIRGE or ELEGY.

thriller \'thril-ər\ One that produces thrills; especially a work of fiction or drama designed to hold the interest by the use of a high degree of intrigue, adventure, or suspense.

ticket name *See* TYPE NAME.

tiercet *See* TERCET.

time-shift A narrative method that shifts back and forth in time from past to present instead of proceeding in strict chronological sequence.

Times Literary Supplement *abbreviation* TLS. Weekly literary journal long famous for its coverage of all aspects of literature and widely considered one of the finest literary reviews in the English language. Founded in 1902 as a supplement to *The Sunday Times* of London, TLS sets the tone and standards of excellence in the field of literary criticism. It presents reviews of major books of fiction and nonfiction published in every language, and its essays are written with sophistication and scholarly authority and in a lively style. It is also noted for its bibliographic thoroughness, for its topical essays by the world's leading scholars, and for the erudition of its readers' published letters to the editor.

title page A page of a book bearing the title and usually the names of the author, editor, or translator (if any) and the publisher and sometimes the place and date of publication. The title page may also carry the edition number if the book is a new edition of a previously published work.

tmesis \tə-'mē-sis, 'mē-sis\ [Late Latin, from Greek *tmêsis* act of cutting] Separation of parts of a compound word by the intervention of one or more words (as in *what place soever* for *whatsoever place*).

topographical poetry Verse genre characterized by the description of a particular landscape. A subgenre, the prospect poem, details the view from a height. The form was established by John Denham in 1642 with the publication of his poem *Cooper's Hill.* Topographical poems were at their peak of popularity in the 17th and 18th centuries, though there are examples from the early 19th century, including several poems by George Crabbe, as well as by such modern writers as John Betjeman and Ted Hughes.

topos \ˈtō-ˌpäs, ˈtä-\ *plural* topoi \-ˌpȯi\ [Greek *tópos,* short for *koinòs tópos,* literally, common place] A conventional literary or rhetorical theme such as the quest or the family.

tornada \tȯr-ˈnäd-ə\ [Old Provençal, from feminine of *tornat,* past participle of *tornar* to turn, return] The refrain of a Provençal poem.

toughie or **toughy** \ˈtəf-ē\ *plural* toughies. A piece of writing characteristic of HARD-BOILED FICTION.

tract \ˈtrakt\ [Middle English *tracte,* modification of Latin *tractatus* action of handling, treatment, discussion] A pamphlet or leaflet of political or religious propaganda.

tractarian \trak-ˈtar-ē-ən\ One who writes, prints, or distributes tracts.

Tractatus Coislinianus \trak-ˈtā-təs-ˌkȯis-ˌlin-e-ˈā-nəs\ Statement of a Greek theory of comedy found in a 10th-century manuscript (published 1839) in the collection of Henri Charles du Cambout de Coislin. The treatment of comedy displays marked Aristotelian influence, even to the point of paralleling the model offered in the *Poetics*. The *Tractatus* is assumed to be either a version of a lost Aristotelian original or a statement of the Aristotelian tradition. Accordingly, as Aristotle stated that tragedy should bring about a catharsis through the arousal of feelings of "terror and pity," comedy must bring about a catharsis through the use of laughter and pleasure. Comic plots include ludicrous mishaps, deception, unexpected developments, and clumsy dances. Characters include impostors, self-deprecators, and buffoons. While the language of comedy should be realistic, it may attain added comic force through the use of puns, dialect, and word malformations.

tradición \ˌträ-dē-ˈsyōn\ [Spanish, literally, tradition] In Latin-American literature, genre of light, short prose sketch in which a historical incident is related in an imaginative and literary style. An evocation of the South American past, the *tradición* may be set in the pre-colonial era, the age of discovery and conquest, the pre-revolutionary era of romance and political intrigue, or the time of the struggle for self-determination in the 19th century. Stimulated by the Romanticists' search for national roots, the Peruvian writer Ricardo Palma created the genre; his *Tradiciones peruanas* (first series, 1872), an entertaining six-volume collection of anecdotes from five centuries of South American history, contains some of the most representative examples of the form.

tradition \trə-ˈdish-ən\ A set of literary or artistic rules or conventions (as of theme, style, symbolism) that is handed down from generation to generation. A writer can be said to be working in a certain tradition, such as the Scottish ballad tradition. Similarly, a specific work or type of writing can belong to a tradition; heroic poetry, for example, is said to be part of the oral tradition. In a more general sense tradition can be seen as the whole of the inherited past or as a continuum into which every writer fits at some point.

tragedy \'traj-ə-dē\ [Greek *tragōidía,* a derivative of *tragōidós* singer in a tragic chorus, performer in tragedy, from *trágos* he-goat + *-ōidos,* a derivative of *aeídein* to sing] A drama of a serious and dignified character that typically describes the development of a conflict between the protagonist and a superior force (such as destiny, circumstance, or society) and reaches a sorrowful or disastrous conclusion. By extension the term may be applied to other literary forms, such as the novel. *Compare* COMEDY.

The origins of the tragic form are Greek, as are those of the term itself, meaning "goat-song" and possibly referring originally to the sacrifice of a goat in the vegetation and fertility rituals associated with the god Dionysus, in whose honor tragedies were performed. To begin with, it seems, these rituals were celebrated in movement and song by a chorus. Later an individual emerged from the chorus to engage in dialogue with it. Aeschylus is credited with the innovation of isolating a second speaker so that dialogue between characters became possible. By the time of Sophocles and Euripides it had become customary for up to three characters to appear on stage at once. The materials of Greek tragedy were drawn from familiar myths of gods and mortals found in the works of Homer and elsewhere; this familiarity focused the dramatic interest on the presentation of the changing awareness and responses of those involved, rather than on plot. Major events, especially death, tended to happen offstage and to be reported and commented on rather than presented directly. The plot, as in Sophocles' *Oedipus the King,* often traces the stages by which the hero or heroine becomes involved in an intolerable and ultimately inescapable situation. Prompted by will or circumstance, fatal ignorance, or binding obligation, the tragic protagonist is confronted in the end by an inexorable fate that ensures an unhappy outcome. In his *Poetics,* Aristotle stated that tragedy should imitate actions that arouse pity and fear and bring about the proper purgation (catharsis) of those emotions.

Roman adaptations of Greek tragedy, particularly by Seneca, tended toward violent sensation and declamatory rhetoric, qualities that were taken up in Elizabethan tragic drama. For Chaucer and the European Middle Ages, tragedy came to mean simply the edifying account of how a great man's fortunes altered from initial prosperity to final wretchedness. Elizabethan England produced a specific type known as the revenge tragedy, of which Thomas Kyd's *The Spanish Tragedie* is an example. Christopher Marlowe's *Tamburlaine the Great* and *Doctor Faustus* introduced the overambitious hero, awe-inspiring in his ambition and magnificent even in his fall. Shakespearean tragedy incorporates elements of the drama of the time but goes further in presenting an imaginative vision of evil and of the resources with which men and women confront it in their extremity.

Seventeenth-century French classical tragedy, unlike Elizabethan tragedy, self-consciously returned both to the legendary subject matter and to the highly conventionalized unities of time, place, and action attributed to Greek tragedy by Aristotle and later critics. The gods of the Greek pantheon became literary and conventional—as represented in the theater of Jean Racine and Pierre Corneille— but the sense of tragic necessity remained; individuals, often confronted with intolerable choices such as that between love and duty, were shown to have achieved human dignity even in keen personal anguish.

A new kind of tragedy emerged in the 19th century in the plays of Henrik Ibsen, August Strindberg, and Anton Chekhov. Written in prose rather than formal verse, they treated painful contemporary situations. Ibsen explored invididual frustration and Strindberg explored compulsive but destructive sexuality, while Chekhov examined the boredom and emptiness of privileged lives in a decaying social order. Tragedy in its fullest dimensions is rarely conspicuous in 20th-century drama, though the American playwright Eugene O'Neill wrote many undeniably successful tragedies. Tragedy did assume prominence in the novel, particularly through such novelists as Fyodor Dostoyevsky, Thomas Hardy, Joseph Conrad, and William Faulkner. *See also* DOMESTIC TRAGEDY; REVENGE TRAGEDY; SENECAN TRAGEDY.

tragic flaw A flaw that brings about the protagonist's downfall. *See* HAMARTIA.

tragicomedy \ˌtraj-i-ˈkäm-ə-dē\ A literary genre consisting of dramas that combine tragic and comic elements with the tragic predominating. Also, a drama of this genre.

When coined by the Roman dramatist Plautus in the 2nd century BC, the Latin word *tragicocomoedia* denoted a play in which gods and mortals, masters and slaves reverse the roles traditionally assigned to them, gods and heroes acting in comic burlesque and slaves adopting tragic dignity. This startling innovation may be seen in Plautus' *Amphitruo*.

In the Renaissance, tragicomedy became a genre of play that mixed tragic elements into drama that was mainly comic. The Italian writer Battista Guarini defined tragicomedy as having most of tragedy's elements—e.g., a certain gravity of diction, the depiction of important public events, and the arousal of compassion—but never carrying the action to tragedy's conclusion, and judiciously including such comic elements as low-born characters, laughter, and jests. Central to this kind of tragicomedy were danger, reversal, and a happy ending. Despite its affront to the strict Neoclassicism of the day, which forbade the mixing of genres, tragicomedy flourished, especially in England. John Fletcher provides a good example of the genre in *The Faithful Shepherdess* (1609?), itself a reworking of Guarini's *Il pastor fido* ("The Faithful Shepherd"), first published in 1590. Nineteenth-century Romantic writers—such as Georg Büchner and Victor Hugo—espoused William Shakespeare's use of tragicomedy in the belief that his plays closely mirrored nature and they used his plays as a model for their works.

With the advent of realism later in the 19th century, the comic interludes of tragicomedy highlighted the ironic counterpoints inherent in a play, making the tragedy seem even more devastating. Such works as Henrik Ibsen's *Ghosts* (1881) and *The Wild Duck* (1884) reflect this technique. Modern tragicomedy is sometimes used synonymously with absurdist drama, which suggests that laughter is the only response left to people who are faced with the tragic emptiness and meaninglessness of existence. Examples of this modern type of tragicomedy are Samuel Beckett's *Endgame* (1958) and Harold Pinter's *The Dumb Waiter* (1960).

Transcendentalism \ˌtran-sen-ˈden-tə-ˌliz-əm\ Movement of writers and philosophers in 19th-century New England who were loosely bound together by adherence to an idealistic system of thought based on a belief in the essential unity of all creation, the innate goodness of humankind, and the supremacy of insight over logic and experience for the revelation of the deepest truths. The writings of the Transcendentalists and those of contemporaries such as Walt Whitman, Herman Melville, and Nathaniel Hawthorne, for whom they prepared the ground, represent the first flowering of the American artistic genius and introduced the American Renaissance in literature.

Sources to which the New England Transcendentalists turned in their search for a liberating philosophy were German transcendentalism, especially as it was refracted by Samuel Taylor Coleridge and Thomas Carlyle; Platonism and Neoplatonism; the Indian and Chinese scriptures; and the writings of such mystics as Emanuel Swedenborg and Jakob Böhme. Eclectic and cosmopolitan in its sources and part of the Romantic movement, New England Transcendentalism originated in the area around Concord, Mass., and from 1830 to 1855 represented a battle between the younger and older generations and the emergence of a new national culture based on native materials. It attracted such diverse and highly individualistic figures as Ralph Waldo Emerson, Henry David Thoreau, Margaret Fuller, Orestes Brownson, Elizabeth Palmer Peabody, and James Freeman Clarke, as well as George Ripley, Bronson Alcott, the younger W.E. Channing, and W.H. Channing. Emerson and Margaret Fuller founded *The Dial* (1840–44), the prototypal "little magazine" wherein some of the best writings by minor Transcendentalists appeared.

The Transcendentalists rejected the conventions of 18th-century thought and what began in a dissatisfaction with Unitarianism developed into a repudiation of the whole established order. They were leaders in such contemporary reform movements as utopian schemes for communal living (Alcott at Fruitlands; Ripley at Brook Farm); suffrage for women; better conditions for workers; temperance for all; modifications of dress and diet; the rise of Free religion; educational innovation; and other humanitarian causes.

transition \tran-ˈsish-ən, -ˈzish-\ English-language literary magazine founded in Paris in 1927 by Eugene and Maria Jolas and Elliot Paul. The magazine, published monthly at first and later quarterly, was dedicated to the original, the revolutionary, and the experimental. Its editors were interested in exploring the role of the unconscious as a source of creation. They published works that used new forms of language to express the world of the imagination, including sections of James Joyce's *Finnegans Wake*. Other authors published in *transition* included Gertrude Stein, Archibald MacLeish, H.D. (Hilda Doolittle), Allen Tate, Samuel Beckett, William Carlos Williams, Ernest Hemingway, Hart Crane, Dylan Thomas, and Franz Kafka. The magazine was an immediate literary success and was published from 1927 to 1930 and 1932 to 1938.

transpose \tranz-ˈpōz, trans-\ To render into another language, style, or manner of expression, or to translate.

transprose \tranz-ˈprōz, trans-\ *archaic* To change from verse into prose.

transumptive \tran-ˈzəmp-tiv, -ˈsəmp-\ [Latin *transumptivus* (used by Quintilian to translate Greek *metálēpsis* use of one word for another), a derivative of *transumere* to take from one position to another] Of, relating to, or characterized by the transfer or substitution of terms. This is equivalent to a metaphorical use of a word, in which one word is used in place of another to suggest an analogy between the two.

transverse \tranz-ˈvərs, trans-\ To turn or render prose into verse.

travel literature Nonfiction prose form that depends largely on the wit, powers of observation, and character of the traveler for its success. In past centuries the traveler tended to be an adventurer or a connoisseur of art, landscapes, or strange customs who may also have been a writer of merit.

The roots of travel literature can be found in the works of ancient Greek geographers, such as Strabo and Pausanias of the 1st and 2nd centuries AD. These were followed by such literary accounts of foreign places as *Il milione* (*Travels*) of Marco Polo and the *Riḥlah* (*Travels*) of the 14th-century Ibn Baṭṭūṭah. Works in a similar vein appeared in the 17th century in the observations of Persia by two French Huguenots, Jean-Baptiste Tavernier and Jean Chardin. Many books of documentary value were written by English gentlemen on their grand tour of Europe. The 18th-century Italian egotist Casanova and his more reliable compatriot Giuseppe Baretti also produced significant travel writings.

The form was particularly suited to the Romantic age. Not only were the Romantics alive to picturesqueness and quaintness but also they were great appreciators of nature. They were eager to study local color and climates and to depict them in the settings for their stories. The record of J.W. von Goethe's journey to Italy in 1786–88 counts more readers than most of his novels. Classics of the genre include *Pismo russkogo puteshestvennika* (1791–92; *Letters of a Russian Traveler, 1789–1790*) by Nikolay Karamzin, one of the earliest documents in the development of Russian Romanticism, *Peterburg* (1913–14) by Andrey Bely, and *Das Reisetagebuch eines Philosophen* (1919; *Travel Diary of a Philosopher*) by Hermann Keyserling. Other travel writers of note include the multinational Lafacadio Hearn, who interpreted Japan with sensitivity and insight. Among the travel books on Italy, there are a few masterpieces including the writings of D.H. Lawrence. Venice, "man's most beautiful artifact," as Bernard Berenson called it, inspired Jean-Jacques Rousseau, François Chateaubriand, Maurice Barrès, and Anatole France. After World War I, there was a yearning for new possibilities of salvation among Europeans, dimly descried in Asia, Russia, or America, and travel literature assumed a metaphysical and semireligious significance. Blaise Cendrars in his novel *Emmène-moi au bout du monde* (1956; "Take Me Away to the End of the World"), epitomizes the urge to seek adventures and a rediscovery of oneself through travels.

The topos of travel, of the protagonist being but a traveler on this earth, has been, from Homer's *Odyssey* onward, one of the most compelling images in literature. An offshoot of the accounts of travelers has been a growing industry of such travel guidebooks as Michelin, Baedeker's, Fodor's, and the Blue Guide.

travesty \'trav-əs-tē\ In literature, the treatment of a noble and dignified subject in an inappropriately light manner. Travesty is a crude form of burlesque in which the original subject matter is changed little but is transformed into something ridiculous through incongruous language and style. An early example of travesty is the humorous treatment of the Pyramus and Thisbe legend in William Shakespeare's play *A Midsummer Night's Dream.* After 1660, travesty became a popular literary device in England as seen in John Phillips' *Don Quixote,* a vulgar mockery of the original work, and Charles Cotton's travesty of Virgil, *Scarronides: or, Virgile Travestie,* an imitation of the French *Virgile travesty* by Paul Scarron. (The use of the word *travesti*—literally, "dressed in disguise"—in the title of Scarron's work gave rise to the English word, first as an adjective.) Later the French developed the *féeries folies,* a musical burlesque that travestied fairy tales. *Compare* BURLESQUE; PARODY.

treatise \'trē-tis, -tiz\ [Middle English *tretis,* from Anglo-French *tretiz,* a derivative of Old French *traitier* to treat] A systematic exposition or argument in writing including a methodical discussion of the facts and principles involved and conclusions reached. The subjects of treatises are often religious, political, philosophical, or scientific. Examples include Geoffrey Chaucer's *Treatise on the Astrolabe,* John Milton's *A Treatise of Civil Power in Ecclesiastical Causes,* and David Hume's *A Treatise of Human Nature.*

treatment \'trēt-mənt\ The manner in which something, such as a subject, is handled in literature, especially in terms of style.

trecento \trā-'chen-tō\ [Italian, literally, three hundred, short for *mille trecento* the year 1300] The 14th century; specifically, the 14th-century period in Italian literature and art.

triad \'trī-ˌad, -əd\ A union or group of three, especially of three closely related persons, beings, or things. In literature the term triad refers specifically to a gnomic literature in medieval Wales and Ireland consisting of short aphorisms grouped in threes. They are written in prose marked by rhythm and assonance and apply to various subjects (such as history, laws, or morals). The term also applies to the structure of a classical ode, which consists of a group of three strophes called the strophe, antistrophe, and epode.

Tribe of Ben \'ben\, *also called* Sons of Ben. A group of young poets and dramatists of the 17th century who were admirers of Ben Jonson, especially his use of classical forms and style. It included many of the Cavalier poets, among them Robert Herrick, Thomas Carew, Sir John Suckling, Richard Lovelace, and Thomas Randolph.

tribrach \'trī-ˌbrak\ [Greek *tríbrachys* having three short syllables, from *tri-* three + *brachýs* short] In classical prosody, a metrical foot of three short syllables. This was usually a resolved iamb (∪ –) or trochee (– ∪), in which the long syllable was broken down into two short ones. The accent was on the first two syllables if the foot was originally a trochee or on the last two if it was originally an iamb.

tricolon \trī-'kō-lən\ [Greek *tríkōlon,* neuter of *tríkōlos* having three members] In classical prosody, a recurrent unit of verse composed of three cola, or a group of three metrical sequences that each constitute a single metrical phrase of not more than about 12 syllables.

trilogy \'tril-ə-jē\ [Greek *trilogía,* from *tri-* three + *lógos* word, speech, account] A series of three dramas or literary or musical compositions that, although each is in one sense complete, have a close mutual relation and form one theme or develop aspects of one basic concept. The term originally referred specifically to a group of three tragedies written by one author for competition. This trilogy constituted the traditional set of plays presented in Athens by a number of competitors at the 5th-century-BC drama festivals known as the Great Dionysia. One of the first authors to present such a trilogy was Aeschylus, whose *Oresteia* is the only surviving example from that time. Modern examples of trilogies include J.R.R. Tolkien's *The Lord of the Rings* and Robertson Davies' *Deptford Trilogy.*

trimeter \'trim-ə-tər\ In prosody, a line of three feet (as in modern English verse) or of three metra, or pairs of feet (as in classical iambic verse). A line of pure iambic trimeter is scanned ∪ – ∪ – ∪ – ∪ – ∪ – ∪ –.

triolet \'trī-ə-let, ˌtrē-ə-'lā\ [Middle French, literally, clover leaf, a derivative of *trefle* clover] A medieval French verse form of eight lines in which the first is repeated as the fourth and seventh and the second as the eighth and the rhyme scheme is *ABaAabAB* (the capital letters indicate the lines that are repeated). The name triolet is taken from the three repetitions of the first line. The great art of the triolet consists in using the refrain line with naturalness and ease and in each repetition slightly altering its meaning, or at least its relation to the rest of the poem. The triolet is preserved in many modern European literatures, especially for light and humorous verse.

Probably invented in the 13th century, the triolet was cultivated as a serious form by such medieval French poets as Adenet le Roi and Jean Froissart. Although its popularity declined in the 15th and 16th centuries, the triolet was revived in the 17th century by Jean de La Fontaine and in the 19th century by

Alphonse Daudet and Théodore de Banville. Triolets are innumerable in French literature and are frequently used in newspapers to give a point and brightness to a brief stroke of satire.

The earliest triolets in English are those of a devotional nature composed in 1651 by Patrick Cary, a Benedictine monk at Douai, France. Reintroduced into English by Robert Bridges in 1873, the triolet has since been cultivated widely in that language, most successfully by Austin Dobson, whose "Rose Kissed Me Today," "I Intended an Ode," and "In the School of Coquettes" are masterpieces of ingenuity and grace.

In Germany, anthologies of triolets were published at Halberstadt in 1795 and at Braunschweig in 1796. Frederich Rassmann made collections in 1815 and 1817 in which he distinguished three species of triolet: the legitimate form; the loose triolet, which only approximately abides by the rules as to number of rhymes and lines; and single-strophe poems, which more or less accidentally approach the true triolet in character. The true form was employed particularly by German Romantic poets of the early 19th century.

triplet \\'trip-lət\\ A unit of three lines of verse. A triplet can be an independent stanza or a group of lines of the same pattern within a stanza of a different pattern, such as three lines that rhyme within a stanza of rhyming couplets. In the latter case, triplets are often set off by a marginal bracket, as in the following lines from John Dryden's *Absalom and Achitophel:*

> His eldest hope, with every grace adorned,
> By me (so Heaven will have it) always mourned,
> And always honored, snatched in manhood's prime
> by unequal fates, and Providence's crime:
> Yet not before the goal of honor won, }
> All parts fulfilled of subject and of son; }
> Swift was the race, but short the time to run. }

Compare TERCET.

tripody \\'trip-ə-dē\\ [Greek *tripodía,* a derivative of *trípous* three-footed, from *tri-* three + *pod-, poús* foot] In classical prosody, a unit or group of three feet. It is used as a measure of trochaic or iambic verse. Trochaic tripody acatalectic is scanned – ∪ – ∪ – ∪, and iambic tripody acatalectic is scanned ∪ – ∪ – ∪ –.

triseme \\'trī-ˌsēm\\ [Greek *trísēmos* having three time units (in music or prosody), from *tri-* three + *sêma* mark, sign] In classical prosody, a foot of three morae (the equivalent of three short syllables) found in answer to one long syllable. It may also be a two- or three-syllable foot (– ∪ ∪ or – ∪ – or – –) that appears associated with and equivalent to the iambic metron ∪ – ∪ –.

tristich \\'tris-tik\\ A strophic unit or stanza of three lines. Edgar Allan Poe used this in his literary criticism, but it is seldom used in the late 20th century. *See* TERCET; TRIPLET.

trithemimer \ˌtrith-ə-ˈmim-ər\ [Greek *trítos* third + *-hēmimerēs* (as in *penthēmimerés* penthemimer)] In classical prosody, a group of three half-feet or a catalectic colon (a colon missing the final syllable) of a foot and a half. Iambic trithemimer scans ∪ – | ∪, trochaic trithemimer scans – ∪ | ∪, and dactylic trithemimer scans – ∪ ∪ | ∪̲ ∪̲.

trithemimeral caesura \ˌtrith-ə-ˈmim-ə-rəl\ *See* CAESURA.

trochaic \trō-ˈkā-ik\ In poetry, of, relating to, or consisting of trochees (feet consisting of a stressed followed by an unstressed syllable in modern poetry or a long followed by a short syllable in classical poetry).

trochee \ˈtrō-kē\ [Greek *trochaîos,* short for *trochaîos poús,* literally, running foot] In prosody, a metrical foot consisting of one long syllable followed by one short syllable in classical verse. In English verse, a trochee is one stressed syllable followed by one unstressed syllable, as in the word

> ´ ∪
> hap | py.

Trochaic meters were extensively used in ancient Greek and Latin tragedy and comedy in a form called trochaic catalectic tetrameter (seven and one half trochees), which was particularly favored by Plautus and Terence. Trochaic meters are not easily adapted to English verse. In long poems, such as Henry Wadsworth Longfellow's *The Song of Hiawatha,* their overall effect is monotonous. But they have been used with great effect in shorter poems, particularly by William Blake, as in his well-known poem "The Tyger":

> ´ ∪ ´ ∪ ´ ∪ ´
> Tyger! | Tyger! | burning | bright
> ´ ∪ ´ ∪ ´ ∪ ´
> In the | forests | of the | night

trope \ˈtrōp\ [Latin *tropus,* from Greek *trópos* figure of speech, manner, style, literally, turn] The use of a word or expression in a figurative sense. *See* FIGURE OF SPEECH.

trot \ˈträt\, *also called* pony. A literal translation of a foreign text.

troubadour or **troubador** \ˈtrü-bə-ˌdȯr, -ˌdu̇r\ [Middle French *troubadour,* from Old Provençal *trobador,* a derivative of *trobar* to compose in verse, invent] One of a class of lyric poets and poet-musicians, often of knightly rank, that flourished from the 11th to the end of the 13th century chiefly in Provence and other regions of southern France, northern Spain, and the north of Italy. They wrote in the *langue d'oc* of southern France and cultivated a lyric poetry intricate in meter and rhyme and usually of a romantic amatory strain. *Compare* TROUVÈRE.

The social influence of the troubadours was unprecedented in the history of medieval poetry. Favored at the courts, they had great freedom of speech, occasionally intervening even in the political arena, but their great achievement was to create around the ladies of the court an aura of cultivation and amenity. Troubadour poetry formed one of the most brilliant schools that ever flourished, and was to influence all later European lyrical poetry.

Much of the troubadours' work has survived, preserved in manuscripts known as chansonniers ("songbooks"), and the rules by which their art was governed are set out in a work called *Leys d'amors* (1340). The verse form they used most often was the canso, consisting of five or six stanzas with a shorter final stanza called an envoi. They also used the *dansa,* or *balada,* a dance song with a refrain; the pastourelle, telling the tale of the love request by a knight to a shepherdess; the *jeu parti,* or débat, a debate on love between two poets; and the alba, or morning song, in which lovers are warned by a night watchman that day approaches and that the jealous husband may at any time surprise them. Other forms included frameworks for a lyrical conversation between two or more persons discussing, as a rule, some point of amorous casuistry or matters of a religious, metaphysical, or satirical character. Troubadour poetry was often set to music, sometimes by the poets themselves. Many of the melodies, however, were furnished by musicians. Most troubador poems have attributions, for the poets valued their originality. As for the music, anonymity was the rule.

trouvère \trü-'ver\ [French, from Old French *troverre, troveor,* a derivative of *trover, trouver* to compose in verse, find] One of a school of poets that flourished in northern France from the 11th to the 14th century. The trouvères were the counterparts in the language of northern France (the *langue d'oïl*) to the Provençal troubadour. The works of the trouvères, including the chansons de geste, are of a prevailingly narrative character. *Compare* TROUBADOUR.

The essence of trouvère rhetoric lies in the combination of traditional themes and the use of established forms in which to express them. The audience gained pleasure from familiarity with these clichés rather than from the poet's originality. It is thus perhaps the least characteristic trouvères who are most appreciated today.

Communication between northern and southern France was facilitated and encouraged by the Crusades and trouvères such as the Châtelaine de Coucy and Conon de Béthune took part in the Crusades. The trouvères, however, developed a lyric poetry distinct from that of the troubadours, and, unlike the latter, they did not prize obscurity of metaphor for its own sake. The poetry of the trouvères was sometimes satirical and sometimes concerned with the pleasures of the good life; but the basic subject of their work was courtly love, in which the poet describes his unrequited passion for an inaccessible lady.

Trouvère lyrics were intended to be sung, probably by the poet alone or with instrumental accompaniment provided by a hired musician. Although originally connected with feudal courts, the trouvères were popular outside aristocratic circles as well, and they tended increasingly to find their patrons in the middle classes. Half the extant trouvère lyrics are the work of a guild of citizen poets of Arras. Many of the trouvères, such as Gace Brûlé (late 12th century), were of aristocratic birth: Thibaut de Champagne (1201–53) was king of Navarre. But others, including Rutebeuf (flourished 1245–85), were of humble origin.

The songs of the trouvères were monophonic (consisting solely of melodic line). The form of the accompaniment is unknown, but it almost certainly included instrumental preludes, postludes, and interludes.

The trouvères used a variety of musical forms, some for any of several of the various poetic categories and some linked to the type of the verse. Four broad categories can be discerned: musical forms based on multiple repetitions of a short phrase, as in a litany; dance songs with refrains; songs based on pairs of repeated lines; and through-composed songs, which used no repetition.

tsa-chü *See* ZAJU.

two-dimensional In literature, lacking depth of characterization.

type name or **ticket name** In dramatic practice, name given to a character to ensure that the personality may be instantly ascertained.

In England the allegorical morality plays of the late Middle Ages presented characters personifying, for example, the seven deadly sins—being named Envy, Sloth, Lust, and so forth. Tudor and Elizabethan dramatists were greatly influenced by the moralities, and Ben Jonson in particular adopted the habit of christening his characters in such a way that whatever "humor" governed them was pointed up. In his play *The Alchemist* are characters named Subtle and Face (two confidence tricksters), Sir Epicure Mammon (a voluptuary), Abel Drugger (a naive tobacconist), and Dol Common (a strumpet). Type names were later a feature of Restoration comedy. In Sir John Vanbrugh's comedy *The Relapse*, there appear, among a gallery of familiar characters with type names, Lord Foppington and his brother Young Fashion. Type names continued to be a fixture of English literature in the latter part of the 18th century, as is evident in some of the characters invented by the dramatist Richard Brinsley Sheridan: Joseph Surface and the dramatist Sir Fretful Plagiary. The most prominent and inventive user of type names in 19th-century English literature was the novelist Charles Dickens, though his are imaginatively suggestive creations rather than explicit labels of a character's occupation, attitudes, or flaws: Josiah Bounderby, Thomas Gradgrind, Mrs. Sparsit, Tulkinghorn, Dr. Blimber, Mrs. Jellyby, and Captain Cuttle. Anthony Trollope and other Victorian novelists also sometimes used type names, especially for comic or flawed characters.

Type names can be found in most other national literatures, and their use has persisted at a diminished level, usually in comedic works or for comic effect.

tz'u *See* CI.

U

Ultima Thule! Utmost Isle!
Here in thy harbors for a while
We lower our sails . . .
—Henry Wadsworth Longfellow

ubi sunt \'ü-bē-'su̇nt\ Derived from the opening words of a number of medieval Latin poems, the term now refers to a verse form in which the poem or its stanzas begin with the Latin words *ubi sunt* ("where are . . .") or their equivalent in another language and which has as a principal theme the transitory nature of all things. A well-known example is François Villon's "Ballade des dames du temps jadis" ("Ballade of the Ladies of Bygone Times"), with its refrain "Mais où sont les neiges d'antan?" ("But where are the snows of yesteryear?").

Ulster cycle \'əl-stər\ or **Ulaid cycle** \'ü-lət͟h^{y}, -ləg^{y}\ In early Irish literature, a group of legends and tales dealing with the heroic age of the Ulaid, a people of northeastern Ireland from whom the English name Ulster ultimately derives. The stories, set in the 1st century BC, were recorded from oral tradition between the 8th and 11th century and are preserved in the 12th-century manuscripts *The Book of the Dun Cow* and *The Book of Leinster* and also in later compilations, such as *The Yellow Book of Lecan* (14th century). They reflect the customs of a free pre-Christian aristocracy who fought from chariots, took heads as trophies, were subject to taboo (*geis*), and were influenced by druids. Mythological elements are freely intermingled with legendary elements that have an air of authenticity. Events center on the reign of the semi-historical King Conor (Conchobar mac Nessa) at Emain Macha (near modern Armagh) and his Knights of the Red Branch (i.e., the palace building in which the heads and arms of vanquished enemies were stored). A rival court at Connaught is ruled by King Ailill and Queen Medb. The chief hero of the Red Branch is the Achilles-like Cú Chulainn, born of a mortal mother, Dechtire, the sister of King Conor, and a divine father, the god Lug (Lugh) of the Long Arm.

Most of the stories are short prose narratives, using verse for description and for scenes of heightened emotion. They fall into types such as destructions, cattle raids, or elopements. The longest tale and the closest approach to an epic is "The Cattle Raid of Cooley," dealing with a conflict between the men of Ulster and of Connaught. One tale portrays the familiar father-son duel, in which Cú Chulainn unknowingly kills his own son, who has come to seek him. Another tale, "Bricriu's Feast," contains a beheading game that is the first appearance in print of a story that was later used in *Sir Gawayne and the Grene Knight* and several other medieval narratives. The tale having the most profound influence on later Irish literature is "The Tragic Death of the Sons of Usnech."

ultima Thule \ˈəl-ti-mə-ˈthü-lē, ˈthyü-lē, ˈthül, ˈthyül\ The furthest possible place in the world, or a remote goal. Thule was the northernmost part of the habitable ancient world. References to ultima Thule in modern literature appear in works by Edgar Allan Poe, Henry Wadsworth Longfellow, and the Australian writer Henry Handel Richardson.

Ultraísmo \ˌül-trä-ˈēz-mō\ or **Ultraism** \ˈəl-trə-ˌiz-əm\ [Spanish *ultraísmo,* a derivative of *ultra-* beyond] Movement in Spanish and Spanish-American poetry after World War I, characterized by a tendency to use free verse, complicated metrical innovations, and daring imagery and symbolism instead of traditional form and content. Influenced by the emphasis on form of the French Symbolists and Parnassians, a distinguished group of poets (*ultraístas*) produced verse that often defied objective analysis and gave the impression of a coldly intellectual experimentation. Launched in Madrid in 1919 by the poet Guillermo de Torre, who coined the name, Ultraísmo found an outlet in the two major avant-garde periodicals, *Grecia* (1919–20) and *Ultra* (1921–22).

Jorge Luis Borges introduced Ultraísmo to South America in 1921. There the movement attracted poets such as the Chileans Pablo Neruda and Vicente Huidobro and the Mexicans Jaime Torres Bodet and Carlos Pellicer. Although the movement had subsided by 1923, the sociopolitical overtones of the writing of the South American *ultraístas,* as seen in the verse of César Vallejo of Peru, flowered into the Marxist poetry of the following decade. Later the verbal techniques of the *ultraístas* were revived by post-World War II avant-garde writers.

Unanimisme \ūē-nȧ-ˈnēz-mᵊ\ or **Unanimism** \yü-ˈnan-i-ˌmiz-əm\ French literary movement based on the psychological concept of group consciousness and collective emotion that posited the need for the poet to merge with this transcendent consciousness. Founded by Jules Romains about 1908, Unanimisme particularly influenced some members of the Abbaye group, a loose organization of young artists and writers who were interested in printing and publicizing new works. *Petit Traité de versification* (1923; "Small Treatise on Versification"), by Romains and Georges Chennevière, and *Notes sur la technique poétique* (1910; "Notes on Poetic Technique"), by Georges Duhamel and Charles Vildrac, outlined the Unanimiste theories of prosody, which resembled those of the American poet Walt Whitman in encouraging the use of strongly accented rhythms and the replacement of symbols and allegory by simple and unadorned diction.

The name *Unanimisme* was based on the title of a poem by Romains, *La Vie unanime* (1908; "Life of One Mind"), that expressed his philosophy.

understate \ˌən-dər-ˈstāt\ **1.** To represent as less than is the case. **2.** To state or present with restraint, especially for effect.

unghosted \ən-ˈgōs-təd\ Not ghostwritten; written firsthand, by the person whose name is on the work.

union \'yün-yən\ Of a literary language, artificially created by a selection of vocabulary and usages from related dialects or languages with the intent of serving all equally, such as Esperanto.

Union of Writers of the U.S.S.R. *also called* Union of Soviet Writers. Organization formed in 1932 by a decree of the Central Committee of the Communist Party of the Soviet Union that abolished existing literary organizations and absorbed all professional Soviet writers into one large union. The union supported Communist Party policies and was the defender and interpreter of the single Soviet literary method, SOCIALIST REALISM. Besides establishing fees, privileges, and other benefits for writers, it maintained institutes for training young writers, provided vacation houses and resorts for its members, and acted as a liaison between the party and its own ranks. The union held its First All-Union Congress in 1934 and thereafter met at irregular intervals. The main union actually encompassed several different local unions, including one for each of the constituent republics of the Soviet Union. After the breakup of the Soviet Union in 1991, the main union was split into several groups and ceased to exist as a single entity.

Uniti \ü-'nē-tē\ (*in full* Compagnia degli Uniti) Company of actors performing commedia dell'arte in Italy in the late 16th and early 17th centuries.

unity \'yü-nə-tē\ *plural* unities. A combination or ordering of parts in a literary or artistic production that constitutes a whole or promotes an undivided total effect; also, the resulting singleness of effect or symmetry and consistency of style and character. *See also* ORGANIC UNITY.

In drama the term refers more specifically to any of three principles derived by French classicists from Aristotle's *Poetics* and requiring a play to have a single action represented as occurring in one place and within one day. They were called respectively *unity of action, unity of place,* and *unity of time.*

These three unities were redefined in 1570 by the Italian humanist Lodovico Castelvetro in his interpretation of Aristotle's *Poetics* and are usually referred to as "Aristotelian rules" for dramatic structure. Actually, Aristotle's observations on tragedy are descriptive rather than prescriptive, and he emphasizes only one unity, that of plot, or action.

In the French classical tragedy, the unities were adhered to literally and became the source of endless critical polemics. Disputes arose over such problems as whether a single day meant 12 or 24 hours and whether a single place meant one room or one city. Some believed that the action represented in the play should occupy no more time than that required for the play's performance—about two hours. In spite of such severe restrictions, the great 17th-century French dramatists Pierre Corneille and Jean Racine, confining the crises of their characters' lives to a single setting and a brief span of hours, produced a unique form of tragedy that derives its austere power from its singleness of concentration. The prestige of the unities continued to dominate French drama until the Romantic era when it was destroyed, in an evening of catcalls and violence, with the opening of Victor Hugo's Romantic tragedy *Hernani* (1830).

In England, however, where playwrights often had two or more plots in a play, they mixed comedy and tragedy and switched to "another part of the forest" freely; the unities were esteemed in theory but ignored in practice.

Universal man *See* RENAISSANCE MAN.

University wit Any of a notable group of pioneer English dramatists writing during the last 15 years of the 16th century. They transformed the native dramatic inheritance of interlude and chronicle play into a potentially great drama by writing plays of quality and diversity. In doing so they prepared the ground for the genius of William Shakespeare. Their forerunner was John Lyly, an Oxford man, and they included Christopher Marlowe and Thomas Nashe (graduates of Cambridge), Thomas Lodge and George Peele (both of Oxford), and Robert Greene (who took degrees from both universities). Another of the wits, though not university trained, was Thomas Kyd. The greatest poetic dramatist was Marlowe, whose handling of blank verse gave the theater its characteristic voice for the next 50 years.

unmeasured \ən-'mezh-ərd, -'māzh-\ Not measured; specifically, not metrical.

unreliable narrator *See* NARRATOR.

unstress *See* SLACK.

Uomo universale *See* RENAISSANCE MAN.

utopia \yü-'tō-pē-ə\ [New Latin *Utopia,* from Greek *ou* not, no + *tópos* place] In literature, a romance or other work describing an ideal commonwealth whose inhabitants exist under seemingly perfect conditions.

The word *utopia* first occurred in Sir Thomas More's book of that name, published in Latin as *Libellus . . . de optimo reipublicae statu, deque nova insula Utopia* (1516; "Concerning the highest state of the republic and the new island Utopia"). It was compounded by More from the Greek words for "not" (ou) and "place" (topos) and thus meant "nowhere." In *Utopia* More describes a pagan and communist city-state in which institutions and policies are entirely governed by reason. The order and dignity of such a state was intended to provide a notable contrast with his description of the unreasonable state of the Europe of his time, which he saw being divided by self-interest and greed for power and riches. The description of Utopia is put in the mouth of a mysterious traveler, Raphael Hythloday, in support of his argument that communism is the only cure against egoism in private and public life. More, in the dialogue, speaks in favor of mitigation of evil rather than cure, human nature being fallible. The reader is thus left guessing as to which parts of the brilliant work's jeu d'esprit are seriously intended and which are mere paradox.

Literary utopias may be practical or satirical, as well as speculative. Utopias are far older than their name. Plato's *Republic* served as a model for many writers, from More to H.G. Wells. A utopian island occurs in the *Sacred History* of Euhemerus (flourished 300 BC), and Plutarch's *Life of Lycurgus* describes a utopian Sparta. The legend of Atlantis inspired many utopian myths; but explorations in the 15th century permitted more realistic settings, and Sir Thomas More associated Utopia with Amerigo Vespucci. Other utopias that were similar to More's in Humanist themes were the *I mondi* (1552) of Antonio Francesco Doni and *La città felice* (1553) of Francesco Patrizi. An early practical utopia was the comprehensive *La città del sole* (written *c.* 1602) of Tommaso Campanella. Francis Bacon's *New Atlantis* (1627) was practical in its scientific program but speculative concerning philosophy and religion. Puritanism produced many literary utopias, both religious and secular, notably, *The Law of Freedom* . . . (1652), in which Gerrard Winstanley advocated the principles of the English agrarian communists known as Diggers. *The Common-Wealth of Oceana* (1656) by James Harrington argued for the distribution of land as the condition of popular independence.

Such works as Gabriel de Foigny's *Terre australe connue* (1676) preached liberty. François Fénelon's *Télémaque* (1699) contained utopian episodes extolling the simple life. *L'An 2440* by Louis-Sébastien Mercier (1770; Eng. trans., 1772) anticipated Revolutionary doctrines. G.A. Ellis' *New Britain* (1820) and Étienne Cabet's *Voyage en Icarie* (1840) were related to experimental communities in the United States that revealed the limitations of purely economic planning. Nathaniel Hawthorne's novel *The Blithedale Romance* (1852) was based partly on his experiences at another such experimental community, that of Brook Farm near Boston, Mass. Edward Bulwer-Lytton, in *The Coming Race* (1871), invented an essence that eliminated economics altogether, and William Morris demonstrated his contempt for economics in *News from Nowhere* (1890). Two influential utopias, however, had economic bases: *Looking Backward* (1888) by Edward Bellamy and *Freiland* (1890; *A Visit to Freeland*) by Theodor Herzka. Wells in *A Modern Utopia* (1905) returned to speculation.

Many utopias are satires that ridicule existent conditions rather than offering practical solutions for them. In this class are Jonathan Swift's *Gulliver's Travels* (1726) and Samuel Butler's *Erewhon* (1872). In the 20th century, when the possibility of a planned society became too imminent, a number of bitterly anti-utopian, or dystopian, novels appeared. Among these are *The Iron Heel* (1907) by Jack London, *My* (1924; *We*) by Yevgeny Zamyatin, *Brave New World* (1932) by Aldous Huxley, and *Nineteen Eighty-four* (1949) by George Orwell. A recent example is Margaret Atwood's *The Handmaid's Tale* (1985). *The Story of Utopias* (1922) by Lewis Mumford is an excellent survey. *See also* ANTI-UTOPIA; DYSTOPIA.

V

With strict regard to Aristotle's rules,
The Vade Mecum *of the true sublime,*
Which makes so many poets . . .
—Lord Byron

valentine \'val-ən-ˌtīn\ A piece of writing or a literary work expressing praise or affection for something—usually used with *to.*

Van nu en straks circle \vän-'nue̅-en-'sträks\ Group of writers associated with an influential Flemish review, *Van nu en straks* ("Of Now and Later"; 1893–94 and 1896–1901). Though holding a variety of opinions, they strove for an art that should comprehend all human activity and give universal significance to individual feelings. Led by the critic August Vermeylen, they included Prosper van Langendonck, Emmanuel Karel de Bom, and Alfred Hegenscheidt. *Van nu en straks* gave Flemish literature a greater significance in Europe as a whole.

variorum or **variorum edition** \ˌvar-ē-'ȯr-əm\ **1.** An edition or text, usually of the complete works of an author, with notes by different people including critics and previous editors of the works. Variorum is short for the Latin phrase *editio cum notis variorum* ("edition with the notes of various people"). **2.** An edition containing variant readings of a text.

Varronian satire \və-'rō-nē-ən\ *See* MENIPPEAN SATIRE.

vatic \'vat-ik\ Of, relating to, or characteristic of a prophet. The Latin word *vates* ("prophet"), from which *vatic* is derived, was applied in classical times to certain poets who were believed to be divinely inspired and therefore prophetic. The Greek Sibyl was one example. Several modern poets, including William Blake, Walt Whitman, and Allen Ginsberg, have been called vatic poets because of the prophetic or oracular nature of their work.

Veda \'vā-də\ Sacred hymn or verse composed in archaic Sanskrit and current among the Indo-European-speaking peoples who entered India from the Iranian regions. No definite date can be ascribed to the composition of the Vedas, but most scholars believe it to have occurred in the period of about 1500–1200 BC. The hymns form a liturgical body that in part grew up around the cult of the soma ritual (the extraction and ingestion of the juice of a plant) and the sacrifice. They extol the hereditary deities, who for the most part personified various natural and cosmic phenomena, such as fire (Agni), the Sun (Sūrya and Savitṛ), dawn (Uṣas), storms (the Rudras), war and rain (Indra), honor (Mitra), divine authority (Varuṇa), and creation (Indra, with some aid of Vishnu). Hymns were composed to these deities, and many were recited or chanted during rituals.

The foremost collection, or Saṃhitā, of such hymns, from which the *hotṛ* (chief priest) drew the material for his recitations, is the Rigveda (Ṛgveda). Sacred formulas known as mantras were recited by the priest responsible for the sacrificial fire and the carrying out of the ceremony; these mantras and verses in time were drawn into Saṃhitās known collectively as Yajurveda. A third group of priests, headed by the *udgātṛ* ("chanter"), performed melodic recitations linked to verses that, although drawn almost entirely from the Rigveda, came to be arranged as a separate Saṃhitā, the Sāmaveda ("Veda of the Chants"). To these three Vedas—Ṛg, Yajur, and Sāma, known as the *trayī-vidyā* ("threefold knowledge")—was added a fourth, the Atharvaveda, a collection of hymns, magic spells, and incantations that represents a more folk level of religion and remains partly outside the Vedic sacrifice.

The entire corpus of Vedic literature—the Saṃhitās and the expositions that came to be attached to them, the Brāhmaṇas, the Āraṇyakas, and the Upanishads—was considered Śruti, the product of divine revelation. The whole of the literature seems to have been preserved orally (although scholars suspect that there were early manuscripts to assist memory).

Vedāṅga \vā-ˈdäŋ-gə\ Any one of six classes of concise, technical, and usually aphoristic Sanskrit works written in the sutra style and designed to teach how to recite, understand, and apply Vedic texts. The word Vedāṅga means literally "limb of the Veda," the Veda being thought of as the body which the limbs support and preserve.

The six areas of study covered by the Vedāṅgas are: (1) *śikṣā* (instruction), which explains the proper articulation and pronunciation of the Vedic texts. Different *śākhā*s (branches) had different ways of pronouncing the texts, and these variations were recorded in *prātiśākhya*s (literally, "Instructions for the *śākhā*s"), four of which are extant; (2) *chandas* (meter), of which there remains only one late representative; (3) *vyākaraṇa* (analysis and derivation), in which the language is grammatically described—Pāṇini's famous grammar (*c.* 400 BC) and the *prātiśākhya*s are the oldest examples of this discipline; (4) *nirukta* (lexicon), which discusses and gives meanings for difficult words, represented by the *Nirukta* of Yāska (*c.* 600 BC); (5) *jyotiṣa* (luminaries), a system of astronomy and astrology used to determine the right times for rituals; and (6) *kalpa* (mode of performance), which studies the correct ways of performing the ritual.

vade mecum \ˌvā-dē-ˈmē-kəm, ˌväd-ā-ˈmā-ˌkům\ **1.** A book for ready reference, a manual. **2.** Something regularly carried about by a person.

V-Effect *See* ALIENATION EFFECT.

vehicle *See* TENOR AND VEHICLE.

vellum \ˈvel-əm\ [Middle English *velim,* from Middle French *velin, veelin,* from *velin, veelin* (adjective) of a calf, a derivative of *veel* calf] An especially fine parchment made from the thinner, more delicate skins of calf or kid or from stillborn or newly born calf or lamb. The term is often used interchangeably with PARCHMENT.

In the preparation of vellum and coarser parchment, the animal skin is washed and divested of hair or wool. Then it is stretched tight on a frame, scraped thin to remove further traces of hair and flesh, whitened with chalk, and smoothed with pumice.

Venus and Adonis stanza \'vē-nəs . . . ə-'dän-is, -'dōn-\ A stanza consisting of an iambic pentameter quatrain and couplet with the rhyme scheme *ababcc*. The stanza was so called because it was used by William Shakespeare in his poem *Venus and Adonis* (1593).

verbal icon *See* ICON.

verbal irony *See* IRONY.

Verfremdungseffekt *See* ALIENATION EFFECT.

verisimilitude \ˌver-i-si-'mil-i-ˌtüd, -ˌtyüd\ [Latin *verisimilitudo* plausibility] The semblance of reality in dramatic or nondramatic fiction. The concept implies that either the action represented must be acceptable or convincing according to the audience's own experience or knowledge or, as in the presentation of science fiction or tales of the supernatural, the audience must be enticed into willingly suspending disbelief and accepting improbable actions as true within the framework of the narrative.

Aristotle in his *Poetics* insisted that literature should reflect nature—that even highly idealized characters should possess recognizable human qualities—and that what was probable took precedence over what was merely possible. Following Aristotle, the 16th-century Italian critic Lodovico Castelvetro pointed out that the nondramatic poet had only words with which to imitate words and things but the dramatic poet could use words to imitate words, things to imitate things, and people to imitate people. His influence on the French neoclassical dramatists of the 17th century is reflected in their preoccupation with *vraisemblance* and their contribution of many refinements to the theory in respect to appropriate diction and gesture.

The concept of verisimilitude was incorporated most fully in the realist writing of the late 19th century, in which works are dominated by well-developed characters who very closely imitate real people in their speech, mannerisms, dress, and material possessions.

verismo \vā-'rēz-mō\ [Italian, realism, a derivative of *vero* true, true to life] Literary realism as it developed in Italy in the late 19th and early 20th centuries. Its primary exponents were the Sicilian novelists Luigi Capuana and Giovanni Verga. The realist movement arose in Europe after the French Revolution, and the realist influence reached Capuana and Verga particularly through the writings of Honoré de Balzac and Émile Zola in France and of the *scapigliatura* group in Italy. Verismo's overriding aim was the objective presentation of life, usually that of the lower classes, using direct, unadorned language, explicit descriptive detail, and realistic dialogue.

Capuana initiated the movement with the short-story collection *Profili di donne* (1877; "Studies of Women") and the novel *Giacinta* (1879) and other psychologically oriented, clinically rendered works, which were objective almost to the point of excising human emotion. Works by his friend Verga, of which the best known are *I Malavoglia* (1881; *The House by the Medlar Tree*) and *Mastro-don Gesualdo* (1889), described with more emotional warmth the dismal conditions in early 19th-century Sicily.

Like Capuana and Verga, most other *veristi* described the life they knew best, that of their native towns or regions. Thus the best of the minor writers of the movement were regionalists, including the Neapolitan novelist Matilde Serao, the Tuscan Renato Fucini, and Grazia Deledda, the novelist of southern Italy who received the Nobel Prize for Literature in 1926.

Verismo faded from the scene in the 1920s but emerged after World War II in a new and explosively vital form, *Neorealismo* (Neorealism).

vers de société \ˌver-də-sōs-yā-ˈtā\ [French, society verse] Witty and typically ironic light verse written to amuse a sophisticated circle of readers.

Vers de société has flourished in cultured societies, particularly in court circles and literary salons, from the time of the Greek poet Anacreon (6th century BC). Its tone is flippant or mildly ironic. Trivial subjects are treated in an intimate, subjective manner, and even when social conditions form the theme, the light mood prevails.

The Roman poets Catullus, Martial, and Horace produced much witty vers de société and have often been translated or closely paraphrased; but much strikingly original verse of this kind has come from poets or other writers known for their serious works. Jean Froissart, the 14th-century historian of feudal chivalry, wrote some of the most charming examples of the late Middle Ages. The English Cavalier poets Robert Herrick, Thomas Carew, and Richard Lovelace wrote much fine vers de société along with their elegant lyrics.

The 18th century was rich in examples, both in French and in English. Among the best English practitioners were John Gay and Alexander Pope, whose poem *The Rape of the Lock* is a masterpiece of the genre. Voltaire, in addition to his political and philosophical works, produced exquisite gems of occasional verse, epistles, and light satires for the enjoyment of his royal friends and patrons.

Vers de société bloomed again in 19th-century literature after the Romantic movement's decline, with the poetry of William Ernest Henley and the scholarly Austin Dobson.

In the 20th century, the American poet Ogden Nash created a new, sophisticated, and urbane vers de société with a theme of self-ironic adult helplessness. In England the tradition was kept alive by the neo-Victorian topical poems of Sir John Betjeman.

verse \ˈvərs\ [Latin *versus* row, line, verse] **1.** A line of metrical writing. **2.** A unit of metrical writing larger than a single line, such as a stanza. **3.** The shortest division of chapters of the Bible. **4.** Poetry. **5.** Metrical writing that is distinguished from poetry especially by its lower level of intensity.

verse-speaking choir A group organized for the choral speaking of poetry.

verset \'vər-sət, vər-'set\ [French, verse in sacred scripture (as the Bible or Qur'ān), group of sentences that form a verselike subdivision in a poetic text, a diminutive of *vers* verse] A short verse, especially from a sacred book, such as those found in the Song of Solomon and the Psalms. Also, a stanza form modeled on such biblical verse. The stanza form is characterized by long lines and powerful, surging rhythms and usually expresses fervent religious or patriotic sentiments. The verset is a flexible form approximating free verse and the prose poem and is open to a wide range of emotional expression. Poetic devices such as repetition, assonance, alliteration, and figures of speech contribute to the overall vigor of the lines. The verset appears mainly in the literature of European Christian countries where it was first used in medieval religious and mystical texts. Friedrich Hölderlin, Charles Péguy, and Paul Claudel have all written poems in this form.

versicle \'vər-si-kəl\ [Latin *versiculus* short line of verse, a diminutive of *versus* line, verse] A little verse. Also, a short response that is spoken or sung during a liturgy.

version \'vər-zhən\ [New Latin *versio,* from Medieval Latin, change, conversion, action of turning, a derivative of Latin *vertere* to turn] **1.** A translation from another language; especially, a translation of the Bible or a part of it. **2.** An adaptation of a literary work.

vers libre \ver-'lēbr, *Angl* 'lē-brə\ *plural* vers libres *same or* 'lē-brəz\ [French, free verse] Nineteenth-century poetic innovation that liberated French poetry from its traditional prosodic rules. In vers libre, the basic metrical unit is the phrase rather than a line of a fixed number of syllables, as was traditional in French versification since the Middle Ages. In vers libre, the lengths of lines may vary according to the sense of the poem, the complete sentence replaces the stanza as a unit of meaning, and rhyme is optional.

Vers libre appears to have been the independent invention of several different French poets in the late 1880s. Among its early advocates and theoreticians were Gustave Kahn, Jules Laforgue, Francis Viélé-Griffin, and Édouard Dujardin. The use of a free prosodic structure in French poetry was not entirely new: it had antecedents in the poems of the Symbolists, the prose poems of Arthur Rimbaud, and, much earlier, in the metrical experiments of Victor Hugo. But the widespread adoption of vers libre at the end of the 19th century influenced poetic trends in other countries, so that verse patterned on irregular metrical designs has become common in the modern poetry of all Western nations. *See also* FREE VERSE.

verso \ˈvər-sō\ [New Latin *verso* (*folio*) the page being turned] **1.** The side of a leaf (such as of a manuscript) that is to be read second. **2.** A left-hand page. *Compare* RECTO.

Victorian literature Body of works written in England during the reign of Victoria (1837–1901), a long period of magnificent achievement. Its leading lights include, in poetry, Robert Browning, Edward Lear, and Alfred, Lord Tennyson; in criticism, Matthew Arnold and John Ruskin; and, above all, in the novel, Charles Dickens, Emily Brontë, George Eliot, Thomas Hardy, William Makepeace Thackeray, and a host of only slightly lesser names.

As the 20th century approached, the romantic, evangelical, and humanitarian impulses that had characterized the era began to lose momentum: poets became aesthetes instead of moral legislators, and novelists began to turn inward for their subject matter rather than looking outward to society. Certain prevailing values of the period (gentility, insularity, materialism, and, especially, censoriousness) have lent to the popular usage of "Victorian" a pejorative connotation that is far too simplistic to characterize the literature of the period.

vignette \vin-ˈyet, vēn-\ A short descriptive literary sketch.

villain \ˈvil-ən\ A character in a story or play who opposes the hero. A villain is also known as an ANTAGONIST.

villanelle \ˌvil-ə-ˈnel\ [French, from Italian *villanella* rustic song, a derivative of *villano* rustic, unrefined] Rustic song in Italy, where the term originated; the term was used in France to designate a short poem of popular character favored by poets in the late 16th century. Joachim du Bellay's "Vanneur de Blé" and Philippe Desportes' "Rozette" are examples of this early type, unrestricted in form. Later poets patterned their villanelles on a highly popular example of the genre written by Jean Passerat. It established a rigorous and somewhat monotonous form: seven-syllable lines using two rhymes, distributed in (normally) five tercets (three-line stanzas) and a final quatrain with line repetitions.

The villanelle was revived in the 19th century by Philoxène Boyer and J. Boulmier. Charles Leconte de Lisle and later Maurice Rollinat also used the form. In England, the villanelle was cultivated by W.E. Henley, Austin Dobson, Andrew Lang, and Edmund Gosse. Examples in English include Henley's "A Dainty Thing's the Villanelle," which itself describes the form, and Dylan Thomas' "Do Not Go Gentle into That Good Night."

virelay or **virelai** \vēr-ˈle\ [Middle French, alteration (influenced by *lai* lay) of *vireli* kind of dance, air accompanying a dance, probably a derivative of *virer* to turn, twist] One of several *formes fixes* ("fixed forms") in French lyric poetry and song of the 14th and 15th centuries.

It probably did not originate in France, and it takes on several different forms even within the French tradition. Similar forms can be found in most of the literatures of medieval and early Renaissance Europe: in the Galician *cantiga,* the Arabic *zajal* and *muwashshah,* the Italian *lauda, ballata,* and *frottola,* the Spanish *villancico,* and the English carol. *Compare* BALLADE; RONDEAU.

The standard virelay form has three stanzas, each preceded and followed by a refrain. Each stanza is in three sections, the first two having the same rhyme scheme and the last having the rhyme scheme of the refrain. In a musical setting the third section of each stanza therefore takes the same music as the refrain, while the first two sections have different music.

The virelay fell out of favor in the first half of the 15th century but then returned in a curtailed form with just one stanza, and without the fixed musical and poetic style previously associated with it. These later virelays with only one stanza are often called *bergerettes.*

vision \'vizh-ən\ A piece of writing (such as a poem) claiming to represent something beheld in a revelatory dream, trance, or ecstasy. These were especially popular in early Celtic literature. *See also* AISLING; DREAM VISION.

volta \'vȯl-tə, 'väl-\ [Italian, turn, act of turning around] The turn in thought in a sonnet that is often indicated by such initial words as "But," "Yet," or "And yet." The volta occurs between the octet and sestet in a Petrarchan sonnet and sometimes between the 8th and 9th or between the 12th and 13th lines of a Shakespearean sonnet, as in William Shakespeare's sonnet number 130:

My mistress' eyes are nothing like the sun;
Coral is far more red than her lips' red;
If snow be white, why then her breasts are dun;
If hairs be wires, black wires grow on her head.
I have seen roses damask'd, red and white,
But no such roses see I in her cheeks;
And in some perfumes is there more delight
Than in the breath that from my mistress reeks.
I love to hear her speak, yet well I know
That music hath a far more pleasing sound;
I grant I never saw a goddess go;
My mistress, when she walks, treads on the ground.
And yet, by heaven, I think my love as rare
As any she belied with false compare.

Vorticism \'vȯr-ti-ˌsiz-əm\ [derivative of *vortex*] Literary and artistic movement that flourished in England from 1912 to 1915, on the brink of World War I. Founded by Wyndham Lewis, Vorticism attempted to relate art to industrialization. It opposed the sentimentality held to be characteristic of the 19th century and extolled the energy of the machine and machine-made products, and it promoted something of a cult of sheer violence.

Artists involved in the movement included the poet Ezra Pound and the sculptor Jacob Epstein. In the visual arts, Vorticist compositions were abstract and sharp-planed, showing the influence of cubism and Futurism. The short-lived magazine *Blast: The Review of the Great English Vortex* (two editions, 1914 and 1915), edited by Lewis, was a typographically arresting, vigorous attempt to create a forum for English literary and plastic artists of the avant-garde. Vorticism went into decline after the Vorticist Exhibition at the Doré Gallery in London in 1915.

vowel rhyme *See* ASSONANCE.

vulgate A commonly accepted text or reading.

vulgus \'vəl-gəs\ A short composition in Latin verse formerly common as an exercise in some English public schools. The word is probably a mock-Latin spelling of *vulgars* (plural of *vulgar*), formerly applied to English sentences to be translated into Latin.

W

. . . the superior author implies more than he says in print. Such is the doctrine of wordsmanship.
—Erskin Caldwell

waka \'wä-kä\ [Japanese] Japanese poetry, specifically the court poetry of the 6th to the 14th century, including such forms as the *chōka* and *sedōka,* in contrast to such later forms as *renga,* haikai, and haiku. The term *waka* also is used, however, as a synonym for tanka, the short poem that is a basic Japanese form.

The *chōka,* or "long poem," is of indefinite length, formed of alternating lines of five and seven syllables ending with an extra seven-syllable line. Many *chōka* have been lost; the shortest of those extant are 7 lines long, while the longest have 150 lines. They may be followed by one or more *hanka* ("envoys"). The amplitude of the *chōka* permitted the poets to treat themes impossible within the compass of the tanka.

The *sedōka,* or "head-repeated poem," consists of two tercets of five, seven, and seven syllables each. An uncommon form, it was sometimes used for dialogues. Hitomaro's *sedōka* are noteworthy. *Chōka* and *sedōka* were seldom written after the 8th century.

The *tanka,* or "short poem," the basic form of Japanese poetry, has existed throughout the history of written verse, outlasting the *chōka* and preceding the haiku. It consists of 31 syllables in five lines of five, seven, five, seven, and seven syllables. The envoys to *chōka* were in tanka form. As a separate form, tanka also served as the progenitor of *renga* and haiku.

Japanese poetry has generally consisted of very small basic units, and its historical development has been one of gradual compression down to the three-line haiku, in which an instantaneous fragment of an emotion or perception takes the place of broader exposition. *See also* HAIKU; RENGA.

Wakefield plays \'wāk-ˌfēld\ A cycle of 32 scriptural (or mystery) plays written in the early 15th century that were performed regularly at Wakefield, a town in the north of England, as part of the summertime religious festival of Corpus Christi. The text of the plays has been preserved in the Towneley Manuscript (so called after a family that once owned it), now in the Huntington Library in California. The plays are sometimes referred to as the Towneley cycle.

The Wakefield cycle probably originated in the later 14th century, when the cycle of plays performed at York was transferred bodily to Wakefield and there established as a Corpus Christi cycle; six of the plays in each are virtually identical, and there are corresponding speeches here and there in others. On the whole, however, each cycle went its own way after the transfer. From a purely literary point of view, the Wakefield plays are considered superior to any other surviving cycle. In particular, the work of a talented reviser, known as the Wakefield Master, is easily recognizable for its brilliant handling of meter, language, and rhyme, and for its wit and satire.

It is not known how long the cycle, which begins with the fall of Lucifer and ends with the Last Judgment, took in performance: the Chester cycle, which is shorter, was given over three days; the York cycle, which is longer, was given in one. Two plays (about Jacob) are peculiar to the Wakefield cycle, which omits many narratives from the New Testament that are found in all the other surviving cycles. The cycle is unusual in that two shepherd's plays are given. *See also* MYSTERY PLAY.

Waldeinsamkeit \'vält-ˌīn-zäm-ˌkīt\ In German Romantic literature, the longing for distant places or times or for a dream world as opposed to reality. The word, which means literally "forest solitude," was coined by Ludwig Tieck, who used it in his short novel *Der blonde Eckbert* ("Fair Eckbert"). Clemens Brentano and J.W. von Goethe were among the other writers who expressed this idea in their works.

war of the theaters In English literary history, conflict involving the English playwrights Ben Jonson, John Marston, and Thomas Dekker. It extended from 1599 to roughly 1603, a period when Jonson was writing for one children's company of players and Marston for a rival group. In 1599 Marston presented a mildly satiric portrait of Jonson in his *Histrio-mastix.* In the same year Jonson replied in *Every Man Out of His Humour,* ridiculing Marston's style as "fustian." Also that same year, Marston's *Jack Drum's Entertainment* presented Jonson, thinly disguised, as a cuckold. The quarrel reached its height about 1600: Jonson wrote *Cynthia's Revels* (performed *c.* 1600), satirizing Marston and Dekker; Marston satirized Jonson in *What You Will;* Jonson, anticipating Marston's attack, wrote *Poetaster* (produced 1601), representing Marston as an inferior poet and a plagiarist and Dekker as a "playdresser" and plagiarist; Dekker and Marston then lampooned Jonson as the laborious poet (Dekker in the play *Satiro-mastix* [produced 1601]). The quarrel was patched up by 1604, when Marston dedicated *The Malcontent* to Jonson.

Some scholars have seen the quarrel as based on a difference of opinion about the nature of drama; it was certainly sharpened by the intense competition that existed between children's companies at the time, which were so popular that in *Hamlet* William Shakespeare refers to the fact that adult actors were forced to undertake provincial tours because of the boys' popularity.

watakushi shōsetsu *See* I NOVEL.

wedge verse *See* RHOPALIC.

weight \'wāt\ In prosody, stress value or quantity of individual sounds, syllables, and units of rhythmic structure in verse.

well-made play *French* pièce bien faite \ˌpyes-byeⁿ-'fet\ A play constructed according to certain strict technical principles and aiming at neatness of plot and theatrical effectiveness. The form dominated the stages of Europe and the United States for most of the 19th century.

The technical formula of the well-made play, developed about 1825 by the French playwright Eugène Scribe, called for complex and highly artificial plotting, a build-up of suspense, a climactic scene in which all problems are resolved, and a happy ending. Conventional romantic conflicts were a staple subject of such plays (for example, the problem of a pretty girl who must choose between a wealthy, unscrupulous suitor and a poor but honest young man). Suspense was created by misunderstandings between characters, mistaken identities, secret information (the poor young man is really of noble birth), lost or stolen documents, and similar contrivances. Later critics, such as Émile Zola and George Bernard Shaw, denounced Scribe's work and that of his successor, Victorien Sardou, for exalting the mechanics of playmaking at the expense of honest characterizations and serious content, but both men's plays were enormously popular in their day. Scribe, with the aid of hack assistants, wrote literally hundreds of plays that were translated, adapted, and imitated all over Europe. In England the well-made play was taken up by such practitioners as Wilkie Collins, who summed up the formula succinctly: "Make 'em laugh; make 'em weep; make 'em wait." Henry Arthur Jones and Arthur Pinero used the technique successfully, with somewhat improved characterizations and emotional tension, and Pinero actually brought it to the level of art with *The Second Mrs. Tanqueray* in 1893. The polished techniques of the well-made play were also turned to serious purposes in the plays of Émile Augier and Alexandre Dumas *fils*, which dealt with social conditions such as prostitution and the emancipation of women and are regarded as the precursors of the PROBLEM PLAY.

Welsh literary renaissance Literary activity in Wales and England in the mid-18th century that attempted to stimulate interest in the Welsh language and in the classical bardic verse forms of Wales. The movement centered on Lewis, Richard, and William Morris, a family of Welsh scholars who preserved ancient texts and encouraged contemporary poets to use the strict meters of the ancient Welsh bards such as the cywydd and awdl. Other scholars also collected and copied bardic manuscripts, laying the groundwork for later research. A new classical school of poetry was led by Goronwy Owen, a poet who wrote verse modeled on that of the medieval bards. The Cymmrodorion Society, established by the Welsh community in London as a center for Welsh literary studies, combined with other such scholarly groups (e.g., the Gwyneddigion and Cymreigyddion societies) to encourage the reestablishment of local eisteddfods (poetic assemblies or contests). As a result, the National Eisteddfod was revived in the early 19th century.

A great number of publications, popular as well as scholarly, resulted from the revival, which also produced religious verse in free meters, lyrical hymns, popular ballads employing cynghanedd (a complex system of accentuation, alliteration, and internal rhyme), and verse dramas based on historical tales, incidents from the Bible, and Welsh mythology and legend.

By the 19th century the arts in Wales had become almost totally dominated by English culture, and the revival subsided. A second revival, based on the scholarly groundwork of the first, occurred at the end of the 19th century, centered in the newly established University of Wales. It brought careful scholarship to bear on the study of ancient texts. Some poets, stimulated by the renaissance, wrote experimental verse that reflects an awareness of the past (especially in the use of cynghanedd) and a solicitude for the survival of the Welsh language.

weltschmerz \ˈvelt-ˌshmerts\ [German, from *Welt* world + *Schmerz* pain, grief] A feeling of melancholy and pessimism or of vague yearning and discontent caused by comparison of the actual state of the world with an ideal state. The term has been used in reference to individuals as well as to the prevailing mood of a whole generation or specific group of people. It is particularly associated with the poets of the Romantic era who refused or were unable to adjust to those realities of the world that they saw as destructive of their right to personal freedom—a phenomenon thought to typify Romanticism. The word was coined by Jean Paul in his pessimistic novel *Selina* (1827) to describe Lord Byron's discontent (especially as shown in *Manfred* and *Childe Harold's Pilgrimage*). In France, where it was called the *mal du siècle,* weltschmerz was expressed during this period by the Viscount de Chateaubriand, Alfred de Vigny, and Alfred de Musset; in Russia by Aleksandr Pushkin and Mikhail Lermontov; in Poland by Juliusz Słowacki; and in America by Nathaniel Hawthorne.

Wenxue yanjiu hui *See* LITERARY RESEARCH ASSOCIATION.

wenyan [Chinese *wényán,* from *wén* character, writing + *yán* speech] *See* GUWEN.

western \ˈwes-tərn\ A genre of novels and short stories, motion pictures, and television and radio shows that are set in the American West, usually in the period from the 1850s to 1900 when the area was fully opened to white settlers. Though basically an American creation, the western has its counterparts in the gaucho literature of Argentina and even in tales of the settlement of the Australian outback. The genre reached its greatest popularity in the early and middle decades of the 20th century and declined somewhat thereafter.

The western has as its setting the immense plains, rugged tablelands, and mountain ranges of that portion of the United States lying west of the Mississippi River, in particular the Great Plains and the Southwest. This area was not truly opened to white settlement until after the American Civil War (1861–65), at which time the Plains Indians were gradually subdued and deprived of most of their lands by white settlers and by the U.S. Cavalry. The conflict between white pioneers and Indians and between cattle ranchers and fence-building farmers form two basic themes. Cowboys were hired by ranchers to drive cattle across hundreds of miles of Western pasturelands to railheads where the animals could be shipped eastward to market. The cattle and mining industries spurred the growth of towns, and the gradual imposition of law and order was accomplished by another class of staple figures in the western, the town sheriff and the U.S. marshal. Actual historical persons in the American West have figured prominently: Wild Bill Hickok, Wyatt Earp, and other lawmen, notorious outlaws such as Billy the Kid and Jesse James, and Indian leaders such as Sitting Bull and Geronimo.

The western has always provided a rich mine for stories of adventure, and indeed a huge number of purely commercial works have capitalized on the basic appeal of gunslinging frontier adventurers, desperadoes, and lawmen. But the western has also furnished the material for a higher form of artistic vehicle, particularly in motion pictures. This was perhaps because the historical western setting lacked the subtly confining web of social conventions and mundane safeties that typify more settled societies. The West's tenuous hold on the rule of law and its fluid social fabric necessitated the settling of individual and group conflicts by the use of violence and the exercise of physical courage, and the moral dramas and dilemmas arising within this elemental, even primeval, framework lent themselves remarkably well to motion-picture treatment.

In literature, the western story had its beginnings in the first adventure narratives that accompanied the opening of the West to white settlement shortly before the Civil War. Accounts of the western plainsmen, scouts, buffalo hunters, and trappers were highly popular in the East. Perhaps the earliest and finest work in this genre was James Fenimore Cooper's *The Prairie* (1827), though the high artistic level of this novel was perhaps atypical in regard to what followed. An early writer to capitalize on the popularity of western adventure narratives was E.Z.C. Judson (Ned Buntline) known as "the father of the dime novel." He wrote dozens of western stories and was responsible for transforming Buffalo Bill into an archetype. Owen Wister, who first saw the West while recuperating from an illness, wrote the first western that won critical praise, *The Virginian* (1902). Classics of the genre have been written by men who actually worked as cowboys; one of the best-loved of these was *Bransford in Arcadia* (1914; reprinted 1917 as *Bransford of Rainbow Range*) by Eugene Manlove Rhodes, a former cowboy and government scout. Andy Adams incorporated many autobiographical incidents in his *Log of a Cowboy* (1903). By far the best-known and one of the most prolific writers of westerns was Zane Grey, an Ohio dentist who became famous with the classic *Riders of the Purple Sage* in 1912. In all, Grey wrote more than 80 books, many of which have retained wide popularity. Another prolific author of westerns was Louis L'Amour.

Notable among the authors of western short stories are A.H. Lewis, Stephen Crane, and Conrad Richter. Many western novels and short stories first appeared in pulp magazines, such as *Ace-High Western Stories* and *Double Action Western*.

Other western classics are Walter van Tilburg Clark's *The Ox-Bow Incident* (1940), who used a Nevada lynching as a metaphor for the struggle for justice, and A.B. Guthrie, Jr.'s *The Big Sky* (1947) about frontier life in the early 1840s, and *The Way West* (1949). Larry McMurtry's *Lonesome Dove* (1985) was a Pulitzer-Prize winning paean to the bygone cowboy. Some western magazines still existed in the late 20th century.

The western film can be dated from Edwin S. Porter's *The Great Train Robbery* (1903), which set the pattern for many films that followed. D.W. Griffith made a series of highly successful westerns in the years before World War I. Most of the hundreds of westerns made from the 1920s to the 1940s were low-budget films that had only slight variations on standard plots. But an increasing number were "big" or "epic westerns," a type introduced in James Cruze's *The Covered Wagon* (1923) and John Ford's *The Iron Horse* (1924).

A new and intently serious western that could treat a wide variety of themes with sensitivity and dramatic realism appeared in the 1950s. These films explored various moral ambiguities and topical problems by means of dramatic allegories set in the Old West, thereby becoming a completely sophisticated genre in the process.This emphasis on human psychology and motivation continued into the 1960s. By the 1980s westerns had almost ceased to be produced in the United States. They were partially replaced by the space epic, a genre in which often all of the aspects of a western were utilized but the setting.

Westerns were also serialized on radio programs during that medium's heyday in the 1930s and '40s. The best-known of these western radio dramas were "The Lone Ranger," featuring the mysterious lawman of that name, and "Death Valley Days," which was set in the Far West. The medium of television also took up westerns in its earlier years. Such long-lived series as "Gunsmoke," "Bonanza," and a half-dozen others captured large viewing audiences during the late 1950s and throughout the '60s, after which their popularity faded.

Whitbread Literary Award \'hwit-ˌbred, 'wit-\ Any of a series of annual awards given to the authors of the most distinguished books first published in the United Kingdom or Ireland within the previous year. Although the rules have varied slightly over the years, the most consistent requirement has been that the authors must have resided in these countries for a specified period of time, at least the previous three years. Since the award was established by the Whitbread Breweries in 1971, the categories have expanded to include the novel, first novel, children's novel, poetry, and biography or autobiography. The Whitbread Book of the Year is chosen from these five category winners. The award is determined by a panel of judges and is presented every winter by the Booksellers Association of Great Britain and Ireland.

whodunit or **whodunnit** \hü-ˈdən-it\ A detective story or a mystery story.

wisdom literature Type of literature that flourished throughout the ancient Middle East, with Egyptian examples dating to before the middle of the 3rd millennium BCE. It revolved around the professional sages and scribes in the service of the court and consisted primarily of maxims about the practical, intelligent way to conduct one's life and of speculations about the worth and meaning of human life. The most common form of these wise sayings, which were intended for oral instruction especially in the schools run by the sages for the young men at the court, was the *mashal* (Hebrew: "comparison" or "parable," although frequently translated "proverb").

The two principal types of wisdom—one practical and utilitarian, the other speculative and frequently pessimistic—arose both within and outside Israel. Practical wisdom consisted chiefly of wise sayings that appealed to experience and offered prudential guidelines for a successful and happy life. Such wisdom is found in a collection of sayings bearing the name of Ptahhotep, a vizier to the Egyptian pharaoh about 2450 BCE, in which the sage counsels his son that the path to material success is by way of proper etiquette, strict discipline, and hard work. Although such instructions were largely materialistic and political, they were moral in character and contributed to a well-ordered society.

Speculative wisdom went beyond maxims of conduct and reflected upon the deeper problems of the value of life and of good and evil. Examples are found in ancient Egyptian and Mesopotamian texts particularly *Ludlul bel nemeqi,* often called the "Babylonian Job"—in which sensitive poets pessimistically addressed such questions as the success of the wicked, the suffering of the innocent, and, in short, the justice of human life.

Hebrew wisdom, which owed much to that of its neighbors, appeared with the establishment of the monarchy and a royal court and found a patron in King Solomon. Through the following centuries the wise men were at times the object of rebuke by the prophets, who disliked their pragmatic realism. The exile, however, brought a change in Hebrew wisdom; it became deeply religious. The wise men were convinced that religion alone possessed the key to life's highest values. It was this mood that dominated the final shaping of the Hebrew wisdom literature. Though dependent on older materials and incorporating documents from before the exile, the wisdom books in their present form were produced after the exile. In the Hebrew Bible the book of Proverbs offers the best example of practical wisdom, while Job and Ecclesiastes give expression to speculative wisdom. Some of the psalms and a few other brief passages are also representative of this type of literature. Among the Apocrypha, the Wisdom of Solomon and Ecclesiasticus are wisdom books.

woman of letters **1.** A woman who is a scholar. **2.** A woman who is an author.

wordsmanship \ˈwərdz-mən-ˌship\ [*word* + *-smanship* (as in *craftsmanship*)] The art or craft of writing.

word value The effectiveness of a word to express the exact shade of meaning desired and to fit into the rhythmic structure of a phrase or sentence.

WPA Federal Theater Project National theater project sponsored and funded by the U.S. government as part of the Works Progress Administration (WPA). Its purpose was to create jobs for unemployed theatrical people in the Great Depression years of 1935–39.

While the project was in operation, some 10,000 professionals were employed in all facets of the theater. The four-year effort involved about 1,000 productions in 40 states; performances were often free to the public. These productions included classical and modern drama, children's plays, puppet shows, musical comedies, and documentary theater known as Living Newspaper. Other projects included the production of plays by young, unknown American playwrights, the promotion of black American theater, and the presentation of radio broadcasts of dramatic works. Following a series of controversial investigations by the House Committee on Un-American Activities and Subcommittee on Appropriations into leftist commentary on social and economic issues, the Federal Theater Project was terminated in 1939 by congressional action.

WPA Federal Writers' Project A program established in 1935 by the Works Progress Administration (WPA) as part of the New Deal struggle against the Great Depression. It provided jobs for unemployed writers, editors, and research workers. Directed by Henry G. Alsberg, it operated in all states and at one time employed 6,600 individuals. The American Guide series, the project's most important achievement, included guidebooks to every state and territory (except Hawaii), as well as to Washington, D.C., New York City, Los Angeles, San Francisco, New Orleans, and Philadelphia; to several major highways (U.S. 1, Ocean Highway, Oregon Trail); and to scores of towns, villages, and counties. The state guides, encyclopedic in scope, combined travel information with essays on geography, architecture, history, and commerce. The project also produced ethnic studies, folklore collections, local histories, and nature studies—totaling more than 1,000 books and pamphlets.

In accordance with WPA regulations, most of the project's personnel came from the relief rolls. They included such already prominent authors as Conrad Aiken, Maxwell Bodenheim, and Claude McKay and such future luminaries as Richard Wright, Ralph Ellison, Nelson Algren, Frank Yerby, Saul Bellow, Loren Eiseley, and Weldon Kees. (Eudora Welty was a photographer for the Mississippi guide.) Congress ended federal sponsorship of the project in 1939 but allowed it to continue under state sponsorship until 1943.

wrenched accent \'rencht\ In prosody, an accent that is forced for the sake of the meter of a verse or that is counter to the regular accent that a given syllable would have in normal speech.

writerly \'rī-tər-lē\ **1.** Of, relating to, or typical of a writer. **2.** Of or relating to a text that demands some effort on the part of the reader, as opposed to a readerly text. The critic Roland Barthes used the terms *lisible* ("readerly") and *scriptible* ("writerly") to distinguish between texts that are straightforward and those whose meaning is not immediately evident. Writerly texts, such as James Joyce's *Ulysses* and William Faulkner's *The Sound and the Fury,* are self-consciously literary works characterized by an emphasis on the mechanics of writing, specifically in their elaborate use of language. *Compare* READERLY.

Y

. . . if she had written nothing but . . . the "Ysopet," she would still deserve not to be forgotten.
—Gustav Masson

Yale school \'yāl\ A group of literary critics, specifically several English professors at Yale University, who became known in the 1970s and '80s for their deconstructionist theories. The Yale school's skeptical, relativistic brand of deconstruction expanded upon the groundwork of French philosopher Jacques Derrida and helped to popularize the deconstruction movement.

The most prominent members of the Yale school were Paul de Man and J. Hillis Miller. Along with Derrida, they contributed essays to the noteworthy collection *Deconstructionism and Criticism* (1979), which analyzed the poem *The Triumph of Life* by P.B. Shelley. De Man, the most influential member, was closely allied to Derrida and based his theories on a system of rhetorical figures. The writings of Geoffrey H. Hartman and Harold Bloom (both of whom were also at Yale) were frequently critical of the Yale school, while Miller, whose work focused on textual opposites and differences, often defended charges that the Yale school was nihilistic. Other American deconstructionists included Barbara Johnson and Jonathan Culler. *See also* DECONSTRUCTION.

yangbanxi \'yäŋ-'bän-'shē\ [Chinese *yàngbǎnxì*, from *yàngbǎn* model + *xì* play, drama] Form of Chinese drama that flourished during the Cultural Revolution (1966–76). The plays were a mixture of Peking opera and modern, Western features, and they dealt with contemporary topics.

Yellow Book, The Short-lived but influential illustrated quarterly magazine devoted to aesthetics, literature, and art, published in London from 1894 to 1897.

From its initial visually arresting issue, for which Aubrey Beardsley was art editor and for which Max Beerbohm wrote an essay, "In Defense of Cosmetics," *The Yellow Book* attained immediate notoriety, largely because of the controversy over Aestheticism that resulted from Oscar Wilde's trial. Published by John Lane and edited by Henry Harland, *The Yellow Book* attracted many outstanding writers and artists of the era, such as Arnold Bennett, Charlotte Mew, Henry James, Edmund Gosse, Richard Le Gallienne, and Walter Sickert.

Yiddish drama The literature, productions, and acting style of the professional Yiddish theater, which developed in Europe beginning in the mid-19th century and rose during its short history to peaks of brilliant artistic expression.

European Jewish drama had its origin in the Middle Ages, when dancers, mimics, and professional jesters entertained at weddings and Purim celebrations with songs and monologues. Purim, the holiday celebrating the downfall of Haman, a persecutor of the Jews in the Bible, became the occasion for increasingly elaborate plays, some of which continue to the present day. By the 16th century these plays, with their interpolated songs and free use of improvisation, were being performed in Yiddish, the language of the majority of central and eastern European Jews.

The beginning of professional Yiddish theater is usually dated to 1876, when Abraham Goldfaden, a former schoolteacher and journalist, joined forces with two traveling musicians to present his own two-act musical sketch in a tavern in Romania. The little play was well received, and Goldfaden went on to organize a full-time professional troupe, for which he eventually wrote songs, dialogues, and, finally, full-length plays. Groups of imitators sprang up, some of them formed by Goldfaden's actors or associates.

Goldfaden and newer Yiddish dramatists, such as Joseph Judah Lerner, became well established in Russia, but the anti-Semitic laws promulgated in 1883 expressly forbade Yiddish plays, and the playwrights and many of their actors immigrated to England and the United States. New York, with its vast immigrant population, became the center of Yiddish drama at the turn of the century.

In the early 1880s Boris Tomashevsky and others went to New York from London and presented the first Yiddish play in the United States. Jacob Gordin is credited with bringing new material and new life into the American Yiddish theater with free adaptations of the works of major European dramatists, such as his *The Jewish King Lear* (1892). Other notable authors are Sholem Asch, Sholem Aleichem, and H. Leivick (pseudonym of Leivick Halpern).

In 1918 Maurice Schwartz founded the Yiddish Art Theatre, in which he served as director and leading actor. Schwartz became the most highly esteemed actor of the Yiddish stage in its heyday, and the theater became the training ground for a generation of actors. Among the notable names associated with it are Rudolph Schildkraut, Jacob Ben-Ami, and Muni Weisenfreund (later known in motion pictures as Paul Muni).

World War II and the Nazi concentration camps destroyed most of the Yiddish culture of Germany and eastern Europe, and the language is rapidly dying out elsewhere, as the children of immigrants are assimilated into new cultures. All of these factors combined have had a devastating impact on the Yiddish theater. In the second half of the 20th century only a few Yiddish theaters of uncertain future survived in New York City, London, Bucharest, Buenos Aires, and Warsaw.

yomihon \ˈyō-mē-ˌhȯn, -ˌhȯŋ\ [Japanese, storybook, literally, book for reading (as opposed to a picture book)] A subgenre of *gesaku,* a type of popular Japanese literature of the Edo, or Tokugawa, period (1603–1867). *Yomihon* were notable for their extended plots culled from Chinese and Japanese historical sources. These novels were openly moralistic romances, and their highly schematized characters often included witches, fairy princesses, and impeccably noble gentlemen. Where *yomihon* succeeded, as in a few works by Takizawa Bakin, they are absorbing as examples of storytelling rather than as moral lessons.

York plays \'yȯrk\ A cycle of 48 plays, dating from the 14th century, of unknown authorship, which were performed during the European Middle Ages by craft guilds in the city of York, in the north of England, on the summer feast day of Corpus Christi. Some of the York plays are almost identical with corresponding plays in the Wakefield cycle and it has been suggested that there was an original (now lost) from which both cycles descended. It is more likely, however, that the York cycle was transferred bodily to Wakefield some time during the later 14th century and there established as a Corpus Christi cycle.

The plays were given in York on one day, in chronological order, on pageant wagons proceeding from one selected place to another. The cycle covers the story of the Fall of Man and his redemption, from the creation of the angels to the Final Judgment; six plays are peculiar to York (the play of Herod's son, of the Transfiguration, of Pilate's wife, of Pilate's majordomo, of the high priests' purchase of the field of blood, and of the appearance of the Virgin to the apostle Thomas).

In the last revision of the York plays, about 14 plays (mainly those concerning Christ's Passion) were redacted into alliterative verse. These powerful adaptations were the work of a dramatic genius, often referred to as the York Realist.

The York plays have been preserved in the Ashburnham Manuscript in the British Library. *See also* MYSTERY PLAY.

Young Germany \'jər-mə-nē\, *also called* Junges Deutschland \'yu̇ŋ-əs-'dȯich-ˌlänt\ A social reform and literary movement in 19th-century Germany (about 1830–50), influenced by French revolutionary ideas, which was opposed to the extreme forms of Romanticism and nationalism then current. The name was first used in Ludolf Wienbarg's *Ästhetische Feldzüge* (1834; "Aesthetic Campaigns"). Members of Young Germany, in spite of their intellectual and literary gifts and penetrating political awareness, failed to command the enthusiasm of their compatriots and, indeed, excited widespread animosity. This was partly due to their lack of social standing and higher education. The Jewish origins of some of the members was also a hindrance. The movement leaders were Wienbarg, Karl Gutzkow, and Theodor Mundt. Heinrich Laube, Georg Herwegh, Ludwig Börne, and Heinrich Heine were also associated with the movement. A resolution of the Diet of the German Confederation passed on Dec. 10, 1835, demanded the suppression of their writings by strict censorship in all the German states. Although several members of the group were gifted poets, they tended in general towards sober prose discourses, in which they tried to scour the dreamier aspects of Romanticism from the public consciousness and to instill a desire for social and political justice. In addition to their interest in social reform, Young Germany also aimed for a vital democratic and national theater and, in what was their most direct influence on literature, prepared the way for dramatic realism in Germany. The revolutionary movements of 1848–49 led to the decline of Young Germany.

Young Poland movement \'pō-lənd\, *Polish* Młoda Polska. Diverse group of late 19th-century and early 20th-century Neoromantic writers brought together in reaction against naturalism and positivism to revive the unfettered expression of feeling and imagination in Polish literature and to extend this reawakening to all the Polish arts. They looked back to the Polish Romantic writers and also to contemporary western European trends, such as Symbolism, for inspiration. Centered in Kraków, the movement was pioneered by the poet Antoni Lange and the editor and critic Zenon Przesmycki ("Miriam").

The most prominent figure of the Young Poland movement was the painter and dramatist Stanisław Wyspiański, whose play *Wesele* (1901; "The Wedding") a masterpiece of evocative allusion, is written in the stylized verse of the traditional puppet theater. Other writers included the peasant poet Jan Kasprowicz, who established a tonic poetic meter that became the characteristic rhythm of modern Polish poetry, and the novelists Stefan Żeromski, Władysław Stanisław Reymont, and Karol Irzykowski.

Ysopet or **Isopet** \ē-zō-'pā\ In French literature, a medieval collection of fables, often versions of Aesop's *Fables*. The word was first applied to a collection of tales written by Marie de France in the late 12th century; they were said to be based directly on an English version of Aesop's *Fables* attributed to King Alfred the Great of Wessex and no longer extant. Another source, better-documented, is the medieval *Romulus* (falsely credited to Romulus, son of Tiberius), which includes fables by the Latin writers Phaedrus and Avienus.

yuefu or **yüeh-fu** \'ywe-'fü\ [Chinese *yuèfŭ*] Form of Chinese poetry derived from the folk-ballad tradition. The *yuefu* takes its name from the Yue Fu ("Music Bureau") created in 120 BC by Emperor Wu for the purpose of collecting songs and their musical scores for ceremonial occasions at court. The music for these songs was later lost, but the words remained, forming a collection of Han dynasty (206 BC–AD 220) folk poetry that served as the basis of the *yuefu* form. These poems were significant because they consisted of lines of varying lengths, some having a regular form of five syllables per line rather than the then-standard four-syllable line. The *yuefu* thus broke ground for the later classic *gushi* ("ancient-style poetry"), with its broader use of rhyme and fewer metrical restrictions. Many later writers, including the great Li Bo (701–762) and Bo Juyi (772–846), continued to create poems derived from the *yuefu* tradition.

Z

"Now I shall throw in some hyperbaton; now we will exhibit a little anadiplosis; this is the occasion surely for a passage of zeugma."
—George Saintsbury

Żagary group \zhȧ-ˈgȧ-ri\ Group of students in Wilno, Poland (now Vilnius, Lithuania) who were associated with the short-lived literary review *Żagary* ("Burning Twigs"; 1931–32), which first appeared as a supplement to the conservative daily *Słowo* ("Word"). The group was representative of the trend known as "catastrophism," the European obsession with cultural cataclysm in the period between the two world wars.

Founded by Teodor Bujnicki, Jerzy Zagórski, and Czesław Miłosz, the group also included Jerzy Putrament and Aleksander Rymkiewicz. Although these writers did not have a clear agenda, they declared their independence from previous literary groups such as Skamander, and were somewhat sympathetic to Marxism.

zaju or **tsa-chü** \ˈdzä-ˈjue̅\ [Chinese *zájù,* from *zá* mixed, sundry + *jù* drama, play] One of the major forms of Chinese drama. The style originated as a short variety play in North China during the Northern Song dynasty (960–1127) and during the Yuan dynasty (1206–1368) developed into a mature four-act dramatic form, in which songs alternate with dialogue. The *zaju,* or northern drama, was distinguished from the *nanxi,* or southern drama (and later the *chuanqi*), by a more rigid form. In the *zaju,* singing was restricted to a single character in each play and each act had a single and distinct rhyme and musical mode. Melodies were those of the Beijing region. Beautiful poetic lyrics were highly valued, while plot incidents were of lesser importance. Of the thousands of romances, religious plays, histories, and domestic, bandit, and lawsuit plays that were composed, only about 200 *zaju* plays survive. *Hsi-hsiang chi* ("The Romance of the Western Chamber"), by Wang Shih-fu, is a 13th-century adaptation of an epic romance of the 12th century. The student Chang and his beautiful sweetheart Ying Ying are models of the tender and melancholy young lovers who figure prominently in Chinese drama. Loyalty is the theme of the history play *Chao-shih ku-erh* ("The Orphan of Chao"), written in the second half of the 13th century. In it the hero sacrifices his son to save the life of young Chao so that Chao can later avenge the death of his family (a situation developed into a major dramatic type in 18th-century popular Japanese drama). *Huilan ji* ("The Chalk Circle"), demonstrating the cleverness of a famous judge, Pao, was adapted in 1948 by Bertolt Brecht in *The Caucasian Chalk Circle*. The life of commoners is portrayed with considerable reality in Yuan drama, though within a highly formalized artistic frame. The lasting worth of *zaju* plays is attested to by their continuous adaptation to new musical styles over the years; stories of *zaju* masterpieces remain a large part of the traditional opera repertory.

zarzuela \thär-ˈthwā-lä, *Angl* zär-ˈzwā-lə\ [Spanish] Spanish musical play consisting of spoken passages, songs, choruses, and dances. It originated in the 17th century as an aristocratic entertainment dealing with mythological or heroic subject matter. The first performances were at the royal residence of La Zarzuela, near Madrid. Writers of zarzuelas included the playwrights Lope de Vega (1562–1635) and Pedro Calderón de la Barca (1600–81) and the composer Juan Hidalgo (*c.* 1600–85). The form declined in the late 17th and the 18th centuries as Italian opera rose in popularity. In the mid-19th century the zarzuela was revived as a popular musical play, an expanded version of the similar 18th-century *tonadilla.* Witty and satirical, it dealt with characters from everyday life and included folk music, dance, and improvisation. Two definite varieties evolved: the *género chico,* a one-act comic zarzuela, and the *género grande,* a serious musical play in two to four acts.

zeugma \ˈzüg-mə\ [Greek *zeûgma,* literally, juncture, joining] The use of a word to modify or govern two or more words usually in such a manner that it applies to each in a different sense (as in "She opened the door and her heart to the homeless boy.") or makes sense with only one (as in "Kill the boys and the luggage!").

Zhdanovshchina \ˈzhdȧ-nəf-shchi-nə\ or **Zhdanovism** \ˈzhdan-ə-ˌviz-əm\ Cultural policy of the Soviet Union during the Cold War period following World War II that called for stricter government control of art and promoted an extreme anti-Western bias. Originally applied to literature, it soon spread to other arts and gradually affected all spheres of intellectual activity in the Soviet Union, including philosophy, biology, medicine, and other sciences. It was initiated by a resolution (1946) of the Central Committee of the Communist Party of the Soviet Union that was formulated by the party secretary and cultural advisor Andrey Aleksandrovich Zhdanov. It was directed against two literary magazines, *Zvezda* and *Leningrad,* which had published supposedly apolitical, bourgeois, individualistic works of the satirist Mikhail Zoshchenko and the poet Anna Akhmatova, who were expelled from the Union of Soviet Writers. The union itself underwent reorganization, but the aims of the resolution were more far-reaching: to free Soviet culture from "servility before the West."

As the campaign accelerated, all vestiges of Westernism, or cosmopolitanism, in Soviet life were ferreted out. Earlier critics and literary historians were denounced for suggesting that Russian classics had been influenced by Jean-Jacques Rousseau, Molière, Lord Byron, or Charles Dickens. Western inventions and scientific theories were claimed to be of Russian origin. Although

Zhdanov died in 1948, the campaign against "cosmopolites" continued until the death of Joseph Stalin in 1953, acquiring increasingly anti-Semitic overtones. This period (1946–53) is generally regarded as the lowest ebb of Soviet literature.

Zhulin qi xian *See* SEVEN SAGES OF THE BAMBOO GROVE.

Index to Proper Names in Text

This index refers to the various entries at which proper names are mentioned. Names are alphabetized by family name without regard to diacritics, spaces, or punctuation, and then by common names. Names of ancient writers are often identified by a placename, and thus are not reversed in alphabetizing, as **Chrétien de Troyes**. Asian names are alphabetized in their original order, in which the family name comes first. In some French and Spanish names, compound surnames are common and these are alphabetized according to common usage, as **Calderón de la Barca, Pedro; García Lorca, Federico;** and **Prévost d'Exiles, Antoine-François**. Names including a connective, such as **de, von, van,** or **le** are alphabetized according to common usage, sometimes by the name after the connective, as **Buffon, Georges-Louis Leclerc de** and sometimes with the connective as part of the surname, as **De Quincey, Thomas**. Names that begin **Mc** or **M'** are alphabetized as spelled.